JOHN CALVIN
GOD THE CREATOR
GOD THE REDEEMER

INSTITUTES OF THE
CHRISTIAN
RELIGION

JOHN CALVIN
GOD THE CREATOR
GOD THE REDEEMER

A New Translation by Henry Beveridge, Esq.

INSTITUTES OF THE
CHRISTIAN
RELIGION

written in Latin by master John Calvin
and translated into English according to the author's last edition.

Bridge-Logos
Gainesville, Florida 32614

Bridge-Logos, Gainesville, FL 32614
Copyright © 2005 by Bridge-Logos Publishers

Printed in the United States of America.

05   1

Library of Congress Catalog Card Number: Pending
International Standard Book Number: 0-88270-927-5

Scripture quotations are from the Holy Bible, King James Version.

Foreword

To read John Calvin is to study the work of some of the finest minds and sharpest pens in Christendom. Calvin was extremely well read and drew heavily from the writings of Turtullian, Origen, the Apostles, Saint Augustine, and Bernard, to name only a few. Befitting his training as an attorney and his passion as a Christian, Calvin devoted years to writing and rewriting his *Institutes of the Christian Religion*, deftly weaving the ideas of his predecessors with his own into a brilliant case for reformation.

That other scholars have enjoined this discussion is no surprise. In the spirit of this partnership of elite brothers that has spanned centuries, the biography of John Calvin in this volume was written by John Foxe (1516-1587), author of *Foxes' Book of Martyrs*. At the end of his piece, we have included some insights from Calvin's personal friends to give you insight into the character of this very human man. Additionally, Charles Haddon Spurgeon (1850-1892), author of *Morning by Morning* and *Evening by Evening*, contributes his treatise, *A Defense of Calvinism*.

We have maintained as much of the original vocabulary as we dare. Calvin wrote in a time when books were rare and owned by only a few. Since Calvin's day, and with the ever widening availability of books and other written media, our culture has developed a distinction between the spoken word and the written word. Their styles are sharply different, with rules that govern each. But Calvin and his contemporaries had no concept of "written" word. That would evolve with readers over the next several centuries. Their work was "spoken" word put to paper. As a consequence, it tends to be oratory in style, filled with flourish and flare. To further complicate the matter of unfamiliar style, Calvin was a Frenchman who wrote in Latin. The work we have today has been translated with careful intention of honoring Calvin's words. If, as a present-day reader, you get tangled up in an occasional sentence that seems to meander maddeningly through a peppering of punctuation marks, merely read it out loud. You will become clear about the meaning, and moreover, you will "hear" Calvin as he thunders. We beg your indulgence, and assure you that the occasional challenge is well worth the result.

Welcome to the mind of Calvin.

The Original Translator's Preface

PREFIXED TO THE FOURTH EDITION 1581
AND REPRINTED VERBATIM IN ALL THE
SUBSEQUENT EDITIONS.
T[HOMAS] N[ORTON], THE TRANSLATOR
TO THE READER.

Good reader, here is now offered you, the fourth time printed in English, M. Calvin's book of the Institutes of the Christian Religion; a book of great labor to the author, and of great profit to the Church of God. M. Calvin first wrote it when he was a young man, a book of small volume, and since that season he has at sundry times published it with new increases, still protesting at every edition himself to be one of those qui scribendo proficiunt, et proficiendo scribunt, which with their writing do grow in profiting, and with their profiting do proceed in writing. At length having, in many [of] his other works, traveled about exposition of sundry books of the Scriptures, and in the same finding occasion to discourse of sundry common-places and matters of doctrine, which being handled according to the occasions of the text that were offered him, and not in any other method, were not so ready for the reader's use, he therefore entered into this purpose to enlarge this book of Institutions, and therein to treat of all those titles and commonplaces largely, with this intent, that whensoever any occasion fell in his other books to treat of any such cause, he would not newly amplify his books of commentaries and expositions therewith, but refer his reader wholly to this storehouse and treasure of that sort of divine learning. As age and weakness grew upon him, so he hastened his labor; and, according to his petition to God, he in manner ended his life with his work, for he lived not long after.

So great a jewel was meet to be made most beneficial, that is to say, applied to most common use. Therefore, in the very beginning of the Queen's Majesty's most blessed reign, I translated it out of Latin into English for the commodity of the Church of Christ, at the special request of my dear friends of worthy memory, Reginald Wolfe and Edward Whitchurch, the one her Majesty's printer for the Hebrew, Greek, and Latin tongues, the other her

Highness' printer of the books of Common Prayer. I performed my work in the house of my said friend, Edward Whitchurch, a man well known of upright heart and dealing, an ancient zealous gospeller, as plain and true a friend as ever I knew living, and as desirous to do anything to common good, especially by the advancement of true religion.

At my said first edition of this book, I considered how the author thereof had of long time purposely labored to write the same most exactly, and to pack great plenty of matter in small room of words; yea, and those so circumspectly and precisely ordered, to avoid the cavillations of such as for enmity to the truth therein contained would gladly seek and abuse all advantages which might be found by any oversight in penning of it, that the sentences were thereby become so full as nothing might well be added without idle superfluity, and again so highly pared, that nothing could be diminished without taking away some necessary substance of matter therein expressed.

This manner of writing, beside the peculiar terms of arts and figures, and the difficulty of the matters themselves, being throughout interlaced with the school men's controversies, made a great hardness in the author's own book, in that tongue wherein otherwise he is both plentiful and easy, insomuch that it sufficeth not to read him once, unless you can be content to read in vain. This consideration encumbered me with great doubtfullness for the whole order and frame of my translation. If I should follow the words, I saw that of necessity the hardness in the translation must needs be greater than was in the tongue wherein it was originally written. If I should leave the course of words, and grant myself liberty after the natural manner of my own tongue, to say that in English which I conceived to be his meaning in Latin, I plainly perceived how hardly I might escape error, and on the other side, in this matter of faith and religion, how perilous it was to err. For I durst not presume to warrant myself to have his meaning without his words. And they that wet what it is to translate well and faithfully, especially in matters of religion, do know that not the only grammatical construction of words sufficeth, but the very building and order to observe all advantages of vehemence or grace, by placing or accent of words, maketh much to the true setting forth of a writer's mind.

In the end, I rested upon this determination, to follow the words so near as the phrase of the English tongue would suffer me. Which purpose I so performed, that if the English book were printed in such paper and letter as the Latin is, it should not exceed the Latin in quantity. Whereby, beside all other commodities that a faithful translation of so good a work may bring, this one benefit is moreover provided for such as are desirous to attain some knowledge of the Latin tongue (which is, at this time, to be wished in many of those men for whose profession this book most fitly serveth), that they shall not find any more English than shall suffice to construe the Latin withal, except in such few places where the great difference of the phrases of the languages enforced me: so that, comparing the one with the other, they shall both profit in good matter, and furnish themselves with understanding of that speech, wherein the greatest treasures of knowledge are disclosed.

In the doing hereof, I did not only trust mine own wit or ability, but examined my whole doing from sentence to sentence throughout the whole book with conference and overlooking of such learned men, as my translation being allowed by their Judgment, I did both satisfy mine own conscience that I had done truly, and their approving of it might be a good warrant to the reader that nothing should herein be delivered him but sound, unmingled, and uncorrupted doctrine, even in such sort as the author himself had first framed it. All that I wrote, the grave, learned, and virtuous man, M. David Whitehead (whom I name with honorable remembrance), did, among others, compare with the Latin, examining every sentence throughout the whole book. Beside all this, I privately required many, and generally all men with whom I ever had any talk of this matter, that if they found anything either not truly translated, or not plainly Englished, they would inform me thereof, promising either to satisfy them or to amend it. Since which time, I have not been advertised by any man of anything, which they would require to be altered. Neither had I myself, by reason of my profession, being otherwise occupied, any leisure to peruse it. And that is the cause, why not only at the second and third time, but also at this impression, you have no change at all in the work, but altogether as it was before.

Indeed, I perceived many men well-minded and studious of this book, to require a table for their ease and furtherance. Their honest desire I have fulfilled in the second edition, and have added thereto a plentiful table, which is also here inserted, which I have translated out of the Latin, wherein the principal matters discoursed in this book are named by their due titles in order of alphabet, and under every title is set forth a brief sum of the whole doctrine taught in this book concerning the matter belonging to that title or common-place; and therewith is added the book, chapter, and section or division of the chapter, where the same doctrine is more largely expressed and proved. And for the readier finding thereof, I have caused the number of the chapters to be set upon every leaf in the book, and quoted the sections also by their due numbers with the usual figures of algorism. And now at this last publishing, my friends, by whose charge it is now newly imprinted in a Roman letter and smaller volume, with divers other Tables which, since my second edition, were gathered by M. Marlorate, to be translated and here added for your benefit.

Moreover, whereas in the first edition the evil manner of my scribbling hand, the interlining of my copy, and some other causes well known among workmen of that faculty, made very many faults to pass the printer, I have, in the second impression, caused the book to be composed by the printed copy, and corrected by the written; whereby it must needs be that it was much more truly done than the other was, as I myself do know above three hundred faults amended. And now at this last printing, the composing after a printed copy bringeth some ease, and the diligence used about the correction having been right faithfully looked unto, it cannot be but much more truly set forth. This also is performed, that the volume being smaller, with a letter fair and legible, it is of more easy price, that it may be of more common use, and so to more large communicating of so great a treasure to those that desire Christian knowledge for instruction of their faith, and guiding of their duties. Thus, on the printer's behalf and mine, your ease and commodity (good readers) provided for. Now resteth your own diligence, for your own profit, in studying it.

To spend many words in commending the work itself were needless; yet thus much I think, I may both not unruly and not vainly say, that though many great learned men have written books of common-places of our religion, as Melancthon, Sarcerius, and others, whose works are very good and profitable to the Church of God, yet by the consenting Judgment of those that understand the same, there is none to be compared to this work of Calvin, both for his substantial sufficiency of doctrine, the sound declaration of truth in articles of our religion, the large and learned confirmation of the same, and the most deep and strong confutation of all old and new heresies; so that (the Holy Scriptures excepted) this is one of the most profitable books for all students of Christian divinity. Wherein (good readers), as I am glad for the glory of God, and for your benefit, that you may have this profit of my travel, so I beseech you let me have this use of your gentleness, that my doings may be construed to such good end as I have meant them; and that if anything mislike you by reason of hardness, or any other cause that may seem to be my default, you will not forthwith condemn the work, but read it after; in which doing you will find (as many have confessed to me that they have found by experience) that those things which at the first reading shall displease you for hardness, shall be found so easy as so hard matter would suffer, and, for the most part, more easy than some other phrase which should with greater looseness and smoother sliding away deceive your understanding. I confess, indeed, it is not finely and pleasantly written, nor carrieth with it such delightful grace of speech as some great wise men have bestowed upon some foolisher things, yet it containeth sound truth set forth with faithful plainness, without wrong done to the author's meaning; and so, if you accept and use it, you shall not fail to have great profit thereby, and I shall think my labor very well employed.

Thomas Norton.

The Printers to the Readers

hereas some men have thought and reported it to be [very great negligence in us for that we have so long kept back from you this,] being so profitable a work for you, namely before the master J[ohnne] Dawes had translated it and delivered it into our hands more than a twelvemonth past: you shall understand for our excuse in that behalf, that we could not well imprint it sooner. For we have been by diverse necessary causes constrained with our earnest entreatance to procure an other frede or oures to translate it whole again. This translation, we trust, you shall well allow. For it hath not only been faithfully done by the translator himself, but also hath been wholly perused by such men, whose ingement and credit all the godly learned in England well know I estheme. But since it is now come forth, we pray you accept it, and see it. If any faults have passed us by oversight, we beseech you let us have your patience, as you have had our diligence.

The Institutes of the Christian Religion, written in Latin by M. John Calvin, and translated into English according to the Author's last edition, with sundry Tables to find the principal matters entreated of in this book, and also the declaration of places of Scripture therein expounded, by Thomas Norton. Whereunto there are newly added in the margen of the book, notes containing in briefs the substance of the matter handled in each Section.

Originally printed at London by Arnold Hatfield, for Bonham Norton. 1599

Prefatory Address

Sire, when I first engaged in this work, nothing was further from my thoughts than to write what should afterwards be presented to your Majesty. My intention was only to furnish a kind of rudiment, by which those who feel some interest in religion might be trained to true godliness. And I toiled at the task chiefly for the sake of my countrymen, the French multitudes of whom I perceived to be hungering and thirsting after Christ, while very few seemed to have been duly imbued with even a slender knowledge of him. That this was the object, which I had in view, is apparent from the work itself, which is written in a simple and elementary form adapted for instruction.

But when I perceived that the fury of certain bad men had risen to such a height in your realm, that there was no place in it for sound doctrine, I thought it might be of service if I were in the same work both to give instruction to my countrymen, and also lay before your Majesty a Confession from which you may learn what the doctrine is that so inflames the rage of those madmen who are this day, with fire and sword, troubling your kingdom. For I fear not to declare that what I have here given may be regarded as a summary of the very doctrine, which, they shout, ought to be punished with confiscation, exile, imprisonment, and flames, as well as exterminated by land and sea.

Indeed, I am aware of how, in order to render our cause as hateful to your Majesty as possible, they have filled your ears and mind with atrocious insinuations; but you will be pleased, of your clemency, to reflect that neither in word nor deed could there be any innocence, were it sufficient merely to accuse. When anyone with the view of exciting prejudice observes that this doctrine, of which I am endeavoring to give your Majesty an account, has been condemned by the suffrages of all the estates, and was long ago stabbed again and again by partial sentences of courts of law, he undoubtedly says nothing more than that it has sometimes been violently oppressed by the power and faction of adversaries, and sometimes fraudulently and insidiously overwhelmed by lies, cavils, and calumny. While a cause is unheard, it is violence to pass sanguinary sentences against it; it is fraud to charge it, contrary to its deserts, with sedition and mischief.

That no one may suppose we are unjust in thus complaining, you yourself, most illustrious Sovereign, can bear us witness with what lying calumnies it is daily traduced in your presence, as aiming at nothing else than to wrest the scepters of kings out of their hands, to overturn all tribunals and seats of justice, to subvert all order and government, to disturb the peace and quiet of society, to abolish all laws, to destroy the distinctions of rank and property, and, in short, to turn all things upside down. And yet, that which you hear is but the smallest portion of what is said; for among the common people are disseminated certain horrible insinuations—insinuations which, if well founded, would justify the whole world in condemning the doctrine with its authors to a thousand fires and gibbets. Who can wonder that the popular hatred is inflamed against it, when credit is given to those most iniquitous accusations? See why all ranks unite with one accord in condemning our persons and our doctrine!

Carried away by this feeling, those who sit in judgment merely give utterance to the prejudices, which they have imbibed at home, and who think they have duly performed their part if they do not order punishment to be inflicted on anyone until convicted, either on his own confession, or on legal evidence. But of what crime convicted? "Of that condemned doctrine," is the answer. But with what justice condemned? The very essence of the defense was not to abjure the doctrine itself, but to maintain its truth. On this subject, however, not a whisper is allowed!

Justice, then, most invincible Sovereign, entitles me to demand that you will undertake a thorough investigation of this cause, which has hitherto been tossed about in any kind of way, and handled in the most irregular manner, without any order of law, and with passionate heat rather than judicial gravity.

Let it not be imagined that I am here framing my own private defense with the view of obtaining a safe return to my native land. Though I cherish towards it the feelings, which become me as a man, still, as matters now are, I can be absent from it without regret. The cause, which I plead, is the common cause of all the godly, and therefore the very cause of Christ—a cause which, throughout your realm, now lies in despair—torn and trampled upon in all kinds of ways, and that more through the tyranny of certain Pharisees than any sanction from yourself. But it matters not to inquire how the thing is done; the fact that it is done cannot be denied. For so far have the wicked prevailed, that the truth of Christ, if not utterly routed and dispersed, lurks as if it were ignobly buried; while the poor Church, either wasted by cruel slaughter or driven into exile or intimidated and terror—struck, scarcely ventures to breathe. Still her enemies press on with their wonted rage and fury over the ruins, which they have made, strenuously assaulting the wall, which is already giving way. Meanwhile, no man comes forth to offer his protection against such furies. Any who would be thought most favorable to the truth, merely talk of pardoning the error and imprudence of ignorant men, for so those modest personages speak: giving the name of *error and imprudence* to that which they know to be the infallible truth of God, and of *ignorant men* to those whose intellect they see that Christ has not despised, seeing he has deigned to entrust them with the mysteries of his heavenly wisdom. Thus, all are ashamed of the Gospel.

Your duty, most serene Prince, is to not shut either your ears or mind against a cause involving such mighty interests as these: how the glory of God is to be maintained on the earth inviolate, how the truth of God is to preserve its dignity, how the kingdom of Christ is to continue amongst us compact and secure. The cause is worthy of your ear, worthy of your investigation, worthy of your throne.

The characteristic of a true sovereign is to acknowledge that in the administration of his kingdom, he is a minister of God. He, who does not make his reign subservient to the divine glory, acts the part not of a king, but a robber. He, moreover, deceives himself who anticipates long prosperity to any kingdom, which is not ruled by the scepter of God—that is, by his divine word. For the heavenly oracle is infallible which has declared, "where there is no vision the people perish" (Proverbs 29:18).

Let not a contemptuous idea of our insignificance dissuade you from the investigation of this cause. We, indeed, are perfectly conscious how poor and abject we are: in the presence of God we are miserable sinners, and in the sight of men most despised—we are, if you will, the mere dregs and off—scouting of the world, or worse, if worse can be named: so that before God there remains nothing of which we can glory save only his mercy, by which, without any merit of our own, we are admitted to the hope of eternal salvation: and before men not even this much remains, since we can glory only in our infirmity, a thing which, in the estimation of men, it is the greatest ignominy even tacitly to confess. But our doctrine must stand sublime above all the glory of the world, and invincible by all its power, because it is not ours, but that of the living God and his Anointed, whom the Father has appointed King, that he may rule from sea to sea, and from the rivers even to the ends of the earth; and so rule as to smite the whole earth and its strength of iron and brass, its splendor of gold and silver, with the mere rod of his mouth, and break them in pieces like a potter's vessel; according to the magnificent predictions of the prophets respecting his kingdom (Daniel 2:34, Isaiah 11:4, Psalm 2:9).

Our adversaries, indeed, clamorously maintain that our appeal to the word of God is a mere pretext—that we are, in fact, its worst corrupters. How far this is not only malicious calumny, but also shameless effrontery, you will be able to decide of your own knowledge by reading our Confession. Here, however, it may be necessary to make some observations which may dispose, or at least assist, you to read and study it with attention.

When Paul declared that all prophecy ought to be according to the analogy of faith (Romans 12:6), he laid down the surest rule for determining the meaning of Scripture. Let our doctrine be tested by this rule, and our victory is secure. For what accords better and more aptly with faith than to acknowledge ourselves divested of all virtue that we may be clothed by God, devoid of all goodness, that we may be filled by him; the slaves of sin, that he may give us freedom; blind, that he may enlighten; lame, that he may cure; and feeble, that he may sustain us; to strip ourselves of all ground of glorying, that he alone may shine forth glorious, and we be glorified in him? When these things and others to the same effect are said by us, they interpose and querulously complain, that in this way we overturn some blind light of nature, fancied preparations, free will, and works meritorious of eternal salvation, with their own supererogation also; because they cannot bear that the entire praise and glory of all goodness, virtue, justice, and wisdom should remain with God. But we read not of any having been blamed for drinking too much of the fountain of living water; on the contrary, those are severely reprimanded who "have hewed them out cisterns, broken cisterns, that can hold no water" (Jeremiah 2:13). Again, what more agreeable to faith than to feel assured that God is a propitious Father when Christ is acknowledged as a brother and propitiator, than confidently to expect all prosperity and gladness from Him, whose ineffable love towards us was such that He "spared not his own Son, but delivered him up for us all" (Romans 8:32), than to rest in the sure hope of salvation and eternal life whenever Christ, in whom such treasures are hid, is conceived to have been given by the Father? Here they attack us, and loudly maintain that this sure confidence is not free from arrogance and presumption. But as nothing is to be presumed of ourselves, so all things are to be presumed of God; nor are we stripped of vainglory for any other reason than that we may learn to glory in the Lord. Why go further? Take but a cursory view, most valiant King, of all the parts of our cause, and count us of all wicked men the most iniquitous, if you do not discover plainly, that "therefore we both labor and suffer reproach because we trust in the living God" (1 Timothy 4:10); because we believe it to be "life eternal" to know "the only true God, and Jesus Christ," whom he has sent (John 17:3). For this hope some of us are in bonds, some beaten with rods, some made a gazing—stock, some proscribed, some most cruelly tortured, some obliged to flee; we are all pressed with straits, loaded with dire execrations, lacerated by slanders, and treated with the greatest indignity.

Look now to our adversaries (I mean the priesthood, at whose beck and pleasure others ply their enmity against us), and consider with me for a little by what zeal they are actuated. The true religion which is delivered in the Scriptures, and which all ought to hold, they readily permit both themselves and others to be ignorant of, to neglect and despise; and they deem it of little moment what each man believes concerning God and Christ, or disbelieves, provided he submits to the judgment of the Church with what they call implicit faith; nor are they greatly concerned though they should see the glow of God dishonored by open blasphemies, provided not a finger is raised against the primacy of the Apostolic See and the authority of holy mother Church. Why, then, do they war for the mass, purgatory, pilgrimage, and similar follies, with such fierceness and acerbity, that though they cannot prove one of them from the word of God, they deny godliness can be safe without faith in these things—faith drawn out, if I may so express it, to its utmost stretch? Why? Just because their belly is their God, and their kitchen their religion, and they believe that if these were away they would not only not be Christians, but not even men. For although some wallow in luxury, and others feed on slender crusts, still they all live by the same pot, which without that fuel might not only cool, but altogether freeze. He, accordingly, who is most anxious about his stomach, proves the fiercest champion of his faith. In short, the object on which all to a man are bent, is to keep their kingdom safe or their belly filled; not one gives even the smallest sign of sincere zeal.

Nevertheless, they cease not to assail our doctrine, and to accuse and defame it in what terms they may, in order to render it either hated or suspected. They call it new, and of recent birth; they carp at it as doubtful and uncertain; they bid us tell by what miracles it has been confirmed; they ask if it be fair to receive it against the consent of so many holy Fathers and the most ancient custom; they urge us to confess either that it is schismatical in giving battle to the Church, or that the Church must have been without life during the many centuries in which nothing of the kind was heard. Lastly, they say there is little need of argument, for its quality may be known by its fruits: namely, the large number of sects, the many seditious disturbances, and the great licentiousness, which it has produced. No doubt, it is a very easy matter for them, in presence of an ignorant and credulous multitude, to insult over an undefended cause; but were an opportunity of mutual discussion afforded, that acrimony which they now pour out upon us in frothy torrents, with as much license as impunity, would assuredly boil dry.

1 First, in calling it new, they are exceedingly injurious to God, whose sacred word deserved not to be charged with novelty. To them, indeed, I very little doubt it is new, as Christ is new, and the Gospel new; but those who are acquainted with the old saying of Paul, that Christ Jesus "died for our sins, and rose again for our justification" (Romans 4:25), will not detect any novelty in us. That it long lay buried and unknown is the guilty consequence of man's impiety; but now when, by the kindness of God, it is restored to us, it ought to resume its antiquity just as the returning citizen resumes his rights.

2 It is owing to the same ignorance that they hold it to be doubtful and uncertain; for this is the very thing of which the Lord complains by his prophet, "The ox knoweth his owner, and the ass his master's crib; but Israel doth not know, my people doth not consider" (Isaiah 1:3). But however

they may sport with its uncertainty, had they to seal their own doctrine with their blood, and at the expense of life, it would be seen what value they put upon it. Very different is our confidence—a confidence that is not appalled by the terrors of death, and therefore not even by the judgment—seat of God.

3 In demanding miracles from us, they act dishonestly. For we have not coined some new gospel, but retain the very one the truth of which is confirmed by all the miracles which Christ and the apostles ever wrought. But they have a peculiarity, which we have not—they can confirm their faith by constant miracles down to the present day! Way rather, they allege miracles, which might produce wavering in minds otherwise well disposed; they are so frivolous and ridiculous, so vain and false. But were they even exceedingly wonderful, they could have no effect against the truth of God, whose name ought to be hallowed always, and everywhere, whether by miracles, or by the natural course of events. The deception would perhaps be more specious if Scripture did not admonish us of the legitimate end and use of miracles. Mark tells us (Mark 16:20) that the signs which followed the preaching of the apostles were wrought in confirmation of it; so Luke also relates that the Lord "gave testimony to the word of his grace, and granted signs and wonders to be done" by the hands of the apostles (Acts 14:3). Very much to the same effect are those words of the apostle, that salvation by a preached gospel was confirmed, "The Lord bearing witness with signs and wonders, and with divers miracles" (Hebrews 2:4). Those things that we are told are seals of the gospel, shall we pervert to the subversion of the gospel? What was destined only to confirm the truth, shall we misapply to the confirmation of lies? The proper course, therefore, is, in the first instance, to ascertain and examine the doctrine, which is said by the Evangelist to precede; then after it, has been proved, but not until then, it may receive confirmation from miracles. But the mark of sound doctrine given by our Savior himself is its tendency to promote the glory not of men, but of God (John 7:18, 8:50). Our Savior having declared this to be test of doctrine, we are in error if we regard as miraculous, works, which are used for any other purpose than to magnify the name of God. And it becomes us to remember that Satan has his miracles, which, although they are tricks rather than true wonders, are still such as to delude the ignorant and unwary. Magicians and enchanters have always been famous for miracles, and miracles of an astonishing description have given support to idolatry: these, however, do not make us converts to the superstitions either of magicians or idolaters. In old times, too, the Donatists used their power of working miracles as a battering ram, with which they shook the simplicity of the common people. We now give to our opponents the answer, which Augustine then gave to the Donatists, "The Lord put us on our guard against those wonder—workers, when he foretold that false prophets would arise, who, by lying signs and divers wonders, would, if it were possible, deceive the very elect" (Matthew 24:24). Paul, too, gave warning that the reign of antichrist would be "with all power, and signs, and lying wonders" (2 Thessalonians 2:9).

But our opponents tell us that their miracles are wrought not by idols, not by sorcerers, not by false prophets, but by saints: as if we did not know it to be one of Satan's wiles to transform himself "into an angel of light" (2 Corinthians 11:14). The Egyptians, in whose neighborhood Jeremiah was buried, anciently sacrificed and paid other divine honors to him. Did they not make an idolatrous abuse of the holy prophet of God? And yet, in recompense for so venerating his tomb, they thought that they were cured of the bite of serpents. What, then, shall we say but that it has been, and always will be, a most just punishment of God, to send on those who do not receive the truth in the love of it, "strong delusion, that they should believe a lie?" (2 Thessalonians 2:11). We, then, have no lack of miracles, sure miracles, that cannot be gainsaid; but those to which our opponents lay claim are mere delusions of Satan, inasmuch as they draw off the people from the true worship of God to vanity.

4 It is slanderous to represent us as opposed to the Fathers (I mean the ancient writers of a purer age), as if the Fathers were supporters of their impiety. Were the contest to be decided by such authority (to speak in the most moderate terms), the better part of the victory would be ours. While there is much that is admirable and wise in the writings of those Fathers, and while in some things it has fared with them as with ordinary men; these pious sons, forsooth, with the peculiar acuteness of intellect, and judgment, and soul, which belongs to them, adore only their slips and errors, while those things which are well said they either overlook, or disguise, or corrupt; so that it may be truly said their only care has been to gather dross among gold. Then, with dishonest clamor, they assail us as enemies and despisers of the Fathers. So far are we from despising them, that if this were the proper place, it would give us no trouble to support the greater part of the doctrines, which we now hold by their suffrages. Still, in studying their writings, we have endeavored to remember (1 Corinthians 3:21-23), that all things are ours, to serve, not lord it over us, but that we axe Christ's only, and must obey him in all things without exception. He who does not draw this distinction will not have any fixed principles in religion; for those holy men were ignorant of many things, are often opposed to each other, and are sometimes at variance with themselves.

It is not without cause (remark our opponents) we are thus warned by Solomon, "Remove not the ancient landmarks which thy fathers have set" (Proverbs 22:28). But the same rule applies not to the measuring of fields and the obedience of faith. The rule applicable to the latter is, "Forget also thine own people, and thy father's house" (Psalm 45:10). But if they are so fond of allegory, why do they not understand the apostles, rather than any other class of Fathers, to be meant by those whose landmarks it is unlawful to remove? This is the interpretation of Jerome, whose words they have quoted in their canons. But as regards those to whom they apply the passage, if they wish the landmarks to be fixed, why do they, whenever it suits their purpose, so freely overleap them?

Among the Fathers there were two, the one of whom said, "Our God neither eats nor drinks, and therefore has no need of chalices and salvers;" and the other, "Sacred rites do not require gold, and things which are not bought with gold, please not by gold." They step beyond the boundary; therefore, when in sacred matters they are so much delighted with gold, driver, ivory, marble, gems, and silks, that unless everything is overlaid with costly show, or rather insane luxury, they think God is not duly worshipped.

It was a Father, who said, "He ate flesh freely on the day on which others abstained from it, because he was a Christian." They overleap the boundaries, therefore, when they doom to perdition every soul that, during Lent, shall have tasted flesh.

There were two Fathers, the one of whom said, "A monk not laboring with his own hands is no better than a violent man and a robber;" and the other, "Monks, however assiduous they may be in study, meditation, and prayer, must not live by others." This boundary, too, they transgressed, when they placed lazy gormandizing monks in dens and stews, to gorge themselves on other men's substance.

It was a Father, who said, "It is a horrid abomination to see in Christian temples a painted image either of Christ or of any saint." Nor was this pronounced by the voice era single individual; but an Ecclesiastical Council also decreed, "Let nothing that is worshipped be depicted on walls." Very far are they from keeping within these boundaries when they leave not a corner without images.

Another Father counseled, "That after performing the office of humanity to the dead in their burial, we should leave them at rest." These limits they burst through when they keep up a perpetual anxiety about the dead.

It is a Father, who testified, "That the substance of bread and wine in the Eucharist does not cease but remains, just as the nature and substance of man remains united to the Godhead in the Lord Jesus Christ." This boundary they pass in pretending that, as soon as the words of our Lord are pronounced, the substance of bread and wine ceases and is transubstantiated into body and blood.

They were Fathers, who, as they exhibited only one Eucharist to the whole Church, and kept back from it the profane and flagitious; so they, in the severest terms, censured all those who, being present, did not communicate How far have they removed these landmarks, in filling not churches only, but also private houses, with their masses, admitting all and sundry to be present, each the more willingly the more largely he pays, however wicked and impure he may be—not inviting anyone to faith in Christ and faithful communion in the sacraments, but rather vending their own work for the grace and merits of Christ!

There were two Fathers, the one of whom decided that those were to be excluded altogether from partaking of Christ's sacred supper, who, contented with communion in one kind, abstained from the other; while the other Father strongly contends that the blood of the Lord ought not to be denied to the Christian people, who, in confessing him, are enjoined to shed their own blood. These landmarks, also, they removed, when, by an unalterable law, they ordered the very thing, which the former Father punished with excommunication, and the latter condemned for a valid reason.

It was a Father, who pronounced it rashness in an obscure question, to decide in either way without clear and evident authority from Scripture. They forgot this landmark when they enacted so many constitutions, so many canons, and so many dogmatic decisions, without sanction from the word of God.

It was a Father, who reproved Montanus, among other heresies, for being the first who imposed laws of fasting. They have gone far beyond this landmark also in enjoining fasting under the strictest laws.

It was a Father, who denied that the ministers of the Church should be interdicted from marrying, and pronounced married life to be a state of chastity; and there were other Fathers, who assented to his decision. These boundaries they overstepped in rigidly binding their priests to celibacy.

It was a Father who thought that Christ only should be listened to, from its being said, "Hear him," and that regard is due not to what others before us have said or done, but only to what Christ, the head of all, has commanded. This landmark they neither observe themselves nor allow to be observed by others, while they subject themselves and others to any master whatever, rather than Christ.

There is a Father, who contends that the Church ought not to prefer herself to Christ, who always judges truly, whereas ecclesiastical judges, who are but men, are generally deceived. Having burst through this barrier also, they hesitate not to suspend the whole authority of Scripture on the judgment of the Church.

All the Fathers with one heart execrated, and with one mouth protested against, contaminating the word of God with subtleties of sophists, and involving it in the brawls of dialecticians. Do they keep within these limits when the sole occupation of their lives is to entwine and entangle the simplicity of Scripture with endless disputes, and worse than sophistical jargon? So much so, that were the Fathers to rise from their graves, and listen to the brawling art which bears the name of speculative theology, there is nothing they would suppose it less to be than a discussion of a religious nature.

But my discourse would far exceed its just limits were I to show, in detail, how petulantly those men shake off the yoke of the Fathers, while they wish to be thought their most obedient sons. Months, nay, years would fail me; and yet so deplorable and desperate is their effrontery, that they presume to chastise us for overstepping the ancient landmarks!

5 Then, again, it is to no purpose they call us to the bar of custom. To make everything yield to custom would be to do the greatest injustice. Were the judgments of mankind correct, custom would be regulated by the good. But it is often far otherwise in point of fact; for, whatever the many are seen to do, forthwith obtains the force of custom. But human affairs have scarcely ever been so happily constituted as that the better course pleased the greater number. Hence, the private vices of the multitude have generally resulted in public error, or rather that common consent in vice which these worthy men would have to be law. Anyone with eyes may perceive that it is not one flood of evils, which has deluged us; that many fatal plagues have invaded the globe; that all things rush headlong; so that either the affairs of men must be altogether despaired of, or we must not only resist, but boldly attack prevailing evils. The cure is prevented by no other cause than the length of time during which we have been accustomed to the disease. But be it so that public error must have a place in human society, still, in the kingdom of God, we must look and listen only to his eternal truth, against which no series of years, no custom, no conspiracy, can plead prescription. Thus Isaiah formerly taught the people of God, "Say ye not, A confederacy, to all to whom this people shall say, A confederacy;" i.e. do not unite with the people in an impious consent; "neither fear ye their fear, nor be afraid. Sanctify the Lord of hosts himself; and let him be your fear, and let him be your dread" (Isaiah 8:12). Now, therefore, let them, if they will, object to us both past ages and present examples; if we sanctify the Lord of hosts, we shall not be greatly afraid. Though many ages should have consented to like ungodliness, He is strong who taketh vengeance to the third and fourth generation; or the whole world should league together in the same iniquity. He taught experimentally what the end is of those who sin with the multitude, when He destroyed the whole human race with a flood, saving Noah with his little family, who, by putting his faith in Him alone, "condemned the world" (Hebrews 11:7). In short, depraved custom is just a kind of general pestilence in which men perish not the less that they fall in a crowd. It would be well, moreover, to ponder the observation of Cyprian: that those who sin in ignorance, though they cannot be entirely exculpated, seem, however, to be, in some sense, excusable; whereas those who obstinately reject the truth, when presented to them by the kindness of God, have no defense to offer.

6 Their dilemma does not push us so violently as to oblige us to confess, either that the Church was a considerable time without life, or that we have now a quarrel with the Church. The Church of Christ assuredly has lived, and will live, as long as Christ shall reign at the right hand of the Father. By his hand it is sustained, by his protection defended, by his mighty power preserved in safety. For what he once undertook he will undoubtedly perform, he will be with iris people always, "even to the end of the world" (Matthew 28:20). With the Church we wage no war, since, with one consent, in common with the whole body of the faithful, we worship and adore one

God, and Christ Jesus the Lord, as all the pious have always adored him. But they themselves err not a little from the truth in not recognizing any church but that which they behold with the bodily eye, and in endeavoring to circumscribe it by limits, within which it cannot be confined.

The hinges on which the controversy turns are these: first, in their contending that the form of the Church is always visible and apparent; and, secondly, in their placing this form in the see of the Church of Rome and its hierarchy. We, on the contrary, maintain, both that the Church may exist without any apparent form, and, moreover, that the form is not ascertained by that external splendor which they foolishly admire, but by a very different mark, namely, by the pure preaching of the word of God, and the due administration of the sacraments. They make an outcry whenever the Church cannot be pointed to with the finger. But how oft was it the fate of the Church among the Jews to be so defaced that no comeliness appeared? What do we suppose to have been the splendid form when Elijah complained that he was left alone? (1 Kings 19:14). How long after the advent of Christ, did it lie hid without form? How often since has it been so oppressed by wars, seditions, and heresies, that it was nowhere seen in splendor? Had they lived at that time, would they have believed there was any Church? But Elijah learned that there remained seven thousand men, who had not bowed the knee to Baal; nor ought we to doubt that Christ has always reigned on earth ever since he ascended to heaven. Had the faithful at that time required some discernible form, must they not have forthwith given way to despondency? And, indeed, Hilary accounted it a very great fault in his day that men were so possessed with a foolish admiration of Episcopal dignity as not to perceive the deadly hydra lurking under that mask. His words are, "One advice I give: Beware of Antichrist; for, unhappily, a love of walls has seized you; unhappily, the Church of God which you venerate exists in houses and buildings; unhappily, under these you find the name of peace. Is it doubtful that in these Antichrist will have his seat? Safer to me are mountains, and woods, and lakes, and dungeons, and whirlpools; since in these prophets, dwelling or immersed, did prophesy."

And what is it at the present day that the world venerates in its horned bishops, unless that it imagines those who are seen presiding over celebrated cities to be holy prelates of religion? Away, then, with this absurd mode of judging! Let us rather reverently admit that, as God alone knows who are his, so he may sometimes withdraw the external manifestation of his Church from the view of men. This, I allow, is a fearful punishment, which God sends on the earth; but if the wickedness of men so deserves, why do we strive to oppose the just vengeance of God? It was thus that God, in past ages, punished the ingratitude of men; for after they had refused to obey his truth, and had extinguished his light, he allowed them, when blinded by sense, both to be deluded by lying vanities and plunged in thick darkness, so that no face of a true Church appeared. Meanwhile, however, though his own people were dispersed and concealed amidst errors and darkness, he saved them from destruction. No wonder; for he knew how to preserve them even in the confusion of Babylon and the flame of the fiery furnace.

But as to the wish that the form of the Church should be ascertained by some kind of vain pomp, how perilous it is I will briefly indicate, rather than explain, that I may not exceed all bounds. What they say is, that the Pontiff, who holds the Apostolic See, and the priests who are anointed and consecrated by him, provided they have the insignia of fillets and miters, represent the Church, and ought to be considered as in the place of the Church, and therefore cannot err. Why so? Because they are pastors of the Church, and consecrated to the Lord. And were not Aaron and other prefects of Israel pastors? But Aaron and his sons, though already set apart to the priesthood, erred notwithstanding when they made the calf (Exodus 32:4). Why, according to this view, should not the four hundred prophets who lied to Ahab represent the Church? (1 Kings 22:11), etc.). The Church, however, stood on the side of Micaiah. He was alone, indeed, and despised, but from his mouth, the truth proceeded. Did not the prophets also exhibit both the name and face of the Church, when, with one accord, they rose up against Jeremiah, and with menaces boasted of it as a thing impossible that the law should perish from the priest, or counsel from the wise, or the word from the prophet? (Jeremiah 19:18). In opposition to the whole body of the prophets, Jeremiah is sent alone to declare from the Lord (Jeremiah 4:9), that a time would come when the law would perish from the priest, counsel from the wise, and the word from the prophet. Was not like splendor displayed in that council when the chief priests, scribes, and Pharisees assembled to consult how they might put Jesus to death? Let them go, then, and cling to the external mask, while they make Christ and all the prophets of God schismatics, and, on the other hand, make Satan's ministers the organs of the Holy Spirit!

But if they are sincere, let them answer me in good faith, —in what place, and among whom, do they think the Church resided, after the Council of Basle degraded and deposed Eugenius from the popedom, and substituted Amadeus in his place? Do their utmost, they cannot deny that that Council was legitimate as far as regards external forms, and was summoned not only by one Pontiff, but by two. Eugenius, with the whole herd of cardinals and bishops who had joined him in plotting the dissolution of the Council, was there condemned of contumacy, rebellion, and schism. Afterwards, however, aided by the favor of princes, he got back his popedom safe. The election of Amadeus, duly made by the authority of a general holy synod, went to smoke; only he himself was appeased with a cardinal's cap, like a piece of offal thrown to a barking dog. Out of the lap of these rebellious and contumacious schismatics proceeded all future popes, cardinals, bishops, abbots, and presbyters. Here they are caught, and cannot escape. For, on which party will they bestow the name of Church? Will they deny it to have been a general Council, though it lacked nothing as regards external majesty, having been solemnly called by two bulls, consecrated by the legate of the Roman See as its president, constituted regularly in all respects, and continuing in possession of all its honors to the last? Will they admit that Eugenius, and his whole train, through whom they have all been consecrated, were schismatic? Let them, then, either define the form of the Church differently, or, however numerous they are, we will hold them all to be schismatics in having knowingly and willingly received ordination from heretics. But had it never been discovered before that the Church is not tied to external pomp, we are furnished with a lengthened proof in their own conduct, in proudly vending themselves to the world under the specious title of Church, notwithstanding that they are the deadly pests of the Church. I speak not of their manners and of those tragic atrocities with which their whole life teems, since it is said that they are Pharisees who should be heard, not imitated. By devoting some portion of your leisure to our writings, you will see, not obscurely, that their doctrine—the very doctrine to which they say it is owing that they are the Church—is a deadly murderer of souls, the firebrand, ruin, and destruction of the Church.

7 Lastly, they are far from candid when they invidiously number up the disturbances, tumults, and disputes, which the preaching of our doctrine has brought in its train, and the fruits which, in many instances, it now produces; for the doctrine itself is undeservedly charged with evils which ought to be ascribed to the malice of Satan. It is one of the characteristics of the divine word, that whenever it appears, Satan ceases to slumber and sleep. This is the surest and most unerring test for distinguishing it from false doctrines, which readily betray themselves, while they are received by all with willing ears, and welcomed by an applauding world. Accordingly, for several ages, during which all things were immersed in profound darkness, almost all mankind were mere jest and sport to the god of this world, who, like any Sardanapalus, idled and luxuriated undisturbed. For what else could he do but laugh and sport while in tranquil and undisputed possession of his kingdom? But when light beaming from above somewhat dissipated the darkness—when the strong man arose and aimed a blow at his kingdom—then, indeed, he began to shake off his wonted torpor, and rush to arms. And first he stirred up the hands of men, that by them he might violently suppress the dawning truth; but when this availed him not, he turned to snares, exciting dissensions and disputes about doctrine by means of his Catabaptists, and other portentous miscreants, that he might thus obscure, and, at length, extinguish the truth. And now be persists in assailing it with both engines, endeavoring to pluck up the true seed by the violent hand of man, and striving, as much as in him lies, to choke it with his tares, that it may not grow and bear knit. But it will be in vain, if we listen to the admonition of the Lord, who long ago disclosed his wiles, that we might not be taken unawares, and armed us with full protection against all his machinations. But how malignant to throw upon the word of God itself the blame either of the seditions which wicked men and rebels, or of the sects which impostors stir up against it! The example, however, is not new. Elijah

was asked if it had been he, who troubled Israel. Christ was seditious, according to the Jews; and the apostles were charged with the crime of popular commotion. What else do those who, in the present day, impute to us all the disturbances, tumults, and contentions, which break out against us? Elijah, however, has taught us our answer (1 Kings 18:17, 18). It is not we who disseminate errors or stir up tumults, but they who resist the mighty power of God.

But while this single answer is sufficient to rebut the rash charges of these men, it is necessary, on the other hand, to consult for the weakness of those who take the alarm at such scandals, and not infrequently waver in perplexity. But that they may not fall away in this perplexity, and forfeit their good degree, let them know that the apostles in their day experienced the very things, which now befall us. There were then unlearned and unstable men who, as Peter tells us (2 Peter 3:16), wrested the inspired writings of Paul to their own destruction. There were despisers of God, who, when they heard that sin abounded in order that grace might more abound, immediately inferred, "We will continue in sin that grace may abound" (Romans 6:1); when they heard that believers were not under the law, but under grace, forthwith sung out, "We will sin because we are not under the law, but under grace" (Romans 6:15). There were some who charged the apostle with being the minister of sin. Many false prophets entered in privately to pull down the churches, which he had reared. Some preached the gospel through envy and strife, not sincerely (Philippians 1:15)—maliciously even—thinking to add affliction to his bonds. Elsewhere the gospel made little progress. All sought their own, not the things which were Jesus Christ's. Others went back like the dog to his vomit, or the sow that was washed to her wallowing in the mire. Great numbers perverted their spiritual freedom to carnal licentiousness. False brethren crept in to the imminent danger of the faithful. Among the brethren themselves various quarrels arose. What, then, were the apostles to do? Were they either to dissemble for the time, or rather lay aside and abandon that gospel which they saw to be the seed—bed of so many strifes, the source of so many perils, the occasion of so many scandals? In straits of this kind, they remembered that "Christ was a stone of stumbling, and a rock of offense," "set up for the fall and rising again of many," and "for a sign to be spoken against" (Luke 2:34); and, armed with this assurance, they proceeded boldly through all perils from tumults and scandals. It becomes us to be supported by the same consideration, since Paul declares that it is a never failing characteristic of the gospel to be a "savor of death unto death in them that perish" (2 Corinthians 2:16), although rather destined to us for the purpose of being a savor of life unto life, and the power of God for the salvation of believers. This we should certainly experience it to be, did we not by our ingratitude corrupt this unspeakable gift of God, and turn to our destruction what ought to be our only saving defense.

But to return, Sire. Be not moved by the absurd insinuations with which our adversaries are striving to frighten you into the belief that nothing else is wished and aimed at by this new gospel (for so they term it), than opportunity for sedition and impunity for all kinds of vice. Our Go is not the author of division, but of peace; and the Son of God, who came to destroy the works of the devil, is not the minister of sin. We, too, are undeservedly charged with desires of a kind for which we have never given even the smallest suspicion. We, forsooth, meditate the subversion of kingdoms; we, whose voice was never heard in faction, and whose life, while passed under you, is known to have been always quiet and simple; even now, when exiled from our home, we nevertheless cease not to pray for all prosperity to your person and your kingdom. We, forsooth, are aiming after an unchecked indulgence in vice, in whose manners, though there is much to be blamed, there is nothing which deserves such an imputation; nor (thank God) have we profited so little in the gospel that our life may not be to these slanderers an example of chastity, kindness, pity, temperance, patience, moderation, or any other virtue. It is plain, indeed, that we fear God sincerely, and worship him in truth, since, whether by life or by death, we desire his name to be hallowed; and hatred herself has been forced to bear testimony to the innocence and civil integrity of some of our people on whom death was inflicted for the very thing which deserved the highest praise. But if any, under pretext of the gospel, excite tumults (none such have as yet been detected in your realm), if any use the liberty of the grace of God as a cloak for licentiousness (I know of numbers who do), there are laws and legal punishments by which they may be punished up to the measure of their deserts—only, in the mean time, let not the gospel of God be evil spoken of because of the iniquities of evil men.

Sire, That you may not lend too credulous an ear to the accusations of our enemies, their virulent injustice has been set before you at sufficient length; I fear even more than sufficient, since this preface has grown almost to the bulk of a full apology. My object, however, was not to frame a defense, but only with a view to the hearing of our cause, to mollify your mind, now indeed turned away and estranged from us—I add, even inflamed against us—but whose good will, we are confident, we should regain, would you but once, with calmness and composure, read this our Confession, which we desire your Majesty to accept instead of a defense. But if the whispers of the malevolent so possess your ear, that the accused are to have no opportunity of pleading their cause; if those vindictive furies, with your connivance, are always to rage with bonds, scourging, torture, maiming, and burnings, we, indeed, like sheep doomed to slaughter, shall be reduced to every extremity; yet so that, in our patience, we will possess our souls, and wait for the strong hand of the Lord, which, doubtless, will appear in its own time, and show itself armed, both to rescue the poor from affliction, and also take vengeance on the despisers, who are now exulting so securely.

Most illustrious King, may the Lord, the King of kings, establish your throne in righteousness, and your scepter in equity.

Epistle to the Reader

[Prefixed to the last edition, revised by the author.]

In the First Edition of this work, having not the least expectation of the success which God, in his boundless goodness, has been pleased to give it, I had, for the greater part, performed my task in a perfunctory manner (as is usual in trivial undertakings); but when I understood that it had been received, by almost all the pious with a favor which I had never dared to ask, far less to hope for, the more I was sincerely conscious that the reception was beyond my deserts, the greater I thought my ingratitude would be, if, to the very kind wishes which had been expressed towards me, and which seemed of their own accord to invite me to diligence, I did not endeavor to respond, at least according to my humble ability. This I attempted not only in the Second Edition, but in every subsequent one the work has received some improvement. But though I do not regret the labor previously expended, I never felt satisfied until the work was arranged in the order in which it now appears. Now I trust it will approve itself to the Judgment of all my readers. As a clear proof of the diligence with which I have labored to perform this service to the Church of God, I may be permitted to mention, that last winter, when I thought I was dying of quartan ague, the more the disorder increased, the less I spared myself, in order that I might leave this book behind me, and thus make some return to the pious for their kind urgency. I could have wished to give it sooner, but it is soon enough if good enough. I shall think it has appeared in good time when I see it more productive of benefit than formerly to the Church of God. This is my only wish.

And truly it would fare ill with me if, not contented with the approbation of God alone, I were unable to despise the foolish and perverse censures of ignorant as well as the malicious and unjust censures of ungodly men. For although, by the blessing of God, my most ardent desire has been to advance his kingdoms and promote the public good, —although I feel perfectly conscious, and take God and his angels to witness, that ever since I began to discharge the office of teacher in the Church, my only object has been to do good to the Church, by maintaining the pure doctrine of godliness, yet I believe there never was a man more assailed, stung, and torn by calumny [as well by the declared enemies of the truth of God, as by many worthless persons who have crept into his Church—as well by monks who have brought forth their frocks from their cloisters to spread infection wherever they come, as by other miscreants not better than they]. After this letter to the reader was in the press, I had undoubted information that, at Augsburg, where the Imperial Diet was held, a rumor of my defection to the papacy was circulated, and entertained in the courts of the princes more readily than might have been expected. This, forsooth, is the return made me by those who certainly are aware of numerous proofs of my constancy—proofs which, while they rebut the foul charge, ought to have defended me against it, with all humane and impartial judges. But the devil, with all his crew, is mistaken if he imagines that, by assailing me with vile falsehoods, he can either cool my zeal, or diminish my exertions. I trust that God, in his infinite goodness, will enable me to persevere with unruffled patience in the course of his holy vocation. Of this, I give the pious reader a new proof in the present edition.

I may further observe, that my object in this work has been, so to prepare and train candidates for the sacred office, for the study of the sacred volume, that they may both have an easy introduction to it, and be able to prosecute it with unfaltering step; for, if I mistake not, I have given a summary of religion in all its parts, and digested it in an order which will make it easy for anyone, who rightly comprehends it, to ascertain both what he ought chiefly to look for in Scripture, and also to what head he ought to refer whatever is contained in it. Having thus paved the way, as it will be unnecessary, in any Commentaries on Scripture which I may afterwards publish, to enter into long discussions of doctrinal points, and enlarge on commonplaces, I will compress them into narrow compass. In this way much trouble and fatigue will be spared to the pious reader, provided he comes prepared with a knowledge of the present work as an indispensable prerequisite. The system here followed being set forth as in a mirror in all my Commentaries, I think it better to let it speak for itself than to give any verbal explanation of it.

Farewell, kind reader: if you derive any benefit from my labors, aid me with your prayers to our heavenly Father.

Geneva, *1st August* 1559.

The zeal of those whose cause I undertook,
Has swelled a short defense into a book.

"I profess to be one of those who, by profiting, write, and by writing profit." —*Augustine*, Epist. 7.

Subject of the Present Work

[Prefixed to the French edition, published at Geneva in 1545.]

In order that my Readers may be the better able to profit by the present work, I am desirous briefly to point out the advantage, which they may derive from it. For by so doing I will show them the end at which they ought to aim, and to which they ought to give their attention in reading it.

Although the Holy Scriptures contain a perfect doctrine, to which nothing can be added—our Lord having been pleased therein to unfold the infinite treasures of his wisdom—still every person, not intimately acquainted with them, stands in need of some guidance and direction, as to what he ought to look for in them, that he may not wander up and down, but pursue a certain path, and so attain the end to which the Holy Spirit invites him.

Hence, it is the duty of those who have received from God more light than others to assist the simple in this matter, and lend them their hand to guide and assist them in finding the sum of what God has been pleased to teach us in his word. Now, this cannot be better done in writing than by treating in succession of the principal matters, which are comprised in Christian philosophy. For he who understands these will be prepared to make more progress in the school of God in one day than any other person in three months, inasmuch as he, in a great measure, knows to what he should refer each sentence, and has a rule by which to test whatever is presented to him.

Seeing, then, how necessary it was in this manner to aid those who desire to be instructed in the doctrine of salvation, I have endeavored, according to the ability which God has given me, to employ myself in so doing, and with this view have composed the present book. And first I wrote it in Latin, that it might be serviceable to all studious persons, from whatever nation they might be; afterwards, desiring to communicate any fruit, which might be in it to my French countrymen, I translated it into our own tongue. I dare not bear too strong a testimony in its favor, and declare how profitable the reading of it will be, lest I should seem to prize my own work too highly. However I may promise this much, that it will be a kind of key opening up to all the children of God a right and ready access to the understanding of the sacred volume. Wherefore, should our Lord give me henceforth means and opportunity of composing some *Commentaries*, I will use the greatest possible brevity, as there will be no occasion to make long digressions, seeing that I have in a manner deduced at length all the articles which pertain to Christianity.

And since we are bound to acknowledge that all truth and sound doctrine proceed from God, I will venture boldly to declare what I think of this work, acknowledging it to be God's work rather than mine. To him, indeed, the praise due to it must be ascribed. My opinion of the work then is this: I exhort all, who reverence the word of the Lord, to read it, and diligently imprint it on their memory, if they would, in the first place, have a summary of Christian doctrine, and, in the second place, an introduction to the profitable reading both of the Old and New Testament. When they shall have done so, they will know by experience that I have not wished to impose upon them with words. Should anyone be unable to comprehend all that is contained in it, he must not, however, give it up in despair; but continue always to read on, hoping that one passage will give him a more familiar exposition of another. Above all things, I would recommend that recourse be had to Scripture in considering the proofs, which I adduce from it.

Method and Arrangement, or Subject of the Whole Work

[From *An Epitome of the Institutions*, by Gaspar Olevian.]

The subject handled by the author of these Christian Institutes is twofold: the former, the knowledge of God, which leads to a blessed immortality; and the latter (which is subordinate to the former), the knowledge of ourselves. With this view, the author simply adopts the arrangement of the Apostles' Creed, as that with which all Christians are most familiar. For as the Creed consists of four parts, the first relating to God the Father, the second to the Son, the third to the Holy Spirit, and the fourth to the Church, so the author, in fulfillment of his task, divides his Institutes into four parts, corresponding to those of the Creed. Each of these parts it will now be proper to explain separately.

Book First

The first article of the Apostles' Creed is concerning *God the Father*, the creation, preservation, and government of the universe, as implied in his omnipotence. Accordingly, the First Book of the Institutes treats of the knowledge of God, considered as the Creator, Preserver, and Governor of the world and of everything contained in it. It shows both wherein the true knowledge of the Creator consists, and what the end of this knowledge is, chapters 1 and 2; that it is not learned at school, but that everyone is self-taught it from the womb, chapter 3. Such, however, is man's depravity, that he stifles and corrupts this knowledge, partly by ignorance, partly by wicked design; and hence does not by means of it either glorify God as he ought, or attain to happiness, chapter 4. This inward knowledge is aided from without, namely by the creatures in which, as in a mirror, the perfections of God may be contemplated. But man does not properly avail himself of this assistance, and hence to those to whom God is pleased to make himself more intimately known for salvation, he communicates his written word. This leads to a consideration of the Holy Scriptures, in which God has revealed that not the Father only, but along with the Father, the Son, and Holy Spirit, is that Creator of heaven and earth, whom, in consequence of our innate depravity we were unable, either from innate natural knowledge, or the beautiful mirror of the world, to know so as to glorify. Here the author treats of the manifestation of God in Scripture; and in connection with it, of the one divine essence in three persons. But, lest man should lay the blame of his voluntary blindness on God, the author shows in what state man was created at first, introducing dissertations on the image of God, free will, and original righteousness. The subject of Creation being thus disposed of, the preservation and government of the world is considered in the three last chapters, which contain a very full discussion of the doctrine of Divine Providence.

Book Second

As man, by sinning, forfeited the privileges conferred on him at his creation, recourse must be had to Christ. Accordingly, the next article in the Creed is, *And in Jesus Christ his only Son, etc.* In like manner, the Second Book of the Institutes treats of the knowledge of God considered as a Redeemer in Christ, and showing man his falls conducts him to Christ the Mediator. Here the subject of original sin is considered, and it is shown that man has no means within himself, by which he can escape from guilt, and the impending curse: that, on the contrary, until he is reconciled and renewed, everything that proceeds from him is of the nature of sin. This subject is considered as far as the sixth chapter. Man being thus utterly undone in himself, and incapable of working out his own cure by thinking a good thought, or doing what is acceptable to God, must seek redemption without himself—viz. in Christ. The end, for which the Law was given, was not to secure worshipers for itself, but to conduct them unto Christ. This leads to an exposition of the Moral Law. Christ was known to the Jews under the Law as the author of salvation, but is more fully revealed under the Gospel in which he was manifested to the world. Hence, arises the doctrine concerning the similarity and difference of the two Testaments, the Old and the New, the Law and the Gospel. These topics occupy as far as the 12th chapter. It is next shown that, in order to secure a complete salvation, it was necessary that the eternal Son of God should become man, and assume a true human nature. It is also shown in what way these two natures constitute one person. In order to purchase a full salvation by his own merits, and effectually apply it, Christ was appointed to the offices of Prophet, Priest, and King. The mode in which Christ performs these offices is considered, and also whether in point of fact he did accomplish the work of redemption. Here an exposition is given of the articles relating to Christ's death, resurrection, and ascension into heaven. In conclusion, it is proved that Christ is rightly and properly said to have merited divine grace and salvation for us.

General Index of Chapters

BOOK FIRST

OF THE KNOWLEDGE OF GOD THE CREATOR
Eighteen Chapters

The Testimony of the Spirit necessary to give full authority to Scripture. The impiety of pretending that the Credibility of Scripture depends on the Judgment of the Church.

BOOK SECOND

OF THE KNOWLEDGE OF GOD THE REDEEMER, IN CHRIST, AS FIRST MANIFESTED TO THE FATHERS UNDER THE LAW, AND THEREAFTER TO US UNDER THE GOSPEL
Seventeen Chapters

Institutes of the Christian Religion

Book First

Book First

OF THE KNOWLEDGE OF
GOD THE CREATOR

ARGUMENT

The First Book treats of the knowledge of God the Creator. But as it is in the creation of man that the divine perfections are best displayed, so man also is made the subject of discourse. Thus, the whole book divides itself into two principal heads—the former relating to the knowledge of God, and the latter to the knowledge of man. In the first chapter, these are considered jointly; and in each of the following chapters, separately: occasionally, however, intermingled with other matters which refer to one or other of the heads; *e.g.*, the discussions concerning Scripture and images, falling under the former head, and the other three concerning the creation of the world, the holy angels and devils, falling under the latter. The last point discussed—viz. the method of the divine government, relates to both.

With regard to the former head—viz. the knowledge of God, it is shown, in the first place, what the kind of knowledge is which God requires, Chapter 2. And, in the second place (Chapters 3-9), where this knowledge must be sought, namely, not in man; because, although naturally implanted in the human mind, it is stifled, partly by ignorance, partly by evil intent, Chapters 3 and 4; not in the frame of the world: because, although it shines most clearly there, we are so stupid that these manifestations, however perspicuous, pass away without any beneficial result, Chapter 5; but in Scripture (Chapter 6), which is treated of, Chapters 7-9. In the third place, it is shown what the character of God is, Chapter 10. In the fourth place, how impious it is to give a visible form to God (here images, the worship of them, and its origin, are considered), Chapter 11. In the fifth place, it is shown that God is to be solely and wholly worshipped, Chapter 12. Lastly, Chapter 13 treats of the unity of the Divine essence, and the distinction of three persons.

With regard to the latter head—viz. the knowledge of man, first, Chapter 14 treats of the creation of the world, and of good and bad angels (these all having reference to man). And then Chapter 15, taking up the subject of man himself, examines his nature and his powers.

The better to illustrate the nature both of God and man, the three remaining Chapters—viz. 16-18, proceed to treat of the general government of the world, and particularly of human actions, in opposition to fortune and fate, explaining both the doctrine and its use. In conclusion, it is shown, that though God employs the instrumentality of the wicked; he is pure from sin and from taint of every kind.

Chapter 1

THE KNOWLEDGE OF GOD AND OF OURSELVES MUTUALLY CONNECTED. NATURE OF THE CONNECTION.

Sections

1. The sum of true wisdom—viz. the knowledge of God and of ourselves. Effects of the latter.

2. Effects of the knowledge of God, in humbling our pride, unveiling our hypocrisy, demonstrating the absolute perfections of God, and our own utter helplessness.

3. Effects of the knowledge of God illustrated by the examples, A. of holy patriarchs; B. of holy angels; C. of the sun and moon.

1 The sum of true wisdom—viz. the knowledge of God and of ourselves. Effects of the latter.

Our wisdom, in so far as it ought to be deemed true and solid Wisdom, consists almost entirely of two parts: the knowledge of God and of ourselves. But as these are connected together by many ties, it is not easy to determine which of the two precedes and gives birth to the other. For, in the first place, no man can survey himself without forthwith turning his thoughts towards the God in whom he lives and moves; because it is perfectly obvious, that the endowments which we possess cannot possibly be from ourselves; nay, that our very being is nothing else than subsistence in God alone. In the second place, those blessings, which unceasingly distil to us from heaven, are like streams conducting us to the fountain. Here, again, the infinitude of good, which resides in God, becomes more apparent from our poverty. In particular, the miserable ruin into which the revolt of the first man has plunged us, compels us to turn our eyes upwards; not only that while hungry and famishing we may thence ask what we want, but being aroused by fear may learn humility. For as there exists in man something like a world of misery, and ever since we were stripped of the divine attire our naked shame discloses an immense series of disgraceful properties every man, being stung by the consciousness of his own unhappiness, in this way necessarily obtains at least some knowledge of God. Thus, our feeling of ignorance, vanity, want, weakness, in short, depravity and corruption, reminds us that in the Lord and none but He, dwell the true light of wisdom, solid virtue, exuberant goodness. We are accordingly urged by our own evil things to consider the good things of God; and, indeed, we cannot aspire to Him in earnest until we have begun to be displeased with ourselves. For what man is not disposed to rest in himself? Who, in fact, does not thus rest, so long as he is unknown to himself; that is, so long as he is contented with his own endowments, and unconscious or unmindful of his misery? Every person, therefore, on coming to the knowledge of himself, is not only urged to seek God, but is also led as by the hand to find him.

2 Effects of the knowledge of God, in humbling our pride, unveiling our hypocrisy, demonstrating the absolute perfections of God, and our own utter helplessness.

On the other hand, it is evident that man never attains to a true self-knowledge until he have previously contemplated the face of God, and come down after such contemplation to look into himself. For (such is our innate pride) we always seem to ourselves just, and upright, and wise, and holy, until we are convinced, by clear evidence, of our injustice, vileness, folly, and impurity. Convinced, however, we are not, if we look to ourselves only, and not to the Lord also —He being the only standard by the application of which this conviction can be produced. For, since we are all naturally prone to hypocrisy, any empty semblance of righteousness is quite enough to satisfy us instead of righteousness itself. And since nothing appears within us or around us that is not tainted with very great impurity, so long as we keep our mind within the confines of human pollution, anything which is in some small degree less defiled delights us as if it were most pure just as an eye, to which nothing but black had been previously presented, deems an object of a whitish, or even of a brownish hue, to be perfectly white. Nay, the bodily sense may furnish a still stronger illustration of the extent to which we are deluded in estimating the powers of the mind. If, at mid-day, we either look down to the ground, or on the surrounding objects which lie open to our view, we think ourselves endued with a very strong and piercing eyesight; but when we look up to the sun, and gaze at it unveiled, the sight which did excellently well for the earth is instantly so dazzled and confounded by the refulgence, as to oblige us to confess that our acuteness in discerning terrestrial objects is mere dimness when applied to the sun. Thus, too, it happens in estimating our spiritual qualities. So long as we do not look beyond the earth, we are quite pleased with our own righteousness, wisdom, and virtue; we address ourselves in the most flattering terms, and seem only less than demigods. But should we once begin to raise our thoughts to God, and reflect what kind of Being he is, and how absolute the perfection of that righteousness, and wisdom, and virtue, to which, as a standard, we are bound to be conformed, what formerly delighted us by its false show of righteousness will become polluted with the greatest iniquity; what strangely imposed upon us under the name of wisdom will disgust by its extreme folly; and what presented the appearance of virtuous energy will be condemned as the most miserable impotence. So far are those qualities in us, which seem most perfect, from corresponding to the divine purity.

3 Effects of the knowledge of God illustrated by the examples, A. of holy patriarchs; B. of holy angels; C. of the sun and moon.

Hence, that dread and amazement with which as Scripture uniformly relates, holy men were struck and overwhelmed whenever they beheld the presence of God. When we see those who previously stood firm and secure so quaking with terror, that the fear of death takes hold of them, nay, they are, in a manner, swallowed up and annihilated, the inference to be drawn is that men are never duly touched and impressed with a conviction of their insignificance, until they have contrasted themselves with the majesty of God. Frequent examples of this consternation occur both in the Book of Judges and the Prophetical Writings; so much so, that it was a common expression among the people of God, "We shall die, for we have seen the Lord." Hence, the Book of Job, also, in humbling men under a conviction of their folly, feebleness, and pollution, always derives its chief argument from descriptions of the Divine wisdom, virtue, and purity. Nor without cause: for we see Abraham the readier to acknowledge himself but dust and ashes the nearer he approaches to behold the glory of the Lord, and Elijah unable to wait with unveiled face for His approach; so dreadful is the sight. And what can man do, man who is but rottenness and a worm, when even the Cherubim themselves must veil their faces in very terror? To this, undoubtedly, the Prophet Isaiah refers, when he says (Isaiah 24:23), "The moon shall be confounded, and the sun ashamed, when the Lord of Hosts shall reign;" i.e., when he shall exhibit his refulgence, and give a nearer view of it, the brightest objects will, in comparison, be covered with darkness.

Although the knowledge of God and the knowledge of ourselves are bound together by a mutual tie, due arrangement requires that we treat of the former in the first place, and then descend to the latter.

Chapter 2

WHAT IT IS TO KNOW GOD. TENDENCY OF THIS KNOWLEDGE.

Sections

1. The knowledge of God the Creator defined. The substance of this knowledge, and the use to be made of it.

2. Further illustration of the use, together with a necessary reproof of vain curiosity, and refutation of the Epicureans. The character of God as it appears to the pious mind, contrasted with the absurd views of the Epicureans. Religion defined.

1 **The knowledge of God the Creator defined. The substance of this knowledge, and the use to be made of it.**

By the knowledge of God, I understand that by which we not only conceive that there is some God, but also apprehend what it is for our interest, and conducive to his glory, what, in short, it is befitting to know concerning him. For, properly speaking, we cannot say that God is known where there is no religion or piety. I am not now referring to that species of knowledge by which men, in themselves lost and under curse, apprehend God as a Redeemer in Christ the Mediator. I speak only of that simple and primitive knowledge, to which the mere course of nature would have conducted us, had Adam stood upright. For although no man will now, in the present ruin of the human race, perceive God to be either a father, or the author of salvation, or propitious in any respect, until Christ interpose to make our peace; still it is one thing to perceive that God our Maker supports us by his power, rules us by his providence, fosters us by his goodness, and visits us with all kinds of blessings, and another thing to embrace the grace of reconciliation offered to us in Christ. Since, then, the Lord first appears, as well in the creation of the world as in the general doctrine of Scripture, simply as a Creator, and afterwards as a Redeemer in Christ,—a twofold knowledge of him hence arises: of these the former is now to be considered, the latter will afterwards follow in its order. But although our mind cannot conceive of God, without rendering some worship to him, it will not, however, be sufficient simply to hold that he is the only being whom all ought to worship and adore, unless we are also persuaded that he is the fountain of all goodness, and that we must seek everything in him, and in none but him. My meaning is: we must be persuaded not only that as he once formed the world, so he sustains it by his boundless power, governs it by his wisdom, preserves it by his goodness, in particular, rules the human race with justice and Judgment, bears with them in mercy, shields them by his protection; but also that not a particle of light, or wisdom, or justice, or power, or rectitude, or genuine truth, will anywhere be found, which does not flow from him, and of which he is not the cause; in this way we must learn to expect and ask all things from him, and thankfully ascribe to him whatever we receive. For this sense of the divine perfections is the proper master to teach us piety, out of which religion springs. By piety, I mean that union of reverence and love to God, which the knowledge of his benefits inspires. For, until men feel that they owe everything to God, that they are cherished by his paternal care, and that he is the author of all their blessings, so that nothing is to be looked for away from him, they will never submit to him in voluntary obedience; nay, unless they place their entire happiness in him, they will never yield up their whole selves to him in truth and sincerity.

2 Further illustration of the use, together with a necessary reproof of vain curiosity, and refutation of the Epicureans. The character of God as it appears to the pious mind, contrasted with the absurd views of the Epicureans. Religion defined.

Those, therefore, who, in considering this question, propose to inquire what the essence of God is, only delude us with frigid speculations, —it being much more our interest to know what kind of being God is, and what things are agreeable to his nature. For, of what use is it to join Epicures in acknowledging some God who has cast off the care of the world, and only delights himself in ease? What avails it, in short, to know a God with whom we have nothing to do? The effect of our knowledge rather ought to be, *first*, to teach us reverence and fear; and, *secondly*, to induce us, under its guidance and teaching, to ask every good thing from him, and, when it is received, ascribe it to him. For how can the idea of God enter your mind without instantly giving rise to the thought, that since you are his workmanship, you are bound, by the very law of creation, to submit to his authority? —that your life is due to him?—that whatever you do ought to have reference to him? If so, it undoubtedly follows that your life is sadly corrupted, if it is not framed in obedience to him, since his will ought to be the law of our lives. On the other hand, your idea of his nature is not clear unless you acknowledge him to be the origin and fountain of all goodness. Hence, would arise both confidence in him, and a desire of cleaving to him, did not the depravity of the human mind lead it away from the proper course of investigation.

For, first of all, the pious mind does not devise for itself any kind of God, but looks alone to the one true God; nor does it feign for him any character it pleases, but is contented to have him in the character in which he manifests himself always guarding, with the utmost diligences against transgressing his will, and wandering, with daring presumptions from the right path. He by whom God is thus known perceiving how he governs all things, confides in him as his guardian and protector, and casts himself entirely upon his faithfulness, —perceiving him to be the source of every blessing, if he is in any strait or feels any want, he instantly recurs to his protection and trusts to his aid, —persuaded that he is good and merciful, he reclines upon him with sure confidence, and doubts not that, in the divine clemency, a remedy will be provided for his every time of need,— acknowledging him as his Father and his Lords he considers himself bound to have respect to his authority in all things, to reverence his majesty aim at the advancement of his glory, and obey his commands,—regarding him as a just judge, armed with severity to punish crimes, he keeps the Judgment-seat always in his view. Standing in awe of it, he curbs himself, and fears to provoke his anger. Nevertheless, he is not so terrified by an apprehension of Judgment as to wish he could withdraw himself, even if the means of escape lay before him; nay, he embraces him not less as the avenger of wickedness than as the rewarder of the righteous; because he perceives that it equally appertains to his glory to store up punishment for the one, and eternal life for the other. Besides, it is not the mere fear of punishment that restrains him from sin. Loving and revering God as his father, honoring and obeying him as his master, although there were no hell, he would revolt at the very idea of offending him.

Such is pure and genuine religion, namely, confidence in God coupled with serious fear—fear, which both includes in it willing reverence, and brings along with it such legitimate worship as is prescribed by the law. And it ought to be more carefully considered that all men promiscuously do homage to God, but very few truly reverence him. On all hands, there is abundance of ostentatious ceremonies, but sincerity of heart is rare.

Chapter 3

THE KNOWLEDGE OF GOD NATURALLY IMPLANTED IN THE HUMAN MIND.

Sections

1. The knowledge of God being manifested to all makes the reprobate without excuse. Universal belief and acknowledgement of the existence of God.

2. Objection—that religion and the belief of a Deity are the inventions of crafty politicians. Refutation of the objection. This universal belief confirmed by the examples of wicked men and Atheists.

3. Confirmed also by the vain endeavors of the wicked to banish all fear of God from their minds. Conclusion, that the knowledge of God is naturally implanted in the human mind.

1 **The knowledge of God being manifested to all makes the reprobate without excuse. Universal belief and acknowledgement of the existence of God.**

That there exists in the human minds and indeed by natural instinct, some sense of Deity, we hold to be beyond dispute, since God himself, to prevent any man from pretending ignorance, has endued all men with some idea of his Godhead, the memory of which he constantly renews and occasionally enlarges, that all to a man being aware that there is a God, and that he is their Maker, may be condemned by their own conscience when they neither worship him nor consecrate their lives to his service. Certainly, if there is any quarter where it may be supposed that God is unknown, the most likely for such an instance to exist is among the dullest tribes farthest removed from civilization. But, as a heathen tells us, there is no nation so barbarous, no race so brutish, as not to be imbued with the conviction that there is a God. Even those who, in other respects, seem to differ least from the lower animals, constantly retain some sense of religion; so thoroughly has this common conviction possessed the mind, so firmly is it stamped on the breasts of all men. Since, then, there never has been, from the very first, any quarter of the globe, any city, any household even, without religion, this amounts to a tacit confession that a sense of Deity is inscribed on every heart. Nay, even idolatry is ample evidence of this fact. For we know how reluctant man is to lower himself, in order to set other creatures above him. Therefore, when he chooses to worship wood and stone rather than be thought to have no God, it is evident how very strong this impression of a Deity must be; since it is more difficult to obliterate it from the mind of man, than to break down the feelings of his nature, —these certainly being broken down, when, in opposition to his natural haughtiness, he spontaneously humbles himself before the meanest object as an act of reverence to God.

2 Objection—that religion and the belief of a Deity are the inventions of crafty politicians. Refutation of the objection. This universal belief confirmed by the examples of wicked men and Atheists.

It is most absurd, therefore, to maintain, as some do, that religion was devised by the cunning and craft of a few individuals, as a means of keeping the body of the people in due subjection, while there was nothing which those very individuals, while teaching others to worship God, less believed than the existence of a God. I readily acknowledge, that designing men have introduced a vast number of fictions into religion, with the view of inspiring the populace with reverence or striking them with terror, and thereby rendering them more obsequious; but they never could have succeeded in this, had the minds of men not been previously imbued with that uniform belief in God, from which, as from its seed, the religious propensity springs. And it is altogether incredible that those who, in the matter of religion, cunningly imposed on their ruder neighbors, were altogether devoid of knowledge of God. For though in old times there were some, and in the present day not a few are found who deny the being of a God, yet, whether they will or not, they occasionally feel the truth which they are desirous not to know. We do not read of any man who broke out into more unbridled and audacious contempt of the Deity than C. Caligula, and yet none showed greater dread when any indication of divine wrath was manifested. Thus, however unwilling, he shook with terror before the God whom he professedly studied to condemn. You may every day see the same thing happening to his modern imitators. The most audacious despiser of God is most easily disturbed, trembling at the sound of a falling leaf. How so, unless in vindication of the divine majesty, which smites their consciences the more strongly the more they endeavor to flee from it. They all, indeed, look out for hiding-places where they may conceal themselves from the presence of the Lord, and again efface it from their mind; but after all their efforts they remain caught within the net. Though the conviction may occasionally seem to vanish for a moment, it immediately returns, and rushes in with new impetuosity, so that any interval of relief from the gnawing of conscience is not unlike the slumber of the intoxicated or the insane, who have no quiet rest in sleep, but are continually haunted with dire horrific dreams. Even the wicked themselves, therefore, are an example of the fact that some idea of God always exists in every human mind.

3 Confirmed also by the vain endeavors of the wicked to banish all fear of God from their minds. Conclusion, that the knowledge of God is naturally implanted in the human mind.

All men of sound Judgment will therefore hold, that a sense of Deity is indelibly engraved on the human heart. And that this belief is naturally engendered in all, and thoroughly fixed in our very bones, is strikingly attested by the contumacy of the wicked, who, though they struggle furiously, are unable to extricate themselves from the fear of God. Though Diagoras, and others of like stamps make themselves merry with whatever has been believed in all ages concerning religion, and Dionysus scoffs at the Judgment of heaven, it is but a Sardonian grin; for the worm of conscience, keener than burning steel, is gnawing them within. I do not say with Cicero, that errors wear out by age, and that religion increases and grows better day-by-day. For the world (as will be shortly seen) labors as much as it can to shake off all knowledge of God, and corrupts his worship in innumerable ways. I only say, that, when the stupid hardness of heart, which the wicked eagerly court as a means of despising God, becomes enfeebled, the sense of Deity, which of all things they wished most to be extinguished, is still in vigour, and now and then breaks forth. Whence we infer, that this is not a doctrine which is first learned at school, but one as to which every man is, from the womb, his own master; one which nature herself allows no individual to forget, though many, with all their might, strive to do so. Moreover, if all are born and live for the express purpose of learning to know God, and if the knowledge of God, in so far as it fails to produce this effect, is fleeting and vain, it is clear that all those who do not direct the whole thoughts and actions of their lives to this end fail to fulfill the law of their being. This did not escape the observation even of philosophers. For it is the very thing, which Plato meant when he taught, as he often does, that the chief good of the soul consists in resemblance to God; *i.e.*, when, by means of knowing him, she is wholly transformed into him. Thus Gryllus, also in Plutarch, reasons most skillfully, when he affirms that, if once religion is banished from the lives of men, they not only in no respect excel, but are, in many respects, much more wretched than the brutes, since, being exposed to so many forms of evil, they continually drag on a troubled and restless existence: that the only thing, therefore, which makes them superior is the worship of God, through which alone they aspire to immortality.

Chapter 4

THE KNOWLEDGE OF GOD STIFLED OR CORRUPTED, IGNORANTLY OR MALICIOUSLY.

Sections

1. The knowledge of God suppressed by ignorance, many falling away into superstition. Such persons, however, inexcusable, because their error is accompanied with pride and stubbornness.

2. Stubbornness the companion of impiety.

3. No pretext can justify superstition. This proved, first, from reason; and, secondly, from Scripture.

4. The wicked never willingly come into the presence of God. Hence, their hypocrisy. Hence, too, their sense of Deity leads to no good result.

1 **The knowledge of God suppressed by ignorance, many falling away into superstition. Such persons, however, inexcusable, because their error is accompanied with pride and stubbornness.**

But though experience testifies that a seed of religion is divinely sown in all, scarcely one in a hundred is found who cherishes it in his heart, and not one in whom it grows to maturity so far is it from yielding fruit in its season. Moreover, while some lose themselves in superstitious observances, and others, of set purpose, wickedly revolt from God, the result is that, in regard to the true knowledge of him, all are so degenerate, that in no part of the world can genuine godliness be found. In saying that some fall away into superstition, I mean not to insinuate that their excessive absurdity frees them from guilt; for the blindness under which they labor is almost invariably accompanied with vain pride and stubbornness. Mingled vanity and pride appear in this, that when miserable men do seek after God, instead of ascending higher than themselves as they ought to do, they measure him by their own carnal stupidity, and, neglecting solid inquiry, fly off to indulge their curiosity in vain speculation. Hence, they do not conceive of him in the character in which he is manifested, but imagine him to be whatever their own rashness has devised. This abyss standing open, they cannot move one footstep without rushing headlong to destruction. With such an idea of God, nothing which they may attempt to offer in the way of worship or obedience can have any value in his sight, because it is not him they worship, but, instead of him, the dream and figment of their own heart. This corrupt procedure is admirably described by Paul when he says that "thinking to be wise, they became fools" (Romans 1:22). He had previously said that "they became vain in their imaginations," but lest any should suppose them blameless, he afterwards adds that they were deservedly blinded, because, not contented with sober inquiry, because, arrogating to themselves more than they have any title to do, they of their own accord court darkness, nay, bewitch themselves with perverse, empty show. Hence, it is that their folly, the result not only of vain curiosity, but of licentious desire and overweening confidence in the pursuit of forbidden knowledge, cannot be excused.

2 Stubbornness the companion of impiety.

The expression of David (Psalm 14:1, 53:1), "The fool hath said in his heart, There is no God," is primarily applied to those who, as will shortly further appear, stifle the light of nature, and intentionally stupefy themselves. We see many, after they have become hardened in a daring course of sin, madly banishing all remembrance of God, though spontaneously suggested to them from within, by natural sense. To show how detestable this madness is, the Psalmist introduces them as distinctly denying that there is a God, because although they do not disown his essence, they rob him of his justice and providence, and represent him as sitting idly in heaven. Nothing being less accordant with the nature of God than to cast off the government of the world, leaving it to chance, and so to wink at the crimes of men that they may wanton with impunity in evil courses; it follows, that every man who indulges in security, after extinguishing all fear of divine Judgment, virtually denies that there is a God. As a just punishment of the wicked, after they have closed their own eyes, God makes their hearts dull and heavy, and hence, seeing, they see not.

David, indeed, is the best interpreter of his own meaning, when he says elsewhere, the wicked has "no fear of God before his eyes" (Psalm 36:1); and, again, "He has said in his heart, God has forgotten; he hideth his face; he will never see it." Thus although they are forced to acknowledge that there is some God, they, however, rob him of his glory by denying his power. For, as Paul declares, "If we believe not, he abideth faithful, he cannot deny himself" (2 Timothy 2:13); so those who feign to themselves a dead and dumb idol, are truly said to deny God. It is, moreover, to be observed, that though they struggle with their own convictions, and would fain not only banish God from their minds, but from heaven also, their stupefaction is never so complete as to secure them from being occasionally dragged before the divine tribunal. Still, as no fear restrains them from rushing violently in the face of God, so long as they are hurried on by that blind impulse, it cannot be denied that their prevailing state of mind about him is brutish oblivion.

3 No pretext can justify superstition. This proved, first, from reason; and, secondly, from Scripture.

In this way, the vain pretext, which many employ to clothe their superstition, is overthrown. They deem it enough that they have some kind of zeal for religion, however preposterous it may be, not observing that true religion must be conformable to the will of God as its unerring standard; that he can never deny himself, and is no spectra or phantom, to be metamorphosed at each individual's caprice. It is easy to see how superstition, with its false glosses, mocks God, while it tries to please him. Usually fastening merely on things on which he has declared he sets no value, it either contemptuously overlooks, or even undisguisedly rejects, the things, which he expressly enjoins, or in which we are assured that he takes pleasure. Those, therefore, who set up a fictitious worship, merely worship and adore their own delirious fancies; indeed, they would never dare so to trifle with God, had they not previously fashioned him after their own childish conceits. Hence, that vague and wandering opinion of Deity is declared by an Apostle to be ignorance of God: "Howbeit, then, when ye knew not God, ye did service unto them which by nature are no gods." And he elsewhere declares, that the Ephesians were "without God" (Ephesians 2:12) at the time when they wandered without any correct knowledge of him. It makes little difference, at least in this respect, whether you hold the existence of one God, or a plurality of gods, since, in both cases alike, by departing from the true God, you have nothing left but an execrable idol. It remains, therefore, to conclude with Lactantius, "No religion is genuine that is not in accordance with truth."

4 The wicked never willingly come into the presence of God. Hence, their hypocrisy. Hence, too, their sense of Deity leads to no good result.

To this fault they add a second—viz. that when they do think of God it is against their will; never approaching him without being dragged into his presence, and when there, instead of the voluntary fear flowing from reverence of the divine majesty, feeling only that forced and servile fear which divine Judgment extorts Judgment which, from the impossibility of escape, they are compelled to dread, but which, while they dread, they at the same time also hate.

To impiety, and to it alone, the saying of Statius properly applies: "Fear first brought gods into the world." Those whose inclinations are at variance with the justice of God, knowing that his tribunal has been erected for the punishment of transgression, earnestly wish that that tribunal were overthrown. Under the influence of this feeling, they are actually warring against God, justice being one of his essential attributes. Perceiving that they are always within reach of his power, that resistance and evasion are alike impossible, they fear and tremble. Accordingly, to avoid the appearance of condemning a majesty by which all are overawed, they have recourse to some species of religious observance, never ceasing meanwhile to defile themselves with every kind of vice, and add crime to crime, until they have broken the holy law of the Lord in everyone of its requirements, and set his whole righteousness at nothing; at all events, they are not so restrained by their semblance of fear as not to luxuriate and take pleasure in iniquity, choosing rather to indulge their carnal propensities than to curb them with the bridle of the Holy Spirit. But since this shadow of religion (it scarcely even deserves to be called a shadow) is false and vain, it is easy to infer how much this confused knowledge of God differs from that piety which is instilled into the breasts of believers, and from which alone true religion springs. And yet hypocrites would fain, by means of tortuous windings, make a show of being near to God at the very time they are fleeing from him.

For while the whole life ought to be one perpetual course of obedience, they rebel without fear in almost all their actions, and seek to appease him with a few paltry sacrifices; while they ought to serve him with integrity of heart and holiness of life, they endeavor to procure his favor by means of frivolous devices and punctilios of no value. Nay, they take greater license in their groveling indulgences, because they imagine that they can fulfill their duty to him by preposterous expiations; in short, while their confidence ought to have been fixed upon him, they put him aside, and rest in themselves or the creatures. At length they bewilder themselves in such a maze of error, that the darkness of ignorance obscures, and ultimately extinguishes, those sparks which were designed to show them the glory of God. Still, however, the conviction that there is some Deity continues to exist, like a plant, which can never be completely eradicated, though so corrupt, that it is only capable of producing the worst of fruit. Nay, we have still stronger evidence of the proposition for which I now contend—viz. that a sense of Deity is naturally engraved on the human heart, in the fact, that the very reprobate are forced to acknowledge it. When at their ease, they can jest about God, and talk pertly and loquaciously in disparagement of his power; but should despair, from any cause, overtake them, it will stimulate them to seek him, and dictate ejaculatory prayers, proving that they were not entirely ignorant of God, but had perversely suppressed feelings which ought to have been earlier manifested.

Chapter 5

THE KNOWLEDGE OF GOD CONSPICUOUS IN THE CREATION, AND CONTINUAL GOVERNMENT OF THE WORLD.

This chapter consists of two parts:

1. The former, which occupies the first ten sections, divides all the works of God into two great classes, and elucidates the knowledge of God as displayed in each class. The one class is treated of in the first six, and the other in the four following sections:

2. The latter part of the chapter shows, that, in consequence of the extreme stupidity of men, those manifestations of God, however perspicuous, lead to no useful result. This latter part, which commences at the eleventh section, is continued to the end of the chapter.

Sections

1. The invisible and incomprehensible essence of God, to a certain extent, made visible in his works.

2. This declared by the first class of works—viz. the admirable motions of the heavens and the earth, the symmetry of the human body, and the connection of its parts; in short, the various objects which are presented to every eye.

3. This more especially manifested in the structure of the human body.

4. The shameful ingratitude of disregarding God, who, in such a variety of ways, is manifested within us. The still more shameful ingratitude of contemplating the endowments of the soul, without ascending to Him who gave them. No objection can be founded on any supposed organism in the soul.

5. The powers and actions of the soul, a proof of its separate existence from the body. Proofs of the soul's immortality. Objection that the whole world is quickened by one soul. Reply to the objection. Its impiety.

6. *Conclusion from what has been said—viz. that the omnipotence, eternity, and goodness of God, may be learned from the first class of works, i.e., those which are in accordance with the ordinary course of nature.*

7. *The second class of works—viz. those above the ordinary course of nature, afford clear evidence of the perfections of God, especially his goodness, justice, and mercy.*

8. *Also his providence, power, and wisdom.*

9. *Proofs and illustrations of the divine Majesty. The use of them—viz. the acquisition of divine knowledge in combination with true piety.*

10. *The tendency of the knowledge of God to inspire the righteous with the hope of future life, and remind the wicked of the punishments reserved for them. Its tendency, moreover, to keep alive in the hearts of the righteous a sense of the divine goodness.*

11. *The second part of the chapter, which describes the stupidity both of learned and unlearned, in ascribing the whole order of things, and the admirable arrangements of divine Providence, to fortune.*

12. *Hence, Polytheism, with all its abominations, and the endless and irreconcilable opinions of the philosophers concerning God.*

13. *All guilty of revolt from God, corrupting pure religion, either by following general custom, or the impious consent of antiquity.*

14. *Though irradiated by the wondrous glories of creation, we cease not to follow our own ways.*

15. *Our conduct altogether inexcusable, the dullness of perception being attributable to ourselves, while we are fully reminded of the true path, both by the structure and the government of the world.*

1 The invisible and incomprehensible essence of God, to a certain extent, made visible in his works.

Since the perfection of blessedness consists in the knowledge of God, he has been pleased, in order that none might be excluded from the means of obtaining felicity, not only to deposit in our minds that seed of religion of which we have already spoken, but so to manifest his perfections in the whole structure of the universe, and daily place himself in our view, that we cannot open our eyes without being compelled to behold him. His essence, indeed, is incomprehensible, utterly transcending all human thought; but on each of his works his glory is engraved in characters so bright, so distinct, and so illustrious, that none, however dull and illiterate, can plead ignorance as their excuse. Hence, with perfect truth, the Psalmist exclaims, "He covereth himself with light as with a garment" (Psalm 104:2); as if he had said, that God for the first time was arrayed in visible attire when, in the creation of the world, he displayed those glorious banners, on which, to whatever side we turn, we behold his perfections visibly portrayed. In the same place, the Psalmist aptly compares the expanded heavens to his royal tent, and says, "He layeth the beams of his chambers in the waters, maketh the clouds his chariot, and walketh upon the wings of the wind," sending forth the winds and lightning as his swift messengers. And because the glory of his power and wisdom is more refulgent in the firmament, it is frequently designated as his palace. And, first, wherever you turn your eyes, there is no portion of the world, however minute, that does not exhibit at least some sparks of beauty; while it is impossible to contemplate the vast and beautiful fabric as it extends around, without being overwhelmed by the immense weight of glory. Hence, the author of the Epistle to the Hebrews elegantly describes the visible worlds as images of the invisible (Hebrews 11:3), the elegant structure of the world serving us as a kind of mirror, in which we may behold God, though otherwise invisible. For the same reason, the Psalmist attributes language to celestial objects, a language which all nations understand (Psalm 19:1), the manifestation of the Godhead being too clear to escape the notice of any people, however obtuse. The Apostle Paul, stating this still more clearly, says, "That which may be known of God is manifest in them, for God has showed it unto them. For the invisible things of him from the creation of the world are clearly seen, being understood by the things that are made, even his eternal power and Godhead" (Romans 1:20).

2 This declared by the first class of works—viz. the admirable motions of the heavens and the earth, the symmetry of the human body, and the connection of its parts; in short, the various objects which are presented to every eye.

In attestation of his wondrous wisdom, both the heavens and the earth present us with innumerable proofs not only those more recondite proofs which astronomy, medicine, and all the natural sciences, are designed to illustrate, but proofs which force themselves on the notice of the most illiterate peasant, who cannot open his eyes without beholding them. It is true, indeed, that those who are more or less intimately acquainted with those liberal studies are thereby assisted and enabled to obtain a deeper insight into the secret workings of divine wisdom. No man, however, though he is ignorant of these, is incapacitated for discerning such proofs of creative wisdom as may well cause him to break forth in admiration of the Creator. To investigate the motions of the heavenly bodies, to determine their positions, measure their distances, and ascertain their properties, demands skill, and a more careful examination; and where these are so employed, as the Providence of God is thereby more fully unfolded, so it is reasonable to suppose that the mind takes a loftier flight, and obtains brighter views of his glory. Still, none who have the use of their eyes can be ignorant of the divine skill manifested so conspicuously in the endless variety, yet distinct and well ordered array, of the heavenly host; and, therefore, it is plain that the Lord has furnished every man with abundant proofs of his wisdom. The same is true in regard to the structure of the human frame. To determine the connection of its parts, its symmetry and beauty, with the skill of a Galen, requires singular acuteness; and yet all men acknowledge that the human body bears on its face such proofs of ingenious contrivance as are sufficient to proclaim the admirable wisdom of its Maker.

3 This more especially manifested in the structure of the human body.

Hence, certain of the philosophers have not improperly called man a *microcosm* (*miniature world*), as being a rare specimen of divine power, wisdom, and goodness, and containing within himself wonders sufficient to occupy our minds, if we are willing so to employ them. Paul, accordingly, after reminding the Athenians that they "might feel after God and find him," immediately adds, that "he is not far from everyone of us" (Acts 17:27); every man having within himself undoubted evidence of the heavenly grace by which he lives, and moves, and has his being. But if, in order to apprehend God, it is unnecessary to go further than ourselves, what excuse can there be for the sloth of any man who will not take the trouble of descending into himself that he may find Him? For the same reason, too, David, after briefly celebrating the wonderful name and glory of God, as everywhere displayed, immediately exclaims, "What is man, that thou art mindful of him?" and again, "Out of the mouths of babes and sucklings thou hast ordained strength" (Psalm 8:2, 4). Thus he declares not only that the human race are a bright mirror of the Creator's works, but that infants hanging on their mothers' breasts have tongues eloquent enough to proclaim his glory without the aid of other orators. Accordingly, he hesitates not to bring them forward as fully instructed to refute the madness of those who, from devilish pride, would fain extinguish the name of God. Hence, too, the passage which Paul quotes from Aratus, "We are his offspring" (Acts 17:28), the excellent gifts with which he has endued us attesting that he is our Father. In the same way also, from natural instinct, and at the dictation of experience, heathen poets called him the father of men. No one, indeed, will voluntarily and willingly devote himself to the service of God unless he has previously tasted his paternal love, and been thereby allured to love and reverence Him.

4 The shameful ingratitude of disregarding God, who, in such a variety of ways, is manifested within us. The still more shameful ingratitude of contemplating the endowments of the soul, without ascending to Him who gave them. No objection can be founded on any supposed organism in the soul.

But herein appears the shameful ingratitude of men. Though they have in their own persons a factory where innumerable operations of God are carried on, and a magazine stored with treasures of inestimable value—instead of bursting forth in his praise, as they are bound to do, they, on the contrary, are the more inflated and swelled with pride. They feel how wonderfully God is working in them, and their own experience tells them of the vast variety of gifts which they owe to his liberality. Whether they will or not, they cannot but know that these are proofs of his Godhead, and yet they inwardly suppress them. They have no occasion to go further than themselves, provided they do not, by appropriating as their own that which has been given them from heaven, put out the light intended to exhibit God clearly to their minds. At this day, however, the earth sustains on her bosom many monster minds—minds that are not afraid to employ the seed of Deity deposited in human nature as a means of suppressing the name of God. Can anything be more detestable than this madness in man, who, finding God a hundred times both in his body and his soul, makes his excellence in this respect a pretext for denying that there is a God? He will not say that chance has made him differ from the brutes that perish; but, substituting nature as the architect of the universe, he suppresses the name of God. The swift motions of the soul, its noble faculties and rare endowments, bespeak the agency of God in a manner which would make the suppression of it impossible, did not the Epicureans, like so many Cyclops, use it as a vantage-ground, from which to wage more audacious war with God. Are so many treasures of heavenly wisdom employed in the guidance of such a worm as man, and shall the whole universe be denied the same privilege? To hold that there are organs in the soul corresponding to each of its faculties is so far from obscuring the glory of God, that it rather illustrates it. Let Epicurus tell what concourse of atoms, cooking meat and drink, can form one portion into refuse and another portion into blood, and make all the members separately perform their office as carefully as if they were so many souls acting with common consent in the superintendence of one body.

5 The powers and actions of the soul, a proof of its separate existence from the body. Proofs of the soul's immortality. Objection that the whole world is quickened by one soul. Reply to the objection. Its impiety.

But my business at present is not with that: I wish rather to deal with those who, led away by absurd subtleties, are inclined, by giving an indirect turn to the frigid doctrine of Aristotle, to employ it for the purpose both of disproving the immortality of the soul, and robbing God of his rights. Under the pretext that the faculties of the soul are organized, they chain it to the body as if it were incapable of a separate existence, while they endeavor as much as in them lies, by pronouncing eulogiums on nature, to suppress the name of God. But there is no ground for maintaining that the powers of the soul are confined to the performance of bodily functions. What has the body to do with your measuring the heavens, counting the number of the stars, ascertaining their magnitudes, their relative distances, the rate at which they move, and the orbits, which they describe? I deny not that Astronomy has its use; all I mean to show is, that these lofty investigations are not conducted by organized symmetry, but by the faculties of the soul itself apart altogether from the body. The single example I have given will suggest many others to the reader. The swift and versatile movements of the soul in glancing from heaven to earth, connecting the future with the past, retaining the remembrance of former years, nay, forming creations of its own—its skill, moreover, in making astonishing discoveries, and inventing so many wonderful arts, are sure indications of the agency of God in man. What shall we say of its activity when the body is asleep, its many revolving thoughts, its many useful suggestions, its many solid arguments, nay, its presentiment of things yet to come? What shall we say but that man bears about with him a stamp of immortality, which can never be effaced? But how is it possible for man to be divine, and yet not acknowledge his Creator? Shall we, by means of a power of judging implanted in our breast, distinguish between justice and injustice, and yet there be no judge in heaven? Shall some remains of intelligence continue with us in sleep, and yet no God keep watch in heaven? Shall we be deemed the inventors of so many arts and useful properties that God may be defrauded of his praise, though experience tells us plainly enough, that whatever we possess is dispensed to us in unequal measures by another hand? The talk of certain persons concerning a secret inspiration quickening the whole world is not only silly, but altogether profane. Such persons are delighted with the following celebrated passage of Virgil: —

> Know, first, that heaven, and earth's compacted frame,
> And flowing waters, and the starry flame,
> And both the radiant lights, one common soul
> Inspires and feeds—and animates the whole.
> This active mind, infused through all the space,
> Unites and mingles with the mighty mass:
> Hence, men and beasts the breath of life obtain,
> And birds of air, and monsters of the main.
> Th' ethereal vigour is in all the same,

And every soul is filled with equal flame."

The meaning of all this is, that the world, which was made to display the glory of God, is its own creator. For the same poet has, in another place, adopted a view common to both Greeks and Latins:

"Hence, to the bee some sages have assigned
A portion of the God, and heavenly mind;
For God goes forth, and spreads throughout the whole,
Heaven, earth, and sea, the universal soul;
Each, at its birth, from him all beings share,
Both man and brute, the breath of vital air;
To him return, and, loosed from earthly chain,
Fly whence they sprung, and rest in God again;
Spurn at the grave, and, fearless of decay,
Dwell in high heaven, art star th' ethereal way."

Here we see how far that jejune speculation, of a universal mind animating and invigorating the world, is fitted to beget and foster piety in our minds. We have a still clearer proof of this in the profane verses, which the licentious Lucretius has written as a deduction from the same principle. The plain object is to form an unsubstantial deity, and thereby banish the true God whom we ought to fear and worship. I admit, indeed that the expressions "Nature is God," may be piously used, if dictated by a pious mind; but as it is inaccurate and harsh (Nature being more properly the order which has been established by God), in matters which are so very important, and in regard to which special reverence is due, it does harm to confound the Deity with the inferior operations of his hands.

6 Conclusion from what has been said—viz. that the omnipotence, eternity, and goodness of God, may be learned from the first class of works, *i.e.*, those which are in accordance with the ordinary course of nature.

Let each of us, therefore, in contemplating his own nature, remember that there is one God who governs all natures, and, in governing, wishes us to have respect to himself, to make him the object of our faith, worship, and adoration. Nothing, indeed, can be more preposterous than to enjoy those noble endowments, which bespeak the divine presence within us, and to neglect him who, of his own good pleasure, bestows them upon us. In regard to his power, how glorious the manifestations by which he urges us to the contemplation of himself; unless, indeed, we pretend not to know whose energy it is that by a word sustains the boundless fabric of the universe—at one time making heaven reverberate with thunder, sending forth the scorching lightning, and setting the whole atmosphere in a blaze; at another, causing the raging tempests to blow, and forthwith, in one moment, when it so pleases him, making a perfect calm; keeping the sea, which seems constantly threatening the earth with devastation, suspended as if it were in air; at one time, lashing it into fury by the impetuosity of the winds; at another, appeasing its rage, and stilling all its waves. Here we might refer to those glowing descriptions of divine power, as illustrated by natural events, which occur throughout Scripture; but more especially in the book of Job, and the prophecies of Isaiah. These, however, I purposely omit, because a better opportunity of introducing them will be found when I come to treat of the Scriptural account of the creation. (*Infra*, chapter 14, sections 1, 2, 20, *sq*). I only wish to observe here, that this method of investigating the divine perfections, by tracing the lineaments of his countenance as shadowed forth in the firmament and on the earth, is common both to those within and to those without the pale of the Church. From the power of God we are naturally led to consider his eternity since that from which all other things derive their origin must necessarily be self existent and eternal. Moreover, if it is asked what cause induced him to create all things at first, and now inclines him to preserve them, we shall find that there could be no other cause than his own goodness. But if this is the only cause, nothing more should be required to draw forth our love towards him; every creature, as the Psalmist reminds us, participating in his mercy. "His tender mercies are over all his works" (Psalm 145:9).

7 The second class of works—viz. those above the ordinary course of nature, afford clear evidence of the perfections of God, especially his goodness, justice, and mercy.

In the second class of God's works, namely those that are above the ordinary course of nature, the evidence of his perfections is in every respect equally clear. For in conducting the affairs of men, he so arranges the course of his providence, as daily to declare, by the clearest manifestations, that though all are in innumerable ways the partakers of his bounty, the righteous are the special objects of his favor, the wicked and profane the special objects of his severity. It is impossible to doubt his punishment of crimes; while at the same time he, in no unequivocal manner, declares that he is the protector, and even the avenger of innocence, by shedding blessings on the good, helping their necessities, soothing and solacing their grief, relieving their sufferings, and in all ways providing for their safety. And though he often permits the guilty to exult for a time with impunity, and the innocent to be driven to and fro in adversity, nay, even to be wickedly and iniquitously oppressed, this ought not to produce any uncertainty as to the uniform justice of all his procedure. Nay, an opposite inference should be drawn. When anyone crime calls forth visible manifestations of his anger, it must be because he hates all crimes; and, on the other hand, his leaving many crimes unpunished, only proves that there is a Judgment in reserve, when the punishment now delayed shall be inflicted. In like manner, how richly does he supply us with the means of contemplating his mercy when, as frequently happens, he continues to visit miserable sinners with unwearied kindness, until he subdues their depravity, and woos them back with more than a parent's fondness?

8 Also his providence, power, and wisdom.

To this purpose the Psalmist (Psalm 107) mentioning how God, in a wondrous manner, often brings sudden and unexpected succor to the miserable when almost on the brink of despair, whether in protecting them when they stray in deserts, and at length leading them back into the right path, or supplying them with food when famishing for want, or delivering them when captive from iron fetters and foul dungeons, or conducting them safe into harbor after shipwreck, or bringing them back from the gates of death by curing their diseases, or, after burning up the fields with heat and drought, fertilizing them with the river of his grace, or exalting the meanest of the people, and casting down the mighty from their lofty seats:—the Psalmist, after bringing forward examples of this description, infers that those things which men call fortuitous events, are so many proofs of divine providence, and more especially of paternal clemency, furnishing ground of joy to the righteous, and at the same time stopping the mouths of the ungodly. But as the greater part of mankind, enslaved by error, walk blindfold in this glorious theatre; he exclaims that it is a rare and singular wisdom to meditate carefully on these works of God, which many, who seem most sharp-sighted in other respects, behold without profit. It is indeed true, that the brightest manifestation of divine glory finds not one genuine spectator among a hundred. Still, neither his power nor his wisdom is shrouded in darkness. His power is strikingly displayed when the rage of the wicked, to all appearance irresistible, is crushed in a single moment; their arrogance subdued, their strongest bulwarks overthrown, their armor dashed to pieces, their strength broken, their schemes defeated without an effort, and audacity which set itself above the heavens is precipitated to the lowest depths of the earth. On the other hand, the poor are raised up out of the dust, and the needy lifted out of the dung hill (Psalm 113:7), the oppressed and afflicted are rescued in extremity, the despairing animated with hope, the unarmed defeat the armed, the few the many, the weak the strong. The excellence of the divine wisdom is manifested in distributing everything in due season, confounding the wisdom of the world, and taking the wise in their own craftiness (1 Corinthians 3:19); in short, conducting all things in perfect accordance with reason.

9 Proofs and illustrations of the divine Majesty. The use of them— viz. the acquisition of divine knowledge in combination with true piety.

We see there is no need of a long and laborious train of argument in order to obtain proofs, which illustrate and assert the Divine Majesty. The few that we have merely touched show them to be so immediately within our reach in every quarter, that we can trace them with the eye, or point to them with the finger. And here we must observe again (see chapter 2, section 2), that the knowledge of God which we are invited to cultivate is not that which, resting satisfied with empty speculation, only flutters in the brain, but a knowledge which will prove substantial and fruitful wherever it is duly perceived, and rooted in the heart. The Lord is manifested by his perfections. When we feel their power within us, and are conscious of their benefits, the knowledge must impress us much more vividly than if we merely imagined a God whose presence we never felt. Hence, it is obvious, that in seeking God, the most direct path and the fittest method is, not to attempt with presumptuous curiosity to pry into his essence, which is rather to be adored than minutely discussed, but to contemplate him in his works, by which he draws near, becomes familiar, and in a manner communicates himself to us. To this the Apostle referred when he said, that we need not go far in search of him (Acts 17:27), because, by the continual working of his power, he dwells in every one of us. Accordingly, David (Psalm 145), after acknowledging that his greatness is unsearchable, proceeds to enumerate his works, declaring that his greatness will thereby be unfolded. It therefore becomes us also diligently to prosecute that investigation of God, which so enraptures the soul with admiration as, at the same time, to make an efficacious impression on it. And, as Augustine expresses it (in Psalm 144), since we are unable to comprehend Him, and are overpowered by his greatness, our proper course is to contemplate his works, and so refresh ourselves with his goodness.

10 The tendency of the knowledge of God to inspire the righteous with the hope of future life, and remind the wicked of the punishments reserved for them. Its tendency, moreover, to keep alive in the hearts of the righteous a sense of the divine goodness.

By the knowledge thus acquired, we ought not only to be stimulated to worship God, but also aroused and elevated to the hope of future life. For, observing that the manifestations, which the Lord gives both of his mercy and severity, are only begun and incomplete, we ought to infer that these are doubtless only a prelude to higher manifestations, of which the full display is reserved for another state. Conversely, when we see the righteous brought into affliction by the ungodly, assailed with injuries, overwhelmed with calumnies, and lacerated by insult and contumely, while, on the contrary, the wicked flourish, prosper, acquire ease and honor, and all these with impunity, we ought forthwith to infer, that there will be a future life in which iniquity shall receive its punishment, and righteousness its reward. Moreover, when we observe that the Lord often lays his chastening rod on the righteous, we may the more surely conclude, that far less will the righteous ultimately escape the scourges of his anger. There is a well-known passage in Augustine, "Were all sin now visited with open punishment, it might be thought that nothing was reserved for the final Judgment; and, on the other hand, were no sin now openly punished, it might be supposed there was no divine providence." It must be acknowledged, therefore, that in each of the works of God, and more especially in the whole of them taken together, the divine perfections are delineated as in a picture, and the whole human race thereby invited and allured to acquire the knowledge of God, and, in consequence of this knowledge, true and complete felicity. Moreover, while his perfections are thus most vividly displayed, the only means of ascertaining their practical operation and tendency is to descend into ourselves, and consider how it is that the Lord there manifests his wisdom, power, and energy, —how he there displays his justice, goodness, and mercy. For although David (Psalm 92:6) justly complains of the extreme infatuation of the ungodly in not pondering the deep counsels of God, as exhibited in the government of the human race, what he elsewhere says (Psalm 40) is most true, that the wonders of the divine wisdom in this respect are more in number than the hairs of our head. But I leave this topic at present, as it will be more fully considered afterwards in its own place (Book I, chapter, sections 6-9).

11 The second part of the chapter, which describes the stupidity both of learned and unlearned, in ascribing the whole order of things, and the admirable arrangements of Divine Providence, to fortune.

Bright, however, as is the manifestation, which God gives both of himself and his immortal kingdom in the mirror of his works, so great is our stupidity, so dull are we in regard to these bright manifestations, that we derive no benefit from them. For in regard to the fabric and admirable arrangement of the universe, how few of us are there who, in lifting our eyes to the heavens, or looking abroad on the various regions of the earth, ever think of the Creator? Do we not rather overlook Him, and sluggishly content ourselves with a view of his works? And then in regard to supernatural events, though these are occurring every day, how few are there who ascribe them to the ruling Providence of God—how many who imagine that they are casual results produced by the blind evolutions of the wheel of chance? Even when under the guidance and direction of these events, we are in a manner forced to the contemplation of God (a circumstance which all must occasionally experience), and are thus led to form some impressions of Deity, we immediately fly off to carnal dreams and depraved fictions, and so by our vanity corrupt heavenly truth. This far, indeed, we differ from each other, in that everyone appropriates to himself some peculiar error; but we are all alike in this, that we substitute monstrous fictions for the one living and true God—a disease not confined to obtuse and vulgar minds, but affecting the noblest, and those who, in other respects, are singularly acute. How lavishly in this respect have the whole body of philosophers betrayed their stupidity and want of sense? To say nothing of the others whose absurdities are of a still grosser description, how completely does Plato, the soberest and most religious of them all, lose himself in his round globe? What must be the case with the rest, when the leaders, who ought to have set them an example, commit such blunders, and labor under such hallucinations? In like manner, while the government of the world places the doctrine of providence beyond dispute, the practical result is the same as if it were believed that all things were carried hither and thither at the caprice of chance; so prone are we to vanity and error. I am still referring to the most distinguished of the philosophers, and not to the common herd, whose madness in profaning the truth of God exceeds all bounds.

12 Hence, Polytheism, with all its abominations, and the endless and irreconcilable opinions of the philosophers concerning God.

Hence, that immense flood of error with which the whole world is overflowed. Every individual mind being a kind of labyrinth, it is not wonderful, not only that each nation has adopted a variety of fictions, but that almost every man has had his own god. To the darkness of ignorance have been added presumption and wantonness, and hence there is scarcely an individual to be found without some idol or phantom as a substitute for Deity. Like water gushing forth from a large and copious spring, immense crowds of gods have issued from the human mind, every man giving himself full license, and devising some peculiar form of divinity, to meet his own views. It is unnecessary here to attempt a catalogue of the superstitions with which the world was overspread. The things were endless; and the corruptions themselves, though not a word should be said, furnish abundant evidence of the blindness of the human mind. I say nothing of the rude and illiterate vulgar; but among the philosophers who attempted, by reason and learning, to pierce the heavens, what shameful disagreement! The higher anyone was endued with genius, and the more he was polished by science and art, the more specious was the coloring which he gave to his opinions. All these, however, if examined more closely, will be found to be vain show. The Stoics plumed themselves on their acuteness, when they said that the various names of God might be extracted from all the parts of nature, and yet that his unity was not thereby divided: as if we were not already too prone to vanity, and had no need of being presented with an endless multiplicity of gods, to lead us further and more grossly into error. The mystic theology of the Egyptians shows how sedulously they labored to be thought rational on this subject. And, perhaps, at the first glance, some show of probability might deceive the simple and unwary; but never did any mortal devise a scheme by which religion was not foully corrupted. This endless variety and confusion emboldened the Epicureans, and other gross despisers of piety, to cut off all sense of God. For when they saw that the wisest contradicted each others they hesitated not to infer from their dissensions, and from the frivolous and absurd doctrines of each, that men foolishly, and to no purpose, brought torment upon themselves by searching for a God, there being none: and they thought this inference safe, because it was better at once to deny God altogether, than to feign uncertain gods, and thereafter engage in quarrels without end. They, indeed, argue absurdly, or rather weave a cloak for their impiety out of human ignorance; though ignorance surely cannot derogate from the prerogatives of God. But since all confess that there is no topic on which such difference exists, both among learned and unlearned, the proper inference is, that the human mind, which thus errs in inquiring after God, is dull and blind in heavenly mysteries. Some praise the answer of Simonides, who being asked by King Hero what God was, asked a day to consider. When the king next day repeated the question, he asked two days; and after repeatedly doubling the number of days, at length replied, "The longer I consider, the darker the subject appears." He, no doubt, wisely suspended his opinion, when he did not see clearly: still his answer shows, that if men are only naturally taught, instead of having any distinct, solid, or certain knowledge, they fasten only on contradictory principles, and, in consequence, worship an unknown God.

13 All guilty of revolt from God, corrupting pure religion, either by following general custom, or the impious consent of antiquity.

Hence, we must hold, that whosoever adulterates pure religion (and this must be the case with all who cling to their own views), make a departure from the one God. No doubt, they will allege that they have a different intention; but it is of little consequence what they intend or persuade themselves to believe, since the Holy Spirit pronounces all to be apostates, who, in the blindness of their minds, substitute demons in the place of God. For this reason Paul declares that the Ephesians were "without God" (Ephesians 2:12), until they had learned from the Gospel, what it is to worship the true God. Nor must this be restricted to one people only, since, in another place, he declares in general, that all men "became vain in their imaginations," after the majesty of the Creator was manifested to them in the structure of the world. Accordingly, in order to make way for the only true God, he condemns all the gods celebrated among the Gentiles as lying and false, leaving no Deity anywhere but in Mount Zion where the special knowledge of God was professed (Habakkuk 2:18, 20). Among the Gentiles in the time of Christ, the Samaritans undoubtedly made the nearest approach to true piety; yet we hear from his own mouth that they worshipped they knew not what (John 4:22); whence it follows that they were deluded by vain errors. In short, though not all gave way to gross vice, or rush headlong into open idolatry, there was no pure and authentic religion founded merely on common belief. A few individuals may not have gone all insane lengths with the vulgar; still Paul's declaration remains true, that the wisdom of God was not apprehended by the princes of this world (1 Corinthians 2:8). But if the most distinguished wandered in darkness, what shall we say of the refuse? No wonder, therefore, that all worship of man's device is repudiated by the Holy Spirit as degenerate. Any opinion which man can form in heavenly mysteries, though it may not beget a long train of errors, is still the parent of error. And though nothing worse should happen, even this is no light sin—to worship an unknown God at random. Of this sin, however, we hear from our Savior's own mouth (John 4:22), that all are guilty who have not been taught out of the law who the God is whom they ought to worship. Nay, even Socrates in Xenophon, lauds the response of Apollo enjoining every man to worship the gods according to the rites of his country, and the particular practice of his own city. But what right have mortals thus to decide of their own authority in a matter which is far above the world; or who can so acquiesce in the will of his forefathers, or the decrees of the people, as unhesitatingly to receive a god at their hands? Everyone will adhere to his own Judgment, sooner than submit to the dictation of others. Since, therefore, in regulating the worship of God, the custom of a city, or the consent of antiquity, is a too feeble and fragile bond of piety; it remains that God himself must bear witness to himself from heaven.

14 Though irradiated by the wondrous glories of creation, we cease not to follow our own ways.

In vain for us, therefore, does Creation exhibit so many bright lamps lighted up to show forth the glory of its Author. Though they beam upon us from every quarter, they are altogether insufficient of themselves to lead us into the right path. Some sparks, undoubtedly, they do throw out; but these are quenched before they can give forth a brighter effulgence. Wherefore, the Apostle, in the very place where he says that the worlds are images of invisible things, adds that it is *by faith* we understand that they were framed by the word of God (Hebrews 11:3); thereby intimating that the invisible Godhead is indeed represented by such displays, but that we have no eyes to perceive it until they are enlightened through faith by internal revelation from God. When Paul says that that which may be known of God is manifested by the creation of the world, he does not mean such a manifestation as may be comprehended by the wit of man (Romans 1:19); on the contrary, he shows that it has no further effect than to render us inexcusable (Acts 17:27). And though he says, elsewhere, that we have not far to seek for God, inasmuch as he dwells within us, he shows, in another passage, to what extent this nearness to God is availing. God, says he, "in times past, suffered all nations to walk in their own ways. Nevertheless, he left not himself without witness, in that he did good, and gave us rain from heaven, and fruitful seasons, filling our hearts with food and gladness" (Acts 14:16, 17). But though God is not left without a witness, while, with numberless varied acts of kindness, he woos men to the knowledge of himself, yet they cease not to follow their own ways, in other words, deadly errors.

15 Our conduct altogether inexcusable, the dullness of perception being attributable to ourselves, while we are fully reminded of the true path, both by the structure and the government of the world.

But though we are deficient in natural powers, which might enable us to rise to a pure and clear knowledge of God, still, as the dullness, which prevents us, is within, there is no room for excuse. We cannot plead ignorance, without being at the same time convicted by our own consciences both of sloth and ingratitude. It would be, indeed, a strange defense for man to pretend that he has no ears to hear the truth, while dumb creatures have voices loud enough to declare it; to allege that he is unable to see that which creatures without eyes demonstrate, to excuse himself on the ground of weakness of mind, while all creatures without reason are able to teach. Wherefore, when we wander and go astray, we are justly shut out from every species of excuse, because all things point to the right path. But while man must bear the guilt of corrupting the seed of divine knowledge so wondrously deposited in his mind, and preventing it from bearing good and genuine fruit, it is still most true that we are not sufficiently instructed by that bare and simple, but magnificent testimony which the creatures bear to the glory of their Creator. For no sooner do we, from a survey of the world, obtain some slight knowledge of Deity, than we pass by the true God, and set up in his stead the dream and phantom of our own brain, drawing away the praise of justice, wisdom, and goodness, from the fountain-head, and transferring it to some other quarter. Moreover, by the erroneous estimate we form, we either so obscure or pervert his daily works, as at once to rob them of their glory and the author of them of his just praise.

Chapter 6

THE NEED OF SCRIPTURE, AS A GUIDE AND TEACHER, IN COMING TO GOD AS A CREATOR.

Sections

1. God gives his elect a better help to the knowledge of himself—viz. the Holy Scriptures. This he did from the very first.

2. First, by oracles and visions, and the ministry of the Patriarchs. Secondly, by the promulgation of the Law, and the preaching of the Prophets. Why the doctrines of religion are committed to writing.

3. This view confirmed, A. By the depravity of our nature making it necessary in everyone who would know God to have recourse to the word; B. From those passages of the Psalms in which God is introduced as reigning.

4. Another confirmation from certain direct statements in the Psalms. Lastly, from the words of our Savior.

1 **God gives his elect a better help to the knowledge of himself—viz. the Holy Scriptures. This he did from the very first.**

Therefore, though the effulgence which is presented to every eye, both in the heavens and on the earth, leaves the ingratitude of man without excuse, since God, in order to bring the whole human race under the same condemnation, holds forth to all, without exception, a mirror of his Deity in his works, another and better help must be given to guide us properly to God as a Creator. Not in vain, therefore, has he added the light of his Word in order that he might make himself known unto salvation, and bestowed the privilege on those whom he was pleased to bring into nearer and more familiar relation to himself. For, seeing how the minds of men were carried to and fro, and found no certain resting-place, he chose the Jews for a peculiar people, and then hedged them in that they might not, like others, go astray. And not in vain does he, by the same means, retain us in his knowledge, since but for this, even those who, in comparison of others, seem to stand strong, would quickly fall away. For as the aged, or those whose sight is defective, when any books however fair, is set before them, though they perceive that there is something written are scarcely able to make out two consecutive words, but, when aided by glasses, begin to read distinctly, so Scripture, gathering together the impressions of Deity, which, until then, lay confused in our minds, dissipates the darkness, and shows us the true God clearly. God therefore bestows a gift of singular value, when, for the instruction of the Church, he employs not dumb teachers merely, but opens his own sacred mouth; when he not only proclaims that some God must be worshipped, but at the same time declares that He is the God to whom worship is due; when he not only teaches his elect to have respect to God, but manifests himself as the God to whom this respect should be paid.

The course, which God followed towards his Church from the very first, was to supplement these common proofs by the addition of his Word, as a surer and more direct means of discovering himself. And there can be no doubt that it was by this help, Adam, Noah, Abraham, and the other patriarchs, attained to that familiar knowledge which, in a manner, distinguished them from unbelievers. I am not now speaking of the peculiar doctrines of faith by which they were elevated to the hope of eternal blessedness. It was necessary, in passing from death unto life, that they should know God, not only as a Creator, but as a Redeemer also; and both kinds of knowledge they certainly did obtain from the Word. In point of order, however, the knowledge first given was that which made them acquainted with the God by whom the world was made and is governed. To this first knowledge was afterwards added the more intimate knowledge which alone quickens dead souls, and by which God is known not only as the Creator of the worlds and the sole author and disposer of all events, but also as a Redeemer, in the person of the Mediator. But as the fall and the corruption of nature have not yet been considered, I now postpone the consideration of the remedy (for which, see Book 2, chapter 6 etc). Let the reader then remember, that I am not now treating of the covenant by which God adopted the children of Abraham, or of that branch of doctrine by which, as founded in Christ, believers have, properly speaking, been in all ages separated from the profane heathen. I am only showing that it is necessary to apply to Scripture, in order to learn the sure marks, which distinguish God, as the Creator of the world, from the whole herd of fictitious gods. We shall afterward, in due course, consider the work of Redemption. In the meantime, though we shall adduce many passages from the New Testament, and some also from the Law and the Prophets, in which express mention is made of Christ, the only object will be to show that God, the Maker of the world, is manifested to us in Scripture, and his true character expounded, so as to save us from wandering up and down, as in a labyrinth, in search of some doubtful deity.

2 First, by oracles and visions, and the ministry of the Patriarchs. Secondly, by the promulgation of the Law, and the preaching of the Prophets. Why the doctrines of religion are committed to writing.

Whether God revealed himself to the fathers by oracles and visions, or, by the instrumentality and ministry of men, suggested what they were to hand down to posterity, there cannot be a doubt that the certainty of what he taught them was firmly engraved on their hearts, so that they felt assured and knew that the things which they learnt came forth from God, who invariably accompanied his word with a sure testimony, infinitely superior to mere opinion. At length, in order that, while doctrine was continually enlarged, its truth might subsist in the world during all ages, it was his pleasure that the same oracles, which he had deposited with the fathers, should be consigned to public records. With this view, the law was promulgated, and prophets were afterwards added to be its interpreters. For though the uses of the law were manifold (Book 2, chapters 7 and 8), and the special office assigned to Moses and all the Prophets was to teach the method of reconciliation between God and man (whence Paul calls Christ "the end of the law" (Romans 10:4); still I repeat that, in addition to the proper doctrine of faith and repentance in which Christ is set forth as a Mediator, the Scriptures employ certain marks and tokens to distinguish the only wise and true God, considered as the Creator and Governor of the world, and thereby guard against his being confounded with the herd of false deities. Therefore, while it becomes man seriously to employ his eyes in considering the works of God, since a place has been assigned him in this most glorious theatre that he may be a spectator of them, his special duty is to give ear to the Word, that he may the better profit. Hence, it is not strange that those who are born in darkness become more and more hardened in their stupidity; because the vast majority instead of confining themselves within due bounds by listening with docility to the Word, exult in their own vanity. If true religion is to beam upon us, our principle must be, that it is necessary to begin with heavenly teaching, and that it is impossible for any man to obtain even the minutest portion of right and sound doctrine without being a disciple of Scripture. Hence, the first step in true knowledge is taken, when we reverently embrace the testimony, which God has been pleased therein to give of himself. For not only does faith, full and perfect faith, but all correct knowledge of God, originate in obedience. And surely, in this respect God has with singular Providence provided for mankind in all ages.

3 This view confirmed, A. By the depravity of our nature making it necessary in everyone who would know God to have recourse to the word; B. From those passages of the Psalms in which God is introduced as reigning.

For if we reflect how prone the human mind is to lapse into forgetfulness of God, how readily inclined to every kind of error, how bent every now and then on devising new and fictitious religions, it will be easy to understand how necessary it was to make such a depository of doctrine as would secure it from either perishing by the neglect, vanishing away amid the errors, or being corrupted by the presumptuous audacity of men. It being thus manifest that God, foreseeing the inefficiency of his image imprinted on the fair form of the universe, has given the assistance of his Word to all whom he has ever been pleased to instruct effectually, we, too, must pursue this straight path, if we aspire in earnest to a genuine contemplation of God;—we must go, I say, to the Word, where the character of God, drawn from his works is described accurately and to the life; these works being estimated, not by our depraved Judgment, but by the standard of eternal truth. If, as I lately said, we turn aside from it, however great the speed with which we move, we shall never reach the goal, because we are off the course. We should consider that the brightness of the Divine countenance, which even an Apostle declares to be inaccessible (1 Timothy 6:16), is a kind of labyrinth,—a labyrinth to us inextricable, if the Word do not serve us as a thread to guide our path; and that it is better to limp in the way, than run with the greatest swiftness out of it. Hence, the Psalmist, after repeatedly declaring (Psalm 93, 96, 97, 99, etc.) that superstition should be banished from the world in order that pure religion may flourish, introduces God as *reigning*; meaning by the term, not the power which he possesses and which he exerts in the government of universal nature, but the doctrine by which he maintains his due supremacy: because error never can be eradicated from the heart of man until the true knowledge of God has been implanted in it.

4 Another confirmation from certain direct statements in the Psalms. Lastly, from the words of our Savior.

Accordingly, the same prophet, after mentioning that the heavens declare the glory of God, that the firmament showed forth the works of his hands, that the regular succession of day and night proclaim his Majesty, proceeds to make mention of the Word: —"The law of the Lord," says he, "is perfect, converting the soul; the testimony of the Lord is sure, making wise the simple. The statutes of the Lord are right, rejoicing the heart; the commandment of the Lord is pure, enlightening the eyes" (Psalm 19:1-9). For though the law has other uses besides (as to which, see Book 2, chapter 7, section 6, 10, 12), the general meaning is, that it is the proper school for training the children of God; the invitation given to all nations, to behold him in the heavens and earth, proving of no avail. The same view is taken in the 29th Psalm, where the Psalmist, after discoursing on the dreadful voice of God, which, in thunder, wind, rain, whirlwind, and tempest, shakes the earth, makes the mountains tremble, and breaks the cedars, concludes by saying, "that in his temple does everyone speak of his glory," unbelievers being deaf to all God's words when they echo in the air. In like manner, another Psalm, after describing the raging billows of the sea, thus concludes, "Thy testimonies are very sure; holiness becometh thine house forever" (Psalm 93:5). To the same effect are the words of our Savior to the Samaritan woman, when he told her that her nation and all other nations worshipped they knew not what; and that the Jews alone gave worship to the true God (John 4:22). Since the human mind, through its weakness, was altogether unable to come to God if not aided and upheld by his sacred word, it necessarily followed that all mankind, the Jews excepted, inasmuch as they sought God without the Word, were laboring under vanity and error.

Chapter 7

THE TESTIMONY OF THE SPIRIT NECESSARY TO GIVE FULL AUTHORITY TO SCRIPTURE. THE IMPIETY OF PRETENDING THAT THE CREDIBILITY OF SCRIPTURE DEPENDS ON THE JUDGMENT OF THE CHURCH.

Section

1. The authority of Scripture derived not from men, but from the Spirit of God. Objection, That Scripture depends on the decision of the Church. Refutation, A. The truth of God would thus be subjected to the will of man. B. It is insulting to the Holy Spirit. C. It establishes a tyranny in the Church. D. It forms a mass of errors. E. It subverts conscience. F. It exposes our faith to the scoffs of the profane.

2. Another reply to the objection drawn from the words of the Apostle Paul. Solution of the difficulties started by opponents. A second objection refuted.

3. A third objection founded on a sentiment of Augustine considered.

4. Conclusion: that the authority of Scripture is founded on its being spoken by God. This confirmed by the conscience of the godly, and the consent of all men of the least candor. A fourth objection common in the mouths of the profane. Refutation.

5. Last and necessary conclusion: that the authority of Scripture is sealed on the hearts of believers by the testimony of the Holy Spirit. The certainty of this testimony. Confirmation of it from a passage of Isaiah, and the experience of believers. Also, from another passage of Isaiah.

1 The authority of Scripture derived not from men, but from the Spirit of God. Objection, That Scripture depends on the decision of the Church. Refutation, A. The truth of God would thus be subjected to the will of man. B. It is insulting to the Holy Spirit. C. It establishes a tyranny in the Church. D. It forms a mass of errors. E. It subverts conscience. F. It exposes our faith to the scoffs of the profane.

Before proceeding further, it seems proper to make some observations on the authority of Scripture, in order that our minds may not only be prepared to receive it with reverence, but be divested of all doubt.

When that which professes to be the Word of God is acknowledged to be so, no person, unless devoid of common sense and the feelings of a man, will have the desperate hardihood to refuse credit to the speaker. But since no daily responses are given from heaven, and the Scriptures are the only records in which God has been pleased to consign his truth to perpetual remembrance, the full authority which they ought to possess with the faithful is not recognized, unless they are believed to have come from heaven, as directly as if God had been heard giving utterance to them. This subject well deserves to be treated more at large, and pondered more accurately. But my readers will pardon me for having more regard to what my plan admits than to what the extent of this topic requires.

A most pernicious error has very generally prevailed—viz. that Scripture is of importance only in so far as conceded to it by the suffrage of the Church; as if the eternal and inviolable truth of God could depend on the will of men. With great insult to the Holy Spirit, it is asked, who can assure us that the Scriptures proceeded from God; who guarantee that they have come down safe and unimpaired to our times; who persuade us that *this* book is to be received with reverence, and *that one* expunged from the list, did not the Church regulate all these things with certainty? On the determination of the Church, therefore, it is said, depend both the reverence, which is due to Scripture, and the books, which are to be admitted into the canon. Thus profane men, seeking, under the pretext of the Church, to introduce unbridled tyranny, care not in what absurdities they entangle themselves and others, provided they extort from the simple this one acknowledgement—viz. that there is nothing which the Church cannot do. But what is to become of miserable consciences in quest of some solid assurance of eternal life, if all the promises with regard to it have no better support than man's Judgment? On being told so, will they cease to doubt and tremble? On the other hand, to what jeers of the wicked is our faith subjected—into how great suspicion is it brought with all, if believed to have only a precarious authority lent to it by the good will of men?

2 Another reply to the objection drawn from the words of the Apostle Paul. Solution of the difficulties started by opponents. A second objection refuted.

These ravings are admirably refuted by a single expression of an Apostle. Paul testifies that the Church is "built on the foundation of the apostles and Prophets" (Ephesians 2:20). If the doctrine of the apostles and Prophets is the foundation of the Church, the former must have had its certainty before the latter began to exist. Nor is there any room for the cavil, that though the Church derives her first beginning from thence, it still remains doubtful what writings are to be attributed to the apostles and Prophets, until her Judgment is interposed. For if the Christian Church was founded at first on the writings of the Prophets, and the preaching of the apostles, that doctrine, wherever it may be found, was certainly ascertained and sanctioned antecedently to the Church, since, but for this, the Church herself never could have existed. Nothing therefore can be more absurd than the fiction that the power of judging Scripture is in the Church, and that on her nod its certainty depends. When the Church receives it, and gives it the stamp of her authority, she does not make that authentic which was otherwise doubtful or refutable but, acknowledging it as the truth of God, she, as in duty bounds shows her reverence by an unhesitating assent. As to the question, How shall we be persuaded that it came from God without recurring to a decree of the Church? it is just the same as if it were asked, How shall we learn to distinguish light from darkness, white from black, sweet from bitter? Scripture bears upon the face of it as clear evidence of its truth, as white and black do of their color, sweet and bitter of their taste.

3 A third objection founded on a sentiment of Augustine considered.

I am aware it is usual to quote a sentence of Augustine in which he says that he would not believe the gospel, were he not moved by the authority of the Church. But it is easy to discover from the context, how inaccurate and unfair it is to give it such a meaning. He was reasoning against the Manichees, who insisted on being implicitly believed, alleging that they had the truth, though they did not show they had. But as they pretended to appeal to the gospel in support of Manes, he asks what they would do if they fell in with a man who did not even believe the gospel—what kind of argument they would use to bring him over to their opinion. He afterwards adds, "But I would not believe the gospel," etc.; meaning, that were he a stranger to the faith, the only thing which could induce him to embrace the gospel would be the authority of the Church. And is it anything wonderful, that one who does not know Christ should pay respect to men?

Augustine, therefore, does not here say that the faith of the godly is founded on the authority of the Church; nor does he mean that the certainty of the gospel depends upon it; he merely says that unbelievers would have no certainty of the gospel, so as thereby to win Christ, were they not influenced by the consent of the Church. And he clearly shows this to be his meaning, by thus expressing himself a little before: "When I have praised my own creed, and ridiculed yours, who do you suppose is to judge between us; or what more is to be done than to quit those who, inviting us to certainty, afterwards command us to believe uncertainty, and follow those who invite us, in the first instance, to believe what we are not yet able to comprehend, that waxing stronger through faith itself, we may become able to understand what we believe—no longer men, but God himself internally strengthening and illuminating our minds? These unquestionably are the words of Augustine; and the obvious inference from them is, that this holy man had no intention to suspend our faith in Scripture on the nod or decision of the Church, but only to intimate (what we too admit to be true) that those who are not yet enlightened by the Spirit of God, become teachable by reverence for the Church, and thus submit to learn the faith of Christ from the gospel. In this way, though the authority of the Church leads us on, and prepares us to believe in the gospel, it is plain that Augustine would have the certainty of the godly to rest on a very different foundation.

At the same time, I deny not that he often presses the Manichees with the consent of the whole Church, while arguing in support of the Scriptures, which they rejected. Hence, he upbraids Faustus for not submitting to evangelical truth—truth so well founded, so firmly established, so gloriously renowned, and handed down by sure succession from the days of the apostles. But he nowhere insinuates that the authority, which we give to the Scriptures, depends on the definitions or devices of men. He only brings forward the universal Judgment of the Church, as a point most pertinent to the cause, and one, moreover, in which he had the advantage of his opponents. Anyone who desires to see this more fully proved may read his short treatises, *De Utilitate Credendi* (The Advantages of Believing), where it will be found that the only facility of believing which he recommends is that which affords an introduction, and forms a fit commencement to inquiry; while he declares that we ought not to be satisfied with opinion, but to strive after substantial truth.

4. Conclusion: that the authority of Scripture is founded on its being spoken by God. This confirmed by the conscience of the godly, and the consent of all men of the least candor. A fourth objection common in the mouths of the profane. Refutation.

It is necessary to attend to what I lately said, that our faith in doctrine is not established until we have a perfect conviction that God is its author. Hence, the highest proof of Scripture is uniformly taken from the character of him whose Word it is. The Prophets and apostles boast not their own acuteness or any qualities, which win credit to speakers, nor do they dwell on reasons;

but they appeal to the sacred name of God, in order that the whole world may be compelled to submission. The next thing to be considered is, how it appears not probable merely, but certain, that the name of God is neither rashly nor cunningly pretended. If, then, we would consult most effectually for our consciences, and save them from being driven about in a whirl of uncertainty, from wavering, and even stumbling at the smallest obstacle, our conviction of the truth of Scripture must be derived from a higher source than human conjectures, Judgments, or reasons; namely, the secret testimony of the Spirit. It is true, indeed, that if we choose to proceed in the way of arguments it is easy to establish, by evidence of various kinds, that if there is a God in heaven, the Law, the Prophecies, and the Gospel, proceeded from him. Nay, although learned men, and men of the greatest talent, should take the opposite side, summoning and ostentatiously displaying all the powers of their genius in the discussion; if they are not possessed of shameless effrontery, they will be compelled to confess that the Scripture exhibits clear evidence of its being spoken by God, and, consequently, of its containing his heavenly doctrine. We shall see a little further on, that the volume of sacred Scripture very far surpasses all other writings. Nay, if we look at it with clear eyes, and unblessed Judgment, it will forthwith present itself with a divine majesty, which will subdue our presumptuous opposition, and force us to do it homage.

Still, however, it is preposterous to attempt, by discussion, to rear up a full faith in Scripture. True, were I called to contend with the craftiest despisers of God, I trust, though I am not possessed of the highest ability or eloquence, I should not find it difficult to stop their obstreperous mouths; I could, without much ado, put down the boastings which they mutter in corners, were anything to be gained by refuting their cavils. But although we may maintain the sacred Word of God against gainsayers, it does not follow that we shall forthwith implant the certainty which faith requires in their hearts. Profane men think that religion rests only on opinion, and, therefore, that they may not believe foolishly, or on slight grounds, desire and insist to have it proved by reason that Moses and the Prophets were divinely inspired. But I answer, that the testimony of the Spirit is superior to reason. For as God alone can properly bear witness to his own words, so these words will not obtain full credit in the hearts of men, until they are sealed by the inward testimony of the Spirit. The same Spirit, therefore, who spoke by the mouth of the Prophets, must penetrate our hearts, in order to convince us that they faithfully delivered the message with which they were divinely entrusted. This connection is most aptly expressed by Isaiah in these words, "My Spirit that is upon thee, and my words which I have put in thy mouth, shall not depart out of thy mouth, nor out of the mouth of thy seed, nor out of the mouth of thy seed's seed, saith the Lord, from henceforth and forever" (Isaiah 59:21). Some worthy persons feel disconcerted, because, while the wicked murmur with impunity at the Word of God, they have not a clear proof at hand to silence them, forgetting that the Spirit is called an earnest and seal to confirm the faith of the godly, for this very reason, that, until he enlightens their minds, they are tossed to and fro in a sea of doubts.

5 Last and necessary conclusion: that the authority of Scripture is sealed on the hearts of believers by the testimony of the Holy Spirit. The certainty of this testimony. Confirmation of it from a passage of Isaiah, and the experience of believers. Also, from another passage of Isaiah.

Let it therefore be held as fixed, that those who are inwardly taught by the Holy Spirit acquiesce implicitly in Scripture; that Scripture, carrying its own evidence along with it, deigns not to submit to proofs and arguments, but owes the full conviction with which we ought to receive it to the testimony of the Spirit. Enlightened by him, we no longer believe, either on our own Judgment or that of others, that the Scriptures are from God; but, in a way superior to human Judgment, feel perfectly assured—as much so as if we beheld the divine image visibly impressed on it—that it came to us, by the instrumentality of men, from the very mouth of God.

We ask not for proofs or probabilities on which to rest our Judgment, but we subject our intellect and Judgment to it as too transcendent for us to estimate. This, however, we do, not in the manner in which some are wont to fasten on an unknown object, which, as soon as known, displeases, but because we have a thorough conviction that, in holding it, we hold unassailable truth; not like miserable men, whose minds are enslaved by superstition, but because we feel a divine energy living and breathing in it— an energy by which we are drawn and animated to obey it, willingly indeed, and knowingly, but more vividly and effectually than could be done by human will or knowledge. Hence, God most justly exclaims by the mouth of Isaiah, "Ye are my witnesses, saith the Lord, and my servant whom I have chosen, that ye may know and believe me, and understand that I am he" (Isaiah 43:10).

Such, then, is a conviction which asks not for reasons; such, a knowledge which accords with the highest reason, namely knowledge in which the mind rests more firmly and securely than in any reasons; such in fine, the conviction which revelation from heaven alone can produce. I say nothing more than every believer experiences in himself, though my words fall far short of the reality. I do not dwell on this subject at present, because we will return to it again: only let us now understand that the only true faith is that which the Spirit of God seals on our hearts. Nay, the modest and teachable reader will find a sufficient reason in the promise contained in Isaiah, that all the children of the renovated Church "shall be taught of the Lord" (Isaiah 54:13). This singular privilege God bestows on his elect only, whom he separates from the rest of mankind. For what is the beginning of true doctrine but prompt alacrity to hear the Word of God? And God, by the mouth of Moses, thus demands to be heard: "It is not in heavens that thou shouldest say, Who shall go up for us to heaven, and bring it unto us, that we may hear and do it? But the word is very nigh unto thee, in thy mouth and in thy heart" (Deuteronomy 30:12, 14). God having been pleased to reserve the treasure of intelligence for his children, no wonder that so much ignorance and stupidity is seen in the *generality* of mankind. In the generality, I include even those specially chosen, until they are engrafted into the body of the Church. Isaiah, moreover, while reminding us that the prophetical doctrine would prove incredible not only to strangers, but also to the Jews, who were desirous to be thought of the household of God, subjoins the reason, when he asks, "To whom has the arm of the Lord been revealed?" (Isaiah 53:1). If at any time, then we are troubled at the small number of those who believe, let us, on the other hand, call to mind, that none comprehend the mysteries of God save those to whom it is given.

Chapter 8

THE CREDIBILITY OF SCRIPTURE SUFFICIENTLY PROVED IN SO FAR AS NATURAL REASON ADMITS.

This chapter consists of four parts. The first contains certain general proofs which may be easily gathered out of the writings both of the Old and New Testament—viz. the arrangement of the sacred volume, its dignity, truth, simplicity, efficacy, and majesty, sections 1, 2. The second part contains special proofs taken from the Old Testament—viz. the antiquity of the books of Moses, their authority, his miracles and prophecies, sections 3-7; also, the predictions of the other Prophets and their wondrous harmony, section 8. There is subjoined a refutation of two objections to the books of Moses and the Prophets, sections 9, 10. The third part exhibits proofs gathered out of the New Testament, *e.g.*, the harmony of the Evangelists in their account of heavenly mysteries, the majesty of the writings of John, Peter, and Paul, the remarkable calling of the Apostles and conversion of Paul, section 11. The last part exhibits the proofs drawn from ecclesiastical history, the perpetual consent of the Church in receiving and preserving divine truth, the invincible force of the truth in defending itself, the agreement of the godly (though otherwise differing so much from one another), the pious profession of the same doctrine by many illustrious men; in fine, the more than human constancy of the martyrs, sections 12, 13. This is followed by a conclusion of the particular topic discussed.

Sections

1. Secondary helps to establish the credibility of Scripture. A. The arrangement of the sacred volume. B. Its dignity. C. Its truth. D. Its simplicity. E. Its efficacy.

2. The majesty conspicuous in the writings of the Prophets.

3. Special proofs from the Old Testament. A. The antiquity of the Books of Moses.

4. This antiquity contrasted with the dreams of the Egyptians. B. The majesty of the Books of Moses.

5. The miracles and prophecies of Moses. A profane objection refuted.

6. Another profane objection refuted.

7. *The prophecies of Moses as to the scepter not departing from Judah, and the calling of the Gentiles.*

8. *The predictions of other Prophets. The destruction of Jerusalem; and the return from the Babylonish captivity. Harmony of the Prophets. The celebrated prophesy of Daniel.*

9. *Objection against Moses and the Prophets. Answer to it.*

10. *Another objection and answer. Of the wondrous Providence of God in the preservation of the sacred books. The Greek Translation. The carefulness of the Jews.*

11. *Special proofs from the New Testament. A. The harmony of the Evangelists, and the sublime simplicity of their writings. B. The majesty of John, Paul, and Peter. C. The calling of the Apostles. D. The conversion of Paul.*

12. *Proofs from Church history. A. Perpetual consent of the Church in receiving and preserving the truth. B. The invincible power of the truth itself. C. Agreement among the godly, not withstanding of their many differences in other respects.*

13. *The constancy of the martyrs. Conclusion. Proofs of this description only of use after the certainty of Scripture has been established in the heart by the Holy Spirit.*

1 **Secondary helps to establish the credibility of Scripture. A. The arrangement of the sacred volume. B. Its dignity. C. Its truth. D. Its simplicity. E. Its efficacy.**

In vain were the authority of Scripture fortified by argument, or supported by the consent of the Church, or confirmed by any other helps, if unaccompanied by an assurance higher and stronger than human Judgment can give. Till this better foundation has been laid, the authority of Scripture remains in suspense. On the other hand, when recognizing its exemption from the common rule, we receive it reverently, and according to its dignity, those proofs which were not so strong as to produce and rivet a full conviction in our minds, become most appropriate helps. For it is wonderful how much we are confirmed in our belief, when we more attentively consider how admirably the system of divine wisdom contained in it is arranged—how perfectly free the doctrine is from everything that savors of earth—how beautifully it harmonizes in all its parts—and how rich it is in all the other qualities which give an air of majesty to composition. Our hearts are still more firmly assured when we reflect that our admiration is elicited more by the dignity of the matter than by the graces of style. For it was not without an admirable arrangement of Providence, that the sublime mysteries of the kingdom of heaven have for the greater part been delivered with a contemptible meanness of words. Had they been adorned with a more splendid eloquence, the wicked might have caviled, and alleged that this constituted all their force. But now, when an unpolished simplicity, almost bordering on rudeness, makes a deeper impression than the loftiest flights of oratory, what does it indicate if not that the Holy Scriptures are too mighty in the power of truth to need the rhetorician's art?

Hence, there was good ground for the Apostle's declaration, that the faith of the Corinthians was founded not on "the wisdom of men," but on "the power of God" (1 Corinthians 2:5), this speech and preaching among them having been "not with enticing words of man's wisdom, but in demonstration of the Spirit and of power" (1 Corinthians 2:5). For the truth is vindicated in opposition to every doubt, when, unsupported by foreign aid, it has its sole sufficiency in itself. How peculiarly this property belongs to Scripture appears from this, that no human writings, however skillfully composed, are at all capable of affecting us in a similar way. Read Demosthenes or Cicero, read Plato, Aristotle, or any other of that class: you will, I admit, feel wonderfully allured, pleased, moved, enchanted; but turn from them to the reading of the Sacred Volume, and whether you will or not, it will so affect you, so pierce your heart, so work its way into your very marrow, that, in comparison of the impression so produced, that of orators and philosophers will almost disappear; making it manifest that in the Sacred Volume there is a truth divine, a something which makes it immeasurably superior to all the gifts and graces attainable by man.

2 The majesty conspicuous in the writings of the Prophets.

I confess, however, that in elegance and beauty, nay, splendor, the style of some of the Prophets is not surpassed by the eloquence of heathen writers. By examples of this description, the Holy Spirit was pleased to show that it was not from want of eloquence he in other instances used a rude and homely style. But whether you read David, Isaiah, and others of the same class, whose discourse flows sweet and pleasant; or Amos the herdsman, Jeremiah, and Zechariah, whose rougher idiom savors of rusticity; that majesty of the Spirit to which I adverted appears conspicuous in all. I am aware, that as Satan often apes God, that he may by a fallacious resemblance the better insinuate himself into the minds of the simple, so he craftily disseminated the impious errors with which he deceived miserable men in an uncouth and semi-barbarous style, and frequently employed obsolete forms of expression in order to cloak his impostures. None possessed of any moderate share of sense need be told how vain and vile such affectation is. But in regard to the Holy Scriptures, however petulant men may attempt to carp at them, they are replete with sentiments, which it is clear that man never could have conceived. Let each of the Prophets be examined, and not one will be found who does not rise far higher than human reach. Those who feel their works insipid must be absolutely devoid of taste.

3 Special proofs from the Old Testament. A. The antiquity of the Books of Moses.

As this subject has been treated at large by others, it will be sufficient here merely to touch on its leading points. In addition to the qualities already mentioned, great weight is due to the antiquity of Scripture. Whatever fables Greek writers may retail concerning the Egyptian Theology, no monument of any religion exists which is not long posterior to the age of Moses. But Moses does not introduce a new Deity. He only sets forth that doctrine concerning the eternal God, which the Israelites had received by tradition from their fathers, by whom it had been transmitted from hand to hand, during a long series of ages. For what else does he do than lead them back to the covenant, which had been made with Abraham? Had he referred to matters of which they had never heard, he never could have succeeded; but their deliverance from the bondage in which they were held must have been a fact of familiar and universal notoriety, the very mention of which must have immediately aroused the attention of all. It is, moreover, probable, that they were intimately acquainted with the whole period of four hundred years. Now, if Moses (who is so much earlier than all other writers) traces the tradition of his doctrine from so remote a period, it is obvious how far the Holy Scriptures must in point of antiquity surpass all other writings.

4 This antiquity contrasted with the dreams of the Egyptians. B. The majesty of the Books of Moses.

Some perhaps may choose to credit the Egyptians in carrying back their antiquity to a period of six thousand years before the world was created. But their garrulity, which even some profane authors have held up to derision, it cannot be necessary for me to refute. Josephus, however, in his work against Appion, produces important passages from very ancient writers, implying that the doctrine delivered in the law was celebrated among all nations from the remotest ages, though it was neither read nor accurately known. And then, in order that the malignant might have no ground for suspicion, and the ungodly have no handle for trivial objection, God has provided, in the most effectual manner, against both dangers. When Moses relates the words, which Jacob, under Divine inspiration, uttered concerning his posterity almost three hundred years before, how does he, ennoble his own tribe? He stigmatizes it with eternal infamy in the person of Levi. "Simon and Levi," says he, "are brethren; instruments of cruelty are in their habitations. O my soul, come not thou into their secret; unto their assembly mine honor be not thou united" (Genesis 49:5, 6). This stigma he certainly might have passed in silence, not only that he might spare his own ancestor, but also save both himself and his whole family from a portion of the disgrace. How can any suspicion attach to him, who, by voluntarily proclaiming that a Divine oracle declared the first founder of his family detestable, neither consults for his own private interest, nor declines to incur obloquy among his tribe, who must have been offended by his statement of the fact? Again, when he relates the wicked murmuring of his brother Aaron, and his sister Miriam (Numbers 12:1), shall we say that he spoke his own natural feelings, or that he obeyed the command of the Holy Spirit? Moreover, when invested with supreme authority, why does he not bestow the office of High Priest on his sons, instead of consigning them to the lowest place? I only touch on a few points out of many; but the Law itself contains throughout numerous proofs, which fully vindicate the credibility of Moses, and place it beyond dispute, that he was in truth a messenger sent forth from God.

5 The miracles and prophecies of Moses. A profane objection refuted.

The many striking miracles, which Moses relates, are so many sanctions of the law delivered, and the doctrine propounded, by him. His being carried up into the mount in a cloud; his remaining there forty days separated from human society; his countenance glistening during the promulgation of the law, as with meridian effulgence; the lightning which flashed on every side; the voices and thundering which echoed in the air; the clang of the trumpet blown by no human mouth; his entrance into the tabernacle, while a cloud hid him from the view of the people; the miraculous vindication of his authority, by the fearful destruction of Korah, Nathan, and Abiram, and all their impious faction; the stream instantly gushing forth from the rock when struck with his rod; the manna which rained from heaven at his prayer;— did not God by all these proclaim aloud that he was an undoubted prophet? If anyone objects that I am taking debatable points for granted, their quibble is easily answered. Moses published all these things in the assembly of the people. How, then, could he possibly impose on the very eyewitnesses of what was done? Is it conceivable that he would have come forward, and, while accusing the people of unbelief, obstinacy, ingratitude, and other crimes, have boasted that his doctrine had been confirmed in their own presence by miracles, which they never saw?

6 Another profane objection refuted.

For it is also worthy of remark, that the miracles which he relates are combined with disagreeable circumstances, which must have provoked opposition from the whole body of the people, if there had been the smallest ground for it. Hence, it is obvious that they were induced to assent, merely because they had been previously convinced by their own experience. But because the fact was too ascribed them to magic (Exodus 9:11). But with what probability is a charge of magic brought against him, who held it in such abhorrence, that he ordered everyone who should consult soothsayers and magicians to be stoned? (Leviticus 20:27). Assuredly, no impostor deals in tricks, without studying to raise his reputation by amazing the common people. But what does Moses do? By crying out, that he and Aaron his brother are nothing (Exodus 16:7), that they merely execute what God has commanded, he clears himself from every approach to suspicion. Again, if the facts are considered in themselves, what kind of incantation could cause manna to rain from heaven every day, and in sufficient quantity to maintain a people, while anyone, who gathered more than the appointed measure, saw his incredulity divinely punished by its turning to worms? To this we may add, that God then suffered his servant to be subjected to so many serious trials, that the ungodly cannot now gain anything by their glamour. When (as often happened) the people proudly and petulantly rose up against him, when individuals conspired, and attempted to overthrow him, how could any impostures have enabled clear to leave it free for heathen writers to deny that Moses did perform miracles, the father of lies suggested a calumny, and him to elude their rage? The event plainly shows that by these means his doctrine was attested to all succeeding ages.

7 The prophecies of Moses as to the scepter not departing from Judah, and the calling of the Gentiles.

Moreover, it is impossible to deny that he was guided by a prophetic spirit in assigning the first place to the tribe of Judah in the person of Jacob, especially if we take into view the fact itself, as explained by the event. Suppose that Moses was the inventor of the prophecy, still, after he committed it to writing, four hundred years pass away, during which no mention is made of a scepter in the tribe of Judah. After Saul is anointed, the kingly office seems fixed in the tribe of Benjamin (1 Samuel 11:15; 16:13). When Samuel anoints David, what apparent ground is there for the transference? Who could have looked for a king out of the plebeian family of a herdsman? And out of seven brothers, who could have thought that the honor was destined for the youngest? And then by what means did he afterwards come within reach of the throne? Who dare say that his anointing was regulated by human art, or skill, or prudence, and was not rather the fulfillment of a divine prophecy? In like manner, do not the predictions, though obscure, of the admission of the Gentiles into the divine covenant, seeing they were not fulfilled until almost two thousand years after, make it palpable that Moses spoke under divine inspiration? I omit other predictions, which so plainly betoken divine revelation, that all men of sound mind must see God spoke them. In short, his Song itself (Deuteronomy 32) is a bright mirror in which God is manifestly seen.

8 The predictions of other Prophets. The destruction of Jerusalem; and the return from the Babylonish captivity. Harmony of the Prophets. The celebrated prophesy of Daniel.

In the case of the other Prophets, the evidence is even clearer. I will only select a few examples, for it was too tedious to enumerate the whole. Isaiah, in his own day, when the kingdom of Judah was at peace, and had even some ground to confide in the protection of the Chaldeans, spoke of the destruction of the city and the captivity of the people (Isaiah 55:1). Supposing it not to be sufficient evidence of divine inspiration to foretell, many years before, events which, at the time, seemed fabulous, but which ultimately turned out to be true, whence shall it be said that the prophecies which he uttered concerning their return proceeded, if it was not from God? He names Cyrus, by whom the Chaldeans were to be subdued and the people restored to freedom. After the prophet thus spoke, more than a hundred years elapsed before Cyrus was born, that being nearly the period which elapsed between the death of the one and the birth of the other. It was impossible at that time to guess that some Cyrus would arise to make war on the Babylonians, and after subduing their powerful monarchy, put an end to the captivity of the children of Israel. Does not this simple, unadorned narrative plainly demonstrate that what Isaiah spoke was not the conjecture of man, but the undoubted oracle of God? Again, when Jeremiah, a considerable time before the people were led away, assigned seventy years as the period of captivity, and fixed their liberation and return, must not his tongue have been guided by the Spirit of God? What effrontery were it to deny that, by these evidences, the authority of the Prophets is established, the very thing being fulfilled to which they appeal in support of their credibility! "Behold, the former things are come to pass, and new things do I declare; before they spring forth I tell you of them" (Isaiah 42:9).

I say nothing of the agreement between Jeremiah and Ezekiel, who, living so far apart, and yet prophesying at the same time, harmonize as completely in all they say as if they had mutually dictated the words to one another. What shall I say of Daniel? Did not he deliver prophecies embracing a future period of almost six hundred years, as if he had been writing of past events generally known? (Daniel 9, etc.). If the pious will duly meditate on these things, they will be sufficiently instructed to silence the cavils of the ungodly. The demonstration is too clear to be gainsaid.

9 Objection against Moses and the Prophets. Answer to it.

I am aware of what is muttered in corners by certain miscreants, when they would display their acuteness in assailing divine truth. They ask, how do we know that Moses and the Prophets wrote the books, which now bear their names? Nay, they even dare to question whether there ever was a Moses. Were anyone to question whether there ever was a Plato, or an Aristotle, or a Cicero, would not the rod or the whip be deemed the fit chastisement of such folly? The law of Moses has been wonderfully preserved, more by divine providence than by human care; and though, owing to the negligence of the priests, it lay for a short time buried, —from the time when it was found by good King Josiah (2 Kings 22:8; 2 Chronicles 34:15), —it has continued in the hands of men, and been transmitted in unbroken succession from generation to generation. Nor, indeed, when Josiah brought it forth, was it as a book unknown or new, but one, which had always been matter of notoriety, and was then in full remembrance. The original writing had been deposited in the temple, and a copy taken from it had been deposited in the royal archives (Deuteronomy 17:18, 19); the only thing which had occurred was, that the priests had ceased to publish the law itself in due form, and the people also had neglected the wonted reading of it. I may add, that scarcely an age passed during which its authority was not confirmed and renewed. Were the books of Moses unknown to those who had the Psalms of David in their hands?

To sum up the whole in one word, it is certain beyond dispute, that these writings passed down, if I may so express it, from hand to hand, being transmitted in an unbroken series from the fathers, who either with their own ears heard them spoken, or learned them from those who had, while the remembrance of them was fresh.

10 Another objection and answer. Of the wondrous Providence of God in the preservation of the sacred books. The Greek Translation. The carefulness of the Jews.

An objection taken from the history of the Maccabees (1 Maccabees 1:57, 58) to impugn the credibility of Scripture is, on the contrary, fitted the best possible to confirm it. First, however, let us clear away the gloss, which is put upon it: having done so, we shall turn the engine, which they erect against us upon themselves. As Antiochus ordered all the books of Scripture to be burnt, it is asked, where did the copies we now have come from? I, in my turn, ask, In what workshop could they have been so quickly fabricated? It is certain that they were in existence the moment the persecution ceased, and that they were acknowledged without dispute by all the pious that had been educated in their doctrine, and were familiarly acquainted with them. Nay, while all the wicked so wantonly insulted the Jews as if they had leagued together for the purpose, not one ever dared to charge them with having introduced spurious books. Whatever, in their opinion, the Jewish religion might be, they acknowledged that Moses was the founder of it. What, then, do those babblers, but betray their snarling petulance in falsely alleging the spuriousness of books whose sacred antiquity is proved by the consent of all history? But not to spend labor in vain in refuting these vile calumnies, let us rather attend to the care which the Lord took to preserve his Word, when against all hope he rescued it from the truculence of a most cruel tyrant as from the midst of the flames—inspiring pious priests and others with such constancy that they hesitated not, though it should have been purchased at the expense of their lives, to transmit this treasure to posterity, and defeating the keenest search of prefects and their satellites.

Who does not recognize it as a signal and miraculous work of God, that those sacred monuments which the ungodly persuaded themselves had utterly perished, immediately returned to resume their former rights, and, indeed, in greater honor? For the Greek translation appeared to disseminate them over the whole world. Nor does it seem so wonderful that God rescued the tables of his covenant from the sanguinary edicts of Antiochus, as that they remained safe and entire amid the manifold disasters by which the Jewish nation was occasionally crushed, devastated, and almost exterminated. The Hebrew language was in no estimation, and almost unknown; and assuredly, had not God provided for religion, it must have utterly perished. For it is obvious from the prophetical writings of that age, how much the Jews, after their return from the captivity, had lost the genuine use of their native tongue. It is of importance to attend to this, because the comparison more clearly establishes the antiquity of the Law and the Prophets. And whom did God employ to preserve the doctrine of salvation contained in the Law and the Prophets, that Christ might manifest it in its own time? The Jews, the bitterest enemies of Christ; and hence Augustine justly calls them the librarians of the Christian Church, because they supplied us with books of which they themselves had not the use.

11 Special proofs from the New Testament. A. The harmony of the Evangelists, and the sublime simplicity of their writings. B. The majesty of John, Paul, and Peter. C. The calling of the Apostles. D. The conversion of Paul.

When we proceed to the New Testament, how solid are the pillars by which its truth is supported! Three evangelists give a narrative in a mean and humble style. The proud often eye this simplicity with disdain, because they attend not to the principal heads of doctrine; for from these they might easily infer that these evangelists treat of heavenly mysteries beyond the capacity of man. Those who have the least particle of candor must be ashamed of their fastidiousness when they read the first chapter of Luke. Even our Savior's discourses, a summary of which is given by these three evangelists, ought to prevent everyone from treating their writings with contempt. John, again, fulminating in majesty, strikes down more powerfully than any thunderbolt the petulance of those who refuse to submit to the obedience of faith.

Let all those acute censors, whose highest pleasure it is to banish a reverential regard of Scripture from their own and other men's hearts, come forward; let them read the Gospel of John, and, willing or unwilling, they will find a thousand sentences which will at least arouse them from their sloth; nay, which will burn into their consciences as with a hot iron, and check their derision. The same thing may be said of Peter and Paul, whose writings, though the greater part read them blindfold, exhibit a heavenly majesty, which in a manner binds and rivets every reader. But one circumstance, sufficient of itself to exalt their doctrine above the world, is, that Matthew, who was formerly fixed down to his money-table, Peter and John, who were employed with their little boats, being all rude and illiterate, had never learned in any human school that which they delivered to others. Paul, moreover, who had not only been an avowed but a cruel and bloody foe, being changed into a new man, shows, by the sudden and unhoped-for change, that a heavenly power had compelled him to preach the doctrine which once he destroyed. Let those dogs deny that the Holy Spirit descended upon the apostles, or, if not, let them refuse credit to the history, still the very circumstances proclaim that the Holy Spirit must have been the teacher of those who, formerly contemptible among the people, all of a sudden began to discourse so magnificently of heavenly mysteries.

12 Proofs from Church history. A. Perpetual consent of the Church in receiving and preserving the truth. B. The invincible power of the truth itself. C. Agreement among the godly, not withstanding of their many differences in other respects.

Add, moreover, that, for the best of reasons, the consent of the Church is not without its weight. For it is not to be accounted of no consequence, that, from the first publication of Scripture, so many ages have uniformly concurred in yielding obedience to it, and that, notwithstanding of the many extraordinary attempts which Satan and the whole world have made to oppress and overthrow it, or completely efface it from the memory of men, it has flourished like the palm tree and continued invincible. Though in old times there was scarcely a sophist or orator of any note who did not exert his powers against it, their efforts proved unavailing. The powers of the earth armed themselves for its destruction, but all their attempts vanished into smoke. When thus powerfully assailed on every side, how could it have resisted if it had trusted only to human aid? Nay, its divine origin is more completely established by the fact, that when all human wishes were against it, it advanced by its own energy. Add that it was not a single city or a single nation that concurred in receiving and embracing it. Its authority was recognized as far and as wide as the world extends—various nations who had nothing else in common entering for this purpose into a holy league. Moreover, while we ought to attach the greatest weight to the agreement of minds so diversified, and in all other things so much at variance with each other—an agreement which a Divine Providence alone could have produced—it adds no small weight to the whole when we attend to the piety of those who thus agree; not of all of them indeed, but of those in whom as lights God was pleased that his Church should shine.

13

The constancy of the martyrs. Conclusion. Proofs of this description only of use after the certainty of Scripture has been established in the heart by the Holy Spirit.

Again, with what confidence does it become us to subscribe to a doctrine attested and confirmed by the blood of so many saints? They, when once they had embraced it, hesitated not boldly and intrepidly, and even with great alacrity, to meet death in its defense. Being transmitted to us with such an earnest, who of us shall not receive it with firm and unshaken conviction? It is therefore no small proof of the authority of Scripture, that it was sealed with the blood of so many witnesses, especially when it is considered that in bearing testimony to the faith, they met death not with fanatical enthusiasm (as erring spirits are sometimes wont to do), but with a firm and constant, yet sober godly zeal. There are other reasons, neither few nor feeble, by which the dignity and majesty of the Scriptures may be not only proved to the pious, but also completely vindicated against the cavils of slanderers. These, however, cannot of themselves produce a firm faith in Scripture until our heavenly Father manifest his presence in it, and thereby secure implicit reverence for it. Then only, therefore, does Scripture suffice to give a saving knowledge of God when its certainty is founded on the inward persuasion of the Holy Spirit.

Still the human testimonies that go to confirm it will not be without effect, if they are used in subordination to that chief and highest proof, as secondary helps to our weakness. But it is foolish to attempt to prove to infidels that the Scripture is the Word of God. This it cannot be known to be, except by faith. Justly, therefore, does Augustine remind us, that every man who would have any understanding in such high matters must previously possess piety and mental peace.

Chapter 9

1 The temper and error of the Libertines, who take to themselves the name of spiritual, briefly described. Their refutation. A. The Apostles and all true Christians have embraced the written Word. This confirmed by a passage in Isaiah; also by the example and words of Paul. B. The Spirit of Christ seals the doctrine of the written Word on the minds of the godly.

Those who, rejecting Scripture, imagine that they have some peculiar way of penetrating to God, are to be deemed not so much under the influence of error as madness. For certain giddy men have lately appeared, who, while they make a great display of the superiority of the Spirit, reject all reading of the Scriptures themselves, and deride the simplicity of those who only delight in what they call the dead and deadly letter. But I wish they would tell me what spirit it is whose inspiration raises them to such a sublime height that they dare despise the doctrine of Scripture as mean and childish.

If they answer that it is the Spirit of Christ, their confidence is exceedingly ridiculous; since they will, I presume, admit that the apostles and other believers in the primitive Church were not illuminated by any other Spirit. None of these thereby learned to despise the word of God, but everyone was imbued with greater reverence for it, as their writings most clearly testify. And, indeed, it had been so foretold by the mouth of Isaiah. For when he says, "My Spirit that is upon thee, and my words which I have put in thy mouth, shall not depart out of thy mouth, nor out of the mouth of thy seed, nor out of the mouth of thy seed's seed, saith the Lord, from henceforth and forever," he does not tie down the ancient Church to external doctrine, as he were a mere teacher of elements; he rather shows that, under the reign of Christ, the true and full felicity of the new Church will consist in their being ruled not less by the Word than by the Spirit of God.

Hence, we infer that these miscreants are guilty of fearful sacrilege in tearing asunder what the prophet joins in indissoluble union. Add to this, that Paul, though carried up even to the third heaven, ceased not to profit by the doctrine of the law and the Prophets, while, in like manner, he exhorts Timothy, a teacher of singular excellence, to give attention to reading (1 Timothy 4:13). And the eulogium, which he pronounces on Scripture well, deserves to be remembered—viz. that "it is profitable for doctrine, for reproof, for correction, and for instruction in righteousness, that the man of God may be perfect" (2 Timothy 3:16). What an infatuation of the devil, therefore, to fancy that Scripture, which conducts the sons of God to the final goal, is of transient and temporary use? Again, I should like those people to tell me whether they have imbibed any other Spirit than that which Christ promised to his disciples. Though their madness is extreme, it will scarcely carry them the length of making this their boast. But what kind of Spirit did our Savior promise to send? One who should not speak of himself (John 16:13), but suggest and instill the truths, which he himself had delivered through the word. Hence, the office of the Spirit promised to us, is not to form new and unheard-of revelations, or to coin a new form of doctrine, by which we may be led away from the received doctrine of the gospel, but to seal on our minds the very doctrine, which the gospel recommends.

2 Refutation continued. C. The impositions of Satan cannot be detected without the aid of the written Word. First Objection. The Answer to it.

Hence, it is easy to understand that we must give diligent heed both to the reading and hearing of Scripture, if we would obtain any benefit from the Spirit of God (just as Peter praises those who attentively study the doctrine of the Prophets (2 Peter 1:19), though it might have been thought to be superseded after the gospel light arose), and, on the contrary, that any spirit which passes by the wisdom of God's Word, and suggests any other doctrine, is deservedly suspected of vanity and falsehood. Since Satan transforms himself into an angel of light, what authority can the Spirit have with us if he is not ascertained by an infallible mark? And assuredly, the Lord points him out to us with sufficient clearness; but these miserable men err as if bent on their own destruction, while they seek the Spirit from themselves rather than from Him. But they say that it is insulting to subject the Spirit, to whom all things are to be subject, to the Scripture: as if it were disgraceful to the Holy Spirit to maintain a perfect resemblance throughout, and be in all respects without variation consistent with himself. True, if he were subjected to a human, an angelical, or to any foreign standard, it might be thought that he was rendered subordinate, or, if you will, brought into bondage, but so long as he is compared with himself, and considered in himself, how can it be said that he is thereby injured? I admit that he is brought to a test, but the very test by which it has pleased him that his majesty should be confirmed. It ought to be enough for us when once we hear his voice; but lest Satan should insinuate himself under his name, he wishes us to recognize him by the image which he has stamped on the Scriptures. The author of the Scriptures cannot vary, and change his likeness. Such as he there appeared at first, such he will perpetually remain. There is nothing contumelious to him in this, unless we are to think it would be honorable for him to degenerate, and revolt against himself.

3 Second Objection from the words of Paul as to the *letter and spirit*. The Answer, with an explanation of Paul's meaning. How the Spirit and the written Word are indissolubly connected.

Their cavil about our cleaving to the dead letter carries with it the punishment, which they deserve for despising Scripture. It is clear that Paul is there arguing against false apostles (2 Corinthians 3:6), who, by recommending the law without Christ, deprived the people of the benefit of the New Covenant, by which the Lord engages that he will write his law on the hearts of believers, and engrave it on their inward parts. The letter therefore is dead, and the law of the Lord kills its readers when it is dissevered from the grace of Christ, and only sounds in the ear without touching the heart. But if the Spirit effectually impresses it on the heart; if it exhibits Christ, it is the word of life converting the soul, and making wise the simple. Nay, in the very same passage, the Apostle calls his own preaching the ministration of the Spirit (2 Corinthians 3:8), intimating that the Holy Spirit so cleaves to his own truth, as he has expressed it in Scripture, that he then only exerts and puts forth his strength when the word is received with due honor and respect.

There is nothing repugnant here to what was lately said (chapter 7) that we have no great certainty of the word itself, until it be confirmed by the testimony of the Spirit. For the Lord has so knit together the certainty of his word and his Spirit, that our minds are duly imbued with reverence for the word when the Spirit shining upon it enables us there to behold the face of God; and, on the other hand, we embrace the Spirit with no danger of delusion when we recognize him in his image, that is, in his word. Thus, indeed, it is. God did not produce his word before men for the sake of sudden display, intending to abolish it the moment the Spirit should arrive; but he employed the same Spirit, by whose agency he had administered the word, to complete his work by the efficacious confirmation of the word. In this way, Christ explained to the two disciples (Luke 24:27), not that they were to reject the Scriptures and trust to their own wisdom, but that they were to understand the Scriptures.

In like manner, when Paul says to the Thessalonians, "Quench not the Spirit," he does not carry them aloft to empty speculation apart from the word; he immediately adds, "Despise not prophesying" (1 Thessalonians 5:19, 20). By this, doubtless, he intimates that the light of the Spirit is quenched the moment prophesying fall into contempt. How is this answered by those swelling enthusiasts, in whose idea the only true illumination consists, in carelessly laying aside, and bidding adieu to the Word of God, while, with no less confidence than folly, they fasten upon any dreaming notion which may have casually sprung up in their minds? Surely, a very different sobriety becomes the children of God. As they feel that without the Spirit of God they are utterly devoid of the light of truth, so they are not ignorant that the word is the instrument by which the illumination of the Spirit is dispensed. They know of no other Spirit than the one who dwelled and spoke in the apostles—the Spirit by whose oracles they are daily invited to the hearing of the word.

Chapter 10

IN SCRIPTURE, THE TRUE GOD OPPOSED, EXCLUSIVELY, TO ALL THE GODS OF THE HEATHEN.

Sections

1. Explanation of the knowledge of God resumed. God as manifested in Scripture, the same as delineated in his works.

2. The attributes of God as described by Moses, David, and Jeremiah. Explanation of the attributes. Summary. Uses of this knowledge.

3. Scripture, in directing us to the true God, excludes the gods of the heathen, who, however, in some sense, held the unity of God.

1 **Explanation of the knowledge of God resumed. God as manifested in Scripture, the same as delineated in his works.**

We formerly observed that the knowledge of God, which, in other respects, is not obscurely exhibited in the frame of the world, and in all the creatures, is more clearly and familiarly explained by the word. It may now be proper to show, that in Scripture the Lord represents himself in the same character in which we have already seen that he is delineated in his works. A full discussion of this subject would occupy a large space. But it will here be sufficient to furnish a kind of index, by attending to which the pious reader may be enabled to understand what knowledge of God he ought chiefly to search for in Scripture, and be directed as to the mode of conducting the search. I am not now adverting to the peculiar covenant by which God distinguished the race of Abraham from the rest of the nations. For when by gratuitous adoption he admitted those who were enemies to the rank of sons, he even then acted in the character of a Redeemer. At present, however, we are employed in considering that knowledge which stops short at the creation of the world, without ascending to Christ the Mediator. But though it will soon be necessary to quote certain passages from the New Testament (proofs being there given both of the power of God the Creator, and of his providence in the preservation of what he originally created), I wish the reader to remember what my present purpose is, that he may not wander from the proper subject. Briefly, then, it will be sufficient for him at present to understand how God, the Creator of heaven and earth, governs the world, which was made by him. In every part of Scripture, we meet with descriptions of his paternal kindness and readiness to do good, and we also meet with examples of severity, which show that he is the just punisher of the wicked, especially when they continue obstinate notwithstanding of all his forbearance.

2 The attributes of God as described by Moses, David, and Jeremiah. Explanation of the attributes. Summary. Uses of this knowledge.

There are certain passages, which contain more vivid descriptions of the divine character, setting it before us as if his genuine countenance were visibly portrayed. Moses, indeed, seems to have intended briefly to comprehend whatever may be known of God by man, when he said, "The Lord, The Lord God, merciful and gracious, long-suffering, and abundant in goodness and truth, keeping mercy for thousands, forgiving iniquity and transgression and sin, and that will by no means clear the guilty; visiting the iniquity of the fathers upon the children, and upon the children's children, unto the third and to the fourth generation" (Exodus 34:6, 7). Here we may observe, *first*, that his eternity and self existence are declared by his magnificent name twice repeated; and, *secondly*, that in the enumeration of his perfections, he is described not as he is in himself, but in relation to us, in order that our acknowledgement of him may be more a vivid actual impression than empty visionary speculation. Moreover, the perfections thus enumerated are just those, which we saw shining in the heavens, and on the earth—compassion, goodness, mercy, justice, Judgment, and truth. For power and energy are comprehended under the name Jehovah.

The Prophets employ similar epithets when they would fully declare his sacred name. Not to collect a great number of passages, it may suffice at present to refer to one Psalm (145) in which a summary of the divine perfections is so carefully given that not one seems to have been omitted. Still, however, every perfection there set down may be contemplated in creation; and, hence, such as we feel him to be when experience is our guide, such he declares himself to be by his word. In Jeremiah, where God proclaims the character in which he would have us to acknowledge him, though the description is not so full, it is substantially the same. "Let him that glorieth," says he, "glory in this, that he understandeth and knoweth me, that I am the Lord which exercise loving-kindness, Judgment, and righteousness, in the earth" (Jeremiah 9:24).

Assuredly, the attributes which are most necessary for us to know are these three: Loving-kindness, on which alone our entire safety depends: Judgment, which is daily exercised on the wicked, and awaits them in a severer form, even for eternal destruction: Righteousness, by which the faithful are preserved, and most benignly cherished. The prophet declares, that when you understand these, you are amply furnished with the means of glorying in God. Nor is there here any omission of his truth, or power, or holiness, or goodness. For how could this knowledge of his loving-kindness, Judgment, and righteousness, exist, if it were not founded on his inviolable truth? How, again, could it be believed that he governs the earth with Judgment and righteousness, without presupposing his mighty power? Whence, too, his loving-kindness, but from his goodness? In fine, if all his ways are loving-kindness, Judgment, and righteousness, his holiness also is thereby conspicuous. Moreover, the knowledge of God, which is set before us in the Scriptures, is designed for the same purpose as that which shines in creation—viz. that we may thereby learn to worship him with perfect integrity of heart and unfeigned obedience, and also to depend entirely on his goodness.

3 Scripture, in directing us to the true God, excludes the gods of the heathen, who, however, in some sense, held the unity of God.

Here, it may be proper to give a summary of the general doctrine. First, then, let the reader observe that the Scripture, in order to direct us to the true God, distinctly excludes and rejects all the gods of the heathen, because religion was universally adulterated in almost every age. It is true, indeed, that the name of one God was everywhere known and celebrated. For those who worshipped a multitude of gods, whenever they spoke the genuine language of nature, simply used the name god, as if they had thought one god sufficient. And this is shrewdly noticed by Justin Martyr, who, to the same effect, wrote a treatise, entitled, On the Monarchy of God, in which he shows, by a great variety of evidence, that the unity of God is engraved on the hearts of all. Tertullian also proves the same thing from the common forms of speech. But as all, without exception, have in the vanity of their minds rushed or been dragged into lying fictions, these impressions, as to the unity of God, whatever they may have naturally been, have had no further effect than to render men inexcusable.

The wisest plainly discover the vague wanderings of their minds when they express a wish for any kind of Deity, and thus offer up their prayers to unknown gods. And then, in imagining a manifold nature in God, though their ideas concerning Jupiter, Mercury, Venus, Minerva, and others, were not so absurd as those of the rude vulgar, they were by no means free from the delusions of the devil. We have elsewhere observed, that however subtle the evasions devised by philosophers, they cannot do away with the charge of rebellion, in that all of them have corrupted the truth of God. For this reason, Habakkuk (2:20), after condemning all idols, orders men to seek God in his temple, that the faithful may acknowledge none but Him, who has manifested himself in his word.

Chapter 11

IMPIETY OF ATTRIBUTING A VISIBLE FORM TO GOD. — THE SETTING UP OF IDOLS A DEFECTION FROM THE TRUE GOD.

There are three leading divisions in this chapter. The first contains a refutation of those who ascribe a visible form to God (s. 1 and 2), with an answer to the objection of those who, because it is said that God manifested his presence by certain symbols, use it as a defense of their error (s. 3 and 4). Various arguments are afterwards adduced, disposing of the trite objection from Gregory's expression, that images are the books of the unlearned (s. 5-7). The second division of the chapter relates to the origin of idols or images, and the adoration of them, as approved by the Papists (s. 8-10). Their evasion refuted (s. 11). The third division treats of the use and abuse of images (s. 12). Whether it is expedient to have them in Christian Churches (s. 13). The concluding part contains a refutation of the second Council of Nice, which very absurdly contends for images in opposition to divine truth, and even to the disparagement of the Christian name.

Sections

1. God is opposed to idols, that all may know he is the only fit witness to himself. He expressly forbids any attempt to represent him by a bodily shape.

2. Reasons for this prohibition from Moses, Isaiah, and Paul. The complaint of a heathen. It should put the worshipers of idols to shame.

3. Consideration of an objection taken from various passages in Moses. The Cherubim and Seraphim show that images are not fit to represent divine mysteries. The Cherubim belonged to the tutelage of the Law.

4. The materials of which idols are made abundantly refute the fiction of idolaters. Confirmation from Isaiah and others. Absurd precaution of the Greeks.

5. *Objection,* —*That images are the books of the unlearned. Objection answered, A. Scripture declares images to be teachers of vanity and lies.*

6. *Answer continued, B. Ancient Theologians condemn the formation and worship of idols.*

7. *Answer continued, —C. The use of images condemned by the luxury and meretricious ornaments given to them in Popish Churches. D. The Church must be trained in true piety by another method.*

8. *The second division of the chapter. Origin of idols or images. Its rise shortly after the flood. Its continual progress.*

9. *Of the worship of images. Its nature. A pretext of idolaters refuted. Pretexts of the heathen. Genius of idolaters.*

10. *Evasion of the Papists. Their agreement with ancient idolaters.*

11. *Refutation of another evasion or sophism—viz. the distinction of* δυλια *and* λατρια.

12. *Third division of the chapter—viz. the use and abuse of images.*

13. *Whether it is expedient to have images in Christian temples.*

14. *Absurd defense of the worship of images by the second so-called Council of Nice. Sophisms or perversions of Scripture in defense of images in churches.*

15. *Passages adduced in support of the worship of images.*

16. *The blasphemous expressions of some ancient idolaters approved by not a few of the more modern, both in word and deed.*

1 God is opposed to idols, that all may know he is the only fit witness to himself. He expressly forbids any attempt to represent him by a bodily shape.

As Scripture, in accommodation to the rude and gross intellect of man, usually speaks in popular terms, so whenever its object is to discriminate between the true God and false deities, it opposes him in particular to idols; not that it approves of what is taught more elegantly and subtly by philosophers, but that it may the better expose the folly, nay, madness of the world in its inquiries after God, so long as everyone clings to his own speculations. This exclusive definition, which we uniformly meet with in Scripture, annihilates every deity which men frame for themselves of their own accord—God himself being the only fit witness to himself. Meanwhile, seeing that this brutish stupidity has overspread the globe, men longing after visible forms of God, and so forming deities of wood and stone, silver and gold, or of any other dead and corruptible matter, we must hold it as a first principle, that as often as any form is assigned to God, his glory is corrupted by an impious lie. In the Law, accordingly, after God had claimed the glory of divinity for himself alone, when he comes to show what kind of worship he approves and rejects, he immediately adds, "Thou shalt not make unto thee any graven image, or any likeness of anything that is in heaven above, or in the earth beneath, or in the water under the earth" (Exodus 20:4). By these words he curbs any licentious attempt we might make to represent him by a visible shape, and briefly enumerates all the forms by which superstition had begun, even long before, to turn his truth into a lie. For we know that the Persian worshipped the Sun. As many stars as the foolish nations saw in the sky, so many gods they imagined them to be. Then to the Egyptians, every animal was a figure of God. The Greeks, again, plumed themselves on their superior wisdom in worshipping God under the human form. But God makes no comparison between images, as if one were more, and another less befitting; he rejects, without exception, all shapes and pictures, and other symbols by which the superstitious imagine they can bring him near to them.

2 Reasons for this prohibition from Moses, Isaiah, and Paul. The complaint of a heathen. It should put the worshipers of idols to shame.

This may easily be inferred from the reasons, which he annexes to his prohibition. First, it is said in the books of Moses (Deuteronomy 4:15), "Take ye therefore good heed unto yourselves; for ye saw no manner of similitude in the day that the Lord spake unto you in Horeb, out of the midst of the fire, lest ye corrupt yourselves, and make you a graven image, the similitude of any figure," etc. We see how plainly God declares against all figures, to make us aware that all longing after such visible shapes is rebellion against him. Of the Prophets, it will be sufficient to mention Isaiah, who is the most copious on this subjects (Isaiah 40:18; 41:7, 29; 45:9; 46:5), in order to show how the majesty of God is defiled by an absurd and indecorous fiction, when he who is incorporeal is assimilated to corporeal matter; he who is invisible to a visible image; he who is a spirit to an inanimate object; and he who fills all space to a bit of paltry wood, or stone, or gold.

Paul, too, reasons in the same way, "Forasmuch, then, as we are the offspring of God, we ought not to think that the Godhead is like unto gold, or silver, or stone, graven by art and man's device" (Acts 17:29). Hence, it is manifest, that whatever statues are set up or pictures painted to represent God, are utterly displeasing to him, as a kind of insults to his majesty. And is it strange that the Holy Spirit thunders such responses from heaven, when he compels even blind and miserable idolaters to make a similar confession

73

on the earth? Seneca's complaint, as given by Augustine, is well known. He says "The sacred immortal, and invisible gods they exhibit in the meanest and most ignoble materials, and dress them in the clothing of men and beasts; some confound the sexes, and form a compound out of different bodies, giving the name of deities to objects, which, if they were met alive, would be deemed monsters." Hence, again, it is obvious, that the defenders of images resort to a paltry quibbling evasion, when they pretend that the Jews were forbidden to use them on account of their proneness to superstition; as if a prohibition which the Lord founds on his own eternal essences and the uniform course of nature could be restricted to a single nation. Besides, when Paul refuted the error of giving a bodily shape to God, he was addressing not Jews, but Athenians.

3. Consideration of an objection taken from various passages in Moses. The Cherubim and Seraphim show that images are not fit to represent divine mysteries. The Cherubim belonged to the tutelage of the Law.

It is true that the Lord occasionally manifested his presence by certain signs, so that he was said to be seen face to face; but all the signs he ever employed were in apt accordance with the scheme of doctrine, and, at the same time, gave plain intimation of his incomprehensible essence. For the cloud, and smoke, and flame, though they were symbols of heavenly glory (Deuteronomy 4:11), curbed men's minds as with a bridle, that they might not attempt to penetrate further. Therefore, even Moses (to whom, of all men, God manifested himself most familiarly) was not permitted though he prayed for it, to behold that face, but received for answer, that the refulgence was too great for man (Exodus 33:20). The Holy Spirit appeared under the form of a dove, but as it instantly vanished, who does not see that in this symbol of a moment, the faithful were admonished to regard the Spirit as invisible, to be contented with his power and grace, and not call for any external figure? God sometimes appeared in the form of a man, but this was in anticipation of the future revelation in Christ, and, therefore, did not give the Jews the least pretext for setting up a symbol of Deity under the human form.

The mercy-seat, also (Exodus 25:17, 18, 21), where, under the Law, God exhibited the presence of his power, was so framed, as to intimate that God is best seen when the mind rises in admiration above itself: the Cherubim with outstretched wings shaded, and the veil covered it, while the remoteness of the place was in itself a sufficient concealment. It is therefore mere infatuation to attempt to defend images of God and the saints by the example of the Cherubim. For what, pray, did these figures mean, if not that images are unfit to represent the mysteries of God, since they were so formed as to cover the mercy-seat with their wings, thereby concealing the view of God, not only from the eye, but from every human sense, and curbing presumption? To this we may add, that the Prophets depict the Seraphim, who are exhibited to us in vision, as having their faces veiled; thus intimating, that the refulgence of the divine glory is so great, that even the angels cannot gaze upon it directly, while the minute beams which sparkle in the face of angels are shrouded from our view.

Moreover, all men of sound Judgment acknowledge that the Cherubim in question belonged to the old tutelage of the law. It is absurd, therefore, to bring them forward as an example for our age. For that period of puerility, if I may so express it, to which such rudiments were adapted, has passed away. Surely, it is disgraceful, that heathen writers should be more skillful interpreters of Scripture than the Papists. Juvenal (Sat. 14) holds up the Jews to derision for worshipping the thin clouds and firmament. This he does perversely and impiously; still, in denying that any visible shape of Deity existed among them, he speaks more accurately than the Papists, who prate about there having been some visible image. In the fact that the people every now and then rushed forth with boiling haste in pursuit of idols, just like water gushing forth with violence from a copious spring, let us learn how prone our nature is to idolatry, that we may not, by throwing the whole blame of a common vice upon the Jews, be led away by vain and sinful enticements to sleep the sleep of death.

4 The materials of which idols are made abundantly refute the fiction of idolaters. Confirmation from Isaiah and others. Absurd precaution of the Greeks.

To the same effect are the words of the Psalmist (Psalm 115:4, 135:15), "Their idols are silver and gold, the works of men's hands." From the materials of which they are made, he infers that they are not gods, taking it for granted that every human device concerning God is a dull fiction. He mentions silver and gold rather than clay or stone, that neither splendor nor cost may procure reverence to idols. He then draws a general conclusion, that nothing is more unlikely than that gods should be formed of any kind of inanimate matter. Man is forced to confess that he is but the creature of a day (see Book 3, chapter 9, section 2), and yet would have the metal, which he has deified to be regarded as God. Whence had idols their origin, but from the will of man? There was ground, therefore, for the sarcasm of the heathen poet, "I was once the trunk of a fig-tree, a useless log, when the tradesman, uncertain whether he should make me a stool, etc., chose rather that I should be a god." In other words, an earth-born creature, who breathes out his life almost every moment, is able by his own device to confer the name and honor of deity on a lifeless trunk. But as that Epicurean poet, in indulging his wit, had no regard for religion, without attending to his jeers or those of his fellows, let the rebuke of the prophet sting, nay, cut us to the heart, when he speaks of the extreme infatuation of those who take a piece of wood to kindle a fire to warm themselves, bake bread, roast or boil flesh, and out of the residue make a god, before which they prostrate themselves as suppliants (Isaiah 44:16). Hence, the same prophet, in another place, not only charges idolaters as guilty in the eye of the law, but upbraids them for not learning from the foundations of the earth, nothing being more incongruous than to reduce the immense and incomprehensible Deity to the stature of a few feet. And yet, experience shows that this monstrous proceeding, though palpably repugnant to the order of nature, is natural to man.

It is, moreover, to be observed, that by the mode of expression that is employed, every form of superstition is denounced. Being works of men, they have no authority from God (Isaiah 2:8, 31:7; Hosea 14:3; Micah 5:13); and, therefore, it must be regarded as a fixed principle, that all modes of worship devised by man are detestable. The infatuation is placed in a still stronger light by the Psalmist (Psalm 115:8), when he shows how aid is implored from dead and senseless objects, by beings who have been endued with intelligence for the very purpose of enabling them to know that the whole universe is governed by Divine energy alone. But as the corruption of nature hurries away all mankind collectively and individually into this madness, the Spirit at length thunders forth a dreadful imprecation, "They that make them are like unto them, so is everyone that trusteth in them." And it is to be observed, that the thing forbidden is *likeness*, whether sculptured or otherwise. This disposes of the frivolous precaution taken by the Greek Church. They think they do admirably, because they have no sculptured shape of Deity, while none go greater lengths in the licentious use of pictures. The Lord, however, not only forbids any image of himself to be erected by a statuary, but to be formed by any artist whatever, because every such image is sinful and insulting to his majesty.

5 Objection, —That images are the books of the unlearned. Objection answered, A. Scripture declares images to be teachers of vanity and lies.

I am not ignorant, indeed, of the assertion, which is now more than threadbare, "that images are the books of the unlearned." So said Gregory: The Holy Spirit makes a very different decision; and had Gregory got his lesson in this matter in the Spirit's school, he never would have spoken as he did. For when Jeremiah declares that "the stock is a doctrine of vanities" (Jeremiah 10:8), and Habakkuk, "that the molten image" is "a teacher of lies," the general doctrine to be inferred certainly is, that everything respecting God which is learned from images is futile and false. If it is objected that the censure of the Prophets is directed against those who perverted images to purposes of impious superstition, I admit it to be so; but I add (what must be obvious to all), that the Prophets utterly condemn what the Papists hold to be an undoubted axiom—viz. that images are substitutes for books. For they contrast images with the true God, as if the two were of an opposite nature, and never could be made to agree. In the passages which I lately quoted, the conclusion drawn is, that seeing there is one true God whom the Jews worshipped, visible shapes made for the purpose of representing him are false and wicked fictions; and all, therefore, who have recourse to them for knowledge are miserably deceived. In short, were it not true that all such knowledge is fallacious and spurious, the Prophets would not condemn it in such general terms. This at least I maintain, that when we teach that all human attempts to give a visible shape to God are vanity and lies, we do nothing more than state *verbatim* what the Prophets taught.

6 Answer continued, B. Ancient Theologians condemn the formation and worship of idols.

Moreover, let Lactantius and Eusebius be read on this subject. These writers assume it as an indisputable fact, that all the beings whose images were erected were originally men. In like manner, Augustine distinctly declares, that it is unlawful not only to worship images, but also to dedicate them. And in this he says no more than had been long before decreed by the Libertine Council, the thirty-sixth Canon of which is, "There must be no pictures used in churches: Let nothing which is adored or worshipped be painted on walls." But the most memorable passage of all is that which Augustine quotes in another place from Varro, and in which he expressly concurs: —"Those who first introduced images of the gods both took away fear and brought in error." Were this merely the saying of Varro, it might perhaps be of little weight, though it might well make us ashamed, that a heathen, groping in darkness, should have attained to such a degree of light, as to see that corporeal images are unworthy of the majesty of God, and that, because they diminish reverential fear and encourage error. The sentiment itself bears witness that it was uttered with no less truth than shrewdness. But Augustine, while he borrows it from Varro, adduces it as conveying his own opinion. At the outset, indeed, he declares that the first errors into which men fell concerning God did not originate with images, but increased with them, as if new fuel had been added. Afterwards, he explains how the fear of God was thereby extinguished or impaired, his presence being brought into contempt by foolish, and childish, and absurd representations. The truth of this latter remark I wish we did not so thoroughly experience. Whosoever, therefore, is desirous of being instructed in the true knowledge of God must apply to some other teacher than images.

7 Answer continued, —C. The use of images condemned by the luxury and meretricious ornaments given to them in Popish Churches. D. The Church must be trained in true piety by another method.

Let Papists, then, if they have any sense of shame, henceforth desist from the futile plea, that images are the books of the unlearned—a plea so plainly refuted by innumerable passages of Scripture. And yet were I to admit the plea, it would not be a valid defense of their peculiar idols. It is well known what kind of monsters they obtrude upon us as divine. For what are the pictures or statues to which they append the names of saints, but exhibitions of the most shameless luxury or obscenity? Were anyone to dress himself after their model, he would deserve the pillory. Indeed, brothels exhibit their inmates more chastely and modestly dressed than churches do images intended to represent virgins. The dress of the martyrs is in no respect more becoming. Let Papists then have some little regard to decency in decking their idols, if they would give the least plausibility to the false allegation, that they are books of some kind of sanctity. But even then, we shall answer, that this is not the method in which the Christian people should be taught in sacred places.

Very different from these follies is the doctrine in which God would have them to be there instructed. His injunction is, that the doctrine common to all should there be set forth by the preaching of the Word, and the administration of the sacraments, —a doctrine to which little heed can be given by those whose eyes are carried too and fro gazing at idols. And who are the unlearned, whose rudeness admits of being taught by images only? Just those whom the Lord acknowledges for his disciples; those whom he honors with a revelation of his celestial philosophy, and desires to be trained in the saving mysteries of his kingdom. Indeed, I confess that, as matters now are, there are not a few in the present day who cannot want such books. But, I ask, whence this stupidity, but just because they are defrauded of the only doctrine which was fit to instruct them? The simple reason that those who had the charge of churches resigned the office of teaching to idols was, because they themselves were dumb. Paul declares, that by the true preaching of the gospel Christ is portrayed and in a manner crucified before our eyes (Galatians 3:1). Of what use, then, were the erection in churches of so many crosses of wood and stone, silver and gold, if this doctrine were faithfully and honestly preached—viz. Christ died that he might bear our curse upon the tree, that he might expiate our sins by the sacrifice of his body, wash them in his blood, and, in short, reconcile us to God the Father? From this one doctrine, the people would learn more than from a thousand crosses of wood and stone. As for crosses of gold and silver, it may be true that the avaricious give their eyes and minds to them more eagerly than to any heavenly instructor.

8 The second division of the chapter. Origin of idols or images. Its rise shortly after the flood. Its continual progress.

In regard to the origin of idols, the statement contained in the Book of Wisdom has been received with almost universal consent—viz. that they originated with those who bestowed this honor on the dead, from a superstitious regard to their memory. I admit that this perverse practice is of very high antiquity, and I deny not that it was a kind of torch by which the infatuated proneness of mankind to idolatry was kindled into a greater blaze. I do not, however, admit that it was the first origin of the practice. That idols were in use before the prevalence of that ambitious consecration of the images of the dead, frequently adverted to by profane writers, is evident from the words of Moses (Genesis 31:19). When he relates that Rachel stole her father's images, he speaks of the use of idols as a common vice. Hence, we may infer, that the human mind is, so to speak, a perpetual forge of idols. There was a kind of renewal of the world at the deluge, but before many years elapse, men are forging gods at will. There is reason to believe, that in the holy Patriarch's lifetime his grandchildren were given to idolatry: so that he must with his own eyes, not without the deepest grief, have seen the earth polluted with idols—that earth whose iniquities God had lately purged with so fearful a Judgment. For Joshua testifies (Joshua 24:2), that Torah and Nachor, even before the birth of Abraham, were the worshipers of false gods. The progeny of Shem having so speedily revolted, what are we to think of the posterity of Ham, who had been cursed long before in their father? Thus, indeed, it is.

The human mind, stuffed as it is with presumptuous rashness, dares to imagine a god suited to its own capacity; as it labors under dullness, nay, is sunk in the grossest ignorance, it substitutes vanity and an empty phantom in the place of God. To these evils, another is added. The god whom man has thus conceived inwardly he attempts to embody outwardly. The mind, in this way, conceives the idol, and the hand gives it birth. That idolatry has its origin in the idea which men have, that God is not present with them unless his presence is carnally exhibited, appears from the example of the Israelites: "Up," said they, "make us gods, which shall go before us; for as for this Moses, the man that brought us up out of the land of Egypt, we wet not what is become of him" (Exodus 22:1). They knew, indeed, that there was a God whose mighty power they had experienced in so many miracles, but they had no confidence of his being near to them, if they did not with their eyes behold a corporeal symbol of his presence, as an attestation to his actual government. They desired, therefore, to be assured by the image, which went before them, that they were journeying under Divine guidance. And daily experience shows, that the flesh is always restless until it has obtained some figment like itself, with which it may vainly solace itself as a representation of God. In consequence of this blind passion men have, almost in all ages since the world began, set up signs on which they imagined that God was visibly depicted to their eyes.

9 Of the worship of images. Its nature. A pretext of idolaters refuted. Pretexts of the heathen. Genius of idolaters.

After such a figment is formed, adoration forthwith ensues: for when once men imagined that they beheld God in images, they also worshipped him as being there. At length their eyes and minds becoming wholly engrossed by them, they began to grow more and more brutish, gazing and wondering as if some divinity were actually before them. It hence appears that men do not fall away to the worship of images until they have imbibed some idea of a grosser description: not that they actually believe them to be gods, but that the power of divinity somehow or other resides in them. Therefore, whether it is God or a creature that is imaged, the moment you fall prostrate before it in veneration, you are so far fascinated by superstition. For this reason, the Lord not only forbade erecting of statues to himself, but also the consecration of titles and stones which might be set up for adoration. For the same reason, also, the second commandment has an additional part concerning adoration. For as soon as a visible form is given to God, his power also is supposed to be annexed to it. So stupid are men, that wherever they figure God, there they fix him, and by necessary consequence proceed to adore him. It makes no difference whether they worship the idol simply, or God in the idol; it is always idolatry when divine honors are paid to an idol, be the color what it may. And because God wills not to be worshipped superstitiously, whatever is bestowed upon idols is so much robbed from him.

Let those attend to this who set about hunting for miserable pretexts in defense of the execrable idolatry in which for many past ages true religion has been buried and sunk. It is said that the images are not accounted gods. Nor were the Jews so utterly thoughtless as not to remember that there was a God whose hand led them out of Egypt before they made the calf. Indeed, Aaron saying, that these were the gods, which had brought them out of Egypt, they intimated, in no ambiguous terms, that they wished to retain God, their deliverer, provided they saw him going before them in the calf. Nor are the heathen to be deemed to have been so stupid as not to understand that God was something else than wood and stone. For they changed the images at pleasure, but always retained the same gods in their minds; besides, they daily consecrated new images without thinking they were making new gods. Augustine tells us that excuses were employed by the idolaters of his time. The vulgar, when accused, replied that they did not worship the visible object, but the Deity which dwelt in it invisibly. Those, again, who had what he calls a more refined religion, said, that they neither worshipped the image, nor any inhabiting Deity, but by means of the corporeal image beheld a symbol of that which it was their duty to worship. What then? All idolaters whether Jewish or Gentile, were actuated in the very way, which has been described. Not contented with spiritual understanding, they thought that images would give them a surer and nearer impression. When once this preposterous representation of God was adopted, there was no limit until, deluded every now and then by new impostures, they came to think that God exerted his power in images. Still the Jews were persuaded, that under such images they worshipped the eternal God, the one true Lord of heaven and earth; and the Gentiles, also, in worshipping their own false gods, supposed them to dwell in heaven.

10 Evasion of the Papists. Their agreement with ancient idolaters.

It is an impudent falsehood to deny that the thing, which was thus anciently done, is also done in our day. For why do men prostrate themselves before images? Why, when in the act of praying, do they turn towards them as to the ears of God? It is indeed true, as Augustine says (in Psalm 113), that no person thus prays or worships, looking at an image, without being impressed with the idea that he is heard by it, or without hoping that what he wishes will be performed by it. Why are such distinctions made between different images of the same God, that while one is passed by, or receives only common honor, another is worshipped with the highest solemnities? Why do they fatigue themselves with votive pilgrimages to images while they have many similar ones at home? Why at the present time do they fight for them to blood and slaughter, as for their altars and hearths, showing more willingness to part with the one God than with their idols? And yet I am not now detailing the gross errors of the vulgar—errors almost infinite in number and in possession of almost all hearts. I am only referring to what those profess who are most desirous to clear themselves of idolatry. They say, "We do not call them our gods." Nor did either the Jews or Gentiles of old so call them; and yet the Prophets never ceased to charge them with their adulteries with wood and stone for the very acts which are daily done by those who would be deemed Christians, namely, for worshipping God carnally in wood and stone.

11 Refutation of another evasion or sophism—viz. the distinction of δυλια and λατρια.

I am not ignorant, however, and I have no wish to disguise the fact, that they endeavor to evade the charge by means of a more subtle distinction, which shall afterwards be fully considered (see *infra*, section 16, and chapter, section 2). The worship, which they pay to their images, they cloak with the name of ει δωλοδυεια (ιδολοδυια), and deny to be ει δωλολατρεια (ιδολατρια). So they speaks holding that the worship which they call δυλια may, without insult to God, be paid to statues and pictures. Hence, they think themselves blameless if they are only the servants, and not the worshippers, of idols; as if it were not a lighter matter to worship than to serve. And yet, while they take refuge in a Greek term, they very childishly contradict themselves. For the Greek word λατρευειν having no other meaning than to worship, what they say is just the same as if they were to confess that they worship their images without worshipping them. They cannot object that I am quibbling upon words. The fact is, that they only betray their ignorance while they attempt to throw dust in the eyes of the simple. But no matter how eloquent they may be, they will never prove by their eloquence that one and the same thing makes two. Let them show how the things differ if they would be thought different from ancient idolaters. For as a murderer or an adulterer will not escape conviction by giving some adventitious name to his crime, so it is absurd for them to expect that the subtle device of a name will exculpate them, if they, in fact, differ in nothing from idolaters whom they themselves are forced to condemn. But so far are they from proving that their case is different, that the source of the whole evil consists in a preposterous rivalry with them, while they with their minds devise, and with their hands execute, symbolical shapes of God.

12 Third division of the chapter—viz. the use and abuse of images.

I am not, however, so superstitious as to think that all visible representations of every kind are unlawful. But as sculpture and painting are gifts of God, what I insist for is, that both shall be used purely and lawfully, —that gifts which the Lord has bestowed upon us, for his glory and our good, shall not be preposterously abused, nay, shall not be perverted to our destruction. We think it unlawful to give a visible shape to God, because God himself has forbidden it, and because it cannot be done without, in some degree, tarnishing his glory. And lest any should think that we are singular in this opinion, those acquainted with the productions of sound divines will find that they have always disapproved of it. If it were unlawful to make any corporeal representation of God, still more unlawful must it be to worship such a representation instead of God, or to worship God in it. The only things, therefore, which ought to be painted or sculptured, are things, which can be presented to the eye; the majesty of God, which is far beyond the reach of any eye, must not be dishonored by unbecoming representations. Visible representations are of two classes—viz. historical, which give a representation of events, and pictorial, which merely exhibit bodily shapes and figures. The former are of some use for instruction or admonition. The latter, so far as I can see, are only fitted for amusement. And yet, it is certain, that the latter are almost the only kind, which have hitherto been exhibited in churches. Hence, we may infer, that the exhibition was not the result of judicious selection, but of a foolish and inconsiderate longing. I say nothing as to the improper and unbecoming form in which they are presented, or the wanton license in which sculptors and painters have here indulged (a point to which I alluded a little ago, *supra*, section 7). I only say, that though they were otherwise faultless, they could not be of any utility in teaching.

13 Whether it is expedient to have images in Christian temples.

But, without reference to the above distinction, let us here consider, whether it is expedient that churches should contain representations of any kind, whether of events or human forms. First, then, if we attach any weight to the authority of the ancient Church, let us remember, that for five hundred years, during which religion was in a more prosperous condition, and a purer doctrine flourished, Christian churches were completely free from visible representations (see Preface, and Book 4, chapter 9, section 9). Hence, their first admission as an ornament to churches took place after the purity of the ministry had somewhat degenerated. I will not dispute as to the rationality of the grounds on which the first introduction of them proceeded, but if you compare the two periods, you will find that the latter had greatly declined from the purity of the times when images were unknown. What then? Are we to suppose that those holy fathers, if they had judged the thing to be useful and salutary, would have allowed the Church to be so long without it? Undoubtedly, because they saw very little or no advantage, and the greatest danger in it, they rather rejected it intentionally and on rational grounds, than omitted it through ignorance or carelessness. This is clearly attested by Augustine in these words, "When images are thus placed aloft in seats of honor, to be beheld by those who are praying or sacrificing, though they have neither sense nor life, yet from appearing as if they had both, they affect weak minds just as if they lived and breathed," etc. And again, in another passage (Psalm 112), he says, "The effect produced, and in a manner extorted, by the bodily shape, is, that the mind, being itself in a body, imagines that a body which is so like its oven must be similarly affected," etc. A little further on he says, "Images are more capable of giving a wrong bent to an unhappy soul, from having mouth, eyes, ears, and feet, than of correcting it, as they neither speak, nor see, nor hear, nor walk." This undoubtedly is the reason that John (1 John 5:21) enjoins us to beware, not only of the worship of idols, but also of idols themselves. And from the fearful infatuation under which the world has hitherto labored, almost to the entire destruction of piety, we know too well from experience that the moment images appear in churches, idolatry has raised its banner; because the folly of manhood cannot moderate itself, but forthwith falls away to superstitious worship. Even were the danger less imminent, still, when I consider the proper end for which churches are erected, it appears to me more unbecoming their sacredness than I well can tell, to admit any other images than those living symbols which the Lord has consecrated by his own word: I mean Baptism and the Lord's Supper, with the other ceremonies. By these, our eyes ought to be more steadily fixed, and more vividly impressed, than to require the aid of any images, which the wit of man may devise. Such, then, is the incomparable blessing of images—a blessing, the want of which, if we believe the Papists, cannot possibly be compensated!

14 Absurd defense of the worship of images by the second so-called Council of Nice. Sophisms or perversions of Scripture in defense of images in churches.

Enough, I believe, would have been said on this subject, were I not in a manner arrested by the Council of Nice; not the celebrated Council which Constantine the Great assembled, but one which was held eight hundred years ago by the orders and under the auspices of the Empress Irene. This Council decreed not only that images were to be used in churches, but also that they were to be worshipped. Everything, therefore, that I have said, is in danger of suffering great prejudice from the authority of this Synod. To confess the truth, however, I am not so much moved by this consideration, as by a wish to make my readers aware of the lengths to which the infatuation has been carried by those who had a greater fondness for images than became Christians. But let us first dispose of this matter. Those who defend the use of images appeal to that Synod for support. But there is a refutation extant which bears the name of Charlemagne, and which is proved by its style to be a production of that period. It gives the opinions delivered by the bishops who were present, and the arguments by which they supported them. John, deputy of the Eastern Churches, said, "God created man in his own image," and thence inferred that images ought to be used. He also thought there was a recommendation of images in the following passage, "Show me thy face, for it is beautiful." Another, in order to prove that images ought to be placed on altars, quoted the passage, "No man, when he has lighted a candle, putteth it under a bushel." Another, to show the utility of looking at images, quoted a verse of the Psalms "The light of thy countenance, O Lord, has shone upon us." Another laid hold of this similitude: As the Patriarchs used the sacrifices of the Gentiles, so ought Christians to use the images of saints instead of the idols of the Gentiles. They also twisted to the same effect the words, "Lord, I have loved the beauty of thy house." But the most ingenious interpretation was the following, "As we have heard, so also have we seen;" therefore, God is known not merely by the hearing of the word, but also by the seeing of images. Bishop Theodore was equally acute: "God," says he, "is to be admired in his saints;" and it is elsewhere said, "To the saints who are on earth;" therefore this must refer to images. In short, their absurdities are so extreme that it is painful even to quote them.

15 Passages adduced in support of the worship of images.

When they treat of adoration, great stress is laid on the worship of Pharaoh, the staff of Joseph, and the inscription, which Jacob set up. In this last case, they not only pervert the meaning of Scripture, but also quote what is nowhere to be found. Then the passages, "Worship at his footstool"— "Worship in his holy mountain"—"The rulers of the people will worship before thy face," seem to them very solid and apposite proofs. Were one, with the view of turning the defenders of images into ridicule, to put words into their mouths, could they be made to utter greater and grosser absurdities?

But to put an end to all doubt on the subject of images, Theodosius Bishop of Mira confirms the propriety of worshipping them by the dreams of his archdeacon, which he adduces with as much gravity as if he were in possession of a response from heaven. Let the patrons of images now go and urge us with the decree of this Synod, as if the venerable Fathers did not bring themselves into utter discredit by handling Scripture so childishly, or wresting it so shamefully and profanely.

16 The blasphemous expressions of some ancient idolaters approved by not a few of the more modern, both in word and deed.

I come now to monstrous impieties, which it is strange they ventured to utter, and twice strange that not all men protested against with the utmost detestation. It is right to expose this frantic and flagitious extravagance, and thereby deprive the worship of images of that gloss of antiquity in which Papists seek to deck it. Theodosius Bishop of Amora fires oft an anathema at all who object to the worship of images. Another attributes all the calamities of Greece and the East to the crime of not having worshipped them. Of what punishment then are the Prophets, Apostles, and Martyrs worthy, in whose day no images existed? They afterwards add, that if the statue of the Emperor is met with odors and incense, much more are the images of saints entitled to the honor. Constantius, Bishop of Constantia in Cyprus, professes to embrace images with reverence, and declares that he will pay them the respect which is due to the ever blessed Trinity: every person refusing to do the same thing he denounces and classes with Marcionites and Manichees. Lest you should think this the private opinion of an individual, they all assent. Nay, John the Eastern legate, carried still further by his zeal, declares it would be better to allow a city to be filled with brothels than be denied the worship of images.

At last, it is resolved with one consent that the Samaritans are the worst of all heretics, and that the enemies of images are worse than the Samaritans. But that the play may not pass off without the accustomed *Plaudite*, the whole thus concludes, "Rejoice and exult, ye who, having the image of Christ, offer sacrifice to it." Where is now the distinction of and with which they would throw dust in all eyes, human and divine? The Council unreservedly relies as much on images as on the living God.

Chapter 12

GOD DISTINGUISHED FROM IDOLS, THAT HE MAY BE THE EXCLUSIVE OBJECT OF WORSHIP.

Sections

1. Scripture, in teaching that there is but one God, does not make a dispute about words, but attributes all honor and religious worship to him alone. This proved, first by the etymology of the term. Second, by the testimony of God himself, when he declares that he is a jealous God, and will not allow himself to be confounded with any fictitious Deity.

2. The Papists in opposing this pure doctrine, gain nothing by their distinction of δυλια and λατρια.

3. Passages of Scripture subversive of the Papistical distinction, and proving that religious worship is due to God alone. Perversions of Divine worship.

1 Scripture, in teaching that there is but one God, does not make a dispute about words, but attributes all honor and religious worship to him alone. This proved, first by the etymology of the term. Second, by the testimony of God himself, when he declares that he is a jealous God, and will not allow himself to be confounded with any fictitious Deity.

We said at the commencement of our work (chapter 2), that the knowledge of God consists not in frigid speculation, but carries worship along with it; and we touched by the way (chapter 5, sections 6, 9, 10) on what will be more copiously treated in other places (Book 2, chapter 8)—viz. how God is duly worshipped. Now I only briefly repeat, that whenever Scripture asserts the unity of God, it does not contend for a mere name, but also enjoins that nothing which belongs to Divinity be applied to any other; thus making it obvious in what respect pure religion differs from superstition. The Greek word ευ σεβεια means "right worship;" for the Greeks, though groping in darkness, were always aware that a certain rule was to be observed, in order that God might not be worshipped absurdly. Cicero truly and shrewdly derives the name *religion* from *relego*, and yet the reason, which he assigns, is forced and farfetched—viz. that honest worshipers *read* and *read again*, and ponder what is true. I rather think the name is used in opposition to *vagrant license* the greater part of mankind rashly taking up whatever first comes in their way, whereas piety, that it may stand with a firm step, confines itself within due bounds. In the same way, superstition seems to take its name from its not being contented with the measure, which reason prescribes, but accumulating a superfluous mass of vanities. But to say nothing more of words, it has been universally admitted in all ages, that religion is vitiated and perverted whenever false opinions are introduced into it, and hence it is inferred, that whatever is allowed to be done from inconsiderate zeal, cannot be defended by any pretext with which the superstitious may choose to cloak it. But although this confession is in every man's mouth, a shameful stupidity is forthwith manifested, inasmuch as men neither cleave to the one God, nor use any selection in their worship, as we have already observed.

But God, in vindicating his own right, first proclaims that he is a jealous God, and will be a stern avenger if he is confounded with any false god; and thereafter defines what due worship is, in order that the human race may be kept in obedience. Both of these he embraces in his Law when he first binds the faithful in allegiance to him as their only Lawgiver, and then prescribes a rule for worshipping him in accordance with his will. The Law, with its manifold uses and objects, I will consider in its own place; at present I only advert to this one, that it is designed as a bridle to curb men, and prevent them from turning aside to spurious worship. But it is necessary to attend to the observation with which I set out—viz. that unless everything peculiar to divinity is confined to God alone, he is robbed of his honor, and his worship is violated.

It may be proper here more particularly to attend to the subtleties which superstition employs. In revolting to strange gods, it avoids the appearance of abandoning the Supreme God, or reducing him to the same rank with others. It gives him the highest place, but at the same time surrounds him with a tribe of minor deities, among whom it portions out his peculiar offices. In this way, though in a dissembling and crafty manner, the glory of the Godhead is dissected, and not allowed to remain entire. In the same way the people of old, both Jews and Gentiles, placed an immense crowd in subordination to the father and ruler of the gods, and gave them, according to their rank, to share with the supreme God in the government of heaven and earth. In the same way, too, for some ages past, departed saints have been exalted to partnership with God, to be worshipped, invoked, and lauded in his stead. And yet we do not even think that the majesty of God is obscured by this abomination, whereas it is in a great measure suppressed and extinguished—all that we retain being a frigid opinion of his supreme power. At the same time, being deluded by these entanglements, we go astray after divers gods.

2 The Papists in opposing this pure doctrine, gain nothing by their distinction of δυλια and λατρια.

The distinction of what is called δυλια and λατρια was invented for the very purpose of permitting divine honors to be paid to angels and dead men with apparent impunity. For it is plain that the worship which Papists pay to saints differs in no respect from the worship of God: for this worship is paid without distinction; only when they are pressed they have recourse to the evasion, that what belongs to God is kept unimpaired, because they leave him λατρια. But since the question relates not to the word, but the thing, how can they be allowed to sport at will with a matter of the highest moment? But not to insist on this, the utmost they will obtain by their distinction is, that they give worship to God, and service to the others. For λατρεια in Greek has the same meaning as *worship* in Latin; whereas δουλεια properly means *service*, though the words are sometimes used in Scripture indiscriminately. But granting that the distinction is invariably preserved, the thing to be inquired into is the meaning of each. Δουλεια unquestionably means *service*, and λατρεια *worship*. But no man doubts that to *serve* is something higher than to *worship*. For it would be often a hard thing to serve him whom you would not refuse to reverence. It is, therefore, an unjust division to assign the greater to the saints and leave the less to God. But several of the ancient fathers observed this distinction. What if they did, when all men see that it is not only improper, but also utterly frivolous?

3 Passages of Scripture subversive of the Papistical distinction, and proving that religious worship is due to God alone. Perversions of Divine worship.

Laying aside subtleties, let us examine the thing. When Paul reminds the Galatians of what they were before they came to the knowledge of Gods he says that they "did service unto them which by nature are no gods" (Galatians 4:8). Because he does not say latria, was their superstition excusable? This superstition, to which he gives the name of dulia, he condemns as much as if he had given it the name of latria. When Christ repels Satan's insulting proposal with the words, "It is written, Thou shalt worship the Lord thy God, and him only shalt thou serve" (Matthew 4:10), there was no question of latria. For all that Satan asked was proskunesiV (homage). In like manners when the angel rebukes John for falling on his knees before him (Revelation 19:10; 22:8, 9), we ought not to suppose that John had so far forgotten himself as to intend to transfer the honor due to God alone to an angel. But because it was impossible that a worship connected with religion should not savor somewhat of divine worship, he could not proskunei n (pay homage to) the angel without derogating from the glory of God. True, we often read that men were worshipped; but that was, if I may so speak, civil honor. The case is different with religious honor, which, the moment it is conjoined with worship, carries profanation of the divine honor along with it. The same thing may be seen in the case of Cornelius (Acts 10:25). He had not made so little progress in piety as not to confine supreme worship to God alone. Therefore, when he prostrates himself before Peter, he certainly does it not with the intention of adoring him instead of God. Yet, Peter sternly forbids him. And why, but just because men never distinguish so accurately between the worship of God and the creatures as not to transfer promiscuously to the creature that which belongs only to God. Therefore, if we would have one God, let us remember that we can never appropriate the minutest portion of his glory without retaining what is his due.

Accordingly, when Zechariah discourses concerning the repairing of the Church, he distinctly says not only that there would be one God, but also that he would have only one name—the reason being, that he might have nothing in common with idols. The nature of the worship which God requires will be seen in its own place (Book 2, chapter 7 and 8). He has been pleased to prescribe in his Law what is lawful and right, and thus restrict men to a certain rule, lest any should allow themselves to devise a worship of their own. But as it is inexpedient to burden the reader by mixing up a variety of topics, I do not now dwell on this one. Let it suffice to remember, that whatever offices of piety are bestowed anywhere else than on God alone, are of the nature of sacrilege. First, superstition attached divine honors to the sun and stars, or to idols: afterwards ambition followed—ambition, which, decking man in the spoils of God, dared to profane all that was sacred. And though the principle of worshipping a supreme Deity continued to be held, still the practice was to sacrifice promiscuously to genii and minor gods, or departed heroes: so prone is the descent to this vice of communicating to a crowd that which God strictly claims as his own peculiar right!

Chapter 13

THE UNITY OF THE DIVINE ESSENCE IN THREE PERSONS TAUGHT, IN SCRIPTURE, FROM THE FOUNDATION OF THE WORLD.

This chapter consists of two parts. The former delivers the orthodox doctrine concerning the Holy Trinity. This occupies from section 1-21, and may be divided into four heads; the first, treating of the meaning of Person, including both the term and the thing meant by it, section 2-6; the second, proving the deity of the Son, section 7-13; the third, the deity of the Holy Spirit, section 14 and 15; and the fourth, explaining what is to be held concerning the Holy Trinity. The second part of the chapter refutes certain heresies, which have arisen, particularly in our age, in opposition to this orthodox doctrine. This occupies from section 21 to the end.

Sections

1. Scripture, in teaching that the essence of God is immense and spiritual, refutes not only idolaters and the foolish wisdom of the world, but also the Manichees and Anthropomorphites. These latter briefly refuted.

2. In this one essence are three persons, yet so that neither is there a triple God, nor is the simple essence of God divided. Meaning of the word Person in this discussion. Three hypostases in God, or the essence of God.

3. Objection of those who, in this discussion, reject the use of the word Person. Answer A. That it is not a foreign term, but is employed for the explanation of sacred mysteries.

4. Answer continued, B. The orthodox compelled to use the terms, Trinity, Subsistence, and Person. Examples from the case of the Asians and Sabellians.

5. Answer continued, C. The ancient Church, though differing somewhat in the explanation of these terms, agree in substance. Proofs from Hilary, Jerome, and Augustine in their use of the words, Essence, Substance, Hypostasis. 4. Provided the orthodox meaning is retained, there should be no dispute about mere terms. But those who object to the terms usually favor the Arian and Sabellian heresy.

6. After the definition of the term follows a definition and explanation of the thing meant by it. The distinction of Persons.

7. Proofs of the eternal Deity of the Son. The Son the Λογος of the Eternal Father, and, therefore, the Son Eternal God. Objection. Reply.

8. Objection, that the Λογος began to be when the creating God spoke. Answer confirmed by Scripture and argument.

9. The Son called God and Jehovah. Other names of the Eternal Father applied to him in the Old Testament. He is, therefore, the Eternal God. Another objection refuted. Case of the Jews explained.

10. The angel who appeared to the fathers under the Law asserts that he is Jehovah. That angel was the Λογος of the Eternal Father. The Son being that Λογος is Eternal God. Impiety of Servetus refuted. Why the Son appeared in the form of an angel.

11. Passages from the New Testament in which the Son is acknowledged to be the Lord of Hosts, the Judge of the world, the God of glory, the Creator of the world, the Lord of angels, the King of the Church, the eternal Λογος, God blessed forever, God manifest in the flesh, the equal of God, the true God and eternal life, the Lord and God of all believers. Therefore, the Eternal God.

12. Christ the Creator, Preserver, Redeemer, and Searcher of hearts. Therefore, the Eternal God.

13. Christ, by his own inherent power, wrought miracles, and bestowed the power of working them on others. Out of the Eternal God, there is no salvation, no righteousness, no life. All these are in Christ. Christ, consequently, is the Eternal God. He in whom we believe and hope, to whom we pray, whom the Church acknowledges as the Savior of the faithful, whom to know is life eternal, in whom the pious glory, and through whom eternal blessings are communicated, is the Eternal God. All these Christ is, and, therefore, he is God.

14. The Divinity of the Spirit proved. A. He is the Creator and Preserver of the world. B. He sent the Prophets. C. He quickeneth all things. D. He is everywhere present. E. He renews the saints, and fits them for eternal life. F. All the offices of Deity belong to him.

15. *The Divinity of the Spirit continued. G. He is called God. H. Blasphemy against him is not forgiven.*

16. *What view to be taken of the Trinity. The form of Christian baptism proves that there are in one essence. The Arian and Macedonian heresies.*

17. *Of the distinction of Persons. They are distinct, but not divided. This proved.*

18. *Analogies taken from human affairs to be cautiously used. Due regard to be paid to those mentioned by Scripture.*

19. *How the Three Persons not only do not destroy, but constitute the most perfect unity*

20. *Conclusion of this part of the chapter, and summary of the true doctrine concerning the unity of Essence and the Three Persons.*

21. *Refutation of Arian, Macedonian, and Anti Trinitarian heresies. Caution to be observed.*

22. *The more modern Anti Trinitarians, and especially Servetus, refuted.*

23. *Other Anti Trinitarians refuted. No good objection that Christ is called the Son of God, since he is also called God. Impious absurdities of some heretics.*

24. *The name of God sometimes given to the Son absolutely as to the Father. Same as to other attributes. Objections refuted.*

25. *Objections further refuted. Caution to be used.*

26. *Previous refutations further explained.*

27. *Reply to certain passages produced from Irenaeus. The meaning of Irenaeus.*

28. *Reply to certain passages produced from Tertullian. The meaning of Tertullian.*

29. *Anti Trinitarians refuted by ancient Christian writers; e.g., Justin, Hilary. Objections drawn from writings improperly attributed to Ignatius. Conclusion of the whole discussion concerning the Trinity.*

1 Scripture, in teaching that the essence of God is immense and spiritual, refutes not only idolaters and the foolish wisdom of the world, but also the Manichees and Anthropomorphites. These latter briefly refuted.

The doctrine of Scripture concerning the immensity and the spirituality of the essence of God should have the effect not only of dissipating the wild dreams of the vulgar, but also of refuting the subtleties of a profane philosophy. One of the ancients thought he spoke shrewdly when he said that everything we see and everything we do not see is God. In this way, he fancied that the Divinity was transfused into every separate portion of the world. But although God, in order to keep us within the bounds of soberness, treats sparingly of his essence, still, by the two attributes which I have mentioned, he at once suppresses all gross imaginations, and checks the audacity of the human mind. His immensity surely ought to deter us from measuring him by our sense, while his spiritual nature forbids us to indulge in carnal or earthly speculation concerning him. With the same view, he frequently represents heaven as his dwelling-place. It is true, indeed, that as he is incomprehensible, he fills the earth also, but knowing that our minds are heavy and grovel on the earth, he raises us above the worlds that he may shake off our sluggishness and inactivity. And here we have a refutation of the error of the Manichees, who, by adopting two first principles, made the devil almost the equal of God. This, assuredly, was to both destroy his unity and restrict his immensity. Their attempt to pervert certain passages of Scripture proved their shameful ignorance, as the very nature of the error did their monstrous infatuation.

The Anthropomorphites also, who dreamed of a corporeal God, because mouth, ears, eyes, hands, and feet, are often ascribed to him in Scripture, are easily refuted. For who is so devoid of intellect as not to understand that God, in so speaking, lisps with us as nurses are wont to do with little children? Such modes of expression, therefore, do not so much express what kind of a being God is, as accommodate the knowledge of him to our feebleness. In doing so, he must, of course, stoop far below his proper height.

2 In this one essence are three persons, yet so that neither is there a triple God, nor is the simple essence of God divided. Meaning of the word Person in this discussion. Three hypostases in God, or the essence of God.

But there is another special mark by which he designates himself, for the purpose of giving a more intimate knowledge of his nature. While he proclaims his unity, he distinctly sets it before us as existing in three persons. These we must hold, unless the bare and empty name of Deity merely is to flutter in our brain without any genuine knowledge. Moreover, lest anyone should dream of a threefold God, or think that the simple essence is divided by the three Persons, we must here seek a brief and easy definition which may effectually guard us from error. But as some strongly inveigh against the term Person as being merely of human inventions let us first consider how far they have any ground for doing so.

When the Apostle calls the Son of God "the express image of his person" (Hebrews 1:3), he undoubtedly does assign to the Father some subsistence in which he differs from the Son. For to hold with some interpreters that the term is equivalent to essence (as if Christ represented the substance of the Father like the impression of a seal upon wax), were not only harsh but also absurd. For the essence of God being simple and undivided, and contained in himself entire, in full perfection, without partition or diminution, it is improper, nay, ridiculous, to call it his express image (χαρακτερ). But because the Father, though distinguished by his own peculiar properties, has expressed himself wholly in the Son, he is said with perfect reason to have rendered his person (hypostasis) manifest in him. And this aptly accords with what is immediately added—viz. that he is "the brightness of his glory."

The fair inference from the Apostle's words is that there is a proper subsistence (hypostasis) of the Father, which shines refulgent in the Son. From this, again it is easy to infer that there is a subsistence (hypostasis) of the Son, which distinguishes him from the Father. The same holds in the case of the Holy Spirit, for we will immediately prove both that he is God, and that he has a separate subsistence from the Father. This, moreover, is not a distinction of essence, which it would be impious to multiply. If credit, then, is given to the Apostle's testimony, it follows that there are three persons (hypostases) in God. The Latins, having used the word *Persona*, betray excessive fastidiousness and even perverseness to quarrel with the term. The most literal translation would be *subsistence*. Many have used *substance* in the same sense. Nor, indeed, was the use of the term Person confined to the Latin Church. For the Greek Church in like manner, perhaps, for the purpose of testifying their consent, have taught that there are three προσωπα in God. All these, however, whether Greeks or Latins, though differing as to the word, are perfectly agreed in substance.

3 Objection of those who, in this discussion, reject the use of the word Person. Answer A. That it is not a foreign term, but is employed for the explanation of sacred mysteries.

Now, then, though heretics may snarl and the excessively fastidious carp at the word Person as inadmissible, in consequence of its human origin, since they cannot displace us from our position that three are named, each of whom is perfect God, and yet that there is no plurality of gods, it is most uncandid to attack the terms which do nothing more than explain what the Scriptures declare and sanction. "It would be better," they say, "to confine not only our meanings but our words within the bounds of Scripture, and not scatter about foreign terms to become the future seedbeds of brawls and dissensions. In this way, men grow tired of quarrels about words; the truth is lost in altercation, and charity melts away amid hateful strife." If they call it a *foreign* term, because it cannot be pointed out in Scripture in so many syllables, they certainly impose an unjust law—a law which would condemn every interpretation of Scripture that is not composed of other words of Scripture. But if by *foreign* they mean that which, after being idly devised, is superstitiously defended, —which tends more to strife than edification, — which is used either out of place, or with no benefit which offends pious ears by its harshness, and leads them away from the simplicity of God's Word, I embrace their soberness with all my heart. For I think, we are bound to speak of God as reverently as we are bound to think of him. As our own thoughts respecting him are foolish, so our own language respecting him is absurd. Still, however, some medium must be observed. The unerring standard both of thinking and speaking must be derived from the Scriptures: by it all the thoughts of ours minds, and the words of our mouths, should he tested. But in regard to those parts of Scripture which, to our capacities, are dark and intricate, what forbids us to explain them in clearer terms— terms, however, kept in reverent and faithful subordination to Scripture truth, used sparingly and modestly, and not without occasion? Of this, we are not without many examples. When it has been proved that the Church was impelled, by the strongest necessity, to use the words Trinity and Person, will not he who still inveighs against novelty of terms be deservedly suspected of taking offense at the light of truth, and of having no other ground for his invective, than that the truth is made plain and transparent?

4 Answer continued, B. The orthodox compelled to use the terms, Trinity, Subsistence, and Person. Examples from the case of the Asians and Sabellians.

Such novelty (if novelty it should be called) becomes most requisite, when the truth is to be maintained against calumniators who evade it by quibbling. Of this, we of the present day have too much experience in being constantly called upon to attack the enemies of pure and sound doctrine. These slippery snakes escape by their swift and tortuous windings, if not strenuously pursued, and when caught, firmly held. Thus the early Christians, when harassed with the disputes which heresies produced, were forced to declare their sentiments in terms most scrupulously exact in order that no indirect subterfuges might remain to ungodly men, to whom ambiguity of expression was a kind of hiding-place. Arius confessed that Christ was God, and the Son of God, because the passages of Scripture to this effect were too clear to be resisted, and then, as if he had done well, pretended to concur with others. But, meanwhile, he ceased not to give out that Christ was created, and had a beginning like other creatures. To drag this man of wiles out of his lurking-places, the ancient Church took a further step, and declared that Christ is the eternal Son of the Father, and consubstantial with the Father. The impiety was fully disclosed when the Arians began to declare their hatred and utter detestation of the term ο μοουσιος. Had their first confession—viz. that Christ was God, been sincere and from the heart, they would not have denied that he was consubstantial with the Father. Who dare charge those ancient writers as men of strife and contention, for having debated so warmly, and disturbed the quiet of the Church for a single word? That little word distinguished between Christians of pure faith and the blasphemous Arians. Next Sabellius arose, who counted the names of Father, Son, and Holy Spirit, as almost nonentities; maintaining that they were not used to mark out some distinction, but that they were different attributes of God, like many others of a similar kind. When the matter was debated, he acknowledged his belief that the Father was God, the Son God, the Spirit God; but then he had the evasion ready, that he had said nothing more than if he had called God powerful, and just, and wise. Accordingly, he sung another note—viz. that the Father was the Son, and the Holy Spirit the Father, without order or distinction. The worthy doctors who then had the interests of piety at heart, in order to defeat it is man's dishonesty, proclaimed that three subsistence were to be truly acknowledged in the one God. That they might protect themselves against tortuous craftiness by the simple open truth, they affirmed that a Trinity of Persons subsisted in the one God, or (which is the same thing) in the unity of God.

5 Answer continued, C. The ancient Church, though differing somewhat in the explanation of these terms, agree in substance. Proofs from Hilary, Jerome, and Augustine in their use of the words, Essence, Substance, Hypostasis. D. Provided the orthodox meaning is retained, there should be no dispute about mere terms. But those who object to the terms usually favor the Arian and Sabellian heresy.

Where names have not been invented rashly, we must beware lest we become chargeable with arrogance and rashness in rejecting them. I wish, indeed, that such names were buried, provided all would concur in the belief that the Father, Son, and Spirit, are one God, and yet that the Son is not the Father, nor the Spirit the Son, but that each has his peculiar subsistence. I am not so minutely precise as to fight furiously for mere words. For I observe, that the writers of the ancient Church, while they uniformly spoke with great reverence on these matters, neither agreed with each other, nor were always consistent with themselves. How strange the formula used by Councils, and defended by Hilary! How extravagant the view, which Augustine sometimes takes! How unlike the Greeks are the Latins! But let one example of variance suffice. The Latins, in translatingGreek, used consubstantialis (consubstantial: meaning having the same substance as something else, for example, another member of the Holy Trinity), intimating that there was one substance of the Father and the Son, and thus using the word Substance for Essence. Hence, Jerome, in his Letter to Damasus, says it is profane to affirm that there are three substances in God. But in Hilary, you will find it said more than a hundred times that there are three substances in God. Then how greatly is Jerome perplexed with the word Hypostasis! He suspects some lurking poison, when it is said that there are three Hypostases in God. And he does not disguise his belief that the expression, though used in a pious sense, is improper if, indeed, he was sincere in saying this, and did not rather designedly endeavor, by an unfounded calumny, to throw odium on the Eastern bishops whom he hated. He certainly shows little candor in asserting that in all heathen schools the Greek word should be equivalent to Hypostasis—an assertion completely refuted by trite and common use.

More courtesy and moderation is shown by Augustine, who, although he says that Hypostasis in this sense is new to Latin ears, is still so far from objecting to the ordinary use of the term by the Greeks, that he is even tolerant of the Latins, who had imitated the Greek phraseology. The purport of what Socrates says of the term, in the Sixth Book of the Tripartite History, is, that it had been improperly applied to this purpose by the unskillful. Hilary charges it upon the heretics as a great crime, that their misconduct had rendered it necessary to subject to the peril of human utterance things which ought to have been reverently confined within the mind, not disguising his opinion that those who do so, do what is unlawful, speak what is ineffable, and pry into what is forbidden. Shortly after, he apologizes at great length for presuming to introduce new terms. For, after putting down the natural names of Father, Son, and Spirit, he adds, that all further inquiry transcends the significance of words, the discernment of sense, and the apprehension of intellect. And in another place (De Conciliis), he congratulates the Bishops of France in not having framed any other confession, but received, without alteration, the ancient and most simple confession received by all Churches from the days of the Apostles. Not unlike this is the apology of Augustine, that the term had been wrung from him by necessity from the poverty of human language in so high a matter: not that the reality could be thereby expressed, but that he might not pass on in silence without attempting to show how the Father, Son, and Spirit, are three.

The modesty of these holy men should be an admonition to us not instantly to dip our pen in gall, and sternly denounce those who may be unwilling to swear to the terms which we have devised, provided they do not in this betray pride, or petulance, or unbecoming heat, but are willing to ponder the necessity which compels us so to speak, and may thus become gradually accustomed to a useful form of expression. Let men also studiously beware, that in opposing the Asians on the one hand, and the Sabellians on the other, and eagerly endeavoring to deprive both of any handle for cavil, they do not bring themselves under some suspicion of being the disciples of either Arius or Sabellius. Arius says that *Christ is God*, and then mutters that *he was made and had a beginning*. He says, that *he is one with the*

Father; but secretly whispers in the ears of his party, *made one*, like other believers, though with special privilege. Say, *he is consubstantial*, and you immediately pluck the mask from this chameleon, though you add nothing to Scripture. Sabellius says that *the Father, Son, and Spirit, indicate some distinction in God*. Say, *they are three*, and he will bawl out that you are making three Gods. Say, that *there is a Trinity of Persons in one Divine essence*, you will only express in one word what the Scriptures say, and stop his empty prattle. Should any be so superstitiously precise as not to tolerate these terms, still do their worst, they will not be able to deny that when *one* is spoken of, a unity of substance must be understood, and when *three* in one essence, the persons in this Trinity are denoted. When this is confessed without equivocations, we dwell not on words. But I was long ago made aware, and, indeed, on more than one occasion, that those who contend persistently about words are tainted with some hidden poison; and, therefore, that it is more expedient to provoke them purposely, than to court their favor by speaking obscurely.

6 After the definition of the term follows a definition and explanation of the thing meant by it. The distinction of Persons.

But to say nothing more of words, let us now attend to the thing signified. By *person*, then, I mean a subsistence in the Divine essence, —a subsistence which, while related to the other two, is distinguished from them by incommunicable properties. By *subsistence*, we wish something else to be understood than *essence*. For if the Word were God simply and had not some property peculiar to himself, John could not have said correctly that he had always been with God. When he adds immediately after, that the Word was God, he calls us back to the one essence. But because he could not be with God without dwelling in the Father, hence arises that subsistence, which, though connected with the essence by an indissoluble tie, being incapable of separation, yet has a special mark by which it is distinguished from it. Now, I say that each of the three subsistences while related to the others is distinguished by its properties. Here relation is distinctly expressed, because, when God is mentioned simply and indefinitely the name belongs not less to the Son and Spirit than to the Father. But whenever the Father is compared with the Son, the peculiar property of each distinguishes the one from the other. Again, whatever is proper to each I affirm to be incommunicable, because nothing can apply or be transferred to the Son that is attributed to the Father as a mark of distinction. I have no objections to adopt the definition of Tertullian, provided it is properly understood, "that there is in God a certain arrangement or economy, which makes no change on the unity of essence."

7 Proofs of the eternal Deity of the Son. The Son the λογος of the Eternal Father, and, therefore, the Son Eternal God. Objection. Reply.

Before proceeding further, it will be necessary to prove the divinity of the Son and the Holy Spirit. Thereafter, we shall see how they differ from each other. When the Word of God is set before us in the Scriptures, it would be certainly most absurd to imagine that it is only a fleeting and evanescent voice, which is sent out into the air, and comes forth beyond God himself, as was the case with the communications made to the patriarchs, and all the prophecies. The reference is rather to the wisdom ever dwelling with God, and by which all oracles and prophecies were inspired. For, as Peter testifies (1 Peter 1:11), the ancient Prophets spoke by the Spirit of Christ just as did the apostles, and all who after them were ministers of the heavenly doctrine. But as Christ was not yet manifested, we necessarily understand that the Word was begotten of the Father before all ages. But if that Spirit, whose organs the Prophets were, belonged to the Word, the inference is irresistible, that the Word was truly God. And this is clearly enough shown by Moses in his account of the creation, where he places the Word as intermediate. For why does he distinctly narrate that God, in creating each of his works, said, Let there be this—let there be that, unless that the unsearchable glory of God might shine forth in his image?

I know prattlers would easily evade this, by saying that *Word* is used for *order* or *command*; but the apostles are better expositors, when they tell us that the worlds were created by the Son, and that he sustains all things by his mighty word (Hebrews 1:2). For we here see that *word* is used for the nod or command of the Son, who is himself the eternal and essential Word of the Father. And no man of sane mind can have any doubt as to Solomon's meaning, when he introduces Wisdom as begotten by God, and presiding at the creation of the world, and all other divine operations (Proverbs 8:22). For it would be trifling and foolish to imagine any temporary command at a time when God was pleased to execute his fixed and eternal counsel, and something more still mysterious. To this our Savior's words refer, "My Father worketh hitherto, and I work" (John 5:17).

In thus affirming, that from the foundation of the world he constantly worked with the Father, he gives a clearer explanation of what Moses simply touched. The meaning therefore is, that God spoke in such a manner as left the Word his peculiar part in the work, and thus made the operation common to both. But the clearest explanation is given by John, when he states that the Word—which was from the beginning, God and with God, was, together with God the Father, the maker of all things. For he both attributes a substantial and permanent essence to the Word, assigning to it a certain peculiarity, and distinctly showing how God spoke the world into being. Therefore, as all revelations from heaven are duly designated by the title of the Word of God, so the highest place must be assigned to that substantial

Word, the source of all inspiration, which, as being liable to no variation, remains forever one and the same with God, and is God.

8 Objection, that the Λογος began to be when the creating God spoke. Answer confirmed by Scripture and argument.

Here, an outcry is made by certain men, who, while they dare not openly deny his divinity, secretly rob him of his eternity. For they contend that the Word only began to be when God opened his sacred mouth in the creation of the world. Thus, with excessive temerity, they imagine some change in the essence of God. For as the names of God, which have respect to external work, began to be ascribed to him from the existence of the work (as when he is called the Creator of heaven and earth), so piety does not recognize or admit any name which might indicate that a change had taken place in God himself. For if anything adventitious took place, the saying of James would cease to be true, that "every good gift, and every perfect gift, is from above, and cometh down from the Father of lights, with whom is no variableness, neither shadow of turning" (James 1:17). Nothing, therefore, is more intolerable than to fancy a beginning to that Word which was always God, and afterwards was the Creator of the world. But they think they argue acutely, in maintaining that Moses, when he says that God then spoke for the first time, must be held to intimate that until then no Word existed in him. This is the merest trifling. It does not surely follow, that because a thing begins to be manifested at a certain time, it never existed previously. I draw a very different conclusion. Since at the very moment when God said, "Let there be light," the energy of the Word-was immediately exerted, it must have existed long before. If any inquire how long, he will find it was without beginning. No certain period of time is defined, when he himself says, "Now O Father, glorify thou me with thine own self with the glory which I had with thee before the world was" (John 17:5). Nor is this omitted by John: for before he descends to the creation of the world, he says, that "in the beginning was the Word, and the Word was with God." We, therefore, again conclude, that the Word was eternally begotten by God, and dwelt with him from everlasting. In this way, his true essence, his eternity, and divinity, are established.

9 The Son called God and Jehovah. Other names of the Eternal Father applied to him in the Old Testament. He is, therefore, the Eternal God. Another objection refuted. Case of the Jews explained.

But though I am not now treating of the office of the Mediator, having deferred it until the subject of redemption is considered, yet because it ought to be clear and incontrovertible to all, that Christ is that Word become incarnate, this seems the most appropriate place to introduce those passages which assert the Divinity of Christ. When it is said in the forty-fifth Psalm, "Thy throne, O God, is forever and ever," the Jews quibble that the name Elohim is applied to angels and sovereign powers. But no passage is to be found in Scripture, where an eternal throne is set up for a creature. For he is not called God simply, but also the eternal Ruler. Besides, the title is not conferred on any man, without some addition, as when it is said that Moses would be a God to Pharaoh (Exodus 7:1). Some read as if it were in the genitive case, but this is too insipid. I admit, that anything possessed of singular excellence is often called divine, but it is clear from the context, that this meaning here were harsh and forced, and totally inapplicable. But if their perverseness still refuses to yield, surely there is no obscurity in Isaiah, where Christ is introduced both as God, and as possessed of supreme powers one of the peculiar attributes of God, "His name shall be called the Mighty God, the Everlasting Father, the Prince of Peace" (Isaiah 9:6). Here, too, the Jews object, and invert the passage thus, "This is the name by which the mighty God, the Everlasting Father, will call him; so that all which they leave to the Son is, 'Prince of Peace.'"

But why should so many epithets be here accumulated on God the Father, seeing the prophet's design is to present the Messiah with certain distinguished properties, which may induce us to put our faith in him? There can be no doubt, therefore, that he who a little before was called Emmanuel, is here called the Mighty God. Moreover, there can be nothing clearer than the words of Jeremiah, "This is the name whereby he shall be called, THE LORD OUR RIGHTEOUSNESS" (Jeremiah 23:6). For as the Jews themselves teach that the other names of God are mere epithets, whereas this, which they call the ineffable name, is substantive, and expresses his essence, we infer, that the only begotten Son is the Eternal God, who elsewhere declares, "My glory will I not give to another" (Isaiah 42:8). An attempt is made to evade this from the fact, that this name is given by Moses to the altar, which he built, and by Ezekiel to the New Jerusalem. But who sees not that the altar was erected as a memorial to show that God was the exalter of Moses, and that the name of God was applied to Jerusalem, merely to testify the Divine presence? For thus the prophet speaks, "The name of the city from that day shall be, The Lord is there" (Ezekiel 48:35). In the same way, "Moses built an altar, and called the name of it JEHOVAH-nissi" (Jehovah my exaltation). But it would seem the point is still more keenly disputed as to another passage in Jeremiah, where the same title is applied to Jerusalem in these words, "In those days shall Judah be saved, and Jerusalem shall dwell safely; and this is the name wherewith she shall be called, The Lord our Righteousness." But so far is this passage from being adverse to the truth, which we defend, that it rather supports it. The prophet having formerly declared that Christ is the true Jehovah from whom righteousness flows, now declares that the Church would be made so sensible of this as to be able to glory in assuming his very name. In the former passage, therefore, the fountain and cause of righteousness is set down, in the latter, the effect is described.

10 The angel who appeared to the fathers under the Law asserts that he is Jehovah. That angel was the Λογος of the Eternal Father. The Son being that Λογος is Eternal God. Impiety of Servetus refuted. Why the Son appeared in the form of an angel.

But if this does not satisfy the Jews, I know not what cavils will enable them to evade the numerous passages in which Jehovah is said to have appeared in the form of an Angel (Judges 6:7; 13:16-23, etc). This Angel claims for himself the name of the Eternal God. Should it be alleged that this is done in respect of the office, which he bears; the difficulty is by no means solved. No servant would rob God of his honor, by allowing sacrifice to be offered to himself. But the Angel, by refusing to eat bread, orders the sacrifice due to Jehovah to be offered to him. Thus, the fact itself proves that he was truly Jehovah. Accordingly, Manoah and his wife infer from the sign, that they had seen not only an angel, but also God. Hence, Manoah's exclamation, "We shall die; for we have seen the Lord." When the woman replies, "If Jehovah had wished to slay us, he would not have received the sacrifice at our hand," she acknowledges that he who is previously called an angel was certainly God. We may add, that the angel's own reply removes all doubt, "Why do ye ask my name, which is wonderful?" Hence, the impiety of Servetus was the more detestable, when he maintained that God was never manifested to Abraham and the Patriarchs, but that an angel was worshipped in his stead.

The orthodox doctors of the Church have correctly and wisely expounded, that the Word of God was the supreme angel, who then began, by anticipation, to perform the office of Mediator. For though he were not clothed with flesh, yet he descended as in an intermediate form, that he might have more familiar access to the faithful. This closer intercourse procured for him the name of the Angel; still, however, he retained the character which justly belonged to him—that of the God of ineffable glory. The same thing is intimated by Hosea, who, after mentioning the wrestling of Jacob with the angel, says, "Even the Lord God of hosts; the Lord is his memorial" (Hosea 12:5). Servetus again insinuates that God personated an angel; as if the prophet did not confirm what had been said by Moses, "Wherefore is it that thou dost ask after my name?" (Genesis 32:29, 30). And the confession of the holy Patriarch sufficiently declares that he was not a created angel, but one in whom the fullness of the Godhead dwelt, when he says, "I have seen God face to face." Hence, also Paul's statement, that Christ led the people in the wilderness (1 Corinthians 10:4). (See *infra*, chapter 14, section 9). Although the time of humiliation had not yet arrived, the eternal Word exhibited a type of the office, which he was to fulfill. Again, if the first chapter of Zechariah (verse 9, etc.) and the second (verse 3, etc.) are candidly considered, it will be seen that the angel who sends the other angel is immediately after declared to be the Lord of hosts, and that supreme power is ascribed to him.

I omit numberless passages in which our faith rests secure, though they may not have much weight with the Jews. For when it is said in Isaiah, "Lo, this is our God; we have waited for him, and he will save us; this is the Lord: we have waited for him, we will be glad and rejoice in his salvation" (Isaiah 25:9), even the blind may see that the God referred to is he who again rises up for the deliverance of his people. And the emphatic description, twice repeated, precludes the idea that reference is made to any other than to Christ. Still clearer and stronger is the passage of Malachi, in which a promise is made that the messenger who was then expected would come to his own temple (Malachi 3:1). The temple certainly was dedicated to Almighty God only, and yet the prophet claims it for Christ. Hence, it follows, that he is the God who was always worshipped by the Jews.

11 Passages from the New Testament in which the Son is acknowledged to be the Lord of Hosts, the Judge of the world, the God of glory, the Creator of the world, the Lord of angels, the King of the Church, the eternal Λογος, God blessed forever, God manifest in the flesh, the equal of God, the true God and eternal life, the Lord and God of all believers. Therefore, the Eternal God.

The New Testament teems with innumerable passages, and our object must therefore be, the selection of a few, rather than an accumulation of the whole. But though the Apostles spoke of him after his appearance in the flesh as Mediator, every passage which I adduce will be sufficient to prove his eternal Godhead. And the first thing deserving of special observation is that predictions concerning the Eternal God are applied to Christ, as either already fulfilled in him, or to be fulfilled at some future period. Isaiah prophesies that, "the Lord of Hosts" shall be "for a stone of stumbling, and for a rock of offense" (Isaiah 8:14). Paul asserts that this prophecy was fulfilled in Christ (Romans 9:33), and, therefore, declares that Christ is that Lord of Hosts. In like manner, he says in another passage, "We shall all stand before the Judgment-seat of Christ. For it is written, As I live, saith the Lord, every knee shall bow to me, and every tongue shall confess to God." Since in Isaiah God predicts this of himself (Isaiah 45:23), and Christ exhibits the reality fulfilled in himself, it follows that he is the very God, whose glory cannot be given to another. It is clear also, that the passage from the Psalms (Psalm 68:19), which he quotes in the Epistle to the Ephesians, is applicable only to God, "When he ascended up on high, he led captivity captive" (Ephesians 4:8). Understanding that such an ascension was shadowed forth when the Lord exerted his power, and gained a glorious victory over heathen nations, he intimates that what was thus shadowed was more fully manifested in Christ.

John testifies that it was the glory of the Son, which was revealed to Isaiah in a vision (John 12:41; Isaiah 6:4), though Isaiah himself expressly says that what he saw was the Majesty of God. Again, there can be no doubt that those qualities which, in the Epistle to the Hebrews, are applied to the Son, are the brightest attributes of God, "Thou, Lord, in the beginning hast laid the foundation of the earth," etc., and, "Let all the angels of God worship him" (Hebrews 1:10, 6). And yet, he does not pervert the passages in thus applying them to Christ, since Christ alone performed the things, which these passages celebrate. It was he who arose and pitied Zion—he who claimed for himself dominion over all nations and islands. And why should John have hesitated to ascribe the Majesty of God to Christ, after saying in his preface that the Word was God? (John 1:14). Why should Paul have feared to place Christ on the Judgment-seat of God (2 Corinthians 5:10), after he had so openly proclaimed his divinity, when he said that he was God over all, blessed forever? And to show how consistent he is in this respect, he elsewhere says, "God was manifest in the flesh" (1 Timothy 3:16). If he is God blessed forever, he therefore it is to whom alone, as Paul affirms in another place, all glory and honor is due. Paul does not disguise this, but openly exclaims, "being in the form of God (he) thought it not robbery to be equal with God, but made himself of no reputation" (Philippians 2:6). And lest the wicked should glamour and say that he was a kind of spurious God, John goes further, and affirms, "This is the true God, and eternal life." Though it ought to be enough for us that he is called God, especially by a witness who distinctly testifies that we have no more gods than one, Paul says, "Though there be that are called gods, whether in heaven or in earth (as there be gods many, and lords many), but to us there is but one God" (1 Corinthians 8:5, 6). When we hear from the same lips that God was manifest in the flesh, that God purchased the Church with his own blood, why do we dream of any second God, to whom he makes not the least allusion? And there is no room to doubt that all the godly entertained the same view. Thomas, by addressing him as his Lord and God, certainly professes that he was the only God whom he had ever adored (John 20:28).

12 Christ the Creator, Preserver, Redeemer, and Searcher of hearts. Therefore, the Eternal God.

The divinity of Christ, if judged by the works, which are ascribed to him in Scripture, becomes still more evident. When he said of himself, "My Father worketh hitherto, and I work," the Jews, though most dull in regard to his other sayings, perceived that he was laying claim to divine power. And, therefore, as John relates (John 5:17), they sought the more to kill him, because he not only broke the Sabbath, but also said that God was his Father, making himself equal with God. What, then, will be our stupidity if we do not perceive from the same passage that his divinity is plainly instructed? To govern the world by his power and providence, and regulate all things by an energy inherent in himself (this an Apostle ascribes to him,

(Hebrews 1:3), surely belongs to none but the Creator. Nor does he merely share the government of the world with the Father, but also each of the other offices, which cannot be communicated to creatures. The Lord proclaims by his Prophets, "I, even I, am he that blotteth out thy transgressions for mine own sake" (Isaiah 43:25). When, in accordance with this declaration, the Jews thought that injustice was done to God when Christ forgave sins, he not only asserted, in distinct terms, that this power belonged to him, but also proved it by a miracle (Matthew 9:6). We thus see that he possessed in himself not the ministry of forgiving sins, but the inherent power, which the Lord declares he will not give to another. What! Is it not the province of God alone to penetrate and interrogate the secret thoughts of the heart? But Christ also had this power, and therefore we infer that Christ is God.

13 Christ, by his own inherent power, wrought miracles, and bestowed the power of working them on others. Out of the Eternal God, there is no salvation, no righteousness, no life. All these are in Christ. Christ, consequently, is the Eternal God. He in whom we believe and hope, to whom we pray, whom the Church acknowledges as the Savior of the faithful, whom to know is life eternal, in whom the pious glory, and through whom eternal blessings are communicated, is the Eternal God. All these Christ is, and, therefore, he is God.

How clearly and transparently does this appear in his miracles? I admit that similar and equal miracles were performed by the Prophets and apostles; but there is this very essential difference, that they dispensed the gifts of God as his ministers, whereas he exerted his own inherent might. Sometimes, indeed, he used prayer, that he might ascribe glory to the Father, but we see that for the most part his own proper power is displayed. And how should not he be the true author of miracles, who, of his own authority, commissions others to perform them? For the Evangelist relates that he gave power to the apostles to cast out devils, cure the lepers, raise the dead, etc. And they, by the mode in which they performed this ministry, showed plainly that their whole power was derived from Christ. "In the name of Jesus Christ of Nazareth," says Peter (Acts 3:6), "rise up and walk." Then it is not surprising that Christ appealed to his miracles in order to subdue the unbelief of the Jews, inasmuch as these were performed by his own energy, and therefore bore the most ample testimony to his divinity.

Again, if out of God there is no salvation, no righteousness, no life, Christ, having all these in him, is certainly God. Let no one object that life or salvation is transfused into him by God. For it is said not that he received, but that he himself is salvation. And if there is none good but God, how could a mere man be pure? I say, how could he be not good and just, but goodness and justice? Then what shall we say to the testimony of the Evangelist, that from the very beginning of the creation "in him was life, and this life was the light of men?" Trusting to such proofs, we can boldly put our hope and faith in him, though we know it is blasphemous impiety to confide in any creature. "Ye believe in God," says he, "believe also in me" (John 14:1). And so Paul (Romans 10:11, and 15:12) interprets two passages of Isaiah "Whose believeth in him shall not be confounded" (Isaiah 28:16); and, "In that day there shall be a root of Jesse, which shall stand for an ensign of the people; to it shall the Gentiles seek" (Isaiah 11:10). But why adduce more passages of Scripture on this head, when we so often meet with the expression, "He that believeth in me has eternal life?"

Again, the prayer of faith is addressed to him—prayer, which specially belongs to the divine majesty, if anything so belongs. For the Prophet Joel says, "And it shall come to pass, that whosoever shall call on the name of the Lord (Jehovah) shall be delivered" (Joel 2:32). And another says, "The name of the Lord (Jehovah) is a strong tower; the righteous runneth into it and is safe" (Proverbs 18:10). But the name of Christ is invoked for salvation, and therefore it follows that he is Jehovah. Moreover, we have an example of invocation in Stephen, when he said, "Lord Jesus, receive my spirit;" and thereafter in the whole Church, when Ananias says in the same book, "Lord, I have heard by many of this man, how much evil he has done to thy saints at Jerusalem; and here he has authority from the chief priests to bind all that call on thy name" (Acts 9:13, 14). And to make it more clearly understood that in Christ dwelt the whole fullness of the Godhead bodily, the Apostle declares that the only doctrine, which he professed to the Corinthians, the only doctrine that he taught, was the knowledge of Christ (1 Corinthians 2:2).

Consider what kind of thing it is, and how great, that the name of the Son alone is preached to us, though God command us to glory only in the knowledge of himself (Jeremiah 9:24). Who will dare to maintain that he, whom to know forms our only ground of glorying, is a mere creature? To this we may add, that the salutations prefixed to the Epistles of Paul pray for the same blessings from the Son as from the Father. By this we are taught, not only that the blessings which our heavenly Father bestows come to us through his intercession, but that by a partnership in power, the Son himself is their author. This practical knowledge is doubtless surer and more solid than any idle speculation. For the pious soul has the best view of God, and may almost be said to handle him, when it feels that it is quickened, enlightened, saved, justified, and sanctified by him.

14 The Divinity of the Spirit proved. A. He is the Creator and Preserver of the world. B. He sent the Prophets. C. He quickeneth all things. D. He is everywhere present. E. He renews the saints, and fits them for eternal life. F. All the offices of Deity belong to him.

In asserting the divinity of the Spirit, the proof must be derived from the same sources. And it is by no means an obscure testimony which Moses bears in the history of the creation, when he says that the Spirit of God was expanded over the abyss or shapeless matter; for it shows not only that the beauty which the world displays is maintained by the invigorating power of the Spirit, but that even before this beauty existed the Spirit was at work cherishing the confused mass. Again, no cavils can explain away the force of what Isaiah says, "And now the Lord God, and his Spirit, has sent me" (Isaiah 48:16), thus ascribing a share in the sovereign power of sending the Prophets to the Holy Spirit. In this, his divine majesty is clear.

But, as I observed, the best proof to us is our familiar experience. For nothing can be more alien from a creature, than the office which the Scriptures ascribe to him, and which the pious actually feel him discharging, —his being diffused over all space, sustaining, invigorating, and quickening all things, both in heaven and on the earth. The mere fact of his not being circumscribed by any limits raises him above the rank of creatures, while his transfusing vigour into all things, breathing into them being, life, and motion, is plainly divine. Again, if regeneration to incorruptible life is higher, and much more excellent than any present quickening, what must be thought of him by whose energy it is produced? Now, many passages of Scripture show that he is the author of regeneration, not by a borrowed, but by an intrinsic energy; and not only so, but that he is also the author of future immortality. In short, all the peculiar attributes of the Godhead are ascribed to him in the same way as to the Son.

He searches the deep things of Gods and has no counselor among the creatures; he bestows wisdom and the faculty of speech, though God declares to Moses (Exodus 4:11) that this is his own peculiar province. In like manner, by means of him we become partakers of the divine nature, so as in a manner to feel his quickening energy within us. Our justification is his work; from him is power, sanctification, truth, grace, and every good thought, since it is from the Spirit alone that all good gifts proceed. Particular attention is due to Paul's expression, that though there are diversities of gifts, "all these worketh that one and the self-same Spirit" (1 Corinthians 12:11), he being not only the beginning or origin, but also the author; as is even more clearly expressed immediately after in these words "dividing to every man severally as he will." For were he not something subsisting in God, will and arbitrary disposal would never be ascribed to him. Most clearly, therefore does Paul ascribe divine power to the Spirit, and demonstrate that he dwells hypostatically in God.

15 The Divinity of the Spirit continued. G. He is called God. H. Blasphemy against him is not forgiven.

Nor does the Scripture, in speaking of him, withhold the name of God. Paul infers that we are the temple of God, from the fact that "the Spirit of God dwelleth in us" (1 Corinthians 3:16; 6:19; and 2 Corinthians 6:16). Now it ought not to be slightly overlooked, that all the promises which God makes of choosing us to himself as a temple, receive their only fulfillment by his Spirit dwelling in us. Surely, as it is admirably expressed by Augustine, "Were we ordered to make a temple of wood and stone to the Spirit, inasmuch as such worship is due to God alone, it would be a clear proof of the Spirit's divinity; how much clearer a proof in that we are not to make a temple to him, but to be ourselves that temple." And the Apostle says at one time that we are the temple of God, and at another time, in the same sense, that we are the temple of the Holy Spirit. Peter, when he rebuked Ananias for having lied to the Holy Spirit, said, that he had not lied unto men, but unto God. And when Isaiah had introduced the Lord of Hosts as speaking, Paul says, it was the Holy Spirit that spoke (Acts 28:25, 26). Nay, words uniformly said by the Prophets to have been spoken by the Lord of Hosts, are by Christ and his apostles ascribed to the Holy Spirit. Hence, it follows that the Spirit is the true Jehovah who dictated the prophecies. Again, when God complains that he was provoked to anger by the stubbornness of the people, in place of Him, Isaiah says that his Holy Spirit was grieved (Isaiah 63:10). Lastly, while blasphemy against the Spirit is not forgiven, either in the present life or that which is to come, whereas he who has blasphemed against the Son may obtain pardon, that majesty must certainly be divine which it is an inexpiable crime to offend or impair.

I designedly omit several passages, which the ancient fathers adduced. They thought it plausible to quote from David, "By the word of the Lord were the heavens made, and all the host of them by the breath (Spirit) of his mouth" (Psalms 33:6), in order to prove that the world was not less the work of the Holy Spirit than of the Son. But seeing it is usual in the Psalms to repeat the same thing twice, and in Isaiah the *spirit* (breath) of the mouth is equivalent to *word*, that proof was weak; and, accordingly, my wish has been to advert briefly to those proofs on which pious minds may securely rest.

16 What view to be taken of the Trinity. The form of Christian baptism proves that there are in one essence. The Arian and Macedonian heresies.

But as God has manifested himself more clearly by the advent of Christ, so he has made himself more familiarly known in three persons. Of many proofs let this one suffice. Paul connects together these three, God, Faith, and Baptism, and reasons from the one to the other—viz. because there is one faith he infers that there is one God; and because there is one baptism, he infers that there is one faith. Therefore, if by baptism we are initiated into the faith and worship of one God, we must of necessity believe that he into whose name we are baptized is the true God. And there cannot be a doubt that our Savior wished to testify, by a solemn rehearsal, that the perfect light of faith is now exhibited, when he said, "Go and teach all nations, baptizing them in the name of the Father, and of the Son, and of the Holy Spirit" (Matthew 28:19), since this is the same thing as to be baptized into the name of the one God, who has been fully manifested in the Father, the Son, and the Spirit. Hence, it plainly appears, that the three persons, in whom alone God is known, subsist in the Divine essence. And since faith certainly ought not to look hither and thither, or run up and down after various objects, but to look, refer, and cleave to God alone, it is obvious that were there various kinds of faith, there behaved also to be various gods. Then, as the baptism of faith is a sacrament, its unity assures us of the unity of God. Hence, also it is proved that it is lawful only to be baptized into one God, because we make a profession of faith in him in whose name we are baptized.

What, then, is our Savior's meaning in commanding baptism to be administered in the name of the Father, and the Son, and the Holy Spirit, if it be not that we are to believe with one faith in the name of the Father, and the Son, and the Holy Spirit? But is this anything else than to declare that the Father, Son, and Spirit, are one God? Wherefore, since it must be held certain that there is one God, not more than one, we conclude that the Word and Spirit are of the very essence of God. Nothing could be more stupid than the trifling of the Arians, who, while acknowledging the divinity of the Son, denied his Divine essence. Equally extravagant were the ravings of the Macedonians, who insisted that by the Spirit would be only meant the gifts of grace poured out upon men. For as wisdom understanding, prudence, fortitude, and the fear of the Lord, proceed from the Spirit, so he is the one Spirit of wisdom, prudence, fortitude, and piety. He is not divided according to the distribution of his gifts, but, as the Apostle assures us (1 Corinthians 12:11), however they are divided, he remains one and the same.

17 Of the distinction of Persons. They are distinct, but not divided. This proved.

On the other hand, the Scriptures demonstrate that there is some distinction between the Father and the Word, the Word and the Spirit; but the magnitude of the mystery reminds us of the great reverence and soberness, which ought to be, employed in discussing it. It seems to me, that nothing can be more admirable than the words of Gregory Nanzianzen: "I cannot think of the unity without being irradiated by the Trinity: I cannot distinguish between the Trinity without being carried up to the unity." Therefore, let us beware of imagining such a Trinity of persons as will distract our thoughts, instead of bringing them instantly back to the unity. The words Father, Son, and Holy Spirit, certainly indicate a real distinction, not allowing us to suppose that they are merely epithets by which God is variously designated from his works. Still they indicate distinction only, not division.

The passages we have already quoted show that the Son has a distinct subsistence from the Father, because the Word could not have been with

God unless he were distinct from the Father; nor but for this could he have had his glory with the Father. In like manner, Christ distinguishes the Father from himself when he says that there is another who bears witness of him (John 5:32; 8:16). To the same effect is it elsewhere said, that the Father made all things by the Word. This could not be, if he were not in some respect distinct from him. Besides, it was not the Father who descended to the earth, but he who came forth from the Father; nor was it the Father who died and rose again, but he whom the Father had sent. This distinction did not take its beginning at the incarnation: for it is clear that the only begotten Son previously existed in the bosom of the Father (John 1:18). For who will dare to affirm that the Son entered his Father's bosom for the first time, when he came down from heaven to assume human nature? Therefore, he was previously in the bosom of the Father, and had his glory with the Father. Christ intimates the distinction between the Holy Spirit and the Father, when he says that the Spirit proceedeth from the Father, and between the Holy Spirit and himself, when he speaks of him as another as he does when he declares that he will send another Comforter; and in many other passages besides (John 14:6; 15:26; 14:16).

18 Analogies taken from human affairs to be cautiously used. Due regard to be paid to those mentioned by Scripture.

I am not sure whether it is expedient to borrow analogies from human affairs to express the nature of this distinction. The ancient fathers sometimes do so, but they at the same time admits that what they bring forward as analogous is very widely different. And hence, it is that I have a great dread of anything like presumption here, lest some rash saying may furnish an occasion of calumny to the malicious, or of delusion to the unlearned. It would be unbecoming, however, to say nothing of a distinction, which we observe that the Scriptures have pointed out. This distinction is, that to the Father is attributed the beginning of action, the fountain and source of all things; to the Son, wisdom, counsel, and arrangement in action, while the energy and efficacy of action is assigned to the Spirit. Moreover, though the eternity of the Father is also the eternity of the Son and Spirit, since God never could be without his own wisdom and energy; and though in eternity there can be no room for first or last, still the distinction of order is not unmeaning or superfluous, the Father being considered first, next the Son from him, and then the Spirit from both. For the mind of every man naturally inclines to consider, first, God, secondly, the wisdom emerging from him, and, lastly, the energy by which he executes the purposes of his counsel. For this reason, the Son is said to be of the Father only, and the Spirit of both the Father and the Son. This is done in many passages, but in none more clearly than in the eighth chapter to the Romans, where the same Spirit is called indiscriminately the Spirit of Christ, and the Spirit of him who raised up Christ from the dead. And not improperly. For Peter also testifies (1 Peter 1:21), that it was the Spirit of Christ which inspired the Prophets, though the Scriptures so often say that it was the Spirit of God the Father.

19 How the Three Persons not only do not destroy, but constitute the most perfect unity

Moreover, this distinction is so far from interfering with the most perfect unity of God, that the Son may thereby be proved to be one God with the Father, inasmuch as he constitutes one Spirit with him, and that the Spirit is not different from the Father and the Son, inasmuch as he is the Spirit of the Father and the Son. In each hypostasis, the whole nature is understood, the only difference being that each has his own peculiar subsistence. The whole Father is in the Son, and the whole Son in the Father, as the Son himself also declares (John 14:10), "I am in the Father, and the Father in me;" nor do ecclesiastical writers admit that the one is separated from the other by any difference of essence. "By those names which denote distinctions" says Augustine "is meant the relation, which they mutually bear to each other, not the very substance by which they are one." In this way, the sentiments of the Fathers, which might sometimes appear to be at variance with each other, are to be reconciled. At one time, they teach that the Father is the beginning of the Son, at another they assert that the Son has both divinity and essence from himself, and therefore is one beginning with the Father. The cause of this discrepancy is well and clearly explained by Augustine, when he says, "Christ, as to himself, is called God, as to the Father he is called Son." And again, "The Father, as to himself, is called God, as to the Son he is called Father. He who, as to the Son, is called Father, is not Son; and he who, as to himself, is called Father, and he who, as to himself, is called Son, is the same God." Therefore, when we speak of the Son simply, without reference to the Father, we truly and properly affirm that he is of himself, and, accordingly, call him the only beginning; but when we denote the relation, which he bears to the Father, we correctly make the Father the beginning of the Son. Augustine's fifth book on the Trinity is wholly devoted to the explanation of this subject. But it is far safer to rest contented with the relation as taught by him, than get bewildered in vain speculation by subtle prying into a sublime mystery.

20 Conclusion of this part of the chapter, and summary of the true doctrine concerning the unity of Essence and the Three Persons.

Let those, then, who love soberness, and are contented with the measure of faith, briefly receive what is useful to be known. It is as follows: —When we profess to believe in one God, by the name God is understood the one simple essence, comprehending three persons or hypostases; and, accordingly, whenever the name of God is used indefinitely, the Son and Spirit, not less than the Father, is meant. But when the Son is joined with the Father, relation comes into view, and so we distinguish between the Persons. But as the Personal subsistence carry an order with them, the principle and origin being in the Father, whenever mention is made of the Father and Son, or of the Father and Spirit together, the name of God is specially given to the Father. In this way, the unity of essence is retained, and respect is had to the order, which, however derogates in no respect from the divinity of the Son and Spirit. And surely since we have already seen how the apostles declare the Son of God to have been He whom Moses and the Prophets declared to be Jehovah, we must always arrive at a unity of essence. We, therefore, hold it detestable blasphemy to call the Son a different God from the Father, because the simple name God admits not of relation, nor can God, considered in himself, be said to be this or that. Then, that the name Jehovah, taken indefinitely, may be applied to Christ, is clear from the words of Paul, "For this thing I besought the Lord thrice." After giving the answer, "My grace is sufficient for thee," he subjoins, "that the power of Christ may rest upon me" (2 Corinthians 12:8, 9). For it is certain that the name of Lord (KurioV) is there put for Jehovah, and, therefore, to restrict it to the person of the Mediator were puerile and frivolous, the words being used absolutely, and not with the view of comparing the Father and the Son. And we know that, in accordance with the received usage of the Greeks, the apostles uniformly substitute the word KurioV for Jehovah.

Not to go far for an example, Paul besought the Lord in the same sense in which Peter quotes the passage of Joel, "Whosoever shall call upon the name of the Lord shall be saved" (Acts 2:21; Joel 2:28). Where this name is specially applied to the Son, there is a different ground for it, as will be seen in its own place; at present it is sufficient to remember, that Paul, after praying to God absolutely, immediately subjoins the name of Christ. Thus, too, the Spirit is called God absolutely by Christ himself. For nothing prevents us from holding that he is the entire spiritual essence of God, in which are comprehended Father, Son, and Spirit. This is plain from Scripture. For as God is there called a Spirit, so the Holy Spirit also, in so far as he is a hypostasis of the whole essence, is said to be both of God and from God.

21 Refutation of Arian, Macedonian, and Anti Trinitarian heresies. Caution to be observed.

But since Satan, in order to pluck up our faith by the roots, has always provoked fierce disputes, partly concerning the Divine essence of the Son and Spirit, and partly concerning the distinction of persons; since in almost every age he has stirred up impious spirits to vex the orthodox doctors on this head, and is attempting in the present day to kindle a new flame out of the old embers, it will be proper here to dispose of some of these perverse dreams. Hitherto our chief object has been to stretch out our hand for the guidance of such as are disposed to learn, not to war with the stubborn and contentious; but now the truth, which was calmly demonstrated, must be vindicated from the calumnies of the ungodly. Still, however it will be our principal study to provide a sure footing for those whose ears are open to the word of God. Here, if anywhere, in considering the hidden mysteries of Scripture, we should speculate soberly and with great moderation, cautiously guarding against allowing either our mind or our tongue to go a step beyond the confines of God's word. For how can the human minds, which has not yet been able to ascertain of what the body of the sun consists, though it is daily presented to the eye, bring down the boundless essence of God to its little measure? Nay, how can it, under its own guidance, penetrate to knowledge of the substance of God while unable to understand its own? Wherefore, let us willingly leave to God the knowledge of himself.

In the words of Hilary, "He alone is a fit witness to himself who is known only by himself." This knowledge, then, if we would leave to God, we must conceive of him as he has made himself known, and in our inquiries make application to no other quarter than his word. On this subject we have five homilies of Chrysostom against the Anomoei, in which he endeavored, but in vain, to check the presumption of the sophists, and curb their garrulity. They showed no more modesty here than they are wont to do in everything else. The very unhappy results of their temerity should be a warning to us to bring more docility than acumen to the discussion of this question, never to attempt to search after God anywhere but in his sacred word, and never to speak or think of him further than we have it for our guide. But if the distinction of Father, Son, and Spirit, subsisting in the one Godhead (certainly a subject of great difficulty), gives more trouble and annoyance to some intellects than is meet, let us remember that the human mind enters a labyrinth whenever it indulges its curiosity, and thus submit to be guided by the divine oracles, no matter how much the mystery may be beyond our reach.

22 The more modern Anti Trinitarians, and especially Servetus, refuted.

It would be tedious, and to no purpose toilsome, to form a catalogue of the errors by which, in regard to this branch of doctrine, the purity of the faith has been assailed. The greater part of heretics have with their gross deliriums made a general attack on the glory of God, deeming it enough if they could disturb and shake the unwary. From a few individuals numerous sects have sprung up, some of them rending the Divine essence, and others confounding the distinction of Persons. But if we hold, what has already been demonstrated from Scripture, that the essence of the one God, pertaining to the Father, Son, and Spirit, is simple and indivisible, and again, that the Father differs in some special property from the Son, and the Son from the Spirit, the door will be shut against Arius and Sabellius, as well as the other ancient authors of error. But as in our day have arisen certain frantic men, such as Servetus and others, who, by new devices, have thrown everything into confusion; it may be worthwhile briefly to discuss their fallacies.

The name of Trinity was so much disliked, nay detested, by Servetus, that he charged all whom he called Trinitarians with being Atheists. I say nothing of the insulting terms in which he thought proper to make his charges. The sum of his speculations was, that a threefold Deity is introduced wherever three Persons are said to exist in his essence, and that this Triad was imaginary, inasmuch as it was inconsistent with the unity of God. At the same time, he would have it that the Persons are certain external ideas which do not truly subsist in the Divine essence, but only figure God to us under this or that form: that at first, indeed, there was no distinction in God, because originally the Word was the same as the Spirit, but ever since Christ came forth God of God, another Spirit, also a God, had proceeded from him. But although he sometimes cloaks his absurdities in allegory, as when he says that the eternal Word of God was the Spirit of Christ with God, and the reflection of the idea, likewise that the Spirit was a shadow of Deity, he at last reduces the divinity of both to nothing; maintaining that, according to the mode of distribution, there is a part of God as well in the Son as in the Spirit, just as the same Spirit substantially is a portion of God in us, and also in wood and stone. His absurd babbling concerning the person of the Mediator will be seen in its own place.

The monstrous fiction that a Person is nothing else than a visible appearance of the glory of God needs not a long refutation. For when John declares that before the world was created the Logos was God (John 1:1), he shows that he was something very different from an idea. But if even then, and from the remotest eternity, that Logos, who was God, was with the Father, and had his own distinct and peculiar glory with the Father (John 17:5), he certainly could not be an external or figurative splendor, but must necessarily have been a hypostasis which dwelt inherently in God himself. But although there is no mention made of the Spirit antecedent to the account of the creation, he is not there introduced as a shadow, but as the essential power of God, where Moses relates that the shapeless mass was unborn by him (Genesis 1:2).

It is obvious that the eternal Spirit always existed in God, seeing he cherished and sustained the confused materials of heaven and earth before they possessed order or beauty. Assuredly, he could not then be an image or representation of God, as Servetus dreams. But he is elsewhere forced to make a more open disclosure of his impiety when he says, that God by his eternal reason decreeing a Son to himself, in this way assumed a visible appearance. For if this be true, no other Divinity is left to Christ than is implied in his having been ordained a Son by God's eternal decree. Moreover, those phantoms, which Servetus substitutes for the hypostases, he so transforms as to make new changes in God. But the most execrable heresy of all is his confounding both the Son and Spirit promiscuously with all the creatures. For he distinctly asserts, that there are parts and partitions in the essence of God, and that every such portion is God. This he does especially when he says, that the spirits of the faithful are co-eternal and consubstantial with God, although he elsewhere assigns a substantial divinity, not only to the soul of man, but also to all created things.

23 Other Anti Trinitarians refuted. No good objection that Christ is called the Son of God, since he is also called God. Impious absurdities of some heretics.

This pool has bred another monster not unlike the former. For certain restless spirits, unwilling to share the disgrace and obloquy of the impiety of Servetus, have confessed that there were indeed three Persons, but added, as a reason, that the Father, who alone is truly and properly God, transfused his Divinity into the Son and Spirit when he formed them. Nor do they refrain from expressing themselves in such shocking terms as these: that the Father is essentially distinguished from the Son and Spirit by this; that he is the only *essentiator*. Their first pretext for this is, that Christ is uniformly called the Son of God. From this they infer, that there is no proper God but the Father. But they forget, that although the name of God is common also to the Son, yet it is sometimes, by way of excellence, ascribed to the Father, as being the source and principle of Divinity; and this is done in order to mark the simple unity of essence. They object, that if the Son is truly God, he must be deemed the Son of a person: which is absurd. I answer, that both are true; namely, that he is the Son of God, because he is the Word, begotten of the Father before all ages; (for we are not now speaking of the Person of the Mediator), and yet, that for the purpose of explanation, regard must be had to the Person, so that the name God may not be understood in its absolute sense, but as equivalent to Father. For if we hold that there is no other God than the Fathers this rank is clearly denied to the Son.

In every case where the Godhead is mentioned, we are by no means to admit that there is an antithesis between the Father and the Son, as if to the former only the name of God could competently be applied. For assuredly, the God who appeared to Isaiah was the one true God, and yet John declares that he was Christ (Isaiah 6; John 12:41). He who declared, by the mouth of Isaiah, that he was to be "for a stone of stumbling" to the Jews, was the one God; and yet Paul declares that he was Christ (Isaiah 8:14; Romans 9:33). He who proclaims by Isaiah, "Unto me every knee shall bow," is the one God; yet Paul again explains that he is Christ (Isaiah 45:23; Romans 14:11). To this we may add the passages quoted by an Apostle, "Thou, Lord, hast laid the foundations of the earth;" "Let all the angels of God worship him" (Hebrews 1:10; 10:6; Psalm 102:26; 97:7). All these apply to the one God; and yet the Apostle contends that they are the proper attributes of Christ.

There is nothing in the cavil, that what properly applies to God is transferred to Christ, because he is the brightness of his glory. Since the name of Jehovah is everywhere applied to Christ, it follows that, in regard to Deity, he is of himself. For if he is Jehovah, it is impossible to deny that he is the same God who elsewhere proclaims by Isaiah, "I am the first, and I am the last; and beside me there is no God" (Isaiah 44:6). We would also do well to ponder the words of Jeremiah, "The gods that have not made the heavens and the earth, even they shall perish from the earth and from under these heavens" (Jeremiah 10:11); whence it follows conversely, that He whose divinity Isaiah repeatedly proves from the creation of the world, is none other than the Son of God. And how is it possible that the Creator, who gives to all should not be of himself, but should borrow his essence from another? Whosoever says that the Son was *essentiated* by the Father, denies his self-existence.

Against this, however, the Holy Spirit protests, when he calls him Jehovah. On the supposition, then, that the whole essence is in the Father only, the essence becomes divisible, or is denied to the Son, who, being thus robbed of his essences will be only a titular God. If we are to believe these triflers, Divine essence belongs to the Father only, on the ground that he is sole God, and *essentiator* of the Son. In this way, the divinity of the Son will be something abstracted from the essence of God, or the derivation of a part from the whole. On the same principle it must also be conceded, that the Spirit belongs to the Father only. For if the derivation is from the primary essence, which is proper to none but the Father, the Spirit cannot justly be deemed the Spirit of the Son. This view, however, is refuted by the testimony of Paul, when he makes the Spirit common both to Christ and the Father. Moreover, if the Person of the Father is expunged from the Trinity, in what will he differ from the Son and Spirit, except in being the only God? They confess that Christ is God, and that he differs from the Father. If he differs, there must be some mark of distinction between them. Those who place it in the essence, manifestly reduce the true divinity of Christ to nothing, since divinity cannot exist without essence, and indeed without entire essence.

The Father certainly cannot differ from the Son, unless he have something peculiar to himself, and not common to him with the Son. What, then, do these men show as the mark of distinction? If it is in the essence, let them tell whether or not he communicated essence to the Son. This he could not do in part merely, for it would be impious to think of a divided God. And besides, on this supposition, there would be a rending of the Divine essence. The whole entire essence must therefore be common to the Father and the Son; and if so, in respect of essence there is no distinction between them. If they reply that the Father, while essentiating, still remains the only God, being the possessor of the essence, then Christ will be a figurative God, one in name or semblance only, and not in reality, because no property can be more peculiar to God than essence, according to the words, "I Am hath sent me unto you" (Exodus 3:4).

117

24 The name of God sometimes given to the Son absolutely as to the Father. Same as to other attributes. Objections refuted.

The assumption, that whenever God is mentioned absolutely, the Father only is meant, may be proved erroneous by many passages. Even in those, which they quote in support of their views, they betray a lamentable inconsistency because the name of Son occurs there by way of contrast, showing that the other name God is used relatively, and in that way confined to the Person of the Father. Their objection may be disposed of in a single word. Were not the Father alone the true God, he would, say they, be his own Father. But there is nothing absurd in the name of God being specially applied, in respect of order and degree, to him who not only of himself begat his own wisdom, but is the God of the Mediator, as I will more fully show in its own place. Forever since Christ was manifested in the flesh, he is called the Son of God, not only because begotten of the Father before all worlds he was the Eternal Word, but also because he undertook the person and office of the Mediator that he might unite us to God. Seeing they are so bold in excluding the Son from the honor of God, I would fain know whether, when he declares that there is "none good but one, that is, God," he deprives himself of goodness.

I speak not of his human nature, lest perhaps they should object, that whatever goodness was in it was derived by gratuitous gift: I ask whether the Eternal Word of God is good, yes or no? If they say no, their impiety is manifest; if yes, they refute themselves. Christ's seeming at the first glance to disclaim the name of good (Matthew 19:17), rather confirms our view. Goodness, being the special property of God alone, and yet being at the time applied to him in the ordinary way of salutation, his rejection of false honor intimates that the goodness in which he excels is Divine. Again, I ask whether, when Paul affirms that God alone is "immortal," "wise, and true" (1 Timothy 1:17), he reduces Christ to the rank of beings mortal, foolish, and false. Is not he immortal, who, from the beginning, had life so as to bestow immortality on angels? Is not he wise who is the eternal wisdom of God? Is not he true who is truth itself?

I ask, moreover, whether they think Christ should be worshipped. If he claims justly, that every knee shall bow to him, it follows that he is the God who, in the law, forbade worship to be offered to any but himself. If they insist on applying to the Father only the words of Isaiah, "I am, and besides me there is none else" (Isaiah 44:6), I turn the passage against themselves, since we see that every property of God is attributed to Christ. There is no room for the cavil that Christ was exalted in the flesh in which he humbled himself, and in respect of which all power is given to him in heaven and on earth. For although the majesty of King and Judge extends to the whole person of the Mediator, yet had he not been God manifested in the flesh, he could not have been exalted to such a height without coming into collision with God. And the dispute is admirably settled by Paul, when he declares that he was equal with God before he humbled himself, and assumed the form of a servants (Philippians 2:6). Moreover, how could such equality exist, if he were not that God whose name is Jah and Jehovah, who rides upon the cherubim, is King of all the earth, and King of ages? Let them glamour as they may, Christ cannot be robbed of the honor described by Isaiah, "Lo, this is our God; we have waited for him" (Isaiah 25:9); for these words describe the advent of God the Redeemer, who was not only to bring back the people from Babylonish captivity, but restore the Church, and make her completely perfect.

Nor does another cavil avail them, that Christ was God in his Father. For though we admit that, in respect of order and gradation, the beginning of divinity is in the Father, we hold it a detestable fiction to maintain that essence is proper to the Father alone, as if he were the deifier of the Son. On this view, either the essence is manifold, or Christ is God only in name and imagination. If they grant that the Son is God, but only in subordination to the Father, the essence, which in the Father is unformed and unbegotten will in him, be formed and begotten. I know that many who would be thought wise deride us for extracting the distinction of persons from the words of Moses when he introduces God as saying, "Let us make man in our own image" (Genesis 1:26).

Pious readers, however, see how frigidly and absurdly the colloquy were introduced by Moses, if there were not several persons in the Godhead. It is certain that those whom the Father addresses must have been untreated. But nothing is untreated except the one God. Now then, unless they concede that the power of creating was common to the Father, Son, and Spirit, and the power of commanding common, it will follow that God did not speak thus inwardly with himself, but addressed other extraneous architects. In fine, there is a single passage, which will at once dispose of these two objections. The declaration of Christ that "God is a Spirit" (John 4:24), cannot be confined to the Father only, as if the Word were not of a spiritual nature. But if the name Spirit applies equally to the Son as to the Father, I infer that under the indefinite name of God the Son is included. He adds immediately after, that the only worshipers approved by the Father are those who worship him in spirit and in truth; and hence I also infer, that because Christ performs the office of teacher under a head, he applies the name God to the Father, not for the purpose of destroying his own Divinity, but for the purpose of raising us up to it as if it were step by step.

25 Objections further refuted. Caution to be used.

The hallucination consists in dreaming of individuals, each of whom possesses a part of the essence. The Scriptures teach that there is essentially but one God, and, therefore, that the essence both of the Son and Spirit is unbegotten;

but inasmuch as the Father is first in order, and of himself begat his own Wisdom, he, as we lately observed, is justly regarded as the principle and fountain of all the Godhead. Thus God, taken indefinitely, is unbegotten, and the Father, in respect of his person, is unbegotten. For it is absurd to imagine that our doctrine gives any ground for alleging that we establish a quaternion of gods. They falsely and calumniously ascribe to us the figment of their own brain, as if we virtually held that three persons emanate from one essence, whereas it is plain, from our writings, that we do not disjoin the persons from the essence, but interpose a distinction between the persons residing in it. If the persons were separated from the essence, there might be some plausibility in their argument; as in this way, there would be a trinity of Gods, not of persons comprehended in one God. This affords an answer to their futile question—whether or not the essence concurs in forming the Trinity, as if we imagined that three Gods were derived from it. Their objection, that there would thus be a Trinity without a God, originates in the same absurdity. Although the essence does not contribute to the distinction, as if it were a part or member, the persons are not without it, or external to it; for the Father, if he were not God, could not be the Father; nor could the Son possibly be Son unless he were God.

We say, then, that the Godhead is absolutely of itself. And hence, also we hold that the Son, regarded as God, and without reference to person, is also of himself; though we also say that, regarded as Son, he is of the Father. Thus his essence is without beginning, while his person has its beginning in God. And, indeed, the orthodox writers, who in former times spoke of the Trinity, used this term only with reference to the Persons. To have included the essence in the distinction would not only have been an absurd error, but gross impiety. For those who class the three thus—Essence, Son, and Spirit—plainly do away with the essence of the Son and Spirit; otherwise, the parts being intermingled would merge into each other—a circumstance which would vitiate any distinction. In short, if God and Father were synonymous terms, the Father would be deifier in a sense which would leave the Son nothing but a shadow; and the Trinity would be nothing more than the union of one God with two creatures.

26 Previous refutations further explained.

To the objection, that if Christ be properly God, he is improperly called the Son of God, it has been already answered, that when one person is compared with another, the name God is not used indefinitely, but is restricted to the Father, regarded as the beginning of the Godhead, not by *essentiating*, as fanatics absurdly express it, but in respect of order. In this sense are to be understood the words which Christ addressed to the Father, "This is life eternal, that they might know thee the only true God, and Jesus Christ whom thou hast sent" (John 17:3). For speaking in the person of the

Mediator, he holds a middle place between God and man; yet so that his majesty is not diminished thereby. For though he humbled (emptied) himself, he did not lose the glory, which he had with the Father, though it was concealed from the world. So, in the Epistle to the Hebrews (Hebrews 1:10; 2:9), though the Apostle confesses that Christ was made a little lower than the angels, he at the same time hesitates not to assert that he is the eternal God who founded the earth.

We must hold, therefore, that as often as Christ, in the character of Mediator, addresses the Father, he, under the term God, includes his own divinity also. Thus, when he says to the apostles, "It is expedient for you that I go away," "My Father is greater than I," he does not attribute to himself a secondary divinity merely, as if in regard to eternal essence he were inferior to the Father; but having obtained celestial glory, he gathers together the faithful to share it with him. He places the Father in the higher degree, inasmuch as the full perfection of brightness conspicuous in heaven differs from that measure of glory, which he himself displayed when clothed in flesh. For the same reason Paul says, that Christ will restore "the kingdom to God, even the Father," "that God may be all in all" (1 Corinthians 15:24, 28). Nothing can be more absurd than to deny the perpetuity of Christ's divinity. But if he will never cease to be the Son of God, but will ever remain the same that he was from the beginning, it follows that under the name of Father the one Divine essence common to both is comprehended. And assuredly Christ descended to us for the very purpose of raising us to the Father, and thereby, at the same time, raising us to himself, inasmuch as he is one with the Father. It is therefore erroneous and impious to confine the name of God to the Father, so as to deny it to the Son. Accordingly, John, declaring that he is the true God, has no idea of placing him beneath the Father in a subordinate rank of divinity. I wonder what these fabricators of new gods mean, when they confess that Christ is truly God, and yet exclude him from the godhead of the Father, as if there could be any true God but the one God, or as if transfused divinity were not a mere modern fiction.

27 Reply to certain passages produced from Irenaeus. The meaning of Irenaeus.

In the many passages, which they collect from Irenaeus, in which he maintains that the Father of Christ is the only eternal God of Israel, they betray shameful ignorance, or very great dishonesty. For they ought to have observed, that that holy man was contending against certain frantic persons, who, denying that the Father of Christ was that God who had in old times spoken by Moses and the Prophets, held that he was some phantom or other produced from the pollution of the world. His whole object, therefore, is to make it plain, that in the Scriptures no other God is announced but the Father of Christ; that it is wicked to imagine any other. Accordingly, there is nothing strange in his so often concluding that the God of Israel was no other than he who is celebrated by Christ and the apostles. Now, when a different heresy is to be resisted, we also say with truth, that the God, who in old times appeared to the fathers, was no other than Christ. Moreover, if it is objected that he was the Father, we have the answer ready, that while we contend for the divinity of the Son, we by no means exclude the Father.

When the reader attends to the purpose of Irenaeus, the dispute is at an end. Indeed, the pious writer insists on this one point, "that he who in Scripture is called God absolutely and indefinitely, is truly the only God; and that Christ is called God absolutely." Let us remember (as appears from the whole work), that the point under discussion was, that the name of Father is not applied enigmatically and parabolically to one who was not truly God. We may add that he contends that the Son as well as the Father united was the God proclaimed by the Prophets and apostles. He afterwards explains how Christ, who is Lord of all, and King and Judge, received power from him who is God of all, namely, in respect of the humiliation by which he humbled himself, even to the death of the cross. At the same time he shortly after affirms, that the Son is the maker of heaven and earth, who delivered the law by the hand of Moses, and appeared to the fathers. Should any babbler now insist that, according to Irenaeus, the Father alone is the God of Israel, I will refer him to a passage in which Irenaeus distinctly says, that Christ is ever one and the same, and also applies to Christ the words of the prophecy of Habakkuk, "God cometh from the south." To the same effect he says, "Therefore, Christ himself, with the Father, is the God of the living." He explains that Abraham believed God, because Christ is the maker of heaven and earth, and very God.

28 Reply to certain passages produced from Tertullian. The meaning of Tertullian.

With no more truth do they claim Tertullian as a patron. Though his style is sometimes rugged and obscure, he delivers the doctrine which we maintain in no ambiguous manner, namely, that while there is one God, his Word, however, is with dispensation or economy; that there is only one God in unity of substance; but that, nevertheless, by the mystery of dispensation, the unity is arranged into Trinity; that there are three, not in state, but in degree—not in substance, but in form—not in power, but in order. He says indeed that he holds the Son to be second to the Father; but he means that the only difference is by distinction. In one place, he says the Son is visible; but after he has discoursed on both views, he declares that he is invisible regarded as the Word. In fine, by affirming that the Father is characterized by his own Person, he shows that he is very far from countenancing the fiction, which we refute. And although he does not acknowledge any other God than the Father, yet, explaining himself in the immediate context, he shows that he does not speak exclusively in respect of the Son, because he denies that he is a different God from the Father; and, accordingly, that the one supremacy is not violated by the distinction of Person. And it is easy to collect his meaning from the whole tenor of his discourse. For he contends against Praxeas, that although God has three distinct Persons, yet there are not several gods, nor is unity divided.

According to the fiction of Praxeas, Christ could not be God without being the Father also; and this is the reason that Tertullian dwells so much on the distinction. When he calls the Word and Spirit a portion of the whole, the expression, though harsh, may be allowed, since it des not refer to the substance, but only (as Tertullian himself testifies) denotes arrangement and economy, which applies to the persons only. Accordingly, he asks, "How many persons, Praxeas, do you think there are, but just as many as there are names for?" In the same way, he shortly after says, "That they may believe the Father and the Son, each in his own name and person." These things, I think, sufficiently refute the effrontery of those who endeavor to blind the simple by pretending the authority of Tertullian.

29 Anti Trinitarians refuted by ancient Christian writers; e.g., Justin, Hilary. Objections drawn from writings improperly attributed to Ignatius. Conclusion of the whole discussion concerning the Trinity.

Assuredly, whosoever will compare the writings of the ancient fathers with each other, will not find anything in Irenaeus different from what is taught by those who come after him. Justin is one of the most ancient, and he agrees with us out and out. Let them object that, by him and others, the Father of Christ is called the one God. The same thing is taught by Hilary, who uses the still harsher expression, that Eternity is in the Father. Is it that he may withhold Divine essence from the Son? His whole work is a defense of the doctrine, which we maintain; and yet these men are not ashamed to produce some kind of mutilated excerpts for the purpose of persuading us that Hilary is a patron of their heresy. With regard to what they pretend as to Ignatius, if they would have it to be of the least importance, let them prove that the apostles enacted laws concerning Lent, and other corruptions. Nothing can be more nauseating, than the absurdities which have been published under the name of Ignatius; and therefore, the conduct of those who provide themselves with such masks for deception is the less entitled to toleration.

Moreover, the consent of the ancient fathers clearly appears from this, that in the Council of Nice, no attempt was made by Arius to cloak his heresy by the authority of any approved author; and no Greek or Latin writer apologizes as dissenting from his predecessors. It cannot be necessary to observe how carefully Augustine, to whom all these miscreants are most violently opposed, examined all ancient writings, and how reverently he embraced the doctrine taught by them. He is most scrupulous in stating the grounds on which he is forced to differ from them, even in the minutest point. On this subject, too, if he finds anything ambiguous or obscure in other writers, he does not disguise it. And he assumes it as an acknowledged fact, that the doctrine opposed by the Arians was received without dispute from the earliest antiquity. At the same time, he was not ignorant of what some others had previously taught. This is obvious from a single expression. When he says that "unity is in the Father," will they pretend that he then forgot himself? In another passage, he clears away every such charge, when he calls the Father the beginning of the Godhead, as being from none—thus wisely inferring that the name of God is specially ascribed to the Father, because, unless the beginning were from him, the simple unity of essence could not be maintained.

I hope the pious reader will admit that I have now disposed of all the calumnies by which Satan has hitherto attempted to pervert or obscure the pure doctrine of faith. The whole substance of the doctrine has, I trust, been faithfully expounded, if my readers will set bounds to their curiosity, and not long more eagerly than they ought for perplexing disputation. I did not undertake to satisfy those who delight in speculate views, but I have not designedly omitted anything, which I thought adverse to me. At the same time, studying the edification of the Church, I have thought it better not to touch on various topics, which could have yielded little profit, while they must have needlessly burdened and fatigued the reader. For instance, what avails it to discuss, as Lombard does at length, Whether or not the Father always generates? This idea of continual generation becomes an absurd fiction from the moment it is seen that from eternity there were three persons in one God.

Chapter 14

IN THE CREATION OF THE WORLD, AND ALL THINGS IN IT, THE TRUE GOD DISTINGUISHED BY CERTAIN MARKS FROM FICTITIOUS GODS.

In this chapter commences the second part of Book First—viz. the knowledge of man. Certain things premised. I. The creation of the world generally (sections 1 and 2). II. The subject of angels considered (sections 3-13). III. Of bad angels or devils (sections 13-20); and, IV. The practical use to be made of the history of the creation (sections 20-22).

Sections

1. *The mere fact of creation should lead us to acknowledge God, but to prevent our falling away to Gentile fictions, God has been pleased to furnish a history of the creation. An impious objection, Why the world was not created sooner? Answer to it. Shrewd saying of an old man.*

2. *For the same reason, the world was created, not in an instant, but in six days. The order of creation described, showing that Adam was not created until God had, with infinite goodness made ample provision for him.*

3. *The doctrine concerning angels expounded. A. That we may learn from them also to acknowledge God. B. That we may be put on our guard against the errors of the worshippers of angels and the Manichees. Manicheeism refuted. Rule of piety.*

4. *The angels created by God. At what time and in what order it is inexpedient to inquire. The garrulity of the Pseudo-Dionysius.*

5. *The nature, offices, and various names of angels.*

6. *Angels, the dispensers of the divine beneficence to us.*

7. *A kind of prefects over kingdoms and provinces, but specially the guardians of the elect. Not certain that every believer is under the charge of a single angel. Enough, that all angels watch over the safety of the Church.*

8. *The number and orders of angels not defined. Why angels said to be winged.*

9. *Angels are ministering spirits and spiritual essences.*

10. *The heathen error of placing angels on the throne of God refuted. A. By passages of Scripture.*

11. *Refutation continued. B. By inferences from other passages. Why God employs the ministry of angels.*

12. *Use of the doctrine of Scripture concerning the holy angels.*

13. *The doctrine concerning bad angels or devils reduced to four heads. That we may guard against their wiles and assaults.*

14. *That we may be stimulated to exercises of piety. Why one angel in the singular number often spoken of.*

15. *The devil being described as the enemy of man, we should perpetually war against him.*

16. *The wickedness of the devil not by creation but by corruption. Vain and useless to inquire into the mode, time, and character of the fall of angels.*

17. *Though the devil is always opposed in will and endeavor to the will of God, he can do nothing without his permission and consent.*

18. *God so overrules wicked spirits as to permit them to try the faithful, and rule over the wicked.*

19. *The nature of bad angels. They are spiritual essences endued with sense and intelligence.*

20. *The latter part of the chapter briefly embracing the history of creation, and showing what it is of importance for us to know concerning God.*

21. *The special object of this knowledge is to prevent us, through ingratitude or thoughtlessness, from overlooking the perfections of God. Example of this primary knowledge.*

22. *Another object of this knowledge—viz. that perceiving how these things were created for our use, we may be excited to trust in God, pray to him, and love him.*

1 The mere fact of creation should lead us to acknowledge God, but to prevent our falling away to Gentile fictions, God has been pleased to furnish a history of the creation. An impious objection, Why the world was not created sooner? Answer to it. Shrewd saying of an old man.

Although Isaiah justly charges the worshipers of false gods with stupidity, in not learning from the foundations of the earth, and the circle of the heavens, who the true God is (Isaiah 40:21); yet so sluggish and groveling is our intellect, that it was necessary he should be more clearly depicted, in order that the faithful might not fall away to Gentile fictions. The idea that God is the soul of the world, though the most tolerable that philosophers have suggested, is absurd; and, therefore, it was of importance to furnish us with a more intimate knowledge in order that we might not wander to and fro in uncertainty. Hence, God was pleased that a history of the creation should exist—a history on which the faith of the Church might lean without seeking any other God than Him whom Moses sets forth as the Creator and Architect of the world. First, in that history, the period of time is marked so as to enable the faithful to ascend by an unbroken succession of years to the first origin of their race and of all things.

This knowledge is of the highest use not only as an antidote to the monstrous fables which anciently prevailed both in Egypt and the other regions of the world, but also as a means of giving a clearer manifestation of the eternity of God as contrasted with the birth of creation, and thereby inspiring us with higher admiration. We must not be moved by the profane jeer, that it is strange how it did not sooner occur to the Deity to create the heavens and the earth, instead of idly allowing an infinite period to pass away, during which thousands of generations might have existed, while the present world is drawing to a close before it has completed its six thousandth year. Why God delayed so long, it is neither fit nor lawful to inquire. Should the human mind presume to do it, it could only fail in the attempt, nor would it be useful for us to know what God, as a trial of the modesty of our faith, has been pleased purposely to conceal. It was a shrewd saying of a good old man, who when some one pertly asked in derision what God did before the world was created, answered he made a hell for the inquisitive. This reproof, not less weighty than severe, should repress the tickling wantonness, which urges many to indulge in vicious and hurtful speculation.

In fine, let us remember that that invisible God, whose wisdom, power, and justice, are incomprehensible, is set before us in the history of Moses as in a mirror, in which his living image is reflected. For as an eye, either dimmed by age or weakened by any other cause, sees nothing distinctly without the aid of glasses, so (such is our imbecility) if Scripture does not direct us in our inquiries after God, we immediately turn vain in our imaginations. Those who now indulge their petulance, and refuse to take warning, will learn, when too late, how much better it had been reverently to regard the secret counsels of God, than to belch forth blasphemies, which pollute the face of heaven. Justly does Augustine complain that God is insulted whenever any higher reason than his will is demanded. He also in another place wisely reminds us that it is just as improper to raise questions about infinite periods of time as about infinite space. However wide the circuit of the heavens may be, it is of some definite extent. But should anyone expostulate with God that vacant space remains exceeding creation by a hundred-fold, must not every pious mind detest the presumption? Similar is the madness of those who charge God with idleness in not having pleased them by creating the world countless ages sooner than he did create it. In their cupidity they affect to go beyond the world, as if the ample circumference of heaven and earth did not contain objects numerous and resplendent enough to absorb all our senses; as if, in the period of six thousand years, God had not furnished facts enough to exercise our minds in ceaseless meditation. Therefore, let us willingly remain hedged in by those boundaries within which God has been pleased to confine our persons, and enclose our minds, so as to prevent them from losing themselves by wandering unrestrained.

2 For the same reason, the world was created, not in an instant, but in six days. The order of creation described, showing that Adam was not created until God had, with infinite goodness made ample provision for him.

With the same view, Moses relates that the work of creation was accomplished not in one moment, but in six days. By this statement we are drawn away from fiction to the one God who thus divided his work into six days, that we may have no reluctance to devote our whole lives to the contemplation of it. For though our eyes, in whatever direction they turn, are forced to behold the works of God, we see how fleeting our attention is, and holy quickly pious thoughts, if any arise, vanish away. Here, too, objection is taken to these progressive steps as inconsistent with the power of God, until human reason is subdued to the obedience of faith, and learns to welcome the calm quiescence to which the sanctification of the seventh day invited us. In the very order of events, we ought diligently to ponder on the paternal goodness of God toward the human race, in not creating Adam until he had liberally enriched the earth with all good things. Had he placed him on an earth barren and unfurnished; had he given life before light, he might have seemed to pay little regard to his interest. But now that he has arranged the motions of the sun and stars for man's use, has replenished the air, earth, and water, with living creatures, and produced all kinds of fruit in abundance for the supply of food, by performing the office of a provident and industrious head of a family, he has shown his wondrous goodness toward us. These subjects, which I only briefly touch, if more attentively pondered, will make it manifest that Moses was a sure witness and herald of the one only Creator. I do not repeat what I have already explained—viz. that mention is here made not of the bare essence of God, but that his eternal Wisdom and Spirit are also set before us, in order that we may not dream of any other God than Him who desires to be recognized in that express image.

3 The doctrine concerning angels expounded. A. That we may learn from them also to acknowledge God. B. That we may be put on our guard against the errors of the worshippers of angels and the Manichees. Manicheeism refuted. Rule of piety.

But before I begin to treat more fully of the nature of man (chapter 15 and Book 2, chapter 1), it will be proper to say something of angels. For although Moses, in accommodation to the ignorance of the generality of men, does not in the history of the creation make mention of any other works of God than those which meet our eye, yet, seeing he afterwards introduces angels as the ministers of God, we easily infer that he for whom they do service is their Creator. Hence, though Moses, speaking in popular language, did not at the very commencement enumerate the angels among the creatures of God, nothing prevents us from treating distinctly and explicitly of what is delivered by Scripture concerning them in other places. For if we desire to know God by his works, we surely cannot overlook this noble and illustrious specimen.

We may add that this branch of doctrine is very necessary for the refutation of numerous errors. The minds of many are so struck with the excellence of angelic natures, that they would think them insulted in being subjected to the authority of God, and so made subordinate. Hence, a fancied divinity has been assigned them. Manes, too, has arisen with his sect, fabricating to himself two principles—God and the devil, attributing the origin of good things to God, but assigning all bad natures to the devil as their author. Were this delirium to take possession of our minds, God would be denied his glory in the creation of the world. For, seeing there is nothing more peculiar to God than eternity and αυ τουσια self-existence, or existence of himself, if I may so speak, do not those who attribute it to the devil in some degree invest him with the honor of divinity? And where is the omnipotence of God, if the devil has the power of executing whatever he pleases against the will, and notwithstanding of the opposition of God? But the only good ground which the Manichees have—viz. that it would be impious to ascribe the creation of anything bad to a good God, militates in no degree against the orthodox faith, since it is not admitted that there is anything naturally bad throughout the universe; the depravity and wickedness whether of man or of the devil, and the sins thence resulting, being not from nature, but from the corruption of nature; nor, at first, did anything whatever exist that did not exhibit some manifestation of the divine wisdom and justice. To obviate such perverse imaginations, we must raise our minds higher than our eyes can penetrate. It was probably with this view that the Nicene Creed, in calling God the creator of all things, makes express mention of things invisible.

My care, however, must be to keep within the bounds which piety prescribes, lest by indulging in speculations beyond my reach, I bewilder the reader, and lead him away from the simplicity of the faith. And since the Holy Spirit always instructs us in what is useful, but altogether omits, or only touches cursorily on matters, which tend little to edification, of all such matters, it certainly is our duty to remain in willing ignorance.

4. The angels created by God. At what time and in what order it is inexpedient to inquire. The garrulity of the Pseudo-Dionysius.

Angels being the ministers appointed to execute the commands of God, must, of course, be admitted to be his creatures, but to stir up questions concerning the time or order in which they were created, bespeaks more perverseness than industry. Moses relates that the heavens and the earth were finished, with all their host; what avails it anxiously to inquire at what time other more hidden celestial hosts than the stars and planets also began to be? Not to dwell on this, let us here remember that on the whole subject of religion one rule of modesty and soberness is to be observed, and it is this, in obscure matters not to speak or think, or even long to know, more than the Word of God has delivered. A second rule is, that in reading the Scriptures we should constantly direct our inquiries and meditations to those things which tend to edification, not indulge in curiosity, or in studying things of no use. And since the Lord has been pleased to instruct us, not in frivolous questions, but in solid piety, in the fear of his name, in true faith, and the duties of holiness, let us rest satisfied with such knowledge. Wherefore, if we would be duly wise, we must renounce those vain babblings of idle men, concerning the nature, ranks, and number of angels, without any authority from the Word of God.

I know that many fasten on these topics more eagerly, and take greater pleasure in them than in those relating to daily practice. But if we decline not to be the disciples of Christ, let us not decline to follow the method, which he has prescribed. In this way, being contented with him for our master, we will not only refrain from, but even feel averse to, superfluous speculations, which he discourages.

None can deny that Dionysus (whoever he may have been) has many shrewd and subtle disquisitions in his Celestial Hierarchy, but on looking at them more closely, everyone must see that they are merely idle talk. The duty of a Theologian, however, is not to tickle the ear, but confirm the conscience, by teaching what is true, certain, and useful. When you read the work of Dionysus, you would think that the man had come down from heaven, and was relating, not what he had learned, but what he had actually seen. Paul, however, though he was carried to the third heaven, so far from delivering anything of the kind, positively declares, that it was not lawful for man to speak the secrets, which he had seen. Bidding adieu, therefore, to that nugatory wisdom, let us endeavor to ascertain from the simple doctrine of Scripture what it is the Lord's pleasure that we should know concerning angels.

5 The nature, offices, and various names of angels.

In Scripture, then, we uniformly read that angels are heavenly spirits, whose obedience and ministry God employs to execute all the purposes, which he has decreed, and hence their name as being a kind of intermediate messengers to manifest his will to men. The names by which several of them are distinguished have reference to the same office. They are called hosts, because they surround their Prince as his court, —adorn and display his majesty, — like soldiers, have their eyes always turned to their leader's standard, and are so ready and prompt to execute his orders, that the moment he gives the nod, they prepare for, or rather are actually at work. In declaring the magnificence of the divine throne, similar representations are given by the Prophets, and especially by Daniel, when he says, that when God stood up to Judgment, "thousand thousands ministered unto him, and ten thousand times ten thousand stood before him" (Daniel 7:10). As by these means the Lord wonderfully exerts and declares the power and might of his hand, they are called virtues. Again, as his government of the world is exercised and administered by them, they are called at one time Principalities, at another Powers, at another Dominions (Colossians 1:16; Ephesians 1:21).

Lastly, as the glory of God in some measure dwells in them, they are also termed Thrones; though as to this last designation I am unwilling to speak positively, as a different interpretation is equally, if not more congruous. To say nothing, therefore, of the name of Thrones, the former names are often employed by the Holy Spirit in commendation of the dignity of angelic service. Nor is it right to pass by without honor those instruments by whom God specially manifests the presence of his power. Nay, they are more than once called Gods, because the Deity is in some measure represented to us in their service, as in a mirror. I am rather inclined, however, to agree with ancient writers, that in those passages wherein it is stated that the angel of the Lord appeared to Abraham, Jacob, and Moses, Christ was that angel. Still it is true, that when mention is made of all the angels, they are frequently so designated. Nor ought this to seem strange. For if princes and rulers have this honor given them, because in their office they are vicegerents of God, the supreme King and Judge, with far greater reason may it be given to angels, in whom the brightness of the divine glory is much more conspicuously displayed.

6 Angels, the dispensers of the divine beneficence to us.

But the point on which the Scriptures specially insist is that which tends most to our comfort, and to the confirmation of our faith, namely, that angels are the ministers and dispensers of the divine bounty towards us. Accordingly, we are told how they watch for our safety, how they undertake our defense, direct our path, and take heed that no evil befall us. There are whole passages, which relate, in the first instance, to Christ, the Head of the Church, and after him to all believers. "He shall give his angels charge over thee, to keep thee in all thy ways. They shall bear thee up in their hands, lest thou dash thy foot against a stone." Again, "The angel of the Lord encampeth round about them that fear him, and delivereth them." By these passages, the Lord shows that the protection of those whom he has undertaken to defend he has delegated to his angels. Accordingly, an angel of the Lord consoles Hagar in her flight, and bids her be reconciled to her mistress. Abraham promises to his servant that an angel will be the guide of his journey.

Jacob, in blessing Ephraim and Manasseh, prays "The angel which redeemed me from all evil bless the lads." Therefore, an angel was appointed to guard the camp of the Israelites; and as often as God was pleased to deliver Israel from the hands of his enemies, he stirred up avengers by the ministry of angels. Thus, in fine (not to mention more), angels ministered to Christ, and were present with him in all straits. To the women they announced his resurrection; to the disciples they foretold his glorious advent. In discharging the office of our protectors, they war against the devil and all our enemies, and execute vengeance upon those who afflict us. Thus, we read that an angel of the Lord, to deliver Jerusalem from siege, slew one hundred and eighty-five thousand men in the camp of the king of Assyria in a single night.

7 A kind of prefects over kingdoms and provinces, but specially the guardians of the elect. Not certain that every believer is under the charge of a single angel. Enough, that all angels watch over the safety of the Church.

Whether or not each believer has a single angel assigned to him for his defense, I dare not positively affirm. When Daniel introduces the angel of the Persian and the angel of the Greeks, he undoubtedly intimates that certain angels are appointed as a kind of presidents over kingdoms and provinces. Again, when Christ says that the angels of children always behold the face of his Father, he insinuates that there are certain angels to whom their safety has been entrusted. But I know not if it can be inferred from this, that each believer has his own angel. This, indeed, I hold for certain, that each of us is cared for, not by one angel merely, but that all with one consent watch for our safety. For it is said of all the angels collectively, that they rejoice "over one sinner that repenteth, more than over ninety and nine just persons which need no repentance." It is also said, that the angels (meaning more than one) carried the soul of Lazarus into Abraham's bosom. Nor was it to no purpose that Elisha showed his servant the many chariots of fire, which were specially allotted him.

There is one passage which seems to intimate somewhat more clearly that each individual has a separate angel. When Peter, after his deliverance from prison, knocked at the door of the house where the brethren were assembled, being unable to think it could be himself, they said that it was his angel. This idea seems to have been suggested to them by a common belief that every believer has a single angel assigned to him. Here, however, it may be alleged, that there is nothing to prevent us from understanding it of anyone of the angels to whom the Lord might have given the charge of Peter at that particular time, without implying that he was to be his, perpetual guardian, according to the vulgar imagination, that two angels a good and a bad, as a kind of genii, are assigned to each individual. After all, it is not worthwhile anxiously to investigate a point, which does not greatly concern us. If no one thinks it enough to know that all the orders of the heavenly host are perpetually watching for his safety, I do not see what he could gain by knowing that he has one angel as a special guardian.

Those, again, who limit the care which God takes of each of us to a single angel, do great injury to themselves and to all the members of the Church, as if there were no value in those promises of auxiliary troops, who on every side encircling and defending us, embolden us to fight more manfully.

8 The number and orders of angels not defined. Why angels said to be winged.

Those who presume to dogmatize on the ranks and numbers of angels would do well to consider on what foundation they rest. As to their rank, I admit that Michael is described by David as a mighty Prince, and by Jude as an Archangel. Paul also tells us, that an archangel will blow the trumpet, which is to summon the world to Judgment. But how is it possible from such passages to ascertain the gradations of honor among the angels to determine the insignia, and assign the place and station of each? Even the two names, Michael and Gabriel, mentioned in Scripture, or a third, if you choose to add it from the history of Tobit, seem to intimate by their meaning that they are given to angels in accommodation to the weakness of our capacity, though I rather choose not to speak positively on the point. As to the number of angels, we learn from the mouth of our Savior that there are many legions, and from Daniel that there are many myriads. Elisha's servant saw a multitude of chariots, and their vast number is declared by the fact, that they encamp round about those that fear the Lord.

It is certain that spirits have no bodily shape, and yet Scripture, in accommodation to us, describes them under the form of winged Cherubim and Seraphim; not without cause, to assure us that when occasion requires, they will hasten to our aid with incredible swiftness, winging their way to us with the speed of lightning. Further than this, in regard both to the ranks and numbers of angels, let us class them among those mysterious subjects, the full revelation of which is deferred to the last day, and accordingly refrain from inquiring too curiously, or talking presumptuously.

9 Angels are ministering spirits and spiritual essences.

There is one point, however, which though called into doubt by certain restless individuals, we ought to hold for certain—viz. that angels are ministering spirits (Hebrews 1:14); whose service God employs for the protection of his people, and by whose means he distributes his favors among men, and also executes other works. The Sadducees of old maintained, that by angels nothing more was meant than the movements, which God impresses on men, or manifestations, which he gives of his own power (Acts 23:8). But this dream is contradicted by so many passages of Scriptures that it seems strange how such gross ignorance could have had any countenance among the Jews. To say nothing of the passages I have already quoted, passages which refer to thousands and legions of angels, speak of them as rejoicing, as bearing up the faithful in their hands, carrying their souls to rest, beholding the face of their Father, and so forth: there are other passages which most clearly prove that they are real beings possessed of spiritual essence.

Stephen and Paul say that the Law was enacted in the hands of angels. Our Savior moreover says that at the resurrection the elect will be like angels; that the Day of Judgment is known not even to the angels; that at that time he himself will come with the holy angels. However much such passages may be twisted, their meaning is plain. In like manner, when Paul beseeches Timothy to keep his precepts as before Christ and his elect angels, it is not qualities or inspirations without substance that he speaks of, but true spirits. And when it is said, in the Epistle to the Hebrews, that Christ was made more excellent than the angels, that the world was not made subject to them, that Christ assumed not their nature, but that of man, it is impossible to give a meaning to the passages without understanding that angels are blessed spirits, as to whom such comparisons may competently be made. The author of that Epistle declares the same thing when he places the souls of believers and the holy angels together in the kingdom of heaven. Moreover, in the passages we have already quoted, the angels of children are said to behold the face of God, to defend us by their protection, to rejoice in our salvation, to admire the manifold grace of God in the Church, to be under Christ their head. To the same effect is their frequent appearance to the holy patriarchs in human form, their speaking, and consenting to be hospitably entertained. Christ, too, in consequence of the supremacy, which he obtains as Mediator, is called the Angel (Malachi 3:1). It was thought proper to touch on this subject in passing, with the view of putting the simple upon their guard against the foolish and absurd imaginations which, suggested by Satan many centuries ago, are always starting up anew

10 The heathen error of placing angels on the throne of God refuted. A. By passages of Scripture.

It remains to give warning against the superstition which usually begins to creep in, when it is said that all blessings are ministered and dispensed to us by angels. For the human mind is apt immediately to think that there is no honor, which they ought not to receive, and hence the peculiar offices of Christ and God are bestowed upon them. In this way, the glory of Christ was for several former ages greatly obscured, extravagant eulogiums being pronounced on angels without any authority from Scripture. Among the corruptions, which we now oppose, there is scarcely anyone of greater antiquity. Even Paul appears to have had a severe contest with some who so exalted angels as to make them almost the superiors of Christ. Hence, he so anxiously urges in his Epistle to the Colossians (Colossians 1:1:16, 20), that Christ is not only superior to all angels, but that all the endowments which they possess are derived from him; thus warning us against forsaking him, by turning to those who are not sufficient for themselves, but must draw with us at a common fountain. As the refulgence of the Divine glory is manifested in them, there is nothing to which we are more prone than to prostrate ourselves before them in stupid adoration, and then ascribe to them the blessings, which we owe to God alone. Even John confesses in the Apocalypse (Revelation 19:10; 22:8, 9), that this was his own case, but he immediately adds the answer which was given to him, "See thou do it not; I am thy fellow servant: worship God."

11 Refutation continued. B. By inferences from other passages. Why God employs the ministry of angels.

This danger we will happily avoid, if we consider why it is that Gods instead of acting directly without their agency, is wont to employ it in manifesting his power, providing for the safety of his people, and imparting the gifts of his beneficence. This he certainly does not from necessity, as if he were unable to dispense with them. Whenever he pleases, he passes them by, and performs his own work by a single nod: so far are they from relieving him of any difficulty. Therefore, when he employs them it is as a help to our weakness, that nothing may be wanting in elevating our hopes or strengthening our confidence.

It ought, indeed, to be sufficient for us that the Lord declares himself our protector. But when we see ourselves beset by so many perils, so many injuries, so many kinds of enemies, such is our frailty and effeminacy, that we might at times be filled with alarm, or driven to despair, did not the Lord proclaim his gracious presence by some means in accordance with our feeble capacities. For this reason, he not only promises to take care of us, but assures us that he has numberless attendants, to whom he has committed the charge of our safety, that whatever dangers may impend, so long as we are encircled by their protection and guardianship, we are placed beyond all hazard of evil. I admit that after we have a simple assurance of the divine protection, it is improper in us still to look round for help. But since for this our weakness the Lord is pleased, in his infinite goodness and indulgence, to provide, it would ill become us to overlook the favor. Of this we have an example in the servant of Elisha (2 Kings 6:17), who, seeing the mountain encompassed by the army of the Assyrians, and no means of escape, was completely overcome with terror, and thought it all over with himself and his master. Then Elisha prayed to God to open the eyes of the servant, who forthwith beheld the mountain filled with horses and chariots of fire; in other words, with a multitude of angels, to whom he and the prophet had been given in charge. Confirmed by the vision he received courage, and could boldly defy the enemy, whose appearance previously filled him with dismay.

12 Use of the doctrine of Scripture concerning the holy angels.

Whatever, therefore, is said as to the ministry of angels, let us employ for the purpose of removing all distrust, and strengthening our confidence in God. Since the Lord has provided us with such protection, let us not be terrified at the multitude of our enemies as if they could prevail notwithstanding of his aid, but let us adopt the sentiment of Elisha, that more are for us than against us. How preposterous, therefore, is it to allow ourselves to be led away from God by angels who have been appointed for the very purpose of assuring us of his more immediate presence to help us? But we are so led away, if angels do not conduct us directly to him—making us look to him, invoke and celebrate him as our only defender—if they are not regarded merely as hands moving to our assistance just as he directs—if they do not direct us to Christ as the only Mediator on whom we must wholly depend and recline, looking towards him, and resting in him.

Our minds ought to give thorough heed to what Jacob saw in his vision (Genesis 28:12), —angels descending to the earth to men, and again mounting up from men to heaven, by means of a ladder, at the head of which the Lord of Hosts was seated, intimating that it is solely by the intercession of Christ that the ministry of angels extends to us, as he himself declares, "Hereafter ye shall see heaven open, and the angels of God ascending and descending upon the Son of man" (John 1:51). Accordingly, the servant of Abraham, though he had been commended to the guardianship of an angel (Genesis 24:7), does not therefore invoke that angel to be present with him, but trusting to the commendation, pours out his prayers before the Lord, and entreats him to show mercy to Abraham. As God does not make angels the ministers of his power and goodness, that he may share his glory with them, so he does not promise his assistance by their instrumentality, that we may divide our confidence between him and them. Away, then, with that Platonic philosophy of seeking access to God by means of angels and courting them with the view of making God more propitious, —a philosophy which presumptuous and superstitious men attempted at first to introduce into our religion, and which they persist in even to this day.

13 The doctrine concerning bad angels or devils reduced to four heads. That we may guard against their wiles and assaults.

The tendency of all that Scripture teaches concerning devils is to put us on our guard against their wiles and machinations, that we may provide ourselves with weapons strong enough to drive away the most formidable foes. For when Satan is called the god and ruler of this world, the strong man armed, the prince of the power of the air, the roaring lion, the object of all these descriptions is to make us more cautious and vigilant, and more prepared for the contest. This is sometimes stated in distinct terms. For Peter, after describing the devil as a roaring lion going about seeking whom he may devour, immediately adds the exhortation, "whom resist steadfast in the faith" (1 Peter 5:9). And Paul, after reminding us that we wrestle not against flesh and blood, but against principalities, against powers, against the rulers of the darkness of this world, against spiritual wickedness in high places, immediately enjoins us to put on armor equal to so great and perilous a contest (Ephesians 6:12). Wherefore, let this be the use to which we turn all these statements. Being forewarned of the constant presence of an enemy the most daring, the most powerful, the most crafty, the most indefatigable, the most completely equipped with all the engines and the most expert in the science of war, let us not allow ourselves to be overtaken by sloth or cowardice, but, on the contrary, with minds aroused and ever on the alert, let us stand ready to resist; and, knowing that this warfare is terminated only by death, let us study to persevere. Above all, fully conscious of our weakness and want of skill, let us invoke the help of God, and attempt nothing without trusting in him, since it is his alone to supply counsel, and strength, and courage, and arms.

14 That we may be stimulated to exercises of piety. Why one angel in the singular number often spoken of.

That we may feel the more strongly urged to do so, the Scripture declares that the enemies who war against us are not one or two, or few in number, but a great host. Mary Magdalene is said to have been delivered from seven devils by which she was possessed; and our Savior assures us that it is an ordinary circumstance, when a devil has been expelled, if access is again given to it, to take seven other spirits, more wicked than itself, and resume the vacant possession. Nay, one man is said to have been possessed by a whole legion. By this, then, we are taught that the number of enemies with whom we have to war is almost infinite, that we may not, from a contemptuous idea of the fewness of their numbers, be more remiss in the contest, or from imagining that an occasional truce is given us, indulge in sloth. In one Satan or devil being often mentioned in the singular number, the thing denoted is that domination of iniquity, which is opposed to the reign of righteousness. For, as the Church and the communion of saints has Christ for its head, so the faction of the wicked and wickedness itself, is portrayed with its prince exercising supremacy. Hence, the expression, "Depart, ye cursed, into everlasting fire, prepared for the devil and his angels" (Matthew 25:41).

15 The devil being described as the enemy of man, we should perpetually war against him.

One thing, which ought to animate us to perpetual contest with the devil, is that he is everywhere called both our adversary and the adversary of God. For, if the glory of God is dear to us, as it ought to be, we ought to struggle with all our might against him who aims at the extinction of that glory. If we are animated with proper zeal to maintain the Kingdom of Christ, v. e must wage irreconcilable war with him who conspires its ruin. Again, if we have any anxiety about our own salvation, we ought to make neither peace nor truce with him who is continually laying schemes for its destruction. But such is the character given to Satan in the third chapter of Genesis, where he is seen seducing man from his allegiance to God, that he may both deprive God of his due honor, and plunge man headlong in destruction. Such, too, is the description given of him in the Gospels (Matthew 13:28), where he is called the enemy, and is said to sow tares in order to corrupt the seed of eternal life. In one word, in all his actions we experience the truth of our Savior's description, that he was "a murderer from the beginning, and abode not in the truth" (John 8:44). Truth he assails with lies, light he obscures with darkness. The minds of men he involves in error; he stirs up hatred, inflames strife and war, and all in order that he may overthrow the kingdom of God, and drown men in eternal perdition with himself. Hence, it is evident that his whole nature is depraved, mischievous, and malignant. There must be extreme depravity in a mind bent on assailing the glory of God and the salvation of man. This is intimated by John in his Epistle, when he says that he "sinneth from the beginning" (1 John 3:8), implying that he is the author, leader, and contriver of all malice and wickedness.

16 The wickedness of the devil not by creation but by corruption. Vain and useless to inquire into the mode, time, and character of the fall of angels.

But as the devil was created by God, we must remember that this malice, which we attribute to his nature, is not from creation, but from depravation. Everything damnable in him he brought upon himself, by his revolt and fall. Of this Scripture reminds us, lest, by believing that he was so created at first, we should ascribe to God what is most foreign to his nature. For this reason, Christ declares (John 8:44), that Satan, when he lies, "speaketh of his own," and states the reason, "...because he abode not in the truth." By saying that he abode not in the truth, he certainly intimates that he once was in the truth, and by calling him the father of lies, he puts it out of his power to charge God with the depravity of which he was himself the cause. But although the expressions are brief and not very explicit, they are amply sufficient to vindicate the majesty of God from every calumny. And what more does it concern us to know of devils? Some murmur because the Scripture does not in various passages give a distinct and regular exposition of Satan's fall, its cause, mode, date, and nature. But as these things are of no consequence to us, it was better, if not entirely to pass them in silence, at least only to touch lightly upon them.

The Holy Spirit could not deign to feed curiosity with idle, unprofitable histories. We see it was the Lord's purpose to deliver nothing in his sacred oracles, which we might not learn for edification. Therefore, instead of dwelling on superfluous matters, let it be sufficient for us briefly to hold, with regard to the nature of devils, that at their first creation, they were the angels of God, but by revolting, they both ruined themselves, and became the instruments of perdition to others. As it was useful to know this much, it is clearly taught by Peter and Jude; "God," they say, "spared not the angels that sinned, but cast them down to hell, and delivered them into chains of darkness to be reserved unto Judgment" (2 Peter 2:4; Jude verse 6). And Paul, by speaking of the elect angels, obviously draws a tacit contrast between them and reprobate angels.

17 Though the devil is always opposed in will and endeavor to the will of God, he can do nothing without his permission and consent.

With regard to the strife and war, which Satan is said to wage with God, it must be understood with this qualification, that Satan cannot possibly do anything against the will and consent of God. For we read in the history of Job, that Satan appears in the presence of God to receive his commands, and dares not proceed to execute any enterprise until he is authorized. In the same way, when Ahab was to be deceived, he undertook to be a lying spirit in the mouth of all the Prophets; and on being commissioned by the

Lord, proceeds to do so. For this reason, also, the spirit, which tormented Saul is said to be an evil spirit from the Lord, because he was the scourge by which the misdeeds of the wicked king were punished.

In another place, it is said that the plagues of Egypt were inflicted by God through the instrumentality of wicked angels. In conformity with these particular examples, Paul declares generally that unbelievers are blinded by God, though he had previously described it as the doing of Satan. It is evident, therefore, that Satan is under the power of God, and is so ruled by his authority, that he must yield obedience to it. Moreover, though we say that Satan resists God, and does works at variance with His works, we at the same time maintain that this contrariety and opposition depend on the permission of God.

I now speak not of Satan's will and endeavor, but only of the result. For the disposition of the devil being wicked, he has no inclination whatever to obey the divine will, but, on the contrary, is wholly bent on contumacy and rebellion. This much, therefore, he has of himself, and his own iniquity, that he eagerly, and of set purpose, opposes God, aiming at those things which he deems most contrary to the will of God. But as God holds him bound and fettered by the curb of his power, he executes those things only for which permission has been given him, and thus, however unwilling, obeys his Creator, being forced, whenever he is required, to do Him service.

18 God so overrules wicked spirits as to permit them to try the faithful, and rule over the wicked.

God thus turning the unclean spirits hither and thither at his pleasure, employs them in exercising believers by warring against them, assailing them with wiles, urging them with solicitations, pressing close upon them, disturbing, alarming, and occasionally wounding, but never conquering or oppressing them; whereas they hold the wicked in thralldom, exercise dominion over their minds and bodies, and employ them as bond-slaves in all kinds of iniquity. Because believers are disturbed by such enemies, they are addressed in such exhortations as these: "Neither give place to the devil;" "Your adversary the devil, as a roaring lion, walketh about seeking whom he may devour; whom resist steadfast in the faith" (Ephesians 4:27; 1 Peter 5:8).

Paul acknowledges that he was not exempt from this species of contest when he says, that for subduing his pride, a messenger of Satan was sent to buffet him (2 Corinthians 12:7). This trial, therefore, is common to all the children of God. But as the promise of bruising Satan's head (Genesis 3:15) applies alike to Christ and to all his members, I deny that believers can ever be oppressed or vanquished by him. They are often, indeed, thrown into alarm, but never so thoroughly as not to recover themselves. They fall by the violence of the blows, but they get up again; they are wounded, but not mortally. In fine, they labor on through the whole course of their lives, so as ultimately to gain the victory, though they meet with occasional defeats.

We know how David, through the just anger of God, was left for a time to Satan, and by his instigation numbered the people (2 Samuel 24:1); nor without cause does Paul hold out a hope of pardon in case any should have become ensnared by the wiles of the devil (2 Timothy 2:26). Accordingly, he elsewhere shows that the promise above quoted commences in this life where the struggle is carried on, and that it is completed after the struggle is ended. His words are, "The God of peace shall bruise Satan under your feet shortly" (Romans 16:20).

In our Head, indeed, this victory was always perfect, because the prince of the world "had nothing" in him (John 14:30); but in us, who are his members, it is now partially obtained, and will be perfected when we shall have put off our mortal flesh, through which we are liable to infirmity, and shall have been filled with the energy of the Holy Spirit. In this way, when the kingdom of Christ is raised up and established, that of Satan falls, as our Lord himself expresses it, "I beheld Satan as lightning fall from heaven" (Luke 10:18). By these words, he confirmed the report that the apostles gave of the efficacy of their preaching. In like manner, he says, "When a strong man armed keepeth his palace, his goods are in peace. But when a stronger than he shall come upon him, and overcome him, he taketh from him all his armor wherein he trusted, and divideth his spoils" (Luke 11:21, 22). And to this end, Christ, by dying, overcame Satan, who had the power of death (Hebrews 2:14), and triumphed over all his hosts that they might not injure the Church, which otherwise would suffer from them every moment. For (such being our weakness, and such his raging fury), how could we withstand his manifold and relentless assaults for any period, however short, if we did not trust to the victory of our leader?

God, therefore, does not allow Satan to have dominion over the souls of believers, but only gives over to his sway the impious and unbelieving, whom he deigns not to number among his flock. For the devil is said to have undisputed possession of this world until he is dispossessed by Christ. In like manner, he is said to blind all who do not believe the Gospel, and to do his own work in the children of disobedience. And justly, for all the wicked are vessels of wrath, and, accordingly, to whom should they be subjected but to the minister of the divine vengeance? In fine, they are said to be of their father the devil. For as believers are recognized to be the sons of God by bearing his image, so the wicked are properly regarded as the children of Satan, from having degenerated into his image.

19 The nature of bad angels. They are spiritual essences endued with sense and intelligence.

Having above refuted that nugatory philosophy concerning the holy angels, which teaches that they are nothing but good motions or inspirations which God excites in the minds of men, we must here likewise refute those who foolishly allege that devils are nothing but bad affections or perturbations suggested by our carnal nature. The brief refutation is to be found in passages of Scripture on this subject, passages neither few nor obscure. First, when they are called unclean spirits and apostate angels (Matthew 12:43; Jude, verse 6), who have degenerated from their original, the very terms sufficiently declare that they are not motions or affections of the mind, but truly, as they are called, minds or spirits endued with sense and intellect.

In like manner, when the children of God are contrasted by John, and also by our Savior, with the children of the devil, would not the contrast be absurd if the term devil meant nothing more than evil inspirations? And John adds still more emphatically, that the devil sinneth from the beginning (1 John 3:8). In like manner, when Jude introduces the archangel Michael contending with the devil (Jude, verse 9), he certainly contrasts a wicked and rebellious with a good angel.

To this corresponds the account given in the Book of Job, that Satan appeared in the presence of God with the holy angels. But the clearest passages of all are those which make mention of the punishment which, from the Judgment of God, they already begin to feel, and are to feel more especially at the resurrection, "What have we to do with thee, Jesus, thou Son of God? Art thou come hither to torment us before the time?" (Matthew 8:29); and again, "Depart, ye cursed, into everlasting fire, prepared for the devil and his angels" (Matthew 25:41). Again, "If God spared not the angels that sinned, but cast them down to hell, and delivered them into chains of darkness to be reserved unto Judgment," etc. (2 Peter 2:4). How absurd the expressions, that devils are doomed to eternal punishment, that fire is prepared for them, that they are even now excruciated and tormented by the glory of Christ, if there were truly no devils at all? But as all discussion on this subject is superfluous for those who give credit to the Word of God, while little is gained by quoting Scripture to those empty speculators whom nothing but novelty can please, I believe I have already done enough for my purpose, which was to put the pious on their guard against the delirious dreams with which restless men harass themselves and the simple. The subject, however, deserved to be touched upon, lest any, by embracing that errors should imagine they have no enemy and thereby be more remiss or less cautious in resisting.

20 The latter part of the chapter briefly embracing the history of creation, and showing what it is of importance for us to know concerning God.

Meanwhile, being placed in this most beautiful theatre, let us not decline to take a pious delight in the clear and manifest works of God. For, as we have elsewhere observed, though not the chief, it is, in point of order, the first evidence of faiths to remember to whichever side we turn, that all which meets the eye is the work of God, and at the same time to meditate with pious care on the end which God had in view in creating it. Wherefore, in order that we may apprehend with true faith what it is necessary to know concerning God, it is of importance to attend to the history of the creation, as briefly recorded by Moses and afterwards more copiously illustrated by pious writers, more especially by Basil and Ambrose.

From this history we learn that God, by the power of his Word and his Spirit, created the heavens and the earth out of nothing; that thereafter he produced things inanimate and animate of every kind, arranging an innumerable variety of objects in admirable order, giving each kind its proper nature, office, place, and station; at the same time, as all things were liable to corruption, providing for the perpetuation of each single species, cherishing some by secret methods, and from time to time instilling new vigour into them, and bestowing on others a power of continuing their race, so preventing it from perishing at their own death. Heaven and earth being thus most richly adorned, and copiously supplied with all things, like a large and splendid mansion gorgeously constructed and exquisitely furnished, at length man was made—man, by the beauty of his person and his many noble endowments, the most glorious specimen of the works of God. But, as I have no intention to give the history of creation in detail, it is sufficient to have again thus briefly touched on it in passing. I have already reminded my reader, that the best course for him is to derive his knowledge of the subject from Moses and others who have carefully and faithfully transmitted an account of the creation.

21 The special object of this knowledge is to prevent us, through ingratitude or thoughtlessness, from overlooking the perfections of God. Example of this primary knowledge.

It is unnecessary to dwell at length on the end that should be aimed at in considering the works of God. The subject has been in a great measure explained elsewhere, and in so far as required by our present work, may now be disposed of in a few words. Undoubtedly were one to attempt to speak in due terms of the inestimable wisdom, power, justice, and goodness of God, in the formation of the world, no grace or splendor of diction could equal the greatness of the subject. Still there can be no doubt that the Lord would have us constantly occupied with such holy meditation, in order that, while we contemplate the immense treasures of wisdom and goodness exhibited in the creatures as in so many mirrors, we may not only run our eye over them with a hasty, and evanescent glance, but dwell long upon them, seriously and faithfully turn them in our minds, and every now and then bring them to recollection. But as the present work is of a didactic nature, we cannot fittingly enter on topics, which require lengthened discourse. Therefore, in order to be compendious, let the reader understand that he has a genuine apprehension of the character of God as the Creator of the world; first, if he attends to the general rule, never thoughtlessly or obliviously to overlook the glorious perfections which God displays in his creatures; and, secondly, if he makes a self application of what he sees, so as to fix it deeply on his heart.

The former is exemplified when we consider how great the Architect must be who framed and ordered the multitude of the starry host so admirably, that it is impossible to imagine a more glorious sight, so stationing some, and fixing them to particular spots that they cannot move; giving a freer course to others yet setting limits to their wanderings; so tempering the movement of the whole as to measure out day and night, months, years, and seasons, and at the same time so regulating the inequality of days as to prevent everything like confusion. The former course is, moreover, exemplified when we attend to his power in sustaining the vast mass, and guiding the swift revolutions of the heavenly bodies, etc. These few examples sufficiently explain what is meant by recognizing the divine perfections in the creation of the world. Were we to attempt to go over the whole subject we should never come to a conclusion, there being as many miracles of divine power, as many striking evidences of wisdom and goodness, as there are classes of objects, nay, as there are individual objects, great or small, throughout the universe.

22 Another object of this knowledge—viz. that perceiving how these things were created for our use, we may be excited to trust in God, pray to him, and love him.

The other course which has a closer relation to faith remains to be considered—viz. that while we observe how God has destined all things for our good and salvation, we at the same time feel his power and grace, both in ourselves and in the great blessings which he has bestowed upon us; thence stirring up ourselves to confidence in him, to invocation, praise, and love. Moreover, as I lately observed, the Lord himself, by the very order of creation, has demonstrated that he created all things for the sake of man. Nor is it unimportant to observe, that he divided the formation of the world into six days, though it had been in no respect more difficult to complete the whole work, in all its parts, in one moment than by a gradual progression. But he was pleased to display his providence and paternal care towards us in this, that before he formed man, he provided whatever he foresaw would be useful and salutary to him. How ungrateful, then, were it to doubt whether we are cared for by this most excellent Parent, who we see cared for us even before we were born! How impious were it to tremble in distrust, lest we should one day be abandoned in our necessity by that kindness which, antecedent to our existence, displayed itself in a complete supply of all good things! Moreover, Moses tells us that everything that the world contains is liberally placed at our disposal. This God certainly did not that he might delude us with an empty form of donation. Nothing, therefore, which concerns our safety, will ever be wanting.

To conclude, as often as we call God the Creator of heaven and earth, let us remember that the distribution of all the things which he created are in his hand and power, but that we are his sons, whom he has undertaken to nourish and bring up in allegiance to him, that we may expect the substance of all good from him alone, and have full hope that he will never suffer us to be in want of things necessary to salvation, so as to leave us dependent on some other source; that in everything we desire we may address our prayers to him, and, in every benefit we receive, acknowledge his hand, and give him thanks; that thus allured by his great goodness and beneficence, we may study with our whole heart to love and serve him.

Chapter 15

STATE IN WHICH MAN WAS CREATED. THE FACULTIES OF THE SOUL—THE IMAGE OF GOD—FREE WILL— ORIGINAL RIGHTEOUSNESS.

This chapter is thus divided: —I. The necessary rules to be observed in considering the state of man before the fall being laid down, the point first considered is the creation of the body, and the lesson taught by its being formed out of the earth, and made alive, section 1. II. The immortality of the human soul is proved by various solid arguments, section 2. III. The image of God (the strongest proof of the soul's immortality) is considered, and various absurd fancies are refuted, section 3. IV. Several errors, which obscure the light of truth being dissipated, follow a philosophical and theological consideration of the faculties of the soul before the fall.

Sections

1. A twofold knowledge of God—viz. before the fall and after it. The former here considered. Particular rules or precautions to be observed in this discussion. What we are taught by a body formed ant of the dust, and tenanted by a spirit.

2. The immortality of the soul proved from, A. The testimony of conscience. B. The knowledge of God. C. The noble faculties with which it is endued. D. Its activity and wondrous fancies in sleep. E. Innumerable passages of Scripture.

3. The image of God one of the strongest proofs of the immortality of the soul. What meant by this image. The dreams of Osiander concerning the image of God refuted. Whether any difference between "image" and "likeness." Another objection of Osiander refuted. The image of God conspicuous in the whole Adam.

4. The image of God is in the soul. Its nature may be learnt from its renewal by Christ. What is comprehended under this renewal. What the image of God in man before the fall. In what things it now appears. When and where it will be seen in perfection.

5. *The dreams of the Manichees and of Servetus, as to the origin of the soul, refuted. Also, of Osiander, who denies that there is any image of God in man without essential righteousness.*

6. *The doctrine of philosophers as to the faculties of the soul generally discordant, doubtful, and obscure. The excellence of the soul described. Only one soul in each man. A brief review of the opinion of philosophers as to the faculties of the soul. What to be thought of this opinion.*

7. *The division of the faculties of the soul into intellect and will, more agreeable to Christian doctrine.*

8. *The power and office of the intellect and will in man before the fall. Man's free will. This freedom lost by the fall—a fact unknown to philosophers. The delusion of Pelagians and Papists. Objection as to the fall of man when free, refuted.*

1 A twofold knowledge of God—viz. before the fall and after it. The former here considered. Particular rules or precautions to be observed in this discussion. What we are taught by a body formed ant of the dust, and tenanted by a spirit.

We have now to speak of the creation of man, not only because of all the works of God, it is the noblest and most admirable specimen of his justice, wisdom, and goodness, but also, as we observed at the outset, we cannot clearly and properly know God unless the knowledge of ourselves be added. This knowledge is twofold, —relating, first, to the condition in which we were at first created; and, secondly to our condition such as it began to be immediately after Adam's fall. For it would little avail us to know how we were created if we remained ignorant of the corruption and degradation of our nature in consequence of the fall. At present, however, we confine ourselves to a consideration of our nature in its original integrity.

Certainly, before we descend to the miserable condition into which man has fallen, it is of importance to consider what he was at first. For there is need of caution, lest we attend only to the natural ills of man, and thereby seem to ascribe them to the Author of nature; impiety deeming it a sufficient defense if it can pretend that everything vicious in it proceeded in some sense from God, and not hesitating, when accused, to plead against God, and throw the blame of its guilt upon Him. Those who would be thought to speak more reverently of the Deity catch at an excuse for their depravity from nature, not considering that they also, though more obscurely, bring a charge against God, on whom the dishonor would fall if anything vicious were proved to exist in nature. Seeing, therefore, that the flesh is continually on the alert for subterfuges, by which it imagines it can remove the blame of its own wickedness from itself to some other quarter, we must diligently guard against this depraved procedure, and accordingly treat of the calamity of the human race in such a way as may cut off every evasion, and vindicate the justice of God against all who would impugn it.

We shall afterwards see, in its own place (Book 2, chapter 1, section 3), how far mankind now is from the purity originally conferred on Adam. And, first, it is to be observed, that when he was formed out of the dust of the ground a curb was laid on his pride—nothing being more absurd than that those should glory in their excellence who not only dwell in tabernacles of clay, but are themselves in part dust and ashes. But God having not only deigned to animate a vessel of clay, but to make it the habitation of an immortal spirit, Adam might well glory in the great liberality of his Maker.

2 The immortality of the soul proved from, A. The testimony of conscience. B. The knowledge of God. C. The noble faculties with which it is endued. D. Its activity and wondrous fancies in sleep. E. Innumerable passages of Scripture.

Moreover, there can be no question that man consists of a body and a soul; meaning by soul, an immortal though created essence, which is his nobler part. Sometimes he is called a spirit. But though the two terms, while they are used together differ in their meaning, still, when spirit is used by itself it is equivalent to soul, as when Solomon speaking of death says, that the spirit returns to God who gave it (Ecclesiastes 12:7). And Christ, in commending his spirit to the Father, and Stephen his to Christ, simply mean, that when the soul is freed from the prison-house of the body, God becomes its perpetual keeper. Those who imagine that the soul is called a spirit because it is a breath or energy divinely infused into bodies, but devoid of essence, err too grossly, as is shown both by the nature of the thing, and the whole tenor of Scripture.

It is true, indeed, that men cleaving too much to the earth are dull of apprehension, nay, being alienated from the Father of Lights, are so immersed in darkness as to imagine that they will not survive the grave; still the light is not so completely quenched in darkness that all sense of immortality is lost. Conscience, which, distinguishing, between good and evil, responds to the Judgment of God, is an undoubted sign of an immortal spirit. How could motion devoid of essence penetrate to the Judgment-seat of God, and under a sense of guilt strike itself with terror? The body cannot be affected by any fear of spiritual punishment. This is competent only to the soul, which must therefore be endued with essence. Then the mere knowledge of a God sufficiently proves that souls, which rise higher than the world, must be immortal, it being impossible that any evanescent vigour could reach the very fountain of life. In fine, while the many noble faculties with which the human mind is endued proclaim that something divine is engraved on it, they are so many evidences of an immortal essence.

For such sense as the lower animals possess goes not beyond the body, or at least not beyond the objects actually presented to it. But the swiftness with which the human mind glances from heaven to earth, scans the secrets of nature, and, after it has embraced all ages, with intellect and memory digests each in its proper order, and reads the future in the past, clearly demonstrates that there lurks in man a something separated from the body. We have intellect by which we are able to conceive of the invisible God and angels—a thing of which body is altogether incapable.

We have ideas of rectitude, justice, and honesty—ideas that the bodily senses cannot reach. The seat of these ideas must therefore be a spirit. Nay, sleep itself, which stupefying the man, seems even to deprive him of life, is no obscure evidence of immortality—not only suggesting thoughts of things that never existed, but foreboding future events. I briefly touch on topics, which even profane writers describe with a more splendid eloquence. For pious readers, a simple reference is sufficient. Were not the soul some kind of essence separated from the body, Scripture would not teach that we dwell in houses of clay, and at death remove from a tabernacle of flesh; that we put off that which is corruptible, in order that, at the last day, we may finally receive according to the deeds done in the body. These, and similar passages which everywhere occur, not only clearly distinguish the soul from the body, but by giving it the name of man, intimate that it is his principal part.

Again, when Paul exhorts believers to cleanse themselves from all filthiness of the flesh and the spirit, he shows that there are two parts in which the taint of sin resides. Peter, also, in calling Christ the Shepherd and Bishop of souls, would have spoken absurdly if there were no souls towards which he might discharge such an office. Nor would there be any ground for what he says concerning the eternal salvation of souls, or for his injunction to purify our souls, or for his assertion that fleshly lusts war against the soul; neither could the author of the Epistle to the Hebrews say, that pastors watch as those who must give an account for our souls, if souls were devoid of essence. To the same effect, Paul calls God to witness upon his soul, which could not be brought to trial before God if incapable of suffering punishment. This is still more clearly expressed by our Savior, when he bids us fear him who, after he has killed the body, is able also to cast into hell fire.

Again, when the author of the Epistle to the Hebrews distinguishes the fathers of our flesh from God, who alone is the Father of our spirits, he could not have asserted the essence of the soul in clearer terms. Moreover, did not the soul, when freed from the fetters of the body, continue to exist, our Savior would not have represented the soul of Lazarus as enjoying blessedness in Abraham s bosom, while, on the contrary, that of Dives was suffering dreadful torments. Paul assures us of the same thing when he says, that so long as we are present in the body, we are absent from the Lord. Not to dwell on a matter as to which there is little obscurity, I will only add, that Luke mentions among the errors of the Sadducees that they believed neither angel nor spirit.

3. The image of God one of the strongest proofs of the immortality of the soul. What meant by this image. The dreams of Osiander concerning the image of God refuted. Whether any difference between "image" and "likeness." Another objection of Osiander refuted. The image of God conspicuous in the whole Adam.

A strong proof of this point may be gathered from its being said, that man was created in the image of God. For though the divine glory is displayed in man's outward appearance, it cannot be doubted that the proper seat of the image is in the soul. I deny not, indeed, that external shape, in so far as it distinguishes and separates us from the lower animals, brings us nearer to God; nor will I vehemently oppose any who may choose to include under the image of God that

While the mute creation downward bend
Their sight, and to their earthly mother tend,
Man looks aloft, and with erected eyes,
Beholds his own hereditary skies."

Only let it be understood, that the image of God which is beheld or made conspicuous by these external marks, is spiritual. For Osiander (whose writings exhibit a perverse ingenuity in futile devices), extending the image of God indiscriminately as well to the body as to the soul, confounds heaven with earth. He says, that the Father, the Son, and the Holy Spirit, placed their image in man, because, even though Adam had stood entire, Christ would still have become man. Thus, according to him, the body, which was destined for Christ, was a model and type of that corporeal figure which was then formed. But where does he find that Christ is an image of the Spirit?

I admit, indeed, that in the person of the Mediator, the glory of the whole Godhead is displayed: but how can the eternal Word, who in order precedes the Spirit, be called his image? In short, the distinction between the Son and the Spirit is destroyed when the former is represented as the image of the latter. Moreover, I should like to know in what respect Christ in the flesh in which he was clothed resembles the Holy Spirit, and by what marks, or lineaments, the likeness is expressed. And since the expression, "Let us make man in our own image," is used in the person of the Son also, it follows that he is the image of himself—a thing utterly absurd. Add that, according to the figment of Osiander, Adam was formed after the model or type of the man Christ. Hence, Christ, in as much as he was to be clothed with flesh, was the idea according to which Adam was formed, whereas the Scriptures teach very differently—viz. that he was formed in the image of

God. There is more plausibility in the imagination of those who interpret that Adam was created in the image of God, because it was conformable to Christ, who is the only image of God; but not even for this is there any solid foundation.

The "image" and "likeness" have given rise to no small discussion: interpreters searching without cause for a difference between the two terms, since "likeness" is merely added by way of exposition. First, we know that repetitions are common in Hebrew, which often gives two words for one thing; and, secondly, there is no ambiguity in the thing itself, man being called the image of God because of his likeness to God. Hence, there is an obvious absurdity in those who indulge in philosophical speculation as to these names, placing the *Zelem*, that is the image, in the substance of the soul, and the *Demuth*, that is the likeness, in its qualities, and so forth. God having determined to create man in his own image, to remove the obscurity which was in this terms adds, by way of explanation, in *his likeness*, as if he had said, that he would make man, in whom he would image himself by means of the marks of resemblance impressed upon him. Accordingly, Moses, shortly after repeating the account, puts down the image of God twice, and makes no mention of the likeness.

Osiander frivolously objects that it is not a part of the man, or the soul with its faculties, which is called the image of God, but the whole Adam, who received his name from the dust out of which he was taken. I call the objection frivolous, as all sound readers will judge. For though the whole man is called mortal, the soul is not therefore liable to death, nor when he is called a rational animal is reason or intelligence thereby attributed to the body. Hence, although the soul is not the man, there is no absurdity in holding that he is called the image of God in respect of the soul; though I retain the principle which I lately laid down, that the image of God extends to everything in which the nature of man surpasses that of all other species of animals.

Accordingly, by this term is denoted the integrity with which Adam was endued when his intellect was clear, his affections subordinated to reason, all his senses duly regulated, and when he truly ascribed all his excellence to the admirable gifts of his Maker. And though the primary seat of the divine image was in the mind and the heart or in the soul and its powers, there was no part even of the body in which some rays of glory did not shine. It is certain that in every part of the world, some lineaments of divine glory are beheld and hence we may infer that when his image is placed in man, there is a kind of tacit antithesis setting man apart from the crowd, and exalting him above all the other creatures. But it cannot be denied that the angels also were created in the likeness of God, since, as Christ declares (Matthew 22:30), our highest perfection will consist in being like them. But it is not without good cause that Moses commends the favor of God towards us by giving us this peculiar title, the more especially that he was only comparing man with the visible creation.

4. The image of God is in the soul. Its nature may be learnt from its renewal by Christ. What is comprehended under this renewal. What the image of God in man before the fall. In what things it now appears. When and where it will be seen in perfection.

But our definition of the image seems not to be complete until it appears more clearly what the faculties are in which man excels, and in which he is to be regarded as a mirror of the divine glory. This, however, cannot be better known than from the remedy provided for the corruption of nature. It cannot be doubted that when Adam lost his first estate he became alienated from God. Wherefore, although we grant that the image of God was not utterly effaced and destroyed in him, it was, however, so corrupted, that anything which remains is fearful deformity; and, therefore, our deliverance begins with that renovation which we obtain from Christ, who is, therefore, called the second Adam, because he restores us to true and substantial integrity. For although Paul, contrasting the quickening Spirit which believers receive from Christ, with the living soul which Adam was created (1 Corinthians 15:45), commends the richer measure of grace bestowed in regeneration, he does not, however, contradict the statement, that the end of regeneration is to form us anew in the image of God.

Accordingly, he elsewhere shows that the new man is renewed after the image of him that created him (Colossians 3:19). To this corresponds another passage, "Put ye on the new man, who after God is created" (Ephesians 4:24). We must now see what particulars Paul comprehends under this renovation. In the first place, he mentions knowledge, and in the second, true righteousness and holiness. Hence, we infer that at the beginning the image of God was manifested by light of intellect, rectitude of heart, and the soundness of every part.

Though I admit that the forms of expression are elliptical, this principle cannot be overthrown—viz. that the leading feature in the renovation of the divine image must also have held the highest place in its creation. To the same effect Paul elsewhere says, that beholding the glory of Christ with unveiled face, we are transformed into the same image. We now see how Christ is the most perfect image of God, into which we are so renewed as to bear the image of God in knowledge, purity, righteousness, and true holiness. This being established, the imagination of Osiander, as to bodily form, vanishes of its own accord. As to that passage of St. Paul (1 Corinthians 11:7), in which the man, alone to the express exclusion of the woman, is called the image and glory of God, it is evident from the context that it merely refers to civil order. I presume it has already been sufficiently proved, that the image comprehends everything, which has any relation to the spiritual and eternal life.

The same thing, in different terms, is declared by St John when he says, that the light which was from the beginning, in the eternal Word of God,

153

was the light of man (John 1:4). His object being to extol the singular grace of God in making man excel the other animals, he at the same time shows how he was formed in the image of God, that he may separate him from the common herd, as possessing not ordinary animal existence, but one which combines with it the light of intelligence. Therefore, as the image of God constitutes the entire excellence of human nature, as it shone in Adam before his fall, but was afterwards vitiated and almost destroyed, nothing remaining but a ruin, confused, mutilated, and tainted with impurity, so it is now partly seen in the elect, in so far as they are regenerated by the Spirit.

Its full luster, however, will be displayed in heaven. But in order to know the particular properties in which it consists, it will be proper to treat of the faculties of the soul. For there is no solidity in Augustine's speculation, that the soul is a mirror of the Trinity, inasmuch as it comprehends within itself, intellect, will, and memory. Nor is there probability in the opinion of those who place likeness to God in the dominion bestowed upon man, as if he only resembled God in this, that he is appointed lord and master of all things. The likeness must be within, in himself. It must be something, which is not external to him but is properly the internal good of the soul.

5 The dreams of the Manichees and of Servetus, as to the origin of the soul, refuted. Also, of Osiander, who denies that there is any image of God in man without essential righteousness.

But before I proceed further, it is necessary to advert to the dream of the Manichees, which Servetus has attempted in our day to revive. Because it is said that God breathed into man's nostrils the breath of life (Genesis 2:7), they thought that the soul was a transmission of the substance of God, as if some portion of the boundless divinity had passed into man. It cannot take long time to show how many gross and foul absurdities this devilish error carries in its train. For if the soul of man is a portion transmitted from the essence of God, the divine nature must not only be liable to passion and change, but also to ignorance, evil desires, infirmity, and all kinds of vice. There is nothing more inconstant than man, contrary movements agitating and distracting his soul. He is always [soon] deluded by want of skill, and overcome by the slightest temptations, while everyone feels that the soul itself is a receptacle for all kinds of pollution. All these things must be attributed to the divine nature, if we hold that the soul is of the essence of God, or a secret influx of divinity. Who does not shudder at a thing so monstrous?

Paul, indeed, quoting from Aratus, tells us we are his offspring (Acts 17:28); not in substance, however, but in quality, in as much as he has adorned us with divine endowments. Meanwhile, to lacerate the essence of the Creator, in order to assign a portion to each individual, is the height of madness. It must, therefore, be held as certain, that souls, notwithstanding of their having the divine image engraved on them, are created just as angels are. Creation, however, is not a transfusion of essence, but a commencement of it out of nothing. Nor, though the spirit is given by God, and when it quits the flesh again returns to him, does it follow that it is a portion withdrawn from his essence.

Here, too, Osiander, carried away by his illusions entangled himself in an impious error, by denying that the image of God could be in man without his essential righteousness; as if God were unable, by the mighty power of his Spirit, to render us conformable to himself, unless Christ were substantially transfused into us. Under whatever color some attempt to gloss these delusions, they can never so blind the eyes of intelligent readers as to prevent them from discerning in them a revival of Manicheism. But from the words of Paul, when treating of the renewal of the image (2 Corinthians 3:18), the inference is obvious, that man was conformable to God, not by an influx of substance, but by the grace and virtue of the Spirit. He says that by beholding the glory of Christ, we are transformed into the same image as by the Spirit of the Lord; and certainly, the Spirit does not work in us to make us of the same substance with God.

6 The doctrine of philosophers as to the faculties of the soul generally discordant, doubtful, and obscure. The excellence of the soul described. Only one soul in each man. A brief review of the opinion of philosophers as to the faculties of the soul. What to be thought of this opinion.

It was vain to seek a definition of the soul from philosophers, not one of whom, with the exception of Plato, distinctly maintained its immortality. Others of the school of Socrates, indeed, lean the same way, but still without teaching distinctly a doctrine of which they were not fully persuaded. Plato, however, advanced still further, and regarded the soul as an image of God. Others so attach its powers and faculties to the present life, that they leave nothing external to the body. Moreover, having already shown from Scripture that the substance of the soul is incorporeal, we must now add, that though it is not properly enclosed by space, it however occupies the body as a kind of habitation, not only animating all its parts, and rendering the organs fit and useful for their actions, but also holding the first place in regulating the conduct.

This it does not merely in regard to the offices of a terrestrial life, but also in regard to the service of God. This, though not clearly seen in our corrupt state, yet the impress of its remains is seen in our very vices. For whence have men such a thirst for glory but from a sense of shame? And whence this sense of shame but from a respect for what is honorable? Of this, the first principle and source is a consciousness that they were born to cultivate righteousness, —a consciousness akin to religion. But as man was undoubtedly created to meditate on the heavenly life, so it is certain that the knowledge of it was engraved on the soul. And, indeed, man would want the principal use of his understanding if he were unable to discern his felicity, the perfection of which consists in being united to God. Hence, the principal action of the soul is to aspire thither, and, accordingly, the more a man studies to approach to God, the more he proves himself to be endued with reason.

Though there is some plausibility in the opinion of those who maintain that man has more than one soul, namely, a sentient and a rational, yet as there is no soundness in their arguments, we must reject it, unless we would torment ourselves with things frivolous and useless. They tell us (see chapter 5, section 4), there is a great repugnance between organic movements and the rational part of the soul. As if reason also were not at variance with herself, and her counsels sometimes conflicting with each other like hostile armies. But since this disorder results from the depravation of nature, it is erroneous to infer that there are two souls, because the faculties do not accord so harmoniously as they ought. But I leave it to philosophers to discourse more subtlety of these faculties. For the edification of the pious, a simple definition will be sufficient. I admit, indeed, that what they ingeniously teach on the subject is true, and not only pleasant, but also useful to be known; nor do I forbid any who are inclined to prosecute the study.

First, I admit that there are five senses, which Plato (in *Theaeteto*) prefers calling organs, by which all objects are brought into a common sensory function, as into a kind of receptacle: Next comes the imagination (*phantasia*), which distinguishes between the objects brought into the sensory function: Next, reason, to which the general power of Judgment belongs: And, lastly, intellect, which contemplates with fixed and quiet look whatever reason discursively revolves. In like manner, to intellect, fancy, and reason, the three cognitive faculties of the soul, correspond three appetite faculties— viz. will—whose office is to choose whatever reason and intellect propound; irascibility, which seizes on what is set before it by reason and fancy; and concupiscence, which lays hold of the objects presented by sense and fancy.

Though these things are true, or at least plausible, still, as I fear they are more fitted to entangle, by their obscurity, than to assist us, I think it best to omit them. If anyone chooses to distribute the powers of the mind in a different manner, calling one appetitive, which, though devoid of reason, yet obeys reason, if directed from a different quarter, and another intellectual, as being by itself participant of reason, I have no great objection. Nor am I disposed to quarrel with the view, that there are three principles of action— viz. sense, intellect, and appetite. But let us rather adopt a division adapted to all capacities—a thing which certainly is not to be obtained from philosophers. For they, when they would speak most plainly, divide the soul into appetite and intellect, but make both double. To the latter they sometimes give the name of *contemplative*, as being contented with mere knowledge and having no active powers (which circumstance makes Cicero designate it by the name of intellect (*ingenii*). At other times they give it the name of *practical*, because it variously moves the will by the apprehension of good or evil. Under this class is included the art of living well and justly. The former—viz. appetite—they divide into will and concupiscence, calling it βουλεσις, so whenever the appetite, which they call ο ρμη, obeys the reason. But when appetite, casting off the yoke of reason, runs to intemperance, they call it πατηος.Thus they always presuppose in man a reason by which he is able to guide himself aright.

7 **The division of the faculties of the soul into intellect and will, more agreeable to Christian doctrine.**

From this method of teaching, we are forced somewhat to dissent. For philosophers, being unacquainted with the corruption of nature, which is the punishment of revolt, erroneously confound two states of man which are very different from each other. Let us therefore hold, for the purpose of the present work, that the soul consists of two parts, the intellect and the will (Book 2 chapter 2, sections 2, 12), —the office of the intellect being to distinguish between objects, according as they seem deserving of being approved or disapproved; and the office of the will, to choose and follow what the intellect declares to be good, to reject and shun what it declares to be bad (Plato, in *Phaedro*).

We dwell not on the subtlety of Aristotle, that the mind has no motion of itself; but that the moving power is choice, which he also terms the appetite intellect. Not to lose ourselves in superfluous questions, let it be enough to know that the intellect is to us the guide and ruler of the soul; that the will always follows its beck, and waits for its decision, in matters of desire. For which reason Aristotle truly taught, that in the appetite there is a pursuit and rejection corresponding in some degree to affirmation and negation in the intellect. Moreover, it will be seen in another place (Book 2, chapter 2, sections 12-26), how surely the intellect governs the will. Here we only wish to observe, that the soul does not possess any faculty, which may not be duly referred to one or other of these members. And in this way, we comprehend sense under intellect. Others distinguish thus: They say that sense inclines to pleasure in the same way as the intellect to good; that hence the appetite of sense becomes concupiscence and lust, while the affection of the intellect becomes will. For the term appetite, which they prefer, I use that of will, as being more common.

8 **The power and office of the intellect and will in man before the fall. Man's free will. This freedom lost by the fall—a fact unknown to philosophers. The delusion of Pelagians and Papists. Objection as to the fall of man when free, refuted.**

Therefore, God has provided the soul of man with intellect, by which he might discern good from evil, just from unjust, and might know what to follow or to shun, reason going before with her lamp; whence philosophers, in reference to her directing power, have called her e gemonikon. To this he has joined will, to which choice belongs. Man excelled in these noble endowments in his primitive condition, when reason, intelligence, prudence, and Judgment, not only sufficed for the government of his earthly life, but also enabled him to rise up to God and eternal happiness. Thereafter choice was added to direct the appetites and temper all the organic motions—the will being thus perfectly submissive to the authority of reason. In this upright state, man possessed freedom of will, by which, if he chose, he was able to obtain eternal life. It would be here unseasonable to introduce the question concerning the secret predestination of God, because we are not considering what might or might not happen, but what the nature of man truly was. Adam, therefore, might have stood if he chose, since it was only by his own will that he fell; but it was because his will was pliable in either directions and he had not received constancy to persevere, that he so easily fell. Still he had a free choice of good and evil; and not only so, but in the mind and will there was the highest rectitude, and all the organic parts were duly framed to obedience, until man corrupted its good properties, and destroyed himself. Hence, the great darkness of philosophers who have looked for a complete building in a ruin, and fit arrangement in disorder. The principle they set out with was that man could not be a rational animal unless he had a free choice of good and evil. They also imagined that the distinction between virtue and vice was destroyed, if man did not of his own counsel arrange his life.

So far well, had there been no change in man. This being unknown to them, it is not surprising that they throw everything into confusion. But those who, while they profess to be the disciples of Christ, still seek for free-will in man, notwithstanding of his being lost and drowned in spiritual destruction, labor under manifold delusion, making a heterogeneous mixture of inspired doctrine and philosophical opinions, and so erring as to both. But it will be better to leave these things to their own place (see Book 2, chapter 2) At present it is necessary only to remember, that man, at his first creation, was very different from all his posterity; who, deriving their origin from him after he was corrupted, received a hereditary taint. At first, every part of the soul was formed to rectitude.

There was soundness of mind and freedom of will to choose the good. If anyone objects that it was placed in a slippery position, because its power was weak, I answer, that the degree conferred was sufficient to take away every excuse. For surely the Deity could not be tied down to this condition, —to make man such, that he either could not or would not sin. Such a nature might have been more excellent; but to expostulate with God as if he had been bound to confer this nature on man, is more than unjust, seeing he had full right to determine how much or how little He would give. Why He did not sustain him by the virtue of perseverance is hidden in his counsel; it is ours to keep within the bounds of soberness. Man had received the power, if he had the will, but he had not the will, which would have given the power; for this will would have been followed by perseverance. Still, after he had received so much, there is no excuse for his having spontaneously brought death upon himself. No necessity was laid upon God to give him more than that intermediate and even transient will, that out of man's fall he might extract materials for his own glory.

Chapter 16

THE WORLD, CREATED BY GOD, STILL CHERISHED AND PROTECTED BY HIM. EACH AND ALL OF ITS PARTS GOVERNED BY HIS PROVIDENCE.

The divisions of this chapter are, I. The doctrine of the special Providence of God over all the creatures, singly and collectively, as opposed to the dreams of the Epicureans about fortune and fortuitous causes. II. The fiction of the Sophists concerning the omnipotence of God, and the error of philosophers, as to a confused and equivocal government of the world, sectionS 1-5. All animals, but especially mankind, from the peculiar superintendence exercised over them, are proofs, evidences, and examples of the Providence of God, sectionS 6, 7. III. A consideration of fate, fortune, chance, contingence, and uncertain events (on which the matter here under discussion turns).

Sections

1. Even the wicked, under the guidance of carnal sense, acknowledge that God is the Creator. The godly acknowledge not this only, but that he is a most wise and powerful governor and preserver of all created objects. In so doing, they lean on the Word of God, some passages from which are produced.

2. Refutation of the Epicureans, who oppose fortune and fortuitous causes to Divine Providence, as taught in Scripture. The sun, a bright manifestation of Divine Providence.

3. Figment of the Sophists as to an indolent Providence refuted. Consideration of the Omnipotence as combined with the Providence of God. Double benefit resulting from a proper acknowledgement of the Divine Omnipotence. Cavils of Infidelity.

4. A definition of Providence refuting the erroneous dogmas of Philosophers. Dreams of the Epicureans and Peripatetics.

5. Special Providence of God asserted and proved by arguments founded on a consideration of the Divine Justice and Mercy. Proved also by passages of Scripture, relating to the sky, the earth, and animals.

6. *Special Providence proved by passages relating to the human race, and the more especially that for its sake the world was created.*

7. *Special Providence proved, lastly, from examples taken from the history of the Israelites, of Jonah, Jacob, and from daily experience.*

8. *Erroneous views as to Providence refuted:* —A. *The sect of the Stoics. B. The fortune and chance of the Heathen.*

9. *How things are said to be fortuitous to us, though done by the determinate counsel of God. Example. Error of separating contingency and event from the secret, but just, and most wise counsel of God. Two examples.*

1 Even the wicked, under the guidance of carnal sense, acknowledge that God is the Creator. The godly acknowledge not this only, but that he is a most wise and powerful governor and preserver of all created objects. In so doing, they lean on the Word of God, some passages from which are produced.

It would be cold and lifeless to represent God as a momentary Creator, who completed his work once for all, and then left it. Here, especially, we must dissent from the profane, and maintain that the presence of the divine power is conspicuous, not less in the perpetual condition of the world then in its first creation. For, although even wicked men are forced, by the mere view of the earth and sky, to rise to the Creator, yet faith has a method of its own in assigning the whole praise of creation to God. To this effect is the passage of the Apostle already quoted that by faith we understand that the worlds were framed by the Word of God (Hebrews 11:3); because, without proceeding to his Providence, we cannot understand the full force of what is meant by God being the Creator, no matter how much we may seem to comprehend it with our mind, and confess it with our tongue.

The carnal mind, when once it has perceived the power of God in the creation, stops there, and, at the farthest, thinks and ponders on nothing else than the wisdom, power, and goodness displayed by the Author of such a work (matters which rise spontaneously, and force themselves on the notice even of the unwilling), or on some general agency on which the power of motion depends, exercised in preserving and governing it. In short, it imagines that all things are sufficiently sustained by the energy divinely infused into them at first. But faith must penetrate deeper. After learning that there is a Creator, it must forthwith infer that he is also a Governor and Preserver, and that, not by producing a kind of general motion in the machine of the globe as well as in each of its parts, but by a special providence sustaining, cherishing, superintending, all the things which he has made, to the very minutest, even to a sparrow. Thus David, after briefly premising that the world was created by God, immediately descends to the continual course of Providence, "By the word of the Lord were the heavens framed, and all the host of them by the breath of his mouth;" immediately adding, "The Lord looketh from heaven, he beholdeth the children of men" (Psalm 33:6, 13, etc.). He subjoins other things to the same effect. For although all do not reason so accurately, yet because it would not be credible that human affairs were superintended by God, unless he were the maker of the world, and no one could seriously believe that he is its Creator without feeling convinced that he takes care of his works; David with good reason, and in admirable order, leads us from the one to the other.

In general, indeed, philosophers teach, and the human mind conceives, that all the parts of the world are invigorated by the secret inspiration of God. They do not, however reach the height to which David rises taking all the pious along with him, when he says, "These wait all upon thee, that thou mayest give them their meat in due season. That thou givest them they gather: thou openest thine hand, they are filled with good. Thou hidest thy face, they are troubled: thou takest away their breath, they die, and return to their dust. Thou sendest forth thy Spirit, they are created, and thou renewest the face of the earth" (Psalm 104:27-30). Nay, though they subscribe to the sentiment of Paul, that in God "we live, and move, and have our being" (Acts 17:28), yet they are far from having a serious apprehension of the grace which he commends, because they have not the least relish for that special care in which alone the paternal favor of God is discerned.

2 Refutation of the Epicureans, who oppose fortune and fortuitous causes to Divine Providence, as taught in Scripture. The sun, a bright manifestation of Divine Providence.

That this distinction may be the more manifest, we must consider that the Providence of God, as taught in Scripture, is opposed to fortune and fortuitous causes. By an erroneous opinion prevailing in all ages, an opinion almost universally prevailing in our own day—viz. that all things happen fortuitously, the true doctrine of Providence has not only been obscured, but almost buried. If one falls among robbers, or ravenous beasts; if a sudden gust of wind at sea causes shipwreck; if one is struck down by the fall of a house or a tree; if another, when wandering through desert paths, meets with deliverance; or, after being tossed by the waves, arrives in port, and makes some wondrous hair-breadth escape from death—all these occurrences, prosperous as well as adverse, carnal sense will attribute to fortune. But whose has learned from the mouth of Christ that all the hairs of his head are numbered

(Matthew 10:30), will look further for the cause, and hold that all events whatsoever are governed by the secret counsel of God.

With regard to inanimate objects, again we must hold that though each is possessed of its peculiar properties, yet all of them exert their force only in so far as directed by the immediate hand of God. Hence, they are merely instruments, into which God constantly infuses what energy he sees meet, and turns and converts to any purpose at his pleasure. No created object makes a more wonderful or glorious display than the sun. For, besides illuminating the whole world with its brightness, how admirably does it foster and invigorate all animals by its heat, and fertilize the earth by its rays, warming the seeds of grain in its lap, and thereby calling forth the verdant blade! This it supports, increases, and strengthens with additional nurture, until it rises into the stalk; and still feeds it with perpetual moisture, until it comes into flower; and from flower to fruit, which it continues to ripen until it attains maturity.

In like manner, by its warmth trees and vines bud, and put forth first their leaves, then their blossom, then and their fruit. And the Lord, that he might claim the entire glory of these things as his own, was pleased that light should exist, and that the earth should be replenished with all kinds of herbs and fruits before he made the sun.

No pious man, therefore, will make the sun either the necessary or principal cause of those things which existed before the creation of the sun, but only the instrument which God employs, because he so pleases; though he can lay it aside, and act equally well by himself: Again, when we read, that at the prayer of Joshua the sun was stayed in its course (Joshua 10:13); that as a favor to Hezekiah, its shadow receded ten degrees (2 Kings 20:11); by these miracles God declared that the sun does not daily rise and set by a blind instinct of nature, but is governed by Him in its course, that he may renew the remembrance of his paternal favor toward us. Nothing is more natural than for spring, in its turns to succeed winter, summer spring, and autumn summer; but in this series the variations are so great and so unequal as to make it very apparent that every single year, month, and day, is regulated by a new and special Providence of God.

3 Figment of the Sophists as to an indolent Providence refuted. Consideration of the Omnipotence as combined with the Providence of God. Double benefit resulting from a proper acknowledgement of the Divine Omnipotence. Cavils of Infidelity.

And truly God claims omnipotence to himself, and would have us to acknowledge it, —not the vain, indolent, slumbering omnipotence which sophists feign, but vigilant, efficacious, energetic, and ever active, —not an omnipotence which may only act as a general principle of confused motion, as in ordering a stream to keep within the channel once prescribed to it, but one which is intent on individual and special movements. God is deemed omnipotent, not because he can act though he may cease or be idle, or because by a general instinct he continues the order of nature previously appointed; but because, governing heaven and earth by his providence, he so overrules all things that nothing happens without his counsel. For when it is said in the Psalms, "He has done whatsoever he has pleased" (Psalm 115:3), the thing meant is his sure and deliberate purpose.

It would be insipid to interpret the Psalmist's words in philosophic fashion, to mean that God is the primary agent, because the beginning and cause of all motion. This rather is the solace of the faithful, in their adversity, that everything, which they endure, is by the ordination and command of God that they are under his hand. But if the government of God thus extends to all his works, it is a childish cavil to confine it to natural influx. Those moreover who confine the Providence of God within narrow limits, as if he allowed all things to be borne along freely according to a perpetual law of nature, do not more defraud God of his glory than themselves of a most useful doctrine; for nothing were more wretched than man if he were exposed to all possible movements of the sky, the air, the earth, and the water.

We may add that by this view the singular goodness of God towards each individual is unbecomingly impaired. David exclaims (Psalm 8:3) that infants hanging at their mothers' breasts are eloquent enough to celebrate the glory of God, because from the very moment of their births, they find an aliment prepared for them by heavenly care. Indeed, if we do not shut our eyes and senses to the fact, we must see that some mothers have full provision for their infants, and others almost none, according as it is the pleasure of God to nourish one child more liberally, and another more sparingly.

Those who attribute due praise to the omnipotence of God thereby derive a double benefit. He to whom heaven and earth belong, and whose nod all creatures must obey, is fully able to reward the homage which they pay to him, and they can rest secure in the protection of Him to whose control everything that could do them harm is subject, by whose authority, Satan, with all his furies and engines, is curbed as with a bridle, and on whose will everything adverse to our safety depends. In this way, and in no other, can the immoderate and superstitious fears, excited by the dangers to which we are exposed, be calmed or subdued. I say superstitious fears. For such they are, as often as the dangers threatened by any created objects inspire us with such terror, that we tremble as if they had in themselves a power to hurt us, or could hurt at random or by chance; or as if we had not in God a sufficient protection against them. For example, Jeremiah forbids the children of God " to be dismayed at the signs of heaven, as the heathen are dismayed at them" (Jeremiah 10:2). He does not, indeed, condemn every kind of fear.

As unbelievers transfer the government of the world from God to the stars, imagining that happiness or misery depends on their decrees or presages, and not on the Divine will, the consequence is, that their fear, which ought to have reference to him only, is diverted to stars and comets. Let him, therefore, who would beware of such unbelief, always bear in mind, that there is no random power, or agency, or motion in the creatures, who are so governed by the secret counsel of God, that nothing happens but what he has knowingly and willingly decreed.

4 A definition of Providence refuting the erroneous dogmas of Philosophers. Dreams of the Epicureans and Peripatetics.

First, then, let the reader remember that the providence we mean is not one by which the Deity, sitting idly in heaven, looks on at what is taking place in the world, but one by which he holds the helms and overrules all events. Hence, his providence extends not less to the hand than to the eye. When Abraham said to his son, *God will provide* (Genesis 22:8), he meant not merely to assert that the future event was foreknown to Gods but to resign the management of an unknown business to the will of Him whose province it is to bring perplexed and dubious matters to a happy result. Hence, it appears that providence consists in action. What many talk of bare prescience is the merest trifling.

Those do not err quite so grossly who attribute government to God, but still, as I have observed, a confused and promiscuous government, which consists in giving an impulse and general movement to the machine of the globe and each of its parts, but does not specially direct the action of every creature. It is impossible, however, to tolerate this error. For, according to its abettors, there is nothing in this providence, which they call universal, to prevent all the creatures from being moved contingently, or to prevent man from turning himself in this direction or in that, according to the mere freedom of his own will.

In this way, they make man a partner with God, —God, by his energy, impressing man with the movement by which he can act, agreeably to the nature conferred upon him while man voluntarily regulates his own actions. In short, their doctrine is that the world, the affairs of men, and men themselves, are governed by the power, but not by the decree of God. I say nothing of the Epicureans (a pest with which the world has always been plagued), who dream of an inert and idle God, and others, not a whit sounder, who of old feigned that God rules the upper regions of the air, but leaves the inferior to Fortune. Against such evident madness, even dumb creatures lift their voice.

My intention now is, to refute an opinion which has very generally obtained—an opinion which, while it concedes to God some blind and equivocal movement, withholds what is of principal moment—viz. the disposing and directing of everything to its proper end by incomprehensible wisdom. By withholding government, it makes God the ruler of the world in name only, not in reality. For what, I ask, is meant by government, if it is not to preside to regulate the destiny of that over which you preside? I do not, however, totally repudiate what is said of an universal providence, provided, on the other hand, it is conceded to me that the world is governed by God, not only because he maintains the order of nature appointed by him, but because he takes a special charge of everyone of his works.

It is true, indeed, that each species of created objects is moved by a secret instinct of nature, as if they obeyed the eternal command of God, and spontaneously followed the course which God at first appointed. And to this we may refer our Savior's words, that he and his Father have always been at work from the beginning (John 5:17); also the words of Paul, that "in him we live, and move, and have our being" (Acts 17:28); also the words of the author of the Epistle to the Hebrews, who, when wishing to prove the divinity of Christ, says, that he upholdeth "all things by the word of his power" (Hebrews 1:3). But some, under pretext of the general, hide and obscure the special providence, which is so surely and clearly taught in Scripture, that it is strange how anyone can bring himself to doubt of it. And, indeed, those who interpose that disguise are themselves forced to modify their doctrine, by adding that many things are done by the special care of God. This, however, they erroneously confine to particular acts. The thing to be proved, therefore, is that single events are so regulated by God, and all events so proceed from his determinate counsel, that nothing happens fortuitously.

5 Special Providence of God asserted and proved by arguments founded on a consideration of the Divine Justice and Mercy. Proved also by passages of Scripture, relating to the sky, the earth, and animals.

Assuming that the beginning of motion belongs to God, but that all things move spontaneously or casually, according to the impulse which nature gives, the vicissitudes of day and nights summer and winter, will be the work of God; inasmuch as he, in assigning the office of each, appointed a certain law, namely, that they should always with uniform tenor observe the same course, day succeeding night, month succeeding month, and year succeeding year. But, as at one time, excessive heat, combined with drought, burns up the fields; at another time excessive rains rot the crops, while sudden devastation is produced by tempests and storms of hail, these will not be the works of God, unless in so far as rainy or fair weather, heat or cold, are produced by the concourse of the stars, and other natural causes.

According to this view, there is no place left either for the paternal favor, or the Judgments of God. If it is said that God fully manifests his beneficence to the human race, by furnishing heaven and earth with the ordinary power of producing food, the explanation is meager and heathenish: as if the fertility of one year were not a special blessing, the penury and dearth of another a special punishment and curse from God. But as it would occupy too much time to enumerate all the arguments, let the authority of God himself suffice.

In the Law and the Prophets he repeatedly declares, that as often as he waters the earth with dew and rain, he manifests his favor, that by his command the heaven becomes hard as iron, the crops are destroyed by mildew and other evils, that storms and hail, in devastating the fields, are signs of sure and special vengeance. This being admitted, it is certain that not a drop of rain falls without the express command of God. David, indeed (Psalm 146:9), extols the general Providence of God in supplying food to the young ravens that cry to him but when God himself threatens living creatures with famine, does he not plainly declare that they are all nourished by him, at one time with scanty, at another with more ample measure?

It is childish, as I have already said, to confine this to particular acts, when Christ says, without reservation, that not a sparrow falls to the ground without the will of his Father (Matthew 10:29). Surely, if the flight of birds is regulated by the counsel of God, we must acknowledge with the prophet, that while he "dwelleth on high," he "humbleth himself to behold the things that are in heaven and in the earth" (Psalm 113:5, 6).

6 Special Providence proved by passages relating to the human race, and the more especially that for its sake the world was created.

But as we know that it was chiefly for the sake of mankind that the world was made, we must look to this as the end which God has in view in the government of it. The prophet Jeremiah exclaims, "O Lord, I know that the way of man is not in himself: it is not in man that walketh to direct his steps" (Jeremiah 10:23). Solomon again says, "Man's goings are of the Lord: how can a man then understand his own way?" (Proverbs 20:24). Will it now be said that God moves man according to the bent of his nature, but that man himself gives the movement any direction he pleases? Were it truly so, man would have the full disposal of his own ways. To this it will perhaps be answered, that man can do nothing without the power of God. But the answer will not avail, since both Jeremiah and Solomon attribute to God not power only, but also election and decree. And Solomon, in another place, elegantly rebukes the rashness of men in fixing their plans without reference to God, as if his hand did not lead them. "The preparations of the heart in man, and the answer of the tongue, is from the Lord" (Proverbs 16:1).

It is a strange infatuation, surely for miserable men, who cannot even give utterance except in so far as God pleases, to begin to act without him! Scriptures moreover, the better to show that everything done in the world is according to his decree, declares that the things that seem most fortuitous are subject to him. For what seems more attributable to chance than the branch which falls from a tree, and kills the passing traveler?

But the Lord sees very differently, and declares that He delivered him into the hand of the slayer (Exodus 21:13). In like manner, who does not attribute the lot to the blindness of Fortune? Not so the Lord, who claims the decision for himself (Proverbs 16:33). He says not, that by his power the lot is thrown into the lap, and taken out, but declares that the only thing which could be attributed to chance is from him. To the same effect are the words of Solomon, "The poor and the deceitful man meet together; the Lord lighteneth both their eyes" (Proverbs 29:13). For although rich and poor are mingled together in the world, in saying that the condition of each is divinely appointed, he reminds us that God, Who enlightens all, has his own eye always open, and thus exhorts the poor to patient endurance, seeing that those who are discontented with their lot endeavor to shake off a burden which God has imposed upon them. Thus, too, another prophet upbraids the profane, who ascribe it to human industry, or to fortune, that some grovel in the mire while others rise to honor. "Promotion cometh neither from the east, nor from the west, nor from the south. But God is the judge: he putteth down ones and setteth up another" (Psalm 75:6, 7). Because God cannot divest himself of the office of judge, it is due to his secret counsel that some are elevated, while others remain without honor.

7 **Special Providence proved, lastly, from examples taken from the history of the Israelites, of Jonah, Jacob, and from daily experience.**

Nay, I affirm in general, that particular events are evidences of the special Providence of God. In the wilderness, God caused a south wind to blow, and brought the people a plentiful supply of birds (Exodus 19:13). When he desired that Jonah should be thrown into the sea, he sent forth a whirlwind. Those who deny that God holds the reins of government will say that this was contrary to ordinary practice, whereas I infer from it that no wind ever rises or rages without his special command. In no way could it be true that "he maketh the winds his messengers, and the flames of fire his ministers;" that "he maketh the clouds his chariot, and walketh upon the wings of the wind" (Psalm 104:3, 4), did he not at pleasure drive the clouds and winds and therein manifest the special presence of his power.

In like manner, we are elsewhere taught, that whenever the sea is raised into a storm, its billows attest the special presence of God. "He commandeth and raiseth the stormy wind, which lifteth up the waves." "He maketh the storm a calm, so that the waves thereof are still" (Psalm 107:25, 29). He also elsewhere declares that he had smitten the people with blasting and mildew (Amos 4:9). Again while man naturally possesses the power of continuing his species, God describes it as a mark of his special favor, that while some continue childless, others are blessed with offspring: for the fruit of the womb is his gift. Hence, the words of Jacob to Rachel, "Am I in God's stead, who has withheld from thee the fruit of the womb?" (Genesis 30:2).

Nothing in nature is more ordinary than that we should be nourished with bread. But the Spirit declares not only that the produce of the earth is God's special gift, but "that man does not live by bread only" (Deuteronomy 8:3), because it is not mere fullness that nourishes him but the secret blessing of God. And hence, on the other hand, he threatens to take away "the stay and the staff, the whole stay of bread, and the whole stay of water" (Isaiah 3:1). Indeed, there could be no serious meaning in our prayer for daily bread, if God did not with paternal hand supply us with food. Accordingly, to convince the faithful that God, in feeding them, fulfills the office of the best of parents, the prophet reminds them that he "giveth food to all flesh" (Psalm 136:25).

In fine, when we hear on the one hand, that "the eyes of the Lord are upon the righteous, and his ears are open unto their cry," and, on the other hand, that "the face of the Lord is against them that do evil, to cut off the remembrance of them from the earth" (Psalm 34:15, 16), let us be assured that all creatures above and below are ready at his service, that he may employ them in whatever way he pleases. Hence, we infer, not only that the general Providence of God, continuing the order of nature, extends over the creatures, but that by his wonderful counsel they are adapted to a certain and special purpose.

8 Erroneous views as to Providence refuted: —A. The sect of the Stoics. B. The fortune and chance of the Heathen.

Those who would cast obloquy on this doctrine, calumniate it as the dogma of the Stoics concerning fate. The same charge was formerly brought against Augustine. We are unwilling to dispute about words; but we do not admit the term Fate, both because it is of the class which Paul teaches us to shun, as profane novelties (1 Timothy 6:20), and also because it is attempted, by means of an odious term, to fix a stigma on the truth of God. But the dogma itself is falsely and maliciously imputed to us. For we do not with the Stoics imagine a necessity consisting of a perpetual chain of causes, and a kind of involved series contained in nature, but we hold that God is the disposer and ruler of all things, —that from the remotest eternity, according to his own wisdom, he decreed what he was to do, and now by his power executes what he decreed. Hence, we maintain, that by his providence, not heaven and earth and inanimate creatures only, but also the counsels and wills of men are so governed as to move exactly in the course, which he has destined.

What, then, you will say; does nothing happen fortuitously, nothing contingently? I answer, it was a true saying of Basil the Great, that Fortune and Chance are heathen terms; the meaning of which ought not to occupy pious minds. For if all success is blessing from God, and calamity and adversity are his curse, there is no place left in human affairs for fortune and chance.

We ought also to be moved by the words of Augustine, "In my writings against the Academics," says he, "I regret having so often used the term Fortune; although I intended to denote by it not some goddess, but the fortuitous issue of events in external matters, whether good or evil. Hence, too, those words, Perhaps, Perchance, Fortuitously, which no religion forbids us to use, though everything must be referred to Divine Providence. Nor did I omit to observe this when I said, Although, perhaps, that which is vulgarly called Fortune, is also regulated by a hidden order, and what we call Chance is nothing else than that the reason and cause of which is secret. It is true, I so spoke, but I repent of having mentioned Fortune there as I did, when I see the very bad custom, which men have of saying, not as they ought to do, 'So God pleased,' but, 'So Fortune pleased.'"

In short, Augustine everywhere teaches that if anything is left to fortune, the world moves at random. And although he elsewhere declares that all things are carried on, partly by the free will of man, and partly by the Providence of God, he shortly after shows clearly enough that his meaning was, that men also are ruled by Providence, when he assumes it as a principle, that there cannot be a greater absurdity than to hold that anything is done without the ordination of God; because it would happen at random. For which reason, he also excludes the contingency which depends on human will, maintaining a little further on, in clearer terms, that no cause must be sought for but the will of God. When he uses the term permission, the meaning that he attaches to it will best appear from a single passage, where he proves that the will of God is the supreme and primary cause of all things, because nothing happens without his order or permission. He certainly does not figure God sitting idly in a watchtower, when he chooses to permit anything. The will which he represents as interposing is, if I may so express it, active (*actualis*), and but for this could not be regarded as a cause.

9 How things are said to be fortuitous to us, though done by the determinate counsel of God. Example. Error of separating contingency and event from the secret, but just, and most wise counsel of God. Two examples.

But since our sluggish minds rest far beneath the height of Divine Providence, we must have recourse to a distinction that may assist them in rising. I say then, that though all things are ordered by the counsel and certain arrangement of God, to us, however, they are fortuitous, —not because we imagine that Fortune rules the world and mankind, and turns all things upside down at random (far be such a heartless thought from every Christian breast); but as the order, method, end, and necessity of events, are, for the most part, hidden in the counsel of God, though it is certain that they are produced by the will of God, they have the appearance of being fortuitous, such being the form under which they present themselves to us, whether considered in their own nature, or estimated according to our knowledge and Judgment.

Let us suppose, for example, that a merchant, after entering a forest in company with trust-worthy individuals, imprudently strays from his companions and wanders bewildered until he falls into a den of robbers and is murdered. His death was not only foreseen by the eye of God, but had been fixed by his decree. For it is said, not that he foresaw how far the life of each individual should extend, but that he determined and fixed the bounds which could not be passed (Job 14:5). Still, in relation to our capacity of discernment, all these things appear fortuitous.

How will the Christian feel? Though he will consider that every circumstance, which occurred in that person's death was indeed in its nature fortuitous, he will have no doubt that the Providence of God, overruled it and guided fortune to his own end. The same thing holds in the case of future contingencies. All future events being uncertain to us, seem in suspense as if ready to take either direction. However, the impression remains seated in our hearts: that nothing will happen which the Lord has not provided. In this sense, the term event is repeatedly used in Ecclesiastes, because, at the first glance, men do not penetrate to the primary cause that lies concealed. And yet, what is taught in Scripture of the secret Providence of God was never so completely effaced from the human heart, as that some sparks did not always shine in the darkness.

Thus, the soothsayers of the Philistine, though they waver in uncertainty, attribute the adverse event partly to God and partly to chance. If the ark, say they, "Goes up by the way of his own coast to Bethshemish, then he has done us this great evil; but if not, then we shall know that it is not his hand that smote us, it was a chance that happened to us." (1 Samuel 6:9). Foolishly, indeed, when divination fails them they flee to fortune. Still we see them constrained, so as not to venture to regard their disaster as fortuitous. But the mode in which God, by the curb of his Providence, turns events in whatever direction he pleases, will appear from a remarkable example. At the very same moment when David was discovered in the wilderness of Maon, the Philistines make an inroad into the country, and Saul is forced to depart (1 Samuel 23:26, 27).

If God, in order to provide for the safety of his servant, threw this obstacle in the way of Saul, we surely cannot say, that though the Philistine took up arms contrary to human expectation, they did it by chance. What seems to us contingence, faith will recognize as the secret impulse of God. The reason is not always equally apparent, but we ought undoubtedly to hold that all the changes that take place in the world are produced by the secret agency of the hand of God. At the same time, that which God has determined, though it must come to pass, is not, however, precisely, or in its own nature, necessary.

We have a familiar example in the case of our Savior's bones. As he assumed a body similar to ours, no sane man will deny that his bones were capable of being broken and yet it was impossible that they should be broken (John 19:33, 36). Hence, again, we see that there was good ground for the distinction that the Schoolmen made between necessity, *secundum quid*, and necessity absolute, also between the necessity of *consequent* and of *consequence*. God made the bones of his Son frangible, though he exempted them from actual fracture; and thus, in reference to the necessity of his counsel, made that impossible which might have naturally taken place.

Chapter 17

USE TO BE MADE OF THE DOCTRINE OF PROVIDENCE.

This chapter may be conveniently divided into two parts: —I. A general explanation is given of the doctrine of Divine Providence, in so far as conducive to the solid instruction and consolation of the godly, section 1, and specially sections 2-12. First, however, those are refuted who deny that the world is governed by the secret and incomprehensible counsel of God; those also who throw the blame of all wickedness upon God, and absurdly pretend that exercises of piety are useless, sections 2-5. Thereafter is added a holy meditation on Divine Providence, which, in the case of prosperity, is painted to the life, sections 6-11. —II. A solution of two objections from passages of Scripture, which attribute repentance to God, and speak of something like an abrogation of his decrees.

Sections

1. Summary of the doctrine of Divine Providence. A. It embraces the future and the past. B. It works by means, without means, and against means. C. Mankind, and particularly the Church, the object of special care. D. The mode of administration usually secret, but always just. This last point more fully considered.

2. The profane denial that the world is governed by the secret counsel of God, refuted by passages of Scripture. Salutary counsel.

3. This doctrine, as to the secret counsel of God in the government of the world, gives no countenance either to the impiety of those who throw the blame of their wickedness upon God, the petulance of those who reject means, or the error of those who neglect the duties of religion.

4. As regards future events, the doctrine of Divine Providence not inconsistent with deliberation on the part of man.

5. In regard to past events, it is absurd to argue that crimes ought not to be punished, because they are in accordance with the divine decrees. A. The wicked resist the declared will of God. B.

They are condemned by conscience. C. The essence and guilt of the crime is in themselves, though God uses them as instruments.

6. A holy meditation on Divine Providence. A. All events happen by the ordination of God. B. All things contribute to the advantage of the godly. C. The hearts of men and all their endeavors are in the hand of God. D. Providence watches for the safety of the righteous. E. God has a special care of his elect.

7. Meditation on Providence continued. F. God in various ways curbs and defeats the enemies of the Church. G. He overrules all creatures, even Satan himself, for the good of his people.

8. Meditation on Providence continued. H. He trains the godly to patience and moderation. Examples. Joseph, Job, and David. I. He shakes off their lethargy, and urges them to repentance.

9. Meditation continued. J. The right use of inferior causes explained. K. When the godly become negligent or imprudent in the discharge of duty, Providence reminds them of their fault. L. It condemns the iniquities of the wicked. M. It produces a right consideration of the future, rendering the servants of God prudent, diligent, and active. N. It causes them to resign themselves to the wisdom and omnipotence of God, and, at the same time, makes them diligent in their calling.

10. Meditation continued. O. Though human life is beset with innumerable evils, the righteous, trusting to Divine Providence, feel perfectly secure.

11. The use of the foregoing meditation.

12. The second part of the chapter, disposing of two objections. First Objection, that Scripture represents God as changing his purpose, or repenting, and that, therefore, his Providence is not fixed. Answer to this first objection. Proof from Scripture that God cannot repent.

13. Why repentance attributed to God.

14. Second objection, that Scripture speaks of an annulment of the divine decrees. Objection answered. Answer confirmed by an example.

1 Summary of the doctrine of Divine Providence. A. It embraces the future and the past. B. It works by means, without means, and against means. C. Mankind, and particularly the Church, the object of special care. D. The mode of administration usually secret, but always just. This last point more fully considered.

Moreover, such is the proneness of the human mind to indulge in vain subtleties, that it becomes almost impossible for those who do not see the sound and proper use of this doctrine, to avoid entangling themselves in perplexing difficulties. It will, therefore, be proper here to advert to the end, which Scripture has in view in teaching that all things are divinely ordained. And it is to be observed, first, that the Providence of God is to be considered with reference both to the past and the future; and, secondly, that in overruling all things, it works at one time with means, at another without means, and at another against means. Lastly, the design of God is to show that He takes care of the whole human race, but is especially vigilant in governing the Church, which he favors with a closer inspection. Moreover, we must add, that although the paternal favor and beneficence, as well as the judicial severity of God, is often conspicuous in the whole course of his Providence, yet occasionally as the causes of events are concealed, the thought is apt to rise, that human affairs are whirled about by the blind impulse of Fortune, or our carnal nature inclines us to speak as if God were amusing himself by tossing men up and down like balls.

It is true, indeed, that if with sedate and quiet minds we were disposed to learn, the issue would at length make it manifest, that the counsel of God was in accordance with the highest reason, that his purpose was either to train his people to patience, correct their depraved affections, tame their wantonness, inure them to self-denial, and arouse them from torpor; or, on the other hand, to cast down the proud, defeat the craftiness of the ungodly, and frustrate all their schemes.

No matter how many causes may escape our notice, we must feel assured that they are deposited with him, and accordingly exclaim with David, "Many, O Lord my God, are thy wonderful works which thou hast done, and thy thoughts which are to us-ward: if I would declare and speak of them, they are more than can be numbered" (Psalm 40:5). For while our adversities ought always to remind us of our sins, that the punishment may incline us to repentance, we see, moreover, how Christ declares there is something more in the secret counsel of his Father than to chastise everyone as he deserves. For he says of the man who was born blind, "Neither has this man sinned, nor his parents: but that the works of God should be made manifest in him" (John 9:3).

Here, where calamity takes precedence even of birth, our carnal sense murmurs as if God were unmerciful in thus afflicting those who have not offended. But Christ declares that, provided we had eyes clear enough, we should perceive that in this spectacle the glory of his Father is brightly displayed. We must use modesty, not as it would be compelling God to render an account, but so revering his hidden Judgments as to account his will the best of all reasons. When the sky is overcast with dense clouds, and a violent tempest arises, the darkness, which is presented to our eye, and the thunder, which strikes our ears, and stupefies all our senses with terror, make us imagine that everything is thrown into confusion, though in the firmament itself all continues quiet and serene. In the same way, when the tumultuous aspect of human affairs unfits us for judging, we should still hold, that God, in the pure light of his justice and wisdom, keeps all these commotions in due subordination, and conducts them to their proper end.

And certainly in this matter many display monstrous infatuation, presuming to subject the works of God to their calculation, and discuss his secret counsels, as well as to pass a precipitate Judgment on things unknown, and that with greater license than on the doings of mortal men. What can be more preposterous than to show modesty toward our equals, and choose rather to suspend our Judgment than incur the blame of rashness, while we petulantly insult the hidden Judgments of God—Judgments, which becomes us to look up to and revere.

2 The profane denial that the world is governed by the secret counsel of God, refuted by passages of Scripture. Salutary counsel.

No man, therefore, will duly and usefully ponder on the Providence of God save he who recollects that he has to do with his own Maker, and the Maker of the world, and in the exercise of the humility which becomes him, manifests both fear and reverence. Hence, it is, that in the present day so many dogs tear this doctrine with envenomed teeth, or, at least, assail it with their bark, refusing to give more license to God than their own reason dictates to themselves. With what petulance, too, are we assailed for not being contented with the precepts of the Law, in which the will of God is comprehended, and for maintaining that his secret counsels govern the world? As if our doctrine were the figment of our own brain, and were not distinctly declared by the Spirit, and repeated in innumerable forms of expression! Since some feeling of shame restrains them from daring to belch forth their blasphemies against heaven, that they may give the freer vent to their rage, they pretend to pick a quarrel with us. But if they refuse to admit that the incomprehensible counsel of God governs every event, which happens in the world, let them explain to what effect Scripture declares, "his Judgments are a great deep" (Psalm 336:7). For when Moses exclaims that the will of God "is not in heaven that thou shouldest say, Who shall go up for us to heaven, and bring it unto us? Neither is it beyond the sea that thou shouldest say, Who shall go over the sea and bring it unto us?" (Deuteronomy 30:12, 13), because it was familiarly expounded in the law, it follows that there must be another hidden will which is compared to " a great deep."

It is of this will Paul exclaims, "O! the depths of the riches of the wisdom and knowledge of God! How unsearchable are his Judgments, and his ways past finding out! For who has known the mind of the Lord, or who has been his counselor?" (Romans 11:33, 34). It is true, indeed, that in the law and the gospel are comprehended mysteries which far transcend the measure of our sense; but since God, to enable his people to understand those mysteries which he has deigned to reveal in his word, enlightens their minds with a spirit of understanding, they are now no longer a deep, but a path in which they can walk safely—a lamp to guide their feet—a light of life—a school of clear and certain truth. But the admirable method of governing the world is justly called a deep, because, while it lies hid from us, it is to be reverently adored.

Both views Moses has beautifully expressed in a few words. "Secret things," saith he, "belong unto the Lord our God, but those things which are revealed belong unto us and to our children forever" (Deuteronomy 29:29). We see how he enjoins us not only studiously to meditate on the law, but also to look up with reverence to the secret Providence of God.

The Book of Job also, in order to keep our minds humble, contains a description of this lofty theme. The author of the Book, after taking an ample survey of the universe, and discoursing magnificently on the works of God, at length adds, "Lo, these are parts of his ways: but how little a portion is heard of him?" (Job 26:14). For which reason he, in another passage, distinguishes between the wisdom, which dwells in God, and the measure of wisdom, which he has assigned to man (Job 28:21, 28). After discoursing of the secrets of nature, he says that wisdom "is hid from the eyes of all living;" that "God understandeth the way thereof." Shortly after, he adds that it has been divulged that it might be investigated; for "unto man he said, Behold the fear of the Lord that is wisdom." To this the words of Augustine refer, "As we do not know all the things which God does respecting us in the best order, we ought, with good intention, to act according to the Law, and in some things be acted upon according to the Law, his Providence being a Law immutable."

Therefore, since God claims to himself the right of governing the world, a right unknown to us, let it be our law of modesty and soberness to acquiesce in his supreme authority regarding his will as our only rule of justice, and the most perfect cause of all things, —not that absolute will, indeed, of which sophists prate, when by a profane and impious divorce, they separate his justice from his power, but that universal overruling Providence from which nothing flows that is not right, though the reasons thereof may be concealed.

3 This doctrine, as to the secret counsel of God in the government of the world, gives no countenance either to the impiety of those who throw the blame of their wickedness upon God, the petulance of those who reject means, or the error of those who neglect the duties of religion.

Those who have learned this modesty will neither murmur against God for adversity in time past, nor charge him with the blame of their own wickedness, as Homer's Agamemnon does: "*Blame not me, but Jupiter and fate.*" On the other hand, they will note like the youth in Plautus, destroy themselves in despairs as if hurried away by the Fates. "Unstable is the condition of affairs; instead of doing as they list, men only fulfill their fate: I will hie me [*hurry to*] to a rock, and there end my fortune with my life." Nor will they, after the example of another, use the name of God as a cloak for their crimes. For in another comedy Lyconides thus expresses himself: —"God was the impeller: I believe the gods wished it. Did they not wish it, it would not be done, I know." They will rather inquire and learn from Scripture what is pleasing to God, and then, under the guidance of the Spirit, endeavor to attain it. Prepared to follow whithersoever God may call, they will show by their example that nothing is more useful than the knowledge of this doctrine, which perverse men undeservedly assail, because it is sometimes wickedly abused.

The profane make such bluster with their foolish puerilities, that they almost, according to the expression, confound heaven and earth. If the Lord has marked the moment of our death, it cannot be escaped, —it is vain to toil and use precaution. Therefore, when one ventures not to travel on a road which he hears is infested by robbers; when another calls in the physician, and annoys himself with drugs, for the sake of his health; a third abstains from coarser food, that he may not injure a sickly constitution; and a fourth fears to dwell in a ruinous house; when all, in short, devise, and, with great eagerness of mind, strike out paths by which they may attain the objects of their desire; either these are all vain remedies, laid hold of to correct the will of God, or his certain decree does not fix the limits of life and death, health and sickness, peace and war, and other matters which men, according as they desire and hate, study by their own industry to secure or avoid. Nay, these trifles even infer, that the prayers of the faithful must be perverse, not to say superfluous, since they entreat the Lord to make a provision for things, which he has decreed from eternity.

Then, imputing whatever happens to the Providence of God, they connive at the man who is known to have expressly designed it. Has an assassin slain an honest citizen? He has, say they, executed the counsel of God. Has some one committed theft or adultery? The deed having been provided and ordained by the Lord, he is the minister of his providence. Has a son waited with indifference for the death of his parent, without trying any remedy? He could not oppose God, who had so predetermined from eternity. Thus, all crimes receive the name of virtues, as being in accordance with divine ordination.

4 As regards future events, the doctrine of Divine Providence not inconsistent with deliberation on the part of man.

As regards future events, Solomon easily reconciles human deliberation with divine providence. For while he derides the stupidity of those who presume to undertake anything without God, as if they were not ruled by his hand, he elsewhere thus expresses himself: "A man's heart deviseth his ways but the Lord directeth his steps" (Proverbs 16:9); intimating, that the eternal decrees of God by no means prevent us from proceeding, under his will, to provide for ourselves, and arrange all our affairs. And the reason for this is clear. For he who has fixed the boundaries of our life, has at the same time entrusted us with the care of it, provided us with the means of preserving it, forewarned us of the dangers to which we are exposed, and supplied cautions and remedies, that we may not be overwhelmed unawares.

Now, our duty is clear, namely, since the Lord has committed to us the defense of our life, —to defend it; since he offers assistance, —to use it; since he forewarns us of danger, —not to rush on heedless; since he supplies remedies, —not to neglect them. But it is said, a danger that is not fatal will not hurt us, and one that is fatal cannot be resisted by any precaution. But what if dangers are not fatal, merely because the Lord has furnished you with the means of warding them off, and surmounting them?

See how far your reasoning accords with the order of divine procedure: You infer that danger is not to be guarded against, because, if it is not fatal, you shall escape without precaution, whereas the Lord enjoins you to guard against its just because he wills it not to be fatal. These insane cavilers overlook what is plainly before their eyes—viz. that the Lord has furnished men with the artful of deliberation and caution, that they may employ them in subservience to his providence, in the preservation of their life; while, on the contrary, by neglect and sloth, they bring upon themselves the evils which he has annexed to them. How comes it that a provident man, while he consults for his safety, disentangles himself from impending evils; while a foolish man, through unadvised temerity, perishes, unless it be that prudence and folly are, in either case, instruments of divine dispensation?

God has been pleased to conceal from us all future events that we may prepare for them as doubtful, and cease not to apply the provided remedies until they have either been overcome, or have proved too much for all our care. Hence, I formerly observed, that the Providence of God does not interpose simply; but, by employing means, assumes, as it would be, a visible form.

5 In regard to past events, it is absurd to argue that crimes ought not to be punished, because they are in accordance with the divine decrees. A. The wicked resist the declared will of God. B. They are condemned by conscience. C. The essence and guilt of the crime is in themselves, though God uses them as instruments.

By the same class of persons, past events are referred improperly and inconsiderately to simple providence. As all contingencies whatsoever depend on it, therefore, neither thefts nor adulteries, nor murders, are perpetrated without an interposition of the divine will. Why, then, they ask, should the thief be punished for robbing him whom the Lord chose to chastise with poverty? Why should the murderer be punished for slaying him whose life the Lord had terminated? If all such persons serve the will of God, why should they be punished? I deny that they serve the will of God. For we cannot say that he who is carried away by a wicked mind performs service on the order of God, when he is only following his own malignant desires. He obeys God, who, being instructed in his will, hastens in the direction in which God calls him.

But how are we so instructed unless by his word? The will declared by his word is, therefore, that which we must keep in view in acting, God requires of us nothing but what he enjoins. If we design anything contrary to his precept, it is not obedience, but contumacy and transgression. But if he did not will it, we could not do it. I admit this. But do we act wickedly for yielding obedience to him? This, assuredly, he does not command. Nay, rather we rush on, not thinking of what he wishes, but so inflamed by our own passionate lust, that, with destined purpose, we strive against him. And in this way, while acting wickedly, we serve his righteous ordination, since in his boundless wisdom he well knows how to use bad instruments for good purposes. And see how absurd this mode of arguing is. They will have it that crimes ought not to be punished in their authors, because they are not committed without the dispensation of God.

I concede more—that thieves and murderers, and other evildoers, are instruments of Divine Providence, being employed by the Lord himself to execute the Judgments, which he has resolved to inflict. But I deny that this forms any excuse for their misdeeds. For how? Will they implicate God in the same iniquity with themselves, or will they cloak their depravity by his righteousness? They cannot exculpate themselves, for their own conscience condemns them: they cannot charge God, since they perceive the whole wickedness in themselves, and nothing in Him save the legitimate use of their wickedness. But it is said he works by their means. And whence, I pray, the fetid odor of a dead body, which has been unconfined and putrefied by the sun's heat? All see that the rays of the sun excite it, but no man therefore says that the fetid odor is in them. In the same way, while the matter and guilt of wickedness belongs to the wicked man, why should it be thought that God contracts any impurity in using it at pleasure as his instrument? Have done, then, with that dog-like petulance which may, indeed, bay from a distance at the justice of God, but cannot reach it!

6 A holy meditation on Divine Providence. A. All events happen by the ordination of God. B. All things contribute to the advantage of the godly. C. The hearts of men and all their endeavors are in the hand of God. D. Providence watches for the safety of the righteous. E. God has a special care of his elect.

These calumnies, or rather frenzied dreams, will easily be dispelled by a pure and holy meditation on Divine Providence, meditation such as piety enjoins, that we may thence derive the best and sweetest fruit. The Christian, then, being most fully persuaded, that all things come to pass by the dispensation of God, and that nothing happens fortuitously, will always direct his eye to him as the principal cause of events, at the same time paying due regard to inferior causes in their own place. Next, he will have no doubt that a special providence is awake for his preservation, and will not suffer anything to happen that will not turn to his good and safety. But as its business is first with men and then with the other creatures, he will feel assured that the Providence of God reigns over both.

In regard to men, good as well as bad, he will acknowledge that their counsels, wishes, aims and faculties are so under his hand, that he has full power to turn them in whatever direction, and constrain them as often as he pleases. The fact that a special providence watches over the safety of believers is attested by a vast number of the clearest promises.

"Cast thy burden upon the Lord, and he shall sustain thee: he shall never suffer the righteous to be moved." "Casting all your care upon him: for he careth for you." "He that dwelleth in the secret place of the Most High shall abide under the shadow of the Almighty." "He that toucheth you, toucheth the apple of mine eye." "We have a strong city: salvation will God appoint for walls and bulwarks." "Can a woman forget her sucking child, that she should not have compassion on the son of her womb? Yea, they may forget, yet will I not forget thee."

Nay, the chief aim of the historical books of Scripture is to show that the Lord, as to prevent them even from dashing their foot against a stone, so carefully guards the ways of his saints. Therefore, as we a little ago justly exploded the opinion of those who feign a universal providence, which does not condescend to take special care of every creature, so it is of the highest moment that we should specially recognize this care towards ourselves. Hence, our Savior, after declaring that even a sparrow falls not to the ground without the will of his Father, immediately makes the application, that being more valuable than many sparrows, we ought to consider that God provides more carefully for us. He even extends this so far, as to assure us that the hairs of our head are all numbered. What more can we wish, if not even a hair of our head can fall, save in accordance with his will? I speak not merely of the human race in general. God having chosen the Church for his abode, there cannot be a doubt, that in governing it, he gives singular manifestations of his paternal care.

7 Meditation on Providence continued. F. God in various ways curbs and defeats the enemies of the Church. G. He overrules all creatures, even Satan himself, for the good of his people.

The servant of God being confirmed by these promises and examples, will add the passages which teach that all men are under his power, whether to conciliate their minds, or to curb their wickedness, and prevent it from doing harm. For it is the Lord who gives us favor, not only with those who wish us well, but also in the eyes of the Egyptians (Exodus 3:21), in various ways defeating the malice of our enemies. Sometimes he deprives them of all presence of mind, so that they cannot undertake anything soundly or soberly. In this ways he sends Satan to be a lie in the mouths of all the Prophets in order to deceive Ahab (1 Kings 22:22), by the counsel of the young men he so infatuates Rehoboam, that his folly deprives him of his kingdom (1 Kings 12:10, 15). Sometimes when he leaves them in possession of intellect, he so fills them with terror and dismays that they can neither will nor plan the execution of what they had designed. Sometimes, too, after permitting them to attempt what lust and rage suggested, he opportunely interrupts them in their career, and allows them not to conclude what they had begun. Thus, the counsel of Ahithophel, which would have been fatal to David, was defeated before its time (2 Samuel 17:7, 14). Thus, for the good and safety of his people, he overrules all the creatures, even the devil himself who, we see, durst not attempt anything against Job without his permission and command.

This knowledge is necessarily followed by gratitude in prosperity, patience in adversity and incredible security for the time to come. Everything, therefore, which turns out prosperous and according to his wish, the Christian will ascribe entirely to God, whether he has experienced his beneficence through the instrumentality of men, or been aided by inanimate creatures. For he will thus consider with himself: Certainly, it was the Lord that disposed the minds of these people in my favor, attaching them to me to make them the instruments of his kindness. In an abundant harvest he will think that it is the Lord who listens to the heaven, that the heaven may listen to the earth, and the earth herself to her own offspring; in other cases, he will have no doubt that he owes all his prosperity to the divine blessing, and, admonished by so many circumstances, will feel it impossible to be ungrateful.

8 Meditation on Providence continued. H. He trains the godly to patience and moderation. Examples. Joseph, Job, and David. I. He shakes off their lethargy, and urges them to repentance.

If anything adverse befalls him, he will forthwith raise his mind to God, whose hand is most effectual in impressing us with patience and placid moderation of mind. Had Joseph kept his thoughts fixed on the treachery of his brethren, he never could have resumed fraternal affection for them. But turning toward the Lord, he forgot the injury, and was so inclined to mildness and mercy, that he even voluntarily comforts his brethren, telling them, "Be not grieved nor angry with yourselves that ye sold me hither; for God did send me before you to preserve life." "As for you, ye thought evil against me; but God meant it unto good" (Genesis 45:5; 50:20).

Had Job turned to the Chaldees, by whom he was plundered, he should instantly have been fired with revenge, but recognizing the work of the Lord, he solaces himself with this most beautiful sentiment: "The Lord gave, and the Lord has taken away; blessed be the name of the Lord" (Job 1:21). So when David was assailed by Shimei with stones and curses, had he immediately fixed his eyes on the man, he would have urged his people to retaliate the injury; but perceiving that he acts not without an impulse from the Lord, he rather calms them. "So let him curse," says he, "because the Lord has said unto him, Curse David."

With the same bridle, he elsewhere curbs the excess of his grief, "I was dumb, I opened not my mouth, because thou didst it" (Psalm 39:9). If there is no more effectual remedy for anger and impatience, he assuredly has not made little progress who has learned so to meditate on Divine Providence, as to be able always to bring his mind to this, The Lord willed it, it must therefore be borne; not only because it is unlawful to strive with him, but because he wills nothing that is not just and befitting.

The whole comes to this. When unjustly assailed by men, overlooking their malice (which could only aggravate our grief, and whet our minds for vengeance), let us remember to ascend to God, and learn to hold it for certain, that whatever an enemy wickedly committed against us was permitted, and sent by his righteous dispensation.

Paul, in order to suppress our desire to retaliate injuries, wisely reminds us that we wrestle not with flesh and blood, but with our spiritual enemy the devil, that we may prepare for the contest (Ephesians 6:12). But to calm all the impulses of passion, the most useful consideration is, that God arms the devil, as well as all the wicked, for conflict, and sits as umpire, that he may exercise our patience. But if the disasters and miseries, which press us, happen without the agency of men, let us call to mind the doctrine of the Law (Deuteronomy 28:1), that all prosperity has its source in the blessing of God, that all adversity is his curse. And let us tremble at the dreadful denunciation, "And if ye will not be reformed by these things, but will walk contrary unto me; then will I also walk contrary unto you" (Leviticus 26:23,

24). These words condemn our torpor, when, according to our carnal sense, deeming that whatever happens in any way is fortuitous, we are neither animated by the kindness of God to worship him, nor by his scourge stimulated to repentance. And it is for this reason that Jeremiah (Lamentations 3:38), and Amos (Amos 3:6), expostulated bitterly with the Jews, for not believing that good as well as evil was produced by the command of God. To the same effect are the words in Isaiah, "I form the light and create darkness: I make peace and create evil. I the Lord do all these things" (Isaiah 45:7).

9 Meditation continued. J. The right use of inferior causes explained. K. When the godly become negligent or imprudent in the discharge of duty, Providence reminds them of their fault. L. It condemns the iniquities of the wicked. M. It produces a right consideration of the future, rendering the servants of God prudent, diligent, and active. N. It causes them to resign themselves to the wisdom and omnipotence of God, and, at the same time, makes them diligent in their calling.

At the same time, the Christian will not overlook inferior causes. For, while he regards those by whom he is benefited as ministers of the divine goodness, he will not, therefore, pass them by, as if their kindness deserved no gratitude, but feeling sincerely obliged to them, will willingly confess the obligation, and endeavor, according to his ability, to return it. In fine, in the blessings which he receives, he will revere and extol God as the principal author, but will also honor men as his ministers, and perceive, as is the truth, that by the will of God he is under obligation to those, by whose hand God has been pleased to show him kindness. If he sustains any loss through negligence or imprudence, he will, indeed, believe that it was the Lord's will, but at the same time, he will impute it to himself. If one for whom it was his duty to care, but whom he has treated with neglect, is carried off by disease, although aware that the person had reached a limit beyond which it was impossible to pass, he will not, therefore, extenuate his fault, but, as he had neglected to do his duty faithfully towards him, will feel as if he had perished by his guilty negligence. Far less where, in the case of theft or murder, fraud and preconceived malice have existed, will he palliate it under the pretext of Divine Providence, but in the same crime will distinctly recognize the justice of God, and the iniquity of man, as each is separately manifested. But in future events, especially, will he take account of such inferior causes. If he is not left destitute of human aid, which he can employ for his safety, he will set it down as a divine blessing; but he will not, therefore, be remiss in taking measures, or slow in employing the help of those whom he sees possessed of the means of assisting him.

Regarding all the aids, which the creatures can lend him, as hands offered him by the Lord, he will avail himself of them as the legitimate instruments of Divine Providence. And as he is uncertain what the result of any business in which he engages is to be (save that he knows, that in all things the Lord will provide for his good), he will zealously aim at what he deems for the best, so far as his abilities enable him. In adopting his measures, he will not be carried away by his own impressions, but will commit and resign himself to the wisdom of God, that under his guidance he may be led into the right path. However, his confidence in external aid will not be such that the presence of it will make him feel secure, the absence of it fill him with dismay, as if he were destitute. His mind will always be fixed on the Providence of God alone, and no consideration of present circumstances will be allowed to withdraw him from the steady contemplation of it.

Joab, while he acknowledges that the issue of the battle is entirely in the hand of God, does not therefore become inactive, but strenuously proceeds with what belongs to his proper calling, "Be of good courage," says he, "and let us play the men for our people, and for the cities of our God; and the Lord do that which seemeth him good" (2 Samuel 10:12). The same conviction keeping us free from rashness and false confidence, will stimulate us to constant prayer, while at the same time filling our minds with good hope, it will enable us to feel secure, and bid defiance to all the dangers by which we are surrounded.

10. Meditation continued. O. Though human life is beset with innumerable evils, the righteous, trusting to Divine Providence, feel perfectly secure.

Here, we are forcibly reminded of the inestimable felicity of a pious mind. Innumerable are the ills, which beset human life, and present death in as many different forms. Not to go beyond ourselves, since the body is a receptacle, nay the nurse, of a thousand diseases, a man cannot move without carrying along with him many forms of destruction. His life is in a manner interwoven with death. For what else can be said where heat and cold bring equal danger? Then, in whatever direction you turn, all surrounding objects not only may do harm, but also almost openly threaten and seem to present immediate death. Go on board a ship, you are but a plank's breadth from death. Mount a horse; the stumbling of a foot endangers your life. Walk along the streets, every tile upon the roofs is a source of danger. If a sharp instrument is in your own hand, or that of a friend, the possible harm is manifest. All the savage beasts you see are so many beings armed for your destruction. Even within a high walled garden, where everything ministers to delight, a serpent will sometimes lurk. Your house, constantly exposed to fire, threatens you with poverty by day, with destruction by night. Your fields, subject to hail, mildew, drought, and other injuries, denounce barrenness, and thereby famine. I say nothing of poison, treachery, robbery, some of which beset us at home. Others follow us abroad.

Amid these perils, must not man be very miserable, as one who, more dead than alive, with difficulty draws an anxious and feeble breath, just as if a drawn sword were constantly suspended over his neck? It may be said that these things happen seldom, at least not always, or to all, certainly never all at once. I admit it; but since we are reminded by the example of others, that they may also happen to us, and that our life is not an exception any more than theirs, it is impossible not to fear and dread as if they were to befall us. What can you imagine more grievous than such trepidation? Add that there is something like an insult to God when it is said, that man, the noblest of the creatures, stands exposed to every blind and random stroke of fortune. Here, however, we were only referring to the misery which man should feel, were he placed under the dominion of chance.

11 The use of the foregoing meditation.

But when once the light of Divine Providence has illumined the believer's soul, he is relieved and set free, not only from the extreme fear and anxiety, which formerly oppressed him, but also from all care. For as he justly shudders at the idea of chance, so he can confidently commit himself to God. This, I say, is his comfort, that his heavenly Father so embraces all things under his power—so governs them at will by his nod—so regulates them by his wisdom, that nothing takes place save according to his appointment; that received into his favor, and entrusted to the care of his angels neither fire, nor water, nor sword, can do him harm, except in so far as God their master is pleased to permit.

For thus sings the Psalm, "Surely he shall deliver thee from the snare of the fowler, and from the noisome pestilence. He shall cover thee with his feathers, and under his wings shalt thou trust; his truth shall be thy shield and buckler. Thou shalt not be afraid for the terror by night; nor for the arrow that flieth by day; nor for the pestilence that walketh in darkness; nor for the destruction that wasteth at noonday" etc. (Psalm 91:2-6). Hence, the exulting confidence of the saints, "The Lord is on my side; I will not fear: what can man do unto me? The Lord taketh my part with them that help me." "Though an host should encamp against me, my heart shall not fear." "Yea, though I walk through the valley of the shadow of death, I will fear no evil." (Psalm 118:6; 27:3; 23:4).

How comes it, I ask, that their confidence never fails, but just that while the world apparently revolves at random, they know that God is everywhere at work, and feel assured that his work will be their safety? When assailed by the devil and wicked men, if they were not confirmed by remembering and meditating on Providence, they should, of necessity, forthwith despair. But when they call to mind that the devil, and the whole train of the ungodly, are, in all directions, held in by the hand of God as with a bridle, so that they can neither conceive any mischief, nor plan what they have conceived, nor however much they may have planned, move a single finger to perpetrate, unless in so far as he permits, nay, unless in so far as he commands; that they are not only bound by his fetters, but are even forced to do him service, —when the godly think of all these things, they have ample sources of consolation.

For, as it belongs to the lord to arm the fury of such foes and turn and intend it at pleasure, so it is his also to determine the measure and the end, so as to prevent them from breaking loose and acting without discipline or restraint as they list. Supported by this conviction, Paul, who had said in one place that Satan hindered his journey (1 Thessalonians 2:18), in another resolves, with the permission of God, to undertake it (1 Corinthians 16:7).

If he had only said that Satan was the obstacle, he might have seemed to give him too much power, as if he were able even to overturn the counsels of God; but now, when he makes God the disposer, on whose permission all journeys depend, he shows, that however Satan may contrive, he can accomplish nothing except in so far as He pleases to give the word. For the same reason, David, considering the various turns which human life undergoes as it rolls, and in a manner whirls around, retakes himself to this asylum, "My times are in thy hand" (Psalm 31:15). He might have said the course of life or *time* in the singular number, but by *times* he meant to express, that no matter how unstable the condition of man may be, the unexpected changes, which are always taking place are under divine regulation.

Hence, Rezin and the king of Israel, after they had joined their forces for the destruction of Israel, and seemed torches, which had been kindled to destroy and consume the land, are termed by the prophet "smoking fire brands." They could only emit a little smoke (Isaiah 7:4). So Pharaoh, when he was an object of dread to all by his wealth and strength, and the multitude of his troops, is compared to the largest of beasts, while his troops are compared to fishes; and God declares that he will take both leader and army with his hooks, and drag them whither he pleases (Ezekiel 29:4).

In one word, not to dwell longer on this, give heed, and you will at once perceive that ignorance of Providence is the greatest of all miseries, and the knowledge of it the highest happiness.

12 The second part of the chapter, disposing of two objections. First Objection, that Scripture represents God as changing his purpose, or repenting, and that, therefore, his Providence is not fixed. Answer to this first objection. Proof from Scripture that God cannot repent.

On the Providence of God, in so far as conducive to the solid instruction and consolation of believers (for, as to satisfying the curiosity of foolish men, it is a thing which cannot be done, and ought not to be attempted), enough would have been said, did not a few passages remain which seem to insinuate, contrary to the view which we have expounded, that the counsel of God is not firm and stable, but varies with the changes of sublunary affairs.

First, in reference to the Providence of God, it is said that he repented of having made man (Genesis 6:6), and of having raised Saul to the kingdom (1 Samuel 15:11), and that he will repent of the evil which he had resolved to inflict on his people as soon as he shall have perceived some amendment in them (Jeremiah 18:8).

Secondly, his decrees are sometimes said to be annulled. He had by Jonah proclaimed to the Ninevites, "Yet forty days and Nineveh shall be overthrown," but, immediately on their repentance, he inclined to a more merciful sentence (Jonah 3:4-10). After he had, by the mouth of Isaiah, given Hezekiah intimation of his death, he was moved by his tears and prayers to defer it (Isaiah 38:15; 2 Kings 20:15). Hence, many argue that God has not fixed human affairs by an eternal decree, but according to the merits of each individual, and as he deems right and just, disposes of each single year, and day, and hour.

As to repentance, we must hold that it can no more exist in God than ignorance, or error, or impotence. If no man knowingly or willingly reduces himself to the necessity of repentance, we cannot attribute repentance to God without saying either that he knows not what is to happen, or that he cannot evade it, or that he rushes precipitately and inconsiderately into a resolution, and then forthwith regrets it. But so far is this from the meaning of the Holy Spirit that in the very mention of repentance, he declares that any feeling of regret does not influence God, and that he is not a man that he should repent. And it is to be observed, that, in the same chapter, both things are so conjoined, that a comparison of the passages admirably removes the appearance of contradiction.

When it is said that God repented of having made Saul king, the term *change* is used figuratively. Shortly after, it is added, "The Strength of Israel will not lie nor repent; for he is not a man, that he should repent" (1 Samuel 15:29). In these words, his immutability is plainly asserted without figure. Wherefore it is certain that, in administering human affairs, the ordination of God is perpetual and superior to everything like repentance. That there might be no doubt of his constancy, even his enemies are forced to bear testimony to it. For, Balaam, even against his will, behaved to break forth into this exclamation, "God is not a man, that he should lie; neither the son of man, that he should repent: has he said, and shall he not do it? Or has he spoken, and shall he not make it good?" (Numbers 23:19).

13 Why repentance attributed to God.

What then is meant by the term repentance? The very same that is meant by the other forms of expression, by which God is described to us humanly. Because our weakness cannot reach his height, any description, which we receive, of him must be lowered to our capacity in order to be intelligible. And the mode of lowering is to represent him not as he really is, but as we conceive of him. Though he is incapable of every feeling of perturbation, he declares that he is angry with the wicked. Wherefore, as when we hear that God is angry, we ought not to imagine that there is any emotion in him, but ought rather to consider the mode of speech accommodated to our sense, God appearing to us like one inflamed and irritated whenever he exercises Judgment, so we ought not to imagine anything more under the term repentance than a change of action, men being wont to testify their dissatisfaction by such a change. Hence, because every change whatever among men is intended as a correction of what displeases, and the correction proceeds from repentance, the same term applied to God simply means that his procedure is changed.

In the meantime, there is no inversion of his counsel or will, no change of his affection. What from eternity he had foreseen, approved, decreed, he prosecutes with unvarying uniformity, however sudden to the eye of man the variation may seem to be.

14. Second objection, that Scripture speaks of an annulment of the divine decrees. Objection answered. Answer confirmed by an example.

Nor does the Sacred History, while it relates that the destruction which had been proclaimed to the Ninevites was remitted, and the life of Hezekiah, after an intimation of death, prolonged, imply that the decrees of God were annulled. Those who think so labor under delusion as to the meaning of *threatening*, which, though they affirm simply, nevertheless contain in them a tacit condition dependent on the result. Why did the Lord send Jonah to the Ninevites to predict the overthrow of their city? Why did he by Isaiah give Hezekiah intimation of his death? He might have destroyed both them and him without a message to announce the disaster. He had something else in view than to give them a warning of death, which might let them see it at a distance before it came. It was because he did not wish them destroyed but reformed, and thereby saved from destruction. When Jonah prophesies that in forty days Nineveh will be overthrown, he does it in order to prevent the overthrow. When Hezekiah is forbidden to hope for longer life, it is that he may obtain longer life.

Who does not now see that, by threatening of this kind, God wished to arouse those to repentance whom he terrified, that they might escape the Judgment, which their sins deserved? If this is so, the very nature of the case obliges us to supply a tacit condition in a simple denunciation. This is even confirmed by analogous cases. The Lord rebuking King Abimelech for having carried off the wife of Abraham, uses these words: "Behold, thou art but a dead man, for the woman which thou hast taken; for she is a man's wife." But, after Abimelech's excuse, he thus speaks: "Restore the man his wife, for he is a prophet, and he shall pray for thee, and thou shalt live; and if thou restore her not, know thou that thou shalt surely die, thou and all that art thine" (Genesis 20:3, 7).

You see that, by the first announcement, he makes a deep impression on his mind, that he may render him eager to give satisfaction, and that by the second he clearly explains his will. Since the other passages may be similarly explained, you must not infer from them that the Lord derogated in any respect from his former counsel, because he recalled what he had promulgated. When, by denouncing punishment, he admonishes to repentance those whom he wishes to spare, he paves the way for his eternal decree, instead of varying it one whit either in will or in language. The only difference is, that he does not express, in so many syllables, what is easily understood. The words of Isaiah must remain true, "The Lord of hosts has purposed, and who shall disannul it? And his hand is stretched out, and who shall turn it back?" (Isaiah 14:27).

Chapter 18

THE INSTRUMENTALITY OF THE WICKED EMPLOYED BY GOD, WHILE HE CONTINUES FREE FROM EVERY TAINT.

This last chapter of the First Book consists of three parts: I. It having been said above that God bends all the reprobate, and even Satan himself, at his will, three objections are started. First, that this happens by the permission, not by the will of God. To this objection there is a twofold reply, the one, that angels and men, good and bad, do nothing but what is appointed by God; the second, that all movements are secretly directed to their end by the hidden inspiration of God, sections 1, 2. II. A second objection is that there are two contrary wills in God, if by a secret counsel he decrees what he openly prohibits by his law. This objection refuted, section 3. III. The third objection is, that God is made the author of all wickedness, when he is said not only to use the agency of the wicked, but also to govern their counsels and affections, and that therefore the wicked are unjustly punished. This objection refuted in the last section.

Sections

1. The carnal mind the source of the objections, which are raised against the Providence of God. A primary objection, making a distinction between the permission and the will of God, refuted. Angels and men, good and bad, do nothing but what has been decreed by God. This proved by examples.

2. All hidden movements directed to their end by the unseen but righteous instigation of God. Examples, with answers to objections.

3. These objections originate in a spirit of pride and blasphemy. Objection, that there must be two contrary wills in God, refuted. Why the one simple will of God seems to us as if it were manifold.

4. Objection, that God is the author of sin, refuted by examples. Augustine's answer and admonition.

1 The carnal mind the source of the objections, which are raised against the Providence of God. A primary objection, making a distinction between the *permission* and the *will* of God, refuted. Angels and men, good and bad, do nothing but what has been decreed by God. This proved by examples.

From other passages, in which God is said to draw or bend Satan himself, and all the reprobate, to his will, a more difficult question arises. For the carnal mind can scarcely comprehend how, when acting by their means, he contracts no taint from their impurity, nay, how, in a common operation, he is exempt from all guilt, and can justly condemn his own ministers. Hence, a distinction has been invented between *doing* and *permitting* because to many it seemed altogether inexplicable how Satan and all the wicked are so under the hand and authority of God, that he directs their malice to whatever end he pleases, and employs their iniquities to execute his Judgments. The modesty of those who are thus alarmed at the appearance of absurdity might perhaps be excused, did they not endeavor to vindicate the justice of God from every semblance of stigma by defending an untruth.

It seems absurd that man should be blinded by the will and command of God, and yet be forthwith punished for his blindness. Hence, recourse is had to the evasion that this is done only by the permission, and not by the will of God. He himself, however, openly declaring that he *does* this, repudiates the evasion. That men do nothing save at the secret instigation of God, and do not discuss and deliberate on anything but what he has previously decreed with himself and brings to pass by his secret direction, is proved by numberless clear passages of Scripture. What we formerly quoted from the Psalms, to the effect that he does whatever pleases him, certainly extends to all the actions of men.

If God is the arbiter of peace and war, as is there said, and that without any exception, who will venture to say that men are borne along at random with a blind impulse, while He is unconscious or quiescent? But the matter will be made clearer by special examples. From the first chapter of Job we learn that Satan appears in the presence of God to receive his orders, just as do the angels who obey spontaneously. The manner and the end are different, but still the fact is, that he cannot attempt anything without the will of God. But though afterwards his power to afflict the saint seems to be only a bare permission, yet as the sentiment is true, "The Lord gave, and the Lord has taken away; as it pleased the Lord, so it has been done," we infer that God was the author of that trial of which Satan and wicked robbers were merely the instruments. Satan's aim is to drive the saint to madness by despair. The Sabeans cruelly and wickedly make a sudden incursion to rob another of his goods. Job acknowledges that he was deprived of all his property, and brought to poverty, because such was the pleasure of God. Therefore, whatever men or Satan himself devise, God holds the helm, and makes all their efforts contribute to the execution of his Judgments. God wills that the perfidious Ahab should be deceived; the devil offers his agency for that purpose, and is sent with a definite command to be a lying spirit in the mouth of all the Prophets (2 Kings 22:20).

If the blinding and infatuation of Ahab is a Judgment from God, the fiction of bare permission is at an end; for it would be ridiculous for a judge only to permit, and not also to decree, what he wishes to be done at the very time that he commits the execution of it to his ministers. The Jews purposed to destroy Christ. Pilate and the soldiers indulged them in their fury; yet the disciples confess in solemn prayer that all the wicked did nothing but what the hand and counsel of God had decreed (Acts 4:28), just as Peter had previously said in his discourse, that Christ was delivered to death by the determinate counsel and foreknowledge of God (Acts 2:23); in other words, that God, to whom all things are known from the beginning, had determined what the Jews had executed. He repeats the same thing elsewhere, "Those things, which God before had showed by the mouth of all his Prophets, that Christ should suffer, he has so fulfilled" (Acts 4:18). Absalom, incestuously defiling his father's bed, perpetrates a detestable crime. God, however, declares that it was his work; for the words are, "Thou midst it secretly, but I will do this thing before all Israel, and before the sun."

The cruelties of the Chaldeans in Judea are declared by Jeremiah to be the work of God. For which reason, Nebuchadnezzar is called the servant of God. God frequently exclaims that by his hiss, by the clang of his trumpet, by his authority and command, the wicked are excited to war. He calls the Assyrian the rod of his anger, and the axe that he wields in his hand. The overthrow of the city and downfall of the temple, he calls his own work. David, not murmuring against God, but acknowledging him a just judge, confesses that the curses of Shimei are uttered by his orders. "The Lord," says he, "has bidden him curse." Often in sacred history, whatever happens is said to proceed from the Lord, as the revolt of the ten tribes, the death of Eli's sons, and very many others of a similar description. Those who have a tolerable acquaintance with the Scriptures see that, with a view to brevity, I am only producing a few out of many passages, from which it is perfectly clear that it is the merest trifling to substitute a bare permission for the Providence of God, as if he sat in a watch-tower waiting for fortuitous events, his Judgments meanwhile depending on the will of man.

2 All hidden movements directed to their end by the unseen but righteous instigation of God. Examples, with answers to objections.

With regard to secret movements, what Solomon says of the heart of a king, that it is turned hither and thither, as God sees meet, certainly applies to the whole human race, and has the same force as if he had said, that whatever we conceive in our minds is directed to its end by the secret inspiration of God. And certainly, did he not work internally in the minds of men, it could not have been properly said, that he takes away the lip from the true, and prudence from the aged—takes away the heart from the princes of the earth, that they wander through devious paths. To the same effect, we often read that men are intimidated when He fills their hearts with terror. Thus, David left the camp of Saul while none knew, because a sleep from God had fallen upon all. But nothing can be clearer than the many passages which declare, that he blinds the minds of men, and smites them with giddiness, intoxicates them with a spirit of stupor, renders them infatuated, and hardens their hearts. Even these expressions many would confine to permissions as if, by deserting the reprobate, he allowed them to be blinded by Satan. But since the Holy Spirit distinctly says, that the blindness and infatuation are inflicted by the just Judgment of God, the solution is altogether inadmissible. He is said to have hardened the heart of Pharaoh, to have hardened it yet more, and confirmed it. Some evade these forms of expression by a silly cavil, because Pharaoh is elsewhere said to have hardened his own heart, thus making his will the cause of hardening it; as if the two things did not perfectly agree with each other, though in different senses—viz. that man, though acted upon by God, at the same time also acts.

But I retort the objection on those who make it. If to harden means only bare permission, the contumacy will not properly belong to Pharaoh. Now, could anything be more feeble and insipid than to interpret as if Pharaoh had only allowed himself to be hardened? We may add, that Scripture cuts off all handle for such cavils: "I," saith the Lord, "will harden his heart" (Exodus 4:21). So also, Moses says of the inhabitants of the land of Canaan, that they went forth to battle because the Lord had hardened their hearts (Joshua 11:20). The same thing is repeated by another prophet, "He turned their hearts to hate his people" (Psalm 105:25). In like manner, in Isaiah, he says of the Assyrian, "I will send him against a hypocritical nation, and against the people of my wrath will I give him a charge to take the spoil, and to take the prey" (Isaiah 10:6); not that he intends to teach wicked and obstinate man to obey spontaneously, but because he bends them to execute his Judgments, just as if they carried their orders engraved on their minds. And hence, it appears that they are impelled by the sure appointment of God.

I admit, indeed, that God often acts in the reprobate by interposing the agency of Satan; but in such a manner, that Satan himself performs his part, just as he is impelled, and succeeds only in so far as he is permitted. The evil spirit that troubled Saul is said to be from the Lord (1 Samuel 16:14), to intimate that Saul's madness was a just punishment from God. Satan is also said to blind the minds of those who believe not (2 Corinthians 4:4). But how so, unless that a spirit of error is sent from God himself, making those who refuse to obey the truth to believe a lie? According to the former view, it is said, "If the prophet be deceived when he has spoken a thing, I the Lord have deceived that prophet" (Ezekiel 14:9). According to the latter view, he is said to have given men over to a reprobate mind (Romans 1:28), because he is the special author of his own just vengeance, whereas Satan is only his minister. But as in the Second Book (Chapter 4, sections 3, 4), in discussing the question of man's freedom, this subject will again be considered; the little that has now been said seems to be all that the occasion requires. The sum of the whole is this, —since the will of God is said to be the cause of all things, all the counsels and actions of men must be held to be governed by his providence; so that he not only exerts his power in the elect, who are guided by the Holy Spirit, but also forces the reprobate to do him service.

3 These objections originate in a spirit of pride and blasphemy. Objection, that there must be two contrary wills in God, refuted. Why the one simple will of God seems to us as if it were manifold.

As I have hitherto stated only what is plainly and unambiguously taught in Scripture, those who hesitate not to stigmatize what the sacred oracles thus teach, had better beware what kind of censure they employ. If, under a pretence of ignorance, they seek the praise of modesty, what greater arrogance can be imagined than to utter one word in opposition to the authority of God—to say, for instance, "I think otherwise,"—"I would not have this subject touched?" But if they openly blaspheme, what will they gain by assaulting heaven? Such petulance, indeed, is not new. In all ages, there have been wicked and profane men, who rabidly assailed this branch of doctrine. But what the Spirit declared of old by the mouth of David (Psalm 51:6), they will feel by experience to be true—God will overcome when he is judged. David indirectly rebukes the infatuation of those whose license is so unbridled, that from their groveling spot of earth they not only plead against God, but also arrogate to themselves the right of censuring him. At the same time, he briefly intimates that the blasphemies that they belch forth against heaven, instead of reaching God, only illustrate his justice, when the mists of their calumnies are dispersed. Even our faith, because founded on the sacred word of God, is superior to the whole world, and is able from its height to look down upon such mists.

Their first objection—that if nothing happens without the will of God, he must have two contrary wills, decreeing by a secret counsel what he has openly forbidden in his law—is easily disposed of. But before I reply to it, I would again remind my readers, that this cavil is directed not against me, but against the Holy Spirit, who certainly dictated this confession to that holy man Job, "The Lord gave, and the Lord has taken away," when, after being plundered by robbers, he acknowledges that their injustice and mischief was a just chastisement from God. And what says the Scripture elsewhere? The sons of Eli "hearkened not unto the voice of their father, because the Lord would slay them" (1 Samuel 2:25). Another prophet also exclaims, "Our God is in the heavens: he has done whatsoever he has pleased" (Psalm 115:3). I have already shown clearly enough that God is the author of all those things which, according to these objectors, happen only by his inactive permission. He testifies that he creates light and darkness, forms good and evil (Isaiah 45:7); that no evil happens which he has not done (Amos 3:6). Let them tell me whether God exercises his Judgments willingly or unwillingly.

As Moses teaches that he who is accidentally killed by the blow of an axe, is delivered by God into the hand of him who smites him (Deuteronomy 19:5), so the Gospel, by the mouth of Luke, declares, that Herod and Pontius Pilate conspired "to do whatsoever thy hand and thy counsel determined before to be done" (Acts 4:28). And, in truth, if Christ was not crucified by the will of God, where is our redemption? Still, however, the will of God is not at variance with itself. It undergoes no change. He makes no pretence of not willing what he wills, but while in himself the will is one and undivided, to us it appears manifold, because, from the feebleness of our intellect, we cannot comprehend how, though after a different manner, he wills and wills not the very same thing. Paul terms the calling of the Gentiles a hidden mystery, and shortly after adds that therein was manifested the manifold wisdom of God (Ephesians 3:10). Since, because of the dullness of our sense, the wisdom of God seems manifold (or, as an old interpreter rendered it, multiform), are we, therefore, to dream of some variation in God, as if he either changed his counsel, or disagreed with himself? Nay, when we cannot comprehend how God can will that to be done which he forbids us to do, let us call to mind our imbecility, and remember that the light in which he dwells is not without cause termed inaccessible (1 Timothy 6:16), because shrouded in darkness. Hence, all pious and modest men will readily acquiesce in the sentiment of Augustine: "Man sometimes with a good will wishes something which God does not will, as when a good son wishes his father to live, while God wills him to die.

Again, it may happen that man with a bad will wishes what God wills righteously, as when a bad son wishes his father to die, and God also wills it. The former wishes what God wills not, the latter wishes what God also wills. And yet the filial affection of the former is more consonant to the good will of God, though willing differently, than the unnatural affection of the latter, though willing the same thing; so much does approbation or condemnation depend on what it is befitting in man, and what in God to will, and to what end the will of each has respect. For the things, which God rightly wills, he accomplishes by the evil wills of bad men." He also said that the apostate angels, by their revolt, and all the reprobate, as far as they themselves were concerned, did what God willed not; but, in regard to his omnipotence, it was impossible for them to do so: for, while they act against the will of God, his will is accomplished in them. Hence, he exclaims, "Great is the work of God, exquisite in all he wills! So that, in a manner wondrous and ineffable, that is not done without his will which is done contrary to it, because it could not be done if he did not permit; nor does he permit it unwillingly, but willingly; nor would He who is good permit evil to be done, were he not omnipotent to bring good out of evil."

4 Objection, that God is the author of sin, refuted by examples. Augustine's answer and admonition.

In the same way is solved, or rather spontaneously vanishes, another objection—viz. If God not only uses the agency of the wicked, but also governs their counsels and affections, he is the author of all their sins; and, therefore, men, in executing what God has decreed, are unjustly condemned, because they are obeying his will. Here *will* is improperly confounded with *precept*, though it is obvious, from innumerable examples, that there is the greatest difference between them. When Absalom defiled his father's bed, though God was pleased thus to avenge the adultery of David, he did not therefore enjoin an abandoned son to commit incest, unless, perhaps, in respect of David, as David himself says of Shimei's curses. For, while he confesses that Shimei acts by the order of God, he by no means commends the obedience, as if that petulant dog had been yielding obedience to a divine command; but recognizing in his tongue the scourge of God, he submits patiently to be chastised. Thus, we must hold, that while by means of the wicked God performs what he had secretly decreed, they are not excusable as if they were obeying his precept, which of set purpose they violate according to their lust.

How these things, which men do perversely, are of God, and are ruled by his secret providence, is strikingly shown in the election of King Jeroboam (1 Kings 12:20), in which the rashness and infatuation of the people are severely condemned for perverting the order sanctioned by God, and perfidiously revolting from the family of David. And yet we know it was God's will that Jeroboam should be anointed. Hence, the apparent contradiction in the words of Hosea (Hosea 8:4; 13:11), because, while God complained that that kingdom was erected without his knowledge, and against his will, he elsewhere declares, that he had given King Jeroboam in his anger. How shall we reconcile the two things, —that Jeroboam's reign was not of God, and yet God appointed him king? In this way: The people could not revolt from the family of David without shaking off a yoke divinely imposed on them, and yet God himself was not deprived of the power of thus punishing the ingratitude of Solomon. We, therefore, see how God, while not willing treachery, with another view justly wills the revolt; and hence Jeroboam, by unexpectedly receiving the sacred unction, is urged to aspire to the kingdom. For this reason, the sacred history says, that God stirred up an enemy to deprive the son of Solomon of part of the kingdom (1 Kings 11:23).

Let the reader diligently ponder both points: how, as it was the will of God that the people should be ruled by the hand of one king, their being rent into two parties was contrary to his will; and yet how this same will originated the revolt. For certainly, when Jeroboam, who had no such thought, is urged by the prophet verbally, and by the oil of unction, to hope for the kingdom, the thing was not done without the knowledge or against the will of God, who had expressly commanded it; and yet the rebellion of the people is justly condemned, because it was against the will of God that they revolted from the posterity of David. For this reason, it is afterwards added, that when Rehoboam haughtily spurned the prayers of the people, "the cause was from the Lord, that he might perform his saying, which the Lord spoke by Ahijah" (1 Kings 12:15). See how sacred unity was violated against the will of God, while, at the same time, with his will the ten tribes were alienated from the son of Solomon. To this might be added another similar example—viz. the murder of the sons of Ahab, and the extermination of his whole progeny by the consent, or rather the active agency, of the people. Jehu says truly "There shall fall unto the earth nothing of the word of the Lord, which the Lord spoke concerning the house of Ahab: for the Lord has done that which he spoke by his servant Elijah" (2 Kings 10:10). And yet, with good reason, he upbraids the citizens of Samaria for having lent their assistance. "Ye be righteous: behold, I conspired against my master, and slew him, but who slew all these?"

If I mistake not, I have already shown clearly how the same act at once betrays the guilt of man, and manifests the righteousness of God. Modest minds will always be satisfied with Augustine's answer, "Since the Father delivered up the Son, Christ his own body, and Judas his Master, how in such a case is God just, and man guilty, but just because in the one act which they did, the reasons for which they did it are different?" If any are not perfectly satisfied with this explanation—viz. that there is no concurrence between God and man, when by His righteous impulse man does what he ought not to do, let them give heed to what Augustine elsewhere observes: "Who can refrain from trembling at those Judgments when God does according to his pleasure even in the hearts of the wicked, at the same time rendering to them according to their deeds?" And certainly, in regard to the treachery of Judas, there is just as little ground to throw the blame of the crime upon God, because He was both pleased that his Son should be delivered up to death, and did deliver him, as to ascribe to Judas the praise of our redemption. Hence, Augustine, in another place, truly observes, that when God makes his scrutiny, he looks not to what men could do, or to what they did, but to what they wished to do, thus taking account of their will and purpose. Those to whom this seems harsh had better consider how far their captiousness is entitled to any toleration, while, on the ground of its exceeding their capacity, they reject a matter which is clearly taught by Scripture, and complain of the enunciation of truths, which, if they were not useful to be known, God never would have ordered his Prophets and apostles to teach. Our true wisdom is to embrace with meek docility, and without reservation, whatever the Holy Scriptures, have delivered. Those who indulge their petulance, petulance manifestly directed against God, do not deserve a longer refutation.

End of Book First

Institutes of the Christian Religion

✠

Book Second

Book Second

OF THE KNOWLEDGE OF GOD, THE REDEEMER, IN CHRIST, AS FIRST MANIFESTED TO THE FATHERS, UNDER THE LAW, AND THEREAFTER TO US UNDER THE GOSPEL

ARGUMENT

The First Part of the Apostles' Creed—viz. the knowledge of God the Creator, being disposed of, we now come to the Second Part, which relates to the knowledge of God as a Redeemer in Christ. The subjects treated of accordingly are, *first*, the Occasion of Redemption—viz. Adam's fall; and, *secondly*, Redemption itself. The first five chapters are devoted to the former subject, and the remainder to the latter.

Under the Occasion of Redemption, the Fall is considered not only in a general way, but also specially in its effects. Hence, the first four chapters treat of original sin, free will, the corruption of human nature, and the operation of God in the heart. The fifth chapter contains a refutation of the arguments usually urged in support of free will.

The subject of redemption may be reduced to five particular heads:

I. The character of him in whom salvation for lost man must be sought, Chapter 6.

II. How he was manifested to the world, namely, in a twofold manner. First, under the Law. Here the Decalogue is expounded, and some other points relating to the law discussed, Chapters 7 and 8. Secondly, under the Gospel. Here the resemblance and difference of the two dispensations are considered, Chapters 9, 10, 11.

III. What kind of person Christ was, and behaved to be, in order to perform the office of Mediator—viz. God and man in one person, Chapters 12, 13, 14.

IV. For what end he was sent into the world by the Father. Here, Christ's prophetical, kingly, and priestly offices are considered, Chapter 15.

V. In what way, or by what successive steps, Christ fulfilled the office of our Redeemer, Chapter 16. Here are considered his crucifixion, death, burial, descent to hell, resurrection, ascension to heaven, and seat at the right hand of the Father, together with the practical use of the whole doctrine. Chapter 17 contains an answer to the question, Whether Christ is properly said to have merited the grace of God for us.

Chapter 1

THROUGH THE FALL AND REVOLT OF ADAM,
THE WHOLE HUMAN RACE MADE ACCURSED
AND DEGENERATE. OF ORIGINAL SIN.

I. How necessary the knowledge of ourselves is, its nature, the danger of mistake, its leading parts, sections 1, 2, 3. II. The causes of Adam's fearful fall, section 4. III. The effects of the fall extending to Adam's posterity, and all the creatures, section 5, to the end of the Chapter, where the nature, propagation, and effect of original sin are considered.

Sections

1. The knowledge of ourselves most necessary. To use it properly we must be divested of pride, and clothed with true humility, which will dispose us to consider our fall, and embrace the mercy of God in Christ.

2. Though there is plausibility in the sentiment, which stimulates us to self-admiration, the only sound sentiment is that which inclines us to true humbleness of mind. Pretexts for pride. The miserable vanity of sinful man.

3. Different views taken by carnal wisdom and by conscience, which appeals to divine justice as its standard. The knowledge of ourselves, consisting of two parts, the former of which having already been discussed, the latter is here considered.

4. In considering this latter part, two points to be considered. How it happened that Adam involved himself and the whole human race in this dreadful calamity. This the result not of sensual intemperance, but of infidelity (the source of other heinous sins), which led to revolt from God, from whom all true happiness must be derived. An enumeration of the other sins produced by the infidelity of the first man.

5. The second point to be considered is the extent to which the contagious influence of the fall extends. It extends A. To all the creatures, though unoffending; and, B. To the whole posterity of Adam. Hence, hereditary corruption, or original sin, and the depravation of a nature which was previously pure and good. This depravation communicated to the whole posterity of Adam, but not in the way supposed by the Pelagians and Celestians.

6. Depravation communicated not merely by imitation, but by propagation. This proved, A. From the contrast drawn between Adam and Christ. Confirmation from passages of Scripture; B. From the general declaration that we are the children of wrath.

7. Objection, that if Adam's sin is propagated to his posterity, the soul must be derived by transmission. Answer. Another objection—viz. that children cannot derive corruption from pious parents. Answer.

8. Definition of original sin. Two parts in the definition. Exposition of the latter part. Original sin exposes us to the wrath of God. It also produces in us the works of the flesh. Other definitions considered.

9. Exposition of the former part of the definition—viz. that hereditary depravity extends to all the faculties of the soul.

10. From the exposition of both parts of the definition, it follows that God is not the author of sin, the whole human race being corrupted by an inherent viciousness.

11. This, however, is not from nature, but is an adventitious quality. Accordingly, the dream of the Manichees as to two principles vanishes.

1 **The knowledge of ourselves most necessary. To use it properly we must be divested of pride, and clothed with true humility, which will dispose us to consider our fall, and embrace the mercy of God in Christ.**

It was not without reason that the ancient proverb so strongly recommended to man the knowledge of himself. For if it is deemed disgraceful to be ignorant of things pertaining to the business of life, much more disgraceful is self-ignorance, in consequence of which we miserably deceive ourselves in matters of the highest moment, and so walk blindfold. But the more useful the precept is, the more careful we must be not to use it preposterously, as we see certain philosophers have done. For they, when exhorting man to know himself, state the motive to be, that he may not be ignorant of his own excellence and dignity. They wish him to see nothing in himself but what will fill him with vain confidence, and inflate him with pride.

But self-knowledge consists in this, *first*, When reflecting on what God gave us at our creation, and still continues graciously to give, we perceive how great the excellence of our nature would have been had its integrity remained, and, at the same time, remember that we have nothing of our own, but depend entirely on God, from whom we hold at pleasure whatever he has seen it meet to bestow; *secondly*, When viewing our miserable condition since Adam's fall, all confidence and boasting are overthrown, we blush for shame, and feel truly humble.

For as God at first formed us in his own image, that he might elevate our minds to the pursuit of virtue, and the contemplation of eternal life, so to prevent us from heartlessly burying those noble qualities which distinguish us from the lower animals, it is of importance to know that we were endued with reason and intelligence, in order that we might cultivate a holy and honorable life, and regard a blessed immortality as our destined aim. At the same time, it is impossible to think of our primeval dignity without being immediately reminded of the sad spectacle of our ignominy and corruption, ever since we fell from our original in the person of our first parent. In this way, we feel dissatisfied with ourselves, and become truly humble, while we are inflamed with new desires to seek after God, in whom each may regain those good qualities of which all are found to be utterly destitute.

2 Though there is plausibility in the sentiment, which stimulates us to self-admiration, the only sound sentiment is that which inclines us to true humbleness of mind. Pretexts for pride. The miserable vanity of sinful man.

In examining ourselves, the search which divine truth enjoins, and the knowledge which it demands, are such as may indispose us to everything like confidence in our own powers, leave us devoid of all means of boasting, and so incline us to submission. This is the course that we must follow if we would attain to the true goal, both in speculation and practice. I am aware how much more plausible the view is, which invites us rather to ponder on our good qualities, than to contemplate what must overwhelm us with shame—our miserable destitution and ignominy.

There is nothing more acceptable to the human mind than flattery, and, accordingly, when told that its endowments are of a high order, it is apt to be excessively credulous. Hence, it is not strange that the greater part of mankind has erred so egregiously in this matter. Owing to the innate self-love by which all are blinded, we most willingly persuade ourselves that we do not possess a single quality which is deserving of hatred; and hence, independent of any countenance from without, general credit is given to the very foolish idea, that man is perfectly sufficient of himself for all the purposes of a good and happy life. If any are disposed to think more modestly, and concede somewhat to God, that they may not seem to arrogate everything as their own, still, in making the division, they apportion matters so, that the chief ground of confidence and boasting always remains with themselves. Then, if a discourse is pronounced which flatters the pride spontaneously springing up in man's inmost heart, nothing seems more delightful. Accordingly, in every age, he, who is most forward in extolling the excellence of human nature, is received with the loudest applause. But be this heralding of human excellence what it may, by teaching man to rest in himself, it does nothing more than fascinate by its sweetness, and, at the same time, so delude as to drown in perdition all who assent to it.

For what avails it to proceed in vain confidence, to deliberate, resolve, plan, and attempt what we deem pertinent to the purpose, and, at the very outset, prove deficient and destitute both of sound intelligence and true virtue, though we still confidently persist until we rush headlong on destruction? But this is the best that can happen to those who put confidence in their own powers. Whosoever, therefore, gives heed to those teachers, who merely employ us in contemplating our good qualities, so far from making progress in self-knowledge, will be plunged into the most pernicious ignorance.

3 Different views taken by carnal wisdom and by conscience, which appeals to divine justice as its standard. The knowledge of ourselves, consisting of two parts, the former of which having already been discussed, the latter is here considered.

While revealed truth concurs with the general consent of mankind in teaching that the second part of wisdom consists in self-knowledge, they differ greatly as to the method by which this knowledge is to be acquired. In the judgment of the flesh man deems his self-knowledge complete, when, with overweening confidence in his own intelligence and integrity, he takes courage, and spurs himself on to virtuous deeds, and when, declaring war upon vice, he uses his utmost endeavor to attain to the honorable and the fair. But he who tries himself by the standard of divine justice, finds nothing to inspire him with confidence; and hence, the more thorough his self-examination, the greater his despondency. Abandoning all dependence on himself, he feels that he is utterly incapable of duly regulating his conduct.

It is not the will of God, however, that we should forget the primeval dignity which he bestowed on our first parents—a dignity which may well stimulate us to the pursuit of goodness and justice. It is impossible for us to think of our first original, or the end for which we were created, without being urged to meditate on immortality, and to seek the kingdom of God. But such meditation, so far from raising our spirits, rather casts them down, and makes us humble. For what is our original? One from which we have fallen. What the end of our creation? One from which we have altogether strayed, so that, weary of our miserable lot, we groan, and groaning sigh for a dignity now lost. When we say that man should see nothing in himself, which can raise his spirits, our meaning is that he possesses nothing on which he can proudly plume himself.

Hence, in considering the knowledge which man ought to have of himself, it seems proper to divide it thus, *first*, to consider the end for which he was created, and the qualities—by no means contemptible qualities—with which he was endued, thus urging him to meditate on divine worship and the future life; and, *secondly*, to consider his faculties, or rather want of faculties—a want which, when perceived, will annihilate all his confidence, and cover him with confusion. The tendency of the former view is to teach him what his duty is, of the latter, to make him aware how far he is able to perform it. We shall treat of both in their proper order.

4 **In considering this latter part, two points to be considered. How it happened that Adam involved himself and the whole human race in this dreadful calamity. This the result not of sensual intemperance, but of infidelity (the source of other heinous sins), which led to revolt from God, from whom all true happiness must be derived. An enumeration of the other sins produced by the infidelity of the first man.**

As the act which God punished so severely must have been not a trivial fault, but a heinous crime, it will be necessary to attend to the peculiar nature of the sin which produced Adam's fall, and provoked God to inflict such fearful vengeance on the whole human race. The common idea of sensual intemperance is childish. The sum and substance of all virtues could not consist in abstinence from a single fruit amid a general abundance of every delicacy that could be desired, the earth, with happy fertility, yielding not only abundance, but also endless variety. We must, therefore, look deeper than sensual intemperance. The prohibition to touch the tree of the knowledge of good and evil was a trial of obedience, that Adam, by observing it, might prove his willing submission to the command of God. For the very term shows the end of the precept to have been to keep him contented with his lot, and not allow him arrogantly to aspire beyond it. The promise, which gave him hope of eternal life as long as he should eat of the tree of life, and, on the other hand, the fearful denunciation of death the moment he should taste of the tree of the knowledge of good and evil, were meant to prove and exercise his faith. Hence, it is not difficult to infer in what way Adam provoked the wrath of God.

Augustine, indeed, is not far from the mark, when he says (Psalm 19), that pride was the beginning of all evil, because, had not man's ambition carried him higher than he was permitted, he might have continued in his first estate. A further definition, however, must be derived from the kind of temptation, which Moses describes. When, by the subtlety of the devil, the woman faithlessly abandoned the command of God, her fall obviously had its origin in disobedience. This Paul confirms, when he says, that, by the disobedience of one man, all were destroyed. At the same time, it is to be observed, that the first man revolted against the authority of God, not only in allowing himself to be ensnared by the wiles of the devil, but also by despising the truth, and turning aside to lies. Assuredly, when the word of God is despised, all reverence for Him is gone. His majesty can neither be duly honored among us nor his worship maintained in its integrity unless we hang upon his lips. Hence, infidelity was at the root of the revolt. From infidelity again sprang ambition and pride, together with ingratitude, because Adam, by longing for more than was allotted him, manifested contempt for the great liberality with which God had enriched him. It was surely monstrous impiety that a son of earth should deem it little to have been made in the likeness, unless he were also made the equal of God.

If the apostasy by which man withdraws from the authority of his Maker, nay, petulantly shakes off his allegiance to him, is a foul and execrable crime, it is in vain to extenuate the sin of Adam. Nor was it simple apostasy. It was accompanied with foul insult to God, the guilty pair assenting to Satan's calumnies when he charged God with malice, envy, and falsehood. In fine, infidelity opened the door to ambition, and ambition was the parent of rebellion, man casting off the fear of God, and giving free vent to his lust. Hence, Bernard truly says, that, in the present day, a door of salvation is opened to us when we receive the Gospel with our ears, just as by the same entrance, when thrown open to Satan, death was admitted. Never would Adam have dared to show any repugnance to the command of God if he had not been incredulous as to his word. The strongest curb to keep all his affections under due restraint, would have been the belief that nothing was better than to cultivate righteousness by obeying the commands of God, and that the highest possible felicity was to be loved by him. Man, therefore, when carried away by the blasphemies of Satan, did his very utmost to annihilate the whole glory of God.

5 The second point to be considered is the extent to which the contagious influence of the fall extends. It extends A. To all the creatures, though unoffending; and, B. To the whole posterity of Adam. Hence, hereditary corruption, or original sin, and the depravation of a nature which was previously pure and good. This depravation communicated to the whole posterity of Adam, but not in the way supposed by the Pelagians and Celestians.

As Adam's spiritual life would have consisted in remaining united and bound to his Maker, so estrangement from him was the death of his soul. Nor is it strange that he who perverted the whole order of nature in heaven and earth deteriorated his race by his revolt. "The whole creation groaned," saith St. Paul, "being made subject to vanity, not willingly" (Romans 8:20, 22). If the reason is asked, there cannot be a doubt that creation bears part of the punishment deserved by man, for whose use all other creatures were made. Therefore, since through man's fault a curse has extended above and below, over all the regions of the world, there is nothing unreasonable in its extending to all his offspring. After the heavenly image in man was effaced, he not only was himself punished by a withdrawal of the ornaments in which he had been arrayed—viz. wisdom, virtue, justice, truth, and holiness, and by the substitution in their place of those dire pests, blindness, impotence, vanity, impurity, and unrighteousness, but he involved his posterity also, and plunged them in the same wretchedness. This is the hereditary corruption to which early Christian writers gave the name of Original Sin, meaning by the term the depravation of a nature formerly good and pure. The subject gave rise to much discussion, there being nothing more remote from common apprehension, than that the fault of one should render all guilty, and so become a common sin. This seems to be the reason that the oldest doctors of the church only glance obscurely at the point, or, at least, do not explain it so clearly as it required. This timidity, however, could not prevent the rise of a Pelagius with his profane fiction—that Adam sinned only to his own hurt, but did no hurt to his posterity.

Satan, by thus craftily hiding the disease, tried to render it incurable. But when it was clearly proved from Scripture that the sin of the first man passed to all his posterity, recourse was had to the trivial objection: that it passed by imitation and not by propagation. The orthodoxy, therefore, and more especially Augustine, labored to show, that we are not corrupted by acquired wickedness, but bring an innate corruption from the very womb. It was the greatest impudence to deny this. But no man will wonder at the presumption of the Pelagians and Celestians, who has learned from the writings of that holy man how extreme the effrontery of these heretics was.

Surely there is no ambiguity in David's confession, "I was shapen in iniquity; and in sin did my mother conceive me" (Psalm 51:5). His object in the passage is not to throw blame on his parents; but the better to commend the goodness of God towards him; he properly reiterates the confession of impurity from his very birth. As it is clear, that there was no peculiarity in David's case, it follows that it is only an instance of the common lot of the whole human race. All of us, therefore, descending from an impure seed, come into the world tainted with the contagion of sin. Nay, before we behold the light of the sun we are in God's sight defiled and polluted. "Who can bring a clean thing out of an unclean? Not one," says the Book of Job (Job 14:4).

6 Depravation communicated not merely by imitation, but by propagation. This proved, A. From the contrast drawn between Adam and Christ. Confirmation from passages of Scripture; B. From the general declaration that we are the children of wrath.

We thus see that the impurity of parents is transmitted to their children, so that all, without exception, are originally depraved. The commencement of this depravity will not be found until we ascend to the first parent of all as the fountainhead. We must, therefore, hold it for certain, that, in regard to human nature, Adam was not merely a progenitor, but a root, and that, accordingly, by his corruption, the whole human race was deservedly vitiated. This is plain from the contrast which the Apostle draws between Adam and Christ, "Wherefore, as by one man sin entered into the world, and death by sin; and so death passed upon all men, for that all have sinned; even so might grace reign through righteousness unto eternal life by Jesus Christ our Lord" (Romans 5:19-21).

To what quibble will the Pelagians here recur? That the sin of Adam was propagated by imitation! Is the righteousness of Christ then available to us only in so far as it is an example held forth for our imitation? Can any man tolerate such blasphemy? But if, out of all controversy, the righteousness of Christ, and thereby life, is ours by communication, it follows that both of these were lost in Adam that they might be recovered in Christ, whereas sin and death were brought in by Adam, that they might be abolished in Christ.

There is no obscurity in the words, "As by one man's disobedience many were made sinners, so by the obedience of one shall many be made righteous." Accordingly, the relation subsisting between the two is this: As Adam, by his ruin, involved and ruined us, so Christ, by his grace, restored us to salvation. In this clear light of truth, I cannot see any need of a longer or more laborious proof. Thus, too, in the First Epistle to the Corinthians, when Paul would confirm believers in the confident hope of the resurrection, he shows that the life is recovered in Christ, which was lost in Adam (1 Corinthians 15:22). Having already declared that all died in Adam, he now also openly testifies, that all are imbued with the taint of sin. Condemnation, indeed, could not reach those who are altogether free from blame. But his meaning cannot be made clearer than from the other member of the sentence, in which he shows that the hope of life is restored in Christ. Everyone knows that the only mode in which this is done is, when by a wondrous communication Christ transfuses into us the power of his own righteousness, as it is elsewhere said, "The Spirit is life because of righteousness" (1 Corinthians 15:22). Therefore, the only explanation which can be given of the expression, "in Adam all died," is, that he by sinning not only brought disaster and ruin upon himself, but also plunged our nature into like destruction; and that not only in one fault, in a matter not pertaining to us, but by the corruption into which he himself fell, he infected his whole seed.

Paul never could have said that all are "by nature the children of wrath" (Ephesians 2:3), if they had not been cursed from the womb. And it is obvious that the nature there referred to is not nature such as God created, but as vitiated in Adam; for it would have been most incongruous to make God the author of death. Adam, therefore, when he corrupted himself, transmitted the contagion to all his posterity. For a heavenly Judge, even our Savior himself, declares that all are by birth vicious and depraved, when he says that "that which is born of the flesh is fleshy" (John 3:6), and that therefore the gate of life is closed against all until they have been regenerated.

7 Objection, that if Adam's sin is propagated to his posterity, the soul must be derived by transmission. Answer. Another objection—viz. that children cannot derive corruption from pious parents. Answer.

To the understanding of this subject, there is no necessity for an anxious discussion (which in no small degree perplexed the ancient doctors), as to whether the soul of the child comes by transmission from the soul of the parent. It should be enough for us to know that Adam was made the depository of the endowments, which God was pleased to bestow on human nature, and that, therefore, when he lost what he had received, he lost not only for himself but also for us all. Why feel any anxiety about the transmission of the soul, when we know that the qualities, which Adam lost, he received for us not less than for himself, that they were not gifts to a single man, but attributes of the whole human race? There is nothing absurd, therefore, in the view, that when he was divested, his nature was left naked and destitute that he having been defiled by sin, the pollution extends to all his seed. Thus, from a corrupt root corrupt branches proceeding, transmit their corruption to the saplings, which spring from them. The children, being damaged and degraded in their parents, conveyed the taint to the grandchildren; in other words, corruption commencing in Adam, is, by perpetual descent, conveyed from those preceding to those coming after them. The cause of the contagion is neither in the substance of the flesh nor the soul, but God was pleased to ordain that those gifts which he had bestowed on the first man, that man should lose as well for his descendants as for himself.

The Pelagian quibble regarding the improbability of children deriving corruption from pious parents, whereas, they ought rather to be sanctified by their purity, is easily refuted. Children come not by spiritual regeneration but carnal descent. Accordingly, as Augustine says, "Both the condemned unbeliever and the acquitted believer beget offspring not acquitted but condemned, because the nature which begets is corrupt." Moreover, though godly parents do in some measure contribute to the holiness of their offspring, this is by the blessing of God; a blessing, however, which does not prevent the primary and universal curse of the whole race from previously taking effect. Guilt is from nature, whereas sanctification is from supernatural grace.

8 Definition of original sin. Two parts in the definition. Exposition of the latter part. Original sin exposes us to the wrath of God. It also produces in us the works of the flesh. Other definitions considered.

But lest the thing itself of which we speak be unknown or doubtful, it will be proper to define original sin. I have no intention, however, to discuss all the definitions that different writers have adopted, but only to adduce the one that seems to me most accordant with truth. Original sin, then, may be defined a hereditary corruption and depravity of our nature, extending to all the parts of the soul, which first makes us obnoxious to the wrath of God, and then produces in us works which in Scripture are termed works of the flesh. This corruption is repeatedly designated by Paul by the term sin (Galatians 5:19); while the works which proceed from it, such as adultery, fornication, theft, hatred, murder, reveling, he terms, in the same way, the fruits of sin, though in various passages of Scripture, and even by Paul himself, they are also termed sins.

The two things, therefore, are to be distinctly observed—viz. that being thus perverted and corrupted in all the parts of our nature, we are, merely on account of such corruption, deservedly condemned by God, to whom nothing is acceptable but righteousness, innocence, and purity. This is not liability for another's fault. For when it is said, that the sin of Adam has made us obnoxious to the justice of God, the meaning is not, that we, who are in ourselves innocent and blameless, are bearing his guilt, but that since by his transgression we are all placed under the curse, he is said to have brought us under obligation. Through him, however, not only has punishment been derived, but also pollution instilled, for which punishment is justly due.

Hence, Augustine, though he often terms it another's sin (that he may more clearly show how it comes to us by descent), at the same time asserts that it is each individual's own sin. And the Apostle most distinctly testifies, "death passed upon all men, for that all have sinned" (Romans 5:12); that is, are involved in original sin, and polluted by its stain. Hence, even infants bringing their condemnation with them from their mother's womb, suffer not for another's, but for their own defect. For although they have not yet produced the fruits of their own unrighteousness, they have the seed implanted in them. Nay, their whole nature is a seedbed of sin, and therefore cannot but be odious and abominable to God. Hence, it follows, that it is properly deemed sinful in the sight of God, for there could be no condemnation without guilt. Next comes the other point—viz. that this perversity in us never ceases, but constantly produces new fruits, in other words, those works of the flesh which we formerly described; just as a lighted furnace sends forth sparks and flames, or a fountain without ceasing pours out water.

Hence, those who have defined original sin as the want of the original righteousness that we ought to have had, though they substantially comprehend the whole case, do not significantly enough express its power and energy. For our nature is not only utterly devoid of goodness, but so prolific in all kinds of evil, that it can never be idle. Those who term it *concupiscence* use a word not very inappropriate, provided it would be added (this, however, many will by no means concede), that everything which is in man, from the intellect to the will, from the soul even to the flesh, is defiled and pervaded with this concupiscence; or, to express it more briefly, that the whole man is in himself nothing else than concupiscence.

9 Exposition of the former part of the definition—viz. that hereditary depravity extends to all the faculties of the soul.

I have said, therefore, that all the parts of the soul were possessed by sin, ever since Adam revolted from the fountain of righteousness. For not only did the inferior appetites entice him, but abominable impiety seized upon the very citadel of the mind, and pride penetrated to his inmost heart (Romans 7:12; Book 4, chapter 15, section 10–12), so that it is foolish and unmeaning to confine the corruption thence proceeding to what are called sensual motions, or to call it an excitement, which allures, excites, and drags the single part which they call sensuality into sin.

Here Peter Lombard has displayed gross ignorance. When investigating the seat of corruption, he says it is in the flesh (as Paul declares), not properly, indeed, but as being more apparent in the flesh, as if Paul had meant that only a part of the soul, and not the whole nature, was opposed to supernatural grace. Paul himself leaves no room for doubt, when he says, that corruption does not dwell in one part only, but that no part is free from its deadly taint. For, speaking of corrupt nature, he not only condemns the inordinate nature of the appetites, but also, in particular, declares that the understanding is subjected to blindness, and the heart to depravity (Ephesians 4:17, 18). The third chapter of the Epistle to the Romans is nothing but a description of original sin; the same thing appears more clearly from the mode of renovation. For the spirit, which is contrasted with the old man, and the flesh, denotes not only the grace by which the sensual or inferior part of the soul is corrected, but includes a complete reformation of all its parts (Ephesians 4:23). And, accordingly, Paul enjoins not only that gross appetites be suppressed, but also that we be renewed in the spirit of our mind (Ephesians 4:23), as he elsewhere tells us to be transformed by the renewing of our mind (Romans 12:2).

Hence, it follows, that that part in which the dignity and excellence of the soul are most conspicuous, has not only been wounded, but also so corrupted, that mere cure is not sufficient. There must be a new nature. How far sin has seized both on the mind and heart, we shall shortly see.

Here I only wished briefly to observe, that the whole man, from the crown of the head to the sole of the foot, is so deluged that no part remains exempt from sin, and, therefore, everything that proceeds from him is imputed as sin. Thus, Paul says, that all carnal thoughts and affections are enmity against God, and consequently death (Romans 8:7).

10 From the exposition of both parts of the definition, it follows that God is not the author of sin, the whole human race being corrupted by an inherent viciousness.

Let us have done, then, with those who dare to inscribe the name of God on their vices, because we say that men are born vicious. The divine workmanship, which they ought to look for in the nature of Adam, when still entire and uncorrupted, they absurdly expect to find in their depravity. The blame of our ruin rests with our own carnality, not with God, its only cause being our degeneracy from our original condition. And let no one here glamour that God might have provided better for our safety by preventing Adam's fall. This objection, which, from the daring presumption implied in it, is odious to every pious mind, relates to the mystery of predestination, which will afterwards be considered in its own place. Meanwhile let us remember that our ruin is attributable to our own depravity, that we may not insinuate a charge against God himself, the Author of nature. It is true that nature has received a mortal wound, but there is a great difference between a wound inflicted from without, and one inherent in our first condition. It is plain that this wound was inflicted by sin; and, therefore, we have no ground of complaint except against ourselves. This is carefully taught in Scripture. For the Preacher says, "Lo, this only have I found, that God made man upright; but they have sought out many inventions" (Ecclesiastes 7:29). Since man, by the kindness of God, was made upright, but by his own infatuation fell away unto vanity, his destruction is obviously attributable only to himself.

11 This, however, is not from nature, but is an adventitious quality. Accordingly, the dream of the Manichees as to two principles vanishes.

We say, then, that man is corrupted by a natural viciousness, but not by one that proceeded from nature. In saying that it proceeded not from nature, we mean that it was more an adventitious event that befell man, than a substantial property assigned to him from the beginning. We, however call it *natural* to prevent anyone from supposing that each individual contracts it by depraved habit, whereas all receive it by a hereditary law. And we have authority for so calling it. For, on the same grounds the apostle says, that we are "by nature the children of wrath" (Ephesians 2:3). How could God, who takes pleasure in the meanest of his works, be offended with the noblest of them all? The offense is not with the work itself, but the corruption of the work. Wherefore, if it is not improper to say, that, in consequence of the corruption of human nature, man is naturally hateful to God, it is not improper to say, that he is naturally vicious and depraved. Hence, in the view of our corrupt nature, Augustine hesitates not to call those sins natural that necessarily reign in the flesh wherever the grace of God is wanting. This disposes of the absurd notion of the Manichees, who, imagining that man was essentially wicked, went the length of assigning him a different Creator, that they might thus avoid the appearance of attributing the cause and origin of evil to a righteous God.

Chapter 2

MAN NOW DEPRIVED OF FREEDOM OF WILL, AND MISERABLY ENSLAVED

Having in the first chapter treated of the fall of man, and the corruption of the human race, it becomes necessary to inquire, Whether the sons of Adam are deprived of all liberty; and if any particle of liberty remains, how far its power extends? The four next chapters are devoted to this question. This second chapter may be reduced to three general heads: I. The foundation of the whole discussion. II. The opinions of others on the subject of human freedom, sections 2–9. III. The true doctrine on the subject, sections 10–27.

Sections

1. Connection of the previous with the four following chapters. In order to lay a proper foundation for the discussion of free will, two obstacles in the way to be removed—viz. sloth and pride. The basis and sum of the whole discussion. The solid structure of this basis, and a clear demonstration of it by the argument a majori ad minus. Also from the inconveniences and absurdities arising from the obstacle of pride.

2. The second part of the chapter containing the opinions of others. The opinions of philosophers.

3. The labyrinths of philosophers. A summary of the opinion common to all the philosophers.

4. The opinions of others continued—viz. The opinions of the ancient theologians on the subject of free will. These composed partly of Philosophy and partly of Theology. Hence, their falsehood, extravagance, perplexity, variety, and contradiction. Too great fondness for philosophy in the Church has obscured the knowledge of God and of ourselves. The better to explain the opinions of philosophers, a definition of Free Will given. Wide difference between this definition and these opinions.

5. *Certain things annexed to Free Will by the ancient theologians, especially the Schoolmen. Many kinds of Free Will according to them.*

6. *Puzzles of scholastic divines in the explanation of this question.*

7. *The conclusion that so trivial a matter ought not to be so much magnified. Objection of those who have a fondness for new terms in the Church. Objection answered.*

8. *Another answer. The Fathers, and especially Augustine, while retaining the term Free Will, yet condemned the doctrine of the heretics on the subject, as destroying the grace of God.*

9. *The language of the ancient writers on the subject of Free Will is, with the exception of that of Augustine, almost unintelligible. Still they set little or no value on human virtue, and ascribe the praise of all goodness to the Holy Spirit.*

10. *The last part of the chapter, containing a simple statement of the true doctrine. The fundamental principle is, that man first begins to profit in the knowledge of himself when he becomes sensible of his ruined condition. This confirmed, A. by passages of Scripture.*

11. *Confirmed, B. by the testimony of ancient theologians.*

12. *The foundation being laid, to show how far the power both of the intellect and will now extends, it is maintained in general, and in conformity with the views of Augustine and the Schoolmen, that the natural endowments of man are corrupted, and the supernatural almost entirely lost. A separate consideration of the powers of the Intellect and the Will. Some general considerations. The intellect possesses some powers of perception. Still it labors under a twofold defect.*

13. *Man's intelligence extends both to things terrestrial and celestial. The power of the intellect in regard to the knowledge of things terrestrial. First, with regard to matters of civil polity.*

14. *The power of the intellect, secondly, with regard to the arts. Particular gifts in this respect conferred on individuals, and attesting the grace of God.*

15. *The rise of this knowledge of things terrestrial, first, that we may see how human nature, notwithstanding of its fall, is still adorned by God with excellent endowments.*

16. *Use of this knowledge continued. Secondly, that we may see that these endowments bestowed on individuals are intended for the*

common benefit of mankind. They are sometimes conferred even on the wicked.

17. *Some portion of human nature still left. This, whatever the amount of it, should be ascribed entirely to the divine indulgence. Reason of this. Examples.*

18. *Second part of the discussion, namely, that which relates to the power of the human intellect in regard to things celestial. These reducible to three heads, namely, divine knowledge, adoption, and will. The blindness of man in regard to these proved and thus tested by a simile.*

19. *Proved, moreover, by passages of Scripture, showing. That the sons of Adam are endued with some light, but not enough to enable them to comprehend God. Reasons.*

20. *Adoption not from nature, but from our heavenly Father, being sealed in the elect by the Spirit of regeneration. Obvious from many passages of Scripture, that, before regeneration, the human intellect is altogether unable to comprehend the things relating to regeneration. This fully proved. First argument. Second argument. Third argument.*

21. *Fourth argument. Scripture ascribes the glory of our adoption and salvation to God only. The human intellect blind as to heavenly things until it is illuminated. Disposal of a heretical objection.*

22. *Human intellect ignorant of the true knowledge of the divine law. This proved by the testimony of an Apostle, by an inference from the same testimony, and from a consideration of the end and definition of the Law of Nature. Plato obviously mistaken in attributing all sins to ignorance.*

23. *Themistius nearer the truth in maintaining, that the delusion of the intellect is manifested not so much in generals as in particulars. Exception to this rule.*

24. *Themistius, however, mistaken in thinking that the intellect is so very seldom deceived as to generals. Blindness of the human intellect when tested by the standard of the Divine Law, with regard to both to the first and second tables. Examples.*

25. *A middle view to be taken—viz. that all sins are not imputable to ignorance, and, at the same time, that all sins do not imply intentional malice. All the human mind conceives and plans in this*

matter is evil in the sight of God. Need of divine direction every moment.

26. The will examined. The natural desire of good, which is universally felt, no proof of the freedom of the human will. Two fallacies as to the use of terms, appetite, and good.

27. The doctrine of the Schoolmen on this subject opposed to and refuted by Scripture. The whole man being subject to the power of sin, it follows that the will, which is the chief seat of sin, requires to be most strictly curbed. Nothing ours but sin.

1 Connection of the previous with the four following chapters. In order to lay a proper foundation for the discussion of free will, two obstacles in the way to be removed—viz. sloth and pride. The basis and sum of the whole discussion. The solid structure of this basis, and a clear demonstration of it by the argument *a majori ad minus*. Also from the inconveniences and absurdities arising from the obstacle of pride.

Having seen that the dominion of sin, ever since the first man was brought under it, not only extends to the whole race, but has complete possession of every soul, it now remains to consider more closely, whether from the period of being thus enslaved, we have been deprived of all liberty; and if any portion still remains, how far its power extends. In order to facilitate the answer to this questions it may be proper in passing to point out the course that our inquiry ought to take. The best method of avoiding error is to consider the dangers that beset us on either side.

Man being devoid of all uprightness, immediately takes occasion from the fact to indulge in sloth, and having no ability in himself for the study of righteousness, treats the whole subject as if he had no concern in it. On the other hand, man cannot arrogate anything, however minute, to himself, without robbing God of his honor, and through rash confidence subjecting himself to a fall. To keep free of both these rocks, our proper course will be, first, to show that man has no remaining good in himself, and is beset on every side by the most miserable destitution; and then teach him to aspire to the goodness of which he is devoid, and the liberty of which he has been deprived: thus giving him a stronger stimulus to exertion than he could have if he imagined himself possessed of the highest virtue. How necessary the latter point is, everybody sees. As to the former, several seem to entertain more doubt than they ought.

For it being admitted as incontrovertible that man is not to be denied anything that is truly his own, it ought also to be admitted, that he is to be deprived of everything like false boasting. If man had no title to glory in himself, when, by the kindness of his Maker, he was distinguished by the noblest ornaments, how much ought he to be humbled now, when his ingratitude has thrust him down from the highest glory to extreme ignominy? At the time when he was raised to the highest pinnacle of honor, all which Scripture attributes to him is, that he was created in the image of God, thereby intimating that the blessings in which his happiness consisted were not his own, but derived by divine communication.

What remains, therefore, now that man is stripped of all his glory, than to acknowledge the God for whose kindness he failed to be grateful, when he was loaded with the riches of his grace? Not having glorified him by the acknowledgment of his blessings, now, at least, he ought to glorify him by the confession of his poverty. In truth, it is no less useful for us to renounce all the praise of wisdom and virtue, than to aim at the glory of God. Those who invest us with more than we possess only add sacrilege to our ruin. For when we are taught to contend in our own strength, what more is done than to lift us up, and then leave us to lean on a reed that immediately gives way? Indeed, our strength is exaggerated when it is compared to a reed. All that foolish men invent and prattle on this subject is mere smoke. Wherefore, it is not without reason that Augustine so often repeats the well-known saying, that free will is more destroyed than established by its defenders. It was necessary to premise this much for the sake of some who, when they hear that human virtue is totally overthrown, in order that the power of God in man may be exalted, conceive an utter dislike to the whole subject, as if it were perilous, not to say superfluous, whereas it is manifestly both most necessary and most useful.

2 The second part of the chapter containing the opinions of others. The opinions of philosophers.

Having lately observed, that the faculties of the soul are seated in the mind and the heart, let us now consider how far the power of each extends. Philosophers generally maintain, that reason dwells in the mind like a lamp, throwing light on all its counsels, and like a queen, governing the will—that it is so pervaded with divine light as to be able to consult for the best, and so endued with vigour as to be able perfectly to command; that, on the contrary, sense is dull and short-sighted, always creeping on the ground, groveling among inferior objects, and never rising to true vision; that the appetite, when it obeys reason, and does not allow itself to be subjugated by sense, is borne to the study of virtue, holds a straight course, and becomes transformed into will; but that when enslaved by sense, it is corrupted and depraved so as to degenerate into lust.

In a word, since, according to their opinion, the faculties which I have mentioned above, namely, intellect, sense, and appetite, or will (the latter being the term in ordinary use), are seated in the soul, they maintain that the intellect is endued with reason, the best guide to a virtuous and happy life, provided it duly avails itself of its excellence, and exerts the power with which it is naturally endued; that, at the same time, the inferior movement, which is termed sense, and by which the mind is led away to error and delusion, is of such a nature, that it can be tamed and gradually subdued by the power of reason. To the will, moreover, they give an intermediate place between reason and sense, regarding it as possessed of full power and freedom, whether to obey the former, or yield itself up to be hurried away by the latter.

3 The labyrinths of philosophers. A summary of the opinion common to all the philosophers.

Sometimes, indeed, convinced by their own experience, they do not deny how difficult it is for man to establish the supremacy of reason in himself, inasmuch as he is at one time enticed by the allurements of pleasure; at another, deluded by a false semblance of good; and, at another, impelled by unruly passions, and pulled away (to use Plato's expression) as by ropes or sinews. For this reason, Cicero says, that the sparks given forth by nature are immediately extinguished by false opinions and depraved manners. They confess that when once diseases of this description have seized upon the mind, their course is too impetuous to be easily checked, and they hesitate not to compare them to fiery steeds, which, having thrown off the charioteer, scamper away without restraint. At the same time, they set it down as beyond dispute, that virtue and vice are in our own power.

For (say they), If it is in our choice to do this thing or that, it must also be in our choice not to do it: Again, If it is in our choice not to act, it must also be in our choice to act: But both in doing and abstaining we seem to act from free choice; and, therefore, if we do good when we please, we can also refrain from doing it; if we commit evil, we can also shun the commission of it. Nay, some have gone the length of boasting (Seneca, *passim*) that it is the gift of the gods that we live, but a gift of our own that we live well and purely. Hence, Cicero says, in the person of Cotta, that as everyone acquires virtue for himself, no wise man ever thanked the gods for it. "We are praised," says he, "for virtue, and glory in virtue, but this could not be, if virtue were the gift of God, and not from ourselves." A little after, he adds, "The opinion of all mankind is, that fortune must be sought from God, wisdom from ourselves." Thus, in short, all philosophers maintain, that human reason is sufficient for right government; that the will, which is inferior to it, may indeed be solicited to evil by sense, but having a free choice, there is nothing to prevent it from following reason as its guide in all things.

4 The opinions of others continued—viz. The opinions of the ancient theologians on the subject of free will. These composed partly of Philosophy and partly of Theology. Hence, their falsehood, extravagance, perplexity, variety, and contradiction. Too great fondness for philosophy in the Church has obscured the knowledge of God and of ourselves. The better to explain the opinions of philosophers, a definition of Free Will given. Wide difference between this definition and these opinions.

Among ecclesiastical writers, although there is none who did not acknowledge that sound reason in man was seriously injured by sin, and the will greatly entangled by vicious desires, yet many of them made too near an approach to the philosophers. Some of the most ancient writers appear to me to have exalted human strengths from a fear that a distinct acknowledgment of its impotence might expose them to the jeers of the philosophers with whom they were disputing, and also furnish the flesh, already too much disinclined to good, with a new pretext for sloth. Therefore, to avoid teaching anything that the majority of mankind might deem absurd, they made it their study, in some measure, to reconcile the doctrine of Scripture with the dogmas of philosophy, at the same time making it their special care not to furnish any occasion to sloth. This is obvious from their words.

Chrysostom says, "God having placed good and evil in our power, has given us full freedom of choice; he does not keep back the unwilling, but embraces the willing." Again, "He who is wicked is often, when he so chooses, changed into good, and he who is good falls through sluggishness, and becomes wicked. For the Lord has made our nature free. He does not lay us under necessity, but furnishing apposite remedies, allows the whole to depend on the views of the patient." Again, "As we can do nothing rightly until aided by the grace of God, so, until we bring forward what is our own, we cannot obtain favor from above." He had previously said, "As the whole is not done by divine assistance, we ourselves must of necessity bring somewhat." Accordingly, one of his common expressions is, "Let us bring what is our own, God will supply the rest." In unison with this, Jerome says, "It is ours to begin, God's to finish: it is ours to offer what we can, his to supply what we cannot."

From these sentences, you see that they have bestowed on man more than he possesses for the study of virtue, because they thought that they could not shake off our innate sluggishness unless they argued that we sin by ourselves alone. With what skill they have thus argued we shall see. Assuredly, we shall soon be able to show that the sentiments just quoted are most inaccurate. Moreover although the Greek Fathers, above others, and especially Chrysostom, have exceeded due bounds in extolling the powers of the human will, yet all ancient theologians, with the exception of Augustine, are so confused, vacillating, and contradictory on this subject, that no certainty can be obtained from their writings. It is needless, therefore, to be more particular in enumerating every separate opinion. It will be sufficient to extract from each as much as the exposition of the subject seems to require. Succeeding writers (everyone courting applause for his acuteness in the defense of human nature) have uniformly, one after the other, gone more widely astray, until the common dogma came to be, that man was corrupted only in the sensual part of his nature, that reason remained entire, and will was scarcely impaired. Still the expression was often on their lips, that man's natural gifts were corrupted, and his supernatural taken away. Of the thing implied by these words, however, scarcely one in a hundred had any distinct idea. Certainly, if I desired clearly to express what the corruption of nature is, I would not seek for any other expression. But it is of great importance attentively to consider what the power of man now is when vitiated in all the parts of his nature, and deprived of supernatural gifts. Persons professing to be the disciples of Christ have spoken too much like the philosophers on this subject. As if human nature were still in its integrity, the term free will has always been in use among the Latins, while the Greeks were not ashamed to assume that man still had full power in himself.

But since the principle entertained by all, even the vulgar, is, that man is endued with free will, while some, who would be thought more skilful, know not how far its power extends; it will be necessary, first to consider the meaning of the term, and afterwards ascertain, by a simple appeal to Scripture, what man's natural power for good or evil is. The thing meant by free will, though constantly occurring in all writers, few have defined. Origen, however, seems to have stated the common opinion when he said, "It is a power of reason to discern between good and evil; of will, to choose the one or other." Nor does Augustine differ from him when he says, "It is a power of reason and will to choose the good, grace assisting; to choose the bad, grace desisting."

Bernard, while aiming at greater acuteness, speaks more obscurely, when he describes it as consent, in regard to the indestructible liberty of the wills and the inalienable judgment of reason. Anselm's definition is not very intelligible to ordinary understanding. He calls it a power of preserving rectitude on its own account. Peter Lombard and the Schoolmen preferred the definition of Augustine, both because it was clearer and that did not exclude divine grace, without which they saw that the will was not sufficient of itself. They however add something of their own, because they deemed it either better or necessary for clearer explanation. First, they agree that the term *will* (arbitrium) has reference to reason, whose office it is to distinguish between good and evil, and that the epithet *free* properly belongs to the will, which may incline either way. Wherefore, since liberty properly belongs to the will, Thomas Aquinas says that the most congruous definition is to call free will an elective power, combining intelligence and appetite, but inclining more to appetite. We now perceive in what it is they suppose the faculty of free will to consist—viz. in reason and will. It remains to see how much they attribute to each.

5 Certain things annexed to Free Will by the ancient theologians, especially the Schoolmen. Many kinds of Free Will according to them.

In general, they are wont to place under the free will of man only intermediate things—viz. those that pertain not to the kingdom of God, while they refer true righteousness to the special grace of God and spiritual regeneration. The author of the work, "De Vocatione Gentium" (On the Calling of the Gentiles), wishing to show this, describes the will as threefold—viz. sensitive, animal, and spiritual. The two former, he says, are free to man, but the last is the work of the Holy Spirit. What truth there is in this will be considered in its own place. Our intention at present is only to mention the opinions of others, not to refute them. When writers treat of free will, their inquiry is chiefly directed not to what its power is in relation to civil or external actions, but to the obedience required by the divine law. The latter I admit to be the great question, but I cannot think the former should be altogether neglected; and I hope to be able to give the best reason for so thinking (sections 12 to 18). The schools, however, have adopted a distinction which enumerates three kinds of freedom; the first, a freedom from necessity; the second, a freedom from sin; and the third, a freedom from misery: the first naturally so inherent in man, that he cannot possibly be deprived of it; while through sin the other two have been lost. I willingly admit this distinction, except in so far as it confounds *necessity* with *compulsion*. How widely the things differ, and how important it is to attend to the difference, will appear elsewhere.

6 Puzzles of scholastic divines in the explanation of this question.

All this being admitted, it will be beyond dispute, that free will does not enable any man to perform good works, unless he is assisted by grace; indeed, the special grace which the elect alone receive through regeneration. For I stay not to consider the extravagance of those, who say that grace is offered equally and promiscuously to all. But it has not yet been shown whether man is entirely deprived of the power of well-doing, or whether he still possesses it in some, though in a very feeble and limited degree—a degree so feeble and limited, that it can do nothing of itself, but when assisted by grace, is able also to perform its part.

The Master of the Sentences, wishing to explain this, teaches that a twofold grace is necessary to fit for any good work. The one he calls Operating. To it, it is owing that we effectually will what is good. The other, which succeeds this good will, and aids it, he calls Co-operating. My objection to this division (see *infra*, chapter 3, section 10, and chapter 7, section 9) is, that while it attributes the effectual desire of good to divine grace, it insinuates that man, by his own nature, desires good in some degree, though ineffectually. Thus Bernard, while maintaining that a good will is the work of God, concedes this much to man—viz. that of his own nature he longs for such a good will. This differs widely from the view of Augustine, though Lombard pretends to have taken the division from him. Besides, there is an ambiguity in the second division, which has led to an erroneous interpretation. For it has been thought that we co-operate with subsequent grace, inasmuch as it pertains to us either to nullify the first grace, by rejecting its or to confirm it, by obediently yielding to it.

The author of the work De Vocatione Gentium expresses it thus: It is free to those who enjoy the faculty of reason to depart from grace, so that the not departing is a reward, and that which cannot be done without the co-operation of the Spirit is imputed as merit to those whose will might have made it otherwise. It seemed proper to make these two observations in passing, that the reader may see how far I differ from the sounder of the Schoolmen. Still further do I differ from more modern sophists, who have departed even more widely than the Schoolmen from the ancient doctrine. The division, however, shows in what respect free will is attributed to man. For Lombard ultimately declares that our freedom is not to the extent of leaving us equally inclined to good and evil in act or in thought, but only to the extent of freeing us from compulsion. This liberty is compatible with our being depraved, the servants of sin, able to do nothing but sin.

7 The conclusion that so trivial a matter ought not to be so much magnified. Objection of those who have a fondness for new terms in the Church. Objection answered.

In this way, then, man is said to have free will, not because he has a free choice of good and evil, but because he acts voluntarily, and not by compulsion. This is perfectly true: but why should so small a matter have been dignified with so proud a title? An admirable freedom! That man is not forced to be the servant of sin, while he is, however, a voluntary slave, his will being bound by the fetters of sin. I abominate mere verbal disputes, by which the Church is harassed to no purpose; but I think we ought religiously to eschew terms that imply some absurdity, especially in subjects where error is of pernicious consequence. How few are there who, when they hear free will attributed to man, do not immediately imagine that he is the master of his mind and will in such a sense, that he can of himself incline himself either to good or evil? It may be said that such dangers are removed by carefully expounding the meaning to the people. But such is the proneness of the human mind to go astray, that it will more quickly draw error from one little word, than truth from a lengthened discourse. Of this, the very term in question furnishes too strong a proof. For the explanation given by ancient Christian writers having been lost sight of, almost all who have come after them, by attending only to the etymology of the term, have been led to indulge a fatal confidence.

8 Another answer. The Fathers, and especially Augustine, while retaining the term Free Will, yet condemned the doctrine of the heretics on the subject, as destroying the grace of God.

As to the Fathers (if their authority weighs with us), they have the term constantly in their mouths; but they, at the same time, declare what extent of meaning they attach to it. In particular, Augustine hesitates not to call the will *a slave*. In another passages, he is offended with those who deny free will; but his chief reason for this is explained when he says, "Only lest anyone should presume so to deny freedom of will, from a desire to excuse sin." It is certain he elsewhere admits, that without the Spirit the will of man is not free, inasmuch as it is subject to lusts which chain and master it. And again, that nature began to want liberty the moment the will was vanquished by the revolt into which it fell. Again, that man, by making a bad use of free will, lost both himself and his will. Again, that free will having been made a captive, can do nothing in the way of righteousness. Again, no will is free which has not been made so by divine grace. Again, that the righteousness of God is not fulfilled when the law orders, and man acts by his own strength, but when the Spirit assists, and the will (not the free will of man, but the will freed by God) obeys. He briefly states the ground of all these observations, when he says, that man at his creation received a great degree of free will, but lost it by sinning.

In another place, after showing that free will is established by grace, he strongly inveighs against those who arrogate anything to themselves without grace. His words are, "How much soever miserable men presume to plume themselves on free will before they are made free, or on their strength after they are made free, they do not consider that, in the very expression *free will*, liberty is implied." "Where the Spirit of the Lord is, there is liberty" (2 Corinthians 3:17). If, therefore, they are the servants of sin, why do they boast of free will? He who has been vanquished is the servant of him who vanquished him. But if men have been made free, why do they boast of it as of their own work? Are they so free that they are unwilling to be the servants of Him who has said, "Without me ye can do nothing" (John 15:5)? In another passage he even seems to ridicule the word, when he says, "That the will is indeed free, but not freed—free of righteousness, but enslaved to sin." The same idea he elsewhere repeats and explains, when he says, "That man is not free from righteousness save by the choice of his will, and is not made free from sin save by the grace of the Savior."

Declaring that the freedom of man is nothing else than emancipation or manumission from righteousness, he seems to jest at the emptiness of the name. If anyone, then, chooses to make use of this terms without attaching any bad meaning to it, he shall not be troubled by me on that account; but as it cannot be retained without very great danger, I think the abolition of it would be of great advantage to the Church. I am unwilling to use it myself; and others if they will take my advice, will do well to abstain from it.

9 The language of the ancient writers on the subject of Free Will is, with the exception of that of Augustine, almost unintelligible. Still they set little or no value on human virtue, and ascribe the praise of all goodness to the Holy Spirit.

It may, perhaps, seem that I have greatly prejudiced my own view by confessing that all the ecclesiastical writers, with the exception of Augustine, have spoken so ambiguously or inconsistently on this subject, that no certainty is attainable from their writings. Some will interpret this to mean, that I wish to deprive them of their right of suffrage, because they are opposed to me. Truly, however, I have had no other end in view than to consult, simply and in good faith, for the advantage of pious minds, which, if they trust to those writers for their opinion, will always fluctuate in uncertainty. At one time, they teach, that man having been deprived of the power of free will must flee to grace alone; at another, they equip or seem to equip him in armor of his own. It is not difficult, however, to show, that notwithstanding of the ambiguous manner in which those writers express themselves, they hold human virtue in little or no account, and ascribe the whole merit of all that is good to the Holy Spirit.

To make this more manifest, I may here quote some passages from them. What, then, is meant by Cyprian in the passage so often lauded by Augustine, "Let us glory in nothing, because nothing is ours," unless it be, that man being utterly destitute, considered in himself, should entirely depend on God? What is meant by Augustine and Eucherius, when they expound that Christ is the tree of life, and that whose puts forth his hand to it shall live; that the choice of the will is the tree of the knowledge of good and evil, and that he who, forsaking the grace of God, tastes of it shall die? What is meant by Chrysostom, When he says, "That every man is not only naturally a sinner, but is wholly sin?"

If there is nothing good in us; if man, from the crown of the head to the sole of the foot, is wholly sin; if it is not even lawful to try how far the power of the will extends, —how can it be lawful to share the merit of a good work between God and man? I might quote many passages to the same effect from other writers; but lest any quibbler should say, that I select those only which serve my purpose, and cunningly pass by those who are against me, I desist. This much, however, I dare affirm, that though they sometimes go too far in extolling free will, the main object which they had in view was to teach man entirely to renounce all self-confidence, and place his strength in God alone. I now proceed to a simple exposition of the truth in regard to the nature of man.

10. The last part of the chapter, containing a simple statement of the true doctrine. The fundamental principle is, that man first begins to profit in the knowledge of himself when he becomes sensible of his ruined condition. This confirmed, A. by passages of Scripture.

Here however, I must again repeat what I premised at the outset of this chapter, that he who is most deeply abased and alarmed, by the consciousness of his disgrace, nakedness, want, and misery, has made the greatest progress in the knowledge of himself. Man is in no danger of taking too much from himself, provided he learns that whatever he wants is to be recovered in God. But he cannot arrogate to himself one particle beyond his due, without losing himself in vain confidence, and, by transferring divine honor to himself, becoming guilty of the greatest impiety. And, assuredly, whenever our minds are seized with a longing to possess a somewhat of our own, which may reside in us rather than in God, we may rest assured that the thought is suggested by no other counselor than he who enticed our first parents to aspire to be like gods, knowing good and evil.

It is sweet, indeed, to have so much virtue of our own as to be able to rest in ourselves; but let the many solemn passages by which our pride is sternly humbled, deter us from indulging this vain confidence: "Cursed be the man that trusteth in man, and maketh flesh his arm" (Jeremiah 17:5). "He delighteth not in the strength of the horse; he taketh not pleasure in the legs of a man. The Lord taketh pleasure in those that fear him, in those that hope in his mercy" (Psalm 147:10, 11). "He giveth power to the faint; and to them that have no might he increaseth strength. Even the youths shall faint and be weary, and the young men shall utterly fall: But they that wait upon the Lord shall renew their strength" (Isaiah 40:29-31). The scope of all these passages is that we must not entertain any opinion whatever of our own strength, if we would enjoy the favor of God, who "resisteth the proud, but giveth grace unto the humble" (James 4:6). Then let us call to mind such promises as these, "I will pour water upon him that is thirsty, and floods upon the dry ground" (Isaiah 44:3); "Ho, everyone that thirsteth, come ye to the waters" (Isaiah 55:1).

These passages declare, that none are admitted to enjoy the blessings of God save those who are pining under a sense of their own poverty. Nor ought such passages as the following to be omitted: "The sun shall no more be thy light by day; neither for brightness shall the moon give light unto thee: but the Lord shall be unto thee an everlasting light, and thy God thy glory" (Isaiah 60:19). The Lord certainly does not deprive his servants of the light of the sun or moon, but as he would alone appear glorious in them, he dissuades them from confidence even in those objects, which they deem most excellent.

11 Confirmed, B. by the testimony of ancient theologians.

I have always been exceedingly delighted with the words of Chrysostom, "The foundation of our philosophy is humility;" and still more with those of Augustine, "As the orator, when asked, What is the first precept in eloquence? Answered, Delivery: What is the second? Delivery: What the third? Delivery: so, if you ask me in regard to the precepts of the Christian Religion, I will answer, first, second, and third, Humility." By humility, he means not when a man, with a consciousness of some virtue, refrains from pride, but when he truly feels that he has no refuge but in humility. This is clear from another passage, "Let no man" says he, "flatter himself: of himself he is a devil: his happiness he owes entirely to God. What have you of your own but sin? Take your sin which is your own; for righteousness is of God." Again, "Why presume so much on the capability of nature? It is wounded, maimed, vexed, lost. The thing wanted is genuine confession, not false defense." "When anyone knows that he is nothing in himself, and has no help from himself, the weapons within himself are broken, and the war is ended." All the weapons of impiety must be bruised, and broken, and burnt in the fire; you must remain unarmed, having no help in yourself. The more infirm you are, the more the Lord will sustain you. So, in expounding the seventieth Psalm, he forbids us to remember our own righteousness, in order that we may recognize the righteousness of God, and shows that God bestows his grace upon us, that we may know that we are nothing; that we stand only by the mercy of God, seeing that in ourselves eve are altogether wicked.

Let us not contend with God for our right, as if anything attributed to him were lost to our salvation. As our insignificance is his exaltation, so the confession of our insignificance has its remedy provided in his mercy. I do not ask, however, that man should voluntarily yield without being convinced, or that, if he has any powers, he should shut his eyes to them, that he may thus be subdued to true humility; but that getting quit of the disease of self-love and ambition under the blinding of which he thinks of himself more highly than he ought to think, he may see himself as he really is, by looking into the faithful mirror of Scripture.

12 The foundation being laid, to show how far the power both of the intellect and will now extends, it is maintained in general, and in conformity with the views of Augustine and the Schoolmen, that the natural endowments of man are corrupted, and the supernatural almost entirely lost. A separate consideration of the powers of the Intellect and the Will. Some general considerations. The intellect possesses some powers of perception. Still it labors under a twofold defect.

I feel pleased with the well-known saying which has been borrowed from the writings of Augustine, that man's natural gifts were corrupted by sin, and his supernatural gifts withdrawn; meaning by supernatural gifts the light of faith and righteousness, which would have been sufficient for the attainment of heavenly life and everlasting felicity. Man, when he withdrew his allegiance to God, was deprived of the spiritual gifts by which he had been raised to the hope of eternal salvation. Hence, it follows, that he is now an exile from the kingdom of God, so that all things which pertain to the blessed life of the soul are extinguished in him until he recover them by the grace of regeneration. Among these are faith, love to God, charity towards our neighbor, the study of righteousness and holiness.

All these, when restored to us by Christ, are to be regarded as adventitious and above nature. If so, we infer that they were previously abolished. On the other hand, soundness of mind and integrity of heart were, at the same time, withdrawn, and it is this that constitutes the corruption of natural gifts. For although there is still some residue of intelligence and judgment as well as will, we cannot call a mind sound and entire which is both weak and immersed in darkness. As to the will, its depravity is but too well known. Therefore, since reason, by which man discerns between good and evil, and by which he understands and judges, is a natural gift, it could not be entirely destroyed; but being partly weakened and partly corrupted, a shapeless ruin is all that remains. In this sense it is said (John 1:5), that "the light shineth in darkness, and the darkness comprehended it not;" these words clearly expressing both points—viz. that in the perverted and degenerate nature of man there are still some sparks which show that he is a rational animal, and differs from the brutes, inasmuch as he is endued with intelligence, and yet, that this light is so smothered by clouds of darkness that it cannot shine forth to any good effect.

In like manner, the will, because inseparable from the nature of man, did not perish, but was so enslaved by depraved lusts as to be incapable of one righteous desire. The definition now given is complete, but there are several points that require to be explained. Therefore, proceeding agreeably to that primary distinction (Book 1, chapter 15, section 7 and 8), by which we divided the soul into intellect and will, we will now inquire into the power of the intellect.

To charge the intellect with perpetual blindness, so as to leave it no intelligence of any description whatever, is repugnant not only to the Word of God, but to common experience. We see that there has been implanted in the human mind a certain desire of investigating truth, to which it never would aspire unless some relish for truth antecedently existed. There is, therefore, now, in the human mind, discernment to this extent, that it is naturally influenced by the love of truth, the neglect of which in the lower animals is a proof of their gross and irrational nature. Still it is true that this love of truth fails before it reaches the goal, forthwith falling away into vanity. As the human mind is unable, from dullness, to pursue the right path of investigation, and, after various wanderings, stumbling every now and then like one groping in darkness, at length gets completely bewildered, so its whole procedure proves how unfit it is to search the truth and find it. Then it labors under another grievous defect, in that it frequently fails to discern what the knowledge is which it should study to acquire.

Hence, under the influence of a vain curiosity, it torments itself with superfluous and useless discussions, either not adverting at all to the things necessary to be known, or casting only a cursory and contemptuous glance at them. At all events, it scarcely ever studies them in sober earnest. Profane writers are constantly complaining of this perverse procedure, and yet almost all of them are found pursuing it. Hence, Solomon, throughout the Book of Ecclesiastes, after enumerating all the studies in which men think they attain the highest wisdom, pronounces them vain and frivolous.

13 Man's intelligence extends both to things terrestrial and celestial. The power of the intellect in regard to the knowledge of things terrestrial. First, with regard to matters of civil polity.

Still, however, man's efforts are not always so utterly fruitless as not to lead to some result, especially when his attention is directed to inferior objects. Nay, even with regard to superior objects, though he is more careless in investigating them, he makes some little progress. Here, however, his ability is more limited, and he is never made more sensible of his weakness than when he attempts to soar above the sphere of the present life. It may therefore be proper, in order to make it more manifest how far our ability extends in regard to these two classes of objects, to draw a distinction between them.

The distinction is that we have one kind of intelligence of earthly things, and another of heavenly things. By earthly things, I mean those that relate not to God and his kingdom, to true righteousness and future blessedness, but have some connection with the present life, and are in a manner confined within its boundaries. By heavenly things, I mean the pure knowledge of God, the method of true righteousness, and the mysteries of the heavenly kingdom. To the former belong matters of policy and economy, all mechanical arts and liberal studies. To the latter (as to which, see the eighteenth and following sections) belong the knowledge of God and of his will, and the means of framing the life in accordance with them. As to the former, the view to be taken is this: Since man is by nature a social animal, he is disposed, from natural instinct, to cherish and preserve society; and accordingly we see that the minds of all men have impressions of civil order and honesty.

Hence, it is that every individual understands how human societies must he regulated by laws, and is able to comprehend the principles of those laws. Hence, the universal agreement in regard to such subjects, both among nations and individuals, the seeds of them being implanted in the breasts of all without a teacher or lawgiver. The truth of this fact is not affected by the wars and dissensions which immediately arise, while some, such as thieves and robbers, would invert the rules of justice, loosen the bonds of law, and give free scope to their lust; and while others (a vice of most frequent occurrence) deem that to be unjust which is elsewhere regarded as just, and, on the contrary, hold that to be praiseworthy which is elsewhere forbidden. For such persons do not hate the laws from not knowing that they are good and sacred, but, inflamed with headlong passion, quarrel with what is clearly reasonable, and licentiously hate what their mind and understanding approve. Quarrels of this latter kind do not destroy the primary idea of justice. For while men dispute with each other as to particular enactments, their ideas of equity agree in substance. This, no doubt, proves the weakness of the human mind, which, even when it seems on the right path, halts and hesitates. Still, however, it is true, that some principle of civil order is impressed on all. And this is ample proof, that, in regard to the constitution of the present life, no man is devoid of the light of reason.

14 The power of the intellect, secondly, with regard to the arts. Particular gifts in this respect conferred on individuals, and attesting the grace of God.

Next, come manual and liberal arts, in learning which, as all have some degree of aptitude, the full force of human acuteness is displayed. But though not all are equally able to learn all the arts, we have sufficient evidence of a common capacity in the fact, that there is scarcely an individual who does not display intelligence in some particular art. And this capacity extends not merely to the learning of the art, but to the devising of something new, or the improving of what had been previously learned. This led Plato to adopt the erroneous idea, that such knowledge was nothing but recollection. So cogently does it oblige us to acknowledge that its principle is naturally implanted in the human mind. But while these proofs openly attest the fact of a universal reason and intelligence naturally implanted, this universality is of a kind that should lead every individual for himself to recognize it as a special gift of God. To this gratitude, we have a sufficient call from the Creator himself, when, in the case of idiots, he shows what the endowments of the soul would be were it not pervaded with his light. Though natural to all, it is so in such a sense that it ought to be regarded as a gratuitous gift of his beneficence to each. Moreover, the invention, the methodical arrangement, and the more thorough and superior knowledge of the arts, being confined to a few individuals cannot be regarded as a solid proof of common shrewdness. Still, however, as they are bestowed indiscriminately on the good and the bad, they are justly classed among natural endowments.

15

The rise of this knowledge of things terrestrial, first, that we may see how human nature, notwithstanding of its fall, is still adorned by God with excellent endowments.

Therefore, in reading profane authors, the admirable light of truth displayed in them should remind us, that the human mind, however much fallen and perverted from its original integrity, is still adorned and invested with admirable gifts from its Creator. If we reflect that the Spirit of God is the only fountain of truth, we will be careful, as we would avoid offering insult to him, not to reject or condemn truth wherever it appears. In despising the gifts, we insult the Giver.

How, then, can we deny that truth must have beamed on those ancient lawgivers who arranged civil order and discipline with so much equity? Shall we say that the philosophers, in their exquisite researches and skillful description of nature, were blind? Shall we deny the possession of intellect to those who drew up rules for discourse, and taught us to speak in accordance with reason? Shall we say that those who, by the cultivation of the medical art, expended their industry in our behalf were only raving? What shall we say of the mathematical sciences? Shall we deem them the dreams of madmen? Nay, we cannot read the writings of the ancients on these subjects without the highest admiration, an admiration that their excellence will not allow us to withhold. But shall we deem anything noble and praiseworthy, without tracing it to the hand of God? Far from us be such ingratitude; an ingratitude not chargeable even on heathen poets, who acknowledged that philosophy and laws, and all useful arts were the inventions of the gods. Therefore, since it is manifest that men whom the Scriptures term carnal, are so acute and clear-sighted in the investigation of inferior things, their example should teach us how many gifts the Lord has left in possession of human nature, notwithstanding of its having been despoiled of the true good.

16

Use of this knowledge continued. Secondly, that we may see that these endowments bestowed on individuals are intended for the common benefit of mankind. They are sometimes conferred even on the wicked.

Moreover, let us not forget that there are most excellent blessings, which the Divine Spirit dispenses to whom he will for the common benefit of mankind. For if the skill and knowledge required for the construction of the Tabernacle behaved to be imparted to Bezaleel and Aholiab, by the Spirit of God (Exodus 31:2; 35:30), it is not strange that the knowledge of those things which are of the highest excellence in human life is said to be communicated to us by the Spirit. Nor is there any ground for asking what concourse the Spirit can have with the ungodly, who are altogether alienated from God? For what is said as to the Spirit dwelling in believers only, is to be understood of the Spirit of holiness by which we are consecrated to God as temples.

Notwithstanding of this, he fills, moves, and invigorates all things by the virtue of the Spirit, and that according to the peculiar nature that each class of beings has received by the Law of Creation. But if the Lord has been pleased to assist us by the work and ministry of the ungodly in physics, dialectics, mathematics, and other similar sciences, let us avail ourselves of it, lest, by neglecting the gifts of God spontaneously offered to us, we be justly punished for our sloth.

Lest anyone, however, should imagine a man to be very happy merely because, with reference to the elements of this world, he has been endued with great talents for the investigation of truth, we ought to add, that the whole power of intellect thus bestowed is, in the sight of God, fleeting and vain whenever it is not based on a solid foundation of truth. Augustine (*supra*, sections 4 and 12), to whom, as we have observed, the Master of Sentences and the Schoolmen are forced to subscribe, says most correctly that as the gratuitous gifts bestowed on man were withdrawn, so the natural gifts which remained were corrupted after the fall. Not that they can be polluted in themselves in so far as they proceed from God, but that they have ceased to be pure to polluted man, lest he should by their means obtain any praise.

17 Some portion of human nature still left. This, whatever the amount of it, should be ascribed entirely to the divine indulgence. Reason of this. Examples.

The sum of the whole is this: From a general survey of the human race, it appears that one of the essential properties of our nature is reason, which distinguishes us from the lower animals, just as these by means of sense are distinguished from inanimate objects. For although some individuals are born without reason, that defect does not impair the general kindness of God, but rather serves to remind us, that whatever we retain ought justly to be ascribed to the Divine indulgence. Had God not so spared us, our revolt would have carried along with it the entire destruction of nature. In that some excel in acuteness, and some in judgment, while others have greater readiness in learning some peculiar art, God, by this variety commends his favor toward us, lest anyone should presume to arrogate to himself that which flows from His mere liberality. For whence is it that one is more excellent than another, but that in a common nature the grace of God is specially displayed in passing by many and thus proclaiming that it is under obligation to none.

We may add that each individual is brought under particular influences according to his calling. Many examples of this occur in the Book of Judges, in which the Spirit of the Lord is said to have come upon those whom he called to govern his people (Judges 6:34). In short, in every distinguished act there is a special inspiration. Thus, it is said of Saul, "there went with him a band of men whose hearts the Lord had touched" (1 Samuel 10:26). And when his inauguration to the kingdom is foretold, Samuel thus addresses him, "The Spirit of the Lord will come upon thee, and thou shalt prophesy with them, and shalt be turned into another man" (1 Samuel 10:6). This extends to the whole course of government, as it is afterwards said of David, "The Spirit of the Lord came upon David from that day forward" (1 Samuel 16:13). The same thing is elsewhere said with reference to particular movements. Nay, even in Homer, men are said to excel in genius, not only according as Jupiter has distributed to each, but according as he leads them day-by-day.

And certainly experience shows when those who were most skillful and ingenious stand stupefied, that the minds of men are entirely under the control of God, who rules them every moment. Hence, it is said, "He poureth contempt upon princes, and causeth them to wander in the wilderness where there is no way" (Psalm 107:40). Still, in this diversity we can trace some remains of the divine image distinguishing the whole human race from other creatures.

18 Second part of the discussion, namely, that which relates to the power of the human intellect in regard to things celestial. These reducible to three heads, namely, divine knowledge, adoption, and will. The blindness of man in regard to these proved and thus tested by a simile.

We must now explain what the power of human reason is, in regard to the kingdom of God, and spiritual discernments that consists chiefly of three things—the knowledge of God, the knowledge of his paternal favor towards us, which constitutes our salvation, and the method of regulating of our conduct in accordance with the Divine Law. With regard to the former two, but more properly the second, men otherwise the most ingenious are blinder than moles. I deny not, indeed, that in the writings of philosophers we meet occasionally with shrewd and apposite remarks on the nature of God, though they invariably savor somewhat of giddy imagination.

As observed above, the Lord has bestowed on them some slight perception of his Godhead that they might not plead ignorance as an excuse for their impiety, and has, at times, instigated them to deliver some truths, the confession of which should be their own condemnation. Still, though seeing, they saw not. Their discernment was not such as to direct them to the truth, far less to enable them to attain it, but resembled that of the bewildered traveler, who sees the flash of lightning glance far and wide for a moment, and then vanish into the darkness of the night, before he can advance a single step. So far is such assistance from enabling him to find the right path. Besides, how many monstrous falsehoods intermingle with those minute particles of truth scattered up and down in their writings as if by chance. In short, not one of them even made the least approach to that assurance of the divine favor, without which the mind of man must ever remain a mere chaos of confusion. To the great truths, What God is in himself, and what he is in relation to us, human reason makes not the least approach. (See Book 3, chapter 2, sections 14, 15, 16).

19 Proved, moreover, by passages of Scripture, showing. That the sons of Adam are endued with some light, but not enough to enable them to comprehend God. Reasons.

But since we are intoxicated with a false opinion of our own discernment, and can scarcely be persuaded that in divine things it is altogether stupid and blind, I believe the best course will be to establish the fact, not by argument, but by Scripture. Most admirable to this effect is the passage that I lately quoted from John, when he says, "In him was life; and the life was the light of men. And the light shineth in darkness; and the darkness comprehended it not" (John 1:4, 5). He intimates that the human soul is indeed irradiated with a beam of divine light, so that it is never left utterly devoid of some small flame, or rather spark, though not such as to enable it to comprehend God. And why so? Because its acuteness is, in reference to the knowledge of God, mere blindness. When the Spirit describes men under the term *darkness*, he declares them void of all power of spiritual intelligence. For this reason, it is said that believers, in embracing Christ, are "born, not of blood, nor of the will of the flesh, nor of the will of man, but of God" (John 1:13); in other words, that the flesh has no capacity for such sublime wisdom as to apprehend God, and the things of God, unless illumined by His Spirit. In like manner our Savior, when he was acknowledged by Peter, declared that it was by special revelation from the Father (Matthew 16:17).

20 Adoption not from nature, but from our heavenly Father, being sealed in the elect by the Spirit of regeneration. Obvious from many passages of Scripture, that, before regeneration, the human intellect is altogether unable to comprehend the things relating to regeneration. This fully proved. First argument. Second argument. Third argument.

If we were persuaded of a truth that ought to be beyond dispute—viz. that human nature possesses none of the gifts that the elect receive from their heavenly Father through the Spirit of regeneration, there would be no room here for hesitation. For thus speaks the congregation of the faithful, by the mouth of the prophet: "With thee is the fountain of life: in thy light shall we see light" (Psalm 36:9). To the same effect is the testimony of the Apostle Paul, when he declares, that "no man can say that Jesus is the Lord, but by the Holy Ghost" (1 Corinthians 12:3).

John Baptist, on seeing the dullness of his disciples, exclaims, "A man can receive nothing, unless it be given him from heaven" (John 3:27). That the gift to which he here refers must be understood not of ordinary natural gifts, but of special illumination, appears from this—that he was complaining how little his disciples had profited by all that he had said to them in commendation of Christ. "I see," says he, "that my words are of no effect in imbuing the minds of men with divine things, unless the Lord enlighten their understandings by His Spirit." Nay, Moses also, while upbraiding the people for their forgetfulness, at the same time observes, that they could not become wise in the mysteries of God without his assistance.

"Ye have seen all that the Lord did before your eyes in the land of Egypt, unto Pharaoh, and unto all his servants, and unto all his land; the great temptations which thine eyes have seen, the signs, and these great miracles: yet the Lord has not given you an heart to perceive, and eyes to see, and ears to hear, unto this, day" (Deuteronomy 29:2, 3, 4). Would the expression have been stronger had he called us mere blocks in regard to the contemplation of divine things?

Hence, the Lord, by the mouth of the Prophet, promises to the Israelites as a singular favor, "I will give them an heart to know me" (Jeremiah 24:7); intimating, that in spiritual things the human mind is wise only in so far as he enlightens it. This was also clearly confirmed by our Savior when he said, "No man can come to me, except the Father which has sent me draw him" (John 6:44). Nay, is not he himself the living image of his Father, in which the full brightness of his glory is manifested to us?

Therefore, how far our faculty of knowing God extends could not be better shown than when it is declared, that though his image is so plainly exhibited, we have not eyes to perceive it. What? Did not Christ descend into the world that he might make the will of his Father manifest to men, and did he not faithfully perform the office? True! He did; but nothing is accomplished by his preaching unless the inner teacher, the Spirit, open the way into our minds. Only those, therefore, come to him who have heard and learned of the Father. And in what is the method of this hearing and learning? It is when the Spirit, with a wondrous and special energy, forms the ear to hear and the mind to understand. Lest this should seem new, our Savior refers to the prophecy of Isaiah, which contains a promise of the renovation of the Church. "For a small moment have I forsaken thee; but with great mercies will I gather thee" (Isaiah 54:7). If the Lord here predicts some special blessing to his elect, it is plain that the teaching to which he refers is not that which is common to them with the ungodly and profane.

It thus appears that none can enter the kingdom of God save those whose minds have been renewed by the enlightening of the Holy Spirit. On this subject the clearest exposition is given by Paul, who, when expressly handling it, after condemning the whole wisdom of the world as foolishness and vanity, and thereby declaring man's utter destitution, thus concludes, "The natural man receiveth not the things of the Spirit of God: for they are foolishness unto him: neither can he know them, for they are spiritually discerned" (1 Corinthians 2:14). Whom does he mean by the "natural man"? The man who trusts to the light of nature. Such a man has no understanding in the spiritual mysteries of God. Why so? Is it because through sloth he neglects them? Nay, though he exerts himself, it is of no avail; they are "spiritually discerned." And what does this mean? That altogether hidden from human discernment, they are made known only by the revelation of the Spirit, so that they are accounted foolishness wherever the Spirit does not give light. The Apostle had previously declared, that "Eye has not seen, nor ear heard, neither have entered into the heart of man, the things which God has prepared for them that love him;" nay, that the wisdom of the world is a kind of veil by which the mind is prevented from beholding God (1 Corinthians 2:9). What would we more? The Apostle declares that God has "made foolish the wisdom of this world" (1 Corinthians 1:20); and shall we attribute to it an acuteness capable of penetrating to God, and the hidden mysteries of his kingdom? Far from us be such presumption!

21 Fourth argument. Scripture ascribes the glory of our adoption and salvation to God only. The human intellect blind as to heavenly things until it is illuminated. Disposal of a heretical objection.

What the Apostle here denies to man, he, in another place, ascribes to God alone, when he prays, "that the God of our Lord Jesus Christ, the Father of glory, may give unto you the spirit of wisdom and revelation" (Ephesians 1:17). You now hear that all wisdom and revelation is the gift of God. What follows? "The eyes of your understanding being enlightened." Surely, if they require a new enlightening, they must in themselves be blind. The next words are, "that ye may know what is the hope of his calling" (Ephesians 1:18). In other words, the minds of men have not capacity enough to know their calling. Let no prating Pelagian here allege that God obviates this rudeness or stupidity, when, by the doctrine of his word, he directs us to a path that we could not have found without a guide.

David had the law, comprehending in it all the wisdom that could be desired, and yet not contented with this, he prays, "Open thou mine eyes, that I may behold wondrous things out of thy law" (Psalms 119:18). By this expression, he certainly intimates, that it is like sunrise to the earth when the word of God shines forth; but that men do not derive much benefit from it until he himself, who is for this reason called the Father of lights (James 1:17), either gives eyes or opens them; because, whatever is not illuminated by his Spirit is wholly darkness.

The Apostles had been duly and amply instructed by the best of teachers. Still, as they wanted the Spirit of truth to complete their education in the very doctrine that they had previously heard, they were ordered to wait for him (John 14:26). If we confess that what we ask of God is lacking to us, and He by the very thing promised intimates our want, no man can hesitate to acknowledge that he is able to understand the mysteries of God, only in so far as illuminated by his grace. He, who ascribes to himself more understanding than this, is the blinder for not acknowledging his blindness.

22 Human intellect ignorant of the true knowledge of the divine law. This proved by the testimony of an Apostle, by an inference from the same testimony, and from a consideration of the end and definition of the Law of Nature. Plato obviously mistaken in attributing all sins to ignorance.

It remains to consider the third branch of the knowledge of spiritual things— viz. the method of properly regulating the conduct. This is correctly termed the knowledge of the works of righteousness, a branch in which the human mind seems to have somewhat more discernment than in the former two, since an Apostle declares, "When the Gentiles, which have not the law, do by nature the things contained in the law, these, having not the law, are a law unto themselves: which show the work of the law written in their hearts, their conscience also bearing witness, and their thoughts the meantime accusing or else excusing one another" (Romans 2:14, 15). If the Gentiles have the righteousness of the law naturally engraved on their minds, we certainly cannot say that they are altogether blind as to the rule of life. Nothing indeed is more common, than for man to be sufficiently instructed in a right course of conduct by natural law, of which the Apostle here speaks.

Let us consider, however, for what end this knowledge of the law was given to men. For from this it will forthwith appear how far it can conduct them in the way of reason and truth. This is even plain from the words of Paul, if we attend to their arrangement. He had said a little before, that those who had sinned in the law will be judged by the law; and those who have sinned without the law will perish without the law. As it might seem unaccountable that the Gentiles should perish without any previous judgment, he immediately subjoins, that conscience served them instead of the law, and was therefore sufficient for their righteous condemnation. The end of the natural law, therefore, is to render man inexcusable, and may be not improperly defined—the judgment of conscience distinguishing sufficiently between just and unjust, and by convicting men on their own testimony depriving them of all pretext for ignorance. So indulgent is man towards himself, that, while doing evil, he always endeavors as much as he can to suppress the idea of sin. It was this, apparently, which induced Plato (in his Protagoras) to suppose that sins were committed only through ignorance. There might be some ground for this, if hypocrisy were so successful in hiding vice as to keep the conscience clear in the sight of God. But since the sinner, when trying to evade the judgment of good and evil implanted in him, is always dragged forward, and not permitted to wink so effectually as not to be compelled at times, whether he will or not, to open his eyes, it is false to say that he sins only through ignorance.

23 Themistius nearer the truth in maintaining, that the delusion of the intellect is manifested not so much in generals as in particulars. Exception to this rule.

Themistius is more accurate in teaching, that the intellect is very seldom mistaken in the general definition or essence of the matter; but that deception begins as it advances further, namely, when it descends to particulars. That homicide, putting the case in the abstract, is an evil, no man will deny; and yet one who is conspiring the death of his enemy deliberates on it as if the thing was good. The adulterer will condemn adultery in the abstract, and yet flatter himself while privately committing it. The ignorance lies here: that man, when he comes to the particular, forgets the rule, which he had laid down in the general case.

Augustine treats most admirably on this subject in his exposition of the first verse of the fifty-seventh Psalm. The doctrine of Themistius, however, does not always hold true: for the turpitude of the crime sometimes presses so on the conscience, that the sinner does not impose upon himself by a false semblance of good, but rushes into sin knowingly and willingly. Hence, the expression, —I see the better course, and approve it: I follow the worse (Medea of Ovid). For this reason, Aristotle seems to me to have made a very shrewd distinction between incontinence and intemperance. Where incontinence reigns, he says that through the passion, particular knowledge is suppressed, so that the individual sees not in his own misdeed the evil that he sees generally in similar cases. But when the passion is over, repentance immediately succeeds. Intemperance again, is not extinguished or diminished by a sense of sin, but on the contrary, persists in the evil choice that it has once made.

24 Themistius, however, mistaken in thinking that the intellect is so very seldom deceived as to generals. Blindness of the human intellect when tested by the standard of the Divine Law, with regard to both to the first and second tables. Examples.

Moreover, when you hear of a universal judgment in man distinguishing between good and evil, you must not suppose that this judgment is, in every respect, sound and entire. For if the hearts of men are imbued with a sense of justice and injustice, in order that they may have no pretext to allege ignorance, it is by no means necessary for this purpose that they should discern the truth in particular cases. It is even more than sufficient if they understand so far as to be unable to practice evasion without being convicted by their own conscience, and beginning even now to tremble at the judgment-seat of God. Indeed, if we would test our reason by the Divine Law, which is a perfect standard of righteousness, we should find how blind it is in many respects. It certainly attains not to the principal heads in the First Table, such as, trust in God, the ascription to him of all praise in virtue and righteousness, the invocation of his name, and the true observance of his day of rest. Did ever any soul, under the guidance of natural sense, imagine that these and the like constitute the legitimate worship of God?

When profane men would worship God, no matter how often they may be drawn off from their vain trifling, they constantly relapse into it. They admit, indeed, that sacrifices are not pleasing, to God, unless accompanied with sincerity of mind; and by this they testify that they have some conception of spiritual worship, though they immediately pervert it by false devices: for it is impossible to persuade them that everything which the law enjoins on the subject is true. Shall I then extol the discernment of a mind that can neither acquire wisdom by itself, nor listen to advice? As to the precepts of the Second Table, there is considerably more knowledge of them, inasmuch as they are more closely connected with the preservation of civil society. Even here, however, there is something defective. Every man of understanding deems it most absurd to submit to unjust and tyrannical domination, provided it can by any means be thrown off, and there is but one opinion among men, that it is the part of an abject and servile mind to bear it patiently, the part of an honorable and high-spirited mind to rise up against it.

Indeed, philosophers do not regard the revenge of injuries as a vice. But the Lord, condemning this too lofty spirit, prescribes to his people that patience which mankind deem infamous. In regard to the general observance of the law, concupiscence altogether escapes our animadversion. For the natural man cannot bear to recognize diseases in his lusts. The light of nature is stifled sooner than take the first step into this profound abyss. For, when philosophers class immoderate movements of the mind among vices, they mean those, which break forth and manifest themselves in grosser forms. Depraved desires, in which the mind can quietly indulge, they regard as nothing (see *infra*, chapter 8, section 49).

25 A middle view to be taken—viz. that all sins are not imputable to ignorance, and, at the same time, that all sins do not imply intentional malice. All the human mind conceives and plans in this matter is evil in the sight of God. Need of divine direction every moment.

As we have above animadverted on Plato's error, in ascribing all sins to ignorance, so we must repudiate the opinion of those who hold that all sins proceed from preconceived gravity and malice. We know too well from experience how often we fall, even when our intention is good. Our reason is exposed to so many forms of delusion, is liable to so many errors, stumbles on so many obstacles, is entangled by so many snares, that it is ever wandering from the right direction. Of how little value it is in the sight of God, in regard to all the parts of life, Paul shows, when he says, that we are not "sufficient of ourselves to think anything as of ourselves" (2 Corinthians 3:5). He is not speaking of the will or affection; he denies us the power of thinking aright how anything can be duly performed. Is it, indeed, true, that all thought, intelligence, discernment, and industry, are so defective, that, in the sight of the Lord, we cannot think or aim at anything that is right? To us, who can scarcely bear to part with acuteness of intellect (in our estimation a most precious endowment), it seems hard to admit this, whereas it is regarded as most just by the Holy Spirit, who "knoweth the thoughts of man, that they are vanity" (Psalm 94:11), and distinctly declares, that "every imagination of the thoughts of his heart was only evil continually" (Genesis 6:5; 8:21).

If everything that our mind conceives, meditates plans, and resolves, is always evil, how can it ever think of doing what is pleasing to God, to whom righteousness and holiness alone are acceptable? It is thus plain, that our mind, in whatever direction it turns, is miserably exposed to vanity. David was conscious of its weakness when he prayed, "Give me understanding, and I shall keep thy law" (Psalm 119:34). By desiring to obtain a new understanding, he intimates that his own was by no means sufficient. This he does not once only, but in one psalm repeats the same prayer almost ten times, the repetition intimating how strong the necessity that urged him to pray. What he thus asked for himself alone, Paul prays for the churches in general. "For this cause," says he, "we also, since the day we heard it, do not cease to pray for you, and to desire that ye might be filled with the knowledge of his will, in all wisdom and spiritual understanding; that you might walk worthy of the Lord," etc. (Colossians 1:9, 10). Whenever he represents this as a blessing from God, we should remember that he at the same time testifies that it is not in the power of man.

Accordingly, Augustine, in speaking of this inability of human reason to understand the things of God, says, that he deems the grace of illumination not less necessary to the mind than the light of the sun to the eye. And, not content with this, he modifies his expression, adding, that we open our eyes to behold the light, whereas the mental eye remains shut, until it is opened by the Lord. Nor does Scripture say that our minds are illuminated in a single day, so as afterwards to see of themselves. The passage, which I lately quoted from the Apostle Paul, refers to continual progress and increase. David, too, expresses this distinctly in these words: "With my whole heart have I sought thee: O let me not wander from thy commandments" (Psalm 119:10). Though he had been regenerated, and so had made no ordinary progress in true piety, he confesses that he stood in need of direction every moment, in order that he might not decline from the knowledge with which he had been endued. Hence, he elsewhere prays for a renewal of a right spirit, which he had lost by his sin, (Psalm 51:12). For that which God gave at first, while temporarily withdrawn, it is equally his province to restore.

26 The will examined. The natural desire of good, which is universally felt, no proof of the freedom of the human will. Two fallacies as to the use of terms, *appetite,* and *good.*

We must now examine the will, on which the question of freedom principally turns, the power of choice belonging to it rather than the intellect, as we have already seen (*supra*, sect. 4). And at the outset, to guard against its being thought that the doctrine taught by philosophers, and generally received—viz. that all things by natural instinct have a desire of good, is any proof of the rectitude of the human will, —let us observe, that the power of free will is not to be considered in any of those desires which proceed more from instinct than mental deliberation. Even the schoolmen admit that there is no act of free will, unless when reason looks at opposites. By this they mean, that the things desired must be such as may be made the object of choice, and that to pave the way for choice, deliberation must precede. And, undoubtedly, if you attend to what this natural desire of good in man is, you will find that it is common to him with the brutes. They, too, desire what is good; and when any semblance of good capable of moving the sense appears, they follow it. Here, however, man does not, in accordance with the excellence of his immortal nature, rationally choose, and studiously pursue, what is truly for his good. He does not admit reason to his counsel, nor exert his intellect; but without reason, without counsel, follows the bent of his nature like the lower animals. The question of freedom, therefore, has nothing to do with the fact of man's being led by natural instinct to desire good. The question is, Does man, after determining by right reason what is good, choose what he thus knows, and pursue what he thus chooses?

Lest any doubt should be entertained as to this, we must attend to the double misnomer. For this *appetite* is not properly a movement of the will, but natural inclination; and this *good* is not one of virtue or righteousness, but of condition—viz. that the individual may feel comfortable. In fine, no matter how much man may desire to obtain what is good, he does not follow it. There is no man who would not be pleased with eternal blessedness; and yet, without the impulse of the Spirit, no man aspires to it. Since, then, the natural desire of happiness in man no more proves the freedom of the will, than the tendency in metals and stones to attain the perfection of their nature, let us consider, in other respects, whether the will is so utterly vitiated and corrupted in every part as to produce nothing but evil, or whether it retains some portion uninjured, and productive of good desires.

27 The doctrine of the Schoolmen on this subject opposed to and refuted by Scripture. The whole man being subject to the power of sin, it follows that the will, which is the chief seat of sin, requires to be most strictly curbed. Nothing ours but sin.

Those who ascribe our willing effectually, to the primary grace of Gods (*supra*, section 6), seem conversely to insinuate that the soul has in itself a power of aspiring to good, though a power too feeble to rise to solid affection or active endeavor. There is no doubt that this opinion, adopted from Origen and certain of the ancient Fathers, has been generally embraced by the schoolmen, who are wont to apply to man in his natural state (*in puris naturalibus*, as they express it) the following description of the apostle: — "For that which I do I allow not: for what I would, that do I not; but what I hate, that do I." "To will is present with me; but how to perform that which is good I find not" (Romans 7:15, 18). But, in this way, the whole scope of Paul's discourse is inverted. He is speaking of the Christian struggle (touched on more briefly in the Epistle to the Galatians), which believers constantly experience from the conflict between the flesh and the Spirit. But the Spirit is not from nature, but from regeneration. That the apostle is speaking of the regenerate is apparent from this, that after saying, "in me dwells no good thing," he immediately adds the explanation, "in my flesh." Accordingly, he declares, "It is no more I that do it, but sin that dwelleth in me."

What is the meaning of the correction, "in me (that is, *in my flesh*)?" It is just as if he had spoken in this way, No good thing dwells in me, of myself, for in my flesh nothing good can be found. Hence, follows the species of excuse, It is not I myself that do evil, but sin that dwelleth in me. This applies to none but the regenerate, who, with the leading powers of the soul, tend towards what is good.

The whole is made plain by the conclusion, "I delight in the law of God after the inward man: but I see another law in my members, warring against the law of my mind" (Romans 7:22, 23). Who has this struggle in himself, save those who, regenerated by the Spirit of God, bear about with them the remains of the flesh?

Accordingly, Augustine, who had at one time thought that the discourse related to the natural man, afterwards retracted his exposition as unsound and inconsistent. And, indeed if we admit that men, without grace, have any motions to good, however feeble, what answer shall we give to the apostles who declares that "we are incapable of thinking a good thought?" (2 Corinthians 3:6). What answer shall we give to the Lord, who declares, by Moses, "every imagination of man's heart is only evil continually?" (Genesis 8:21). Since the blunder has thus arisen from an erroneous view of a single passage, it seems unnecessary to dwell upon it.

Let us rather give due weight to our Savior's words, "Whosoever committeth sin is the servant of sin" (John 8:34). We are all sinners by nature, therefore we are held under the yoke of sin. But if the whole man is subject to the dominion of sin, surely the will, which is its principal seat, must be bound with the closest chains. And, indeed, if divine grace were preceded by any will of ours, Paul could not have said, "it is God which worketh in us both to will and to do" (Philippians 2:13). Away, then, with all the absurd trifling which many have indulged in with regard to preparation. Although believers sometimes ask to have their heart trained to the obedience of the divine law, as David does in several passages (Psalm 51:12), it is to be observed, that even this longing in prayer is from God. This is apparent from the language used. When he prays, "Create in me a clean heart," he certainly does not attribute the beginning of the creation to himself. Let us therefore rather adopt the sentiment of Augustine, "God will prevent you in all things, but do you sometimes prevent his anger. How? Confess that you have all these things from God, that all the good you have is from him, all the evil from yourself." Shortly after he says, "Of our own we have nothing but sin."

Chapter 3

EVERYTHING PROCEEDING FROM THE CORRUPT NATURE OF MAN DAMNABLE

The principal matters in this chapter are—I. A recapitulation of the former chapter, proving, from passages of Scriptures that the intellect and will of man are so corrupted, that no integrity, no knowledge or fear of God, can now be found in him, sections 1 and 2. II. Objections to this doctrine, from the virtues, which shone in some of the heathen, refuted, sections 3 and 4. III. What kind of will remains in man, the slave of sin, section 5. The remedy and cure, section 6. IV. The opinion of Neo-Pelagian sophists concerning the preparation and efficacy of the will, and also concerning perseverance and co-operating grace, refuted, both by reason and Scripture, sections 7–12. V. Some passages from Augustine confirming the truth of this doctrine, sections 13 and 14.

Sections

1. The intellect and will of the whole man corrupt. The term flesh applies not only to the sensual, but also to the higher part of the soul. This demonstrated from Scripture.

2. The heart also involved in corruption, and hence in no part of man can integrity, or knowledge or the fear of God, be found.

3. Objection, that some of the heathen were possessed of admirable endowments, and, therefore, that the nature of man is not entirely corrupt. Answer, Corruption is not entirely removed, but only inwardly restrained. Explanation of this answer.

4. Objection still urged, that the virtuous and vicious among the heathen must be put upon the same level, or the virtuous prove that human nature, properly cultivated, is not devoid of virtue. Answer, That these are not ordinary properties of human nature, but special gifts of God. These gifts defiled by ambition, and hence the actions proceeding from them, however esteemed by man, have no merit with God.

5. Though man has still the faculty of willing there is no soundness in it. He falls under the bondage of sin necessarily, and yet voluntarily. Necessity must be distinguished from compulsion. The ancient Theologians acquainted with this necessity. Some passages condemning the vacillation of Lombard.

6. Conversion to God constitutes the remedy or soundness of the human will. This not only begun, but continued and completed; the beginning, continuance, and completion, being ascribed entirely to God. This proved by Ezekiel's description of the stony heart, and from other passages of Scripture.

7. Various Objections. —A. The will is converted by God, but, when once prepared, does its part in the work of conversion. Answer from Augustine. B. Grace can do nothing without will, nor the will without grace. Answer. Grace itself produces will. God prevents the unwilling, making him willing, and follows up this preventing grace that he may not will in vain. Another answer gathered from various passages of Augustine.

8. Answer to the second Objection continued. No will inclining to good except in the elect. The cause of election out of man. Hence, right will, as well as election, are from the good pleasure of God. The beginning of willing and doing well is of faith; faith again is the gift of God; and hence mere grace is the cause of our beginning to will well. This proved by Scripture.

9. Answer to second Objection continued. That good will is merely of grace proved by the prayers of saints. Three axioms A. God does not prepare man's heart, so that he can afterwards do some good of himself, but every desire of rectitude, every inclination to study, and every effort to pursue it, is from Him. B. This desire, study, and effort, do not stop short, but continue to effect. C. This progress is constant. The believer perseveres to the end. A third Objection, and three answers to it.

10. A fourth Objection. Answer. Fifth Objection. Answer. Answer confirmed by many passages of Scripture, and supported by a passage from Augustine.

11. Perseverance not of ourselves, but of God. Objection. Two errors in the objection. Refutation of both.

1 **The intellect and will of the whole man corrupt. The term** *flesh* **applies not only to the sensual, but also to the higher part of the soul. This demonstrated from Scripture.**

The nature of man, in both parts of his soul—viz. intellect and will—cannot be better ascertained than by attending to the epithets applied to him in Scripture. If he is fully depicted (and it may easily be proved that he is) by the words of our Savior, "that which is born of the flesh is flesh" (John 3:6), he must be a very miserable creature. For, as an apostle declares, "to be carnally minded is death" (Romans 8:8), "It is enmity against God, and is not subject to the law of God, neither indeed can be." Is it true that the flesh is so perverse, that it is perpetually striving with all its might against God? That it cannot accord with the righteousness of the divine law? That, in short, it can beget nothing but the materials of death? Grant that there is nothing in human nature but flesh, and then extract something good out of it if you can. But it will be said, that the word *flesh* applies only to the sensual, and not to the higher part of the soul. This, however, is completely refuted by the words both of Christ and his apostle.

The statement of our Lord is that a man must be born again, because he is flesh. He requires not to be born again, with reference to the body. But a mind is not born again merely by having some portion of it reformed. It must be totally renewed. This is confirmed by the antithesis used in both passages.

In the contrast between the Spirit and the flesh, there is nothing left of an intermediate nature. In this way, everything in man, which is not spiritual, falls under the denomination of carnal. But we have nothing of the Spirit except through regeneration. Everything, therefore, which we have from nature, is flesh. Any possible doubt which might exist on the subject is removed by the words of Paul (Ephesians 4:23), where, after a description of the old man, who, he says, "is corrupt according to the deceitful lusts," he bids us "be renewed in the spirit" of our mind. You see that he places unlawful and depraved desires not in the sensual part merely, but in the mind itself, and therefore requires that it should be renewed.

Indeed, he had a little before drawn a picture of human nature, which shows that there is no part in which it is not perverted and corrupted.

For when he says that the "Gentiles walk in the vanity of their mind, having the understanding darkened being alienated from the life of God through the ignorance that is in them, because of the blindness of their heart" (Ephesians 4:17, 18), there can be no doubt that his words apply to all whom the Lord has not yet formed anew both to wisdom and righteousness. This is rendered more clear by the comparison which immediately follows, and by which he reminds believers that they "have not so learned Christ" these words implying that the grace of Christ is the only remedy for that blindness and its evil consequences. Thus, too, had Isaiah prophesied of the kingdom of Christ, when the Lord promised to the Church, that though darkness should "cover the earth, and gross darkness the people," yet that he should "arise" upon it, and "his glory" should be seen upon it (Isaiah 40:2). When it is thus declared that divine light is to arise on the Church alone, all without the Church is left in blindness and darkness. I will not enumerate all that occurs throughout Scripture, and particularly in the Psalms and Prophetical writings, as to the vanity of man. There is much in what David says, "Surely men of low degree are vanity, and men of high degree are a lie: to be laid in the balance, they are altogether lighter than vanity" (Psalm 62:10).

The human mind receives a humbling blow when all the thoughts that proceed from it are derided as foolish, frivolous, perverse, and insane.

2 The heart also involved in corruption, and hence in no part of man can integrity, or knowledge or the fear of God, be found.

In no degree more lenient is the condemnation of the heart, when it is described as "deceitful above all things, and desperately wicked" (Jeremiah 17:9). But as I study brevity, I will be satisfied with a single passage, one, however, in which as in a bright mirror, we may behold a complete image of our nature. The Apostle, when he would humble man's pride, uses these words: "There is none righteous no, not one: there is none that understandeth, there is none that seeketh after God. They are all gone out of the way, they are together become unprofitable; there is none that does good, no, not one. Their throat is an open sepulcher; with their tongues they have used deceit; the poison of asps is under their lips: Whose mouth is full of cursing and bitterness: their feet are swift to shed blood: destruction and misery are in their ways: and the way of peace have they not known: there is no fear of God before their eyes" (Romans 3:10-18).

Thus, he thunders not against certain individuals, but against the whole posterity of Adam—not against the depraved manners of any single age, but the perpetual corruption of nature. His object in the passage is not merely to upbraid men in order that they may repent, but to teach that all are overwhelmed with inevitable calamity, and can be delivered from it only by the mercy of God. As this could not be proved without previously proving the overthrow and destruction of nature, he produced those passages to show that its ruin is complete.

Let it be a fixed point, then, that men are such as is here described, not by vicious custom, but by depravity of nature. The reasoning of the Apostle, that there is no salvation for man, except in the mercy of God, because in himself he is desperate and undone, could not otherwise stand. I will not here labor to prove that the passages apply, with the view of removing the doubts of any who might think them quoted out of place.

I will take them as if they had been used by Paul for the first time, and not taken from the Prophets. First, then, he strips man of righteousness, that is, integrity and purity; and, secondly, he strips him of sound intelligence. He argues, that defect of intelligence is proved by apostasy from God. To seek Him is the beginning of wisdom, and, therefore, such defect must exist in all who have revolted from Him. He subjoins, that all have gone astray, and become mere corruption; that there is none that does good. He then enumerates the crimes by which those who have once given loose to their wickedness pollute every member of their bodies. Lastly, he declares that they have no fear of God, according to whose rule all our steps should be directed. If these are the hereditary properties of the human race, it is vain to look for anything good in our nature.

I confess indeed, that not all these iniquities break out in every individual. Still it cannot be denied that the hydra lurks in every breast. For as a body, while it contains and fosters the cause and matter of disease, cannot be called healthy, although pain is not actually felt; so a soul, while teeming with such seeds of vice, cannot be called sound. This similitude, however, does not apply throughout. In a body however morbid, the functions of life are performed; but the soul, when plunged into that deadly abyss, not only labors under vice, but is altogether devoid of good.

3. Objection, that some of the heathen were possessed of admirable endowments, and, therefore, that the nature of man is not entirely corrupt. Answer, Corruption is not entirely removed, but only inwardly restrained. Explanation of this answer.

Here, again we are met with a question very much the same as that which was previously solved. In every age there have been some who, under the guidance of nature, were all their lives devoted to virtue. It is of no consequence, that many blots may be detected in their conduct; by the mere study of virtue, they evinced that there was somewhat of purity in their nature. The value that virtues of this kind have in the sight of God will be considered more fully when we treat of the merit of works.

Meanwhile however, it will be proper to consider it in this place also, in so far as necessary for the exposition of the subject in hand. Such examples, then, seem to warn us against supposing that the nature of man is utterly vicious, since, under its guidance, some have not only excelled in illustrious deeds, but also conducted themselves most honorably through the whole course of their lives. But we ought to consider, that, notwithstanding of the corruption of our nature, there is some room for divine grace, such grace as, without purifying it, may lay it under internal restraint. For, did the Lord let every mind loose to wanton in its lusts, doubtless there is not a man who would not show that his nature is capable of all the crimes with which Paul charges it (Romans 3 compared with Psalm 14:3, etc.). What? Can you exempt yourself from the number of those whose feet are swift to shed blood; whose hands are foul with rapine and murder; whose throats are like open sepulchers; whose tongues are deceitful; whose lips are venomous; whose actions are useless, unjust, rotten, deadly; whose soul is without God; whose inward parts are full of wickedness; whose eyes are on the watch for deception; whose minds are prepared for insult; whose every part, in short, is framed for endless deeds of wickedness?

If every soul is capable of such abominations (and the Apostle declares this boldly), it is surely easy to see what the result would be, if the Lord were to permit human passion to follow its bent. No ravenous beast would rush so furiously, no stream, however rapid and violent, so impetuously burst its banks. In the elect, God cures these diseases in the mode which will shortly be explained; in others, he only lays them under such restraint as may prevent them from breaking forth to a degree incompatible with the preservation of the established order of things. Hence, no matter how much men may disguise their impurity, some are restrained only by shame, others by a fear of the laws, from breaking out into many kinds of wickedness. Some aspire to an honest life, as deeming it most conducive to their interest, while others are raised above the vulgar lot, that, by the dignity of their station, they may keep inferiors to their duty. Thus God, by his providence, curbs the perverseness of nature, preventing it from breaking forth into action, yet without rendering it inwardly pure.

4 Objection still urged, that the virtuous and vicious among the heathen must be put upon the same level, or the virtuous prove that human nature, properly cultivated, is not devoid of virtue. Answer, That these are not ordinary properties of human nature, but special gifts of God. These gifts defiled by ambition, and hence the actions proceeding from them, however esteemed by man, have no merit with God.

The objection, however, is not yet solved. For we must either put Cataline on the same footing with Camillus, or hold Camillus to be an example that nature, when carefully cultivated, is not wholly void of goodness. I admit that the specious qualities, which Camillus possessed, were divine gifts, and appear entitled to commendation when viewed in themselves. But in what way will they be proofs of a virtuous nature? Must we not go back to the mind, and from it begin to reason thus? If a natural man possesses such integrity of manners, nature is not without the faculty of studying virtue. But what if his mind was depraved and perverted, and followed anything rather than rectitude? Such it undoubtedly was, if you grant that he was only a natural man. How then will you laud the power of human nature for good, if, even where there is the highest semblance of integrity, a corrupt bias is always detected? Therefore, as you would not commend a man for virtue whose vices impose upon you by a show of virtue, so you will not attribute a power of choosing rectitude to the human will while rooted in depravity.

Still, the surest and easiest answer to the objection is that those are not common endowments of nature, but special gifts of God, which he distributes in divers forms, and, in a definite measure, to men otherwise profane. For which reason, we hesitate not, in common language, to say, that one is of a good, another of a vicious nature; though we cease not to hold that both are placed under the universal condition of human depravity.

All we mean is that God has conferred on the one a special grace that he has not seen it meet to confer on the other. When he was pleased to set Saul over the kingdom, he made him a new man. This is the thing meant by Plato, when, alluding to a passage in the Iliad, he says, that the children of kings are distinguished at their birth by some special qualities—God, in kindness to the human race, often giving a spirit of heroism to those whom he destines for empire. In this way, the great leaders celebrated in history were formed. The same judgment must be given in the case of private individuals. But as those endued with the greatest talents were always impelled by the greatest ambitions (a stain which defiles all virtues and makes them lose all favor in the sight of God), so we cannot set any value on anything that seems praiseworthy in ungodly men. We may add, that the principal part of rectitude is wanting, when there is no zeal for the glory of God, and there is no such zeal in those whom he has not regenerated by his Spirit. Nor is it without good cause said in Isaiah, that on Christ should rest "the spirit of knowledge, and of the fear of the Lord" (Isaiah 11:2); for by this we are taught that all who are strangers to Christ are destitute of that fear of God which is the beginning of wisdom (Psalm 111:10).

The virtues that deceive us by an empty show may have their praise in civil society and the common intercourse of life, but before the judgment-seat of God, they will be of no value to establish a claim of righteousness.

5 Though man has still the faculty of willing there is no soundness in it. He falls under the bondage of sin necessarily, and yet voluntarily. Necessity must be distinguished from compulsion. The ancient Theologians acquainted with this necessity. Some passages condemning the vacillation of Lombard.

When the will is enchained as the slave of sin, it cannot make a movement towards goodness, far less steadily pursue it. Every such movement is the first step in that conversion to God, which in Scripture is entirely ascribed to divine grace. Thus, Jeremiah prays, "Turn thou me, and I shall be turned" (Jeremiah 31:18). Hence, too, in the same chapter, describing the spiritual redemption of believers, the Prophet says, "The Lord has redeemed Jacob, and ransomed him from the hand of him that was stronger than he" (Jeremiah 31:11); intimating how close the fetters are with which the sinner is bound, so long as he is abandoned by the Lord, and acts under the yoke of the devil. Nevertheless, there remains a will which both inclines and hastens on with the strongest affection towards sin; man, when placed under this bondage, being deprived not of will, but of soundness of will.

Bernard says not improperly, that all of us have a will; but to will well is proficiency, to will ill is defect. Thus simply to will is the part of man, to will ill the part of corrupt nature, to will well the part of grace.

Moreover, when I say that the will, deprived of liberty, is led or dragged by necessity to evil, it is strange that any should deem the expression harsh, seeing there is no absurdity in it, and it is not at variance with pious use. It does, however, offend those who know not how to distinguish between necessity and compulsion. Were anyone to ask them, "Is not God necessarily good, is not the devil necessarily wicked," what answer would they give? The goodness of God is so connected with his Godhead, that it is not more necessary to be God than to be good; whereas the devil, by his fall, was so estranged from goodness, that he can do nothing but evil. Should anyone give utterance to the profane jeer, that little praise is due to God for a goodness to which he is forced, is it not obvious to every man to reply, It is owing not to violent impulse, but to his boundless goodness, that he cannot do evil? Therefore, if the free will of God in doing good is not impeded, because he necessarily must do good; if the devil, who can do nothing but evil, nevertheless sins voluntarily; can it be said that man sins less voluntarily because he is under a necessity of sinning?

This necessity is uniformly proclaimed by Augustine, who, even when pressed by the invidious cavil of Celestius, hesitated not to assert it in the following terms: "Man through liberty became a sinner, but corruption, ensuing as the penalty, has converted liberty into necessity." Whenever mention is made of the subject, he hesitates not to speak in this way of the necessary bondage of sin. Let this, then, be regarded as the sum of the distinction. Man, since he was corrupted by the fall, sins not forced or unwilling, but voluntarily, by a most forward bias of the mind; not by violent compulsion, or external force, but by the movement of his own passion; and yet such is the depravity of his nature, that he cannot move and act except in the direction of evil. If this is true, the thing not obscurely expressed is, that he is under a necessity of sinning.

Bernard, assenting to Augustine, thus writes: "Among animals, man alone is free, and yet sin intervening, he suffers a kind of violence, but a violence proceeding from his will, not from nature, so that it does not even deprive him of innate liberty." For that which is voluntary is also free. A little after he adds, "Thus, by some means strange and wicked, the will itself, being deteriorated by sin, makes a necessity; but so that the necessity, in as much as it is voluntary, cannot excuse the will, and the will, in as much as it is enticed, cannot exclude the necessity." For this necessity is in a manner voluntary. He afterwards says, "we are under a yoke, but no other yoke than that of voluntary servitude; therefore, in respect of servitude, we are miserable, and in respect of will, inexcusable; because the will, when it was free, made itself the slave of sin." At length he concludes, "Thus the soul, in some strange and evil way, is held under this kind of voluntary, yet sadly free necessity, both bond and free; bond in respect of necessity, free in respect of will: and what is still more strange, and still more miserable, it is guilty because free, and enslaved because guilty, and therefore enslaved because free."

My readers hence perceive that the doctrine, which I deliver, is not new, but the doctrine which of old Augustine delivered with the consent of all the godly, and which was afterwards shut up in the cloisters of monks for almost a thousand years. Lombard, by not knowing how to distinguish between necessity and compulsion, gave occasion to a pernicious error.

6 Conversion to God constitutes the remedy or soundness of the human will. This not only begun, but continued and completed; the beginning, continuance, and completion, being ascribed entirely to God. This proved by Ezekiel's description of the stony heart, and from other passages of Scripture.

On the other hand, it may be proper to consider what the remedy is which divine grace provides for the correction and cure of natural corruption. Since the Lord, in bringing assistance, supplies us with what is lacking, the nature of that assistance will immediately make manifest its converse—viz. our penury. When the Apostle says to the Philippians, "Being confident of this very thing, that he which has begun a good work in you, will perform it until the day of Jesus Christ" (Philippians 1:6), there cannot be a doubt, that by the good work thus begun, he means the very commencement of conversion in the will. God, therefore, begins the good work in us by exciting in our hearts a desire, a love, and a study of righteousness, or (to speak more correctly) by turning, training, and guiding our hearts unto righteousness; and he completes this good work by confirming us unto perseverance.

But lest anyone should cavil that the good work thus begun by the Lord consists in aiding the will, which is in itself weak, the Spirit elsewhere declares what the will, when left to itself, is able to do. His words are, "A new heart also will I give you, and a new spirit will I put within you: and I will take away the stony heart out of your flesh, and I will give you an heart of flesh. And I will put my Spirit within you, and cause you to walk in my statutes, and ye shall keep my judgments, and do them" (Ezekiel 36:26, 27). How can it be said that the weakness of the human will is aided to enable it to aspire effectually to the choice of good, when the fact is, that it must be wholly transformed and renovated?

If there is any softness in a stone; if you can make it tender, and flexible into any shape, then it may be said, that the human heart may be shaped for rectitude, provided that which is imperfect in it is supplemented by divine grace. But if the Spirit, by the above similitude, meant to show that no good can ever be extracted from our heart until it is made altogether new, let us not attempt to share with Him what He claims for himself alone. If it is like turning a stone into flesh when God turns us to the study of rectitude, everything proper to our own will is abolished, and that which succeeds in its place is wholly of God. I say the will is abolished, but not in so far as it is will, for in conversion everything essential to our original nature remains: I also say, that it is created anew, not because the will then begins to exist, but because it is turned from evil to good.

This, I maintain, is wholly the work of God, because, as the Apostle testifies, we are not "sufficient of ourselves to think anything as of ourselves" (2 Corinthians 3:5). Accordingly, he elsewhere says, not merely that God assists the weak or corrects the depraved will, but that he worketh in us to will (Philippians 2:13). From this it is easily inferred, as I have said, that everything good in the will is entirely the result of grace. In the same sense, the Apostle elsewhere says, "It is the same God which worketh all in all" (1 Corinthians 12:6). For he is not there treating of universal government, but declaring that all the good qualities which believers possess are due to God. In using the term "all," he certainly makes God the author of spiritual life from its beginning to its end. This he had previously taught in different terms, when he said that there is "one Lord Jesus Christ, by whom are all things, and we by him" (1 Corinthians 8:6); thus plainly extolling the new creation, by which everything of our common nature is destroyed. There is here a tacit antithesis between Adam and Christ, which he elsewhere explains more clearly when he says, "We are his workmanship, created in Christ Jesus unto good works, which God has before ordained that we should walk in them" (Ephesians 2:10). His meaning is to show in this way that our salvation is gratuitous because the beginning of goodness is from the second creation, which is obtained in Christ.

If any, even the minutest, ability were in ourselves, there would also be some merit. But to show our utter destitution, he argues that we merit nothing, because we are created in Christ Jesus unto good works, which God has prepared; again intimating by these words, that all the fruits of good works are originally and immediately from God.

Hence, the Psalmist, after saying that the Lord "has made us," to deprive us of all share in the work, immediately adds, "not we ourselves." That he is speaking of regeneration, which is the commencement of the spiritual life, is obvious from the context, in which the next words are, "we are his people, and the sheep of his pasture" (Psalm 100:3). Not contented with simply giving God the praise of our salvation, he distinctly excludes us from all share in it, just as if he had said that not one particle remains to man as a ground of boasting. The whole is of God.

7 Various Objections. —A. The will is converted by God, but, when once prepared, does its part in the work of conversion. Answer from Augustine. B. Grace can do nothing without will, nor the will without grace. Answer. Grace itself produces will. God prevents the unwilling, making him willing, and follows up this preventing grace that he may not will in vain. Another answer gathered from various passages of Augustine.

But perhaps there will be some who, while they admit that the will is in its own nature averse to righteousness, and is converted solely by the power of God, will yet hold that, when once it is prepared, it performs a part in acting. This they found upon the words of Augustine, that grace precedes every good work; the will accompanying, not leading; a handmaid, and not a guide. The words thus not improperly used by this holy writer, Lombard preposterously wrests to the above effect. But I maintain, that as well in the words of the Psalmist which I have quoted, as in other passages of Scripture, two things are clearly taught—viz. that the Lord both corrects, or rather destroys, our depraved will, and also substitutes a good will from himself. In as much as it is prevented by grace, I have no objection to your calling it a handmaid; but in as much as when formed again, it is the work of the Lord, it is erroneous to say, that it accompanies preventing grace as a voluntary attendant. Therefore, Chrysostom is inaccurate in saying, that grace cannot do anything without will, nor will anything without grace, as if grace did not, in terms of the passage lately quoted from Paul, produce the very will itself.

The intention of Augustine, in calling the human will the handmaid of grace, was not to assign it a kind of second place to grace in the performance of good works. His object merely was to refute the pestilential dogma of Pelagius, who made human merit the first cause of salvation. As was sufficient for his purpose at the time, he contends that grace is prior to all merit, while, in the meantime, he says nothing of the other question as to the perpetual effect of grace, which, however, he handles admirably in other places. For in saying, as he often does, that the Lord prevents the unwilling in order to make him willing, and follows after the willing that he may not will in vain, he makes him the sole author of good works. Indeed, his sentiments on this subject are too clear to need any lengthened illustration. "Men," says he, "labor to find in our will something that is our own, and not God's; how they can find it, I cannot reason." In his First Book against Pelagius and Celestius, expounding the saying of Christ, "Every man therefore that has heard, and has learned of the Father, cometh unto me" (John 6:45), he says, "The will is aided not only so as to know what is to be done, but also to do what it knows." And thus, when God teaches not by the letter of the Law, but by the grace of the Spirit, he so teaches, that everyone who has learned, not only knowing, sees, but also willing, desires, and acting, performs.

8 Answer to the second Objection continued. No will inclining to good except in the elect. The cause of election out of man. Hence, right will, as well as election, are from the good pleasure of God. The beginning of willing and doing well is of faith; faith again is the gift of God; and hence mere grace is the cause of our beginning to will well. This proved by Scripture.

Since we are now occupied with the chief point on which the controversy turns, let us give the reader the sum of the matter in a few, and those most unambiguous, passages of Scripture; thereafter, lest anyone should charge us with distorting Scripture, let us show that the truth, which we maintain to be derived from Scripture, is not unsupported by the testimony of this holy man (I mean Augustine). I deem it unnecessary to bring forward every separate passage of Scripture in confirmation of my doctrine. A selection of the choicest passages will pave the way for the understanding of all those that lie scattered up and down in the sacred volume.

On the other hand, I thought it not out of place to show my accordance with a man whose authority is justly of so much weight in the Christian world. It is certainly easy to prove that the commencement of good is only with God, and that none but the elect have a will inclined to good. But the cause of election must be sought out of man; and hence it follows that a right will is derived not from man himself, but from the same good pleasure by which we were chosen before the creation of the world. Another argument much akin to this may be added.

The beginning of right will and action being of faith, we must see whence faith itself is. But since Scripture proclaims throughout that it is the free gift of God, it follows, that when men, who are with their whole soul naturally prone to evil, begin to have a good will, it is owing to mere grace. Therefore, when the Lord, in the conversion of his people, sets down these two things as requisite to be done—viz. to take away the heart of stone, and give a heart of flesh, he openly declares, that, in order to our conversion to righteousness, what is ours must be taken away, and that what is substituted in its place is of himself. Nor does he declare this in one passage only. For he says in Jeremiah "I will give them one heart, and one way, that they may fear me forever;" and a little after he says, "I will put my fear in their hearts, that they shall not depart from me" (Jeremiah 32:39, 40). Again, in Ezekiel, "I will give them one heart, and I will put a new spirit within you; and I will take the stony heart out of their flesh, and will give them an heart of flesh" (Ezekiel 11:19). He could not more clearly claim to himself, and deny to us, everything good and right in our will, than by declaring, that in our conversion there is the creation of a new spirit and a new heart. It always follows, both that nothing good can proceed from our will until it be formed again, and that after it is formed again in so far as it is good, it is of God, and not of us.

9 Answer to second Objection continued. That good will is merely of grace proved by the prayers of saints. Three axioms A. God does not prepare man's heart, so that he can afterwards do some good of himself, but every desire of rectitude, every inclination to study, and every effort to pursue it, is from Him. B. This desire, study, and effort, do not stop short, but continue to effect. C. This progress is constant. The believer perseveres to the end. A third Objection, and three answers to it.

With this view, likewise the prayers of the saints correspond. Thus Solomon prays that the Lord may "incline our hearts unto him, to walk in his ways, and keep his commandments" (1 Kings 8:58); intimating that our heart is perverse, and naturally indulges in rebellion against the Divine law, until it be turned. Again, it is said in the Psalms, "Incline my heart unto thy testimonies" (Psalm 119:36). For we should always note the antithesis between the rebellious movement of the heart, and the correction by which it is subdued to obedience. David feeling for the time that he was deprived of directing grace, prays, "Create in me a clean heart, O God; and renew a right spirit within me" (Psalm 51:10).

Is not this an acknowledgment that all the parts of the heart are full of impurity, and that the soul has received a twist, which has turned it from straight to crooked? And then, in describing the cleansing, which he earnestly demands as a thing to be created by God, does he not ascribe the work entirely to Him? If it is objected, that the prayer itself is a symptom of a pious and holy affection, it is easy to reply, that although David had already in some measure repented, he was here contrasting the sad fall which he had experienced with his former state. Therefore, speaking in the person of a man alienated from God, he properly prays for the blessings that God bestows upon his elect in regeneration. Accordingly, like one dead, he desires to be created anew, to become, instead of a slave of Satan, an instrument of the Holy Spirit. Strange and monstrous are the longings of our pride.

There is nothing which the Lord enjoins more strictly than the religious observance of his Sabbath, in other words resting from our works; but in nothing do we show greater reluctance than to renounce our own works, and give due place to the works of God. Did not arrogance stand in the way, we could not overlook the clear testimony, which Christ has borne to the efficacy of his grace. "I," said he, "am the true vine, and my Father is the husband man." "As the branch cannot bear fruit of itself, except it abide in the vine; no more can ye, except ye abide in me" (John 15:1, 4). If we can no more bear fruit of ourselves than a vine can bud when rooted up and deprived of moisture, there is no longer any room to ask what the aptitude of our nature is for good. There is no ambiguity in the conclusion, "For without me ye can do nothing." He says not that we are too weak to suffice for ourselves; but, by reducing us to nothing, he excludes the idea of our possessing any, even the least ability.

If, when engrafted into Christ, we bear fruit like the vine, which draws its vegetative power from the moisture of the ground, and the dew of heaven, and the fostering warmth of the sun, I see nothing in a good work, which we can call our own, without trenching upon what is due to God.

It is vain to have recourse to the frivolous cavil, that the sap and the power of producing are already contained in the vine, and that, therefore, instead of deriving everything from the earth or the original root, it contributes something of its own. Our Savior's words simply mean, that when separated from him, we are nothing but dry, useless wood, because, when so separated, we have no power to do good, as he elsewhere says, "Every plant which my heavenly Father has not planted, shall be rooted up" (Matthew 15:13).

Accordingly, in the passage already quoted from the Apostle Paul, he attributes the whole operation to God, "It is God which worketh in you both to will and to do of his good pleasure" (Philippians 2:13). The first part of a good work is the will; the second is vigorous effort in the doing of it. God is the author of both. It is, therefore, robbery from God to attribute anything to us, either in the will or the act. Were it said that God gives assistance to a weak will, something might be left us; but when it is said that he makes the will, everything good in it is placed without us. Moreover, since even a good will is still weighed down by the burden of the flesh, and prevented from rising, it is added, that, to meet the difficulties of the contest, God supplies the persevering effort until the effect is obtained.

Indeed, the Apostle could not otherwise have said, as he elsewhere does, that "it is the same God which worketh all in all" (1 Corinthians 12:6)—words comprehending, as we have already observed (section 6), the whole course of the spiritual life. For which reason, David, after praying, "Teach me thy way, O Lord, I will walk in thy truths" adds, "unite my heart to fear thy name" (Psalm 86:11); by these words intimating, that even those who are well-affected are liable to so many distractions that they easily become vain, and fall away, if not strengthened to persevere. And hence, in another passage, after praying, "Order my steps in thy word," he requests that strength also may be given him to carry on the war, "Let not any iniquity have dominion over me" (Psalm 119:133).

In this way, the Lord both begins and perfects the good work in us, so that it is due to Him, first, that the will conceives a love of rectitude, is inclined to desire, is moved and stimulated to pursue it; secondly, that this choice, desire, and endeavor fail not, but are carried forward to effect; and, lastly, that we go on without interruption, and persevere even to the end.

10. A fourth Objection. Answer. Fifth Objection. Answer. Answer confirmed by many passages of Scripture, and supported by a passage from Augustine.

This movement of the will is not of that description which was for many ages taught and believed—viz. a movement which thereafter leaves us the choice to obey or resist it, but one which affects us efficaciously. We must, therefore, repudiate the oft-repeated sentiment of Chrysostom, "Whom he draws, he draws willingly;" insinuating that the Lord only stretches out his hand, and waits to see whether we will be pleased to take his aid. We grant that, as man was originally constituted, he could incline to either side, but since he has taught us by his example how miserable a thing free will is if God works not in us to will and to do, of what use to us were grace imparted in such scanty measure? Nay, by our own ingratitude, we obscure and impair divine grace.

The Apostle's doctrine is not, that the grace of a good will is offered to us if we will accept of it, but that God himself is pleased so to work in us as to guide, turn, and govern our heart by his Spirit, and reign in it as his own possession. Ezekiel promises that a new spirit will be given to the elect, not merely that they may be able to walk in his precepts, but that they may really walk in them (Ezekiel 11:19; 36:27). And the only meaning which can be given to our Savior's words, "Every man, therefore, that has heard and learned of the Father, cometh unto me" (John 6:45), is, that the grace of God is effectual in itself. This Augustine maintains in his book, *De Praedestinatione Sancta*. This grace is not bestowed on all promiscuously, according to the common, proverbial principle (of Occam, if I mistake not), that it is not denied to anyone who does what in him lies.

Men are indeed to be taught that the favor of God is offered, without exception, to all who ask it; but since those only begin to ask whom heaven by grace inspires, even this minute portion of praise must not be withheld from him. It is the privilege of the elect to be regenerated by the Spirit of God, and then placed under his guidance and government. Wherefore Augustine justly derides some who arrogate to themselves a certain power of willing, as well as censures others who imagine that that which is a special evidence of gratuitous election is given to all. He says, "Nature is common to all, but not grace;" and he calls it a showy acuteness "which shines by mere vanity, when that which God bestows, on whom he will is attributed generally to all."

Elsewhere he says, "How came you? By believing. Fear, lest by arrogating to yourself the merit of finding the right way, you perish from the right way.

I came, you say, by free choice, came by my own will. Why do you boast? Would you know that even this was given you? Hear Christ exclaiming, 'No man comets unto me, except the Father which has sent me draw him.'" And from the words of John (6:44), he infers it to be an incontrovertible fact that the hearts of believers are so effectually governed from above, that they follow with undeviating affection. "Whosoever is born of God does not commit sin; for his seed remaineth in him" (1 John 3:9). That intermediate movement, which the sophists imagine, a movement, which everyone is free to obey or to reject, is obviously excluded by the doctrine of effectual perseverance.

11 Perseverance not of ourselves, but of God. Objection. Two errors in the objection. Refutation of both.

As to perseverance, it would undoubtedly have been regarded as the gratuitous gift of God, had not the very pernicious error prevailed, that it is bestowed in proportion to human merit, according to the reception, which each individual gives to the first grace. This having given rise to the idea that it was entirely in our own power to receive or reject the offered grace of God, that idea is no sooner exploded than the error founded on it must fall.

The error, indeed, is twofold. For, besides teaching that subsequent supplies of grace reward our gratitude for the first grace and our legitimate use of it, its abettors add that, after this, grace does not operate alone, but only co-operates with us. As to the former, we must hold that the Lord, while he daily enriches his servants, and loads them with new gifts of his grace, because he approves of and takes pleasure in the work, which he has begun, finds that in them, which he may follow up with larger measures of grace. To this effect are the sentences, "To him that has shall be given." "Well done, good and faithful servant: thou hast been faithful over a few things, I will make thee ruler over many things" (Matthew 25:21, 23, 29; Luke 19:17, 16).

But here two precautions are necessary. It must not be said that the legitimate use of the first grace is rewarded by subsequent measures of grace, as if man rendered the grace of God effectual by his own industry, nor must it be thought that there is any such remuneration as to make it cease to be the gratuitous grace of God.

I admit, then, that believers may expect as a blessing from God, that the better the use they make of previous, the larger the supplies they will receive of future grace; but I say that even this use is of the Lord, and that this remuneration is bestowed freely of mere good will. The trite distinction of operating and co-operating grace is employed no less sinisterly than unhappily. Augustine, indeed, used it, but softened it by a suitable definition— viz. that God, by co-operating, perfects what he begins by operating, —that both graces are the same, but obtain different names from the different manner in which they produce their effects. Whence it follows, that he does not make an apportionment between God and man, as if a proper movement on the part of each produced a mutual concurrence. All he does is to mark a multiplication of grace. To this effect, accordingly, he elsewhere says that in man good will precedes many gifts from God; but among these gifts is this good will itself. Whence it follows, that nothing is left for the will to arrogate as its own. This Paul has expressly stated. For, after saying, "It is God which worketh in you both to will and to do," he immediately adds, "of his good pleasure" (Philippians 2:13); indicating by this expression, that the blessing is gratuitous.

As to the common saying, that after we have given admission to the first grace, our efforts co-operate with subsequent grace, this is my answer: —If it is meant that after we are once subdued by the power of the Lord to the obedience of righteousness, we proceed voluntarily, and are inclined to follow the movement of grace, I have nothing to object. For it is most certain, that where the grace of God reigns, there is also this readiness to obey. And whence this readiness, but just that the Spirit of God being everywhere consistent with himself, after first begetting a principle of obedience, cherishes and strengthens it for perseverance? If, again, it is meant that man is able of himself to be a fellow-laborer with the grace of God, I hold it to be a most pestilential delusion.

12 An objection founded on the distinction of co-operating grace. Answer. Answer confirmed by the testimony of Augustine and Bernard.

In support of this view, some make an ignorant and false application of the Apostle's words: "I labored more abundantly than they all: yet not I, but the grace of God which was with me" (1 Corinthians 15:10). The meaning they give them is, that as Paul might have seemed to speak somewhat presumptuously in preferring himself to all the other apostles, he corrects the expression so far by referring the praise to the grace of God, but he, at the same time, calls himself a co-operator with grace. It is strange that this should have proved an obstacle to so many writers, otherwise respectable.

The Apostle says not that the grace of God labored with him to make him a co-partner in the labor. He rather transfers the whole merit of the labor to grace alone, by thus modifying his first expression, "It was not I," says he, "that labored, but the grace of God that was present with me." Those who have adopted the erroneous interpretation have been misled by an ambiguity in the expression, or rather by a preposterous translation, in which the force of the Greek article is overlooked.

For to take the words literally, the Apostle does not say that grace was a fellow-worker with him, but that the grace, which was with him, was sole worker. And this is taught not obscurely, though briefly, by Augustine when he says, "Good will in man precedes many gifts from God, but not all gifts, seeing that the will which precedes is itself among the number." He adds the reason, "for it is written, 'the God of my mercy shall prevent me,' (Psalm 59:10), and 'Surely goodness and mercy shall follow me,' (Psalm 23:6); it prevents him that is unwilling, and makes him willing; it follows him that is willing, that he may not will in vain."

To this Bernard assents, introducing the Church as praying thus, "Draw me, who am in some measure unwilling, and make me willing; draw me, who am sluggishly lagging, and make me run."

13 Last part of the chapter, in which it is proved by many passages of Augustine, that he held the doctrine here taught.

Let us now hear Augustine in his own words, lest the Pelagians of our age, I mean the sophists of the Sorbonne, charge us after their wont with being opposed to all antiquity. In this, indeed, they imitate their father Pelagius, by whom of old a similar charge was brought against Augustine. In the second chapter of his *Treatise De Correptione et Gratis*, addressed to Valentinus, Augustine explains at length what I will state briefly, but in his own words, that to Adam was given the grace of persevering in goodness if he had the will; to us it is given to will, and by will overcome concupiscence: that Adam, therefore, had the power if he had the will, but did not will to have the power, whereas to us is given both the will and the power; that the original freedom of man was to be able not to sin, but that we have a much greater freedom—viz. not to be able to sin. And lest it should be supposed, as Lombard erroneously does, that he is speaking of the perfection of the future state, he shortly after removes all doubt when he says, "For so much is the will of the saints inflamed by the Holy Spirit, that they are able, because they are willing; and willing, because God worketh in them so to will." For if, in such weakness (in which, however, to suppress pride, "strength" must be made "perfect,") their own will is left to them, in such sense that, by the help of God, they are able, if they will, while at the same time God does not work in them so as to make them will; among so many temptations and infirmities the will itself would give way, and, consequently, they would not be able to persevere.

Therefore, to meet the infirmity of the human will and to prevent it from failing, however weak it might be, divine grace was made to act on it inseparably and uninterruptedly.

Augustine next entering fully into the question, how our hearts follow the movement when God affects them, necessarily says, indeed, that the Lord draws men by their own wills; wills, however, which he himself has produced. We have now an attestation by Augustine to the truth which we are specially desirous to maintain—viz. that the grace offered by the Lord is not merely one which every individual has full liberty of choosing to receive or reject, but a grace which produces in the heart both choice and will: so that all the good works which follow after are its fruit and effect; the only will which yields obedience being the will which grace itself has made. In another place, Augustine uses these words, "Every good work in us is performed only by grace."

14 An objection, representing Augustine at variance with himself and other Theologians, removed. A summary of Augustine's doctrine on free will.

In saying elsewhere that the will is not taken away by grace, but out of bad is changed into good, and after it is good is assisted, he means that man is not drawn as if by an extraneous impulse without the movement of the heart, but is inwardly affected so as to obey from the heart. Declaring that grace is given specially and gratuitously to the elect, he writes in this way to Boniface: "We know that Divine grace is not given to all men, and that to those to whom it is given, it is not given either according to the merit of works, or according to the merit of the will, but by free grace: in regard to those to whom it is not given, we know that the not giving of it is a just judgment from God." In the same epistle, he argues strongly against the opinion of those who hold that subsequent grace is given to human merit as a reward for not rejecting the first grace. For he presses Pelagius to confess that gratuitous grace is necessary to us for every action, and that merely from the fact of its being truly grace, it cannot be the recompense of works.

But the matter cannot be more briefly summed up than in the eighth chapter of his *Treatise De Correptione et Gratis*, where he shows, *First*, that human will does not by liberty obtain grace, but by grace obtains liberty. *Secondly*, that by means of the same grace, the heart being impressed with a feeling of delight, is trained to persevere, and strengthened with invincible fortitude. *Thirdly*, that while grace governs the will, it never falls; but when grace abandons it, it falls forthwith. *Fourthly*, that by the free mercy of God, the will is turned to good, and when turned, perseveres. *Fifthly*, that the direction of the will to good, and its constancy after being so directed, depend entirely on the will of God, and not on any human merit. Thus the will (free will, if you choose to call it so), which is left to man, is, as he in another place, describes it, a will which can neither be turned to God, nor continue in God, unless by grace; a will which, whatever its ability may be, derives all that ability from grace.

Chapter 4

HOW GOD WORKS IN THE HEARTS OF MEN

The leading points discussed in this chapter are, I. Whether in bad actions anything is to be attributed to God; if anything, how much. Also, what is to be attributed to the devil and to man, sections 1–5. II. In indifferent matters, how much is to be attributed to God, and how much is left to man, section 6. III. Two objections refuted, sections 7, 8.

Sections

1. Connection of this chapter with the preceding. Augustine's similitude of a good and bad rider. Question answered in respect to the devil.

2. Question answered in respect to God and man. Example from the history of Job. The works of God distinguished from the works of Satan and wicked men. A. By the design or end of acting. How Satan acts in the reprobate. B. How God acts in them.

3. Old Objection, that the agency of God in such cases is referable to prescience or permission, not actual operation. Answer, showing that God blinds and hardens the reprobate, and this in two ways; A. By deserting them; B. By delivering them over to Satan.

4. Striking passages of Scripture, proving that God acts in both ways, and disposing of the objection with regard to prescience. Confirmation from Augustine.

5. A modification of the former answer, proving that God employs Satan to instigate the reprobate, but, at the same time, is free from all taint.

6. How God works in the hearts of men in indifferent matters. Our will in such matters not so free as to be exempt from the overruling providence of God. This confirmed by various examples.

7. Objection, that these examples do not form the rule. An answer, fortified by the testimony of universal experience, by Scripture, and a passage of Augustine.

8. Some, in arguing against the error of free will, draw an argument from the event. How this is to be understood.

1 Connection of this chapter with the preceding. Augustine's similitude of a good and bad rider. Question answered in respect to the devil.

That man is so enslaved by the yoke of sin, that he cannot of his own nature aim at good either in wish or actual pursuit, has, I think, been sufficiently proved. Moreover, a distinction has been drawn between compulsion and necessity, making it clear that man, though he sins necessarily, nevertheless sins voluntarily. But since, from his being brought into bondage to the devil, it would seem that he is actuated more by the devil's will than his own, it is necessary, first, to explain what the agency of each is, and then solve the question, Whether in bad actions anything is to be attributed to God, Scripture intimating that there is some way in which he interferes?

Augustine (in Psalm 31 and 33) compares the human will to a horse preparing to start, and God and the devil to riders. "If God mounts, he, like a temperate and skillful rider, guides it calmly, urges it when too slow, reins it in when too fast, curbs its forwardness and over-action, checks its bad temper, and keeps it on the proper course; but if the devil has seized the saddle, like an ignorant and rash rider, he hurries it over broken ground, drives it into ditches, dashes it over precipices, spurs it into obstinacy or fury."

With this simile, since a better does not occur, we shall for the present be contented. When it is said, then, that the will of the natural man is subject to the power of the devil, and is actuated by him, the meaning is not that the wills while reluctant and resisting, is forced to submit (as masters oblige unwilling slaves to execute their orders), but that, fascinated by the impostures of Satan, it necessarily yields to his guidance, and does him homage.

Those whom the Lord favors not with the direction of his Spirit, he, by a righteous judgment, consigns to the agency of Satan. Wherefore, the Apostle says, "the god of this world has blinded the minds of them which believe not, lest the light of the glorious Gospel of Christ, who is the image of God, should shine into them." And, in another passage, he describes the devil as "the spirit that now worketh in the children of disobedience" (Ephesians 2:2). The blinding of the wicked, and all the iniquities consequent upon it, are called the works of Satan; works the cause of which is not to be sought in anything external to the will of man, in which the root of the evil lies, and in which the foundation of Satan's kingdom, in other words, sin, is fixed.

2 Question answered in respect to God and man. Example from the history of Job. The works of God distinguished from the works of Satan and wicked men. A. By the design or end of acting. How Satan acts in the reprobate. B. How God acts in them.

The nature of the divine agency in such cases is very different. For the purpose of illustration, let us refer to the calamities brought upon holy Job by the Chaldeans. They having slain his shepherds, carry off his flocks. The wickedness of their deed is manifest, as is also the hand of Satan, who, as the history informs us, was the instigator of the whole. Job, however, recognizes it as the work of God, saying, that what the Chaldeans had plundered, "the Lord" had "taken away."

How can we attribute the same work to God, to Satan, and to man, without either excusing Satan by the interference of God, or making God the author of the crime? This is easily done, if we look first to the end, and then to the mode of acting. The Lord designs to exercise the patience of his servant by adversity. Satan's plan is to drive him to despair, while the Chaldeans are bent on making unlawful gain by plunder. Such diversity of purpose makes a wide distinction in the act. In the mode, there is not less difference. The Lord permits Satan to afflict his servant; and the Chaldeans, who had been chosen as the ministers to execute the deed, he hands over to the impulses of Satan, who, pricking on the already depraved Chaldeans with his poisoned darts, instigates them to commit the crime. They rush furiously on to the unrighteous deed, and become its guilty perpetrators. Here Satan is properly said to act in the reprobate, over whom he exercises his sway, which is that of wickedness. God also is said to act in his own way; because even Satan when he is the instrument of divine wrath, is completely under the command of God, who turns him as he will in the execution of his just judgments.

I say nothing here of the universal agency of God, which, as it sustains all the creatures, also gives them all their power of acting. I am now speaking only of that special agency which is apparent in every act. We thus see that there is no inconsistency in attributing the same act to God, to Satan, and to man, while, from the difference in the end and mode of action, the spotless righteousness of God shines forth at the same time that the iniquity of Satan and of man is manifested in all its deformity.

3 Old Objection, that the agency of God in such cases is referable to prescience or permission, not actual operation. Answer, showing that God blinds and hardens the reprobate, and this in two ways; A. By deserting them; B. By delivering them over to Satan.

Ancient writers sometimes manifest a superstitious dread of making a simple confession of the truth in this matter, from a fear of furnishing impiety with a handle for speaking irreverently of the works of God. While I embrace such soberness with all my heart, I cannot see the least danger in simply holding what Scripture delivers. When Augustine was not always free from this superstition, as when he says, that blinding and hardening have respect not to the operation of God, but to prescience. But this subtlety is repudiated by many passages of Scriptures, which clearly show that the divine interference amounts to something more than prescience.

Augustine himself, in his book against Julian, contends at length that sins are manifestations not merely of divine permission or patience, but also of divine power, that thus former sins may be punished. In like manner, what is said of permission is too weak to stand. God is very often said to blind and harden the reprobate, to turn their hearts, to incline and impel them, as I have elsewhere fully explained (Book 1, chapter 18).

The extent of this agency can never be explained by having recourse to prescience or permission. We, therefore, hold that there are two methods in which God may so act. When his light is taken away, nothing remains but blindness and darkness: when his Spirit is taken away, our hearts become hard as stones: when his guidance is withdrawn, we immediately turn from the right path: and hence he is properly said to incline, harden, and blind those whom he deprives of the faculty of seeing, obeying, and rightly executing. The second method, which comes much nearer to the exact meaning of the words, is when executing his judgments by Satan as the minister of his anger, God both directs men's counsels, and excites their wills, and regulates their efforts as he pleases. Thus when Moses relates that Simon, king of the Amorites, did not give the Israelites a passage, because the Lord "had hardened his spirit, and made his heart obstinate," he immediately adds the purpose which God had in view—viz. that he might deliver him into their hand (Deuteronomy 2:30). As God had resolved to destroy him, the hardening of his heart was the divine preparation for his ruin.

4 Striking passages of Scripture, proving that God acts in both ways, and disposing of the objection with regard to prescience. Confirmation from Augustine.

In accordance with the former methods it seems to be said, "The law shall perish from the priests and counsel from the ancients." "He poureth contempt upon princes, and causeth them to wander in the wilderness, where there is no way." Again "O Lord, why hast thou made us to err from thy ways, and hardened our heart from thy fear?" These passages rather indicate what men become when God deserts them, than what the nature of his agency is when he works in them. But there are other passages, which go further, such as those concerning the hardening of Pharaoh: "I will harden his heart, that he shall not let the people go."

The same thing is afterwards repeated in stronger terms. Did he harden his heart by not softening it? This is, indeed, true; but he did something more: he gave it in charge to Satan to confirm him in his obstinacy. Hence, he had previously said, "I am sure he will not let you go." The people come out of Egypt, and the inhabitants of a hostile region come forth against them. How were they instigated? Moses certainly declares of Sihon, that it was the Lord who "had hardened his spirit, and made his heart obstinate" (Deuteronomy 2:30). The Psalmists relating the same history says, "He turned their hearts to hate his people" (Psalm 105:25). You cannot now say that they stumbled merely because they were deprived of divine counsel. For if they are *hardened* and *turned*, they are purposely bent to the very end in view.

Moreover, whenever God saw it meet to punish the people for their transgression, in what way did he accomplish his purpose by the reprobate? In such a way as shows that the efficacy of the action was in him, and that they were only ministers. At one time he declares, "that he will lift an ensign to the nations from far, and will hiss unto them from the end of the earth;" at another, that he will take a net to ensnare them; and at another, that he will be like a hammer to strike them. But he specially declared that he was not inactive among theme when he called Sennacherib an axe, which was formed and destined to be wielded by his own hand.

Augustine is not far from the mark when he states the matter thus, That men sin, is attributable to themselves: that in sinning they produce this or that result, is owing to the mighty power of God, who divides the darkness as he pleases.

5 A modification of the former answer, proving that God employs Satan to instigate the reprobate, but, at the same time, is free from all taint.

Moreover, that the ministry of Satan is employed to instigate the reprobate, whenever the Lord, in the course of his providence, has any purpose to accomplish in them, will sufficiently appear from a single passage. It is repeatedly said in the First Book of Samuel, that an evil spirit from the Lord came upon Saul, and troubled him (1 Samuel 16:14; 18:10; 19:9). It would be impious to apply this to the Holy Spirit. An impure spirit must therefore be called a spirit from the Lord, because completely subservient to his purpose, being more an instrument in acting than a proper agent. We should also add what Paul says, "God shall send them strong delusion, that they should believe a lie: that they all might be damned who believed not the truth" (2 Thessalonians 2:11, 12). But in the same transaction there is always a wide difference between what the Lord does, and what Satan and the ungodly design to do. The wicked instruments, which he has under his hand and can turn as he pleases, he makes subservient to his own justice. They, as they are wicked, give effect to the iniquity conceived in their wicked minds. Everything necessary to vindicate the majesty of God from calumny, and cut off any subterfuge on the part of the ungodly, has already been expounded in the Chapters on Providence (Book 1, Chapters 16–18). Here I only meant to show, in a few words, how Satan reigns in the reprobate, and how God works in both.

6 How God works in the hearts of men in indifferent matters. Our will in such matters not so free as to be exempt from the overruling providence of God. This confirmed by various examples.

In those actions, which in themselves are neither good nor bad, and concern the corporeal rather than the spiritual life, the liberty which man possesses, although we have above touched upon it (*supra*, Chapter 2, sections 13–17), has not yet been explained. Some have conceded a free choice to man in such actions; more, I suppose, because they were unwilling to debate a matter of no great moment, than because they wished positively to assert what they were prepared to concede. While I admit that those who hold that man has no ability in himself to do righteousness, hold what is most necessary to be known for salvation, I think it ought not to be overlooked that we owe it to the special grace of God, whenever, on the one hand, we choose what is for our advantage, and whenever our will inclines in that direction; and on the other, whenever with heart and soul we shun what would otherwise do us harm. And the interference of Divine Providence goes to the extent not only of making events turn out as was foreseen to be expedient, but also of giving the wills of men the same direction.

If we look at the administration of human affairs with the eye of sense, we will have no doubt that, so far, they are placed at man's disposal; but if we lend an ear to the many passages of Scripture which proclaim that even in these matters the minds of men are ruled by God, they will compel us to place human choice in subordination to his special influence. Who gave the Israelites such favor in the eyes of the Egyptians, that they lent them all their most valuable commodities? (Exodus 11:3). They never would have been so inclined of their own accord. Their inclinations, therefore, were more overruled by God than regulated by themselves. And surely, had not Jacob been persuaded that God inspires men with divers affections as seemeth to him good, he would not have said of his son Joseph (whom he thought to be some heathen Egyptian), "God Almighty give you mercy before the man" (Genesis 43:14). In like manner, the whole Church confesses that when the Lord was pleased to pity his people, he made them also to be pitied of all them that carried them captives Psalm 106:46). In like manner, when his anger was kindled against Saul, so that he prepared himself for battle, the cause is stated to have been, that a spirit from God fell upon him (1 Samuel 11:6) who dissuaded Absalom from adopting the counsel of Ahithophel, which was wont to be regarded as an oracle (2 Samuel 17:14).

Who disposed Rehoboam to adopt the counsel of the young men (1 Kings 12:10)? Who caused the approach of the Israelites to strike terror into nations formerly distinguished for valor? Even the harlot Rahab recognized the hand of the Lord. Who, on the other hand, filled the hearts of the Israelites with fear and dread (Leviticus 262:36), but gave a "trembling heart" to him who threatened in the Law? (Deuteronomy 28:65).

7 Objection, that these examples do not form the rule. An answer, fortified by the testimony of universal experience, by Scripture, and a passage of Augustine.

It may be objected, that these are special examples, which cannot be regarded as a general rule. They are sufficient, at all events, to prove the point for which I contend—viz. that whenever God is pleased to make way for his providence, he even in external matters so turns and bends the wills of men, that whatever the freedom of their choice may be, it is still subject to the disposal of God. That your mind depends more on the agency of God than the freedom of your own choice, daily experience teaches. Your judgment often fails, and in matters of no great difficulty, your courage flags; at other times, in matters of the greatest obscurity, the mode of explicating them at once suggests itself, while in matters of moment and danger, your mind rises superior to every difficulty.

In this way, I interpret the words of Solomon, "The hearing ear, and the seeing eye, the Lord hath made even both of them" (Proverbs 20:12). For they seem to me to refer not to their creation, but to peculiar grace in the use of them, when he says, "The king's heart is in the hand of the Lord as the rivers of water; he turneth it whithersoever he will" (Proverbs 21:1), he comprehends the whole race under one particular class. If any will is free from subjection, it must be that of one possessed of regal power, and in a manner exercising dominion over other wills. But if it is under the hand of God, ours surely cannot be exempt from it.

On this subject there is an admirable sentiment of Augustine, "Scripture, if it be carefully examined, will show not only that the good wills of men are made good by God out of evil, and when so made, are directed to good acts, even to eternal life, but those which retain the elements of the world are in the power of God, to turn them whither he pleases, and when he pleases, either to perform acts of kindness, or by a hidden, indeed, but, at the same time, most just judgment to inflict punishment."

8 Some, in arguing against the error of free will, draw an argument from the event. How this is to be understood.

Let the reader here remember, that the power of the human will is not to be estimated by the event, as some unskillful persons are absurdly wont to do. They think it an elegant and ingenious proof of the bondage of the human will, that even the greatest monarchs are sometimes thwarted in their wishes. But the ability of which we speak must be considered as within the man, not measured by outward success. In discussing the subject of free will, the question is not, whether external obstacles will permit a man to execute what he has internally resolved, but whether, in any matter whatever, he has a free power of judging and of willing. If men possess both of these, Attilius Regulus, shut up in a barrel studded with sharp nails, will have a will no less free than Augustus Caesar ruling with imperial sway over a large portion of the globe.

Chapter 5

THE ARGUMENTS USUALLY ALLEGED
IN SUPPORT OF FREE WILL REFUTED

Objections reduced to three principal heads: —I. Four absurdities advanced by the opponents of the orthodox doctrine concerning the slavery of the will, stated and refuted, sections 1–5. II. The passages of Scripture which they pervert in favor of their error, reduced to five heads, and explained, sections 6–15. III. Five other passages quoted in defense of free will expounded, sections 16–19.

Sections

1. Absurd fictions of opponents first refuted, and then certain passages of Scripture explained. Answer by a negative. Confirmation of the answer.

2. Another absurdity of Aristotle and Pelagius. Answer by a distinction. Answer fortified by passages from Augustine, and supported by the authority of an Apostle.

3. Third absurdity borrowed from the words of Chrysostom. Answer by a negative.

4. Fourth absurdity urged of old by the Pelagians. Answer from the works of Augustine. Illustrated by the testimony of our Savior. Another answer, which explains the use of exhortations.

5. A third answer, which contains a fuller explanation of the second. Objection to the previous answers. Objection refuted. Summary of the previous answers.

6. First class of arguments, which the Neo-Pelagians draw from Scripture in defense of free will. The Law demands perfect obedience and therefore God either mocks us, or requires things, which are not in our power. Answer by distinguishing precepts into three sorts. The first of these considered in this and the following section.

7. This general argument from the Law of no avail to the patrons of free will. Promises conjoined with precepts, prove that our salvation is to be found in the grace of God. *Objection, that the Law was given to the persons living at the time. Answer, confirmed by passages from Augustine.*

8. *A special consideration of the three classes of precepts of no avail to the defenders of free will. A. Precepts enjoining us to turn to God. B. Precepts, which simply speak of the observance of the Law. C. Precepts, which enjoin us to persevere in the grace of God.*

9. *Objection. Answer. Confirmation of the answer from Jeremiah. Another objection refuted.*

10. *A second class of arguments in defense of free will drawn from the promises of God—viz. that the promises which God makes to those who seek him are vain if it is not in our power to do, or not do, the thing required. Answer, which explains the use of promises, and removes the supposed inconsistency.*

11. *Third class of arguments drawn from the divine upbraiding, —that it is in vain to upbraid us for evils which it is not in our power to avoid. Answer. Sinners are condemned by their own consciences, and, therefore, the divine upbraiding is just. Moreover, there is a twofold use in this upbraiding. Various passages of Scripture explained by means of the foregoing answers.*

12. *Objection founded on the words of Moses. Refutation by the words of an Apostle. Confirmation by argument.*

13. *Fourth class of arguments by the defenders of free will. God waits to see whether or not sinners will repent; therefore, they can repent. Answer by a dilemma. Passage in Hosea explained.*

14. *Fifth class of arguments in defense of free will. God and bad works described as our own, and therefore we are capable of both. Answer by an exposition, which shows that this argument is unavailing. Objection drawn from analogy. Answer. The nature and mode of divine agency in the elect.*

15. *Conclusion of the answer to the last class of arguments.*

16. *Third and last division of the chapter discussing certain passages of Scripture. A. A passage from Genesis. Its true meaning explained.*

17. *B. Passage from the Epistle to the Romans. Explanation. Refutation of an objection. Another refutation. A third refutation from Augustine. C. A passage from First Corinthians. Answer to it.*

18. D. A passage from Ecclesiastes. Explanation. Another explanation.

19. E. A passage from Luke. Explanation. Allegorical arguments weak. Another explanation. A third explanation. A fourth from Augustine. Conclusion and summary of the whole discussion concerning free will.

1 Absurd fictions of opponents first refuted, and then certain passages of Scripture explained. Answer by a negative. Confirmation of the answer.

Enough would seem to have been said on the subject of man's will, were there not some who endeavor to urge him to his ruin by a false opinion of liberty, and at the same time, in order to support their own opinion, assail ours. First, they gather some absurd inferences, by which they endeavor to bring odium upon our doctrine, as if it were abhorrent to common sense, and then they oppose it with certain passages of Scripture (*infra*, section 6). Both devices we shall dispose of in their order. If sin, say they, is necessary, it ceases to be sin; if it is voluntary, it may be avoided. Such, too, were the weapons with which Pelagius assailed Augustine. But we are unwilling to crush them by the weight of his name, until we have satisfactorily disposed of the objections themselves.

I deny, therefore, that sin ought to be the less imputed because it is necessary; and, on the other hand, I deny the inference, that sin may be avoided because it is voluntary. If anyone will dispute with God, and endeavor to evade his judgment, by pretending that he could not have done otherwise, the answer already given is sufficient, that it is owing not to creation, but the corruption of nature, that man has become the slave of sin, and can will nothing but evil. For whence that impotence of which the wicked so readily avail themselves as an excuse, but just because Adam voluntarily subjected himself to the tyranny of the devil?

Hence, the corruption by which we are held bound as with chains, originated in the first man's revolt from his Maker. If all men are justly held guilty of this revolt, let them not think themselves excused by a necessity in which they see the clearest cause of their condemnation.

But this I have fully explained above; and in the case of the devil himself, have given an example of one who sins not less voluntarily that he sins necessarily. I have also shown, in the case of the elect angels, that though their will cannot decline from good, it does not therefore cease to be will. This Bernard shrewdly explains when he says that we are the more miserable in this, that the necessity is voluntary; and yet this necessity so binds us who are subject to it, that we are the slaves of sin, as we have already observed.

The second step in the reasoning is vicious, because it leaps from *voluntary* to *free*; whereas we have proved above, that a thing may be done voluntarily, though not subject to free choice.

2 Another absurdity of Aristotle and Pelagius. Answer by a distinction. Answer fortified by passages from Augustine, and supported by the authority of an Apostle.

They add, that unless virtue and vice proceed from free choice, it is absurd either to punish man or reward him. Although this argument is taken from Aristotle, I admit that Chrysostom and Jerome also use it. Jerome, however, does not disguise that it was familiar to the Pelagians. He even quotes their words, "If grace acts in us, grace, and not we who do the work, will be crowned."

With regard to punishment, I answer, that it is properly inflicted on those by whom the guilt is contracted. What matters it whether you sin with a free or an enslaved judgment, so long as you sin voluntarily, especially when man is proved a sinner because he is under the bondage of sin? In regard to the rewards of righteousness, is there any great absurdity in acknowledging that they depend on the kindness of God rather than our own merits? How often do we meet in Augustine with this expression, — "God crowns not our merits but his own gifts; and the name of reward is given not to what is due to our merits, but to the recompense of grace previously bestowed?" Some seem to think there is acuteness in the remark, that there is no place at all for the mind, if good works do not spring from free will as their proper source; but in thinking this unreasonable, they are widely mistaken.

Augustine does not hesitate uniformly to describe as necessary the very thing, which they count it impious to acknowledge. Thus, he asks, "What is human merit? He who came to bestow not due recompense but free grace, though himself free from sin, and the giver of freedom, found all men sinners." Again, "If you are to receive your due, you must be punished. What then is done? God has not rendered you due punishment, but bestows upon you unmerited grace. If you wish to be an alien from grace, boast your merits" (in Psalm 70). Again, "You are nothing in yourself, sin is yours, merit God's.

Punishment is your due; and when the reward shall come, God shall crown his own gifts, not your merits." To the same effect, he elsewhere says that grace is not of merit, but merit of grace. And shortly after he concludes, that God by his gifts anticipates all our merit, that he may thereby manifest his own merit, and give what is absolutely free, because he sees nothing in us that can be a ground of salvation. But why extend the list of quotations, when similar sentiments are always recurring in his works?

The abettors of this error would see a still better refutation of it, if they would attend to the source from which the apostle derives the glory of the saints, —"Moreover, whom he did predestinate, them he also called; and whom he called, them he also justified; and whom he justified, them he also glorified" (Romans 8:30). On what ground, then, the apostle being judge (2 Timothy 4:8), are believers crowned? Because by the mercy of God, not their own exertions, they are predestinated, called, and justified. Away, then, with the vain fear, that unless free will stands, there will no longer be any merit! It is most foolish to take alarm, and recoil from that which Scripture inculcates. "If thou didst receive it, why dost thou glory as if thou hadst not received it?" (1 Corinthians 4:7).

You see how everything is denied to free will, for the very purpose of leaving no room for merit. And yet, as the beneficence and liberality of God are manifold and inexhaustible, the grace that he bestows upon us, inasmuch as he makes it our own, he recompenses as if the virtuous acts were our own.

3 Third absurdity borrowed from the words of Chrysostom. Answer by a negative.

But it is added, in terms which seem to be borrowed from Chrysostom that if our will possesses not the power of choosing good or evil, all who are partakers of the same nature must be alike good or alike bad. A sentiment akin to this occurs in the work *De Vocatione Gentium*, usually attributed to Ambrose, who argues that no one would ever decline from faith, did not the grace of God leave us in a mutable state. It is strange that such men should have so blundered. How did it fail to occur to Chrysostom, that it is divine election, which distinguishes among men? We have not the least hesitation to admit what Paul strenuously maintains, that all, without exception, are depraved and given over to wickedness; but at the same time we add, that through the mercy of God all do not continue in wickedness. Therefore, while we all labor naturally under the same disease, those only recover health to whom the Lord is pleased to put forth his healing hand. The others, whom he passes over in just judgment, pine and rot away until they are consumed. And this is the only reason that some persevere to the end, and others, after beginning their course, fall away.

Perseverance is the gift of God, which he does not lavish promiscuously on all, but imparts to whom he pleases. If it is asked how the difference arises—why some steadily persevere, and others prove deficient in steadfastness, we can give no other reason than that the Lord, by his mighty power, strengthens and sustains the former, so that they perish not, while he does not furnish the same assistance to the latter, but leaves them to be monuments of instability.

4

Fourth absurdity urged of old by the Pelagians. Answer from the works of Augustine. Illustrated by the testimony of our Savior. Another answer, which explains the use of exhortations.

Still it is insisted, that exhortations are vain, warnings superfluous, and rebukes absurd, if the sinner possesses not the power to obey. When similar objections were urged against Augustine, he was obliged to write his book, *De Correptione et Gratia*, where he has fully disposed of them. The substance of his answer to his opponents is this: "O, man! Learn from the precept what you ought to do; learn from correction, that it is your own fault you have not the power; and learn in prayer, whence it is that you may receive the power." Very similar is the argument of his book, *De Spiritu et Litera*, in which he shows that God does not measure the precepts of his law by human strength, but, after ordering what is right, freely bestows on his elect the power of fulfilling it.

The subject, indeed, does not require a long discussion. For we are not singular in our doctrine, but have Christ and all his apostles with us. Let our opponents, then, consider how they are to come off victorious in a contest, which they wage with such antagonists. Christ declares, "without me ye can do nothing,"(John 20:5). Does he the less censure and chastise those who, without him, did wickedly? Does he the less exhort every man to be intent on good works? How severely does Paul inveigh against the Corinthians for want of charity (1 Corinthians 3:3); and yet at the same time, he prays that charity may be given them by the Lord. In the Epistle to the Romans, he declares that "it is not of him that willeth, nor of him that runneth, but of God that showeth mercy" (Romans 9:16). Still he ceases not to warn, exhort, and rebuke them.

Why then do they not expostulate with God for making sport with men, by demanding of them things that he alone can give, and chastising them for faults committed through want of his grace? Why do they not admonish Paul to spare those who have it not in their power to will or to run, unless the mercy of God, which has forsaken them, precedes?

As if the doctrine were not founded on the strongest reason—reason which no serious inquirer can fail to perceive. The extent to which doctrine, and exhortation, and rebuke, are in themselves able to change the mind, is indicated by Paul when he says, "Neither is he that planteth anything, neither he that watereth; but God that giveth the increase" (1 Corinthians 3:7) in like manner, we see that Moses delivers the precepts of the Law under a heavy sanction, and that the prophets strongly urge and threaten transgressors though they at the same time confess, that men are wise only when an understanding heart is given them; that it is the proper work of God to circumcise the heart, and to change it from stone into flesh; to write his law on their inward parts; in short, to renew souls so as to give efficacy to doctrine.

5 A third answer, which contains a fuller explanation of the second. Objection to the previous answers. Objection refuted. Summary of the previous answers.

What purpose, then, is served by exhortations? It is this: As the wicked, with obstinate hearts, despise them, they will be a testimony against them when they stand at the judgment-seat of God. Nay, they even now strike and lash their consciences. For, however they may petulantly deride, they cannot disapprove them. "But what," you will ask, "can a miserable mortal do, when softness of heart, which is necessary to obedience, is denied him?"

I ask, in reply, "Why have recourse to evasion, since hardness of heart cannot be imputed to any but the sinner himself?"

The ungodly, though they would gladly evade the divine admonitions, are forced, whether they will or not, to feel their power. But their chief use is to be seen in the case of believers, in whom the Lord, while he always acts by his Spirit, also omits not the instrumentality of his word, but employs it, and not without effect.

Let this, then, be a standing truth, that the whole strength of the godly consists in the grace of God, according to the words of the prophet, "I will give them one heart, and I will put a new spirit within you; and I will take the stony heart out of their flesh, and will give them an heart of flesh, that they may walk in my statutes" (Ezekiel 11:19, 20). But it will be asked, why are they now admonished of their duty, and not rather left to the guidance of the Spirit? Why are they urged with exhortations when they cannot hasten any faster than the Spirit impels them? And why are they chastised, if at any time they go astray, seeing that this is caused by the necessary infirmity of the flesh? "O, man! Who art thou that replies against God?"

If, in order to prepare us for the grace that enables us to obey exhortation, God sees fit to employ exhortation, what is there in such an arrangement for you to carp and scoff at? Had exhortations and reprimands no other profit with the godly than to convince them of sin, they could not be deemed altogether useless. Now, when, by the Spirit of God acting within, they have the effect of inflaming their desire of good, of arousing them from lethargy, of destroying the pleasure and honeyed sweetness of sin, making it hateful and loathsome, who will presume to quibble about them as superfluous?

Should anyone wish a clearer reply, let him take the following: —God works in his elect in two ways: inwardly, by his Spirit, outwardly, by his Word. By his Spirit illuminating their minds, and training their hearts to the practice of righteousness, he makes them new creatures, while, by his Word, he stimulates them to long and seek for this renovation. In both, he exerts the might of his hand in proportion to the measure in which he dispenses them. The Word, when addressed to the reprobate, though not effectual for their amendment, has another use. It urges their consciences now, and will render them more inexcusable on the Day of Judgment.

Thus, our Savior, while declaring that none can come to him but those whom the Father draws, and that the elect come after they have heard and learned of the Father (John 6:44, 45), does not lay aside the office of teacher, but carefully invites those who must be taught inwardly by the Spirit before they can make any profit. The reprobate, again, are admonished by Paul, that the doctrine is not in vain; because, while it is in them a savor of death unto death, it is still a sweet savor unto God (2 Corinthians 2:16).

6 First class of arguments, which the Neo-Pelagians draw from Scripture in defense of free will. The Law demands perfect obedience and therefore God either mocks us, or requires things, which are not in our power. Answer by distinguishing precepts into three sorts. The first of these considered in this and the following section.

The enemies of this doctrine are at great pains in collecting passages of Scripture, as if, unable to accomplish anything by their weight, they were to overwhelm us by their number. But as in battle, when it is come to close quarters, an unwarlike multitude, however great the pomp and show they make, give way after a few blows, and take to flight, so we shall have little difficulty here in disposing of our opponents and their host. All the passages which they pervert in opposing us are very similar in their import; and hence, when they are arranged under their proper heads, one answer will suffice for several; it is not necessary to give a separate consideration to each. Precepts seem to be regarded as their stronghold. These they think so accommodated to our abilities, as to make it follow as a matter of course, that whatever they enjoin we are able to perform. Accordingly, they run over all the precepts, and by them fix the measure of our power. For, say they, when God enjoins meekness, submission, love, chastity, piety, and holiness, and when he forbids anger, pride, theft, uncleanness, idolatry, and the like, he either mocks us, or only requires things which are in our power.

All the precepts, which they thus heap together, may be divided into three classes. Some enjoin a first conversion unto God, others speak simply of the observance of the law, and others inculcate perseverance in the grace, which has been received. We shall first treat of precepts in general, and then proceed to consider each separate class. That the abilities of man are equal to the precepts of the divine law, has long been a common idea, and has some show of plausibility. It is founded, however, on the grossest ignorance of the law. Those who deem it a kind of sacrilege to say, that the observance of the law is impossible, insist, as their strongest argument, that, if it is so, the Law has been given in vain (*infra*, Chapter 7, section 5). For they speak just as if Paul had never said anything about the Law. But what, pray, is meant by saying, that the Law "was added because of transgressions;" "by the law is the knowledge of sin;" "I had not known sin but by the law;" "the law entered that the offense might abound?" (Galatians 3:19; Romans 3:20; 7:7; 5:20). Is it meant that the Law was to be limited to our strength, lest it should be given in vain? Is it not rather meant that it was placed far above us, in order to convince us of our utter feebleness? Paul indeed declares that charity is the end and fulfilling of the Law (1 Timothy 1:5). But when he prays that the minds of the Thessalonians may be filled with it, he clearly enough acknowledges that the Law sounds in our ears without profit, if God do not implant it thoroughly in our hearts (1 Thessalonians 3:12).

7 This general argument from the Law of no avail to the patrons of free will. Promises conjoined with precepts, prove that our salvation is to be found in the grace of God. Objection, that the Law was given to the persons living at the time. Answer, confirmed by passages from Augustine.

I admit, indeed, that if the Scripture taught nothing else on the subject than that the Law is a rule of life by which we ought to regulate our pursuits, I should at once assent to their opinion; but since it carefully and clearly explains that the use of the Law is manifold, the proper course is to learn from that explanation what the power of the Law is in man.

In regard to the present question, while it explains what our duty is it teaches that the power of obeying it is derived from the goodness of God, and it accordingly urges us to pray that this power may be given us. If there were merely a command and no promise, it would be necessary to try whether our strength were sufficient to fulfill the command; but since promises are annexed, which proclaim not only that aid, but that our whole power is derived from divine grace, they at the same time abundantly testify that we are not only unequal to the observance of the Law, but mere fools in regard to it. Therefore, let us hear no more of a proportion between our ability and the divine precepts, as if the Lord had accommodated the standard of justice, which he was to give in the Law to our feeble capacities. We should rather gather from the promises hove ill provided we are, having in everything so much need of grace. But say they, "Who will believe that the Lord designed his Law for blocks and stones?" There is no wish to make anyone believe this. The ungodly are neither blocks nor stones, when, taught by the Law that their lusts are offensive to God, they are proved guilty by their own confession; nor are the godly blocks or stones, when admonished of their powerlessness, they take refuge in grace.

To this effect are the pithy sayings of Augustine, "God orders what we cannot do, that we may know what we ought to ask of him. There is a great utility in precepts, if all that is given to free will is to do greater honor to divine grace. Faith acquires what the Law requires; nay, the Law requires, in order that faith may acquire what is thus required; nay, more, God demands of us faith itself, and finds not what he thus demands, until by giving he makes it possible to find it." Again, he says, "Let God give what he orders, and order what he wills."

8 A special consideration of the three classes of precepts of no avail to the defenders of free will. A. Precepts enjoining us to turn to God. B. Precepts, which simply speak of the observance of the Law. C. Precepts, which enjoin us to persevere in the grace of God.

This will be more clearly seen by again attending to the three classes of precepts to which we above referred. Both in the Law and in the Prophets, God repeatedly calls upon us to turn to him. But, on the other hand, a prophet exclaims, "Turn thou me, and I shall be turned; for thou art the Lord my God. Surely after that I was turned, I repented." He orders us to circumcise the foreskins of our hearts; but Moses declares that his own hand makes that circumcision. In many passages, he demands a new heart, but in others, he declares that he gives it.

As Augustine says, "What God promises, we ourselves do not through choice or nature, but he himself does by grace." The same observation is made, when, in enumerating the rules of Tichonius, he states the third in effect to be—that we distinguish carefully between the Law and the promises, or between the commands and grace. Let them now go and gather from precepts what man's power of obedience is, when they would destroy the divine grace by which the precepts themselves are accomplished. The precepts of the second class are simply those that enjoin us to worship God, to obey and adhere to his will, to do his pleasure, and follow his teaching. But innumerable passages testify that every degree of purity, piety, holiness, and justices that we possess, is his gift. Of the third class of precepts is the exhortation of Paul and Barnabas to the proselytes, as recorded by Luke; they "persuaded them to continue in the grace of God" (Acts 13:43). But the source from which this power of continuance must be sought is elsewhere explained by Paul, when he says, "Finally, my brethren, be strong in the Lord" (Ephesians 6:10). In another passage he says, "Grieve not the Holy Spirit of God, whereby ye are sealed unto the day of redemption" (Ephesians 4:30).

As the thing here enjoined could not be performed by man, he prays in behalf of the Thessalonians, that God would count them "worthy of this calling, and fulfill all the good pleasure of his goodness, and the work of faith with power" (2 Thessalonians 1:11). In the same way, in the Second Epistle to the Corinthians, when treating of alms, he repeatedly commends their good and pious inclination. A little further on, however, he exclaims, "Thanks be to God, which put the same earnest care into the heart of Titus for you. For indeed he accepted the exhortation" (2 Corinthians 8:16, 17).

If Titus could not even perform the office of being a mouth to exhort others, except in so far as God suggested, how could the others have been voluntary agents in acting, if the Lord Jesus had not directed their hearts?

9 Objection. Answer. Confirmation of the answer from Jeremiah. Another objection refuted.

Some, who would be thought more acute, endeavor to evade all these passages, by the quibble, that there is nothing to hinder us from contributing our part, while God, at the same time, supplies our deficiencies. They, moreover, offer passages from the Prophets as evidence, in which the work of our conversion seems to be shared between God and us: "Turn ye unto me, saith the Lord of hosts, and I will turn unto you, saith the Lord of hosts" (Zechariah 1:3). The kind of assistance that God gives us has been shown above (sect. 7, 8), and need not now be repeated.

One thing only I ask to be conceded to me, that it is vain to think we have a power of fulfilling the Law, merely because we are enjoined to obey it. Since, in order to our fulfilling the divine precepts, the grace of the Lawgiver is both necessary, and has been promised to us, this much at least is clear, that more is demanded of us than we are able to pay. Nor can any cavil evade the declaration in Jeremiah, that the covenant which God made with his ancient people was broken, because it was only of the letter—that to make it effectual, it was necessary for the Spirit to interpose and train the heart to obedience (Jeremiah 31:32).

The opinion we now combat is not aided by the words, "Turn unto me, and I will turn unto you." The turning there spoken of is not that by which God renews the heart unto repentance; but that in which, by bestowing prosperity, he manifests his kindness and favor, just in the same way as he sometimes expresses his displeasure by sending adversity. The people complaining under the many calamities which befell them, that they were forsaken by God, he answers, that his kindness would not fail them, if they would return to a right course, and to himself, the standard of righteousness. The passage, therefore, is wrested from its proper meaning when it is made to countenance the idea that the work of conversion is divided between God and man (*supra*, Chapter 2, section 27). We have only glanced briefly at this subject, as the proper place for it will occur when we come to treat of the Law (Chapter 7, sections 2 and 3).

10 A second class of arguments in defense of free will drawn from the promises of God—viz. that the promises which God makes to those who seek him are vain if it is not in our power to do, or not do, the thing required. Answer, which explains the use of promises, and removes the supposed inconsistency.

The second class of objections is akin to the former. They allege the promises in which the Lord makes a pact with our will. Such are the following: "Seek good, and not evil, that ye may live" (Amos 5:14). "If ye be willing and obedient, ye shall eat the good of the land: but if ye refuse and rebel, ye shall be devoured with the sword; for the mouth of the Lord has spoken it" (Isaiah 1:19, 20). "If thou wilt put away thine abominations out of my sight, then thou shalt not remove" (Jeremiah 4:1). "It shall come to pass, if thou shalt hearken diligently unto the voice of the Lord thy God, to observe and do all the commandments which I command thee this days that the Lord thy God will set thee on high above all nations of the earth" (Deuteronomy 28:1).

There are other similar passages (Leviticus 26:3, etc.). They think that the blessings contained in these promises are offered to our will absurdly and in mockery, if it is not in our power to secure or reject them. It is, indeed, an easy matter to indulge in declamatory complaint on this subject, to say that we are cruelly mocked by the Lord, when he declares that his kindness depends on our wills if we are not masters of our wills—that it would be a strange liberality on the part of God to set his blessings before us, while we have no power of enjoying them, —a strange certainty of promises, which, to prevent their ever being fulfilled, are made to depend on an impossibility. Of promises of this description, which have a condition annexed to them, we shall elsewhere speak, and make it plain that there is nothing absurd in the impossible fulfillment of them. In regard to the matter in hand, I deny that God cruelly mocks us when he invites us to merit blessings, which he knows we are altogether unable to merit.

The promises being offered alike to believers and to the ungodly have their use in regard to both. As God by his precepts stings the consciences of the ungodly, to prevent them from enjoying their sins while they have no remembrance of his judgments, so, in his promises, he in a manner takes them to witness how unworthy they are of his kindness. Who can deny that it is most just and most becoming in God to do good to those who worship him, and to punish with due severity those who despise his majesty? God, therefore, proceeds in due order, when, though the wicked are bound by the fetters of sin, he lays down the law in his promises, that he will do them good only if they depart from their wickedness. This would be right, though His only object were to let them understand that they are deservedly excluded from the favor due to his true worshipers.

On the other hand, as he desires by all means to stir up believers to supplicate his grace, it surely should not seem strange that he attempts to accomplish by promises the same thing that, as we have shown, he to their great benefit accomplishes by means of precepts. Being taught by precepts what the will of God is, we are reminded of our wretchedness in being so completely at variance with that will, and, at the same time, are stimulated to invoke the aid of the Spirit to guide us into the right path. But as our indolence is not sufficiently aroused by precepts, promises are added, that they may attract us by their sweetness, and produce a feeling of love for the precept. The greater our desire of righteousness, the greater will be our earnestness to obtain the grace of God. And thus, it is that in the protestations, *if we are willing, if thou shalt hearken,* the Lord neither attributes to us a full power of willing and hearkening, nor yet mocks us for our impotence.

11 Third class of arguments drawn from the divine upbraiding, — that it is in vain to upbraid us for evils which it is not in our power to avoid. Answer. Sinners are condemned by their own consciences, and, therefore, the divine upbraiding is just. Moreover, there is a twofold use in this upbraiding. Various passages of Scripture explained by means of the foregoing answers.

The third class of objections is not unlike the other two. For they produce passages in which God upbraids his people for their ingratitude, intimating that it was not his fault that they did not obtain all kinds of favor from his indulgence. Of such passages, the following are examples: "The Amalekites and the Canaanites are before you, and ye shall fall by the sword: because ye are turned away from the Lord, therefore the Lord will not be with you" (Numbers 14:43). "Because ye have done all these works, saith the Lord, and I spake unto you, rising up early and speaking, but ye heard not; and I called you, but ye answered not; therefore will I do unto this house, which is called by my name, wherein ye trust, and unto the place which I gave to you and to your fathers, as I have done to Shiloh" (Jeremiah 7:13, 14). "They obeyed not thy voice, neither walked in thy law; they have done nothing of all that thou commandedst them to do: therefore thou hast caused all this evil to come upon them" (Jeremiah 32:23).

How, they ask, can such upbraiding be directed against those who have it in their power immediately to reply, —Prosperity was dear to us: we feared adversity; that we did not, in order to obtain the one and avoid the other, obey the Lord, and listen to his voice, is owing to its not being free for us to do so in consequence of our subjection to the dominion of sin; in vain, therefore, are we upbraided with evils which it was not in our power to escape. But to say nothing of the pretext of necessity, which is but a feeble and flimsy defense of their conduct, can they, I ask, deny their guilt? If they are held convicted of any fault, the Lord is not unjust in upbraiding them for having, by their own perverseness, deprived themselves of the advantages of his kindness. Let them say, then, whether they can deny that their own will is the depraved cause of their rebellion.

If they find within themselves a fountain of wickedness, why do they stand declaiming about extraneous causes, with the view of making it appear that they are not the authors of their own destruction? If it is true that it is not for another's faults that sinners are both deprived of the divine favor, and visited with punishment, there is good reason that they should hear these rebukes from the mouth of God. If they obstinately persist in their vices, let them learn in their calamities to accuse and detest their own wickedness, instead of charging God with cruelty and injustice. If they have not manifested docility, let them, under a feeling of disgust at the sins, which they see to be the cause of their misery and ruin, return to the right path, and, with serious contrition, confess the very thing of which the Lord by his rebuke reminds them.

Of what use the harsh criticisms of the prophets above quoted are to believers, appears from the solemn prayer of Daniel, as given in his ninth chapter. Of their use in regard to the ungodly, we see an example in the Jews, to whom Jeremiah was ordered to explain the cause of their miseries, though the event could not be otherwise than the Lord had foretold. "Therefore thou shalt speak these words unto them; but they will not hearken unto thee: thou shalt also call unto them; but they will not answer thee" (Jeremiah 7:27). Of what use, then, was it to talk to the deaf? It was, that even against their will they might understand that what they heard was true, and that it was impious blasphemy to transfer the blame of their wickedness to God, when it resided in themselves.

These few explanations will make it very easy for the reader to disentangle himself from the immense heap of passages (containing both precepts and reprimands) which the enemies of divine grace are in the habit of piling up, that they may thereon erect their statue of free will. The Psalmist upbraids the Jews as "a stubborn and rebellious generation; a generation that set not their heart aright" (Psalm 78:8); and in another passage, he exhorts the men of his time, "Harden not your heart" (Psalm 95:8). This implies that the whole blame of the rebellion lies in human depravity. But it is foolish thence to infer, that the heart, the preparation of which is from the Lord, may be equally bent in either direction. The Psalmist says, "I have inclined my heart to perform thy statutes alway" (Psalm 119:112), meaning that with willing and cheerful readiness of mind he had devoted himself to God. He does not boast, however, that he was the author of that disposition, for in the same psalm he acknowledges it the gift of God.

We must, therefore, attend to the admonition of Paul, when he thus addresses believers, "Work out your own salvation with fear and trembling. For it is God which worketh in you both to will and to do of his good pleasure" (Philippians 2:12, 13). He ascribes to them a part in acting that they may not indulge in carnal sloth, but by enjoining fear and trembling, he humbles them so as to keep them in remembrance, that the very thing which they are ordered to do is the proper work of God—distinctly intimating, that believers act (if I may so speak) *passively* in as much as the power is given them from heaven, and cannot in any way be arrogated to themselves. Accordingly, when Peter exhorts us to "add to faith virtue" (2 Peter 1:5), he does not concede to us the possession of a second place, as if we could do anything separately. He only arouses the sluggishness of our flesh, by which faith itself is frequently stifled.

To the same effect are the words of Paul. He says, "Quench not the Spirit" (1 Thessalonians 5:19); because a spirit of sloth, if not guarded against, is always creeping in upon believers. But should any thence infer that it is entirely in their own power to foster the offered light, his ignorance will easily be refuted by the fact that the very diligence that Paul enjoins is derived only from God (2 Corinthians 7:1). We are often commanded to purge ourselves of all impurity, though the Spirit claims this as his peculiar office.

In fine, that what properly belongs to God is transferred to us only by way of concession, is plain from the words of John, "He that is begotten of God keepeth himself" (1 John 5:18). The advocates of free will fasten upon the expression as if it implied, that we are kept partly by the power of God, partly by our own, whereas the very keeping of which the Apostle speaks is itself from heaven. Hence, Christ prays his Father to keep us from evil (John 17:15), and we know that believers, in their warfare against Satan, owe their victory to the armor of God.

Accordingly, Peter, after saying, "Ye have purified your souls in obeying the truth," immediately adds by way of correction, "through the Spirit" (1 Peter 1:22). In fine, John briefly shows the nothingness of human strength in the spiritual contest, when he says, "Whosoever is born of God does not commit sin; for his seed remaineth in him" (1 John 3:9). He elsewhere gives the reasons "This is the victory that overcometh the world, even our faith" (1 John 5:4).

12 Objection founded on the words of Moses. Refutation by the words of an Apostle. Confirmation by argument.

But a passage is produced from the Law of Moses, which seems very adverse to the view now given. After promulgating the Law, he takes the people to witness in these terms: "This commandment which I command thee this day, it is not hidden from thee, neither is it far off. It is not in heaven, that thou shouldest say, Who shall go up for us to heaven, and bring it unto us, that we may hear it, and do it? But the word is very nigh unto thee, in thy mouth, and in thy heart, that thou mayest do it" (Deuteronomy 30:11, 12, 14). Certainly, if this is to be understood of mere precepts, I admit that it is of no little importance to the matter in hand. For, though it would be easy to evade the difficulty by saying, that the thing here treated of is not the observance of the law, but the facility and readiness of becoming acquainted with it, some scruple, perhaps, would still remain.

The Apostle Paul, however, no mean interpreter, removes all doubt when he affirms, that Moses here spoke of the doctrine of the Gospel (Romans 10:8). If anyone is so refractory as to contend that Paul violently wrested the words in applying them to the Gospel, though his hardihood is chargeable with impiety, we are still able, independently of the authority of the Apostle, to repel the objection. For, if Moses spoke of precepts merely, he was only inflating the people with vain confidence. Had they attempted the observance of the law in their own strength, as a matter in which they should find no difficulty, what else could have been the result than to throw them headlong? Where, then, was that easy means of observing the law, when the only access to it was over a fatal precipice? Accordingly, nothing is more certain than that under these words is comprehended the covenant of mercy, which had been promulgated along with the demands of the law.

A few verses before, he had said, "The Lord thy God will circumcise thine heart, and the heart of thy seed, to love the Lord thy God with all thine heart, and with all thy soul, that thou mayest live" (Deuteronomy 30:6). Therefore, the readiness of which he immediately after speaks was placed not in the power of man, but in the protection and help of the Holy Spirit, who mightily performs his own work in our weakness. The passage, however, is not to be understood of precepts simply, but rather of the Gospel promises, which, so far from proving any power in us to fulfill righteousness, utterly disprove it.

This is confirmed by the testimony of Paul, when he observes that the Gospel holds forth salvation to us, not under the harsh arduous, and impossible terms on which the law treats with us (namely, that those shall obtain it who fulfill all its demands), but on terms easy, expeditious, and readily obtained. This passage, therefore, tends in no degree to establish the freedom of the human will.

13 Fourth class of arguments by the defenders of free will. God waits to see whether or not sinners will repent; therefore, they can repent. Answer by a dilemma. Passage in Hosea explained.

They are wont also to adduce certain passages in which God is said occasionally to try men, by withdrawing the assistance of his grace, and to wait until they turn to him, as in Hosea, "I will go and return to my place, until they acknowledge their offense, and seek my face" (Hosea 5:15). It would be absurd (say they), that the Lord should wait until Israel should seek his face, if their minds were not flexible, to turn in either direction of their own accord. As if anything were more common in the prophetical writings than for God to put on the semblance of rejecting and casting off his people until they reform their lives.

But what can our opponents extract from such threats? If they mean to maintain that people, when abandoned by God, are able of themselves to think of turning unto him, they will do it in the very face of Scripture. On the other hand, if they admit that divine grace is necessary to conversion, why do they dispute with us? But while they admit that grace is so far necessary, they insist on reserving some ability for man. How do they prove it? Certainly not from this or any similar passage, for it is one thing to withdraw from man, and look to what he will do when thus abandoned and left to himself, and another thing to assist his powers (whatever they may be), in proportion to their weakness.

What, then, it will be asked, is meant by such expressions? I answer, just the same as if God were to say, "Since nothing is gained by admonishing, exhorting, rebuking this stubborn people, I will withdraw for a little, and silently leave them to be afflicted; I shall see whether, after long calamity, any remembrance of me will return, and induce them to seek my face."

But by the departure of the Lord to a distance is meant the withdrawal of prophecy. By his waiting to see what men will do is meant that he, while silent, and in a manner hiding himself, tries them for a season with various afflictions. Both he does that he may humble us the more; for we shall sooner be broken than corrected by the strokes of adversity, unless his Spirit train us to docility. Moreover, when the Lord, offended and fatigued with our obstinate perverseness, leaves us for a while (by withdrawing his word, in which he is wont in some degree to manifest his presence), and makes trial of what we will do in his absence, from this it is erroneously inferred, that there is some power of free will, the extent of which is to be considered and tried, whereas the only end which he has in view is to bring us to an acknowledgment of our utter nothingness.

14. Fifth class of arguments in defense of free will. God and bad works described as our own, and therefore we are capable of both. Answer by an exposition, which shows that this argument is unavailing. Objection drawn from analogy. Answer. The nature and mode of divine agency in the elect.

Another objection is founded on a mode of speaking which is constantly observed both in Scripture and in common discourse. God works are said to be ours, and we are said to do what is holy and acceptable to God, just as we are said to commit sin. But if sins are justly imputed to us, as proceeding from ourselves, for the same reason (say they) some share must certainly be attributed to us in works of righteousness. It could not be accordant with reason to say, that we do those things, which we are incapable of doing of our own motion, God moving us, as if we were stones.

These expressions, therefore, it is said, indicate that while, in the matter of grace, we give the first place to God, and a secondary place must be assigned to our agency. If the only thing here insisted on were, that good works are termed *ours*, I, in my turn, would reply, that the bread, which we ask God to give us, is also termed *ours*. What, then, can be inferred from the title of possession, but simply that, by the kindness and free gift of Gods that becomes ours which in other respects is by no means due to us?

Therefore, let them either ridicule the same absurdity in the Lord's Prayer, or let them cease to regard it as absurd, that good works should be called ours, though our only property in them is derived from the liberality of

God. But there is something stronger in the fact, that we are often said in Scripture to worship God, do justice, obey the law, and follow good works. These being proper offices of the mind and will, how can they be consistently referred to the Spirit, and, at the same time, attributed to us, unless there be some concurrence on our part with the divine agency? This difficulty will be easily disposed of if we attend to the manner in which the Holy Spirit acts in the righteous.

The similitude with which they invidiously assail us is foreign to the purpose; for who is so absurd, as to imagine that movement in man differs in nothing from the impulse given to a stone? Nor can anything of the kind be inferred from our doctrine. To the natural powers of man we ascribe approving and rejecting, willing and not willing, striving and resisting—viz. approving vanity, rejecting solid good, willing evil and not willing good, striving for wickedness and resisting righteousness.

What then does the Lord do? If he sees meet to employ depravity of this description as an instrument of his anger, he gives it whatever aim and direction he pleases, that, by a guilty hand, he may accomplish his own good work. A wicked man thus serving the power of God, while he is bent only on following his own lust, can we compare to a stone, which, driven by an external impulse, is borne along without motion, or sense, or will of its own? We see how wide the difference is. But how stands the case with the godly, as to whom chiefly the question is raised?

When God erects his kingdom in them, he, by means of his Spirit, curbs their will, that it may not follow its natural bent, and be carried hither and thither by vagrant lusts; bends, frames trains, and guides it according to the rule of his justice, so as to incline it to righteousness and holiness, and establishes and strengthens it by the energy of his Spirit, that it may not stumble or fall.

For which reason Augustine thus expresses himself, "It will be said we are therefore acted upon, and do not act. Nay, you act and are acted upon, and you then act well when you are acted upon by one that is good. The Spirit of God who actuates you is your helper in acting, and bears the name of helper, because you, too, do something." In the former member of this sentence, he reminds us that the motion of the Holy Spirit does not destroy the agency of man, because nature furnishes the will, which is guided to aspire to good. As to the second member of the sentence, in which he says that the very idea of help implies that we also do something, we must not understand it as if he were attributing to us some independent power of action; but not to foster a feeling of sloth, he reconciles the agency of God with our own agency, by saying, that to wish is from nature, to wish well is from grace. Accordingly, he had said a little before, "Did not God assist us, we should not only not be able to conquer, but not able even to fight."

15 Conclusion of the answer to the last class of arguments.

Hence, it appears that the grace of God (as this name is used when regeneration is spoken of) is the rule of the Spirit, in directing and governing the human will. Govern he cannot, without correcting, reforming, renovating (hence we say that the beginning of regeneration consists in the abolition of what is ours); in like manner, he cannot govern without moving, impelling, urging, and restraining. Accordingly, all the actions, which are afterwards done, are truly said to be wholly his.

Meanwhile, we deny not the truth of Augustine's doctrine, that the will is not destroyed, but rather repaired, by grace—the two things being perfectly consistent—viz. that the human will may be said to be renewed when its depravity and perverseness being corrected, it is conformed to the true standard of righteousness and that, at the same time, the will may be said to be made new, being so vitiated and corrupted that its nature must be entirely changed. There is nothing then to prevent us from saying that our will does what the Spirit does in us, although the will contributes nothing of itself apart from grace. We must, therefore, remember what we quoted from Augustine, that some men labor in vain to find in the human will some good quality properly belonging to it. Any intermixture which men attempt to make by conjoining the effort of their own will with divine grace is corruption, just as when unwholesome and muddy water is used to dilute wine. But though everything good in the will is entirely derived from the influence of the Spirit, yet, because we have naturally an innate power of willing, we are not improperly said to do the things of which God claims for himself all the praise; first, because everything which his kindness produces in us is our own (only we must understand that it is not of ourselves); and, secondly, because it is our mind, our will, our study which are guided by him to what is good.

16 Third and last division of the chapter discussing certain passages of Scripture. A. A passage from Genesis. Its true meaning explained.

The other passages which they gather together from different quarters will not give much trouble to any person of tolerable understanding, who pays due attention to the explanations already given. They adduce the passage of Genesis, "Unto thee shall be his desire, and thou shalt rule over him" (Genesis 4:7).

This they interpret of sin, as if the Lord were promising Cain that the dominion of sin should not prevail over his mind, if he would labor in subduing it. We, however, maintain that it is much more agreeable to the context to understand the words as referring to Abel, it being there the purpose of God to point out the injustice of the envy which Cain had conceived against his brother.

And this He does in two ways, by showing, first, that it was vain to think he could, by means of wickedness, surpass his brother in the favor of God, by whom nothing is esteemed but righteousness; and, secondly, how ungrateful he was for the kindness he had already received, in not being able to bear with a brother who had been subjected to his authority. But lest it should be thought that we embrace this interpretation because the other is contrary to our view, let us grant that God does here speak of sin. If so, his words contain either an order or a promise. If an order, we have already demonstrated that this is no proof of man's ability; if a promise, where is the fulfillment of the promise when Cain yielded to the sin over which he ought to have prevailed? They will allege a tacit condition in the promise, as if it were said that he would gain the victory if he contended. This subterfuge is altogether unavailing. For, if the dominion spoken of refers to sin, no man can have any doubt that the form of expression is imperative, declaring not what we are able, but what it is our duty to do, even if beyond our ability.

Although both the nature of the case, and the rule of grammatical construction, require that it be regarded as a comparison between Cain and Abel, we think the only preference given to the younger brother was, that the elder made himself inferior by his own wickedness.

17 B. Passage from the Epistle to the Romans. Explanation. Refutation of an objection. Another refutation. A third refutation from Augustine. C. A passage from First Corinthians. Answer to it.

They appeal, moreover, to the testimony of the Apostle Paul, because he says, "It is not of him that willeth, nor of him that runneth, but of God that showeth mercy" (Romans 9:15). From this they infer that there is something in will and endeavor, which, though weak in themselves, still, being mercifully aided by God, are not without some measure of success. But if they would attend in sober earnest to the subject there handled by Paul, they would not so rashly pervert his meaning. I am aware they can quote Origen and Jerome in support of this exposition.

To these I might, in my turn, oppose Augustine. But it is of no consequence what they thought, if it is clear what Paul meant. He teaches that salvation is prepared for those only on whom the Lord is pleased to bestow his mercy—that ruin and death await all whom he has not chosen. He had proved the condition of the reprobate by the example of Pharaoh, and confirmed the certainty of gratuitous election by the passage in Moses, "I will have mercy on whom I will have mercy." Thereafter he concludes, that it is not of him that willeth, nor of him that runneth, but of God that showeth mercy. If these words are understood to mean that the will or endeavor are not sufficient, because unequal to such a task, the Apostle has not used them very appropriately. We must therefore abandon this absurd mode of arguing, "It is not of him that willeth, nor of him that runneth;" therefore, there is some will, some running.

Paul's meaning is simpler—there is neither will nor running by which we can prepare the way for our salvation—it is wholly of the divine mercy. He indeed says nothing more than he says to Titus, when he writes, "After that the kindness and love of God our Savior toward man appeared, not by works of righteousness which we have done, but according to his mercy he saved us" (Titus 3:4, 5).

Those who argue that Paul insinuated there was some will and some running when he said, "It is not of him that willeth, nor of him that runneth," would not allow me to argue after the same fashion, that we have done some righteous works, because Paul says that we have attained the divine favor, "not by works of righteousness which we have done." But if they see a flaw in this mode of arguing, let them open their eyes, and they will see that their own mode is not free from a similar fallacy.

The argument which Augustine uses is well founded, "If it is said, 'It is not of him that willeth, nor of him that runneth,' because neither will nor running are sufficient; it may, on the other hand, be retorted, it is not 'of God that showeth mercy,' because mercy does not act alone." This second proposition being absurd, Augustine justly concludes the meaning of the words to be, that there is no good will in man until it is prepared by the Lord; not that we ought not to will and run, but that both are produced in us by God. Some, with equal lack of skill, wrest the saying of Paul, "We are laborers together with God" (1 Corinthians 3:9). There cannot be a doubt that these words apply to ministers only, who are called "laborers with God"—not from bringing anything of their own, but because God makes use of their instrumentality after he has rendered them fit, and provided them with the necessary endowments.

18 D. A passage from Ecclesiastes. Explanation. Another explanation.

They appeal also to Ecclesiasticus, who is well known to be a writer of doubtful authority. But, though we might justly decline his testimony, let us see what he says in support of free will. His words are, "He himself made man from the beginning, and left him in the hand of his counsel; If thou wilt, to keep the commandments, and perform acceptable faithfulness. He has set fire and water before thee: stretch forth thy hand unto whether thou wilt. Before man is life and death; and whether him liketh shall be given him" (Ecclesiastes 15:14-17).

Grant that man received at his creation a power of acquiring life or death; what, then, if we, on the other hand, can reply that he has lost it?

Assuredly, I have no intention to contradict Solomon, who asserts, "God has made man upright;" that "they have sought out many inventions" (Ecclesiastes 7:29). But since man, by degenerating, has made shipwreck of himself and all his blessings, it certainly does not follow, that everything attributed to his nature, as originally constituted, applies to it now when vitiated and degenerate.

Therefore, not only to my opponents, but to the author of Ecclesiasticus himself (whoever he may have been), this is my answer: If you mean to tell man that in himself there is a power of acquiring salvation, your authority with us is not so great as, in the least degree, to prejudice the undoubted word of God; but if only wishing to curb the malignity of the fleshy which by transferring the blame of its own wickedness to God, is wont to catch at a vain defense, you say that rectitude was given to man, in order to make it apparent he was the cause of his own destruction, I willingly assent. Only agree with me in this, that it is by his own fault he is stripped of the ornaments in which the Lord at first attired him, and then let us unite in acknowledging that what he now wants is a physician, and not a defender.

19 E. A passage from Luke. Explanation. Allegorical arguments weak. Another explanation. A third explanation. A fourth from Augustine. Conclusion and summary of the whole discussion concerning free will.

There is nothing more frequent in their mouths than the parable of the traveler who fell among thieves, and was left half dead (Luke 10:32). I am aware that it is a common idea with almost all writers, that under the figure of the traveler is represented the calamity of the human race. Hence, our opponents argue that man was not so mutilated by the robbery of sin and the devil as not to preserve some remains of his former endowments; because it is said, he was left half dead. For where is the half living, unless some portion of right will and reason remain?

First, if I were I to deny that there is any room for their allegory, what could they say? There can be no doubt that the Fathers invented it contrary to the genuine sense of the parable. Allegories ought to be carried no further than Scripture expressly sanctions: so far are they from forming a sufficient basis to found doctrines upon. And were I so disposed I might easily find the means of tearing up this fiction by the roots. The Word of God leaves no half-life to man, but teaches, that, in regard to life and happiness, he has utterly perished.

Paul, when he speaks of our redemption, says not that the half dead are cured (Ephesians 2:5, 6; 5:14) but that those who were dead are raised up. He does not call upon the half dead to receive the illumination of Christ, but upon those who are asleep and buried. In the same way our Lord himself says, "The hour is coming, and now is, when the dead shall hear the voice of the Son of God" (John 5:25). How can they presume to set up a flimsy allegory in opposition to so many clear statements? But be it that this allegory is good evidence, what can they extort out of it?

Man is half dead; therefore, there is some soundness in him. True! He has a mind capable of understanding, though incapable of attaining to heavenly and spiritual wisdom; he has some discernment of what is honorable; he has some sense of the Divinity, though he cannot reach the true knowledge of God. But to what do these amount? They certainly do not refute the doctrine of Augustine—a doctrine confirmed by the common suffrages even of the Schoolmen, that after the fall, the gifts on which salvation depends were withdrawn, and natural gifts corrupted and defiled (*supra*, chapter 2 section 2).

Let it stand, therefore, as an indubitable truth, which no engines can shake, that the mind of man is so entirely alienated from the righteousness of God that he cannot conceive, desire, or design anything but what is wicked, distorted, foul, impure, and iniquitous; that his heart is so thoroughly envenomed by sin that it can breathe out nothing but corruption and rottenness; that if some men occasionally make a show of goodness, their mind is ever interwoven with hypocrisy and deceit, their soul inwardly bound with the fetters of wickedness.

Chapter 6

REDEMPTION FOR MAN LOST
TO BE SOUGHT IN CHRIST

The parts of this chapter are, I. The excellence of the doctrine of Christ the Redeemer—a doctrine always entertained by the Church, section 1. II. Christ, the Mediator in both dispensations, was offered to the faith of the pious Israelites and people of old, as is plain from the institution of sacrifice, the calling of Abraham's family, and the elevation of David and his posterity, section 2. III. Hence, the consolation, strength, hope, and confidence of the godly under the Law, Christ being offered to them in various ways by their heavenly Father.

Sections

1. The knowledge of God the Creator of no avail without faith in Christ the Redeemer. First reason. Second reason strengthened by the testimony of an Apostle. Conclusion. This doctrine entertained by the children of God in all ages from the beginning of the world. Error of throwing open heaven to the heathen, who know nothing of Christ. The pretexts for this refuted by passages of Scripture.

2. God never was propitious to the ancient Israelites without Christ the Mediator. First reason founded on the institution of sacrifice. Second reason founded on the calling of Abraham. Third reason founded on the elevation of David's family to regal dignity, and confirmed by striking passages of Scripture.

3. Christ the solace ever promised to the afflicted; the banner of faith and hope always erected. This confirmed by various passages of Scripture.

4. The Jews taught to have respect to Christ. This teaching sanctioned by our Savior himself. The common saying, that God is the object of faith, requires to be explained and modified. Conclusion of this discussion concerning Christ. No saving knowledge of God in the heathen.

1 The knowledge of God the Creator of no avail without faith in Christ the Redeemer. First reason. Second reason strengthened by the testimony of an Apostle. Conclusion. This doctrine entertained by the children of God in all ages from the beginning of the world. Error of throwing open heaven to the heathen, who know nothing of Christ. The pretexts for this refuted by passages of Scripture.

The whole human race having been undone in the person of Adam, the excellence and dignity of our origin, as already described, is so far from availing us, that it rather turns to our greater disgrace, until God, who does not acknowledge man when defiled and corrupted by sin as his own work, appear as a Redeemer in the person of his only begotten Son. Since our fall from life unto death, all that knowledge of God the Creator, of which we have discoursed, would be useless, were it not followed up by faith, holding forth God to us as a Father in Christ.

The natural course undoubtedly was that the fabric of the world should be a school in which we might learn piety, and from it, to pass to eternal life and perfect felicity. But after looking at the perfection beheld wherever we turn our eye, above and below, we are met by the divine malediction, which, while it involves innocent creatures in our fault, of necessity fills our own souls with despair. For although God is still pleased in many ways to manifest his paternal favor towards us, we cannot, from a mere survey of the world, infer that he is a Father. Conscience urging us within, and showing that sin is a just ground for our being forsaken, will not allow us to think that God accounts or treats us as sons.

In addition to this are our sloth and ingratitude. Our minds are so blinded that they cannot perceive the truth, and all our senses are so corrupt that we wickedly rob God of his glory. Wherefore, we must conclude with Paul, "After that in the wisdom of God the world by wisdom knew not God, it pleased God by the foolishness of preaching to save them that believe" (1 Corinthians 1:21). By the "wisdom of God," he designates this magnificent theatre of heaven and earth replenished with numberless wonders, the wise contemplation of which should have enabled us to know God. But this we do with little profit; and, therefore, he invites us to faith in Christ, —faith which, by a semblance of foolishness, disgusts the unbeliever.

Therefore, although the preaching of the cross is not in accordance with human wisdom, we must, however, humbly embrace it if we would return to God our Maker, from whom we are estranged, that he may again become our Father. It is certain that after the fall of our first parent, no knowledge of God without a Mediator was effectual to salvation.

Christ speaks not of his own age merely, but embraces all ages, when he says, "This is life eternal that they might know thee the only true God, and Jesus Christ, whom thou hast sent" (John 17:3). The more shameful therefore is the presumption of those who throw heaven open to the unbelieving and profane, in the absence of that grace which Scripture uniformly describes as the only door by which we enter into life. Should any confine our Savior's words to the period subsequent to the promulgation of the Gospel, the refutation is at hand; since on a ground common to all ages and nations, it is declared, that those who are estranged from God, and as such, are under the curse, the children of wrath, cannot be pleasing to God until they are reconciled. To this we may add the answer which our Savior gave to the Samaritan woman "Ye worship ye know not what; we know what we worship: for salvation is of the Jews" (John 4:22). By these words, he both charges every Gentile religion with falsehood, and assigns the reason—viz. that under the Law the Redeemer was promised to the chosen people only, and that, consequently, no worship was ever pleasing to God in which respect was not had to Christ.

Hence, also Paul affirms that all the Gentiles were "without God," and deprived of the hope of life. Now, since John teaches that there was life in Christ from the beginning, and that the whole world had lost it (John 1:4), it is necessary to return to that fountain. And, accordingly, Christ declares that inasmuch as he is a propitiator, he is life. And, indeed, the inheritance of heaven belongs to none but the sons of God (John 15:6). Now, it was most incongruous to give the place and rank of sons to any who have not been engrafted into the body of the only begotten Son. And John distinctly testifies that those who believe in his name become the sons of God. But as it is not my intention at present formally to discuss the subject of faith in Christ, it is enough to have thus touched on it in passing.

2 God never was propitious to the ancient Israelites without Christ the Mediator. First reason founded on the institution of sacrifice. Second reason founded on the calling of Abraham. Third reason founded on the elevation of David's family to regal dignity, and confirmed by striking passages of Scripture.

Hence, it is that God never showed himself propitious to his ancient people, nor gave them any hope of grace without a Mediator. I say nothing of the sacrifices of the Law, by which believers were plainly and openly taught that salvation was not to be found anywhere but in the expiation, which Christ alone completed. All I maintain is that the prosperous and happy state of the Church was always founded in the person of Christ. For although God embraced the whole posterity of Abraham in his covenant, yet Paul properly argues (Galatians 3:16), that Christ was truly the seed in which all the nations of the earth were to be blessed, since we know that all who were born of Abraham, according to the flesh, were not accounted the seed. To omit Ishmael and others, how came it that of the two sons of Isaac, the twin brothers, Esau and Jacob, while yet in the womb, the one was chosen and the other rejected? Nay, how came it that the first-born was rejected, and the younger alone admitted? Moreover, how happens it that the majority is rejected?

It is plain, therefore, that the seed of Abraham is considered chiefly in one head, and that the promised salvation is not attained without coming to Christ, whose office it is to gather together those which were scattered abroad. Thus, the primary adoption of the chosen people depended on the grace of the Mediator. Although it is not expressed in very distinct terms in Moses, it, however, appears to have been commonly known to all the godly. For before a king was appointed over the Israelites, Hannah, the mother of Samuel, describing the happiness of the righteous, speaks thus in her song, "He shall give strength unto his king, and exalt the horn of his anointed;" meaning by these words, that God would bless his Church. To this corresponds the prediction, which is afterwards added, "I will raise me up a faithful priest, and he shall walk before mine anointed forever" (1 Samuel 2:10, 35).

And there can be no doubt that our heavenly Father intended that a living image of Christ should be seen in David and his posterity. Accordingly, exhorting the righteous to fear Him, he bids them "Kiss the Son" (Psalm 2:12). Corresponding to this is the passage in the Gospel, "He that honoreth not the Son, honoreth not the Father" (John 5:23). Therefore, though the kingdom was broken up by the revolt of the ten tribes, yet the covenant which God had made in David and his successors behaved to stand, as is also declared by his Prophets, "Howbeit I will not take the whole kingdom out of his hand: but I will make him prince all the days of his life for David my servant's sake" (1 Kings 11:34). The same thing is repeated a second and third time. It is also expressly said, "I will for this afflict the seed of David, but not forever" (1 Kings 11:39). Some time afterwards it was said, "Nevertheless, for David's sake did the Lord his God give him a lamp in Jerusalem, to set up his son after him, and to establish Jerusalem" (1 Kings 15:4). And when matters were bordering on destruction, it was again said, "Yet the Lord would not destroy Judah for David his servant's sake, as he had promised to give him always a light, and to his children" (2 Kings 8:19).

The sum of the whole comes to this—David, all others being excluded, was chosen to be the person in whom the good pleasure of the Lord should dwell; as it is said elsewhere, "He forsook the tabernacle of Shiloh;" "Moreover, he refused the tabernacle of Joseph, and chose not the tribe of Ephraim;" "But chose the tribe of Judah, the Mount Zion which he loved;" "He chose David also his servant, and took him from the sheep folds: from following the ewes great with young he brought him to feed Jacob his people, and Israel his inheritance" (Psalm 78:60, 67, 70, 71). In fine, God, in thus preserving his Church, intended that its security and salvation should depend on Christ as its head.

Accordingly, David exclaims, "The Lord is their strength, and he is the saving strength of his anointed;" and then prays "Save thy people, and bless thine inheritance;" intimating, that the safety of the Church was indissolubly connected with the government of Christ. In the same sense he elsewhere says, "Save, Lord: let the king hear us when we call" (Psalm 20:9).

These words plainly teach that believers, in applying for the help of God, had their sole confidence in this—that they were under the unseen government of the King. This may be inferred from another psalm, "Save now, I beseech thee O Lord: Blessed be he that cometh in the name of the Lord" (Psalm 118:25, 26).

Here it is obvious that believers are invited to Christ, in the assurance that they will be safe when entirely in his hand. To the same effect is another prayer, in which the whole Church implores the divine mercy "Let thy hand be upon the Man of thy right hand, upon the Son of man, whom thou madest strong (or best fitted) for thyself" (Psalm 80:17). For though the author of the psalm laments the dispersion of the whole nations, he prays for its revival in him who is sole Head. After the people were led away into captivity, the land laid waste, and matters to appearance desperate, Jeremiah, lamenting the calamity of the Church, especially complains, that by the destruction of the kingdom the hope of believers was cut off; "The breath of our nostrils, the anointed of the Lord, was taken in their pits, of whom we said, Under his shadow we shall live among the heathen" (Lamentations 4:20).

From all this it is abundantly plain, that as the Lord cannot be propitious to the human race without a Mediator, Christ was always held forth to the holy Fathers under the Law as the object of their faith.

3 Christ the solace ever promised to the afflicted; the banner of faith and hope always erected. This confirmed by various passages of Scripture.

Moreover, when comfort is promised in affliction, especially when the deliverance of the Church is described, the banner of faith and hope in Christ is unfurled. "Thou wentest forth for the salvation of thy people, even for salvation with thine anointed" (Habakkuk 3:13). And whenever mention is made in the Prophets of the renovation of the Church, the people are directed to the promise made to David, that his kingdom would be forever. And there is nothing strange in this, since otherwise there would have been no stability in the covenant.

To this purpose is the remarkable prophecy in (Isaiah 7:14). After seeing that the unbelieving King Ahab repudiated what he had testified regarding the deliverance of Jerusalem from siege and its immediate safety, he passes as if it were abruptly to the Messiah, "Behold, a virgin shall conceive and bear a son, and shall call his name Emmanuel;" intimating indirectly, that though the king and his people wickedly rejected the promise offered to them, as if they were bent on causing the faith of God to fail, the covenant would not be defeated—the Redeemer would come in his own time. In fine, all the prophets, to show that God was easily placated, were always careful to bring forward that kingdom of David, on which redemption and eternal salvation depended. Thus in Isaiah it is said, "I will make an everlasting covenant with you, even the sure mercies of David. Behold, I have given him for a witness to the people" (Isaiah 55:3, 4); intimating, that believers, in calamitous circumstances, could have no hope, had they not this testimony that God would be ready to hear them.

In the same way, to revive their drooping spirits, Jeremiah says, "Behold, the days come, saith the Lord, that I will raise unto David a righteous Branch, and a King shall reign and prosper, and shall execute judgment and justice in the earth. In his days Judah shall be saved, and Israel shall dwell safely" (Jeremiah 23:5, 6).

In Ezekiel also it is said, "I will set up one Shepherd over them, and he shall feed them, even my servant David; he shall feed them, and he shall be their shepherd. And I the Lord will be their God, and my servant David a prince among them: I the Lord have spoken it. And I will make with them a covenant of peace" (Ezekiel 34:23, 24, 25). And again, after discoursing of this wondrous renovation, he says, "David my servant shall be king over them: and they all shall have one shepherd." "Moreover, I will make a covenant of peace with them; it shall be an everlasting covenant with them" (Ezekiel 37:24-26).

I select a few passages out of many, because I merely wish to impress my readers with the fact that the hope of believers was ever treasured up in Christ alone. All the other prophets concur in this. Thus Hosea, "Then shall the children of Judah and the children of Israel be gathered together, and appoint themselves one head" (Hosea 1:11). This he afterwards explains in clearer terms, "Afterward shall the children of Israel return, and seek the Lord their God, and David their king" (Hosea 3:5). Micah, also speaking of the return of the people, says expressly, "Their king shall pass before them, and the Lord on the head of them" (Micah 2:13). So Amos, in predicting the renovation of the people, says "In that day will I raise up the tabernacle of David that is fallen, and close up the breaches thereof; and I will raise up the ruins, and I will build it as in the days of old" (Amos 9:11); in other words, the only banner of salvation was, the exaltation of the family of David to regal splendor, as fulfilled in Christ. Hence, too, Zechariah, as nearer in time to the manifestation of Christ, speaks more plainly, "Rejoice greatly, O daughter of Zion; shout, O daughter of Jerusalem: behold, thy King cometh unto thee: he is just, and having salvation" (Zechariah 9:9). This corresponds to the passage already quoted from the Psalms, "The Lord is their strength, and he is the saving health of their anointed." Here salvation is extended from the head to the whole body.

4 **The Jews taught to have respect to Christ. This teaching sanctioned by our Savior himself. The common saying, that God is the object of faith, requires to be explained and modified. Conclusion of this discussion concerning Christ. No saving knowledge of God in the heathen.**

By familiarizing the Jews with these prophecies, God intended to teach them, that in seeking for deliverance, they should turn their eyes directly towards Christ. And though they had sadly degenerated, they never entirely lost the knowledge of this general principle, that God, by the hand of Christ, would be the deliverer of the Church, as he had promised to David; and that in this way only the free covenant by which God had adopted his chosen people would be fulfilled. Hence, it was, that on our Savior's entry into Jerusalem, shortly before his death, the children shouted, "Hosannah to the son of David" (Matthew 21:9). For there seems to have been a hymn known to all, and in general use, in which they sung that the only remaining pledge, which they had of the divine mercy, was the promised advent of a Redeemer.

For this reason, Christ tells his disciples to believe in him, in order that they might have a distinct and complete belief in God, "Ye believe in God, believe also in me" (John 14:1).

For although, properly speaking, faith rises from Christ to the Father, he intimates that even when it leans on God, it gradually vanishes away, unless he himself interposes to give it solid strength. The majesty of God is too high to be scaled up to by mortals, who creep like worms on the earth. Therefore, the common saying that God is the object of faith requires to be received with some modification. When Christ is called the image of the invisible God (Colossians 1:15), the expression is not used without cause, but is designed to remind us that we can have no knowledge of our salvation, until we behold God in Christ. For although the Jewish scribes had by their false glosses darkened what the Prophets had taught concerning the Redeemer, yet Christ assumed it to be a fact, received with public consent, that there was no other remedy in desperate circumstances, no other mode of delivering the Church than the manifestation of the Mediator.

It is true, that the fact adverted to by Paul was not so generally known as it ought to have been—viz. that Christ is the end of the Law (Romans 10:4), though this is both true, and clearly appears both from the Law and the Prophets. I am not now, however, treating of faith, as we shall elsewhere have a fitter place (Book 3, chapter 2), but what I wish to impress upon my readers in this way is, that the first step in piety is, to acknowledge that God is a Father, to defend, govern, and cherish us, until he brings us to the eternal inheritance of his kingdom; that hence it is plain, as we lately observed, there is no saving knowledge of God without Christ, and that, consequently, from the beginning of the world Christ was held forth to all the elect as the object of their faith and confidence.

In this sense, Irenaeus says, that the Father, who is boundless in himself, is bounded in the Son, because he has accommodated himself to our capacity, lest our minds should be swallowed up by the immensity of his glory. Fanatics, not attending to this, distort a useful sentiment into an impious dream, as if Christ had only a share of the Godhead, as a part taken from a whole, whereas the meaning merely is, that God is comprehended in Christ alone.

John is correct: "Whosoever denieth the Son, the same has not the Father" (1 John 1:23). For though in old time there were many who boasted that they worshipped the Supreme Deity, the Maker of heaven and earth, yet as they had no Mediator, it was impossible for them truly to enjoy the mercy of God, so as to feel persuaded that he was their Father. Not holding the head, that is, Christ, their knowledge of God was evanescent; and hence they at length fell away to gross and foul superstitions betraying their ignorance, just as the Turks in the present day, who, though proclaiming, with full throat, that the Creator of heaven and earth is their God, yet by their rejection of Christ, substitute an idol in his place.

Chapter 7

THE LAW GIVEN, NOT TO RETAIN A PEOPLE FOR ITSELF, BUT TO KEEP ALIVE THE HOPE OF SALVATION IN CHRIST UNTIL HIS ADVENT

The divisions of this chapter are, I. The Moral and Ceremonial Law a schoolmaster to bring us to Christ, sections 1, 2. II. This true of the Moral Law, especially its conditional promises. These given for the best reasons. In what respect the observance of the Moral Law is said to be impossible, sections 3–5. III. Of the threefold office and use of the Moral Law, sections 6–12. Antinomians refuted, section 13. IV. What the abrogation of the Law, Moral and Ceremonial, sections 14–17.

Sections
1. The whole system of religion delivered by the hand of Moses, in many ways pointed to Christ. This exemplified in the case of sacrifices, ablutions, and an endless series of ceremonies. This proved, A. By the declared purpose of God; B. By the nature of the ceremonies themselves; C. From the nature of God; D. From the grace offered to the Jews; E. From the consecration of the priests.

2. Proof continued. F. From a consideration of the kingdom erected in the family of David. G. From the end of the ceremonies. H. From the end of the Moral Law.

3. A more ample exposition of the last proof. The Moral Law leads believers to Christ. Showing the perfect righteousness required by God, it convinces us of our inability to fulfil it. It thus denies us life, adjudges us to death, and so urges us to seek deliverance in Christ.

4. The promises of the Law, though conditional, founded on the best reason. This reason explained.

5. No inconsistency in giving a law, the observance of which is impossible. This proved from reason, and confirmed by Scripture. Another confirmation from Augustine.

6. *A consideration of the office and use of the Moral Law shows that it leads to Christ. The Law, while it describes the righteousness, which is acceptable to God, proves that every man is unrighteous.*

7. *The Law fitly compared to a mirror, which shows us our wretchedness. This derogates not in any degree from its excellence.*

8. *When the Law discloses our guilt, we should not despond, but flee to the mercy of God. How this may be done.*

9. *Confirmation of the first use of the Moral Law from various passages in Augustine.*

10. *A second use of the Law is to curb sinners. This most necessary for the good of the community at large; and this in respect not only of the reprobate, but also of the elect, previous to regeneration. This confirmed by the authority of an Apostle.*

11. *The Law showing our wretchedness disposes us to admit the remedy. It also tends to keep us in our duty. Confirmation from general experience.*

12. *The third and most appropriate use of the Law respects the elect. A. It instructs and teaches them to make daily progress in doing the will of God. B. Urges them by exhortation to obedience. Testimony of David. How he is to be reconciled with the Apostle.*

13. *The profane heresy of the Antinomians must be exploded. Argument founded on a passage in David, and another in Moses.*

14. *Last part of the chapter treating of the abrogation of the Law. In what respect any part of the Moral Law abrogated.*

15. *The curse of the Law how abrogated.*

16. *Of the abrogation of the Ceremonial Law in regard to the observance only.*

17. *The reason assigned by the Apostle applicable not to the Moral Law, but to ceremonial observances only. These abrogated, not only because they separated the Jews from the Gentiles, but still more because they were a kind of formal instruments to attest our guilt and impunity. Christ, by destroying these, is justly said to have taken away the handwriting that was against us, and nailed it to his cross.*

1 The whole system of religion delivered by the hand of Moses, in many ways pointed to Christ. This exemplified in the case of sacrifices, ablutions, and an endless series of ceremonies. This proved, A. By the declared purpose of God; B. By the nature of the ceremonies themselves; C. From the nature of God; D. From the grace offered to the Jews; E. From the consecration of the priests.

From the whole course of the observations now made, we may infer, that the Law was not superadded about four hundred years after the death of Abraham in order that it might lead the chosen people away from Christ, but, on the contrary, to keep them in suspense until his advent; to inflame their desire, and confirm their expectation, that they might not become dispirited by the long delay.

By the Law, I understand not only the Ten Commandments, which contain a complete rule of life, but the whole system of religion delivered by the hand of Moses. Moses was not appointed as a Lawgiver, to do away with the blessing promised to the race of Abraham; nay, we see that he is constantly reminding the Jews of the free covenant which had been made with their fathers, and of which they were heirs; as if he had been sent for the purpose of renewing it.

This is most clearly manifested by the ceremonies. For what could be more vain or frivolous than for men to reconcile themselves to God, by offering him the foul odor produced by burning the fat of beasts? Or to wipe away their own impurities by be sprinkling themselves with water or blood? In short, the whole legal worship (if considered by itself apart from the types and shadows of corresponding truth) is a mere mockery. Wherefore, both in Stephen's address (Acts 7:44), and in the Epistle to the Hebrews, great weight is justly given to the passage in which God says to Moses, "Look that thou make them after the pattern which was showed thee in the mount" (Exodus 25:40).

Had there not been some spiritual end to which they were directed, the Jews, in the observance of them, would have deluded themselves as much as the Gentiles in their vanities. Profane men, who have never made religion their serious study, cannot bear without disgust to hear of such a multiplicity of rites. They not merely wonder why God fatigued his ancient people with such a mass of ceremonies, but they despise and ridicule them as childish toys. This they do, because they attend not to the end; from which, if the legal figures are separated, they cannot escape the charge of vanity.

But the type shows that God did not enjoin sacrifice, in order that he might occupy his worshippers with earthly exercises, but rather that he might raise their minds to something higher. This is clear even from His own nature. Being a spirit, he is delighted only with spiritual worship.

The same thing is testified by the many passages in which the Prophets accuse the Jews of stupidity, for imagining that mere sacrifices have any value in the sight of God. Did they by this mean to derogate in any respect from the Law? By no means; but as interpreters of its true meaning, they wished in this way to turn the attention of the people to the end which they ought to have had in view, but from which they generally wandered.

From the grace offered to the Jews we may certainly infer, that the law was not a stranger to Christ. Moses declared the end of the adoption of the Israelites to be, that they should be "a kingdom of priests, and an holy nation" (Exodus 19:6). This they could not attain, without a greater and more excellent atonement than the blood of beasts. For what could be less in accordance with reason, than that the sons of Adams who, from hereditary taint, are all born the slaves of sin, should be raised to royal dignity, and in this way made partakers of the glory of God, if the noble distinction were not derived from some other source? How, moreover, could the priestly office exist in vigour among those whose vices rendered them abominable in the sight of God, if they were not consecrated in a holy head?

Wherefore, Peter elegantly transposes the words of Moses, teaching that the fullness of grace, of which the Jews had a foretaste under the Law, is exhibited in Christ, "Ye are a chosen generation, a royal priesthood" (1 Peter 2:9). The transposition of the words intimates that those to whom Christ has appeared in the Gospel, have obtained more than their fathers, inasmuch as they are all endued with priestly and royal honor, and can, therefore, trusting to their Mediator, appear with boldness in the presence of God.

2 Proof continued. F. From a consideration of the kingdom erected in the family of David. G. From the end of the ceremonies. H. From the end of the Moral Law.

And it is to be observed, by the way, that the kingdom, which was at length erected in the family of David, is part of the Law, and is comprehended under the dispensation of Moses; whence it follows, that, as well in the whole tribe of Levi as in the posterity of David, Christ was exhibited to the eyes of the Israelites as in a double mirror. For, as I lately observed (section 1), in no other way could those who were the slaves of sin and death, and defiled with corruption, be either kings or priests. Hence, appears the perfect truth of Paul's statement, "The law was our schoolmaster to bring us unto Christ," "until the seed should come to whom the promise was made" (Galatians 3:24, 19).

For Christ not yet having been made familiarly known to the Jews, they were like children whose weakness could not bear a full knowledge of heavenly things. How they were led to Christ by the ceremonial law has already been adverted to, and may be made more intelligible by several passages in the Prophets. Although they were required, in order to appease God, to approach him daily with new sacrifices, yet Isaiah promises, that all their sins would be expiated by one single sacrifice, and with this Daniel concurs (Isaiah 53:5; Daniel 9:26, 27)). The priests appointed from the tribe of Levi entered the sanctuary, but it was once said of a single priest, "The Lord has sworn, and will not repent, Thou art a priest forever, after the order of Melchizedek" (Psalm 110:4). The unction of oil was then visible, but Daniel in vision declares that there will be another unction.

Not to dwell on this, the author of the Epistle to the Hebrews proves clearly, and at length, from the fourth to the eleventh chapter, that ceremonies were vain, and of no value, unless as bringing us to Christ.

In regard to the Ten Commandments, we must, in like manner, attend to the statement of Paul, that "Christ is the end of the law for righteousness to everyone that believeth" (Romans 10:4); and, again, that ministers of the new testament were "not of the letter, but of the spirit: for the letter killeth, but the split giveth life" (2 Corinthians 3:6).

The former passage intimates, that it is in vain to teach righteousness by precept, until Christ bestow it by free imputation, and the regeneration of the Spirit. Hence, he properly calls Christ the end or fulfilling of the Law, because it would avail us nothing to know what God demands did not Christ come to the succor of those who are laboring, and oppressed under an intolerable yoke and burden. In another place, he says that the Law "was added because of transgressions" (Galatians 3:19), that it might humble men under a sense of their condemnation.

Moreover, inasmuch as this is the only true preparation for Christ, the statements, though made in different words, perfectly agree with each other. But because he had to dispute with perverse teachers, who pretended that men merited justification by the works of the Law, he was sometimes obliged, in refuting their error, to speak of the Law in a more restricted sense, merely as law, though, in other respects, the covenant of free adoption is comprehended under it.

3 A more ample exposition of the last proof. The Moral Law leads believers to Christ. Showing the perfect righteousness required by God, it convinces us of our inability to fulfill it. It thus denies us life, adjudges us to death, and so urges us to seek deliverance in Christ.

But in order that a sense of guilt may urge us to seek for pardon, it is of importance to know how our being instructed in the Moral Law renders us more inexcusable. If it is true, that a perfect righteousness is set before us in the Law, it follows, that the complete observance of it is perfect righteousness in the sight of God; that is, a righteousness by which a man may be deemed and pronounced righteous at the divine tribunal. Wherefore Moses, after promulgating the Law, hesitates not to call heaven and earth to witness, that he had set life and death, good and evil, before the people. Nor can it be denied, that the reward of eternal salvation, as promised by the Lord, awaits the perfect obedience of the Law (Deuteronomy 30:19). Again, however, it is of importance to understand in what way we perform that obedience for which we justly entertain the hope of that reward.

For of what use is it to see that the reward of eternal life depends on the observance of the Law, unless it moreover appears whether it be in our power in that way to attain to eternal life? Herein, then, the weakness of the Law is manifested; for, in none of us is that righteousness of the Law manifested, and, therefore, being excluded from the promises of life, we again fall under the curse.

I state not only what happens, but also what must necessarily happen. The doctrine of the Law transcending our capacity, a man may indeed look from a distance at the promises held forth, but he cannot derive any benefit from them. The only thing, therefore, remaining for him is, from their excellence to form a better estimate of his own misery, while he considers that the hope of salvation is cut off, and he is threatened with certain death. On the other hand, those fearful denunciations which strike not at a few individuals, but at every individual without exceptions rise up; rise up, I say, and, with inexorable severity, pursue us; so that nothing but instant death is presented by the Law.

4 The promises of the Law, though conditional, founded on the best reason. This reason explained.

Therefore, if we look merely to the Law, the result must be despondency, confusion, and despair, seeing that by it we are all cursed and condemned, while we are kept far away from the blessedness which it holds forth to its observers. Is the Lord, then, you will ask, only sporting with us? Is it not the next thing to mockery, to hold out the hope of happiness, to invite and exhort us to it, to declare that it is set before us, while all the while the entrance to it is precluded and quite shut up?

I answer, Although the promises, in so far as they are conditional, depend on a perfect obedience of the Law, which is nowhere to be found, they have not, however, been given in vain. For when we have learned, that the promises would be fruitless and unavailing, did not God accept us of his free goodness, without any view to our works, and when, having so learned, we, by faith, embrace the goodness thus offered in the Gospel, the promises, with all their annexed conditions, are fully accomplished. For God, while bestowing all things upon us freely, crowns his goodness by not disdaining our imperfect obedience; forgiving its deficiencies, accepting it as if it were complete, and so bestowing upon us the full amount of what the Law has promised. But as this point will be more fully discussed in treating of justification by faith, we shall not follow it further at present.

5 No inconsistency in giving a law, the observance of which is impossible. This proved from reason, and confirmed by Scripture. Another confirmation from Augustine.

What has been said as to the impossible observance of the Law, it will be proper briefly to explain and confirm, the general opinion being, that nothing can be more absurd. Hence, Jerome has not hesitated to denounce anathema against it. What Jerome thought, I care not; let us inquire what is the truth.

I will not here enter into a long and intricate discussion on the various kinds of possibility. By impossible, I mean, that which never was, and, being prevented by the ordination and decree of God, never will be. I say, that if we go back to the remotest period, we shall not find a single saint who, clothed with a mortal body, ever attained to such perfection as to love the Lord with all his heart, and soul, and mind, and strength; and, on the other hand, not one who has not felt the power of concupiscence. Who can deny this?

I am aware, indeed of a kind of saints whom a foolish superstition imagines, and whose purity the angels of heaven scarcely equal. This, however, is repugnant both to Scripture and experience. But I say further, that no saint ever will attain to perfection, so long as he is in the body. Scripture bears clear testimony to this effect: "There is no man that sinneth not," saith Solomon (1 King 8:46). David says, "In thy sight shall no man living be justified" (Psalm 143:2). Job also, in numerous passages, affirms the same thing. But the clearest of all is Paul, who declares, "the flesh lusteth against the Spirit, and the Spirit against the flesh" (Galatians 5:17). And he proves, that "as many as are of the works of the law are under the curse," for the simple reason, that it is written, "Cursed is everyone that continueth not in all things which are written in the book of the law to do them" (Galatians 3:10; Deuteronomy 27:26); intimating, or rather assuming it as confessed, that none can so continue. But whatever Scripture has declared must be regarded as perpetual, and hence necessary.

The Pelagians annoyed Augustine with the sophism, that it was insulting to God to hold, that he orders more than believers are able, by his grace, to perform; and he, in order to evade it, acknowledged that the Lord was able, if he chose, to raise a mortal man to angelic purity; but that he had never done, and never would do it, because so the Scripture had declared. This I deny not: but I add, that there is no use in absurdly disputing concerning the power of God in opposition to his truth; and therefore there is no ground for quibbling, when it is said that that thing cannot be, which the Scriptures declare will never be. But if it is the word that is objected to, I refer to the answer that our Savior gave to his disciples when they asked, "Who then can be saved?" "With men," said he, "this is impossible; but with God all things are possible" (Matthew 19:25).

Augustine argues in the most convincing manner, that while in the flesh, we never can give God the love, which we owe him. "Love so follows knowledge, that no man can perfectly love God who has not previously a full comprehension of his goodness." So long as we are pilgrims in the world, we see through a glass darkly, and therefore our love is imperfect. Let it therefore be held incontrovertible, that, in consequence of the feebleness of our nature, it is impossible for us, so long as we are in the flesh, to fulfill the law. This will also be proved elsewhere from the writings of Paul (Romans 8:3).

6 A consideration of the office and use of the Moral Law shows that it leads to Christ. The Law, while it describes the righteousness, which is acceptable to God, proves that every man is unrighteous.

That the whole matter may be made clearer, let us take a succinct view of the office and use of the Moral Law. Now this office and use seems to me to consist of three parts. First, by exhibiting the righteousness of God, —in other words, the righteousness, which alone is acceptable to God, —it admonishes everyone of his own unrighteousness, informs, convicts, and finally condemns him. This is necessary, in order that man, who is blind and intoxicated with self-love, may be brought at once to know and to confess his weakness and impurity. For until his vanity is made perfectly manifest, he is puffed up with infatuated confidence in his own powers, and never can be brought to feel their feebleness so long as he measures them by a standard of his own choice. So soon, however, as he begins to compare them with the requirements of the Law, he has something to tame his presumption. However high his opinion of his own powers may be, he immediately feels that they pant under the heavy load, then totter and stumble, and finally fall and give way. He, then, who is schooled by the Law, lays aside the arrogance, which formerly blinded him.

In like manner must he be cured of pride, the other disease under which we have said that he labors. So long as he is permitted to appeal to his own judgment, he substitutes a hypocritical for a real righteousness, and, contented with this, sets up certain factitious observances in opposition to the grace of God. But after he is forced to weigh his conduct in the balance of the Law, renouncing all dependence on this fancied righteousness, he sees that he is at an infinite distance from holiness, and, on the other hand, that he teems with innumerable vices of which he formerly seemed free. The recesses in which concupiscence lies hid are so deep and tortuous that they easily elude our view; and hence the Apostle had good reason for saying, "I had not known lust, except the law had said, Thou shalt not covet." For, if it is not brought forth from its lurking places, it miserably destroys in secret before its fatal sting is discerned.

7 The Law fitly compared to a mirror, which shows us our wretchedness. This derogates not in any degree from its excellence.

Thus the Law is a kind of mirror. As in a mirror we discover any stains upon our face, so in the Law we behold, first, our impotence; then, in consequence of it, our iniquity; and, finally, the curse, as the consequence of both. He who has no power of following righteousness is necessarily plunged in the mire of iniquity, and this iniquity is immediately followed by the curse. Accordingly, the greater the transgression of which the Law convicts us, the severer the judgment to which we are exposed. To this effect is the Apostle's declaration, that "by the law is the knowledge of sin" (Romans 3:20). By these words, he only points out the first office of the Law as experienced by sinners not yet regenerated. In conformity to this, it is said, "The law entered that the offense might abound;" and, accordingly, that it is "the ministration of death;" that it "worketh wrath" and kills (Romans 5:20; 2 Corinthians 3:7; Romans 4:15).

For there cannot be a doubt that the clearer the consciousness of guilt, the greater the increase of sin, because then a rebellious feeling against the Lawgiver is added to the transgression. All that remains for the Law is to arm the wrath of God for the destruction of the sinner; for by itself it can do nothing but accuse, condemn, and destroy him.

Thus, Augustine says, "If the Spirit of grace be absent, the law is present only to convict and slay us." But to say this neither insults the law, nor derogates in any degree from its excellence. Assuredly, if our whole will were formed and disposed to obedience, the mere knowledge of the law would be sufficient for salvation; but since our carnal and corrupt nature is at enmity with the Divine law, and is in no degree amended by its discipline, the consequence is, that the law which, if it had been properly attended to, would have given life, becomes the occasion of sin and death.

When all are convicted of transgression, the more it declares the righteousness of God, the more, on the other hand, it discloses our iniquity; the more certainly it assures us that life and salvation are treasured up as the reward of righteousness, the more certainly it assures us that the unrighteous will perish. So far, however are these qualities from throwing disgrace on the Law, that their chief tendency is to give a brighter display of the divine goodness. For they show that it is only our weakness and depravity that prevents us from enjoying the blessedness, which the law openly sets before us. Hence, additional sweetness is given to divine grace, which comes to our aid without the law, and additional loveliness to the mercy which confers it, because they proclaim that God is never weary in doing good, and in loading us with new gifts.

8 When the Law discloses our guilt, we should not despond, but flee to the mercy of God. How this may be done.

But while the law attests the unrighteousness and condemnation of all, it does not follow (if we make the proper use of it) that we are immediately to give up all hope and rush headlong on despair. No doubt, it has some such effect upon the reprobate, but this is owing to their obstinacy. With the children of God, the effect is different. The Apostle testifies that the law pronounces its sentence of condemnation in order "that every mouth may be stopped, and all the world may become guilty before God" (Romans 3:19). In another place, however, the same Apostle declares, that "God has concluded them all in unbelief;" not that he might destroy all, or allow all to perish, but that "he might have mercy upon all" (Romans 11:32); in other words, that divesting themselves of an absurd opinion of their own virtue, they may perceive how they are wholly dependent on the hand of God; that feeling how naked and destitute they are, they may take refuge in his mercy, rely upon it, and cover themselves up entirely with it; renouncing all righteousness and merit, and clinging to mercy alone, as offered in Christ to all who long and look for it in true faith. In the precepts of the law, God is seen as the rewarder only of perfect righteousness (a righteousness of which all are destitute), and, on the other hand, as the stern avenger of wickedness. But in Christ his countenance beams forth full of grace and gentleness towards poor unworthy sinners.

9 Confirmation of the first use of the Moral Law from various passages in Augustine.

There are many passages in Augustine, as to the utility of the law in leading us to implore Divine assistance. Thus, he writes to Hilary, "The law orders, that we, after attempting to do what is ordered and so feeling our weakness under the law, may learn to implore the help of grace." In like manner, he writes to Asellius, "The utility of the law is that it convinces man of his weakness, and compels him to apply for the medicine of grace, which is in Christ."

In like manner, he says to Innocentius Romanus, "The law orders; grace supplies the power of acting." Again, to Valentinus, "God enjoins what we cannot do, in order that we may know what we have to ask of him." Again, "The law was given, that it might make you guilty—being made guilty might fear; fearing, might ask indulgence, not presume on your own strength." Again, "The law was given, in order to convert a great into a little man—to show that you have no power of your own for righteousness; and might thus, poor, needy, and destitute, flee to grace."

He afterwards thus addresses the Almighty, "So do, O Lord, so do, O merciful Lord; command what cannot be fulfilled; nay, command what cannot be fulfilled, unless by thy own grace: so that when men feel they have no strength in themselves to fulfill it, every mouth may be stopped, and no man seem great in his own eyes. Let all be little ones; let the whole world become guilty before God."

But I am forgetting myself in producing so many passages, since this holy man wrote a distinct treatise, which he entitled *De Spiritu et Litera*. The other branch of this first use he does not describe so distinctly, either because he knew that it depended on the former, or because he was not so well aware of it, or because he wanted words in which he might distinctly and clearly explain its proper meaning. But even in the reprobates themselves, this first office of the law is not altogether wanting. They do not, indeed, proceed so far with the children of God as, after the flesh is cast down, to be renewed in the inner man, and revive again, but stunned by the first terror, give way to despair. Still it tends to manifest the equity of the Divine judgment, when their consciences are thus heaved upon the waves. They would always willingly carp at the judgment of God; but now, though that judgment is not manifested, still the alarm produced by the testimony of the law and of their conscience bespeaks their deserts.

10. **A second use of the Law is to curb sinners. This most necessary for the good of the community at large; and this in respect not only of the reprobate, but also of the elect, previous to regeneration. This confirmed by the authority of an Apostle.**

The second office of the Law is, by means of its fearful denunciations and the consequent dread of punishment, to curb those who, unless forced, have no regard for rectitude and justice. Such persons are curbed not because their mind is inwardly moved and affected, but because, as if a bridle were laid upon them, they refrain their hands from external acts, and internally check the depravity, which would otherwise petulantly burst forth. It is true; they are not on this account either better or more righteous in the sight of God. For although restrained by terror or shame, they dare not proceed to what their mind has conceived, or give full license to their raging lust, their heart is by no means trained to fear and obedience. Nay, the more they restrain themselves, the more they are inflamed, the more they rage and boil, prepared for any act or outbreak whatsoever were it not for the terror of the law. And not only so, but they thoroughly detest the law itself, and execrate the Lawgiver; so that if they could, they would most willingly annihilate him, because they cannot bear either his ordering what is right, or his avenging the despisers of his Majesty.

The feeling of all who are not yet regenerate, though in some more, in others less lively, is, that in regard to the observance of the law, they are not led by voluntary submission, but dragged by the force of fear. Nevertheless, this forced and extorted righteousness is necessary for the good of society, its peace being secured by a provision but for which all things would be thrown into tumult and confusion. Nay, this tuition is not without its use, even to the children of God, who, before their effectual calling, being destitute of the Spirit of holiness, freely indulge the lusts of the flesh.

When, by the fear of Divine vengeance, they are deterred from open outbreaks, though, from not being subdued in mind, they profit little at present, still they are in some measure trained to bear the yoke of righteousness, so that when they are called, they are not like mere novices, studying a discipline of which previously they had no knowledge.

This office seems to be especially in the view of the Apostle, when he says, "That the law is not made for a righteous man, but for the lawless and disobedient, for the ungodly and for sinners, for unholy and profane, for murderers of fathers and murderers of mothers, for manslayers, for whoremongers, for them that defile themselves with mankind, for men-stealers, for liars, for perjured persons, and if there be any other thing that is contrary to sound doctrine" (1 Timothy 1:9, 10). He thus indicates that it is a restraint on unruly lusts that would otherwise burst all bonds.

11 The Law showing our wretchedness disposes us to admit the remedy. It also tends to keep us in our duty. Confirmation from general experience.

To both may be applied the declaration of the Apostle in another place, that "The law was our schoolmaster to bring us unto Christ" (Galatians 3:24); since there are two classes of persons, whom by its training it leads to Christ. Some (of whom we spoke in the first place), from excessive confidence in their own virtue or righteousness, are unfit to receive the grace of Christ, until they are completely humbled. This the law does by making them sensible , of their misery, and so disposing them to long for what they previously imagined they did not want. Others have need of a bridle to restrain them from giving full scope to their passions, and thereby utterly losing all desire after righteousness. For where the Spirit of God rules not, the lusts sometimes so burst forth, as to threaten to drown the soul subjected to them in forgetfulness and contempt of God; and so they would, did not God interpose with this remedy. Those, therefore, whom he has destined to the inheritance of his kingdom, if he does not immediately regenerate, he, through the works of the law, preserves in fear, against the time of his visitation, not, indeed, that pure and chaste fear which his children ought to have, but a fear useful to the extent of instructing them in true piety according to their capacity. Of this, we have so many proofs, that there is not the least need of an example.

For all who have remained for some time in ignorance of God will confess, as the result of their own experience, that the law had the effect of keeping them in some degree in the fear and reverence of God, until, being regenerated by his Spirit, they began to love him from the heart.

12 The third and most appropriate use of the Law respects the elect. A. It instructs and teaches them to make daily progress in doing the will of God. B. Urges them by exhortation to obedience. Testimony of David. How he is to be reconciled with the Apostle.

The third use of the Law (being also the principal use, and more closely connected with its proper end) has respect to believers in whose hearts the Spirit of God already flourishes and reigns. For although the Law is written and engraved on their hearts by the finger of God, that is, although they are so influenced and actuated by the Spirit, that they desire to obey God, they still profit in the Law in two ways. For it is the best instrument for enabling them daily to learn with greater truth and certainty what that will of the Lord is which they aspire to follow, and to confirm them in this knowledge; just as a servant who desires with all his soul to approve himself to his master, must still observe, and be careful to ascertain his master's dispositions, that he may comport himself in accommodation to them.

Let none of us deem ourselves exempt from this necessity, for none have as yet attained to such a degree of wisdom, as that they may not, by the daily instruction of the Law, advance to a purer knowledge of the Divine will. Then, because we need not doctrine merely, but exhortation also, the servant of God will derive this further advantage from the Law: by frequently meditating upon it, he will be excited to obedience, and confirmed in it, and so drawn away from the slippery paths of sin. In this way, must the saints press onward, since, however great the alacrity with which, under the Spirit, they hasten toward righteousness, they are retarded by the sluggishness of the flesh, and make less progress than they ought.

The Law acts like a whip to the flesh, urging it on as men do a lazy sluggish ass. Even in the case of a spiritual man, inasmuch as he is still burdened with the weight of the flesh, the Law is a constant stimulus, pricking him forward when he would indulge in sloth. David had this use in view when he pronounced this high eulogium on the Law, "The law of the Lord is perfect, converting the soul: the testimony of the Lord is sure, making wise the simple. The statutes of the Lord are right, rejoicing the heart: the commandment of the Lord is pure, enlightening the eyes" (Psalm 19:7, 8). Again, "Thy word is a lamp unto my feet, and a light unto my path" (Psalm 119:105). The whole psalm abounds in passages to the same effect.

Such passages are not inconsistent with those of Paul, which show not the utility of the law to the regenerate, but what it is able of itself to bestow. The object of the Psalmist is to celebrate the advantages, which the Lord, by means of his law, bestows on those whom he inwardly inspires with a love of obedience. And he adverts not to the mere precepts, but also to the promise annexed to them, which alone makes that sweet, which in itself is bitter. For what is less attractive than the law, when, by its demands and threatening, it overawes the soul, and fills it with terror? David specially shows that in the law he saw the Mediator, without whom it gives no pleasure or delight.

13 The profane heresy of the Antinomians must be exploded. Argument founded on a passage in David, and another in Moses.

Some unskillful persons, from not attending to this, boldly discard the whole Law of Moses, and do away with both its Tables, imagining it unchristian to adhere to a doctrine, which contains the ministration of death. Far from our thoughts is this profane notion. Moses has admirably shown that the Law, which can produce nothing but death in sinners, ought to have a better and more excellent effect upon the righteous. When about to die, he thus addressed the people, "Set your hearts unto all the words which I testify among you this day, which ye shall command your children to observe to do, all the words of this law. For it is not a vain thing for you; because it is your life" (Deuteronomy 32:46, 47).

If it cannot be denied that it contains a perfect pattern of righteousness, then, unless we ought not to have any proper rule of life, it must be impious to discard it. There are not various rules of life, but one perpetual and inflexible rule; and, therefore, when David describes the righteous as spending their whole lives in meditating on the Law (Psalm 1:2), we must not confine to a single age, an employment which is most appropriate to all ages, even to the end of the world. Nor are we to be deterred or to shun its instructions, because the holiness, which it prescribes, is stricter than we are able to render, so long as we bear about the prison of the body. It does not now perform toward us the part of a hard taskmaster, who will not be satisfied without full payment; but, in the perfection to which it exhorts us, points out the goal at which, during the whole course of our lives, it is not less our interest than our duty to aim. It is well if we thus press onward. Our whole life is a race, and after we have finished our course, the Lord will enable us to reach that goal to which, at present, we can only aspire in wish.

14 Last part of the chapter treating of the abrogation of the Law. In what respect any part of the Moral Law abrogated.

Since, in regard to believers, the law has the force of exhortation, not to bind their consciences with a curse, but by urging them, from time to time, to shake off sluggishness and chastise imperfection, —many, when they would express this exemption from the curse, say, that in regard to believers the Law (I still mean the Moral Law) is abrogated: not that the things which it enjoins are no longer right to be observed, but only that it is not to believers what it formerly was; in other words, that it does not, by terrifying and confounding their consciences, condemn and destroy.

It is certainly true that Paul shows, in clear terms, that there is such an abrogation of the Law. And that our Lord preached the same appears from this, that he would not have refuted the opinion of his destroying the Law, if it had not been prevalent among the Jews. Since such an opinion could not have arisen at random without some pretext, there is reason to presume that it originated in a false interpretation of his doctrine, in the same way in which all errors generally arise from a perversion of the truth. But lest we should stumble against the same stone, let us distinguish accurately between what has been abrogated in the Law, and what still remains in force. When the Lord declares, that he came not to destroy the Law, but to fulfill (Matthew 5:17); that until heaven and earth pass away, not one jot or little shall remain unfulfilled; he shows that his advent was not to derogate, in any degree, from the observance of the Law. And justly, since the very end of his coming was to remedy the transgression of the Law. Therefore, the doctrine of the Law has not been infringed by Christ, but remains, that, by teaching, admonishing, rebuking, and correcting, it may fit and prepare us for every good work.

15 The curse of the Law how abrogated.

What Paul says, as to the abrogation of the Law, evidently applies not to the Law itself, but merely to its power of constraining the conscience. For the Law not only teaches, but also imperiously demands. If obedience is not yielded, nay, if it is omitted in any degree, it thunders forth its curse. For this reason, the Apostle says, that "as many as are of the works of the law are under the curse: for it is written, Cursed is everyone that continueth not in all things which are written in the book of the law to do them" (Galatians 3:10; Deuteronomy 27:26).

Those he describes as under the works of the Law, who do not place righteousness in that forgiveness of sins by which we are freed from the rigor of the Law. He therefore shows that we must be freed from the fetters of the Law, if we would not perish miserably under them. But what fetters? Those of rigid and austere exaction, which remits not one iota of the demand, and leaves no transgression unpunished. To redeem us from this curse, Christ was made a curse for us: for it is written, Cursed is everyone that hangeth on a tree (Deuteronomy 21:23, compared with (Galatians 3:13, 4:4). In the following chapter, indeed, he says, that "Christ was made under the law, in order that he might redeem those who are under the law;" but the meaning is the same. For he immediately adds, "That we might receive the adoption of sons."

What does this mean? That we might not be, all our lifetime, subject to bondage, having our consciences oppressed with the fear of death. Meanwhile, it must ever remain an indubitable truth, that the Law has lost none of its authority, but must always receive from us the same respect and obedience.

16 Of the abrogation of the Ceremonial Law in regard to the observance only.

The case of ceremonies is different, these having been abrogated not in effect but in use only. Though Christ by his advent put an end to their use, so far is this from derogating from their sacredness, that it rather commends and illustrates it. For as these ceremonies would have given nothing to God's ancient people but empty show, if the power of Christ's death and resurrection had not been prefigured by them, —so, if the use of them had not ceased, it would, in the present day, be impossible to understand for what purpose they were instituted. Accordingly, Paul, in order to prove that the observance of them was not only superfluous, but pernicious also, says that they "are a shadow of things to come; but the body is of Christ" (Colossians 2:17). We see, therefore, that the truth is made clearer by their abolition than if Christ, who has been openly manifested, were still figured by them as at a distance and as under a veil.

By the death of Christ, the veil of the temple was rent in vain, the living and express image of heavenly things, which had begun to be dimly shadowed forth, being now brought fully into view, as is described by the author of the Epistle to the Hebrews (Hebrews 10:1). To the same effect, our Savior declares, that "the law and the prophets were until John: since that time the kingdom of God is preached, and every man presseth into it" (Luke 16:16); not that the holy fathers were left without the preaching of the hope of salvation and eternal life, but because they only saw at a distance, and under a shadow, what we now behold in full light.

Why it behooved the Church to ascend higher than these elements is explained by John the Baptist, when he says, "The law was given by Moses, but grace and truth came by Jesus Christ" (John 1:17). For though it is true that expiation was promised in the ancient sacrifices, and the ark of the covenant was a sure pledge of the paternal favor of God, the whole would have been delusory had it not been founded on the grace of Christ, wherein true and eternal stability is found. It must be held as a fixed point, that though legal rites ceased to be observed, their end serves to show more clearly, how great their utility was before the advent of Christ, who, while he abolished the use, sealed their force and effect by his death.

17 The reason assigned by the Apostle applicable not to the Moral Law, but to ceremonial observances only. These abrogated, not only because they separated the Jews from the Gentiles, but still more because they were a kind of formal instruments to attest our guilt and impunity. Christ, by destroying these, is justly said to have taken away the handwriting that was against us, and nailed it to his cross.

There is a little more difficulty in the following passage of Paul: "You, being dead in your sins and the uncircumcision of your flesh, has he quickened together with him, having forgiven you all trespasses; blotting out the handwriting of ordinances that was against us, which was contrary to us, and took it out of the way, nailing it to his cross," etc. (Colossians 2:13, 14). He seems to extend the abolition of the Law considerably further, as if we had nothing to do with its injunctions.

Some err in interpreting this simply of the Moral Law, as implying the abolition not of its injunctions, but of its inexorable rigor. Others examining Paul's words more carefully, see that they properly apply to the Ceremonial Law, and show that Paul repeatedly uses the term *ordinance* in this sense. He thus writes to the Ephesians: "He is our peace, who has made both one, and has broken down the middle wall of partition between us; having abolished in his flesh the enmity, even the law of commandments contained in ordinances; for to make in himself of twain one new man" (Ephesians 2:14).

There can be no doubt that he is there treating of ceremonies, as he speaks of "the middle wall of partition" which separated Jews and Gentiles. I therefore hold that the former view is erroneous; but, at the same time, it does not appear to me that the latter comes fully up to the Apostle's meaning.

For I cannot admit that the two passages are perfectly parallel. As his object was to assure the Ephesians that they were admitted to fellowship with the Jews, he tells them that the obstacle, which formerly stood in the way, was removed. This obstacle was in the ceremonies. For the rites of ablution and sacrifice, by which the Jews were consecrated to the Lord, separated them from the Gentiles.

But who sees not that, in the Epistle to the Colossians, a more sublime mystery is adverted to? No doubt, a question is raised there as to the Mosaic observances, to which false apostles were endeavoring to bind the Christian people. But as in the Epistle to the Galatians he takes a higher view of this controversy, and in a manner traces it to its fountain, so he does in this passage also. For if the only thing considered in rites is the necessity of observing them, of what use was it to call it handwriting, which was contrary to us? Besides, how could the bringing in of it be set down as almost the whole sum of redemption? Wherefore, the very nature of the case clearly shows that reference is here made to something more internal.

I cannot doubt that I have ascertained the genuine interpretation, provided I am permitted to assume what Augustine has somewhere most truly affirmed, nay, derived from the very words of the Apostle—viz. that in the Jewish ceremonies there was more a confession than an expiation of sins. For what more was done in sacrifice by those who substituted purifications instead of themselves, than to confess that they were conscious of deserving death? What did these purifications testify but that they themselves were impure? By these means, therefore, the handwriting both of their guilt and impurity was always renewed. But the attestation of these things was not the removal of them. Wherefore, the Apostle says that Christ is "the mediator of the new testament, —by means of death, for the redemption of the transgressions that were under the first testament" (Hebrews 9:15). Justly, therefore, does the Apostle describe these handwritings as against the worshipers, and contrary to them, since by means of them their impurity and condemnation were openly sealed.

There is nothing contrary to this in the fact that they were partakers of the same grace with ourselves. This they obtained through Christ, and not through the ceremonies, which the Apostle there contrasts with Christ: showing that by the continued use of them, the glory of Christ was obscured. We perceive how ceremonies, considered in themselves, are elegantly and appositely termed handwritings, and contrary to the salvation of man, in as much as they were a kind of formal instruments, which attested his liability.

On the other hand, when false apostles wished to bind them on the Christian Church, Paul, entering more deeply into their signification, with good reason warned the Colossians how seriously they would relapse if they allowed a yoke to be in that way imposed upon them. By so doing, they, at the same time, deprived themselves of all benefit from Christ, who, by his eternal sacrifice once offered, had abolished those daily sacrifices, which were indeed powerful to attest sin, but could do nothing to destroy it.

Chapter 8

EXPOSITION OF THE MORAL LAW.

This chapter consists of four parts. I. Some general observations necessary for the understanding of the subject are made by way of preface, section 1–5. II. Three things always to be attended to in ascertaining and expounding the meaning of the Moral Law, section 6–12. III. Exposition of the Moral Law, or the Ten Commandments, section 13–15. IV. The end for which the whole Law is intended—viz. to teach not only elementary principles, but perfection, section 51, to the end of the chapter.

Sections

1. The Law was committed to writing, in order that it might teach more fully and perfectly that knowledge, both of God and of ourselves, which the law of nature teaches meagerly and obscurely. Proof of this, from an enumeration of the principal parts of the Moral Law; and also from the dictate of natural law, written on the hearts of all, and, in a manner, effaced by sin.

2. Certain general maxims. From the knowledge of God, furnished by the Law, we learn that God is our Father and Ruler. Righteousness is pleasing; iniquity is an abomination in his sight. Hence, how weak soever we may be, our duty is to cultivate the one, and shun the other.

3. From the knowledge of ourselves, furnished by the Law, we learn to discern our own utter powerlessness, we are ashamed; and seeing it is in vain to seek for righteousness in ourselves, are induced to seek it elsewhere.

4. Hence, God has annexed promises and threatening to his promises. These not limited to the present life, but embrace things heavenly and eternal. They, moreover, attest the spotless purity of God, his love of righteousness, and also his kindness towards us.

5. The Law shows, moreover, that there is nothing more acceptable to God than obedience. Hence, all superstitious and hypocritical modes of worship are condemned. A remedy against superstitious worship and human presumption.

6. *The second part of the chapter, containing three observations or rules. First rule, Our life must be formed by the Law, not only to external honesty, but to inward and spiritual righteousness. In this respect, the Law of God differs from civil laws, he being a spiritual Lawgiver, man not. This rule of great extent, and not sufficiently attended to.*

7. *This first rule confirmed by the authority of Christ, and vindicated from the false dogma of Sophists, who say that Christ is only another Moses.*

8. *Second observation or rule to be carefully attended to—viz. that the end of the command must be inquired into, until it is ascertained what the Lawgiver approves or disapproves. Example. Where the Law approves, its opposite is condemned, and vice versa.*

9. *Full explanation of this latter point. Example.*

10. *The Law states what is most impious in each transgression, in order to show how heinous the transgression is. Example.*

11. *Third observation or rule regards the division of the Law into Two Tables: the former comprehending our duty to God; the latter, our duty to our neighbor. The connection between these necessary and inseparable. Their invariable order. Sum of the Law.*

12. *Division of the Law into Ten Commandments. Various distinctions made with regard to them, but the best distinction that which divides them into Two Tables. Four commandments belong to the First, and six to the Second Table.*

13. *The third part of the chapter, containing an exposition of the Decalogue. The preface vindicates the authority of the Law. This it does in three ways. First, by a declaration of its majesty.*

14. *The preface to the Law vindicates its authority. Secondly, by calling to mind God's paternal kindness.*

15. *Thirdly, by calling to mind the deliverance out of the land of Egypt. Why God distinguishes himself by certain epithets. Why mention is made of the deliverance from Egypt. In what way, and how far, the remembrance of this deliverance should still affect us.*

16. *Exposition of the First Commandment. Its end. What it is to have God, and to have strange gods. Adoration due to God, trust,*

invocation, thanksgiving, and also true religion, required by the Commandment. Superstition, Polytheism, and Atheism, forbidden. What meant by the words, "before me."

17. Exposition of the Second Commandment. The end and sum of it. Two parts. Short enumeration of forbidden shapes.

18. Why a threatening is added. Four titles applied to God, to make a deeper impression. He is called Mighty, Jealous, an Avenger, Merciful. Why said to be jealous. Reason drawn from analogy.

19. Exposition of the threatening, which is added. First, as to visiting the iniquity of the fathers upon the children. A misinterpretation on this head refuted, and the genuine meaning of the threatening explained.

20. Whether this visiting of the sins of parents inconsistent with the divine justice. Apparently conflicting passages reconciled.

21. Exposition of the latter part—viz. the showing mercy to thousands. The use of this promise. Consideration of an exception of frequent occurrence. The extent of this blessing.

22. Exposition of the Third Commandment. The end and sum of it. Three parts. These considered. What it is to use the name of God in vain. Swearing. Distinction between this commandment and the Ninth.

23. An oath defined. It is a species of divine worship. This explained.

24. Many modes in which this commandment is violated. A. By taking God to witness, what we know is false. The insult thus offered.

25. Modes of violation continued. B. Taking God to witness in trivial matters. Contempt thus shown. When and how an oath should be used. C. Substituting the servants of God instead of himself when taking an oath.

26. The Anabaptists, who condemn all oaths, refuted By the authority of Christ, who cannot be opposed in anything to the Father. A passage perverted by the Anabaptists explained. The design of our Savior in the passage. What meant by his there prohibiting oaths.

27. The lawfulness of oaths confirmed by Christ and the apostles. Some approve of public, but not of private oaths. The lawfulness of the latter proved both by reason and example. Instances from Scripture.

rudiments and first principles, but a perfect standard of righteousness, modeled on the divine purity.

52. Why, in the Gospels and Epistles, the latter table only mentioned, and not the first. The same thing occurs in the Prophets.

53. An objection to what is said in the former section removed.

54. A conduct duly regulated by the divine Law, characterized by charity toward our neighbor. This subverted by those who give the first place to self-love. Refutation of their opinion.

55. Who our neighbor. Double error of the Schoolmen on this point.

56. This error consists in converting precepts into counsels to be observed by monks.

57. Refutation of this error from Scripture and the ancient Theologians. Sophistical objection obviated.

58. Error of the Schoolmen consists in calling hidden impiety and covetousness venial sins. Refutation drawn, A. From a consideration of the whole Decalogue. B. The testimony of an Apostle. C. The authority of Christ. D. The nature and majesty of God. E. The sentence pronounced against sin. Conclusion.

59. Refutation drawn, A. From a consideration of the whole Decalogue. B. The testimony of an Apostle. C. The authority of Christ. D. The nature and majesty of God. E. The sentence pronounced against sin. Conclusion.

1 The Law was committed to writing, in order that it might teach more fully and perfectly that knowledge, both of God and of ourselves, which the law of nature teaches meagerly and obscurely. Proof of this, from an enumeration of the principal parts of the Moral Law; and also from the dictate of natural law, written on the hearts of all, and, in a manner, effaced by sin.

I believe it will not be out of place here to introduce the Ten Commandments of the Law, and give a brief exposition of them. In this way it will be made more clear, that the worship which God originally prescribed is still in force (a point to which I have already adverted); and then a second point will be confirmed—viz. that the Jews not only learned from the law wherein true piety consisted, but from feeling their inability to observe it would be overawed by the fear of judgments and so drawn, even against their will, towards the Mediator.

In giving a summary of what constitutes the true knowledge of God, we showed that we cannot form any just conception of the character of God, without feeling overawed by his majesty, and bound to do him service.

In regard to the knowledge of ourselves, we showed that it principally consists in renouncing all idea of our own strength, and divesting ourselves of all confidence in our own righteousness, while, on the other hand, under a full consciousness of our wants, we learn true humility and self-abasement. Both of these the Lord accomplishes by his Law, first, when, in assertion of the right which he has to our obedience, he calls us to reverence his majesty, and prescribes the conduct by which this reverence is manifested; and, secondly, when, by promulgating the rule of his justice (a rule, to the rectitude of which our nature, from being depraved and perverted, is continually opposed, and to the perfection of which our ability, from its infirmity and nervelessness for good, is far from being able to attain), he charges us both with impotence and unrighteousness.

Moreover, the very things contained in the two tables are, in a manner, dictated to us by that internal law, which, as has been already said, is in a manner written and stamped on every heart. For conscience, instead of allowing us to stifle our perceptions, and sleep on without interruption, acts as an inward witness and monitor, reminds us of what we owe to God, points out the distinction between good and evil, and thereby convicts us of departure from duty. But man, being immured in the darkness of error, is scarcely able, by means of that natural law, to form any tolerable idea of the worship, which is acceptable to God. At all events, he is very far from forming any correct knowledge of it. In addition to this, he is so swollen with arrogance and ambition, and so blinded with self-love, that he is unable to survey, and descend into himself, that he may so learn to humble and abase himself, and confess his misery.

Therefore, as a necessary remedy, both for our dullness and our contumacy, the Lord has given us his written Law, which, by its sure attestations, removes the obscurity of the law of nature, and also, by shaking off our lethargy, makes a more lively and permanent impression on our minds.

2 Certain general maxims. From the knowledge of God, furnished by the Law, we learn that God is our Father and Ruler. Righteousness is pleasing; iniquity is an abomination in his sight. Hence, how weak soever we may be, our duty is to cultivate the one, and shun the other.

It is now easy to understand the doctrine of the law—viz. that God, as our Creator, is entitled to be regarded by us as a Father and Master, and should, accordingly, receive from us fear, love, reverence, and glory; nay, that we are not our own, to follow whatever course passion dictates, but are bound to obey him implicitly, and to acquiesce entirely in his good pleasure. Again, the Law teaches, that justice and rectitude are a delight, injustice an abomination to him, and, therefore, as we would not with impious ingratitude revolt from our Maker, our whole life must be spent in the cultivation of righteousness. For if we manifest becoming reverence only when we prefer his will to our own, it follows, that the only legitimate service to him is the practice of justice, purity, and holiness. Nor can we plead as an excuse, that we want the power, and, like debtors, whose means are exhausted, are unable to pay.

We cannot be permitted to measure the glory of God by our ability; whatever we may be, he ever remains like himself, the friend of righteousness, the enemy of unrighteousness, and whatever his demands from us may be, as he can only require what is right, we are necessarily under a natural obligation to obey. Our inability to do so is our own fault. If lust, in which sin has its dominion, so enthralls us, that we are not free to obey our Father, there is no ground for pleading necessity as a defense, since this evil necessity is within, and must be imputed to ourselves.

3 From the knowledge of ourselves, furnished by the Law, we learn to discern our own utter powerlessness, we are ashamed; and seeing it is in vain to seek for righteousness in ourselves, are induced to seek it elsewhere.

When, under the guidance of the Law, we have advanced thus far, we must, under the same guidance, proceed to descend into ourselves. In this way, we at length arrive at two results: First, contrasting our conduct with the righteousness of the Law, we see how very far it is from being in accordance with the will of God, and, therefore, how unworthy we are of holding our place among his creatures, far less of being accounted his sons; and, secondly, taking a survey of our powers, we see that they are not only unequal to fulfill the Law, but are altogether null. The necessary consequence must be, to produce distrust of our own ability, and also anxiety and trepidation of mind.

Conscience cannot feel the burden of its guilt, without forthwith turning to the judgment of God, while the view of this judgment cannot fail to excite a dread of death. In like manner, the proofs of our utter powerlessness must instantly beget despair of our own strength. Both feelings are productive of humility and abasement, and hence the sinner, terrified at the prospect of eternal death (which he sees justly impending over him for his iniquities), turns to the mercy of God as the only haven of safety. Feeling his utter inability to pay what he owes to the Law, and thus despairing of himself, he rethinks him of applying and looking to some other quarter for help.

4 Hence, God has annexed promises and threatening to his promises. These not limited to the present life, but embrace things heavenly and eternal. They, moreover, attest the spotless purity of God, his love of righteousness, and also his kindness towards us.

But the Lord does not count it enough to inspire a reverence for his justice. To imbue our hearts with love to himself, and, at the same time, with hatred to iniquity, he has added promises and threatening. The eye of our mind being too dim to be attracted by the mere beauty of goodness, our most merciful Father has been pleased, in his great indulgence, to allure us to love and long after it by the hope of reward. He accordingly declares that rewards for virtue are treasured up with him, that none who yield obedience to his commands will labor in vain.

On the other hand, he proclaims not only that iniquity is hateful in his sight, but also that it will not escape with impunity, because he will be the avenger of his insulted majesty. That he may encourage us in every way, he promises present blessings, as well as eternal felicity, to the obedience of those who shall have kept his commands, while he threatens transgressors with present suffering, as well as the punishment of eternal death.

The promise, "Ye shall therefore keep my statutes, and my judgments; which if a man do, he shall live in them" (Leviticus 18:5), and corresponding to this the threatening, "The souls that sinneth, it shall die" (Ezekiel 18:4, 20); doubtless point to a future life and death, both without end. But though in every passage where the favor or anger of God is mentioned, the former comprehends eternity of life and the latter eternal destruction, the Law, at the same time, enumerates a long catalogue of present blessings and curses (Leviticus 26:4; Deuteronomy 28:1). The threatening attest the spotless purity of God, which cannot bear iniquity, while the promises attest at once his infinite love of righteousness (which he cannot leave unrewarded), and his wondrous kindness.

Being bound to do him homage with all that we have, he is perfectly entitled to demand everything which he requires of us as a debt; and as a debt, the payment is unworthy of reward. He therefore foregoes his right, when he holds forth reward for services, which are not offered spontaneously, as if they were not due. The amount of these services, in themselves, has been partly described and will appear more clearly in its own place.

For the present, it is enough to remember that the promises of the Law are no mean commendation of righteousness as they show how much God is pleased with the observance of them, while the threatening denounced are intended to produce a greater abhorrence of unrighteousness, lest the sinner should indulge in the blandishments of vice, and forget the judgment which the divine Lawgiver has prepared for him.

5 The Law shows, moreover, that there is nothing more acceptable to God than obedience. Hence, all superstitious and hypocritical modes of worship are condemned. A remedy against superstitious worship and human presumption.

The Lord, in delivering a perfect rule of righteousness, has reduced it in all its parts to his mere will, and in this way has shown that there is nothing more acceptable to him than obedience. There is the more necessity for attending to this, because the human mind, in its wantonness, is always inventing different modes of worship as a means of gaining his favor. This irreligious affectation of religion being innate in the human mind, has betrayed itself in every age, and is still doing so, men always longing to devise some method of procuring righteousness without any sanction from the Word of God.

Hence, in those observances, which are generally regarded as good works, the precepts of the Law occupy a narrow space, almost the whole being usurped by this endless host of human inventions. But was not this the very license which Moses meant to curb, when, after the promulgation of the Law, he thus addressed the people: "Observe and hear all these words which I command thee, that it may go well with thee, and with thy children after thee forever, when thou does that which is good and right in the sight of the Lord thy God." "What thing soever I command you, observe to do it: thou shalt not add thereto, nor diminish from it" (Deuteronomy 12:28-32).

Previously, after asking "what nation is there so great, that has statutes and judgments so righteous as all this law, which I set before you this day?" he had added, "Only take heed to thyself, and keep thy soul diligently, lest thou forget the things which thine eyes have seen, and lest they depart from thy heart all the days of thy life" (Deuteronomy 4:8, 9).

God foreseeing that the Israelites would not rest, but after receiving the Law, would, unless sternly prohibited give birth to new kinds of righteousness, declares that the Law comprehended a perfect righteousness. This ought to have been a most powerful restraint, and yet they desisted not from the presumptuous course so strongly prohibited. How do we act? We are certainly under the same obligation as they were; for there cannot be a doubt that the claim of absolute perfection, which God made for his Law, is perpetually in force. Not contented with it, however, we labor prodigiously in feigning and coining an endless variety of good works, one after another. The best cure for this vice would be a constant and deep-seated conviction that the Law was given from heaven to teach us a perfect righteousness; that the only righteousness so taught is that which the divine will expressly enjoins; and that it is, therefore, vain to attempt, by new forms of worship, to gain the favor of God, whose true worship consists in obedience alone; or rather, that to go a wandering after good works which are not prescribed by the Law of God, is an intolerable violation of true and divine righteousness. Most truly, does Augustine say in one place, that the obedience, which is rendered to God, is the parent and guardian; in another, that it is the source of all the virtues.

6 The second part of the chapter, containing three observations or rules. First rule, Our life must be formed by the Law, not only to external honesty, but to inward and spiritual righteousness.

In this respect, the Law of God differs from civil laws, he being a spiritual Lawgiver, man not. This rule of great extent, and not sufficiently attended to.

After we shall have expounded the Divine Law, what has been previously said of its office and use will be understood more easily, and with greater benefit. But before we proceed to the consideration of each separate commandment, it will be proper to take a general survey of the whole. At the outset, it was proved that in the Law human life is instructed not merely in outward decency but in inward spiritual righteousness. Though none can deny this, yet very few duly attend to it, because they do not consider the Lawgiver, by whose character that of the Law must also be determined. Should a king issue an edict prohibiting murder, adultery, and theft, the penalty, I admit, will not be incurred by the man who has only felt a longing in his mind after these vices, but has not actually committed them. The reason is that a human lawgiver does not extend his care beyond outward order, and, therefore, his injunctions are not violated without outward acts.

But God, whose eye nothing escapes, and who regards not the outward appearance so much as purity of heart, under the prohibition of murder, adultery, and thefts includes wrath, hatred, lust, covetousness, and all other things of a similar nature. Being a spiritual Lawgiver, he speaks to the soul not less than the body. The murder, which the soul commits, is wrath and hatred; the theft, covetousness and avarice; and the adultery, lust.

It may be alleged that human laws have respect to intentions and wishes, and not fortuitous events. I admit this but then these must manifest themselves externally. They consider the *animus* with which the act was done, but do not scrutinize the secret thoughts. Accordingly, their demand is satisfied when the hand merely refrains from transgression. On the contrary, the law of heaven being enacted for our minds, the first thing necessary to a due observance of the Law is to put them under restraint. But the generality of men, even while they are most anxious to conceal their disregard of the Law, only frame their hands and feet and other parts of their body to some kind of observance, but in the meanwhile keep the heart utterly estranged from everything like obedience. They think it enough to have carefully concealed from man what they are doing in the sight of God. Hearing the commandments, "Thou shalt not kill," "Thou shalt not commit adultery," "Thou shalt not steal," they do not unsheathe their sword for slaughter, nor defile their bodies with harlots, nor put forth their hands to other men's goods. So far well; but with their whole soul they breathe out slaughter, boil with lust, cast a greedy eye at their neighbor's property, and in wish devour it.

Here the principal thing, which the Law requires, is wanting. Whence then, this gross stupidity, but just because they lose sight of the Lawgiver, and form an idea of righteousness in accordance with their own disposition?

Against this Paul strenuously protests, when he declares that the *law is spiritual* (Romans 7:14); intimating that it not only demands the homage of the soul, and mind, and will, but requires an angelic purity, which, purified from all filthiness of the flesh, savors only of the Spirit.

7 This first rule confirmed by the authority of Christ, and vindicated from the false dogma of Sophists, who say that Christ is only another Moses.

In saying that this is the meaning of the Law, we are not introducing a new interpretation of our own; we are following Christ, the best interpreter of the Law (Matthew 5:22, 28, 44). The Pharisees having instilled into the people the erroneous idea that everyone fulfilled the Law who did not in external act do anything against the Law, he pronounces this a most dangerous delusion, and declares that an immodest look is adultery, and that hatred of a brother is murder.

"Whosoever is angry with his brother without a cause, shall be in danger of the judgment;" whosoever by whispering or murmuring gives indication of being offended, "shall be in danger of the council;" whosoever by reproaches and evil-speaking gives way to open anger, "shall be in danger of hell-fire."

Those, who have not perceived this, have pretended that Christ was only a second Moses, the giver of an evangelical, to supply the deficiency of the Mosaic Law. Hence, the common axiom as to the perfection of the Evangelical Law, and its great superiority to that of Moses. This idea is in many ways most pernicious. For it will appear from Moses himself, when we come to give a summary of his precepts, that great indignity is thus done to the Divine Law. It certainly insinuates that the holiness of the fathers under the Law was little else than hypocrisy, and leads us away from that one unvarying rule of righteousness.

It is very easy, however, to confute this error, which proceeds on the supposition that Christ added to the Law, whereas he only restored it to its integrity by maintaining and purifying it when obscured by the falsehood, and defiled by the leaven of the Pharisees.

8 Second observation or rule to be carefully attended to—viz. that the end of the command must be inquired into, until it is ascertained what the Lawgiver approves or disapproves. Example. Where the Law approves, its opposite is condemned, and *vice versa*.

The next observation we would make is that there is always more in the requirements and prohibitions of the Law than is expressed in words. This, however, must be understood so as not to convert it into a kind of Lesbian code; and thus, by licentiously wresting the Scriptures, make them assume any meaning that we please. By taking this excessive liberty with Scripture, its authority is lowered with some, and all hope of understanding it abandoned by others. We must, therefore, if possible, discover some path, which may conduct us with direct and firm step to the will of God.

We must consider, I say, how far interpretation can be permitted to go beyond the literal meaning of the words, still making it apparent that no appending of human glosses is added to the Divine Law, but that the pure and genuine meaning of the Lawgiver is faithfully exhibited. It is true that, in almost all the commandments, there are elliptical expressions, and that, therefore, any man would make himself ridiculous by attempting to restrict the spirit of the Law to the strict letter of the words.

It is plain that a sober interpretation of the Law must go beyond these, but how far is doubtful, unless some rule is adopted. The best rule, in my opinion, would be, to be guided by the principle of the commandment— viz. to consider in the case of each what the purpose is for which it was given. For example, every commandment either requires or prohibits; and the nature of each is instantly discerned when we look to the principle of the commandment as its end. Thus, the end of the Fifth Commandment is to render honor to those on whom God bestows it. The sum of the commandment, therefore, is that it is right in itself, and pleasing to God, to honor those on whom he has conferred some distinction; that to despise and rebel against such persons is offensive to Him.

The principle of the First Commandment is that God only is to be worshipped. The sum of the commandment, therefore, is that true piety, in other words, the worship of the Deity, is acceptable, and impiety is an abomination, to him. So in each of the commandments we must first look to the matter of which it treats, and then consider its end, until we discover what it properly is that the Lawgiver declares to be pleasing or displeasing to him. Only, we must reason from the precept to its contrary in this way: If this pleases God, its opposite displeases; if that displeases, its opposite pleases: if God commands this, he forbids the opposite; if he forbids that, he commands the opposite.

9 Full explanation of this latter point. Example.

What is now touched on somewhat obscurely will become perfectly clear as we proceed and get accustomed to the exposition of the Commandments. It is sufficient thus to have adverted to the subject; but perhaps our concluding statement will require to be briefly confirmed, as it might otherwise not be understood, or, though understood mighty perhaps, at the outset appear unsound. There is no need of proving, that when good is ordered the evil which is opposed to it is forbidden. This everyone admits. It will also be admitted, without much difficulty, that when evil is forbidden, its opposite is enjoined. Indeed, it is a common saying, that censure of vice is commendation of virtue.

We, however, demand somewhat more than is commonly understood by these expressions. When the particular virtue opposed to a particular vice is spoken of, all that is usually meant is abstinence from that vice. We maintain that it goes further, and means opposite duties and positive acts. Hence, the commandment, "Thou shalt not kill," the generality of men will merely consider as an injunction to abstain from all injury and all wish to inflict injury. I hold that it moreover means that we are to aid our neighbor's life by every means in our power. And not to assert without giving my reasons I prove it thus: God forbids us to injure or hurt a brother, because he would have his life to be dear and precious to us; and, therefore, when he so forbids, he, at the same time, demands all the offices of charity which can contribute to his preservation.

10 The Law states what is most impious in each transgression, in order to show how heinous the transgression is. Example.

But why did God thus deliver his commandments by halves, using elliptical expressions with a larger meaning than that actually expressed? Other reasons are given, but the following seems to me the best: —As the flesh is always on the alert to extenuate the heinousness of sin (unless it is made perceptible to the touch), and to cover it with specious pretexts, the Lord sets forth, by way of example, whatever is foulest and most iniquitous in each species of transgression, that the delivery of it might produce a shudder in the hearer, and impress his mind with a deeper abhorrence of sin.

In forming an estimate of sins, we are often imposed upon by imagining that the more hidden the less heinous they are. This delusion the Lord dispels by accustoming us to refer the whole multitude of sins to particular heads, which admirably show how great a degree of heinousness there is in each. For example, wrath and hatred do not seem so very bad when they are designated by their own names; but when they are prohibited under the name of murder, we understand better how abominable they are in the sight of God, who puts them in the same class with that horrid crime. Influenced by his judgment, we accustom ourselves to judge more accurately of the heinousness of offenses, which previously seemed trivial.

11 Third observation or rule regards the division of the Law into Two Tables: the former comprehending our duty to God; the

latter, our duty to our neighbor. The connection between these necessary and inseparable. Their invariable order. Sum of the Law.

It will now be proper to consider what the division of the divine Law into Two Tables means. It will be judged by all men of sense from the formal manner in which these are sometimes mentioned, that it has not been done at random, or without reason. Indeed, the reason is so obvious as not to allow us to remain in doubt with regard to it. God thus divided his Law into two parts, containing a complete rule of righteousness, that he might assign the first place to the duties of religion which relate especially to His worship, and the second to the duties of charity which have respect to man.

The first foundation of righteousness undoubtedly is the worship of God. When it is subverted, all the other parts of righteousness, like a building rent asunder, and in ruins, are racked and scattered.

What kind of righteousness do you call it, not to commit theft and rapine, if you, in the meantime, with impious sacrilege, rob God of his glory? Or not to defile your body with fornication, if you profane his holy name with blasphemy? Or not to take away the life of man, if you strive to cut off and destroy the remembrance of God?

It is vain, therefore, to talk of righteousness apart from religion. Such righteousness has no more beauty than the trunk of a body deprived of its head. Nor is religion the principal part merely: it is the very soul by which the whole lives and breathes. Without the fear of God, men do not even observe justice and charity among themselves. We say, then, that the worship of God is the beginning and foundation of righteousness; and that wherever it is wanting, any degree of equity, or continence, or temperance, existing among men themselves, is empty and frivolous in the sight of God.

We call it the source and soul of righteousness, in as much as men learn to live together temperately, and without injury, when they revere God as the judge of right and wrong. In the First Table, accordingly, he teaches us how to cultivate piety, and the proper duties of religion in which his worship consists; in the second, he shows how, in the fear of his name, we are to conduct ourselves towards our fellow-men.

Hence, as related by the Evangelists (Matthew 22:37; Luke 10:27), our Savior summed up the whole Law in two heads—viz. to love the Lord with all our heart, with all our soul, and with all our strength, and our neighbor as ourselves. You see how, of the two parts under which he comprehends the whole Law, he devotes the one to God, and assigns the other to mankind.

12 Division of the Law into Ten Commandments. Various distinctions made with regard to them, but the best distinction that which divides them into Two Tables. Four commandments belong to the First, and six to the Second Table.

But although the whole Law is contained in two heads, yet, in order to remove every pretext for excuse, the Lord has been pleased to deliver more fully and explicitly in Ten Commandments, everything relating to his own honor, fear, and love, as well as everything relating to the charity which, for his sake, he enjoins us to have towards our fellowmen. Nor is it an unprofitable study to consider the division of the commandments, provided we remember that it is one of those matters in which every man should have full freedom of judgment, and on account of which, difference of opinion should not lead to contention. We are, indeed, under the necessity of making this observation, lest the division, which we are to adopt, should excite the surprise or derision of the reader, as novel or of recent invention.

There is no room for controversy as to the fact that the Law is divided into ten heads since divine authority repeatedly sanctions this. The question, therefore, is not as to the number of the parts, but the method of dividing them. Those who adopt a division which gives three commandments to the First Table, and throws the remaining seven into the Second Table, expunge the commandment concerning images from the list, or at least conceal it under the first, though there cannot be a doubt that it was distinctly set down by the Lord as a separate commandment; whereas the tenth, which prohibits the coveting of what belongs to our neighbor, they absurdly break down into two. Moreover, it will soon appear that this method of dividing was unknown in a purer age.

Others count four commandments in the First Table as we do, but for the first set down the introductory promise, without adding the precept. But because I must hold, unless I am convinced by clear evidence to the contrary, that the "ten words" mentioned by Moses are Ten Commandments and because I see that number arranged in most admirable order, I must, while I leave them to hold their own opinion, follow what appears to me better established—viz. that what they make to be the first commandment is of the nature of a preface to the whole Law, that thereafter follow four commandments in the First Table, and six in the Second, in the order in which they will here be reviewed.

This division Origen adopts without discussion, as if it had been everywhere received in his day. It is also adopted by Augustine, in his book addressed to Boniface, where, in enumerating the commandments, he follows this order, Let one God be religiously obeyed, let no idol be worshipped, let the name of God be not used in vain; while previously he had made separate mention of the typical commandment of the Sabbath.

Elsewhere, indeed, he expresses approbation of the first division, but on too slight grounds, because, by the number three (making the First Table consist of three commandments), the mystery of the Trinity would be better manifested. Even here, however, he does not disguise his opinion, that in other respects, our division is more to his mind. Besides these, the author of an unfinished work on Matthew supports us. Josephus, no doubt with the general consent of his age, assigns five commandments to each table. This, while repugnant to reason, inasmuch as it confounds the distinction between piety and charity, is also refuted by the authority of our Savior, who in Matthew places the command to honor parents in the list of those belonging to the Second Table (Matthew 19:19). Let us now hear God speaking in his own words.

FIRST COMMANDMENT

I AM THE LORD THY GOD, WHICH BROUGHT THEE OUT OF
THE LAND OF EGYPT, OUT OF THE HOUSE OF BONDAGE.
THOU SHALT HAVE NO OTHER GODS
BEFORE ME.

13 **The third part of the chapter, containing an exposition of the Decalogue. The preface vindicates the authority of the Law. This it does in three ways. First, by a declaration of its majesty.**

Whether you take the former sentence as a part of the commandment, or read it separately is to me a matter of indifference, provided you grant that it is a kind of preface to the whole Law. In enacting laws, the first thing to be guarded against is their being forthwith abrogated by contempt. The Lord, therefore, takes care, in the first place, that this shall not happen to the Law about to be delivered, by introducing it with a triple sanction. He claims to himself power and authority to command, that he may impress the chosen people with the necessity of obedience; he holds forth a promise of favor, as a means of alluring them to the study of holiness; and he reminds them of his kindness, that he may convict them of ingratitude, if they fail to make a suitable return.

By the name, Lord, are denoted power and lawful dominion. If all things are from him, and by him consist, they ought in justice to bear reference to him, as Paul says (Romans 11:36). This name, therefore, is in itself sufficient to bring us under the authority of the divine majesty: for it was monstrous for us to wish to withdraw from the dominion of him, out of whom we cannot even exist.

14 **The preface to the Law vindicates its authority. Secondly, by calling to mind God's paternal kindness.**

After showing that he has a right to command, and to be obeyed, he next, in order not to seem to drag men by mere necessity, but to allure them, graciously declares, that he is the God of the Church. For the mode of expression implies, that there is a mutual relation included in the promise, "I will be their God, and they shall be my people" (Jeremiah 31:33). Hence, Christ infers the immortality of Abraham, Isaac, and Jacob, from the fact that God had declared himself to be their God (Matthew 22:32). It is, therefore, the same as if he had said, I have chosen you to myself, as a people to whom I shall not only do good in the present life, but also bestow felicity in the life to come. The end contemplated in this is adverted to in the Law, in various passages. For when the Lord condescends in mercy to honor us so far as to admit us to partnership with his chosen people, he chooses us, as Moses says, "to be a holy people," "a peculiar people unto himself," to "keep all his commandments" (Deuteronomy 7:6; 14:2; 26:18). Hence, the exhortation, "Ye shall be holy; for I the Lord your God am holy" (Leviticus 19:2). These two considerations form the ground of the remonstrance, "A son honoreth his father, and a servant his master; if then I be a father, where is mine honor? And if I be a master, where is my fear? saith the Lord of hosts" (Malachi 1:6).

15 Thirdly, by calling to mind the deliverance out of the land of Egypt. Why God distinguishes himself by certain epithets. Why mention is made of the deliverance from Egypt. In what way, and how far, the remembrance of this deliverance should still affect us.

Next follows a commemoration of his kindness, which ought to produce upon us an impression strong in proportion to the detestation in which ingratitude is held even among men. It is true, indeed, he was reminding Israel of a deliverance then recent, but one which, on account of its wondrous magnitude, was to be forever memorable to the remotest posterity. Moreover, it is most appropriate to the matter in hand. For the Lord intimates that they were delivered from miserable bondage, that they might learn to yield prompt submission and obedience to him as the author of their freedom. In like manners to keep us to his true worship, he often describes himself by certain epithets, which distinguish his sacred Deity from all idols and fictitious gods. For, as I formerly observed, such is our proneness to vanity and presumption, that as soon as God is named, our minds, unable to guard against error, immediately fly off to some empty delusion.

In applying a remedy to this disease, God distinguishes his divinity by certain titles, and thus confines us within distinct boundaries, that we may not wander hither and thither, and feign some new deity for ourselves, abandoning the living God, and setting up an idol. For this reason, whenever the Prophets would bring him properly before us, they invest, and surround him with those characters under which he had manifested himself to the people of Israel. When he is called the God of Abraham, or the God of Israel, when he is stationed in the temple of Jerusalem, between the Cherubim, these, and similar modes of expression, do not confine him to one place or one people, but are used merely for the purpose of fixing our thoughts on that God who so manifested himself in the covenant which he made with Israel, as to make it unlawful on any account to deviate from the strict view there given of his character.

Let it be understood, then, that mention is made of deliverance, in order to make the Jews submit with greater readiness to that God who justly claims them as his own. We again, instead of supposing that the matter has no reference to us, should reflect that the bondage of Israel in Egypt was a type of that spiritual bondage, in the fetters of which we are all bound, until the heavenly avenger delivers us by the power of his own arm, and transports us into his free kingdom. Therefore, as in old times, when he would gather together the scattered Israelites to the worship of his name, he rescued them from the intolerable tyranny of Pharaoh; so all who profess him now are delivered from the fatal tyranny of the devil, of which that of Egypt was only a type. There is no man, therefore, whose mind ought not to be aroused to give heed to the Law, which, as he is told, proceeded from the supreme King, from him who, as he gave all their being, justly destines and directs them to himself as their proper end. There is no man, I say, who should not hasten to embrace the Lawgiver, whose commands, he knows, he has been specially appointed to obey, from whose kindness he anticipates an abundance of all good, and even a blessed immortality, and to whose wondrous power and mercy he is indebted for deliverance from the jaws of death.

16 Exposition of the First Commandment. Its end. What it is to have God, and to have strange gods. Adoration due to God, trust, invocation, thanksgiving, and also true religion, required by the Commandment. Superstition, Polytheism, and Atheism, forbidden. What meant by the words, "before me."

The authority of the Law being founded and established, God delivers his First Commandment—

THOU SHALT HAVE NO OTHER GODS BEFORE ME.

The purport of this commandment is that the Lord will have himself alone to be exalted in his people, and claims the entire possession of them as his own. That it may be so, he orders us to abstain from ungodliness and superstition of every kind, by which the glory of his divinity is diminished or obscured; and, for the same reason, he requires us to worship and adore him with truly pious zeal. The simple terms used obviously amount to this. For seeing we cannot have God without embracing everything, which belongs to him, the prohibition against having strange gods means, that nothing, which belongs to him, is to be transferred to any other.

The duties, which we owe to God, are innumerable, but they seem to admit of being not improperly reduced to four heads: Adoration, with its accessory spiritual submission of conscience, Trust, Invocation, Thanksgiving. By Adoration, I mean the veneration and worship which we render to him when we do homage to his majesty; and hence I make part of it to consist in bringing our consciences into subjection to his Law. Trust, is secure resting in him under a recognition of his perfections, when, ascribing to him all power, wisdom, justice, goodness, and truth, we consider ourselves happy in having been brought into intercourse with him. Invocation, may be defined the retaking of ourselves to his promised aid as the only resource in every case of need. Thanksgiving is the gratitude, which ascribes to him the praise of all our blessings. As the Lord does not allow these to be derived from any other quarter, so he demands that they shall be referred entirely to himself. It is not enough to refrain from other gods. We must, at the same time, devote ourselves wholly to him, not acting like certain impious despisers, who regard it as the shortest method, to hold all religious observance in derision. But here precedence must be given to true religion, which will direct our minds to the living God.

When duly imbued with the knowledge of him, the whole aim of our lives will be to revere, fear, and worship his majesty, to enjoy a share in his blessings, to have recourse to him in every difficulty, to acknowledge, laud, and celebrate the magnificence of his works, to make him the sole aim of all our actions. Next, we must beware of superstition, by which our minds are turned aside from the true God, and carried to and fro after a multiplicity of gods. Therefore, if we are contented with one God, let us call to mind what was formerly observed, that all fictitious gods are to be driven far away, and that the worship, which he claims for himself, is not to be mutilated. Not a particle of his glory is to be withheld: everything belonging to him must be reserved to him entire. The words, "before me," go to increase the indignity, God being provoked to jealousy whenever we substitute our fictions in his stead; just as an unfaithful wife stings her husband's heart more deeply when her adultery is committed openly before his eyes. Therefore, God having by his present power and grace declared that he had respect to the people whom he had chosen, now, in order to deter them from the wickedness of revolt, warns them that they cannot adopt strange gods without his being witness and spectator of the sacrilege. To the audacity of so doing is added the very great impiety of supposing that they can mock the eye of God with their evasions. Far from this, the Lord proclaims that everything, which we design, plan, or execute, lies open to his sight. Our conscience must, therefore, keep aloof from the most distant thought of revolt, if we would have our worship approved by the Lord. The glory of his Godhead must be maintained entire and incorrupt, not merely by external profession, but as under his eye, which penetrates the inmost recesses of his heart.

SECOND COMMANDMENT

THOU SHALT NOT MAKE UNTO THEE ANY GRAVEN IMAGE,
OR ANY LIKENESS OF ANYTHING THAT IS IN HEAVEN ABOVE,

OR THAT IS IN THE EARTH BENEATH, OR THAT IS IN THE
WATER UNDER THE EARTH: THOU SHALT NOT BOW DOWN
THYSELF TO THEM, NOR SERVE THEM.

17 Exposition of the Second Commandment. The end and sum
of it. Two parts. Short enumeration of forbidden shapes.

As in the first commandment the Lord declares that he is one, and that
besides him no gods must be either worshipped or imagined, so he here
more plainly declares what his nature is, and what the kind of worship with
which he is to be honored, in order that we may not presume to form any
carnal idea of him. The purport of the commandment, therefore, is that he
will not have his legitimate worship profaned by superstitious rites.
Wherefore, in general, he calls us entirely away from the carnal frivolous
observances which our stupid minds are wont to devise after forming some
gross idea of the divine nature, while, at the same time, he instructs us in the
worship which is legitimate, namely, spiritual worship of his own
appointment. The grossest vice here prohibited is external idolatry.

This commandment consists of two parts. The former curbs the
licentious daring, which would subject the incomprehensible God to our
senses, or represent him under any visible shape. The latter forbids the
worship of images on any religious ground. There is, moreover, a brief
enumeration of all the forms by which the Deity was usually represented by
heathen and superstitious nations. By "anything which is in heaven above"
is meant the sun, the moon, and the stars, perhaps also birds, as in
Deuteronomy, where the meaning is explained, there is mention of birds as
well as stars (Deuteronomy 4:15). I would not have made this observation,
had I not seen that some absurdly apply it to the angels. The other particulars
I pass, as requiring no explanation. We have already shown clearly enough
(Book 1, chapters 11, 12) that every visible shape of Deity which man devises
is diametrically opposed to the divine nature; and, therefore, that the moment
idols appear, true religion is corrupted and adulterated.

18 Why a threatening is added. Four titles applied to God, to
make a deeper impression. He is called Mighty, Jealous, an
Avenger, Merciful. Why said to be jealous. Reason drawn from
analogy.

The threatening subjoined ought to have no little effect in shaking off our
lethargy. It is in the following terms: —

I THE LORD THY GOD AM A JEALOUS GOD, VISITING THE
INIQUITY OF THE FATHERS UPON THE CHILDREN UNTO THE
THIRD AND FOURTH GENERATION OF THEM THAT HATE ME;

AND SHOWING MERCY UNTO THOUSANDS OF THEM THAT LOVE ME, AND KEEP MY COMMANDMENTS.

The meaning here is the same as if he had said, that our duty is to cleave to him alone. To induce us to this, he proclaims his authority, which he will not permit to be impaired or despised with impunity. It is true, the word used is *El*, which means God; but as it is derived from a word meaning *strength*, I have had no hesitations in order to express the sense more fully, so to render it as inserted on the margin. Secondly, he calls himself *jealous*, because he cannot bear a partner. Thirdly, he declares that he will vindicate his majesty and glory, if any transfer it either to the creatures or to graven images; and that not by a simple punishment of brief duration, but one extending to the third and fourth generation of such as imitate the impiety of their progenitors. In like manner, he declares his constant mercy and kindness to the remote posterity of those who love him, and keep his Law. The Lord very frequently addresses us in the character of a husband; the union by which he connects us with himself, when he receives us into the bosom of the Church, having some resemblance to that of holy wedlock, because founded on mutual faith. As he performs all the offices of a true and faithful husband, so he stipulates for love and conjugal chastity from us; that is, that we do not prostitute our souls to Satan, to be defiled with foul carnal lusts.

Hence, when he rebukes the Jews for their apostasy, he complains that they have cast off chastity, and polluted themselves with adultery. Therefore, as the purer and more chaste the husband is, the more grievously is he offended when he sees his wife inclining to a rival; so the Lord, who has betrothed us to himself in truth, declares that he burns with the hottest jealousy whenever, neglecting the purity of his holy marriage, we defile ourselves with abominable lusts, and especially when the worship of his Deity, which ought to have been most carefully kept unimpaired, is transferred to another, or adulterated with some superstition; since, in this way, we not only violate our plighted troth, but defile the nuptial couch, by giving access to adulterers.

19 Exposition of the threatening, which is added. First, as to visiting the iniquity of the fathers upon the children. A misinterpretation on this head refuted, and the genuine meaning of the threatening explained.

In the threatening we must attend to what is meant when God declares that he will visit the iniquity of the fathers upon the children unto the third and fourth generation. It seems inconsistent with the equity of the divine procedure to punish the innocent for another's fault; and the Lord himself declares, that "the son shall not bear the iniquity of the father" (Ezekiel 18:20). But still we meet more than once with a declaration as to the postponing of the punishment of the sins of fathers to future generations. Thus, Moses repeatedly addresses the Lord as "visiting the iniquity of the fathers upon the children unto the third and fourth generation" (Numbers 14:18). In like manner, Jeremiah, "Thou showest loving-kindness unto thousands, and recompenses the iniquity of the fathers into the bosom of their children after them" (Jeremiah 32:18).

Some feeling sadly perplexed how to solve this difficulty, think it is to be understood of temporal punishments only, which it is said sons may properly bear for the sins of their parents, because they are often inflicted for their own safety. This is indeed true; for Isaiah declared to Hezekiah, that his children should be stripped of the kingdom, and carried away into captivity, for a sin which he had committed (Isaiah 39:7); and the households of Pharaoh and Abimelech were made to suffer for an injury done to Abraham (Genesis 12:17; 20:3–18). But the attempt to solve the question in this way is an evasion rather than a true interpretation. For the punishment denounced here and in similar passages is too great to be confined within the limits of the present life.

We must therefore understand it to mean, that a curse from the Lord righteously falls not only on the head of the guilty individual, but also on his entire lineage. When it has fallen, what can be anticipated but that the father, being deprived of the Spirit of God, will live most flagitiously; that the son, being in like manner forsaken of the Lord, because of his father's iniquity, will follow the same road to destruction; and be followed in his turn by succeeding generations, forming a seed of evil-doers?

20 Whether this visiting of the sins of parents inconsistent with the divine justice. Apparently conflicting passages reconciled.

First, let us examine whether such punishment is inconsistent with the divine justice. If human nature is universally condemned, those on whom the Lord does not bestow the communication of his grace must be doomed to destruction; nevertheless, they perish by their own iniquity, not by unjust hatred on the part of God. There is no room to expostulate, and ask why the grace of God does not forward their salvation as it does that of others. Therefore, when God punishes the wicked and flagitious for their crimes, by depriving their families of his grace for many generations, who will dare to bring a charge against him for this most righteous vengeance? But it will be said, the Lord, on the contrary, declares, that the son shall not suffer for the father's sin (Ezekiel 18:20).

Observe the scope of that passage. The Israelites, after being subjected to a long period of uninterrupted calamities, had begun to say, as a proverb, that their fathers had eaten the sour grape, and thus set the children's teeth on edge; meaning that they, though in themselves righteous and innocent, were paying the penalty of sins committed by their parents, and this more from the implacable anger than the duly tempered severity of God. The prophet declares it was not so: that they were punished for their own wickedness; that it was not in accordance with the justice of God that a righteous son should suffer for the iniquity of a wicked father; and that nothing of the kind was exemplified in what they suffered. For, if the visitation of which we now speak is accomplished when God withdraws from the children of the wicked the light of his truth and the other helps to salvation, the only way in which they are accursed for their fathers' wickedness is in being blinded and abandoned by God, and so left to walk in their parents' steps. The misery which they suffer in time, and the destruction to which they are finally doomed, are thus punishments inflicted by divine justice, not for the sins of others, but for their own iniquity.

21 Exposition of the latter part—viz. the showing mercy to thousands. The use of this promise. Consideration of an exception of frequent occurrence. The extent of this blessing.

On the other hand, there is a promise of mercy to thousands—a promise, which is frequently mentioned in Scripture, and forms an article in the solemn covenant made with the Church—I will be "a God unto thee, and to thy seed after thee" (Genesis 17:7). With reference to this, Solomon says, "The just man walketh in his integrity: his children are blessed after him," Proverbs 20:7); not only in consequence of a religious education (though this certainly is by no means unimportant), but in consequence of the blessing promised in the covenant—viz. that the divine favor will dwell forever in the families of the righteous. Herein is excellent consolation to believers, and great ground of terror to the wicked; for if, after death, the mere remembrance of righteousness and iniquity have such an influence on the divine procedure, that his blessing rests on the posterity of the righteous, and his curse on the posterity of the wicked, much more must it rest on the heads of the individuals themselves.

Notwithstanding of this, however, the offspring of the wicked sometimes amends, while that of believers degenerates, because the Almighty has not here laid down an inflexible rule, which might derogate from his free election. For the consolation of the righteous, and the dismay of the sinner, it is enough that the threatening itself is not vain or nugatory, although it does not always take effect. For, as the temporal punishments inflicted on a few of the wicked are proofs of the divine wrath against sin, and of the future judgment that will ultimately overtake all sinners, though many escape with impunity even to the end of their lives, so, when the Lord gives one example of blessing a son for his father's sake, by visiting him in mercy and kindness, it is a proof of constant and unfailing favor to his worshipers. On the other hand, when, in any single instance, he visits the iniquity of the father on the son, he gives intimation of the judgment, which awaits all the reprobates for their own iniquities. The certainty of this is the principal thing here taught. Moreover, the Lord, by the way, commends the riches of his mercy by extending it to thousands, while he limits his vengeance to four generations.

Third Commandment

THOU SHALT NOT TAKE THE NAME OF THE LORD THY GOD IN VAIN.

22 Exposition of the Third Commandment. The end and sum of it. Three parts. These considered. What it is to use the name of God in vain. Swearing. Distinction between this commandment and the Ninth.

The purport of this Commandment is that the majesty of the name of God is to be held sacred. In sum, therefore, it means, that we must not profane it by using it irreverently or contemptuously. This prohibition implies a corresponding precept—viz. that it be our study and care to treat his name with religious veneration. Wherefore it becomes us to regulate our minds and our tongues, so as never to think or speak of God and his mysteries without reverence and great soberness, and never, in estimating his works, to have any feeling towards him but one of deep veneration.

We must, I say, steadily observe the three following things: —*First*, Whatever our mind conceives of him, whatever our tongue utters, must bespeak his excellence, and correspond to the sublimity of his sacred name; in short, must be fitted to extol its greatness. *Secondly*, We must not rashly and preposterously pervert his sacred word and adorable mysteries to purposes of ambition, or avarice, or amusement, but, according as they bear the impress of his dignity, must always maintain them in due honor and esteem. *Lastly*, We must not detract from or throw obloquy upon his works, as miserable men are wont insultingly to do, but must laud every action which we attribute to him as wise, and just, and good. This is to sanctify the name of God. When we act otherwise, his name is profaned with vain and wicked abuse, because it is applied to a purpose foreign to that to which it is consecrated.

Were there nothing worse, in being deprived of its dignity, it is gradually brought into contempt. But if there is so much evil in the rash and unseasonable employment of the divine name, there is still more evil in its being employed for nefarious purposes, as is done by those who use it in necromancy, cursing, illicit exorcisms, and other impious incantations. But the Commandment refers especially to the case of oaths, in which a perverse employment of the divine name is particularly detestable; and this it does the more effectually to deter us from every species of profanation.

That the thing here commanded relates to the worship of God, and the reverence due to his name, and not to the equity which men are to cultivate towards each other, is apparent from this, that afterwards, in the Second Table, there is a condemnation of the perjury and false testimony by which human society is injured, and that the repetition would be superfluous, if, in this Commandment, the duty of charity were handled. Moreover, this is necessary even for distinction, because, as was observed, God has, for good reason, divided his Law into two tables. The inference then is that God here vindicates his own right, and defends his sacred name, but does not teach the duties which men owe to men.

23 An oath defined. It is a species of divine worship. This explained.

In the first place, we must consider what an oath is. An oath, then, is calling God to witness that what we say is true. Execrations being manifestly insulting to God are unworthy of being classed among oaths. That an oath, when duly taken, is a species of divine worship, appears from many passages of Scripture, as when Isaiah prophesies of the admission of the Assyrians and Egyptians to a participation in the covenant, he says, "In that day shall five cities in the land of Egypt speak the language of Canaan, and swear to the Lord of hosts" (Isaiah 19:18). Swearing by the name of the Lord here means, that they will make a profession of religion. In like manner, speaking of the extension of the Redeemer's kingdom, it is said, "He who blesseth himself in the earth shall bless himself in the God of truth: and he that sweareth in the earth shall swear by the God of truth" (Isaiah 65:16). In Jeremiah it is said, "If they will diligently learn the ways of my people, to swear by my name, The Lord liveth; as they taught my people to swear by Baal; then shall they be built in the midst of my people" (Jeremiah 12:16).

By appealing to the name of the Lord, and calling him to witness, we are justly said to declare our own religious veneration of him. For we thus acknowledge that he is eternal and unchangeable truth, inasmuch as we not only call upon him, in preference to others, as a fit witness to the truth, but as its only assertor, able to bring hidden things to light, a discerner of the hearts.

When human testimony fails, we appeal to God as witness, especially when the matter to be proved lies hid in the conscience. For which reason, the Lord is grievously offended with those who swear by strange gods, and construes such swearing as a proof of open revolt, "Thy children have forsaken me, and sworn by them that are no gods" (Jeremiah 5:7). The heinousness of the offense is declared by the punishment denounced against it, "I will cut off them that swear by the Lord, and that swear by Malcham" (Zephaniah 1: 4, 5).

24 Many modes in which this commandment is violated. A. By taking God to witness, what we know is false. The insult thus offered.

Understanding that the Lord would have our oaths to be a species of divine worship, we must be the more careful that they do not, instead of worship, contain insult, or contempt, and vilification. It is no slight insult to swear by him and do it falsely: hence, in the Law this is termed profanation (Leviticus 19:12). For if God is robbed of his truth, what is it that remains? Without truth, he could not be God. But assuredly, he is robbed of his truth, when he is made the approver and attester of what is false. Hence, when Joshua is endeavoring to make Achan confess the truth, he says, "My son, give, I pray thee, glory to the Lord God of Israel" (Joshua 7:19); intimating, that grievous dishonor is done to God when men swear by him falsely. And no wonder; for, as far as in them lies, his sacred name is in a manner branded with falsehood. That this mode of expression was common among the Jews whenever anyone was called upon to take an oath, is evident from a similar supplication used by the Pharisees, as given in John (John 9:24); Scripture reminds us of the caution which we ought to use by employing such expressions as the following: —"As the Lord liveth;" "God do so and more also;" "I call God for a record upon my soul." Such expressions intimate, that we cannot call God to witness our statement, without imprecating his vengeance for perjury if it is false.

25 Modes of violation continued. B. Taking God to witness in trivial matters. Contempt thus shown. When and how an oath should be used. C. Substituting the servants of God instead of himself when taking an oath.

The name of God is vulgarized and vilified when used in oaths, which, though true, are superfluous. This, too, is to take his name in vain. Wherefore, it is not sufficient to abstain from perjury, unless we, at the same time, remember that an oath is not appointed or allowed for passion or pleasure, but for necessity; and that, therefore, he who uses it on any other than necessary occasions makes a licentious use of it.

Moreover, no case of ecessity can be pretended, unless where some purpose of religion or charity is to be served. Inthis matter, great sin is committed in the present day—sin the more intolerable in this, that its frequency has made it cease to be regarded as a fault, though it certainly is not accounted trivial before the judgment-seat of God. Introducing it indiscriminately in frivolous discourse everywhere profanes the name of God; and the evil is disregarded, because it has been long and audaciously persisted in with impunity.

The commandment of the Lord, however, stands; the penalty also stands, and will one day receive effect. Special vengeance will be executed on those who have taken the name of God in vain. Another form of violation is exhibited, when, with manifest impiety, we, in our oaths, substitute the holy servants of God for God himself, thus conferring upon them the glory of his Godhead. It is not without cause the Lord has, by a special commandment, required us to swear by his name, and, by a special prohibition, forbidden us to swear by other gods. The Apostle gives a clear attestation to the same effect, when he says, that "men verily swear by the greater;" but that "when God made promiseto Abraham, because he could swear by nogreater, he sware by himself;" (Hebrews 6:16, 13).

26 The Anabatists, who condemn all oaths, refuted By the authority of Christ, who cannot be opposed in anything to the Father. A passage perverted by the Anabaptists explained. The design of our Savior in the passage. What meant by his there prohibiting oaths.

The Anabaptists, not content with this moderate use of oaths, condemn all, without exception, on the ground of our Savior's general prohibition, "I say unto you, Swear not at all:" "Let your speech be Yea, yea; Nay, nay: for whatsoever is more than these cometh of evil" (Matthew 5:34; James 5:12). In this way, they inconsiderately make a stumbling-stone of Christ, setting him in opposition to the Father, as if he had descended into the world to annul his decrees. In the Law, the Almighty not only permits an oath as a thing that is lawful (this were amply sufficient), but, in a case of necessity, actually commands it (Exodus 22:11). Christ again declares, that he and his Father are one; that he only delivers what was commanded of his Father; that his doctrine is not his own, but his that sent him (John 10:18, 30; 7:16).

What then? Will they make God contradict himself, by approving and commanding at one time, what he afterwards prohibits and condemns? But as there is some difficulty in what our Savior says on the subject of swearing, it may be proper to consider it a little. Here, however, we shall never arrive at the true meaning, unless we attend to the design of Christ, and the subject of which he is treating. His purpose was, neither to relax nor to curtail the Law, but to restore the true and genuine meaning, which had been greatly corrupted by the false glosses of the Scribes and Pharisees. If we attend to this, we shall not suppose that Christ condemned all oaths but those only, which transgressed the rule of the Law.

It is evident, from the oaths themselves, that the people were accustomed to think it enough if they avoided perjury, whereas the Law prohibits not perjury merely, but also vain and superfluous oaths. Therefore, our Lord, who is the best interpreter of the Law, reminds them that there is a sin not only in perjury, but also in swearing. How in swearing? Namely, by swearing vainly.

Those oaths, however, which are authorized by the Law, he leaves safe and free. Those who condemn oaths think their argument invincible when they fasten on the expression, *not at all*. The expression applies not to the word *swear*, but to the subjoined forms of oaths. For part of the error consisted in their supposing, that when they swore by the heaven and the earth, they did not touch the name of God. The Lord, therefore, after cutting off the principal source of prevarication, deprives them of all subterfuges, warning them against supposing that they escape guilt by suppressing the name of God, and appealing to heaven and earth. For it ought here to be observed in passing, that although the name of God is not expressed, yet men swear by him in using indirect forms, as when they swear by the light of life, by the bread they eat, by their baptism, or any other pledges of the divine liberality towards them.

Some erroneously suppose that our Savior, in that passage, rebukes superstition, by forbidding men to swear by heaven and earth, and Jerusalem. He rather refutes the sophistical subtlety of those who thought it nothing vainly to utter indirect oaths, imagining that they thus spared the holy name of God, whereas that name is inscribed on each of his mercies.

The case is different, when any mortal living or dead, or an angel, is substituted in the place of God, as in the vile form devised by flattery in heathen nations, *"By the life or genius of the king;* for, in this case, the false apotheosis obscures and impairs the glory of the one God. But when nothing else is intended than to confirm what is said by an appeal to the holy name of God, although it is done indirectly, yet his majesty is insulted by all frivolous oaths.

Christ strips this abuse of every vain pretext when he says, "Swear not at all." To the same effect is the passage in which James uses the words of our Savior above quoted (James 5:12). For this rash swearing has always prevailed in the world, notwithstanding that it is a profanation of the name of God. If you refer the words, *not at all*, to the act itself, as if every oath, without exception, were unlawful, what will be the use of the explanation, which immediately follows—Neither by heaven, neither by the earth, etc.? These words make it clear, that the object in view was to meet the cavils by which the Jews thought they could extenuate their fault.

27 The lawfulness of oaths confirmed by Christ and the apostles. Some approve of public, but not of private oaths. The lawfulness of the latter proved both by reason and example. Instances from Scripture.

Every person of sound judgment must now see that in that passage our Lord merely condemned those oaths, which were forbidden by the Law. For he who in his life exhibited a model of the perfection, which he taught, did not object to oaths whenever the occasion required them; and the disciples, who doubtless in all things obeyed their Master, followed the same rule.

Who will dare to say that Paul would have sworn (Romans 1:9; 2 Corinthians 1:23) if an oath had been altogether forbidden? But when the occasion calls for it, he adjures without any scruple, and sometimes even imprecates. The question, however, is not yet disposed of. For some think that the only oaths exempted from the prohibition are public oaths, such as those which are administered to us by the magistrate, or independent states employ in ratifying treaties, or the people take when they swear allegiance to their sovereign, or the soldier in the case of the military oath, and others of a similar description. To this class they refer (and justly) those protestations in the writings of Paul, which assert the dignity of the Gospel; since the Apostles, in discharging their office, were not private individuals, but the public servants of God. I certainly deny not that such oaths are the safest because they are most strongly supported by passages of Scripture.

The magistrate is enjoined, in a doubtful matter, to put the witness upon oath; and he in his turn to answer upon oath; and an Apostle says, that in this way there is an end of all strife (Hebrews 6:16). In this commandment, both parties are fully approved. Nay, we may observe, that among the ancient heathens a public and solemn oath was held in great reverence, while those common oaths, which were indiscriminately used, were in little or no estimation, as if they thought that, in regard to them, the Deity did not interpose. Private oaths used soberly, sacredly, and reverently, on necessary occasions, it would be perilous to condemn, supported as they are by reason and example. For if private individuals are permitted, in a grave and serious matter, to appeal to God as a judge, much more may they appeal to him as a witness. Your brother charges you with perfidy. You, as bound by the duties of charity, labor to clear yourself from the charge. He will on no account be satisfied. If, through his obstinate malice, your good name is brought into jeopardy, you can appeal, without offense, to the judgment of God, that he may in time manifest your innocence. If the terms are weighed, it will be found that it is a less matter to call upon him to be witness; and I therefore see not how it can be called unlawful to do so.

And there is no want of examples. If it is pretended that the oath, which Abraham and Isaac made with Abimelech, was of a public nature, and that by which Jacob and Laban bound themselves in mutual league was private. Boaz, though a private man, confirmed his promise of marriage to Ruth in the same way. Obadiah, too, a just man, and one that feared God, though a private individual, in seeking to persuade Elijah, asseverates with an oath.

I hold, therefore, that there is no better rule than so to regulate our oaths that they shall neither be rash, frivolous, promiscuous, nor passionate, but be made to serve a just necessity; in other words, to vindicate the glory of God, or promote the edification of a brother. This is the end of the Commandment.

FOURTH COMMANDMENT

REMEMBER THE SABBATH DAY TO KEEP IT HOLY. SIX DAYS
SHALT THOU LABOR AND DO ALL THY WORK: BUT THE
SEVENTH DAY IS THE SABBATH OF THE LORD THY GOD. IN IT
THOU SHALT NOT DO ANY WORK, etc.

28 **Exposition of the Fourth Commandment. Its end. Three purposes.**

The purport of the commandment is, that being dead to our own affections and works, we meditate on the kingdom of God, and in order to such meditation, have recourse to the means which he has appointed. But as this commandment stands in peculiar circumstances apart from the others, the mode of exposition must be somewhat different.

Early Christian writers are wont to call it typical, as containing the external observance of a day which was abolished with the other types on the advent of Christ. This is indeed true; but it leaves the half of the matter untouched. Wherefore, we must look deeper for our exposition, and attend to three cases in which it appears to me that the observance of this commandment consists.

First, under the rest of the seventh days the divine Lawgiver meant to furnish the people of Israel with a type of the spiritual rest by which believers were to cease from their own works, and allow God to work in them. Secondly, he meant that there should be a stated day on which they should assemble to hear the Law, and perform religious rites, or which, at least, they should specially employ in meditating on his works, and be thereby trained to piety. Thirdly, he meant that servants and those who lived under the authority of others should be indulged with a day of rest, and thus have some intermission from labor.

29 **Explanation of the first purpose—viz. a shadowing forth of spiritual rest. This the primary object of the precept. God is therein set forth as our sanctifier; and hence we must abstain from work, that the work of God in us may not be hindered.**

We are taught in many passages that this adumbration of spiritual rest held a primary place in the Sabbath. Indeed, there is no commandment the observance of which the Almighty more strictly enforces. When he would intimate by the Prophets that religion was entirely subverted, he complains that his Sabbaths were polluted, violated, not kept, not hallowed; as if, after it was neglected, there remained nothing in which he could be honored. The observance of it he eulogizes in the highest terms, and hence, among other divine privileges, the faithful set an extraordinary value on the revelation of the Sabbath.

In Nehemiah, the Levites, in the public assembly, thus speak: "Thou madest known unto them thy holy Sabbath, and commandedst them precepts, statutes, and laws, by the hand of Moses thy servant." You see the singular honor, which it holds among all the precepts of the Law. All this tends to celebrate the dignity of the mystery, which is most admirably expressed by Moses and Ezekiel.

Thus in Exodus: "Verily my Sabbaths shall ye keep: for it is a sign between me and you throughout your generations; that ye may know that I am the Lord that does sanctify you. Ye shall keep my Sabbath therefore; for it is holy unto you: everyone that defileth it shall surely be put to death: for whosoever does any work therein, that soul shall be cut off from among his people. Six days may work be done; but in the seventh is the Sabbath of rest, holy to the Lord: whosoever does any work in the Sabbath day, he shall surely be put to death. Wherefore the children of Israel shall keep the Sabbath, to observe the Sabbath throughout their generations, for a perpetual covenant. It is a sign between me and the children of Israel forever" (Exodus 31:13-17).

Ezekiel is still more full, but the sum of what he says amounts to this: that the Sabbath is a sign by which Israel might know that God is their sanctifier. If our sanctification consists in the mortification of our own will, the analogy between the external sign and the thing signified is most appropriate. We must rest entirely, in order that God may work in us; we must resign our own will, yield up our heart, and abandon all the lusts of the flesh. In short, we must desist from all the acts of our own mind, that God working in us, we may rest in him, as the Apostle also teaches (Hebrews 3:13; 4:3, 9).

30 The number seven denoting perfection in Scripture, this commandment may, in that respect, denote the perpetuity of the Sabbath, and its completion at the last day.

This complete cessation was represented to the Jews by the observance of one day in seven, which, that it might be more religiously attended to, the Lord recommended by his own example. For it is no small incitement to the zeal of man to know that he is engaged in imitating his Creator. Should anyone expect some secret meaning in the number seven, this being in Scripture the number for perfection, it may have been selected, not without cause, to denote perpetuity. In accordance with this, Moses concludes his description of the succession of day and night on the same day on which he relates that the Lord rested from his works.

Another probable reason for the number may be that the Lord intended that the Sabbath never should be completed before the arrival of the last day. We here begin our blessed rest in him, and daily make new progress in it; but because we must still wage an incessant warfare with the flesh, it shall not be consummated until the fulfillment of the prophecy of Isaiah: "From one new moon to another, and from one Sabbath to another, shall all flesh come to worship before me, saith the Lord" (Isaiah 66:23); in other words, when God shall be "all in all" (1 Corinthians 15:28). It may seem, therefore, that by the seventh day the Lord delineated to his people the future perfection of his Sabbath on the last day, that by continual meditation on the Sabbath, they might throughout their whole lives aspire to this perfection.

31 Taking a simpler view of the commandment, the number is of no consequence, provided we maintain the doctrine of a perpetual rest from all our works, and, at the same time, avoid a superstitious observance of days. The ceremonial part of the commandment abolished by the advent of Christ.

Should these remarks on the number seem to any somewhat far-fetched, I have no objection to their taking it more simply: that the Lord appointed a certain day on which his people might be trained, under the tutelage of the Law, to meditate constantly on the spiritual rest, and fixed upon the seventh, either because he foresaw it would be sufficient, or in order that his own example might operate as a stronger stimulus; or, at least to remind men that the Sabbath was appointed for no other purpose than to render them conformable to their Creator. It is of little consequence which of these be adopted, provided we lose not sight of the principal thing delineated—viz. the mystery of perpetual resting from our works. The prophets every now and then called the Jews to contemplate this, lest they should think a carnal cessation from labor sufficient.

Beside the passages already quoted, there is the following: "If thou turn away thy foot from the Sabbath, from doing thy pleasure on my holy day; and call the Sabbath a delight, the holy of the Lord, honorable; and shalt honor him, not doing thine own ways, nor finding thine own pleasure, nor speaking thine own words: then shalt thou delight thyself in the Lord" (Isaiah 58:13, 14).

Still there can be no doubt, that, on the advent of our Lord Jesus Christ, the ceremonial part of the commandment was abolished. He is the truth, at whose presence all the emblems vanish; and the body, at the sight of which the shadows disappear. He, I say, is the true completion of the Sabbath: "We are buried with him by baptism unto death: that like as Christ was raised up from the dead by the glory of the Father, even so we should walk in newness of life" (Romans 6:4). Hence, as the Apostle elsewhere says, "Let no man therefore judge you in meat, or in drink, or in respect of an holiday, or of the new moon, or of the Sabbath days; which are a shadow of things to come; but the body is of Christ" (Colossians 2:16, 17); meaning by body the whole essence of the truth, as is well explained in that passage.

This is not contented with one day, but requires the whole course of our lives, until being completely dead to ourselves, we are filled with the life of God. Christians, therefore, should have nothing to do with a superstitious observance of days.

32 The second and third purposes of the Commandment explained. These twofold and perpetual. This confirmed. Of religious assemblies.

The two other cases ought not to be classed with ancient shadows, but are adapted to every age. The Sabbath being abrogated, there is still room among us, first, to assemble on stated days for the hearing of the Word, the breaking of the mystical bread, and public prayer; and, secondly, to give our servants and laborers relaxation from labor. It cannot be doubted that the Lord provided for both in the commandment of the Sabbath. The former is abundantly evinced by the mere practice of the Jews. The latter Moses has expressed in Deuteronomy in the following terms: "The seventh day is the Sabbath of the Lord thy God: in it thou shalt not do any work, thou, nor thy son, nor thy daughter, nor thy manservant, nor thy maidservant; —that thy manservant and thy maidservant may rest as well as thou" (Deuteronomy 5:14).

Likewise in Exodus, "That thine ox and thine ass may rest, and the son of thy handmaid, and the stranger, may be refreshed" (Exodus 23:12).

Who can deny that both are equally applicable to us as to the Jews? Religious meetings are enjoined us by the word of God; their necessity, experience itself sufficiently demonstrates. But unless these meetings are stated, and have fixed days allotted to them, how can they be held? We must, as the apostle expresses it, do all things decently and in orders (1 Corinthians 14:40). So impossible, however, would it be to preserve decency and order without this politic arrangements that the dissolution of it would instantly lead to the disturbance and ruin of the Church. But if the reason for which the Lord appointed a Sabbath to the Jews is equally applicable to us, no man can assert that it is a matter with which we have nothing to do. Our most provident and indulgent Parent has been pleased to provide for our wants not less than for the wants of the Jews.

Why, it may be asked, do we not hold daily meetings, and thus avoid the distinction of days? Would that we were privileged to do so! Spiritual wisdom undoubtedly deserves to have some portion of every day devoted to it. But if, owing to the weakness of many, daily meetings cannot be held, and charity will not allow us to exact more of them, why should we not adopt the rule, which the will of God has obviously imposed upon us?

33

Of the observance of the Lord's Day, in answer to those who complain that the Christian people are thus trained to Judaism. Objection.

I am obliged to dwell a little longer on this because some restless spirits re now making an outcry about the observance of the Lord's Day. They complain that Christian people are trained in Judaism, because some observance of days is retained. My reply is that we observe those days without Judaism, because in this matter we differ widely from the Jews. We do not celebrate it with most minute formality, as a ceremony by which we imagine that a spiritual mystery is typified, but we adopt it as a necessary remedy for preserving order in the Church. Paul informs us that Christians are not to be judged in respect of its observance, because it is a shadow of something to come (Colossians 2:16); and, accordingly, he expresses a fear lest his labor among the Galatians should prove in vain, because they still observed days (Galatians 4:10, 11). And he tells the Romans that it is superstitious to make one day differ from another (Romans 14:5).

But who, except those restless men, does not see what the observance is to which the Apostle refers? Those persons had no regard to that politic and ecclesiastical arrangement, but by retaining the days as types of spiritual things, they in so far obscured the glory of Christ, and the light of the Gospel. They did not desist from manual labor on the ground of its interfering with sacred study and meditation, but as a kind of religious observance; because they dreamed that by their cessation from labor, they were cultivating the mysteries which had of old been committed to them.

It was, I say, against this preposterous observance of days that the Apostle inveighs, and not against that legitimate selection which is subservient to the peace of Christian society. For in the churches established by him, this was the use for which the Sabbath was retained. He tells the Corinthians to set the first day apart for collecting contributions for the relief of their brethren at Jerusalem (1 Corinthians 16:2).

If superstition is dreaded, there was more danger in keeping the Jewish Sabbath than the Lord's Day as Christians now do. It being expedient to overthrow superstition, the Jewish holy day was abolished; and as a thing necessary to retain decency, orders, and peace, in the Church, another day was appointed for that purpose.

34

Ground of this institution. There is no kind of superstitious necessity. The sum of the Commandment.

It was not, however, without a reason that the early Christians substituted what we call the Lord's Day for the Sabbath. The resurrection of our Lord being the end and accomplishment of that true rest which the ancient Sabbath typified, this day, by which types were abolished serves to warn Christians against adhering to a shadowy ceremony. I do not cling so to the number seven as to bring the Church under bondage to it, nor do I condemn churches for holding their meetings on other solemn days, provided they guard against superstition. This they will do if they employ those days merely for the observance of discipline and regular order.

The whole may be thus summed up: As the truth was delivered typically to the Jews, so it is imparted to us without figure; first, that during our whole lives we may aim at a constant rest from our own works, in order that the Lord may work in us by his Spirit; secondly that every individual, as he has opportunity, may diligently exercise himself in private, in pious meditation on the works of God, and, at the same time, that all may observe the legitimate order appointed by the Church, for the hearing of the word, the administration of the sacraments, and public prayer: And, thirdly, that we may avoid oppressing those who are subject to us.

In this way, we get quit of the trifling of the false prophets, who in later times instilled Jewish ideas into the people, alleging that nothing was abrogated but what was ceremonial in the commandment, (this they term in their language the taxation of the seventh day), while the moral part remains—viz. the observance of one day in seven. But this is nothing else than to insult the Jews, by changing the day, and yet mentally attributing to it the same sanctity; thus retaining the same typical distinction of days as had place among the Jews. And of a truth, we see what profit they have made by such a doctrine. Those who cling to their constitutions go thrice as far as the Jews in the gross and carnal superstition of sabbatism; so that the rebukes which we read in Isaiah (Isaiah 1:13; 58:13) apply as much to those of the present day, as to those to whom the Prophet addressed them.

We must be careful, however, to observe the general doctrine—viz. in order that religion may neither be lost nor languish among us, we must diligently attend on our religious assemblies, and duly avail ourselves of those external aids, which tend to promote the worship of God.

FIFTH COMMANDMENT

HONOR THY FATHER AND THY MOTHER:
THAT THY DAYS MAY BE LONG UPON THE LAND WHICH
THE LORD THY GOD GIVETH THEE.

35 The Fifth Commandment (the first of the Second Table), expounded. Its end and substance. How far honor due to parents. To whom the term *father* applies.

The end of this commandment is that since the Lord takes pleasure in the preservation of his own ordinance, the degrees of dignity appointed by him must be held inviolable. The sum of the commandment, therefore, will be, that we are to look up to those whom the Lord has set over us, yielding them honor, gratitude, and obedience. Hence, it follows, that everything in the way of contempt, ingratitude, or disobedience, is forbidden. For the term *honor* has this extent of meaning in Scripture. Thus when the Apostle says, "Let the elders that rule well be counted worthy of double honor" (Timothy 5:17), he refers not only to the reverence, which is due to them, but also to the recompense to which their services are entitled. But as this command to submit is very repugnant to the perversity of the human mind (which, puffed up with ambitious longings will scarcely allow itself to be subject), that superiority which is most attractive and least invidious is set forth as an example calculated to soften and bend our minds to habits of submission.

From that subjection which is most easily endured, the Lord gradually accustoms us to every kind of legitimate subjection, the same principle regulating all. For to those whom he raises to eminences he communicates his authority, in so far as necessary to maintain their station. The titles of Father, God, and Lord, all meet in him alone and hence whenever anyone of them is mentioned, our mind should be impressed with the same feeling of reverence. Those, therefore, to whom he imparts such titles, he distinguishes by some small spark of his refulgence, to entitle them to honor, each in his own place. In this way, we must consider that our earthly father possesses something of a divine nature in him, because there is some reason for his bearing a divine title, and that he who is our prince and ruler is admitted to some communion of honor with God.

36 It makes no difference whether those to whom this honor is required are worthy or unworthy. The honor is claimed especially for parents. It consists of three parts. A. Reverence.

Wherefore, we ought to have no doubt that the Lord here lays down this universal rule—viz. that knowing how every individual is set over us by his appointment, we should pay him reverence, gratitude, obedience, and every duty in our power. And it makes no difference whether or not those on whom the honor is conferred deserve it. Be they what they may, the Almighty, by conferring their station upon them, shows that he would have them honored. The commandment specifies the reverence due to those to whom we owe our being. This Nature herself should in some measure teach us. For they are monsters, and not men, who petulantly and contemptuously violate the paternal authority.

Hence, the Lord orders all who rebel against their parents to be put to death, they being, as it where, unworthy of the light in paying no deference to those to whom they are indebted for beholding it. And it is evident, from the various appendices to the Law that we were correct in stating, that the honor here referred to consists of three parts, reverence, obedience, and gratitude. The first of these the Lord enforces, when he commands that whose curse his father or his mother shall be put to death. In this way, he avenges insult and contempt. The second he enforces, when he denounces the punishment of death on disobedient and rebellious children. To the third belongs our Savior's declaration, that God requires us to do good to our parents (Matthew 15). And whenever Paul mentions this commandment, he interprets it as enjoining obedience.

37 Honor due to parents continued. B. Obedience. C. Gratitude. Why a promise added. In what sense it is to be taken. The present life a testimony of divine blessing. The reservation considered and explained.

A promise is added by way of recommendation: the better to remind us how pleasing to God is the submission, which is here required. Paul applies that stimulus to rouse us from our lethargy, when he calls this the first commandment with promise; the promise contained in the First Table not being specially appropriated to anyone commandment, but extended to the whole law. Moreover, the sense in which the promise is to be taken is as follows: —The Lord spoke to the Israelites especially of the land that he had promised them for an inheritance. If, then, the possession of the land was an earnest of the divine favor, we cannot wonder if the Lord was pleased to testify his favor, by bestowing long life, as in this way they were able long to enjoy his kindness.

The meaning therefore is: Honor thy father and thy mother, that thou may be able, during the course of a long life, to enjoy the possession of the land which is to be given thee in testimony of my favor. But, as the whole earth is blessed to believers, we justly class the present life among the number of divine blessings.

Whence this promise has, in like manner, reference to us also, inasmuch as the duration of the present life is a proof of the divine benevolence toward us. It is not promised to us, nor was it promised to the Jews, as if in itself it constituted happiness, but because it is an ordinary symbol of the divine favor to the pious.

Wherefore, if anyone who is obedient to parents happens to be cut off before mature age (a thing which not infrequently happens), the Lord nevertheless adheres to his promise as steadily as when he bestows a hundred acres of land where he had promised only one. The whole lies in this: We must consider that long life is promised only in so far as it is a blessing from God, and that it is a blessing only in so far as it is a manifestation of divine favor. This, however, he testifies and truly manifests to his servants more richly and substantially by death.

38 Conversely a curse denounced on disobedient children. How far obedience due to parents, and those in the place of parents.

Moreover, while the Lord promises the blessing of present life to children who show proper respect to their parents, he, at the same time, intimates that an inevitable curse is impending over the rebellious and disobedient; and, that it may not fail of execution, he, in his Law, pronounces sentence of death upon theme and orders it to be inflicted. If they escape the judgment, he, in some way or other, will execute vengeance. For we see how great a number of this description of individuals fall either in battle or in brawls; others of them are overtaken by unwonted disasters, and almost all are a proof that the threatening is not used in vain. But if any do escape until extreme old age, yet, because deprived of the blessing of God in this life, they only languish on in wickedness, and are reserved for severer punishment in the world to come, they are far from participating in the blessing promised to obedient children. It ought to be observed by the way, that we are ordered to obey parents only in the Lord. This is clear from the principle already laid down: for the place that they occupy is one to which the Lord has exalted them, by communicating to them a portion of his own honor.

Therefore the submission yielded to them should be a step in our ascent to the Supreme Parent, and hence, if they instigate us to transgress the law, they deserve not to be regarded as parents, but as strangers attempting to seduce us from obedience to our true Father.

The same holds in the case of rulers, masters, and superiors of every description. For it would be unbecoming and absurd that the honor of God should be impaired by their exaltation—an exaltation which, being derived from him, ought to lead us up to him.

SIXTH COMMANDMENT

THOU SHALT NOT KILL.

39 Sixth Commandment expounded. Its end and substance. God, as a spiritual Lawgiver, forbids the murder of the heart, and requires a sincere desire to preserve the life of our neighbor.

The purport of this commandment is that since the Lord has bound the whole human race by a kind of unity, the safety of all ought to be considered as entrusted to each. In general, therefore, all violence and injustice, and every kind of harm from which our neighbor's body suffers, is prohibited. Accordingly, we are required faithfully to do what in us lies to defend the life of our neighbor; to promote whatever tends to his tranquility, to be vigilant in warding off harm, and, when danger comes, to assist in removing it.

Remembering that the Divine Lawgiver thus speaks, consider, moreover, that he requires you to apply the same rule in regulating your mind. It is ridiculous, that he, who sees the thoughts of the heart, and has special regard to them, should train the body only to rectitude.

This commandment, therefore, prohibits the murder of the heart, and requires a sincere desire to preserve our brother's life. The hand, indeed, commits the murder, but the mind, under the influence of wrath and hatred, conceives it.

How can you be angry with your brother, without passionately longing to do him harm? If you must not be angry with him, neither must you hate him, hatred being nothing but inveterate anger. However you may disguise the fact, or endeavor to escape from it by vain pretexts. Where either wrath or hatred is, there is an inclination to do mischief. If you still persist in tergiversation, the mouth of the Spirit has declared, that "whosoever hateth his brother is a murderer" (1 John 3:15); and the mouth of our Savior has declared, that "whosoever is angry with his brother without a cause shall be in danger of the judgment: and whosoever shall say to his brother, Raca, shall be in danger of the council: but whosoever shall say, Thou fool, shall be in danger of hell fire" (Matthew 5:22).

40 A twofold ground for this Commandment. A. Man is the image of God. B. He is our flesh.

Scripture notes a twofold equity on which this commandment is founded. Man is both the image of God and our flesh. Wherefore, if we would not violate the image of God, we must hold the person of man sacred—if we would not divest ourselves of humanity we must cherish our own flesh. The practical inference to be drawn from the redemption and gift of Christ will be elsewhere considered. The Lord has been pleased to direct our attention to these two natural considerations as inducements to watch over our neighbor's preservation—viz. to revere the divine image impressed upon him, and embrace our own flesh. To be clear of the crime of murder, it is not enough to refrain from shedding man's blood. If in act you perpetrate, if in endeavor you plot, if in wish and design you conceive what is adverse to another's safety, you have the guilt of murder. On the other hand, if you do not according to your means and opportunity study to defend his safety, by that inhumanity you violate the law. But if the safety of the body is so carefully provided for, we may hence infer how much care and exertion is due to the safety of the soul, which is of immeasurably higher value in the sight of God.

SEVENTH COMMANDMENT

THOU SHALT NOT COMMIT ADULTERY.

41 Exposition of the Seventh Command. The end and substance of it. Remedy against fornication.

The purport of this commandment is that as God loves chastity and purity, we ought to guard against all uncleanness. The substance of the commandment therefore is that we must not defile ourselves with any impurity or libidinous excess. To this corresponds the affirmative, that we must regulate every part of our conduct chastely and continently. The thing expressly forbidden is adultery, to which lust naturally tends, that its filthiness (being of a grosser and more palpable form, in as much as it casts a stain even on the body) may dispose us to abominate every form of lust. As the law under which man was created was not to lead a life of solitude, but enjoy a help meet for him, and ever since he fell under the curse the necessity for this mode of life is increased; the Lord made the requisite provision for us in this respect by the institution of marriage, which, entered into under his authority, he has also sanctified with his blessing. Hence, it is evident, that any mode of cohabitation different from marriage is cursed in his sight, and that the conjugal relation was ordained as a necessary means of preventing us from giving way to unbridled lust. Let us beware, therefore, of yielding to indulgence, seeing we are assured that the curse of God lies on every man and woman cohabiting without marriage.

42 Continence an excellent gift, when under the control of God only. Altogether denied to some; granted only for a time to others. Argument in favor of celibacy refuted.

Now, since natural feeling and the passions unnamed by the fall make the marriage tie doubly necessary, save in the case of those whom God has by special grace exempted, let every individual consider how the case stands with himself. Virginity, I admit, is a virtue not to be despised; but since it is denied to some, and to others granted only for a season, those who are assailed by incontinence, and unable successfully to war against it, should retake themselves to the remedy of marriage, and thus cultivate chastity in the way of their calling. Those incapable of self-restraint, if they apply not to the remedy allowed and provided for intemperance, war with God and resist his ordinance. And let no man tell me (as many in the present day do) that he can do all things, God helping! The help of God is present with those only who walk in his ways (Psalm 91:14), that is, in his callings from which all withdraw themselves who, omitting the remedies provided by God, vainly and presumptuously strive to struggle with and surmount their natural feelings. That continence is a special gift from God, and of the class of those which are not bestowed indiscriminately on the whole body of the Church, but only on a few of its members, our Lord affirms (Matthew 19:12). He first describes a certain class of individuals who have made themselves eunuchs for the kingdom of heavenly sake; that is, in order that they may be able to devote themselves with more liberty and less restraint to the things of heaven.

But lest anyone should suppose that such a sacrifice was in every man's power, he had shown a little before that not all are capable, but those only to whom it is specially given from above. Hence, he concludes, "He that is able to receive it, let him receive it." Paul asserts the same thing still more plainly when he says, "Every man has his proper gift of God, one after this manner, and another after that" (1 Corinthians 7:7).

43 Each individual may refrain from marriage so long as he is fit to observe celibacy. True celibacy and the proper use of it. Any man not gifted with continence wars with God and with nature, as constituted by him, in remaining unmarried. Chastity defined.

Since we are reminded by an express declaration, that it is not in every man's power to live chaste in celibacy although it may be his most strenuous study and aim to do so—that it is a special grace which the Lord bestows only on certain individuals, in order that they may be less encumbered in his service, do we not oppose God, and nature as constituted by him, if we do not accommodate our mode of life to the measure of our ability? The Lord prohibits fornication; therefore, he requires purity and chastity. The only method which each has of preserving it is to measure himself by his capacity.

Let no man rashly despise matrimony as a thing useless or superfluous to him; let no man long for celibacy unless he is able to dispense with the married state. Nor even here let him consult the tranquility or convenience of the flesh, save only that, freed from this tie, he may be the readier and more prepared for all the offices of piety. And since there are many on whom this blessing is conferred only for a time, let everyone, in abstaining from marriage, do it so long as he is fit to endure celibacy. If he has not the power of subduing his passion, let him understand that the Lord has made it obligatory on him to marry.

The Apostle shows this when he enjoins: "Nevertheless, to avoid fornication, let every man have his own wife and let every woman have her own husband." "If they cannot contain, let them marry." He first intimates that the greater part of men are liable to incontinence; and then of those so liable, he orders all, without exception, to have recourse to the only remedy by which lack of chastity may be rendered unnecessary. The incontinent, therefore, neglecting to cure their infirmity by this means, sin by the very circumstance of disobeying the Apostle's command. And let not a man flatter himself, that because he abstains from the outward act he cannot be accused of lack of chastity. His mind may in the meantime be inwardly inflamed with lust. For Paul's definition of chastity is purity of mind, combined with purity of body.

"The unmarried woman careth for the things of the Lord, that she may be holy both in body and spirit" (1 Corinthians 7:34). Therefore when he gives a reason for the former precept, he not only says that it is better to marry than to live in fornication, but that it is better to marry than to burn.

44 Precautions to be observed in married life. Everything repugnant to chastity here condemned.

Moreover, when spouses are made aware that the Lord blesses their union, they are thereby reminded that they must not give way to intemperate and unrestrained indulgence. For though honorable wedlock veils the turpitude of incontinence, it does not follow that it ought forthwith to become a stimulus to it. Wherefore, let spouses consider that not all things are lawful for them. Let there be sobriety in the behavior of the husband toward the wife, and of the wife in her turn toward the husband; each so acting as not to do anything unbecoming the dignity and temperance of married life.

Marriage contracted in the Lord ought to exhibit measure and modesty—not run to the extreme of wantonness. This excess Ambrose censured gravely, but not undeservedly, when he described the man who shows no modesty or comeliness in conjugal intercourse, as committing adultery with his wife. Lastly let us consider who the Lawgiver is that thus condemns fornication: even He who, as he is entitled to possess us entirely, requires integrity of body, soul, and spirit. Therefore, while he forbids fornication, he at the same time forbids us to lay snares for our neighbor's chastity by lascivious attire, obscene gestures, and impure conversation.

There was reason in the remark made by Archelaus to a youth clothed effeminately and over-luxuriously, that it mattered not in what part his wantonness appeared. We must have respect to God, who abhors all contaminations whatever be the part of soul or body in which it appears. And that there may be no doubt about it, let us remember, that what the Lord here commends is chastity. If he requires chastity, he condemns everything, which is opposed to it. Therefore, if you aspire to obedience, let not your mind burn within with evil concupiscence, your eyes wanton after corrupting objects, nor your body be decked for allurement; let neither your tongue by filthy speeches, nor your appetite by intemperance, entice the mind to corresponding thoughts. All vices of this description are a kind of stains, which despoil chastity of its purity.

EIGHTH COMMANDMENT

THOU SHALT NOT STEAL.

45 Exposition of the Eighth Commandment. Its end and substance. Four kinds of theft. The bad acts condemned by this Commandment. Other peculiar kinds of theft.

The purport is, that injustice being an abomination to God, we must render to every man his due. In substance, then, the commandment forbids us to long after other men's goods, and, accordingly, requires every man to exert himself honestly in preserving his own. For we must consider, that what each individual possesses has not fallen to him by chance, but by the distribution of the sovereign Lord of all, that no one can pervert his means to bad purposes without committing a fraud on a divine dispensation.

There are very many kinds of theft. One consists in violence, as when a man's goods are forcibly plundered and carried off; another in malicious imposture, as when they are fraudulently intercepted; a third in the more hidden craft which takes possession of them with a semblance of justice; and a fourth in sycophancy, which wiles them away under the pretence of donation. But not to dwell too long in enumerating the different classes, we know that all the arts by which we obtain possession of the goods and money of our neighbors, for sincere affection substituting an eagerness to deceive or injure them in any way, are to be regarded as thefts. Though they may be obtained by an action at law, God gives a different decision. He sees the long train of deception by which the man of craft begins to lay nets for his more simple neighbor, until he entangles him in its meshes—sees the harsh and cruel laws by which the more powerful oppresses and crushes the feeble—sees the enticements by which the more wily baits the hook for the less wary, though all these escape the judgment of man, and no cognizance is taken of them. Nor is the violation of this commandment confined to money, or merchandise, or lands, but extends to every kind of right, for we defraud our neighbors to their hurt if we decline any of the duties, which we are bound to perform towards them.

If an agent or an indolent steward wastes the substance of his employer, or does not give due heed to the management of his property; if he unjustly squanders or luxuriously wastes the means entrusted to him; if a servant holds his master in derision, divulges his secrets, or in any way is treacherous to his life or his goods; if, on the other hand, a master cruelly torments his household, he is guilty of theft before God; since everyone who, in the exercise of his calling, performs not what he owes to others, keeps back, or makes away with what does not belong to him.

46 Proper observance of this Commandment. Four heads. Application. A. To the people and the magistrate. B. To the pastors of the Church and their flocks. C. To parents and children. D. To the old and the young. E. To servants and masters. F. To individuals.

This commandment, therefore, we shall duly obey, if, contented with our own lot, we study to acquire nothing but honest and lawful gain; if we long not to grow rich by injustice, nor to plunder our neighbor of his goods, that our own may thereby be increased; if we hasten not to heap up wealth cruelly wrung from the blood of others; if we do not, by means lawful and unlawful, with excessive eagerness scrape together whatever may glut our avarice or meet our prodigality.

On the other hand, let it be our constant aim faithfully to lend our counsel and aid to all so as to assist them in retaining their property; or if we have to do with the perfidious or crafty, let us rather be prepared to yield somewhat of our right than to contend with them. And not only so, but let us contribute to the relief of those whom we see under the pressure of difficulties, assisting their want out of our abundance.

Lastly, let each of us consider how far he is bound in duty to others, and in good faith pay what we owe. In the same way, let the people pay all due honor to their rulers, submit patiently to their authority, obey their laws and orders, and decline nothing which they can bear without sacrificing the favor of God.

Let rulers, again, take due charge of their people, preserve the public peace, protect the good, curb the bad, and conduct themselves throughout as those who must render an account of their office to God, the Judge of all.

Let the ministers of churches faithfully give heed to the ministry of the word, and not corrupt the doctrine of salvation, but deliver it purely and sincerely to the people of God. Let them teach not merely by doctrine, but by example; in short, let them act the part of good shepherds towards their flocks.

Let the people, in their turn, receive them as the messengers and apostles of God, render them the honor which their Supreme Master has bestowed on them, and supply them with such things as are necessary for their livelihood.

Let parents be careful to bring up, guide, and teach their children as a trust committed to them by God. Let them not exasperate or alienate them by cruelty, but cherish and embrace them with the levity and indulgence, which becomes their character. The regard due to parents from their children has already been adverted to.

Let the young respect those advanced in years, as the Lord has been pleased to make that age honorable.

Let the aged also, by their prudence and their experience (in which they are far superior), guide the feebleness of youth, not assailing them with harsh and clamorous invectives but tempering strictness with ease and affability.

Let servants show themselves diligent and respectful in obeying their masters, and this not with eye-service, but from the heart, as the servants of God. Let masters also not be stern and disobliging to their servants, nor harass them with excessive asperity, nor treat them with insult, but rather let them acknowledge them as brethren and fellow-servants of our heavenly Master, whom, therefore, they are bound to treat with mutual love and kindness.

Let everyone, I say, thus consider what in his own place and order he owes to his neighbors, and pay what he owes.

Moreover, we must always have a reference to the Lawgiver, and so remember that the law requiring us to promote and defend the interest and convenience of our fellow men applies equally to our minds and our hands.

NINTH COMMANDMENT

THOU SHALT NOT BEAR FALSE WITNESS AGAINST THY NEIGHBOR.

47 Exposition of the ninth Commandment. Its end and substance. The essence of the Commandment—detestation of falsehood, and the pursuit of truth. Two kinds of falsehood. Public and private testimony. The equity of this Commandment.

The purport of the commandment is, since God, who is truth, abhors falsehood, we must cultivate unfeigned truth towards each other. The sum, therefore, will be, that we must not by calumnies and false accusations injure our neighbor's name, or by falsehood impair his fortunes; in fine, that we must not injure anyone from petulance, or a love of evil-speaking. To this prohibition corresponds the command, that we must faithfully assist everyone, as far as in us lies, in asserting the truth, for the maintenance of his good name and his estate.

The Lord seems to have intended to explain the commandment in these words: "Thou shalt not raise a false report: put not thine hand with the wicked to be an unrighteous witness." "Keep thee far from a false matter" (Exodus 23:1, 7). In another passage, he not only prohibits that species of falsehood, which consists in acting the part of talebearers among the people, but also says, "Neither shalt thou stand against the blood of thy neighbor" (Leviticus 19:16). Both transgressions are distinctly prohibited. Indeed, there can be no doubt, that as in the previous commandment he prohibited cruelty, lack of chastity, and avarice, so here he prohibits falsehood, which consists of the two parts to which we have adverted.

By malignant or vicious detraction, we sin against our neighbor's good name: by lying, sometimes even by casting a slur upon him, we injure him in his estate. It makes no difference whether you suppose that formal and judicial testimony is here intended, or the ordinary testimony, which is given, in private conversation. For we must always recur to the consideration, that for each kind of transgression one species is set forth by way of example, that to it the others may be referred, and that the species chiefly selected, is that in which the turpitude of the transgression is most apparent. It seems proper, however, to extend it more generally to calumny and sinister insinuations by which our neighbors are unjustly aggrieved. For falsehood in a court of justice is always accompanied with perjury. But against perjury, in so far as it profanes and violates the name of God, there is a sufficient provision in the third commandment.

Hence, the legitimate observance of this precept consists in employing the tongue in the maintenance of truth, to promote both the good name and the prosperity of our neighbor. The equity of this is perfectly clear. For if a good name is more precious than riches, a man, in being robbed of his good name, is no less injured than if he were robbed of his goods; while, in the latter case, false testimony is sometimes not less injurious than rapine committed by the hand.

48 How numerous the violations of this Commandment. A. By detraction. B. By evil speaking—a thing contrary to the offices of Christian charity. C. By scurrility or irony. D. By prying curiosity, and proneness to harsh judgments.

And yet it is strange, with what supine security men everywhere sin in this respect. Indeed, very ew are found who do not notoriously labor under this disease: such is the envenomed delight we take both in prying into and exposing our neighbor's faults. Let us not imagine it is a sufficient excuse to say that on many occasions our statements are not false. He, who forbids us to defame our neighbor's reputation by falsehood, desires us to keep it untarnished in so far as truh will permit.

Though the commandment is only directed against falsehood, it intimates that the preservation of our neighbor's good name is recommended. It ought to be a sufficient inducement to us to guard our neighbor's good name, that God takes an interest in it. Wherefore, evil speaking in general is undoubtedly condemned. Moreover, by evil-speaking, we understand not the rebuke which is administered with a view of correcting; not accusation or judicial decision, by which evil is sought to be remedied; not public censure, which tends to strike terror into other offenders; not the disclosure made to those whose safety depends on being forewarned, lest unawares they should be brought into danger, but the odious crimination which springs from a malicious and petulant love of slander.

Nay, the commandment extends so far as to include that scurrilous affected urbanity, instinct with invective, by which the failings of others, under an appearance of sportiveness, are bitterly assailed, as some are wont to do, who court the praise of wit, though it should call forth a blush, or inflict a bitter pang. By petulance of this description, our brethren are sometimes grievously wounded. But if we turn our eye to the Lawgiver, whose just authority extends over the ears and the mind, as well as the tongue, we cannot fail to perceive that eagerness to listen to slander, and an unbecoming proneness to censorious judgments are here forbidden. It is absurd to suppose that God hates the disease of evil speaking in the tongue, and yet disapproves not of its malignity in the mind. Wherefore, if the true fear and love of God dwell in us, we must endeavor, as far as is lawful and expedient, and as far as charity admits, neither to listen nor give utterance to bitter and acrimonious charges, nor rashly entertain sinister suspicions. As just interpreters of the words and the actions of other men, let us candidly maintain the honor due to them by our judgment, our ear, and our tongue.

TENTH COMMANDMENT

THOU SHALT NOT COVET THY NEIGHBOR'S HOUSE;
THOU SHALT NOT COVET THY NEIGHBOR'S WIFE
NOR HIS MANSERVANT, NOR HIS MAIDSERVANT,
NOR HIS OX NOR HIS ASS, NOR ANYTHING THAT IS
THY NEIGHBOR'S.

49 Exposition of the Tenth Commandment. Its end and substance. What meant by the term *Covetousness*. Distinction between counsel and the covetousness here condemned.

The purport is: Since the Lord would have the whole soul pervaded with love, any feeling of an adverse nature must be banished from our minds. The sum, therefore, will be, that no thought be permitted to insinuate itself into our minds, and inhale them with a noxious concupiscence tending to our neighbor's loss. To this corresponds the contrary precept, that everything that we conceive, deliberate, will, or design, be conjoined with the good and advantage of our neighbor. But here it seems we are met with a great and perplexing difficulty. For if it was correctly said above, that under the words adultery and theft, lust and an intention to injure and deceive are prohibited, it may seem superfluous afterwards to employ a separate commandment to prohibit a covetous desire of our neighbor's goods. The difficulty will easily be removed by distinguishing between *design* and *covetousness*. Design, such as we have spoken of in the previous commandments, is a deliberate consent of the will, after passion has taken possession of the mind.

Covetousness may exist without such deliberation and assent, when the mind is only stimulated and tickled by vain and perverse objects. As, therefore, the Lord previously ordered that charity should regulate our wishes, studies, and actions, so he now orders us to regulate the thoughts of the mind in the same way, that none of them may be depraved and distorted, so as to give the mind a contrary bent. Having forbidden us to turn and incline our mind to wrath, hatred, adultery, theft, and falsehood, he now forbids us to give our thoughts the same direction.

50 Why God requires so much purity. Objection. Answer. Charity toward our neighbor here principally commended. Why house, wife, manservant, maidservant, ox, and ass, etc., are mentioned. Improper division of this Commandment into two.

Nor is such rectitude demanded without reason. For who can deny the propriety of occupying all the powers of the mind with charity? If it ceases to have charity for its aim, who can question that it is diseased? How comes it that so many desires of a nature hurtful to your brother enter your mind, but just because, disregarding him, you think only of yourself? Were your mind wholly imbued with charity, no portion of it would remain for the entrance of such thoughts. In so far, therefore, as the mind is devoid of charity, it must be under the influence of concupiscence. Some one will object that those fancies, which casually rise up in the mind and then vanish, cannot properly be condemned as concupiscences [*powerful feelings of physical desire*], which have their seat in the heart. I answer, That the question here relates to a description of fancies which while they present themselves to our thoughts, at the same time impress and stimulate the mind with cupidity, since the mind never thinks of making some choice, but the heart is excited and tends towards it. God therefore commands a strong and ardent affection, an affection not to be impeded by any portion, however minute, of concupiscence. He requires a mind so admirably arranged as not to be prompted in the slightest degree contrary to the law of love.

Lest you should imagine that this view is not supported by any grave authority, I may mention that Augustine first suggested it to me. But although it was the intention of God to prohibit every kind of perverse desire, he, by way of example, sets before us those objects which are generally regarded as most attractive: thus leaving no room for cupidity of any kind, by the interdiction of those things in which it especially delights and loves to revel.

Such, then, is the Second Table of the Law, in which we are sufficiently instructed in the duties which we owe to man for the sake of God, on a consideration of whose nature the whole system of love is founded. It would be vain, therefore, to inculcate the various duties taught in this table, without placing your instructions on the fear and reverence to God as their proper foundation. I need not tell the considerate reader, that those who make two precepts out of the prohibition of covetousness, perversely split one thing into two. There is nothing in the repetition of the words, "Thou shalt not covet." The "house" being first put down, its different parts are afterwards enumerated, beginning with the "wife;" and hence it is clear, that the whole ought to be read consecutively, as is properly done by the Jews. The sum of the whole commandment, therefore, is that whatever each individual possesses, remains entire and secure not only from injury, or the wish to injure, but also from the slightest feeling of covetousness, which can spring up in the mind.

51 The last part of the chapter. The end of the Law. Proof. A summary of the Ten Commandments. The Law delivers not merely rudiments and first principles, but a perfect standard of righteousness, modeled on the divine purity.

It will not now be difficult to ascertain the general end contemplated by the whole Law—viz. the fulfillment of righteousness, that man may form his life on the model of the divine purity. For therein God has so delineated his own character, that anyone exhibiting in action what is commanded, would in some measure exhibit a living image of God. Wherefore Moses, when he wished to fix a summary of the whole in the memory of the Israelites, thus addressed them, "And now, Israel, what does the Lord thy God require of thee, but to fear the Lord thy God, to walk in all his ways, and to love him, and to serve the Lord thy God with all thy heart, and with all thy soul, to keep the commandments of the Lord and his statutes which I command thee this day for thy good?" (Deuteronomy 10:12, 13). And he ceased not to reiterate the same thing, whenever he had occasion to mention the end of the Law. To this the doctrine of the Law pays so much regard, that it connects man, by holiness of life, with his God; and, as Moses elsewhere expresses it (Deuteronomy 6:5; 11:13), and makes him cleave to him. Moreover, this holiness of life is comprehended under the two heads above mentioned. "Thou shalt love the Lord thy God with all thy heart, and with all thy soul, and with all thy mind, and with all thy strength, and thy neighbor as thyself."

First, our mind must be completely filled with love to God, and then this love must forthwith flow out toward our neighbor. The Apostle shows this when he says, "The end of the commandment is charity out of a pure heart, and a good conscience, and of faith unfeigned" (1 Timothy 1:5). You see that conscience and faith unfeigned are placed at the head, in other words, true piety; and that from this charity is derived. It is a mistake then to suppose, that merely the rudiments and first principles of righteousness are delivered in the Law, to form a kind of introduction to good works, and not to guide to the perfect performance of them.

For complete perfection, nothing more can be required than is expressed in these passages of Moses and Paul. How far, pray, would he wish to go, who is not satisfied with the instruction which directs man to the fear of

God, to spiritual worship, practical obedience; in fine, purity of conscience, faith unfeigned, and charity? This confirms that interpretation of the Law, which searches out, and finds in its precepts, all the duties of piety and charity. Those who merely search for dry and meager elements, as if it taught the will of God only by halves, by no means understand its end, the Apostle being witness.

52 Why, in the Gospels and Epistles, the latter table only mentioned, and not the first. The same thing occurs in the Prophets.

As, in giving a summary of the Law, Christ and the Apostles sometimes omit the First Table, very many fall into the mistake of supposing that their words apply to both tables. In Matthew, Christ calls "judgment, mercy, and faith," the "weightier matters of the Law." I think it clear, that by *faith* is here meant veracity towards men. But in order to extend the words to the whole Law, some take it for piety towards God. This is surely to no purpose. For Christ is speaking of those works by which a man ought to approve himself as just. If we attend to this, we will cease to wonder why, elsewhere, when asked by the young man, "What good thing shall I do, that I may have eternal life?" he simply answers, that he must keep the commandments, "Thou shalt do no murder, Thou shalt not commit adultery, Thou shalt not steal, Thou shalt not bear false witness, Honor thy father and thy mother: and, Thou shalt love thy neighbor as thyself" (Matthew 19:16, 18).

The obedience of the First Table consisted almost entirely either in the internal affection of the heart, or in ceremonies. The affection of the heart was not visible, and hypocrites were diligent in the observance of ceremonies; but the works of charity were of such a nature as to be a solid attestation of righteousness. The same thing occurs so frequently in the Prophets, that it must be familiar to everyone who has any tolerable acquaintance with them. For, almost on every occasion, when they exhort men to repentance, omitting the First Table, they insist on faith, judgment, mercy, and equity. Nor do they, in this way, omit the fear of God. They only require a serious proof of it from its signs. It is well known, indeed, that when they treat of the Law, they generally insist on the Second Table, because therein the cultivation of righteousness and integrity is best manifested. There is no occasion to quote passages. Everyone can easily for himself perceive the truth of my observation.

53 An objection to what is said in the former section removed.

Is it then true, you will ask, that it is a more complete summary of righteousness to live innocently with men, than piously towards God? By no means; but because no man, as a matter of course, observes charity in all respects, unless he seriously fear God, such observance is a proof of piety also. To this we may add, that the Lord, well knowing that none of our good deeds can reach him (as the Psalmist declares, (Psalm 16:2), does not demand from us duties towards himself, but exercises us in good works towards our neighbor.

Hence, the Apostle, not without cause, makes the whole perfection of the saints to consist in charity (Ephesians 3:19; Colossians 3:14). And in another passage, he not improperly calls it the "fulfilling of the law," adding, "he that loveth another has fulfilled the law" (Romans 13:8). And again, "All the law is fulfilled in this: Thou shalt love thy neighbor as thyself" (Galatians 5:14). For this is the very thing which Christ himself teaches when he says, "All things whatsoever ye would that men should do to you, do ye even so to them: for this is the law and the prophets" (Matthew 7:12). It is certain that, in the law and the prophets, faith, and whatever pertains to the due worship of God, holds the first place, and that to this charity is made subordinate; but our Lord means, that in the Law the observance of justice and equity towards men is prescribed as the means which we are to employ in testifying a pious fear of God, if we truly possess it.

54 A conduct duly regulated by the divine Law, characterized by charity toward our neighbor. This subverted by those who give the first place to self-love. Refutation of their opinion.

Let us therefore hold, that our life will be framed in best accordance with the will of God, and the requirements of his Law, when it is, in every respect, most advantageous to our brethren. But in the whole Law, there is not one syllable, which lays down a rule as to what man is to do or avoid for the advantage of his own carnal nature. And, indeed, since men are naturally prone to excessive self-love, which they always retain, however great their departure from the truth may be, there was no need of a law to inflame a love already existing in excess.

Hence, it is perfectly plain, that the observance of the Commandments consists not in the love of ourselves, but in the love of God and our neighbor; and that he leads the best and holiest life who as little as may be studies and lives for himself; and that none lives worse and more unrighteously than he who studies and lives only for himself, and seeks and thinks only of his own.

Nay, the better to express how strongly we should be inclined to love our neighbor, the Lord has made self-love the standard, there being no feeling in our nature of greater strength and vehemence. The force of the expression ought to be carefully weighed. He does not (as some sophists have stupidly dreamed) assign the first place to self-love, and the second to charity. He rather transfers to others the love, which we naturally feel for ourselves. Hence, the Apostle declares, that charity "seeketh not her own" (1 Corinthians 13:5). Nor is the argument worth a straw, that the thing regulated must always be inferior to the rule. The Lord did not make self-love the rule, as if love towards others was subordinate to it; but whereas, through natural gravity, the feeling of love usually rests on ourselves, he shows that it ought to diffuse itself in another direction—that we should be prepared to do good to our neighbor with no less alacrity, ardor, and solicitude, than to ourselves.

55 Who our neighbor. Double error of the Schoolmen on this point.

Our Savior having shown, in the parable of the Samaritan (Luke 10:36), that the term *neighbor* comprehends the most remote stranger, there is no reason for limiting the precept of love to our own connections. I deny not that the closer the relation the more frequent our offices of kindness should be. For the condition of humanity requires that there be more duties in common between those who are more nearly connected by the ties of relationship, or friendship, or neighborhood. And this is done without any offense to God, by whose providence we are in a manner impelled to do it. But I say that the whole human race, without exception, are to be embraced with one feeling of charity: that here there is no distinction of Greek or Barbarian, worthy or unworthy, friend or foe, since all are to be viewed not in themselves, but in God. If we turn aside from this view, there is no wonder that we entangle ourselves in error. Wherefore, if we would hold the true course in love, our first step must be to turn our eyes not to man, the sight of whom might oftener produce hatred than love, but to God, who requires that the love which we bear to him be diffused among all mankind, so that our fundamental principle must ever be, Let a man be what he may, he is still to be loved, because God is loved.

56 This error consists in converting precepts into counsels to be observed by monks.

Wherefore, nothing could be more pestilential than the ignorance or wickedness of the Schoolmen in converting the precepts respecting revenge and the love of enemies (precepts which had formerly been delivered to all the Jews, and were then delivered universally to all Christians) into counsels which it was free to obey or disobey, confining the necessary observance of them to the monks, who were made more righteous than ordinary Christians, by the simple circumstance of voluntarily binding themselves to obey counsels. The reason they assign for not receiving them as laws is, that they seem too heavy and burdensome, especially to Christians, who are under the law of grace.

Have they, indeed, the hardihood to remodel the eternal law of God concerning the love of our neighbor? Is there a page of the Law in which any such distinction exists; or rather do we not meet in every page with commands, which, in the strictest terms, require us to love our enemies? What is meant by commanding us to feed our enemy if he is hungry, to bring back his ox or his ass if we meet it going astray, or help it up if we see it lying under its burden? (Proverbs 25:21; Exodus 23:4). Shall we show kindness to cattle for man's sake, and have no feeling of good will to himself? What? Is not the word of the Lord eternally true: "Vengeance is mine, I will repay?" (Deuteronomy 32:35). This is elsewhere more explicitly stated: "Thou shalt not avenge, nor bear any grudge against the children of thy people" (Leviticus 19:18). Let them either erase these passages from the Law, or let them acknowledge the Lord as a Lawgiver, not falsely feign him to be merely a counselor.

57 Refutation of this error from Scripture and the ancient Theologians. Sophistical objection obviated.

And what, pray, is meant by the following passage, which they have dared to insult with this absurd gloss? "Love your enemies, bless them that curse you, do good to them that hate you, and pray for them which despitefully use you, and persecute you; that ye may be the children of your Father which is in heaven" (Matthew 5:44, 45).

Who does not here concur in the reasoning of Chrysostom, that the nature of the motive makes it plain that these are not exhortations, but precepts? For what is left to us if we are excluded from the number of the children of God? According to the Schoolmen, monks alone will be the children of our Father in heaven—monks alone will dare to invoke God as their Father. And in the meantime, how will it fare with the Church?

By the same rule, she will be confined to heathens and publicans. For our Savior says, "If ye love them which love you, what reward have ye? do not even the publicans the same?" It will truly be well with us if we are left only the name of Christians, while we are deprived of the inheritance of the kingdom of heaven!

Nor is the argument of Augustine less forcible: "When the Lord forbids adultery, he forbids it in regard to the wife of a foe not less than the wife of a friend; when he forbids theft, he does not allow stealing of any description, whether from a friend or an enemy."

Now, these two commandments, "Thou shalt not steal, Thou shalt not commit adultery," Paul brings under the rule of love; nay, he says that they are briefly comprehended in this saying; "Thou shalt love thy neighbor as thyself" (Romans 13:9). Therefore, Paul must either be a false interpreter of the Law, or we must necessarily conclude, that under this precept we are bound to love our enemies just as our friends. Those, then, show themselves to be in truth the children of Satan who thus licentiously shake off a yoke common to the children of God. It may be doubted whether, in promulgating this dogma, they have displayed greater stupidity or impudence.

There is no ancient writer who does not hold it as certain that these are pure precepts. It was not even doubted in the age of Gregory, as is plain from his decided assertion; for he holds it to be incontrovertible that they are precepts. And how stupidly they argue! The burden, say they, was too difficult for Christians to hear! As if anything could be imagined more difficult than to love the Lord with all the heart, and soul, and strength. Compared with this Law, there is none that may not seem easy, whether it be to love our enemy, or to banish every feeling of revenge from our minds. To our weakness, indeed, everything, even to the minutest tittle of the Law, is arduous and difficult.

In the Lord, we have strength. It is his to give what he orders, and to order what he wills. That Christians are under the law of grace means not that they are to wander unrestrained without law, but that they are engrafted into Christ, by whose grace they are freed from the curse of the Law, and by whose Spirit they have the Law written in their hearts. This grace Paul has termed, but not in the proper sense of the term, a law, alluding to the Law of God, with which he was contrasting it. The Schoolmen, laying hold of the term *Law*, make it the groundwork of their vain speculations.

58 Error of the Schoolmen consists in calling hidden impiety and covetousness venial sins. Refutation drawn, A. From a consideration of the whole Decalogue. B. The testimony of an Apostle. C. The authority of Christ. D. The nature and majesty of God. E. The sentence pronounced against sin. Conclusion.

The same must be said of their application of the term, venial sin, both to the hidden impiety, which violates the First Table, and the direct transgression of the last commandment of the Second Table. They define venial sin to be, desire unaccompanied with deliberate assent, and not remaining long in the heart. But I maintain that it cannot even enter the heart unless through a want of those things which are required in the Law. We are forbidden to have strange gods. When the mind, under the influence of distrust, looks elsewhere or is seized with some sudden desire to transfer its blessedness to some other quarter, whence are these movements, however evanescent, but just because there is some empty corner in the soul to receive such temptations? And, not to lengthen out the discussion, there is a precept to love God with the whole heart, and mind, and soul; and, therefore, if all the powers of the soul are not directed to the love of God, there is a departure from the obedience of the Law; because those internal enemies which rise up against the dominion of God, and countermand his edicts prove that his throne is not well established in our consciences.

It has been shown that the last commandment goes to this extent. Has some undue longing sprung up in our mind? Then we are chargeable with covetousness, and stand convicted as transgressors of the Law. For the Law forbids us not only to meditate and plan our neighbor's loss, but also to be stimulated and inflamed with covetousness. But every transgression of the Law lays us under the curse, and therefore even the slightest desires cannot be exempted from the fatal sentence. "In weighing our sins," says Augustine, "let us not use a deceitful balance, weighing at our own discretion what we will, and how we will, calling this heavy and that light: but let us use the divine balance of the Holy Scriptures, as taken from the treasury of the Lord, and by it weigh every offense, nay, not weigh, but rather recognize what has been already weighed by the Lord." And what saith the Scripture? Certainly when Paul says, that "the wages of sin is death" (Romans 6:23), he shows that he knew nothing of this vile distinction. As we are but too prone to hypocrisy, there was very little occasion for this sop to soothe our torpid consciences.

59 Refutation drawn, A. From a consideration of the whole Decalogue. B. The testimony of an Apostle. C. The authority of Christ. D. The nature and majesty of God. E. The sentence pronounced against sin. Conclusion.

I wish they would consider what our Savior meant when he said, "Whosoever shall break one of these least commandments, and shall teach men so, he shall be called the least in the kingdom of heaven" (Matthew 5:19). Are they not of this number when they presume to extenuate the transgression of the Law, as if it were unworthy of death? The proper course had been to consider not simply what is commanded, but who it is that commands, because every least transgression of his Law derogates from his authority. Do they count it a small matter to insult the majesty of God in anyone respect? Again, since God has explained his will in the Law, everything contrary to the Law is displeasing to him. Will they feign that the wrath of God is so disarmed that the punishment of death will not forthwith follow upon it? He has declared plainly (if they could be induced to listen to his voice, instead of darkening his clear truth by their insipid subtleties), "The soul that sinneth it shall die" (Ezekiel 18:20). Again, in the passage lately quoted, "The wages of sin is death."

What these men acknowledge to be sin, because they are unable to deny it, they contend is not mortal. Having already indulged this madness too long, let them learn to repent; or, if they persist in their infatuation, taking no further notice of them, let the children of God remember that all sin is mortal, because it is rebellion against the will of God, and necessarily provokes his anger; and because it is a violation of the Law, against every violation of which, without exception, the judgment of God has been pronounced. The faults of the saints are indeed venial, not, however, in their own nature, but because, through the mercy of God, they obtain pardon.

Chapter 9

CHRIST, THOUGH KNOWN TO THE JEWS UNDER THE LAW, YET ONLY MANIFESTED UNDER THE GOSPEL.

There are three principal heads in this chapter. I. Preparatory to a consideration of the knowledge of Christ, and the benefits procured by him; the 1st and 2nd sections are occupied with the dispensation of this knowledge, which, after the manifestation of Christ in the flesh, was more clearly revealed than under the Law. II. A refutation of the profane dream of Servetus, that the promises are entirely abrogated, section 3. Likewise, a refutation of those who do not properly compare the Law with the Gospel, section 4. III. A necessary and brief exposition of the ministry of John Baptist, which occupies an intermediate place between the law and the Gospel.

Sections

1. *The holy fathers under the Law saw the day of Christ, though obscurely. He is more fully revealed to us under the Gospel. A reason for this, confirmed by the testimony of Christ and his Apostles.*

2. *The term Gospel, used in its most extensive sense, comprehends the attestations of mercy, which God gave to the fathers. Properly, however, it means the promulgation of grace exhibited in the God-man Jesus Christ.*

3. *The notion of Servetus, that the promises are entirely abolished, refuted. Why we must still trust to the promises of God. Another reason. Solution of a difficulty.*

4. *Refutation of those who do not properly compare the Law and the Gospel. Answer to certain questions here occurring. The Law and the Gospel briefly compared.*

5. *Third part of the chapter. Of the ministry of John the Baptist.*

1 The holy fathers under the Law saw the day of Christ, though obscurely. He is more fully revealed to us under the Gospel. A reason for this, confirmed by the testimony of Christ and his Apostles.

Since God was pleased (and not in vain) to testify in ancient times by means of expiations and sacrifices that he was a Father, and to set apart for himself a chosen people, he was doubtless known even then in the same character in which he is now fully revealed to us. Accordingly Malachi, having enjoined the Jews to attend to the Law of Moses (because after his death there was to be an interruption of the prophetical office), immediately after declares that the Sun of righteousness should arise (Malachi 4:2); thus intimating, that though the Law had the effect of keeping the pious in expectation of the coming Messiah, there was ground to hope for much greater light on his advent. For this reason, Peter, speaking of the ancient prophets, says, "Unto whom it was revealed, that not unto themselves, but unto us, they did minister the things which are now reported unto you by them that have preached the Gospel unto you, with the Holy Ghost sent down from heaven" (1 Peter 1:12). Not that the prophetical doctrine was useless to the ancient people, or unavailing to the prophets themselves, but that they did not obtain possession of the treasure which God has transmitted to us by their hands. The grace of which they testified is now set familiarly before our eyes. They had only a slight foretaste; to us is given a fuller fruition.

Our Savior, accordingly, while he declares that Moses testified of him, extols the superior measure of grace bestowed upon us (John 5:46). Addressing his disciples, he says, "Blessed are your eyes, for they see, and your ears, for they hear. For verily I say unto you, That many prophets and righteous men have desired to see those things which ye see, and have not seen them, and to hear those things which ye hear, and have not heard them" (Matthew 13:15; Luke 10:23).

It is no small commendation of the Gospel revelation, that God has preferred us to holy men of old, so much distinguished for piety. There is nothing in this view inconsistent with another passage, in which our Savior says, "Your father Abraham rejoiced to see my day, and he saw it and was glad" (John 8:56). For though the event being remote, his view of it was obscure, he had full assurance that it would one day be accomplished; and hence the joy which the holy patriarch experienced even to his death. Nor does John Baptist, when he says, "No man has seen God at any time; the only begotten Son, which is in the bosom of the Father, he has declared him" (John 1:18), exclude the pious who had previously died from a participation in the knowledge and light which are manifested in the person of Christ; but comparing their condition with ours, he intimates that the mysteries which they only beheld dimly under shadows are made clear to us; as is well explained by the author of the Epistle to the Hebrews, in these words, "God, who at sundry times and in divers manners spake in time past unto the fathers by the prophets, has in these last days spoken unto us by his Son" (Hebrews 1:1, 2).

Hence, although this only begotten Son, who is now to us the brightness of his Father's glory and the express image of his person, was formerly made known to the Jews, as we have elsewhere shown from Paul, that he was the Deliverer under the old dispensation; it is nevertheless true, as Paul himself elsewhere declares, that "God, who commanded the light to shine out of darkness, has shined in our hearts, to give the light of the knowledge of the glory of God in the face of Jesus Christ" (2 Corinthians 4:6); because, when he appeared in this his image, he in a manner made himself visible, his previous appearance having been shadowy and obscure. More shameful and more detestable, therefore, is the ingratitude of those who walk blindfold in this meridian light. Accordingly, Paul says, "The god of this world has blinded their minds, lest the light of the glorious Gospel of Christ should shine unto them" (2 Corinthians 4:4).

2 The term Gospel, used in its most extensive sense, comprehends the attestations of mercy, which God gave to the fathers. Properly, however, it means the promulgation of grace exhibited in the God-man Jesus Christ.

By the Gospel, I understand the clear manifestation of the mystery of Christ. I confess, indeed, that inasmuch as the term Gospel is applied by Paul to the doctrine of faith (2 Timothy 4:10), it includes all the promises by which God reconciles men to himself, and which occur throughout the Law. For Paul there opposes faith to those terrors, which vex and torment the conscience when salvation is sought by means of works. Hence, it follows that *Gospel*, taken in a large sense, comprehends the evidences of mercy and paternal favor, which God bestowed on the Patriarchs. Still, by way of excellence, it is applied to the promulgation of the grace manifested in Christ. This is not only founded on general use, but has the sanction of our Savior and his Apostles. Hence, it is described as one of his peculiar characteristics, that he preached the Gospel of the kingdom (Matthew 4:23; 9:35; Mark 1:14).

Mark, in his preface to the Gospel, calls it "*The beginning of the Gospel of Jesus Christ.* There is no use of collecting passages to prove what is already perfectly known. Christ at his advent "brought life and immortality to light through the Gospel" (2 Timothy 1:10). Paul does not mean by these words that the Fathers were plunged in the darkness of death before the Son of God became incarnate; but he claims for the Gospel the honorable distinction of being a new and extraordinary kind of embassy, by which God fulfilled what he had promised, these promises being realized in the person of the Son. For though believers have at all times experienced the truth of Paul's declaration, that "all the promises of God in him are yea and amen," inasmuch as these promises were sealed upon their hearts; yet because he has in his flesh completed all the parts of our salvation, this vivid manifestation of realities was justly entitled to this new and special distinction.

Accordingly, Christ says, "Hereafter ye shall see heaven open, and the angels of God ascending and descending upon the Son of man." For though he seems to allude to the ladder which the Patriarch Jacob saw in vision, he commends the excellence of his advent in this, that it opened the gate of heaven, and gave us familiar access to it.

3 The notion of Servetus, that the promises are entirely abolished, refuted. Why we must still trust to the promises of God. Another reason. Solution of a difficulty.

Here, we must guard against the diabolical imagination of Servetus, who, from a wish, or at least the pretence of a wish, to extol the greatness of Christ, abolishes the promises entirely, as if they had ended at the same time with the Law. He pretends that by the faith of the Gospel, all the promises have been fulfilled as if there were no distinction between Christ and us. I lately observed that Christ had not left any part of our salvation incomplete; but from this it is erroneously inferred, that we are now put in possession of all the blessings purchased by him; thereby implying, that Paul was incorrect in saying, "We are saved by hope" (Romans 3:24).

I admit, indeed, that by believing in Christ we pass from death unto life; but we must at the same time remember the words of John, that though we know we are "the sons of God," "it does not yet appear what we shall be: but we know that, when he shall appear, we shall be like him; for we shall see him as he is" (1 John 3:2). Therefore, although Christ offers us in the Gospel a present fullness of spiritual blessings, fruition remains in the keeping of hope, until we are divested of corruptible flesh, and transformed into the glory of him who has gone before us.

Meanwhile, in leaning on the promises, we obey the command of the Holy Spirit, whose authority ought to have weight enough with us to silence all the barking of that impure dog. We have it on the testimony of Paul: "Godliness is profitable unto all things, having promise of the life that now is, and of that which is to come" (1 Timothy 4:8). For this reason, he glories in being "an apostle of Jesus Christ, according to the promise of life which is in Christ Jesus" (2 Timothy 1:1). And he elsewhere reminds us, that we have the same promises that were given to the saints in ancient time (2 Corinthians 7:1). In fine, he makes the sum of our felicity consist in being sealed with the Holy Spirit of promise. Indeed we have no enjoyment of Christ, unless by embracing him as clothed with his own promises. Hence, it is that he indeed dwells in our hearts and yet we are as pilgrims in regard to him, because "we walk by faith, not by sight" (2 Corinthians 5:6, 7).

There is no inconsistency in the two things—viz. that in Christ we possess everything pertaining to the perfection of the heavenly life, and yet that faith is only a vision "of things not seen" (Hebrews 11:1). Only there is this difference to be observed in the nature or quality of the promises: that the Gospel points with the finger to what the Law shadowed under types.

4 **Refutation of those who do not properly compare the Law and the Gospel. Answer to certain questions here occurring. The Law and the Gospel briefly compared.**

Hence, also, we see the error of those who, in comparing the Law with the Gospel, represent it merely as a comparison between the merit of works, and the gratuitous imputation of righteousness. The contrast thus made is by no means to be rejected, because, by the term Law, Paul frequently understands that rule of holy living in which God exacts what is his due, giving no hope of life unless we obey in every respect; and, on the other hand, denouncing a curse for the slightest failure. This Paul does when showing that we are freely accepted of God, and accounted righteous by being pardoned, because that obedience of the Law to which the reward is promised is nowhere to be found. Hence, he appropriately represents the righteousness of the Law and the Gospel as opposed to each other. But the Gospel has not succeeded the whole Law in such a sense as to introduce a different method of salvation. It rather confirms the Law, and proves that everything that it promised is fulfilled. What was shadow, it has made substance. When Christ says that the Law and the Prophets were until John, he does not consign the fathers to the curse, which, as the slaves of the Law, they could not escape. He intimates that they were only imbued with the rudiments, and remained far beneath the height of the Gospel doctrine.

Accordingly Paul, after calling the Gospel "the power of God unto salvation to everyone that believeth," shortly after adds, that it was "witnessed by the Law and the Prophets" (Romans 1:16; 3:21). And in the end of the same Epistle, though he describes "the preaching of Jesus Christ" as "the revelation of the mystery which was kept secret since the world began," he modifies the expression by adding, that it is "now made manifest" "by the scriptures of the prophets" (Romans 16:25, 26). Hence, we infer that when the whole Law is spoken of, the Gospel differs from it only in respect of clearness of manifestation. Still, because of the inestimable riches of grace set before us in Christ, there is good reason for saying, that by his advent the kingdom of heaven was erected on the earth (Matthew 12:28).

5 Third part of the chapter. Of the ministry of John the Baptist.

John stands between the Law and the Gospel, holding an intermediate office allied to both. For though he gave a summary of the Gospel when he pronounced Christ to be "the Lamb of God who taketh away the sin of the world," yet, inasmuch as he did not unfold the incomparable power and glory which shone forth in his resurrection, Christ says that he was not equal to the Apostles. For this is the meaning of the words: "Among them that are born of woman, there has not risen a greater than John the Baptist: notwithstanding, he that is least in the kingdom of heaven is greater than he" (Matthew 11:28). He is not there commending the persons of men, but after preferring John to all the Prophets, he gives the first place to the preaching of the Gospel, which is elsewhere designated by the kingdom of heaven. When John himself, in answer to the Jews, says that he is only "a voice" (John 1:23), as if he were inferior to the Prophets it is not in pretended humility but he means to teach that the proper embassy was not entrusted to him, that he only performed the office of a messenger, as had been foretold by Malachi, "Behold, I will send you Elijah the prophets before the coming of the great and dreadful day of the Lord" (Malachi 4:5). And, indeed, during the whole course of his ministry, he did nothing more than prepare disciples for Christ. He even proves from Isaiah that this was the office to which he was divinely appointed. In this sense, he is said by Christ to have been "a burning and a shining light" (John 5:35), because full day had not yet appeared. And yet, this does not prevent us from classing him among the preachers of the Gospel, since he used the same baptism that was afterwards committed to the Apostles. Still, however, he only began that which had freer course under the Apostles, after Christ was taken up into the heavenly glory.

Chapter 10

THE RESEMBLANCE BETWEEN THE OLD TESTAMENT AND THE NEW.

This chapter consists of four parts. I. The sum, utility, and necessity of this discussion, section 1. II. A proof that, generally speaking, the old and new dispensations are in reality one, although differently administered. Three points in which the two dispensations entirely agree, sections 2–4. III. The Old Testament, as well as the New, had regard to the hope of immortality and a future life, whence two other resemblances or points of agreement follow—viz. that both were established by the free mercy of God, and confirmed by the intercession of Christ. This proved by many arguments, passages of Scripture, and examples, sections 5–23. IV. Conclusion of the whole chapter, where, for fuller confirmation, certain passages of Scripture are produced. Refutation of the cavils of the Sadducees and other Jews.

Sections

1. Introduction, showing the necessity of proving the similarity of both dispensations in opposition to Servetus and the Anabaptists.

2. This similarity in general. Both covenants truly one, though differently administered. Three things in which they entirely agree.

3. First general similarity, or agreement—viz. that the Old Testament, equally with the New, extended its promises beyond the present life, and held out a sure hope of immortality. Reason for this resemblance. Objection answered.

4. The other two points of resemblance—viz. that both covenants were established in the mercy of God, and confirmed by the mediation of Christ.

5. The first of these points of resemblance being the foundation of the other two, a lengthened proof is given of it. The first argument taken from a passage, in which Paul, showing that the sacraments of both dispensations had the same meaning, proves that the condition of the ancient church was similar to ours.

6. *An objection from John 6:49—viz. that the Israelites ate manna in the wilderness, and are dead, whereas Christians eat the flesh of Christ, and die not. Answer reconciling this passage of the Evangelist with that of the Apostle.*

7. *Another proof from the Law and the Prophets—viz. the power of the divine word in quickening souls before Christ was manifested. Hence, the believing Jews were raised to the hope of eternal life.*

8. *Third proof from the form of the covenant, which shows that it was in reality one both before and after the manifestation of Christ in the flesh.*

9. *Confirmation of the former proof from the clear terms in which the form is expressed. Another confirmation derived from the former and from the nature of God.*

10. *Fourth proof from examples. Adam, Abel, and Noah, when tried with various temptations, neglecting the present, aspired with living faith and invincible hope to a better life. They, therefore, had the same aim as believers under the Gospel.*

11. *Continuation of the fourth proof from the example of Abraham, whose call and whole course of life shows that he ardently aspired to eternal felicity. Objection disposed of.*

12. *Continuation of the fourth proof from the examples of Isaac and Jacob.*

13. *Conclusion of the fourth proof. Adam, Abel, Noah, Abraham, Isaac, Jacob, and others under the Law, looked for the fulfillment of the divine promises not on the earth, but in heaven. Hence, they termed this life an earthly pilgrimage, and desired to be buried in the land of Canaan, which was a figure of eternal happiness.*

14. *A fifth proof from Jacob's earnestness to obtain the birthright. This shows a prevailing desire of future life. This perceived in some degree by Balaam.*

15. *A sixth proof from David, who expects such great things from the Lord, and yet declares the present life to be mere vanity.*

16. *A seventh proof also from David. His descriptions of the happiness of believers could only be realized in a future state.*

17. *An eighth proof from the common feeling and confession of all the pious who sought by faith and hope to obtain in heaven what they did not see in the present shadowy life.*

18. A continuation and confirmation of the former proof from the exultation of the righteous, even amid the destruction of the world.

19. A ninth proof from Job, who spoke most distinctly of this hope. Two objections disposed of.

20. A tenth proof from the later Prophets, who taught that the happiness of the righteous was placed beyond the limits of the present life.

21. This clearly established by Ezekiel's vision of the dry bones, and a passage in Isaiah.

22. Last proof from certain passages in the Prophets, which clearly show the future immortality of the righteous in the kingdom of heaven.

23. Conclusion of the whole discussion concerning the similarity of both dispensations. For fuller confirmation, four passages of Scripture produced. Refutation of the error of the Sadducees and other Jews, who denied eternal salvation and the sure hope of the Church.

1 **Introduction, showing the necessity of proving the similarity of both dispensations in opposition to Servetus and the Anabaptists.**

From what has been said above, it must now be clear, that all whom, from the beginning of the world, God adopted as his peculiar people, were taken into covenant with him on the same conditions, and under the same bond of doctrine, as ourselves; but as it is of no small importance to establish this point, I will here add it by way of appendix, and show, since the Fathers were partakers with us in the same inheritance, and hoped for a common salvation through the grace of the same Mediator, how far their condition in this respect was different from our own. For although the passages which we have collected from the Law and the Prophets for the purpose of proof, make it plain that there never was any other rule of piety and religion among the people of God; yet as many things are written on the subject of the difference between the Old and New Testaments in a manner which may perplex ordinary readers, it will be proper here to devote a special place to the better and more exact discussion of this subject.

This discussion, which would have been most useful at any rate, has been rendered necessary by that monstrous miscreant, Servetus, and some madmen of the sect of the Anabaptists, who think of the people of Israel just as they would do of some herd of swine, absurdly imagining that the Lord gorged them with temporal blessings here, and gave them no hope of a blessed immortality. Let us guard pious minds against this pestilential error, while we at the same time remove all the difficulties that are wont to start up when mention is made of the difference between the Old and the New Testaments. By the way also, let us consider what resemblance and what difference there is between the covenant which the Lord made with the Israelites before the advent of Christ, and that which he has made with us now that Christ is manifested.

2 This similarity in general. Both covenants truly one, though differently administered. Three things in which they entirely agree.

It is possible, indeed, to explain both in one word. The covenant made with all the fathers is so far from differing from ours in reality and substance, that it is altogether one and the same: still the administration differs. But because this brief summary is insufficient to give anyone a full understanding of the subject, our explanation to be useful must extend to greater length. It was superfluous, however, in showing the similarity, or rather identity, of the two dispensations, again to treat of the particulars that have already been discussed, as it was unseasonable to introduce those that are still to be considered elsewhere. What we propose to insist upon here may be reduced to three heads: —First, That temporal opulence and felicity was not the goal to which the Jews were invited to aspire, but that they were admitted to the hope of immortality, and that assurance of this adoption was given by immediate communications, by the Law and by the Prophets. *Secondly*, That the covenant by which they were reconciled to the Lord was founded on no merits of their own, but solely on the mercy of God, who called them; and, *thirdly*, That they both had and knew Christ the Mediator, by whom they were united to God, and made capable of receiving his promises. The second of these, as it is not yet perhaps sufficiently understood, will be fully considered in its own place (Book 3, chapters 15–18). For we will prove by many clear passages in the Prophets, that all which the Lord has ever given or promised to his people is of mere goodness and indulgence. The third also has, in various places, been not obscurely demonstrated. Even the first has not been left unnoticed.

3 First general similarity, or agreement—viz. that the Old Testament, equally with the New, extended its promises beyond the present life, and held out a sure hope of immortality. Reason for this resemblance. Objection answered.

As the first is most pertinent to the present subject, and is most contradicted, we shall enter more fully into the consideration of it, taking care, at the same time, where any of the others requires explanations to supply it by the way, or afterwards add it in its proper place. The Apostle, indeed, removes all doubt when he says that the Gospel which God gave concerning his Son, Jesus Christ, "he had promised aforetime by his prophets in the holy Scriptures" (Romans 1:2). And again, that "the righteousness of God without the law is manifested, being witnessed by the law and the prophets" (Romans 3:21). For the Gospel does not confine the hearts of men to the enjoyment of the present life, but raises them to the hope of immortality; does not fix them down to earthly delights, but announcing that there is a treasure laid up in heaven, carries the heart thither also. For in another place he thus explains, "After that ye believed [the Gospel,] ye were sealed with that Holy Spirit of promise, which is the earnest of our inheritance unto the redemption of the purchased possession" (Ephesians 1:13, 14). Again, "Since we heard of your faith in Christ Jesus, and of the love which ye have to all the saints, for the hope which is laid up for you in heaven, whereof ye heard before in the word of the truth of the Gospel" (Colossians 1:4). Again, "Whereunto he called you by our Gospel to the obtaining of the glory of our Lord Jesus Christ" (2 Thessalonians 2:14).

Whence also it is called the word of salvation and the power of God, with salvation to everyone that believes, and the kingdom of heaven. But if the doctrine of the Gospel is spiritual, and gives access to the possession of incorruptible life, let us not suppose that those to whom it was promised and declared altogether neglected the care of the soul, and lived stupidly like cattle in the enjoyment of bodily pleasures. Let no one here quibble and say, that the promises concerning the Gospel, which are contained in the Law and the Prophets, were designed for a new people. Paul, shortly after making that statement concerning the Gospel promised in the Law, adds that, "whatsoever things the law saith, it saith to those who are under the law." I admit, indeed, he is there treating of a different subject, but when he said that everything contained in the Law was directed to the Jews, he was not so oblivious as not to remember what he had said a few verses before of the Gospel promised in the Law. Most clearly, therefore, does the Apostle demonstrate that the Old Testament had special reference to the future life, when he says that the promises of the Gospel were comprehended under it.

4 The other two points of resemblance—viz. that both covenants were established in the mercy of God, and confirmed by the mediation of Christ.

In the same way, we infer that the Old Testament was both established by the free mercy of God and confirmed by the intercession of Christ. For the preaching of the Gospel declares nothing more than sinners, without any merit of their own, are justified by the paternal indulgence of God. It is wholly summed up in Christ. Who, then, will presume to represent the Jews as destitute of Christ, when we know that they were parties to the Gospel covenant, which has its only foundation in Christ? Who will presume to make them aliens to the benefit of gratuitous salvation, when we know that they were instructed in the doctrine of justification by faith? And not to dwell on a point which is clear, we have the remarkable saying of our Lord, "Your father Abraham rejoiced to see my day, and he saw it and was glad" (John 8:56)). What Christ here declares of Abraham, an apostle shows to be applicable to all believers, when he says that Jesus Christ is the "same yesterday, today, and forever" (Hebrews 13:8). For he is not there speaking merely of the eternal divinity of Christ, but of his power, of which believers always had full proof. Hence, both the blessed Virgin and Zachariah, in their hymns, say that the salvation revealed in Christ was a fulfillment of the mercy promised "to our fathers, to Abraham, and to his seed forever" (Luke 1:55, 72). If, by manifesting Christ, the Lord fulfilled his ancient oath, it cannot be denied that the subject of that oath must ever have been Christ and eternal life.

5 The first of these points of resemblance being the foundation of the other two, a lengthened proof is given of it. The first argument taken from a passage, in which Paul, showing that the sacraments of both dispensations had the same meaning, proves that the condition of the ancient church was similar to ours.

Nay, the Apostle makes the Israelites our equals, not only in the grace of the covenant, but also in the signification of the Sacraments. For employing the example of those punishments, which the Scripture states to have been of old inflicted on the Jews, in order to deter the Corinthians from falling into similar wickedness, he begins with premising that they have no ground to claim for themselves any privilege which can exempt them from the divine vengeance which overtook the Jews, since the Lord not only visited them with the same mercies, but also distinguished his grace among them by the same symbols: as if he had said, If you think you are out of danger, because the Baptism which you received, and the Supper of which you daily partake, have excellent promises, and if, in the meantime, despising the goodness of God, you indulge in licentiousness, know that the Jews, on whom the Lord inflicted his severest judgments, possessed similar symbols. They were baptized in passing through the sea, and in the cloud that protected them from the burning heat of the sun. It is said, that this passage was a carnal baptism, corresponding in some degree to our spiritual baptism. But if so, there would be a want of conclusiveness in the argument of the Apostle, whose object is to prevent Christians from imagining that they excelled the Jews in the matter of baptism. Besides, the cavil cannot apply to what immediately follows—viz. that they did "all eat the same spiritual meat; and did all drink the same spiritual drink: for they drank of that spiritual Rock that followed them: and that Rock was Christ" (1 Corinthians 10:3, 4).

6 An objection from John 6:49—viz. that the Israelites ate manna in the wilderness, and are dead, whereas Christians eat the flesh of Christ, and die not. Answer reconciling this passage of the Evangelist with that of the Apostle.

To take off the force of this passage of Paul, an objection is founded on the words of our Savior, "Your fathers did eat manna in the wilderness, and are dead." "If any man eat of this bread, he shall live forever" (John 6:49, 51). There is no difficulty in reconciling the two passages. The Lord, as he was addressing hearers who only desired to be filled with earthly food, while they cared not for the true food of the soul, in some degree adapts his speech to their capacity, and, in particular, to meet their carnal view, draws a comparison between manna and his own body. They called upon him to prove his authority by performing some miracle, such as Moses performed in the wilderness when he obtained manna from heaven. In this manna, they saw nothing but a relief of the bodily hunger from which the people were then suffering; they did not penetrate to the more sublime mystery to which Paul refers. Christ, therefore, to demonstrate that the blessing which they ought to expect from him was more excellent than the lauded one which Moses had bestowed upon their fathers, draws this comparison: If, in your opinion, it was a great and memorable miracle when the Lord, by Moses, supplied his people with heavenly food that they might be supported for a season, and not perish in the wilderness from famine; from this infer how much more excellent is the food which bestows immortality. We see why our Lord omitted to mention what was of principal virtue in the manna, and mentioned only its meanest use. Since the Jews had, by way of upbraiding, cast up Moses to him as one who had relieved the necessity of the people by means of manna, he answers, that he was the minister of a much larger grace, one compared with which the bodily nourishment of the people, on which they set so high a value, ought to be held worthless. Paul, again, knowing that the Lords when he rained manna from heaven, had not merely supplied their bodies with food, but had also dispensed it as containing a spiritual mystery to typify the spiritual quickening which is obtained in Christ, does not overlook that quality which was most deserving of consideration. Wherefore it is surely and clearly proved, that the same promises of celestial and eternal life, which the Lord now gives to us, were not only communicated to the Jews, but also sealed by truly spiritual sacraments. This subject is copiously discussed by Augustine in his work against Faustus the Manichee.

7 Another proof from the Law and the Prophets—viz. the power of the divine word in quickening souls before Christ was manifested. Hence, the believing Jews were raised to the hope of eternal life.

But if my readers would rather have passages quoted from the Law and the Prophets, from which they may see, as we have already done from Christ and the Apostles, that the spiritual covenant was common also to the Fathers, I will yield to the wish, and the more willingly, because opponents will thus be more surely convinced, that henceforth there will be no room for evasion. And I will begin with a proof that, though I know it will seem futile and almost ridiculous to supercilious Anabaptists, will have very great weight with the docile and sober-minded. I take it for granted that the word of God has such an inherent efficacy, that it quickens the souls of all whom he is pleased to favor with the communication of it. Peter's statement has ever been true, that it is an incorruptible seed, "which liveth and abideth forever" (1 Peter 1:23), as he infers from the words of Isaiah (Isaiah 40:6).

Now when God, in ancient times, bound the Jews to him by this sacred bond, there cannot be a doubt that he separated them unto the hope of eternal life. When I say that they embraced the word, which brought them nearer to God, I refer not to that general method of communication, which is diffused through heaven and earth, and all the creatures of the world, and which, though it quickens all things, each according to its nature, rescues none from the bondage of corruption. I refer to that special mode of communication by which the minds of the pious are both enlightened in the knowledge of God, and, in a manner, linked to him. Adam, Abel, Noah, Abraham, and the other patriarchs, having been united to God by this illumination of the word, I say there cannot be the least doubt that entrance was given them into the immortal kingdom of God. They had that solid participation in God, which cannot exist without the blessing of everlasting life.

8 Third proof from the form of the covenant, which shows that it was in reality one both before and after the manifestation of Christ in the flesh.

If the point still seems somewhat involved, let us pass to the form of the covenant, which will not only satisfy calm thinkers, but also sufficiently establish the ignorance of gainsayers. The covenant, which God always made with his servants, was this, "I will walk among you, and will be your God, and ye shall be my people" (Leviticus 26:12). These words, even as the prophets are wont to expound them, comprehend life and salvation, and the whole sum of blessedness. For David repeatedly declares, and with good reason, "Happy is that people whose God is the Lord." "Blessed is the nation whose God is the Lord; and the people whom he has chosen for his own inheritance" (Psalm 144:15; 33:12); and this not merely in respect of earthly happiness, but because he rescues from death, constantly preserves, and, with eternal mercy, visits those whom he has adopted for his people.

As is said in other prophets, "Art not thou from everlasting, O Lord my God, mine Holy One? we shall not die." "The Lord is our judge, the Lord is our lawgiver, the Lord is our king; he will save us" "Happy art thou,

O Israel: who is like unto thee, O people saved by the Lord?" (Hebrews 1:12; Isaiah 33:22; Deuteronomy 33:29). But not to labor superfluously, the prophets are constantly reminding us that no good thing and, consequently, no assurance of salvation, is wanting, provided the Lord is our God. And justly. For if his face, the moment it hath shone upon us, is a perfect pledge of salvation, how can he manifest himself to anyone as his God, without opening to him the treasures of salvation? The terms on which God makes himself ours is to dwell in the midst of us, as he declared by Moses (Leviticus 26:11). But such presence cannot be enjoyed without life being, at the same time, possessed along with it.

And though nothing more had been expressed, they had a sufficiently clear promise of spiritual life in these words, "I am your God" (Exodus 6:7). For he declared that he would be a God not to their bodies only, but especially to their souls. Souls, however, if not united to God by righteousness, remain estranged from him in death. On the other hand, that union, wherever it exists, will bring perpetual salvation with it.

9 Confirmation of the former proof from the clear terms in which the form is expressed. Another confirmation derived from the former and from the nature of God.

To this we may add, that he not only declared he was, but also promised that he would be, their God. By this, their hope was extended beyond present good, and stretched forward into eternity. Moreover, that this observance of the future had the effect appears from the many passages in which the faithful console themselves not only in their present evils, but also for the future, by calling to mind that God was never to desert them. Moreover, in regard to the second part of the promise—viz. the blessing of God, its extending beyond the limits of the present life was still more clearly confirmed by the words, I will be the God of your seed after you (Genesis 17:7). If he was to manifest his favor to the dead by doing good to their posterity, much less would he deny his favor to them. God is not like men, who transfer their love to the children of their friends, because the opportunity of bestowing kind offices as they wished upon themselves is interrupted by death. But God, whose kindness is not impeded by death, does not deprive the dead of the benefit of his mercy, which, on their account, he continues to a thousand generations.

God, therefore, was pleased to give a striking proof of the abundance and greatness of his goodness, which they were to enjoy after death, when he described it as overflowing to all their posterity (Exodus 20:6). The truth of this promise was sealed, and in a manner completed, when, long after the death of Abraham, Isaac, and Jacob, he called himself their God (Exodus 20:6). And why? Was not the name absurd if they had perished? It would have been just the same as if he had said, I am the God of men who exist not. Accordingly, the Evangelists relate that, by this very argument, our Savior refuted the Sadducees (Matthew 22:23; Luke 20:32), who were, therefore, unable to deny that the resurrection of the dead was attested by Moses, inasmuch as he had taught them that all the saints are in his hand (Deuteronomy 33:3). Whence it is easy to infer that death is not the extinction of those who are taken under the tutelage, guardianship, and protection of him who is the disposer of life and death.

10 Fourth proof from examples. Adam, Abel, and Noah, when tried with various temptations, neglecting the present, aspired with living faith and invincible hope to a better life. They, therefore, had the same aim as believers under the Gospel.

Let us now see (and on this the controversy principally turns) whether or not believers themselves were so instructed by the Lord, as to feel that they had elsewhere a better life, and to aspire to it while disregarding the present. First, the mode of life which heaven had imposed upon them made it a constant exercise, by which they were reminded, that if in this world only they had hope, they were of all men the most miserable. Adam, most unhappy even in the mere remembrance of his lost felicity, with difficulty supplies his wants by anxious labors; and that the divine curse might not be restricted to bodily labor, his only remaining solace becomes a source of the deepest grief: Of two sons, the one is torn from him by the parricidal hand of his brother; while the other, who survives, causes detestation and horror by his very look. Abel, cruelly murdered in the very flower of his days, is an example of the calamity, which had come upon man.

While the whole world are securely living in luxury, Noah, with much fatigue, spends a great part of his life in building an ark. He escapes death, but by greater troubles than a hundred deaths could have given. Besides his ten months' residence in the ark, as in a kind of sepulcher, nothing could have been more unpleasant than to have remained so long pent up among the filth of beasts. After escaping these difficulties, he falls into a new cause of sorrow. He sees himself mocked by his own son, and is forced, with his own mouth, to curse one whom, by the great kindness of God, he had received safe from the deluge.

11 Continuation of the fourth proof from the example of Abraham, whose call and whole course of life shows that he ardently aspired to eternal felicity. Objection disposed of.

Abraham alone ought to be to us equal to tens of thousands if we consider his faith, which is set before us as the best model of believing, to whose race also we must be held to belong in order that we may be the children of God. What could be more absurd than that Abraham should be the father of all the faithful, and not even occupy the meanest corner among them? He cannot be denied a place in the list; nay, he cannot be denied one of the most honorable places in it, without the destruction of the whole Church. Now, as regards his experience in life, the moment he is called by the command of God, he is torn away from friends, parents, and country, objects in which the chief happiness of life is deemed to consist, as if it had been the fixed purpose of the Lord to deprive him of all the sources of enjoyment. No sooner does he enter the land in which he was ordered to dwell, than he is driven from it by famine. In the country to which he retires to obtain relief, he is obliged, for his personal safety, to expose his wife to prostitution. This must have been more bitter than many deaths. After returning to the land of his habitation, he is again expelled by famine. What is the happiness of inhabiting a land where you must so often suffer from hunger, nay, perish from famine, unless you flee from it? Then, again, with Abimelech, he is reduced to the same necessity of saving his head by the loss of his wife (Genesis 12:12). While he wanders up and down uncertain for many years, he is compelled, by the constant quarrelling of servants to part with his nephew, who was to him as a son. This departure must doubtless have cost him a pang something like the cutting off of a limb. Shortly after, he learns that his nephew is carried off, captive by the enemy. Wherever he goes, he meets with savage-hearted neighbors, who will not even allow him to drink of the wells, which he has dug with great labor. For he would not have purchased the use from the king of Gerar if he had not been previously prohibited. After he had reached the verge of life, he sees himself childless (the bitterest and most unpleasant feeling to old age), until, beyond expectation, Ishmael is born; and yet he pays dearly for his birth in the reproaches of Sarah, as if he was the cause of domestic disturbance by encouraging the contumacy of a female slave. At length Isaac is born, but in return, the first-born Ishmael is displaced, and almost hostilely driven forth and abandoned. Isaac remains alone, and the good man, now worn out with age, has his heart upon him, when shortly after he is ordered to offer him up in sacrifice.

What can the human mind conceive more dreadful than for the father to be the murderer of his son? Had he been carried off by disease, who would not have thought the old man much to be pitied in having a son given to him in mockery, and in having his grief for being childless doubled to him? Had he been slain by some stranger, this would, indeed, have been much worse than natural death. But all these calamities are little compared with the murder of him by his father's hand. Thus, in fine, during the whole course of his life, he was harassed and tossed in such a way, that anyone desirous to give a picture of a calamitous life could not find one more appropriate. Let it not be said that he was not so very distressed, because he at length escaped from all these tempests. He is not said to lead a happy life who, after infinite difficulties during a long period, at last laboriously works out his escape, but he who calmly enjoys present blessings without any alloy of suffering.

12 Continuation of the fourth proof from the examples of Isaac and Jacob.

Isaac is less afflicted, but he enjoys very few of the sweets of life. He also meets with those vexations, which do not permit a man to be happy on the earth. Famine drives him from the land of Canaan; his wife is torn from his bosom; his neighbors are always annoying and vexing him in all kinds of ways, so that he is even obliged to fight for water. At home, he suffers great annoyance from his daughters-in-law; he is stung by the dissension of his sons, and has no other cure for this great evil than to send the son whom he had blessed into exile (Genesis 26:27); Jacob, again, is nothing but a striking example of the greatest wretchedness. His boyhood is passed most uncomfortably at home amidst the threats and alarms of his elder brother, and to these he is at length forced to give way (Genesis 27:28); A fugitive from his parents and his native soil, in addition to the hardships of exile, the treatment he receives from his uncle Laban is in no respect milder and more humane (Genesis 29). As if it had been little to spend seven years of hard and rigorous servitude, he is cheated in the matter of a wife. For the sake of another wife, he must undergo a new servitude, during which, as he himself complains, the heat of the sun scorches him by day, while in frost and cold he spends the sleepless night (Genesis 31:40, 41). For twenty years, he spends this bitter life, and daily suffers new injuries from his father-in-law. Nor is he quiet at home, which he sees disturbed and almost broken up by the hatreds, quarrels, and jealousies of his wives. When he is ordered to return to his native land, he is obliged to take his departure in a manner resembling an ignominious flight. Even then, he is unable to escape the injustice of his father-in-law, but in the midst of his journey is assailed by him with contumely and reproach (Genesis 31:20) By and by a much greater difficulty befalls him (Genesis 32, 33). For as he approaches his brother, he has as many forms of death in prospect as a cruel foe could invent. Hence, while waiting for his arrival, he is distracted and excruciated by direful terrors; and when he comes into his sight, he falls at his feet like one half dead, until he perceives him to be more placable than he had ventured to hope. Moreover, when he first enters the land, he is bereaved of Rachel his only beloved wife. Afterwards he hears that the son whom she had borne him, and whom he loved more than all his other children, is devoured by a wild beast (Genesis 37:33).

How deep the sorrow caused by his death he himself evinces, when, after long tears, he obstinately refuses to be comforted, declaring that he will go down to the grave to his son mourning. In the meantime, what vexation, anxiety, and grief, must he have received from the carrying off and dishonor of his daughter, and the cruel revenge of his sons, which not only brought him into bad odor with all the inhabitants of the country, but exposed him to the greatest danger of extermination? (Genesis 34) Then follows the horrid wickedness of Reuben his first-born, wickedness than which none could be committed more grievous (Genesis 36:22). The dishonor of a wife being one of the greatest of calamities, what must be said when a son perpetrates the atrocity? Some time after, the family is again polluted with incest (Genesis 38:18).

All these disgraces might have crushed a mind otherwise the most firm and unbroken by misfortune. Towards the end of his life, when he seeks relief for himself and his family from famine, he is struck by the announcement of a new misfortune, that one of his sons is detained in prison, and that to recover him he must entrust to others his dearly beloved Benjamin (Genesis 42, 43). Who can think that in such a series of misfortunes, one moment was given him in which he could breathe secure? Accordingly, his own best witness, he declares to Pharaoh, "Few and evil have the days of the years of my life been" (Genesis 47:9). In declaring that he had spent his life in constant wretchedness, he denies that he had experienced the prosperity, which had been promised him by the Lord. Jacob, therefore, either formed a malignant and ungrateful estimate of the Lord's favor, or he truly declared that he had lived miserable on the earth. If so, it follows that his hope could not have been fixed on earthly objects.

13 Conclusion of the fourth proof. Adam, Abel, Noah, Abraham, Isaac, Jacob, and others under the Law, looked for the fulfillment of the divine promises not on the earth, but in heaven. Hence, they termed this life an earthly pilgrimage, and desired to be buried in the land of Canaan, which was a figure of eternal happiness.

If these holy Patriarchs expected a happy life from the hand of God (and it is indubitable that they did), they viewed and contemplated a different happiness from that of a terrestrial life. This is admirably shown by an Apostle, "By faith he [Abraham] sojourned in the land of promise, as in a strange country, dwelling in tabernacles with Isaac and Jacob, the heirs with him of the same promise: for he looked for a city which has foundations, whose builder and maker is God." "These all died in faith, not having received the promises, but having seen them afar off, and were persuaded of them, and embraced them, and confessed that they were strangers and pilgrims on the earth. For they that say such things declare plainly that they seek a country. And truly, if they had been mindful of that country from whence they came out, they might have had opportunity to return. But now they desire a better country, that is, a heavenly: wherefore God is not ashamed to be called their God: for he has prepared for them a city" (Hebrews 11:9, 10, 13–16). They had been duller than blocks in so persistently pursuing promises, no hope of which appeared upon the earth, if they had not expected their completion elsewhere. They called this world a pilgrimage. The Apostle specifically and with reason urges this, as does Moses. (Genesis 47:9). If they were pilgrims and strangers in the land of Canaan, where is the promise of the Lord that appointed them heirs of it? It is clear, therefore, that the promise of possession that they had received looked further. Hence, they did not acquire a foot breadth in the land of Canaan, except for sepulture; thus testifying that they hoped not to receive the benefit of the promise until after death. And this is the reason that Jacob set so much value on being buried there, that he took Joseph bound by oath to see it done; and why Joseph wished that his bones should some ages later, long after they had moldered into dust, be carried thither (Genesis 47:29, 30; 50:25).

14 **A fifth proof from Jacob's earnestness to obtain the birthright. This shows a prevailing desire of future life. This perceived in some degree by Balaam.**

In short, it is manifest, that in the whole course of their lives, they had an eye to future blessedness. Why should Jacob have aspired so earnestly to primogeniture, and intrigued for it at so much risk, if it was to bring him only exile and destitution, and no good at all, unless he looked to some higher blessing? And that this was his feeling, he declared in one of the last sentences he uttered, "I have waited for thy salvation, O God" (Genesis 49:18). What salvation could he have waited for, when he felt himself breathing his last, if he did not see in death the beginning of a new life? And why talk of saints and the children of God, when even one, who otherwise strove to resist the truth, was not devoid of some similar impression? For what did Balaam mean when he said, "Let me die the death of the righteous, and let my last end be like his" (Numbers 23:10), unless he felt convinced of what David afterward declares, "Precious in the sight of the Lord is the death of his saints?" (Psalm 116:15; 34:12). If death were the goal and ultimate limit, no distinction could be observed between the righteous and the wicked. The true distinction is the different lot, which awaits them after death.

15 **A sixth proof from David, who expects such great things from the Lord, and yet declares the present life to be mere vanity.**

We have not yet come further down than the books of Moses, whose only office, according to our opponents, was to induce the people to worship God, by setting before them the fertility of the land, and its general abundance; and yet to everyone who does not voluntarily shun the light, there is clear evidence of a spiritual covenant. But if we come down to the Prophets, the kingdom of Christ and eternal life are there exhibited in the fullest splendor. First, David, as earlier in time, in accordance with the order of the Divine procedure, spoke of heavenly mysteries more obscurely than they, and yet with what clearness and certainty does he point to it in all he says.

The value he put upon his earthly habitation is attested by these words, "I am a stranger with thee, and a sojourner, as all my fathers were. Verily every man at his best estate is altogether vanity. Surely every man walketh in a vain show. And now, Lord, what wait I for? My hope is in thee" (Psalm 39:12, 5, 6, 7). He who confesses that there is nothing solid or stable on the earth, and yet firmly retains his hope in God, undoubtedly contemplates happiness reserved for him elsewhere. To this contemplation, he is wont to invite believers whenever he would have them to be truly comforted. For, in another passages after speaking of human life as a fleeting and evanescent show, he adds, "The mercy of the Lord is from everlasting to everlasting upon them that fear him" (Psalm 103:17). To this there is a corresponding passage in another psalm, "Of old thou hast laid the foundation of the earth; and the heavens are the work of thy hands. They shall perish, but thou shalt endure; yea, all of them shall wax old like a garment; as a vesture shalt thou change them, and they shall be changed; but thou art the same, and thy years shall have no end. The children of thy servants shall continue, and their seed shall be established before thee" (Psalm 102:25-28).

If, notwithstanding of the destruction of the heavens and the earth, the godly cease not to be established before God, it follows, that their salvation is connected with his eternity. But this hope could have no existence, if it did not lean upon the promise as expounded by Isaiah, "The heavens shall vanish away like smoke, and the earth shall wax old like a garment, and they that dwell therein shall die in like manner; but my salvation shall be forever, and my righteousness shall not be abolished" (Isaiah 51:6). Perpetuity is here attributed to righteousness and salvation, not as they reside in God, but as men experience them.

16 A seventh proof also from David. His descriptions of the happiness of believers could only be realized in a future state.

Nor can those things, which are everywhere said as to the prosperous success of believers, be understood in any other sense than as referring to the manifestation of celestial glory. Of this nature are the following passages: "He preserveth the souls of his saints; he delivereth them out of the hand of the wicked. Light is sown for the righteous, and gladness for the upright in heart." "His righteousness endureth forever; his horn shall be exalted with honor—the desire of the wicked shall perish." "Surely the righteous shall give thanks unto thy name; the upright shall dwell in thy presence." "The righteous shall be in everlasting remembrance." "The Lord redeemeth the soul of his servants." But the Lord often leaves his servants, not only to be annoyed by the violence of the wicked, but to be lacerated and destroyed; allows the good to languish in obscurity and squalid poverty, while the ungodly shine forth among the stars; and even by withdrawing the light of his countenance does not leave them lasting joy. Wherefore, David by no means disguises the fact, that if believers fix their eyes on the present condition of the world, they will be grievously tempted to believe that with God integrity has neither favor nor reward; so much does impiety prosper and flourish, while the godly are oppressed with ignominy, poverty, contempt, and every kind of cross. The Psalmist says, "But as for me, my feet were almost gone; my steps had well nigh slipped. For I was envious of the foolish, when I saw the prosperity of the wicked." At length, after a statement of the case, he concludes, "When I thought to know this, it was too painful for me: until I went into the sanctuary of God; then understood I their end" (Psalm 73:2, 3, 16, 17).

17 An eighth proof from the common feeling and confession of all the pious who sought by faith and hope to obtain in heaven what they did not see in the present shadowy life.

Therefore, even from this confession of David, let us learn that the holy fathers under the Old Testament were not ignorant that in this world God seldom or never gives his servants the fulfillment of what is promised them, and therefore has directed their minds to his sanctuary, where the blessings not exhibited in the present shadowy life are treasured up for them. This sanctuary was the final judgment of God, which, as they could not at all discern it by the eye, they were contented to apprehend by faith. Inspired with this confidence, they doubted not that whatever might happen in the world, a time would at length arrive when the divine promises would be fulfilled.

This is attested by such expressions as these: "As for me, I will behold thy face in righteousness: I shall be satisfied, when I awake, with thy likeness" (Psalm 17:15). "I am like a green olive tree in the house of God" (Psalm 52:8). Again, "The righteous shall flourish like the palm tree: he shall grow like a cedar in Lebanon. Those that be planted in the house of the Lord shall flourish in the courts of our God. They shall still bring forth fruit in old age; they shall be fat and flourishing" (Psalm 92:12-14). He had exclaimed a little before "O Lord, how great are thy works! And thy thoughts are very deep." "When the wicked spring as the grass, and when all the workers of iniquity do flourish: it is that they shall be destroyed forever."

Where was this splendor and beauty of the righteous, unless when the appearance of this world was changed by the manifestation of the heavenly kingdom? Lifting their eyes to the eternal world, they despised the momentary hardships and calamities of the present life, and confidently broke out into these exclamations: "He shall never suffer the righteous to be moved. But thou, O God, shalt bring them down into the pit of destruction: bloody and deceitful men shall not live out half their days" (Psalm 55:22, 23). Where in this world is there a pit of eternal destruction to swallow up the wicked, of whose happiness it is elsewhere said, "They spend their days in wealth, and in a moment go down to the grave?" (Job 21:13).

On the other hand, is the great stability of the saints, who, as David complains, are not only disturbed, but also everywhere utterly bruised and oppressed? It is here. He set before his eyes not merely the unstable vicissitudes of the world, tossed like a troubled sea, but what the Lord is to do when he shall one day sit to fix the eternal constitution of heaven and earth, as he in another place elegantly describes: "They that trust in their wealth, and boast themselves in the multitude of their riches; none of them can by any means redeem his brother, nor give to God a ransom for him." "For he sees that wise men die, likewise the fool and the brutish person perish, and leave their wealth to others. Their inward thought is, that their houses shall continue forever, and their dwelling-places to all generations; they call their lands after their own names. Nevertheless, man being in honor abideth not: he is like the beasts that perish. This their way is their folly: yet their posterity approve their sayings. Like sheep they are laid in the grave; death shall feed on them; and the upright shall have dominion over them in the morning; and their beauty shall consume in the grave from their dwelling" (Psalm 49:6, 7 10–14).

By this derision of the foolish for resting satisfied with the slippery and fickle pleasures, of the world, he shows that the wise must seek for a very different felicity. But he more clearly unfolds the hidden doctrine of the resurrection when he sets up a kingdom to the righteous after the wicked are cast down and destroyed. For what, pray, are we to understand by the "morning," unless it is the revelation of a new life, commencing when the present comes to an end?

18 A continuation and confirmation of the former proof from the exultation of the righteous, even amid the destruction of the world.

Hence, the consideration which believers employed as a solace for their sufferings, and a remedy for their patience: "His anger endureth but a moment: in his favor is life" (Psalm 30:5). How did their afflictions, which continued almost throughout the whole course of life, terminate in a moment? Where did they see the long duration of the divine benignity, of which they had only the slightest taste? Had they clung to earth, they could have found nothing of the kind; but looking to heaven, they saw that the period during which the Lord afflicted his saints was but a moment, and that the mercies with which he gathers them are everlasting: on the other hand, they foresaw that for the wicked, who only dreamed of happiness for a day, there was reserved an eternal and never-ending destruction.

Hence, those expressions: "The memory of the just is blessed, but the name of the wicked shall rot" (Proverbs 10:7). "Precious in the sight of the Lord is the death of his saints" (Psalm 116:15). Again in Samuel: "The Lord will keep the feet of his saints, and the wicked shall be silent in darkness" (1 Samuel 2:9); showing they knew well, that however much the righteous might be tossed about, their latter end was life and peace; that however pleasant the delights of the wicked, they gradually lead down to the chambers of death. They accordingly designated the death of such persons as the death "of the uncircumcised," that is, persons cut off from the hope of resurrection (Ezekiel 28:10; 31:18). Hence, David could not imagine a greater curse than this: "Let them be blotted out of the book of the living, and not be written with the righteous" (Psalm 69:28).

19 A ninth proof from Job, who spoke most distinctly of this hope. Two objections disposed of.

The most remarkable passage of all is that of Job: "I know that my Redeemer liveth, and that he shall stand at the latter day upon the earth: and though after my skin worms destroy this body, yet in my flesh shall I see God: whom I shall see for myself, and mine eyes shall behold, and not another" (Job 19:25-7). Those who would make a display of their acuteness, pretend that these words are to be understood not of the last resurrection, but of the day when Job expected that God would deal more gently with him. Granting that this is partly meant, we shall, however, compel them, whether they will or not, to admit that Job never could have attained to such fullness of hope if his thoughts had risen no higher than the earth. It must, therefore, be confessed, that he who saw that the Redeemer would be present with him when lying in the grave, must have raised his eyes to a future immortality. To those who think only of the present life, death is the extremity of despair; but it could not destroy the hope of Job. "Though he slay me," said he, "yet will I trust in him" (Job 13:15). Let no trifler here burst in with the objection that these are the sayings of a few, and do not by any means prove that there was such a doctrine among the Jews. To this my instant answer is, that these few did not in such passages give utterance to some hidden wisdom, to which only distinguished individuals were admitted privately and apart from others, but that having been appointed by the Holy Spirit to be the teachers of the people, they openly promulgated the mysteries of God, which all in common behaved to learn as the principles of public religion. When, therefore, we hear that those passages in which the Holy Spirit spoke so distinctly and clearly of the spiritual life were public oracles in the Jewish Church, it would be intolerably perverse to confine them entirely to a carnal covenant relating merely to the earth and earthly riches.

20 A tenth proof from the later Prophets, who taught that the happiness of the righteous was placed beyond the limits of the present life.

When we descend to the later prophets, we have it in our power to expatiate freely as in our own field. If, when David, Job, and Samuel, were in question, the victory was not difficult, much easier is it here; for the method and economy which God observed in administering the covenant of his mercy was, that the nearer the period of its full exhibition approached, the greater the additions which were daily made to the light of revelation.

Accordingly, at the beginning, when the first promise of salvation was given to Adam (Genesis 3:15), only a few slender sparks beamed forth: additions being afterwards made, a greater degree of light began to be displayed, and continued gradually to increase and shine with greater brightness, until at length all the clouds being dispersed, Christ the Sun of righteousness arose, and with full refulgence illumined all the earth (Malachi 4). In appealing to the Prophets, therefore, we can have no fear of any deficiency of proof; but as I see an immense mass of materials, which would occupy us much longer than compatible with the nature of our present work (the subject, indeed, would require a large volume), and as I trust, that by what has already been said, I have paved the way, so that every reader of the very least discernment may proceed without stumbling, I will avoid a prolixity, for which at present there is little necessity; only reminding my readers to facilitate the entrance by means of the key which was formerly put into their hands (*supra*, Chapter 4, sections 3, 4); namely, that whenever the Prophets make mention of the happiness of believers (a happiness of which scarcely any vestiges are discernible in the present life), they must have recourse to this distinction: that the better to commend the Divine goodness to the people, they used temporal blessings as a kind of lineaments to shadow it forth, and yet gave such a portrait as might lift their minds above the earth, the elements of this world, and all that will perish, and compel them to think of the blessedness of a future and spiritual life.

21 This clearly established by Ezekiel's vision of the dry bones, and a passage in Isaiah.

One example will suffice. When the Israelites were carried away to Babylon, their dispersion seemed to be the next thing to death, and they could scarcely be dissuaded from thinking that Ezekiel's prophecy of their restoration (Ezekiel 37:4) was a mere fable, because it seemed to them the same thing as if he had prophesied that putrid caresses would be raised to life. The Lord, in order to show that, even in that case, there was nothing to prevent him from making room for his kindness, set before the prophet in vision a field covered with dry bones, to which, by the mere power of his word, he in one moment restored life and strength. The vision served, indeed, to correct the unbelief of the Jews at the time, but it also reminded them how much further the power of the Lord extended than to the bringing back of the people, since by a single nod it could so easily give life to dry scattered bones. Wherefore, the passage may be fitly compared with one in Isaiah, "Thy dead men shall live, together with my dead body shall they arise. Awake and sing, ye that dwell in dust: for thy dew is as the dew of herbs, and the earth shall cast out the dead. Come, my people, enter thou into thy chambers, and shut thy doors about thee: hide thyself for a little moment, until the indignation be overpast. For, behold, the Lord cometh out of his place to punish the inhabitants of the earth for their iniquity: the earth also shall disclose her blood, and shall no more cover her slain" (Isaiah 26:19-21).

22 Last proof from certain passages in the Prophets, which clearly show the future immortality of the righteous in the kingdom of heaven.

It would be absurd however to interpret all the passages on a similar principle, for there are several which point without any veil to the future immortality which awaits believers in the kingdom of heaven. Some of them we have already quoted, and there are many others, but especially the following two. The one is in Isaiah, "As the new heavens and the new earth, which I will make, shall remain before me, saith the Lord, so shall your seed and your name remain. And it shall come to pass, that from one new moon to another, and from one Sabbath to another, shall all flesh come to worship before me, saith the Lord. And they shall go forth, and look upon the caresses of the men that have transgressed against me: for their worm shall not die, neither shall their fire be quenched; and they shall be an abhorring unto all flesh" ((Isaiah 66:22-24). The other passage is in Daniel. "At that time shall Michael stand up, the great prince which standeth for the children of thy people: and there shall be a time of trouble, such as there never was since there was a nation even to that same time: and at that time thy people shall be delivered, everyone shall be found written in the book. And many of them that sleep in the dust of the earth shall awake, some to everlasting life, and some to shame and everlasting contempt" (Daniel 12:1, 2).

23 Conclusion of the whole discussion concerning the similarity of both dispensations. For fuller confirmation, four passages of Scripture produced. Refutation of the error of the Sadducees and other Jews, who denied eternal salvation and the sure hope of the Church.

In proving the two remaining points—viz. that the Patriarchs had Christ as the pledge of their covenant, and placed all their hope of blessing in him, as they are clearer, and not so much refuted, I will be less particular. Let us then lay it down confidently as a truth which no engines of the devil can destroy—that the Old Testament or covenant which the Lord made with the people of Israel was not confined to earthly objects, but contained a promise of spiritual and eternal life, the expectation of which behaved to be impressed on the minds of all who truly consented to the covenant. Let us put far from us the senseless and pernicious notion, that the Lord proposed nothing to the Jews, or that they sought nothing but full supplies of food, carnal delights, abundance of wealth, external influence, a numerous offspring, and all those things which our animal nature deems valuable. For, even now, the only kingdom of heaven which our Lord Jesus Christ promises to his followers, is one in which they may sit down with Abraham, and Isaac and Jacob (Matthew 8:11); and Peter declared of the Jews of his day, that they were heirs of Gospel grace because they were the sons of the prophets, and comprehended in the covenant which the Lord of old made with his people (Acts 3:25). And that this might not be attested by words merely, our Lord approved it by act (Matthew 27:52). At the moment when he rose again, he deigned to make many of the saints partakers of his resurrection, and allowed them to be seen in the city; thus giving a sure earnest, that everything which he did and suffered in the purchase of eternal salvation belonged to believers under the Old Testament, just as much as to us. Indeed, as Peter testifies, they were endued with the same spirit of faith by which we are regenerated to life (Acts 15:8). When we hear that that spirit, which is a kind of spark of immortality in us (whence it is called the "earnest" of our inheritance, (Ephesians 1:14), dwelt in like manner in them, how can we presume to deny them the inheritance? Hence, it is the more wonderful how the Sadducees of old fell into such a degree of drunkenness as to deny both the resurrection and the substantive existence of spirits, both of which where attested to them by so many striking passages of Scripture. Nor would the stupidity of the whole nation in the present day, in expecting an earthly reign of the Messiah, be less wonderful, had not the Scriptures foretold this long before as the punishment which they were to suffer for rejecting the Gospel, God, by a just judgment, blinding minds which voluntarily invite darkness, by rejecting the offered light of heaven. They read, and are constantly turning over the pages of Moses, but a veil prevents them from seeing the light which beams forth in his countenance (2 Corinthians 3:14); and thus to them he will remain covered and veiled until they are converted to Christ, between whom and Moses they now study, as much as in them lies, to maintain a separation.

Chapter 11

THE DIFFERENCE BETWEEN THE
TWO TESTAMENTS.

This chapter consists principally of three parts. I. Five points of difference between the Old and the New Testament, sections 1–11. II. The last of these points being, that the Old Testament belonged to the Jews only, whereas the New Testament belongs to all; the calling of the Gentiles is shortly considered, section 12. III. A reply to two objections usually taken to what is here taught concerning the difference between the Old and the New Testaments, sections 13, 14.

Sections

1. Five points of difference between the Old and the New Testaments. These belong to the mode of administration rather than the substance. First difference. In the Old Testament, the heavenly inheritance is exhibited under temporal blessings; in the New, aids of this description are not employed.

2. Proof of this first difference from the simile of an heir in pupillarity, as in Galatians 4:1.

3. This the reason that the Patriarchs, under the Law, set a higher value on this life and the blessings of it, and dreaded the punishments, these being even more striking. Why severe and sudden punishments existed under the Law.

4. A second difference. The Old Testament typified Christ under ceremonies. The New exhibits the immediate truth and the whole body. The scope of the Epistle to the Hebrews in explaining this difference. Definition of the Old Testament.

5. Hence, the Law our Schoolmaster to bring us unto Christ.

6. Notwithstanding, among those under the Law, some of the strongest examples of faith are exhibited, their equals being scarcely to be found in the Christian Church. The ordinary method of the divine dispensation to be here attended to. These excellent individuals placed under the Law, and aided by ceremonies, that they might behold and hail Christ afar off.

7. *Third difference. The Old Testament is literal, the New spiritual. This difference considered first generally.*

8. *Next treated specially, on a careful examination of the Apostle's text. A threefold antithesis. The Old Testament is literal, deadly, and temporary. The New is spiritual, quickening, and eternal. Difference between the letter and the spirit.*

9. *Fourth difference. The Old Testament belongs to bondage, the New to liberty. This confirmed by three passages of Scripture. Two objections answered.*

10. *Distinction between the three last differences and the first. Confirmation of the above from Augustine. Condition of the patriarchs under the Old Testament.*

11. *Fifth difference. The Old Testament belonged to one people only, the New to all.*

12. *The second part of the chapter depending on the preceding section. Of the calling of the Gentiles. Why the calling of the Gentiles scented to the Apostles so strange and new.*

13. *The last part of the chapter. Two objections considered. A. God, being immutable, cannot consistently disapprove what he once ordered. Answer confirmed by a passage of Scripture.*

14. *Objections. B. God could at first have transacted with the Jews as he now does with Christians. Answer, showing the absurdity of this objection. Another answer founded on a just consideration of the divine will and the dispensation of grace*

1 Five points of difference between the Old and the New Testaments. These belong to the mode of administration rather than the substance. First difference. In the Old Testament, the heavenly inheritance is exhibited under temporal blessings; in the New, aids of this description are not employed.

What, then? you will say, Is there no difference between the Old and the New Testaments? What is to become of the many passages of Scripture in which they are contrasted as things differing most widely from each other? I readily admit the differences which are pointed out in Scripture, but still hold that they derogate in no respect from their established unity, as will be seen after we have considered them in their order. These differences (so far as I have been able to observe them and can remember) seem to be chiefly four, or, if you choose to add a fifth, I have no objections. I hold and think I will be able to show, that they all belong to the mode of administration rather than to the substance. In this way, there is nothing in them to prevent the promises of the Old and New Testament from remaining the same, Christ being the foundation of both. The first difference then is, that though, in old time, the Lord was pleased to direct the thoughts of his people, and raise their minds to the heavenly inheritance, yet, that their hope of it might be the better maintained, he held it forth, and, in a manner, gave a foretaste of it under earthly blessings, whereas the gift of future life, now more clearly and lucidly revealed by the Gospel, leads our minds directly to meditate upon it, the inferior mode of exercise formerly employed in regard to the Jews being now laid aside. Those who attend not to the divine purpose in this respect, suppose that God's ancient people ascended no higher than the blessings, which were promised, to the body. They hear the land of Canaan so often named as the special, and the only, reward of the Divine Law to its worshipers; they hear that the severest punishment which the Lord denounces against the transgressors of the Law is expulsion from the possession of that land and dispersion into other countries; they see that this forms almost the sum of the blessings and curses declared by Moses; and from these things they confidently conclude that the Jews were separated from other nations not on their own account, but for another reason—viz. that the Christian Church might have an emblem in whose outward shape might be seen an evidence of spiritual things.

But since the Scripture sometimes demonstrates that the earthly blessings thus bestowed were intended by God himself to guide them to a heavenly hope, it shows great lack of skill, not to say dullness, not to attend to this mode of dispensation. The ground of controversy is this: our opponents hold that the land of Canaan was considered by the Israelites as supreme and final happiness, and now, since Christ was manifested, typifies to us the heavenly inheritance; whereas we maintain that, in the earthly possession which the Israelites enjoyed, they beheld, as in a mirror, the future inheritance which they believed to be reserved for them in heaven.

2 Proof of this first difference from the simile of an heir in pupillarity, as in Galatians 4:1.

This will better appear from the similitude, which Paul uses in Galatians (Galatians 4:1). He compares the Jewish nation to an heir in pupillarity, who, as yet unfit to govern himself, follows the direction of a tutor or guide to whose charge he has been committed. Though this simile refers especially to ceremonies, there is nothing to prevent us from applying it most appropriately here also. The same inheritance was destined to them as to us, but from nonage, they were incapable of entering to it, and managing it.

They had the same Church, though it was still in puerility. The Lord, therefore kept them under this tutelage, giving them spiritual promises, not clear and simple, but typified by earthly objects. Hence, when he chose Abraham, Isaac, and Jacob, and their posterity, to the hope of immortality, he promised them the land of Canaan for an inheritance, not that it might be the limit of their hopes, but that the view of it might train and confirm them in the hope of that true inheritance, which, as yet, appeared not. And, to guard against delusion, they received a better promise, which attested that this earth was not the highest measure of the divine kindness. Thus, Abraham is not allowed to keep down his thoughts to the Promised Land: by a greater promise, his views are carried upward to the Lord. He is thus addressed, "Fear not, Abram: I am thy shield, and thy exceeding great reward" (Genesis 15:1). Here we see that the Lord is the final reward promised to Abraham that he might not seek a fleeting and evanescent reward in the elements of this world, but look to one which was incorruptible. A promise of the land is afterwards added for no other reason than that it might be a symbol of the divine benevolence, and a type of the heavenly inheritance, as the saints declare their understanding to have been. Thus David rises from temporal blessings to the last and highest of all, "My flesh and my heart faileth: but God is the strength of my heart, and my portion forever." "My heart and my flesh crieth out for the living God" (Psalm 73:26; 84:2). Again, "The Lord is the portion of mine inheritance and of my cup: thou maintainest my lot" (Psalm 16:5). Again "I cried unto thee O Lord: I said Thou art my refuge and my portion in the land of the living" (Psalm 142:5).

Those who can venture to speak thus, assuredly declare that their hope rises beyond the world and worldly blessings. This future blessedness, however, the prophets often describe under a type, which the Lord had taught them. In this way are to be understood the many passages in Job (Job 18:17) and Isaiah, to the effect, That the righteous shall inherit the earth, that the wicked shall be driven out of it, that Jerusalem will abound in all kinds of riches, and Zion overflow with every species at abundance. In strict propriety, all these things obviously apply not to the land of our pilgrimage, or to the earthly Jerusalem, but to the true country, the heavenly city of believers, in which the Lord has commanded blessing and life forevermore (Psalm 133:3).

3 This the reason that the Patriarchs, under the Law, set a higher value on this life and the blessings of it, and dreaded the punishments, these being even more striking. Why severe and sudden punishments existed under the Law.

Hence, the reason that the saints under the Old Testament set a higher value on this mortal life and its blessings than would now be meet. For, though they well knew, that in their race they were not to halt at it as the goal, yet, perceiving that the Lord, in accommodation to their feebleness, had there imprinted the lineaments of his favor, it gave them greater delight than it could have done if considered only in itself. For, as the Lord, in testifying his good will towards believers by means of present blessings, then exhibited spiritual felicity under types and emblems, so, on the other hand, by temporal punishments he gave proofs of his judgment against the reprobate.

Hence, by earthly objects, the favor of the Lord was displayed, as well as his punishment inflicted. The unskillful, not considering this analogy and correspondence (if I may so speak) between rewards and punishments, wonder that there is so much variance in God, that those who, in old time, were suddenly visited for their faults with severe and dreadful punishments, he now punishes much more rarely and less severely, as if he had laid aside his former anger, and, for this reason, they can scarcely help imagining, like the Manichees, that the God of the Old Testament was different from that of the New. But we shall easily disencumber ourselves of such doubts if we attend to that mode of divine administration to which I have adverted—that God was pleased to indicate and typify both the gift of future and eternal felicity by terrestrial blessings, as well as the dreadful nature of spiritual death by bodily punishments, at that time when he delivered his covenant to the Israelites as under a kind of veil.

4 A second difference. The Old Testament typified Christ under ceremonies. The New exhibits the immediate truth and the whole body. The scope of the Epistle to the Hebrews in explaining this difference. Definition of the Old Testament.

Another distinction between the Old and New Testaments is in the types, the former exhibiting only the image of truth, while the reality was absent, the shadow instead of the substance, the latter exhibiting both the full truth and the entire body. Mention is usually made of this, whenever the New Testament is contrasted with the Old, but it is nowhere so fully treated as in the Epistle to the Hebrews (chapters 7–10). The Apostle is there arguing against those who thought that the observances of the Mosaic Law could not be abolished without producing the total ruin of religion. In order to refute this error, he adverts to what the Psalmist had foretold concerning the priesthood of Christ (Psalm 110:4). Seeing that an eternal priesthood is assigned to him, it is clear that the priesthood in which there was a daily succession of priests is abolished. And he proves that the institution of this new Priest must prevail, because confirmed by an oath. He afterwards adds that a change of the priest necessarily led to a change of the covenant. And the necessity of this he confirms by the reason, that the weakness of the law was such, that it could make nothing perfect. He then goes on to show in what this weakness consists, namely, that it had external carnal observances which could not render the worshipers perfect in respect of conscience, because its sacrifices of beasts could neither take away sins nor procure true holiness. He therefore concludes that it was a shadow of good things to come, and not the very image of the things, and accordingly had no other office than to be an introduction to the better hope, which is exhibited in the Gospel.

Here we may see in what respect the legal is compared with the evangelical covenant, the ministry of Christ with that of Moses. If the comparison referred to the substance of the promises, there would be a great repugnance between the two covenants; but since the nature of the case leads to a different view, we must follow it in order to discover the truth. Let us, therefore bring forward the covenant, which God once ratified as eternal and unending. Its completion, whereby it is fixed and ratified, is Christ. Till such completion takes place, the Lord, by Moses, prescribes ceremonies that are formal symbols of confirmation. The point brought under discussion was, Whether or not the ceremonies ordained in the Law behaved to give way to Christ. Although these were merely accidents of the covenant, or at least additions and appendages, and, as they are commonly called, accessories, yet because they were the means of administering it, the name of covenant is applied to them, just as is done in the case of other sacraments.

Hence, in general, the Old Testament is the name given to the solemn method of confirming the covenant comprehended under ceremonies and sacrifices. Since there is nothing substantial in it, until we look beyond it, the Apostle contends that it behaved to be annulled and become antiquated (Hebrews 7:22), to make room for Christ, the surety and mediator of a better covenant, by whom the eternal sanctification of the elect was once purchased, and the transgressions which remained under the Law wiped away. But if you prefer it, take it thus: the covenant of the Lord was old, because veiled by the shadowy and ineffectual observance of ceremonies; and it was therefore temporary, being, in suspense until it received a firm and substantial confirmation. Then only did it become new and eternal when it was consecrated and established in the blood of Christ. Hence, the Savior, in giving the cup to his disciples in the last supper, calls it the cup of the new testament in his blood; intimating, that the covenant of God was truly realized, made new, and eternal, when it was sealed with his blood.

5 Hence, the Law our Schoolmaster to bring us unto Christ.

It is now clear in what sense the Apostle said (Galatians 3:24; 4:1) that, by the tutelage of the Law, the Jews were conducted to Christ before he was exhibited in the flesh. He confesses that they were sons and heirs of God, though, because of nonage, they were placed under the guardianship of a tutor. It was fit, the Sun of Righteousness not yet having risen, that there should neither be so much light of revelation nor such clear understanding. The Lord dispensed the light of his word, so that they could behold it at a distance, and obscurely. Accordingly, Paul designates this slender measure of intelligence by the term *childhood*, which the Lord was pleased to train by the elements of this world, and external observances, until Christ should appear. Through him, the knowledge of believers was to be matured. This distinction was noted by our Savior himself when he said that the Law and the Prophets were until John, that from that time the Gospel of the kingdom was preached (Matthew 11:13). What did the Law and the Prophets deliver to the men of their time? They gave a foretaste of that wisdom which was one day to be clearly manifested, and showed it afar off. But where Christ can be pointed to with the finger, there the kingdom of God is manifested. In him are contained all the treasures of wisdom and understanding, and by these we penetrate almost to the very shrine of heaven.

6 Notwithstanding, among those under the Law, some of the strongest examples of faith are exhibited, their equals being scarcely to be found in the Christian Church. The ordinary method of the divine dispensation to be here attended to. These excellent individuals placed under the Law, and aided by ceremonies, that they might behold and hail Christ afar off.

There is nothing contrary to this in the fact, that in the Christian Church scarcely one is to be found who, in excellence of faith, can be compared to Abraham, and that the Prophets were so distinguished by the power of the Spirit, that even in the present day they give light to the whole world. For the question here is, not what grace the Lord conferred upon a few, but what was the ordinary method which he followed in teaching the people, and which even was employed in the case of those very prophets who were endued with special knowledge above others. For their preaching was both obscure as relating to distant objects, and was included in types. Moreover, however wonderful the knowledge displayed in them, as they were under the necessity of submitting to the tutelage common to all the people, they must also be ranked among children. Lastly, none of them ever had such a degree of discernment as not to savor somewhat of the obscurity of the age. Whence the words of our Savior, "Many kings and prophets have desired to see the things which you see, and have not seen them, and to hear the things which ye hear, and have not heard them. Blessed are your eyes, for they see, and your ears, for they hear" (Matthew 13:17). And it was right that the presence of Christ should have this distinguishing feature, that by means of it the revelation of heavenly mysteries should be made more transparent. To the same effect is the passage, which we formerly quoted from the First Epistle of Peter, that to them it was revealed that their labor should be useful not so much to themselves as to our age.

7
Third difference. The Old Testament is literal, the New spiritual. This difference considered first generally.

I proceed to the third distinction, which is thus expressed by Jeremiah: "Behold, the days come, saith the Lord, that I will make a new covenant with the house of Israel, and with the house of Judah; not according to the covenant that I made with their fathers, in the day that I took them by the hand, to bring them out of the land of Egypt; (which my covenant they brake, although I was an husband unto them, saith the Lord); but this shall be the covenant that I will make with the house of Israel; After those days, saith the Lord, I will put my law in their inward parts, and write it in their hearts; and will be their God, and they shall be my people. And they shall teach no more every man his neighbor, and every man his brother, saying, know the Lord: for they shall all know me, from the least of them unto the greatest of them" (Jeremiah 31:31-34). From these words, the Apostle took occasion to institute a comparison between the Law and the Gospel, calling the one a doctrine of the letter, the other a doctrine of the spirit; describing the one as formed on tables of stone, the other on tables of the heart; the one the preaching of death, the other of life; the one of condemnation, the other of justification; the one made void, the other permanent (2 Corinthians 3:5, 6). The object of the Apostle being to explain the meaning of the Prophet, the worlds of the one furnish us with the means of ascertaining what both understood. And yet, there is some difference between them.

The Apostle speaks of the Law more disparagingly than the Prophet. This he does not simply in respect of the Law itself, but because there were some false zealots of the Law who, by a perverse zeal for ceremonies, obscured the clearness of the Gospel, he treats of the nature of the Law with reference to their error and foolish affection. It will, therefore, be proper to attend to this peculiarity in Paul. Both, however, as they are contrasting the Old and New Testament, consider nothing in the Law but what is peculiar to it. For example, the Law everywhere contains promises of mercy; but as these are adventitious to it, they do not enter into the account of the Law as considered only in its own nature. All which is attributed to it is, that it commands what is right, prohibits crimes, holds forth rewards to the cultivators of righteousness, and threatens transgressors with punishment, while at the same time it neither changes nor amends that depravity of heart which is naturally inherent in all.

8
Next treated specially, on a careful examination of the Apostle's text. A threefold antithesis. The Old Testament is literal, deadly, and temporary. The New is spiritual, quickening, and eternal. Difference between the letter and the spirit.

Let us now explain the Apostle's contrast step by step. The Old Testament is literal, because promulgated without the efficacy of the Spirit: the New spiritual, because the Lord has engraved it on the heart. The second antithesis is a kind of exposition of the first. The Old is deadly, because it can do nothing but involve the whole human race in a curse; the New is the instrument of life, because those who are freed from the curse it restores to favor with God. The former is the ministry of condemnation, because it charges the whole sons of Adam with transgression; the latter the ministry of righteousness, because it unfolds the mercy of God, by which we are justified. The last antithesis must be referred to the Ceremonial Law. Being a shadow of things to come, it behaved in time to perish and vanish away, whereas the Gospel, inasmuch as it exhibits the very body, is firmly established forever. Jeremiah indeed calls the Moral Law also a weak and fragile covenant; but for another reason, namely, because it was immediately broken by the sudden defection of an ungrateful people; but as the blame of such violation is in the people themselves, it is not properly alleged against the covenant. The ceremonies, again, inasmuch as through their very weakness they were dissolved by the advent of Christ, had the cause of weakness from within. Moreover, the difference between the spirit and the letter must not be understood as if the Lord had delivered his Law to the Jews without any good result; i.e. as if none had been converted to him. When we consider the multitude of those whom, by the preaching of the Gospel, he has regenerated by his, Spirit, and gathered out of all nations into the communion of his Church, we may say that those of ancient Israel who, with sincere and heartfelt affections embraced the covenant of the Lord, were few or none, though the number is great when they are considered in themselves without comparison.

9 Fourth difference. The Old Testament belongs to bondage, the New to liberty. This confirmed by three passages of Scripture. Two objections answered.

Out of the third distinction, a fourth arises. In Scripture, the term bondage is applied to the Old Testaments because it begets fear, and the term freedom to the New, because productive of confidence and security. Thus, Paul says to the Romans, "Ye have not received the spirit of bondage again to fear; but ye have received the Spirit of adoption whereby we cry, Abba, Father" (Romans 8:15). To the same effect is the passage in the Hebrews, "For ye are not come unto the mount that might be touched, and that burned with fire, nor unto blackness, and darkness, and tempest, and the sound of a trumpet, and the voice of words; which voice they that heard entreated that the word should not be spoken to them any more: (for they could not endure that which was commanded, And if so much as a beast touch the mountain, it shall be stoned, or thrust through with a dart: and so terrible was the sight, that Moses said, I exceedingly fear and quake); but ye are come unto

Mount Zion, and unto the city of the living God, the heavenly Jerusalem," etc. (Hebrews 12:18-22).

What Paul briefly touches on in the passage which we have quoted from the Romans, he explains more fully in the Epistles to the Galatians, where he makes an allegory of the two sons of Abraham in this way: "Agar is mount Sinai in Arabia, and answereth to Jerusalem which now is, and is in bondage with her children. But Jerusalem which is above is free, which is the mother of us all" (Galatians 4:25, 26). As the offspring of Agar was born in slavery, and could never attain to the inheritances while that of Sara was free and entitled to the inheritance, so by the Law we are subjected to slavery, and by the Gospel alone regenerated into liberty. The sum of the matter comes to this: The Old Testament filled the conscience with fear and trembling—The New inspires it with gladness. By the former the conscience is held in bondage, by the latter it is manumitted and made free. If it be objected, that the holy fathers among the Israelites, as they were endued with the same spirit of faith, must also have been partakers of the same liberty and joy, we answer, that neither was derived from the Law; but feeling that by the Law they were oppressed like slaves, and vexed with a disquieted conscience, they fled for refuge to the (Gospel; and, accordingly, the peculiar advantage of the Gospel was, that, contrary to the common rule of the Old Testament, it exempted those who were under it from those evils. Then, again, we deny that they did possess the spirit of liberty and security in such a degree as not to experience some measure of fear and bondage.

However they might enjoy the privilege, which they had obtained through the grace of the Gospel, they were under the same bonds and burdens of observances as the rest of their nation. Therefore, seeing they were obliged to the anxious observance of ceremonies (which were the symbols of a tutelage bordering on slavery, and handwritings by which they acknowledged their guilt, but did not escape from it), they are justly said to have been, comparatively, under a covenant of fear and bondage, in respect of that common dispensation under which the Jewish people were then placed.

10 Distinction between the three last differences and the first. Confirmation of the above from Augustine. Condition of the patriarchs under the Old Testament.

The three last contrasts to which we have adverted (section 4, 7, 9), are between the Law and the Gospel, and hence in these the Law is designated by the name of the Old, and the Gospel by that of the New Testament. The first is of wider extent (section 1), comprehending under it the promises, which were given even before the Law. When Augustine maintained that these were not to be included under the name of the Old Testament, he took a most correct view, and meant nothing different from what we have now taught; for he had in view those passages of Jeremiah and Paul in which the

Old Testament is distinguished from the word of grace and mercy. In the same passage, Augustine, with great shrewdness remarks, that from the beginning of the world the sons of promise, the divinely regenerated, who, through faith working by love, obeyed the commandments, belonged to the New Testament; entertaining the hope not of carnal, earthly, temporal, but spiritual, heavenly, and eternal blessings, believing especially in a Mediator, by whom they doubted not both that the Spirit was administered to them, enabling them to do good, and pardon imparted as often as they sinned.

The thing, which he thus intended to assert, was that all the saints mentioned in Scripture from the beginning of the world, as having been specially selected by God, were equally with us partakers of the blessing of eternal salvation. The only difference between our division and that of Augustine is, that ours (in accordance with the words of our Savior, "All the prophets and the law prophesied until John" (Matthew 11:13) distinguishes between the Gospel light and that more obscure dispensation of the word which preceded it, while the other division simply distinguishes between the weakness of the Law and the strength of the Gospel. And here also, with regard to the holy fathers, it is to be observed, that though they lived under the Old Testament, they did not stop there, but always aspired to the New, and so entered into sure fellowship with it. Those contented with existing shadows did not carry their thoughts to Christ, the Apostle charges with blindness and malediction. To say nothing of other matters, what greater blindness can be imagined, than to hope for the expiation of sin from the sacrifice of a beast, or to seek mental purification in external washing with water, or to attempt to appease God with cold ceremonies, as if he were greatly delighted with them? Such are the absurdities into which those fall who cling to legal observances, without respect to Christ.

11 Fifth difference. The Old Testament belonged to one people only, the New to all.

The fifth distinction, which we have to add, consists in this, that until the advent of Christ, the Lord set apart one nation, to which he confined the covenant of his grace. Moses says, "When the Most High divided to the nations their inheritance, when he separated the sons of Adam, he set the bounds of the people according to the number of the children of Israel. For the Lord's portion is his people; Jacob is the lot of his inheritance" (Deuteronomy 32:8, 9). In another passage, he thus addresses the people: "Behold, the heaven and the heaven of heavens is the Lord's thy God, the earth also, with all that therein is. Only the Lord had a delight in thy fathers to love them, and he chose their seed, after them, even you, above all people, as it is this day" (Deuteronomy 10:14, 15). That people, therefore, as if they had been the only part of mankind belonging to him he favored exclusively with the knowledge of his name, depositing his covenant in their bosom, manifesting to them the presence of his divinity and honoring them with all privileges. But to say nothing of other favors, the only one here considered is his binding them to him by the communion of his word, so that he was called and regarded as their God. Meanwhile, other nations, as if they had had no kind of intercourse with him, he allowed to wander in vanity not even supplying them with the only means of preventing their destructions— viz. the preaching of his word. Israel was thus the Lord's favorite child the others were aliens. Israel was known and admitted to trust and guardianship, the others left in darkness; Israel was made holy, the others were profane; Israel was honored with the presence of God, the others kept far aloof from him. But on the fullness of the time destined to renew all things, when the Mediator between God and man was manifested the middle wall of partition, which had long kept the divine mercy within the confines of Israel, was broken down, peace was preached to them who were afar off, as well as to those who were nigh, that being, together reconciled to God, they might unite as one people. Wherefore, there is now no respect of Jew or Greek, of circumcision or uncircumcision, but Christ is all and in all. To him the heathen have been given for his inheritance, and the uttermost parts of the earth for his possession (Psalm 2:8), that he may rule without distinction "from sea to sea, and from the river unto the ends of the earth" (Psalm 72:8).

12 The second part of the chapter depending on the preceding section. Of the calling of the Gentiles. Why the calling of the Gentiles scented to the Apostles so strange and new.

The calling of the Gentiles, therefore, is a distinguishing feature illustrative of the superiority of the New over the Old Testament. This, it is true, had been previously declared by the prophets, in passages both numerous and clear, but still the fulfillment of it was deferred to the reign of the Messiah. Even Christ did not acknowledge it at the very outset of his ministry, but delayed it until having completed the whole work of redemption in all its parts, and finished the period of his humiliation, he received from the Father "a name which is above every name, that at the name of Jesus every knee should bow" (Philippians 2:9, 10). Hence, the period being not yet completed, he declared to the woman of Canaan, "I am not sent but unto the lost sheep of the house of Israel" (Matthew 15:24). Nor in his first commission to the Apostles does he permit them to pass the same limits, "Go not into the way of the Gentiles, and into any city of the Samaritans enter ye not: but go rather to the lost sheep of the house of Israel" (Matthew 10:5, 6).

However plainly the thing may have been declared in numerous passages, when it was announced to the Apostles, it seemed to them so new and extraordinary, that they were horrified at it as something monstrous. At length, when they did act upon it, it was timorously, and not without reluctance. Nor is this strange; for it seemed by no means in accordance with reason, that the Lord, who for so many ages had selected Israel from the rest of the nations should suddenly change his purpose, and abandon his choice. Prophecy, indeed, had foretold it, but they could not be so attentive to prophecies, as not to be somewhat startled by the novel spectacle thus presented to their eye. It was not enough that God had in old times given specimens of the future calling of the Gentiles. Those whom he had so called were very few in number, and, moreover, he in a manner adopted them into the family of Abraham, before allowing them to approach his people. But by this public call, the Gentiles were not only made equal to the Jews, but also seemed to be substituted into their place, as if the Jews had been dead. We may add, that any strangers whom God had formerly admitted into the body of the Church, had never been put on the same footing with the Jews. Wherefore, it is not without cause that Paul describes it as the mystery which has been hid from ages and from generations, but now is made manifest to his saints (Colossians 1:26).

13 The last part of the chapter. Two objections considered. A. God, being immutable, cannot consistently disapprove what he once ordered. Answer confirmed by a passage of Scripture.

The whole difference between the Old and New Testaments has, I think, been fully and faithfully explained, under these four or five heads in so far as requisite for ordinary instruction. But since this variety in governing the Church, this diversity in the mode of teaching, this great change in rites and ceremonies, is regarded by some as an absurdity, we must reply to them before passing to other matters. And this can be done briefly, because the objections are not so strong as to require a very careful refutation. It is said to be unreasonable to suppose that God, who is always consistent with himself, permitted such a change as afterwards to disapprove what he had once ordered and commended. I answer, that God ought not to be deemed mutable, because he adapts different forms to different ages, as he knows to be expedient for each. If the husbandman prescribes one set of duties to his household in winter and another in summer, we do not therefore charge him with fickleness or think he deviates from the rules of good husbandry, which depends on the regular course of nature. In like manner, if a father of a family, in educating, governing, and managing his children, pursues one course in boyhood another in adolescence and another in manhood we do not therefore say that he is fickle, or abandons his opinions.

Why, then do we charge God with inconstancy when he makes fit and congruous arrangements for diversities of times? The latter similitude ought to be completely satisfactory. Paul likens the Jews to children, and Christians to grown men (Galatians 4:1). What irregularity is there in the Divine arrangement, which confined them to the rudiments, which were suitable to their age, and trains us by a firmer and manlier discipline? The constancy of God is conspicuous in this: that he delivered the same doctrine to all ages, and persists in requiring that worship of his name, which he commanded at the beginning. His changing the external form and manner does not show that he is liable to change. In so far he has only accommodated himself to the mutable and diversified capacities of man.

14 Objections. B. God could at first have transacted with the Jews as he now does with Christians. Answer, showing the absurdity of this objection. Another answer founded on a just consideration of the divine will and the dispensation of grace.

But it is said, Why this diversity, save that God chose to make it? Would it not have been as easy for him from the first, as after the advent of Christ, to reveal eternal life in clear terms without any figures, to instruct his people by a few clear sacraments, to bestow his Holy Spirit, and diffuse his grace over the whole globe? This is very much the same as to bring a charge against God, because he created the world at so late a period, when he could have done it at the first, or because he appointed the alternate changes of summer and winter, of clay and night. With the feeling common to every pious mind, let us not doubt that everything that God has done has been done wisely and justly, although we may be ignorant of the cause, which required that it should be so done. We should arrogate too much to ourselves if we were not to concede to God that he might have reasons for his counsel, which we are unable to discern. It is strange, they say, that he now repudiates and abominates the sacrifices of beasts, and the whole apparatus of that Levitical priesthood in which he formerly delighted. As if those external and transient matters could delight God, or affect him in any way! It has already been observed that he appointed none of these things on his own account, but instituted them all for the salvation of men. If a physician, adopting the best method, effects a cure upon a youth, and afterwards, when the same individual has grown old, and is again subject to the same disease, employs a different method of cure, can it be said that he repudiates the method which he formerly approved? Nay, continuing to approve of it, he only adapts himself to the different periods of life. In like manner, it was necessary in representing Christ in his absence, and predicting his future advent, to employ a different set of signs from those, which are employed, now that his actual manifestation is exhibited.

It is true, that since the advent of Christ, the calling of God is more widely addressed to all nations, and the graces of the Spirit more liberally bestowed than they had previously been. But who, I ask, can deny the right of God to have the free and uncontrolled disposal of his gifts, to select the nations which he may be pleased to illuminate, the places which he may be pleased to illustrate by the preaching of his word, and the mode and measure of progress and success which he may be pleased to give to his doctrine, —

to punish the world for its ingratitude by withdrawing the knowledge of his name for certain ages, and again, when he so pleases, to restore it in mercy? We see, then, that in the calumnies, which the ungodly employ in this matter, to perplex the minds of the simple, there is nothing that ought to throw doubt either on the justice of God or the veracity of Scripture.

Chapter 12

CHRIST, TO PERFORM THE OFFICE OF MEDIATOR, BEHOOVED TO BECOME MAN.

The two divisions of this chapter are, I. The reasons why our Mediator behooved to be very God, and to become man, sections 1–3. II. Disposal of various objections by some fanatics, and especially by Osiander, to the orthodox doctrine concerning the Mediator, section 4–7.

Sections

1. *Necessary, not absolutely, but by divine decree, that the Mediator should be God, and become man. Neither man nor angel, though pure, could have sufficed. The Son of God behooved to come down. Man in innocence could not penetrate to God without a Mediator, much less could he after the fall.*

2. *A second reason that the Mediator behooved to be God and man—viz. that he had to convert those who were heirs of hell into children of God.*

3. *Third reason, that in our flesh he might yield a perfect obedience, satisfy the divine justice, and pay the penalty of sin. Fourth reason, regarding the consolation and confirmation of the whole Church.*

4. *First objection against the orthodox doctrine: Answer to it. Conformation from the sacrifices of the Law, the testimony of the Prophets, Apostles, Evangelists, and even Christ himself.*

5. *Second objection: Answer: Answer confirmed. Third objection: Answer. Fourth objection by Osiander: Answer.*

6. *Fifth objection, forming the basis of Osiander's errors on this subject: Answer. Nature of the divine image in Adam. Christ the head of angels and men.*

7. *Sixth objection: Answer. Seventh objection: Answer. Eighth objection: Answer. Ninth objection: Answer. Tenth objection: Answer. Eleventh objection: Answer. Twelfth objection: Answer. The sum of the doctrine.*

1 Necessary, not absolutely, but by divine decree, that the Mediator should be God, and become man. Neither man nor angel, though pure, could have sufficed. The Son of God behooved to come down. Man in innocence could not penetrate to God without a Mediator, much less could he after the fall.

It deeply concerned us, that he who was to be our Mediator should be very God and very man. If the necessity were inquired into, it was not what is commonly termed simple or absolute, but flowed from the divine decree on which the salvation of man depended. What was best for us, our most merciful Father determined. Our iniquities, like a cloud intervening between Him and us, having utterly alienated us from the kingdom of heaven, none but a person reaching to him could be the medium of restoring peace. But who could thus reach to him? Could any of the sons of Adam? All of them, with their parents, shuddered at the sight of God. Could any of the angels? They had need of a head, by connection with which they might adhere to their God entirely and inseparably. What then? The case was certainly desperate, if the Godhead itself did not descend to us, it being impossible for us to ascend. Thus the Son of God behooved to become our Emmanuel, the God with us; and in such a way, that by mutual union his divinity and our nature might be combined; otherwise, neither was the proximity near enough, nor the affinity strong enough, to give us hope that God would dwell with us; so great was the repugnance between our pollution and the spotless purity of God. Had man remained free from all taint, he was of too humble a condition to penetrate to God without a Mediator.

What, then, must it have been, when by fatal ruin he was plunged into death and hell, defiled by so many stains, made loathsome by corruption; in fine, overwhelmed with every curse? It is not without cause, therefore, that Paul, when he would set forth Christ as the Mediator, distinctly declares him to be man. There is, says he, "one Mediator between God and man, the man Christ Jesus" (1 Timothy 2:5). He might have called him God, or at least, omitting to call him God he might also have omitted to call him man; but because the Spirit, speaking by his mouth, knew our infirmity, he opportunely provides for it by the most appropriate remedy, setting the Son of God familiarly before us as one of ourselves. That no one, therefore, may feel perplexed where to seek the Mediator, or by what means to reach him, the Spirit, by calling him man, reminds us that he is near, nay, contiguous to us, inasmuch as he is our flesh. And, indeed, he intimates the same thing in another place, where he explains at greater length that he is not a High Priest who "cannot be touched with the feeling of our infirmities; but was in all points tempted like as we are, yet without sin" (Hebrews 4:15).

2 A second reason that the Mediator behooved to be God and man—viz. that he had to convert those who were heirs of hell into children of God.

This will become still clearer if we reflect, that the work to be performed by the Mediator was of no common description: being to restore us to the divine favor, so as to make us, instead of sons of men, sons of God; instead of heirs of hell, heirs of a heavenly kingdom. Who could do this unless the Son of God should also become the Son of man, and so receive what is ours as to transfer to us what is his, making that which is his by nature to become ours by grace? Relying on this earnest, we trust that we are the sons of God, because the natural Son of God assumed to himself a body of our body, flesh of our flesh, bones of our bones, that he might be one with us; he declined not to take what was peculiar to us, that he might in his turn extend to us what was peculiarly his own, and thus might be in common with us both Son of God and Son of man.

Hence, that holy brotherhood which he commends with his own lips, when he says, "I ascend to my Father, and your Father, to my God, and your God" (John 20:17). In this way, we have a sure inheritance in the heavenly kingdom, because the only Son of God, to whom it entirely belonged, has adopted us as his brethren; and if brethren, then partners with him in the inheritance (Romans 8:17). Moreover, it was especially necessary for this cause also that he who was to be our Redeemer should be truly God and man. It was his to swallow up death: who but Life could do so? It was his to conquer sin: who could do so save Righteousness itself? It was his to put to flight the powers of the air and the world: who could do so but the mighty power superior to both? But who possesses life and righteousness, and the dominion and government of heaven, but God alone? Therefore, God, in his infinite mercy, having determined to redeem us, became himself our Redeemer in the person of his only begotten Son.

3 Third reason, that in our flesh he might yield a perfect obedience, satisfy the divine justice, and pay the penalty of sin. Fourth reason, regarding the consolation and confirmation of the whole Church.

Another principal part of our reconciliation with God was, that man, who had lost himself by his disobedience, should, by way of remedy, oppose to it obedience, satisfy the justice of God, and pay the penalty of sin. Therefore, our Lord came forth very man, adopted the person of Adam, and assumed his name, that he might in his stead obey the Father; that he might present our flesh as the price of satisfaction to the just judgment of God, and in the same flesh pay the penalty which we had incurred. Finally, since as God only he could not suffer, and as man only could not overcome death, he united the human nature with the divine, that he might subject the weakness of the one to death as an expiation of sin, and by the power of the other, maintaining a struggle with death, might gain us the victory. Those, therefore, who rob Christ of divinity or humanity either detract from his majesty and glory, or obscure his goodness. On the other hand, they are no less injurious to men, undermining and subverting their faith, which cannot stand unless it rests on this foundation. Moreover, the expected Redeemer was that son of Abraham and David whom God had promised in the Law and in the Prophets. Here believers have another advantage. Tracing up his origin in regular series to David and Abraham, they more distinctly recognize him as the Messiah celebrated by so many oracles. But special attention must be paid to what I lately explained, namely, that a common nature is the pledge of our union with the Son of God; that, clothed with our flesh, he warred to death with sin that he might be our triumphant conqueror; that the flesh which he received of us he offered in sacrifice, in order that by making expiation he might wipe away our guilt, and appease the just anger of his Father.

4 First objection against the orthodox doctrine: Answer to it. Conformation from the sacrifices of the Law, the testimony of the Prophets, Apostles, Evangelists, and even Christ himself.

He who considers these things with due attention, will easily disregard vague speculations, which attract giddy minds and lovers of novelty. One speculation of this class is, that Christ, even though there had been no need of his interposition to redeem the human race, would still have become man. I admit that in the first ordering of creation, while the state of nature was entire, he was appointed head of angels and men; for which reason Paul designates him "the first-born of every creature" (Colossians 1:15). But since the whole Scripture proclaims that he was clothed with flesh in order to become a Redeemer, it is presumptuous to imagine any other cause or end. We know well why Christ was at first promised—viz. that he might renew a fallen world, and succor lost man. Hence, under the Law he was typified by sacrifices, to inspire believers with the hope that God would be propitious to them after he was reconciled by the expiation of their sins. Since from the earliest age, even before the Law was promulgated, there was never any promise of a Mediator without blood, we justly infer that he was destined in the eternal counsel of God to purge the pollution of man, the shedding of blood being the symbol of expiation. Thus, too, the prophets, in discoursing of him, foretold that he would be the Mediator between God and man. It is sufficient to refer to the very remarkable prophecy of Isaiah (Isaiah 53:4, 5), in which he foretells that he was "smitten for our iniquities;" that "the chastisement of our peace was upon him;" that as a priest "he was made an offering for sin;" "that by his stripes we are healed;" that as all "like lost sheep have gone astray," "it pleased the Lord to bruise him, and put him to grief," that he might "bear our iniquities." After hearing that

Christ was divinely appointed to bring relief to miserable sinners, whose overleaps these limits gives too much indulgence to a foolish curiosity.

Then when he actually appeared, he declared the cause of his advent to be, that by appeasing God he might bring us from death unto life. To the same effect was the testimony of the Apostles concerning him (John 1:9; 10:14). Thus John, before teaching that the Word was made flesh, narrates the fall of man. But above all, let us listen to our Savior himself when discoursing of his office: "God so loved the world, that he gave his only begotten Son, that whosoever believeth in him should not perish, but have everlasting life." Again, "The hour is coming, and now is, when the dead shall hear the voice of the Son of God: and they that hear shall live." "I am the resurrection and the life: he that believeth in me, though he were dead, yet shall he live." "The Son of man is come to save that which was lost." Again, "They that be whole need not a physician." I should never have done were I to quote all the passages. Indeed, the Apostles, with one consent, lead us back to this fountain; and assuredly, if he had not come to reconcile God, the honor of his priesthood would fall, seeing it was his office as priest to stand between God and men, and "offer both gifts and sacrifices for sins" (Hebrews 5:1); nor could he be our righteousness, as having been made a propitiation for us in order that God might not impute to us our sins (2 Corinthians 5:19). In short, he would be stripped of all the titles with which Scripture invests him. Nor could Paul's doctrine stand "What the law could not do, in that it was weak through the flesh, God sending his own Son in the likeness of sinful flesh, and for sin, condemned sin in the flesh" (Romans 8:3). Nor what he states in another passage: "The grace of God that bringeth salvation has appeared to all men" (Titus 2:11).

In fine, the only end which the Scripture uniformly assigns for the Son of God voluntarily assuming our nature, and even receiving it as a command from the Father, is, that he might propitiate the Father to us by becoming a victim. "Thus it is written, and thus it behooved Christ to suffer;"—"and that repentance and remission of sins should be preached in his name." "Therefore does my Father love me, because I lay down my life, that I might take it again."—"This commandment have I received of my Father." "As Moses lifted up the serpent in the wilderness, even so must the Son of man be lifted up." "Father, save me from this hour: but for this cause came I unto this hour. Father, glorify thy name." Here he distinctly assigns as the reason for assuming our nature, that he might become a propitiatory victim to take away sin. For the same reason Zacharias declares (Luke 1:79), that he came "to perform the mercy promised to our fathers," "to give light to them that sit in darkness, and in the shadow of death." Let us remember that all these things are affirmed of the Son of God, in who, as Paul elsewhere declares, were "hid all the treasures of wisdom and knowledge," and save whom it was his determination "not to know anything" (Colossians 2:3; 1 Corinthians 2:2).

5 Second objection: Answer: Answer confirmed. Third objection: Answer. Fourth objection by Osiander: Answer.

Should anyone object, that in this there is nothing to prevent the same Christ who redeemed us when condemned from also testifying his love to us when safe by assuming our nature, we have the brief answer, that when the Spirit declares that by the eternal decree of God the two things were connected together—viz. that Christ should be our Redeemer, and, at the same time, a partaker of our nature, it is unlawful to inquire further. He who is tickled with a desire of knowing something more, not contented with the immutable ordination of God, shows also that he is not even contented with that Christ who has been given us as the price of redemption. And, indeed, Paul not only declares for what end he was sent, but rising to the sublime mystery of predestination, seasonably represses all the wantonness and prurience of the human mind. "He has chosen us in him before the foundation of the world, that we should be holy and without blame before him in love: having predestinated us unto the adoption of children by Jesus Christ to himself, according to the good pleasure of his will, to the praise of the glory of his grace, wherein he has made us accepted in the Beloved: In whom we have redemption through his blood" (Ephesians 1:4-7). Here certainly the fall of Adam is not presupposed as anterior in point of time, but our attention is directed to what God predetermined before all ages, when he was pleased to provide a cure for the misery of the human race. If, again, it is objected that this counsel of God depended on the fall of man, which he foresaw, to me it is sufficient and more to reply, that those who propose to inquire, or desire to know more of Christ than God predestinated by his secret decree, are presuming with impious audacity to invent a new Christ.

Paul, when discoursing of the proper office of Christ, justly prays for the Ephesians that God would strengthen them "by his Spirit in the inner man," that they might "be able to comprehend with all saints what is the breadth and length, and depth and height; and to know the love of Christ which passeth knowledge" (Ephesians 3:16, 18); as if he intended of set purpose to set barriers around our minds, and prevent them from declining one iota from the gift of reconciliation whenever mention is made of Christ.

Wherefore, seeing it is as Paul declares it to be, "a faithful saying, and worthy of all acceptation, that Christ Jesus came into the world to save sinners" (1 Timothy 1:15), in it I willingly acquiesce. And since the same Apostle elsewhere declares that the grace which is now manifested by the Gospel "was given us in Christ Jesus before the world began" (2 Timothy 1:9), I am resolved to adhere to it firmly even to the end. This moderation is unjustly vituperated by Osiander, who has unhappily, in the present day, again agitated this question that a few had formerly raised. He brings a charge of overweening confidence against those who deny that the Son of God would have appeared in the flesh if Adam had not fallen, because this

432

notion is not repudiated by any passage of Scripture. As if Paul did not lay a curb on perverse curiosity when after speaking of the redemption obtained by Christ, he bids us "avoid foolish questions" (Titus 3:9). To such insanity have some proceeded in their preposterous eagerness to seem acute, that they have made it a question whether the Son of God might not have assumed the nature of an ass. This blasphemy, at which all pious minds justly shudder with detestation, Osiander excuses by the pretext that it is no where distinctly refuted in Scripture; as if Paul, when he counted nothing valuable or worth knowing "save Jesus Christ and him crucified" (1 Corinthians 2:2), were admitting, that the author of salvation is an ass. He who elsewhere declares that Christ was by the eternal counsel of the Father appointed "head over all things to the church," would never have acknowledged another to whom no office of redemption had been assigned.

6 Fifth objection, forming the basis of Osiander's errors on this subject: Answer. Nature of the divine image in Adam. Christ the head of angels and men.

The principle on which Osiander founds is altogether frivolous. He will have it that man was created in the image of God, inasmuch as he was formed on the model of the future Messiah, in order to resemble him whom the Father had already determined to clothe with flesh. Hence, he infers that though Adam had never fallen from his first and pure original, Christ would still have been man. How silly and distorted this view is, all men of sound judgment at once discern; still he thinks he was the first to see what the image of God was, namely, that not only did the divine glory shine forth in the excellent endowments with which he was adorned, but God dwelt in him essentially. But while I grant that Adam bore the image of God, inasmuch as he was united to God (this being the true and highest perfection of dignity), yet I maintain, that the likeness of God is to be sought for only in those marks of superiority with which God has distinguished Adam above the other animals. And likewise, with one consent, acknowledge that Christ was even then the image of God, and, accordingly, whatever excellence was engraved on Adam had its origin in this, that by means of the only begotten Son he approximated to the glory of his Maker.

Man, therefore, was created in the image of God (Genesis 1:27), and in him the Creator was pleased to behold, as in a mirror, his own glory. To this degree of honor he was exalted by the kindness of the only begotten Son. But I add that as the Son was the common head both of men and angels, so the dignity that was conferred on man belonged to the angels also. For when we hear them called the sons of God (Psalm 82:6), it would be incongruous to deny that they were endued with some quality in which they resembled the Father. But if he was pleased that his glory should be represented in men and angels, and made manifest in both natures, it is ignorant trifling in Osiander to say, that angels were postponed to men, because they did not bear the image of Christ. They could not constantly enjoy the immediate presence of God if they were not like to him; nor does Paul teach (Colossians 3:10) that men are renewed in the image of God in any other way than by being associated with angels, that they may be united together under one head. In fine, if we believe Christ, our felicity will be perfected when we shall have been received into the heavens, and made like the angels. But if Osiander is entitled to infer that the primary type of the image of God was in the man Christ, on the same ground may anyone maintain that Christ behooved to partake of the angelic nature, seeing that angels also possess the image of God.

7 Sixth objection: Answer. Seventh objection: Answer. Eighth objection: Answer. Ninth objection: Answer. Tenth objection: Answer. Eleventh objection: Answer. Twelfth objection: Answer. The sum of the doctrine.

Osiander has no reason to fear that God would be found a liar, if the decree to incarnate the Son had not been previously immutably fixed in his mind. Even had Adam not lost his integrity, he would, with the angels, have been like to God; and yet it would not therefore have been necessary that the Son of God should become either a man or an angel. In vain does he entertain the absurd fear, that unless it had been determined by the immutable counsel of God, before man was created, that Christ should be born, not as the Redeemer, but as the first man, he might lose his precedence, since he would not have been born, except for an accidental circumstance, namely, that he might restore the lost race of man; and in this way would have been created in the image of Adam. For why should he be alarmed at what the Scripture plainly teaches, that "he was in all points tempted like as we are, yet without sin?" (Hebrews 4:15).

Hence, Luke, also, hesitates not to reckon him in his genealogy as a son of Adam (Luke 3:38). I should like to know why Christ is termed by Paul the second Adam (1 Corinthians 15:47), unless it be that a human condition was decreed him, for the purpose of raising up the ruined posterity of Adam. For if in point of order, that condition was antecedent to creation, he ought to have been called the first Adam. Osiander confidently affirms that because Christ was in the purpose of God foreknown as man, men were formed after him as their model. But Paul, by calling him the second Adam, gives that revolt which made it necessary to restore nature to its primitive condition an intermediate place between its original formation and the restitution which we obtain by Christ: hence it follows, that it was this restitution which made the Son of God be born, and thereby become man. Moreover, Osiander argues ill and absurdly, that as long as Adam maintained his integrity, he would have been the image of himself, and not of Christ.

I maintain, on the contrary, that although the Son of God had never become incarnate, nevertheless the image of God was conspicuous in Adam, both in his body and his soul; in the rays of this image it always appeared that Christ was truly head, and had in all things the pre-eminence. In this way we dispose of the futile sophism put forth by Osiander, that the angels would have been without this head, had not God purposed to clothe his Son with flesh, even independent of the sin of Adam. He inconsiderately assumes what no rational person will grant, that Christ could have had no supremacy over the angels, so that they might enjoy him as their prince, unless in so far as he was man. But it is easy to infer from the words of Paul (Colossians 1:15), that inasmuch as he is the eternal Word of God, he is the first-born of every creature, not because he is created, or is to be reckoned among the creatures, but because the entire structure of the world, such as it was from the beginning, when adorned with exquisite beauty had no other beginning; then, inasmuch as he was made man, he is the first-born from the dead. For in one short passage (Colossians 1:16-18), the Apostle calls our attention to both views: that by the Son all things were created, so that he has dominion over angels; and that he became man, in order that he might begin to be a Redeemer.

Owing to the same ignorance, Osiander says that men would not have had Christ for their king unless he had been a man; as if the kingdom of God could not have been established by his eternal Son, though not clothed with human flesh, holding the supremacy while angels and men were gathered together to participate in his celestial life and glory. But he is always deluded, or imposes upon himself by this false principle, that the church would have been akefalon—without a head—had not Christ appeared in the flesh. In the same way as angels enjoyed him for their head, could he not by his divine energy preside over men, and by the secret virtue of his Spirit quicken and cherish them as his body, until they were gathered into heaven to enjoy the same life with the angels? The absurdities, which I have been refuting, Osiander regards as infallible oracles. Taking an intoxicating delight in his own speculations, his wont is to extract ridiculous plans out of nothing. He afterwards says that he has a much stronger passage to produce, namely, the prophecy of Adam, who, when the woman was brought to him, said, "This is now bone of my bone, and flesh of my flesh" (Genesis 2:23). But how does he prove it a prophecy? Because in Matthew Christ attributes the same expression to God! As if everything, which God has spoken by man contained a prophecy.

On the same principle, as the law proceeded from God, let Osiander in each precept find a prophecy. Add that our Savior's exposition would have been harsh and groveling, had he confined himself to the literal meaning. He was not referring to the mystical union with which he has honored the Church, but only to conjugal fidelity, and states, that the reason that God declared man and wife to be one flesh, was to prevent anyone from violating that indissoluble tie by divorce. If this simple meaning is too low for Osiander, let him censure Christ for not leading his disciples to the hidden sense, by interpreting his Father's words with more subtlety

Paul gives no countenance to Osiander's dream, when, after saying that "we are members of his body, of his flesh, and of his bones," he immediately adds, "This is a great mystery" (Ephesians 5:30-32). For he meant not to refer to the sense, in which Adam used the words, but sets forth, under the figure and similitude of marriage, the sacred union, which makes us one with Christ. His words have this meaning; for reminding us that he is speaking of Christ and the Church, he, by way of correction, distinguishes between the marriage tie and the spiritual union of Christ with his Church. Wherefore, this subtlety vanishes at once; I deem it unnecessary to discuss similar absurdities: for from this very brief refutation, the vanity of them all will be discovered. Abundantly sufficient for the solid nurture of the children of God is this sober truth, that "when the fullness of the time was come, God sent forth his Son, made of a woman, made under the law, to redeem them who were under the law" (Galatians 4:4, 5).

Chapter 13

CHRIST CLOTHED WITH THE TRUE SUBSTANCE
OF HUMAN NATURE.

The heads of this chapter are, I. The orthodoxy doctrine as to the true humanity of our Savior, proved from many passages of Scripture, section 1. II. Refutation of the impious objections of the Marcionites, Manichees, and similar heretics, sections 2–4.

Sections

1. Proof of the true humanity of Christ, against the Manichees and Marcionites.

2. Impious objections of heretics further discussed. Six objections answered.

3. Other eight objections answered.

4. Other three objections answered.

1 **Proof of the true humanity of Christ, against the Manichees and Marcionites.**

Of the divinity of Christ, which has elsewhere been established by clear and solid proofs, I presume it would be superfluous again to treat. It remains, therefore, to see how, when clothed with our flesh, he fulfilled the office of Mediator. In ancient times, the reality of his human nature was impugned by the Manichees and Marcionites, the latter figuring to themselves a phantom instead of the body of Christ, and the former dreaming of his having been invested with celestial flesh. The passages of Scripture contradictory to both are numerous and strong. The blessing is not promised in a heavenly seed, or the mask of a man, but the seed of Abraham and Jacob; nor is the everlasting throne promised to an aerial man, but to the Son of David, and the fruit of his loins.

Hence, when manifested in the flesh, he is called the Son of David and Abraham, not because he was born of a virgin, and yet created in the air, but because, as Paul explains, he was "made of the seed of David, according to the flesh" (Romans 1:3), as the same apostle elsewhere says, that he came of the Jews (Romans 9:5). Wherefore, our Lord himself not contented with the name of man, frequently calls himself the Son of man, wishing to express more clearly that he was a man by true human descent. The Holy Spirit having so often, by so many organs, with so much care and plainness, declared a matter, which in itself is not abstruse, who could have thought that mortals would have had the effrontery to darken it with their glosses?

Many other passages are at hand, were it wished to produce more: for instance, that one of Paul, that "God sent forth his Son, made of a woman" (Galatians 4:4), and innumerable others, which show that he was subject to hunger, thirst, cold, and the other infirmities of our nature. But from the many, we must select those which may conduce to build up our minds in true faith, as when it is said, "Verily, he took not on him the nature of angels, but he took on him the seed of Abraham," and "that through death he might destroy him that had the power of death" (Hebrews 2:16, 14). Again, "Both he that sanctifieth and they who are sanctified are all of one: for which cause he is not ashamed to call them brethren." "Wherefore in all things it behooved him to be made like unto his brethren, that he might be a merciful and faithful High Priest" (Hebrews 2:11, 17). Again, "We have not an High Priest which cannot be touched with the feeling of our infirmities" (Hebrews 4:15), and the like. To the same effect is the passage to which we lately referred, in which Paul distinctly declares, that the sins of the world behooved to be expiated in our flesh (Romans 8:3). And certainly everything which the Father conferred on Christ pertains to us for this reason, that "he is the head," that from him the whole body is "fitly joined together, and compacted by that which every joint supplieth" (Ephesians 4:16). Nay, in no other way could it hold true as is said, that the Spirit was given to him without measure (John 1:16), and that out of his fullness have all we received; since nothing could be more absurd than that God, in his own essence, should be enriched by an adventitious gift. For this reason also, Christ himself elsewhere says, "For their sakes I sanctify myself" (John 17:19).

2 Impious objections of heretics further discussed. Six objections answered.

The passages, which they produce in confirmation of their error, are absurdly wrested. They gain nothing by their frivolous subtleties when they attempt to do away with what I have now adduced in opposition to them. Marcion imagines that Christ, instead of a body, assumed a phantom, because it is elsewhere said, that he was made in the likeness of man, and found in fashion as a man. Thus, he altogether overlooks what Paul is then discussing (Philippians 2:7). His object is not to show what kind of body Christ assumed, but that, when he might have justly asserted his divinity he was pleased to exhibit nothing but the attributes of a mean and despised man. For, in order to exhort us to submission by his example, he shows, that when as God he might have displayed to the world the brightness of his glory, he gave up his right, and voluntarily emptied himself; that he assumed the form of a servant, and, contented with that humble condition, suffered his divinity to be concealed under a veil of flesh. Here, unquestionably, he explains not what Christ was, but in what way he acted. Nay, from the whole context it is easily gathered, that it was in the true nature of man that Christ humbled himself. For what is meant by the words, he was "found in fashion as a man," but that for a time, instead of being resplendent with divine glory, the human form only appeared in a mean and abject condition? Nor would the words of Peter, that he was "put to death in the flesh, but quickened by the Spirits" (1 Peter 3:18), hold true, unless the Son of God had become weak in the nature of man.

This is explained more clearly by Paul, when he declares that, "he was crucified through weakness" (2 Corinthians 13:4). And hence his exaltation; for it is distinctly said, that Christ acquired new glory after he humbled himself. This could fitly apply only to a man endued with a body and a soul. Manes dreams of an aerial body, because Christ is called the second Adam, the Lord from heaven. But the apostle does not there speak of the essence of his body as heavenly, but of the spiritual life, which derived from Christ, quickens us (1 Corinthians 15:47). This life Paul and Peter, as we have seen, separate from his flesh. Nay, that passage admirably confirms the doctrine of the orthodox, as to the human nature of Christ. If his body were not of the same nature with ours, there would be no soundness in the argument, which Paul pursues with so much earnestness, —If Christ is risen we shall rise also; if we rise not, neither has Christ risen. Whatever be the cavils by which the ancient Manichees, or their modern disciples, endeavor to evade this, they cannot succeed.

It is a frivolous and despicable evasion to say, that Christ is called the Son of man, because he was promised to men; it being obvious that, in the Hebrew idiom, the Son of man means a true man: and Christ, doubtless, retained the idiom of his own tongue. Moreover, there cannot be a doubt as to what is to be understood by the sons of Adam. Not to go further, a passage in the eighth psalm, which the apostles apply to Christ, will abundantly suffice: "What is man, that thou art mindful of him? and the son of man, that thou visitest him?" (Psalm 8:4). Under this figure is expressed the true humanity of Christ. Although he was not immediately descended of an earthly father, yet he originally sprang from Adam.

Nor could it otherwise be said in terms of the passage, which we have already quoted, "Forasmuch, then, as the children are partakers of flesh and blood, he also himself likewise took part of the same;" these words plainly proving that he was an associate and partner in the same nature with ourselves. In this sense also it is said, that "both he that sanctifieth and they who are sanctified are all of one." The context proves that this refers to a community of nature; for it is immediately added, "For which cause he is not ashamed to call them brethren" (Hebrews 2:11). Had he said at first that believers are of God, where could there have been any ground for being ashamed of persons possessing such dignity? But when Christ of his boundless grace associates himself with the mean and ignoble, we see why it was said, "He is not ashamed." It is vain to object, that in this way the wicked will be the brethren of Christ; for we know that the children of God are not born of flesh and blood, but of the Spirit through faith. Therefore, flesh alone does not constitute the union of brotherhood. But although the apostle assigns to believers only the honor of being one with Christ, it does not however follow, that unbelievers have not the same origin according to the flesh; just as when we say that Christ became man, that he might make us sons of God, the expression does not extend to all classes of persons; the intervention of faith being necessary to our being spiritually engrafted into the body of Christ.

A dispute is also ignorantly raised as to the term *first-born*. It is alleged that Christ ought to have been the first son of Adam, in order that he might be the first-born among the brethren (Romans 8:29). But primogeniture refers not to age, but to degree of honor and pre-eminence of virtue. There is just as little color for the frivolous assertion that Christ assumed the nature of man, and not that of angels (Hebrews 2:16), because it was the human race that he restored to favor. The apostle, to magnify the honor, which Christ has conferred upon us, contrasts us with the angels, to whom we are in this respect preferred. And if due weight is given to the testimony of Moses (Genesis 3:15), when he says that the seed of the woman would bruise the head of the serpent, the dispute is at an end. For the words there used, refer not to Christ alone, but to the whole human race. Since the victory was to be obtained for us by Christ, God declares generally, that the posterity of the woman would overcome the devil. From this it follows, that Christ is a descendant of the human race, the purpose of God in thus addressing Eve being to raise her hopes, and prevent her from giving way to despair.

3 Other eight objections answered.

Those persons, with no less folly than wickedness, wrap up in allegory the passages in which Christ is called the seed of Abraham and the fruit of the loins of David. Had the term *seed* been used allegorically, Paul surely would not have omitted to notice it, when he affirms clearly, and without figure, that the promise was not given "to seeds, as of many; but as of one, And to thy seed, which is Christ" (Galatians 3:16). With similar absurdity they pretend that he was called the Son of David for no other reason but because he had been promised, and was at length in due time manifested. For Paul, after he had called him the Son of David, by immediately subjoining "*according to the flesh,*" certainly designates his nature. So also (Romans

9:5), while declaring him to be "God blessed forever," he mentions separately, that, "as concerning the flesh, he was descended from the Jews." Again, if he had not been truly begotten of the seed of David, what is the meaning of the expression, that he is the "fruit of his loins;" or what the meaning of the promise, "Of the fruit of thy body will I set upon thy throne?" (Psalm 132:11).

Moreover, their mode of dealing with the genealogy of Christ, as given by Matthew, is mere sophistry; for though he reckons up the progenitors not of Mary, but of Joseph, yet as he was speaking of a matter then generally understood, he deems it enough to show that Joseph was descended from the seed of David, since it is certain that Mary was of the same family. Luke goes still further, showing that the salvation brought by Christ is common to the whole human race, inasmuch as Christ, the author of salvation, is descended from Adam, the common father of us all.

I confess, indeed, that the genealogy proves Christ to be the Son of David only as being descended of the Virgin; but the new Marcionites, for the purpose of giving a gloss to their heresy, namely to prove that the body which Christ assumed was unsubstantial, too confidently maintain that the expression as to seed is applicable only to males, thus subverting the elementary principles of nature. But as this discussion belongs not to theology, and the arguments, which they adduce, are too futile to require any labored refutation, I will not touch on matters pertaining to philosophy and the medical art. It will be sufficient to dispose of the objection drawn from the statement of Scripture, that Aaron and Jehoiadah married wives out of the tribe of Judah, and that thus the distinction of tribes was confounded, if proper descent could come through the female. It is well known, that in regard to civil order, descent is reckoned through the male; and yet the superiority on his part does not prevent the female from having her proper share in the descent. This solution applies to all the genealogies.

When Scripture gives a list of individuals, it often mentions males only. Must we therefore say that females go for nothing? Nay, the very children know that they are classified with men. For this reason wives are said to give children to their husbands, the name of the family always remaining with the males. Then, as the male sex has this privilege, that sons are deemed of noble or ignoble birth, according to the condition of their fathers, so, on the other hand, in slavery, that of the mother determines the condition of the child, as lawyers say, *partus sequitur ventrem*. Whence we may infer, that offspring is partly procreated by the seed of the mother. According to the common custom of nations, mothers are deemed progenitors, and with this, the divine law agrees, which could have had no ground to forbid the marriage of the uncle with the niece, if there was no consanguinity between them. It would also be lawful for a brother and sister uterine to intermarry, when their fathers are different.

While I admit that the power assigned to the woman is passive, I hold that the same thing is affirmed indiscriminately of her and of the male.

Christ is not said to have been made by a woman, but of a woman (Galatians 4:4). But some of this herd, laying aside all shame, publicly ask whether we mean to maintain that Christ was procreated of the proper seed of a Virgin. I, in my turn, ask whether they are not forced to admit that he was nourished to maturity in the Virgin's womb. Justly, therefore, we infer from the words of Matthew, that Christ, inasmuch as he was begotten of Mary, was procreated of her seed; as a similar generation is denoted when Boaz is said to have been begotten of Rachab (Matthew 1:5, 16). Matthew does not here describe the Virgin as the channel through which Christ flowed, but distinguishes his miraculous from an ordinary birth, in that she of the seed of David begot Christ. For the same reason for which Isaac is said to be begotten of Abraham, Joseph of Jacob, Solomon of David, is Christ said to have been begotten of his mother. The Evangelist has arranged his discourse in this way. Wishing to prove that Christ derives his descent from David, he deems it enough to state, that he was begotten of Mary. Hence, it follows, that he assumed it as an acknowledged fact that Mary was of the same lineage as Joseph.

4 Other three objections answered.

The absurdities, which they wish to fasten upon us, are mere puerile calumnies. They reckon it base and dishonoring to Christ to have derived his descent from men; because, in that case, he could not be exempted from the common law which includes the whole offspring of Adam, without exception, under sin. But this difficulty is easily solved by Paul's antithesis, "As by one man sin entered into the world, and death by sin"—"even so by the righteousness of one the free gift came upon all men unto justification of life" (Romans 5:12, 18). Corresponding to this is another passage, "The first man is of the earth, earthy: the second man is the Lord from heaven" (1 Corinthians 15:47). Accordingly, the same apostle, in another passage, teaching that Christ was sent "in the likeness of sinful flesh, that the righteousness of the law might be fulfilled in us," distinctly separates him from the common lot, as being true man, and yet without fault and corruption (Romans 8:3).

It is childish trifling to maintain, that if Christ is free from all taint, and was begotten of the seed of Mary, by the secret operation of the Spirit, it is not therefore the seed of the woman that is impure, but only that of the man. We do not hold Christ to be free from all taint, merely because he was born of a woman unconnected with a man, but because the Spirit sanctified him, so that the generation was pure and spotless, such as it would have been before Adam's fall. Let us always bear in mind, that wherever Scripture adverts to the purity of Christ, it refers to his true human nature, since it would be superfluous to say that God is pure. Moreover, the sanctification of which John speaks in his seventeenth chapter is inapplicable to the divine nature. This does not suggest the idea of a twofold seed in Adam, although no contamination extended to Christ, the generation of man not being in itself vicious or impure, but an accidental circumstance of the fall.

Hence, it is not strange that Christ, by whom our integrity was to be restored, was exempted from the common corruption. Another absurdity, which they obtrude upon us—viz. that if the Word of God became incarnate, it must have been enclosed in the narrow tenement of an earthly body, is sheer petulance. For although the boundless essence of the Word was united with human nature into one person, we have no idea of any enclosing. The Son of God descended miraculously from heaven, yet without abandoning heaven; was pleased to be conceived miraculously in the Virgin's womb, to live on the earth, and hang upon the cross, and yet always filled the world as from the beginning.

Chapter 14

HOW TWO NATURES CONSTITUTE THE PERSON OF THE MEDIATOR.

This chapter contains two principal heads: I. A brief exposition of the doctrine of Christ's two natures in one person, sections 1–4. II. A refutation of the heresies of Servetus, which destroy the distinction of natures in Christ, and the eternity of the divine nature of the Son, sections 5-8.

Sections

1. Proof of two natures in Christ a human and a divine. Illustrated by analogy, from the union of body and soul. Illustration applied.

2. Proof from passages of Scripture, which distinguish between the two natures. Proof from the communication of properties.

3. Proof from passages showing the union of both natures. A rule to be observed in this discussion.

4. Utility and use of the doctrine concerning the two natures. The Nestorians. The Eutychians. Both justly condemned by the Church.

5. The heresies of Servetus refuted. General answer or sum of the orthodox doctrine concerning Christ. What meant by the hypostatic union. Objections of Servetus to the deity of Christ. Answer.

6. Another objection and answer. A twofold filiation of Christ.

7. Other objections answered.

8. Conclusion of the former objections. Other pestilential heresies of Servetus.

1 Proof of two natures in Christ—a human and a divine. Illustrated by analogy, from the union of body and soul. Illustration applied.

When it is said that the Word was made flesh, we must not understand it as if he were either changed into flesh, or confusedly intermingled with flesh, but that he made choice of the Virgin's womb as a temple in which he might dwell. He who was the Son of God became the Son of man, not by confusion of substance, but by unity of person. For we maintain, that the divinity was so conjoined and united with the humanity, that the entire properties of each nature remain entire, and yet the two natures constitute only one Christ. If, in human affairs, anything analogous to this great mystery can be found, the most apposite similitude seems to be that of man, who obviously consists of two substances, neither of which however is so intermingled with the other as that both do not retain their own properties. For neither is soul body, nor is body soul. Wherefore that is said separately of the soul which cannot in any way apply to the body; and that, on the other hand, of the body which is altogether inapplicable to the soul; and that, again, of the whole man, which cannot be affirmed without absurdity either of the body or of the soul separately. Lastly, the properties of the soul are transferred to the body, and the properties of the body to the soul, and yet these form only one man, not more than one. Such modes of expression intimate both that there is in man one person formed of two compounds, and that these two different natures constitute one person. Thus, the Scriptures speak of Christ. They sometimes attribute to him qualities, which should be referred specially to his humanity, and sometimes qualities applicable peculiarly to his divinity, and sometimes qualities that embrace both natures, and do not apply specially to either. This combination of a twofold nature in Christ they express so carefully, that they sometimes communicate them with each other, a figure of speech which the ancients termed a "communication of properties."

2 Proof from passages of Scripture, which distinguish between the two natures. Proof from the communication of properties.

Little dependence could be placed on these statements, were it not proved by numerous passages throughout the sacred volume that none of them is of man's devising. What Christ said of himself, "Before Abraham was I am" (John 8:58), was very foreign to his humanity. I am aware of the cavil by which erroneous spirits distort this passage—viz. that he was before all ages, inasmuch as he was foreknown as the Redeemer, as well in the counsel of the Father as in the minds of believers. But seeing he plainly distinguishes the period of his manifestation from his eternal existence, and professedly founds on his ancient government, to prove his precedence to Abraham, he undoubtedly claims for himself the peculiar attributes of divinity.

Paul's assertion that he is "the first-born of every creature," that "he is before all things, and by him all things consist" (Colossians 1:15, 17); his own declaration, that he had glory with the Father before the world was, and that he worketh together with the Father, are equally inapplicable to man. These and similar properties must be specially assigned to his divinity. Again, his being called the servant of the Father, his being said to grow in stature, and wisdom, and favor with God and man, not to seek his own glory, not to know the last day, not to speak of himself, not to do his own will, his being seen and handled, apply entirely to his humanity; since, as God, he cannot be in any respect said to grow, works always for himself, knows everything, does all things after the counsel of his own will, and is incapable of being seen or handled. And yet, he not merely ascribes these things separately to his human nature, but applies them to himself as suitable to his office of Mediator. There is a communication of or properties, when Paul says, that God purchased the Church "with his own blood" (Acts 20:28), and that the Jews crucified the Lord of glory (1 Corinthians 2:8).

In like manner, John says, that the Word of God was "handled." God certainly has no blood, suffers not, cannot be touched with hands; but since that Christ, who was true God and true man, shed his blood on the cross for us, the acts which were performed in his human nature are transferred improperly, but not ceaselessly, to his divinity. We have a similar example in the passage where John says that God laid down his life for us (1 John 3:16). Here a property of his humanity is communicated with his other nature. On the other hand, when Christ, still living on the earth, said, "No man has ascended up to heaven but he that came down from heaven, even the Son of man, which is in heaven" (John 3:13), certainly regarded as man in the flesh which he had put on, he was not then in heaven, but inasmuch as he was both God and man, he, on account of the union of a twofold nature, attributed to the one what properly belonged to the other.

3 Proof from passages showing the union of both natures. A rule to be observed in this discussion.

But, above all, the true substance of Christ is most clearly declared in those passages that comprehend both natures at once. Numbers of these exist in the Gospel of John. What we there read as to his having received power from the Father to forgive sins; as to his quickening whom he will; as to his bestowing righteousness, holiness, and salvation; as to his being appointed judge both of the quick and the dead; as to his being honored even as the Father, are not peculiar either to his Godhead or his humanity, but applicable to both. In the same way, he is called the Light of the world, the good Shepherd, the only Door, the true Vine. With such prerogatives, the Son of God was invested on his manifestation in the flesh, and though he possessed the same with the Father before the world was created, still it was not in the same manner or respect; neither could they be attributed to one who was a man and nothing more.

In the same sense, we ought to understand the saying of Paul: that at the end, Christ shall deliver up "the kingdom to God, even the Father" (1 Corinthians 15:24). The kingdom of God assuredly had no beginning, and will have no end: but because he was hid under a humble clothing of flesh, and took upon himself the form of a servant, and humbled himself (Philippians 2:8), and, laying aside the insignia of majesty, became obedient to the Father; and after undergoing this subjection was at length crowned with glory and honor (Hebrews 2:7), and exalted to supreme authority, that at his name every knee should bow (Philippians 2:19); so at the end he will subject to the Father both the name and the crown of glory, and whatever he received of the Father, that God may be all in all (1 Corinthians 15:28).

For what end were that power and authority given to him, save that the Father might govern us by his hand? In the same sense, also, he is said to sit at the right hand of the Father. But this is only for a time, until we enjoy the immediate presence of his Godhead. And here we cannot excuse the error of some ancient writers, who, by not attending to the office of Mediator, darken the genuine meaning of almost the whole doctrine which we read in the Gospel of John, and entangle themselves in many snares.

Let us, therefore, regard it as the key of true interpretation, that those things, which refer to the office of Mediator, are not spoken of the divine or human nature simply. Christ, therefore, shall reign until he appear to judge the world, inasmuch as, according to the measure of our feeble capacity, he now connects us with the Father. But when, as partakers of the heavenly glory, we shall see God as he is, then Christ, having accomplished the office of Mediator, shall cease to be the vicegerent of the Father, and will be content with the glory which he possessed before the world was. Nor is the name of Lord especially applicable to the person of Christ in any other respect than in so far as he holds a middle place between God and us. To this effect are the words of Paul, "To us there is but one God, the Father, of whom are all things, and we in him; and one Lord Jesus Christ, by whom are all things, and we by him" (1 Corinthians 8:6); that is, to the latter a temporary authority has been committed by the Father until his divine majesty shall be beheld face to face. His giving up of the kingdom to the Father, so far from impairing his majesty, will give a brighter manifestation of it. God will then cease to be the head of Christ, and Christ's own Godhead will then shine forth of itself, whereas it is now in a manner veiled.

4 Utility and use of the doctrine concerning the two natures. The Nestorians. The Eutychians. Both justly condemned by the Church.

This observation, if the readers apply it properly, will be of no small use in solving a vast number of difficulties. For it is strange how the ignorant, nay, some who are not altogether without learning, are perplexed by these modes of expression which they see applied to Christ, without being properly adapted either to his divinity or his humanity, not considering their accordance with the character in which he was manifested as God and man, and with his office of Mediator. It is very easy to see how beautifully they accord with each other, provided they have a sober interpreter, one who examines these great mysteries with the reverence, which is meet. But there is nothing, which furious and frantic spirits cannot throw into confusion. They fasten on the attributes of humanity to destroy his divinity; and, on the other hand, on those of his divinity to destroy his humanity: while those which, spoken conjointly of the two natures, apply to neither, they employ to destroy both. But what else is this than to contend that Christ is not man because he is God, not God because he is man, and neither God nor man because he is both at once.

Christ, therefore, as God and man, possessing natures which are united, but not confused, we conclude that he is our Lord and the true Son of God, even according to his humanity, though not by means of his humanity. We must put far from us the heresy of Nestorius, who, presuming to dissect rather than distinguish between the two natures, devised a double Christ. But we see the Scripture loudly protesting against this, when the name of the Son of God is given to him who is born of a Virgin, and the Virgin herself is called the mother of our Lord (Luke 1:32, 43). We must beware also of the insane fancy of Eutyches, lest, when we would demonstrate the unity of person, we destroy the two natures.

The many passages we have already quoted, in which the divinity is distinguished from the humanity, and the many other passages existing throughout Scripture, may well stop the mouth of the most contentious. I will shortly add a few observations, which will still better dispose of this fiction. For the present, one passage will suffice—Christ would not have called his body a temple (John 2:19), had not the Godhead distinctly dwelt in it. Wherefore, as Nestorius had been justly condemned in the Council of Ephesus, so afterwards was Eutyches in those of Constantinople and Chalcedony, it being not more lawful to confound the two natures of Christ than to divide them.

5 The heresies of Servetus refuted. General answer or sum of the orthodox doctrine concerning Christ. What meant by the hypostatic union. Objections of Servetus to the deity of Christ. Answer.

But in our age, also, has arisen a not less fatal monster, Michael Servetus, who for the Son of God has substituted a figment, composed of the essence of God, spirit, flesh, and three untreated elements. First, indeed, he denies that Christ is the Son of God, for any other reason than because the Holy Spirit begot him in the womb of the Virgin. The tendency of this crafty device is to make out, by destroying the distinction of the two natures, that Christ is somewhat composed of God and man, and yet is not to be deemed God and man. His aim throughout is to establish, that before Christ was manifested in the flesh there were only shadowy figures in God, the truth or effect of which existed for the first time, when the Word who had been destined to that honor truly began to be the Son of God. We indeed acknowledge that the Mediator who was born of the Virgin is properly the Son of God. And how could the man Christ be a mirror of the inestimable grace of God, had not the dignity been conferred upon him both of being and of being called the only begotten Son of God?

Meanwhile, however, the definition of the Church stands unmoved, that he is accounted the Son of God, because the Word begotten by the Father before all ages assumed human nature by hypostatic union, —a term used by ancient writers to denote the union which of two natures constitutes one person, and invented to refute the dream of Nestorius, who pretended that the Son of God dwelt in the flesh in such a manner as not to be at the same time man.

Servetus calumniously charges us with making the Son of God double, when we say that the eternal Word before he was clothed with flesh was already the Son of God: as if we said anything more than that he was manifested in the flesh. Although he was God before he became man, he did not therefore begin to be a new God. Nor is there any greater absurdity in holding that the Son of God, who by eternal generation ever had the property of being a Son, appeared in the flesh. This is intimated by the angel's word to Mary: "That holy thing which shall be born of thee shall be called the Son of God" (Luke 1:35); as if he had said that the name of Son, which was more obscure under the law, would become celebrated and universally known. Corresponding to this is the passage of Paul, that being now the sons of God by Christ, we "have received the Spirit of adoption, whereby we cry, Abba, Father" (Romans 8:15).

Were not also the holy patriarchs of old reckoned among the sons of God? Yea, trusting to this privilege, they invoked God as their Father. But because ever since the only begotten Son of God came forth into the world, his celestial paternity has been more clearly manifested, Paul assigns this to the kingdom of Christ as its distinguishing feature. We must, however, constantly hold, that God never was a Father to angels and men save in respect of his only begotten Son: that men, especially, who by their iniquity were rendered hateful to God, are sons by gratuitous adoption, because he is a Son by nature. Nor is there anything in the assertion of Servetus that this depends on the paternity that God had decreed with himself. Here we deal not with figures, as expiation by the blood of beasts was shown to be; but since they could not be the sons of God in reality, unless their adoption was founded in the head, it is against all reason to deprive the head of that which is common to the members.

I go further: since the Scripture gives the name of sons of God to the angels, whose great dignity in this respect depended not on the future redemption, Christ must in order take precedence of them that he may reconcile the Father to them. I will again briefly repeat and add the same thing concerning the human race. Since angels as well as men were at first created on the condition that God should be the common Father of both; if it is true, as Paul says, that Christ always was the head, "the first-born of every creature—that in all things he might have the pre-eminence" (Colossians 1:15, 18), I think I may legitimately infer, that he existed as the Son of God before the creation of the world.

6 Another objection and answer. A twofold filiation of Christ.

But if his paternity (if I may so express it) had a beginning at the time when he was manifested in the flesh, it follows that he was a Son in respect of human nature also. Servetus and others similarly frenzied hold that Christ who appeared in the flesh is the Son of God, inasmuch as but for his incarnation, he could not have possessed this name. Let them now answer me, whether, according to both natures, and in respect of both, he is a Son? So indeed they prate; but Paul's doctrine is very different. We acknowledge, indeed, that Christ in human nature is called a Son, not like believers by gratuitous adoption merely, but the true, natural, and, therefore, only Son, this being the mark which distinguishes him from all others. Those of us who are regenerated to a new life God honors with the name of sons; the name of true and only begotten Son he bestows on Christ alone.

But how is he an only Son in so great a multitude of brethren, except that he possesses by nature what we acquire by gift? This honor we extend to his whole character of Mediator, so that He who was born of a Virgin, and on the cross offered himself in sacrifice to the Father, is truly and properly the Son of God; but still in respect of his Godhead: as Paul teaches when he says, that he was "separated unto the Gospel of God (which he had promised afore by his prophets in the Holy Scriptures), concerning his Son Jesus Christ our Lord, which was made of the seed of David according to the flesh; and declared to be the Son of God with power" (Romans 1:1-4). When distinctly calling him the Son of David according to the flesh, why should he also say that he was "declared to be the Son of God," if he meant not to intimate, that this depended on something else than his incarnation? For in the same sense in which he elsewhere says, that "though he was crucified through weakness, yet he liveth by the power of God" (2 Corinthians 13:4), so he now draws a distinction between the two natures.

They must certainly admit, that as because of his mother he is called the Son of David, so, because of his Father, he is the Son of God, and that in some respect differing from his human nature. The Scripture gives him both names, calling him at one time the Son of God, at another the Son of Man. As to the latter, there can be no question that he is called a Son in accordance with the phraseology of the Hebrew language, because he is of the offspring of Adam. On the other hand, I maintain that he is called a Son because of his Godhead and eternal essence, because it is no less congruous to refer to his divine nature his being called the Son of God, than to refer to his human nature his being called the Son of Man. In fine, in the passage which I have quoted, Paul does not mean, that he who according to the flesh was begotten of the seed of David, was declared to be the Son of God in any other sense than he elsewhere teaches that Christ, who descended of the Jews according to the flesh, is "over all, God blessed forever" (Romans 9:5). But if in both passages the distinction of two natures is pointed out, how can it be denied, that he who according to the flesh is the Son of Man, is also in respect of his divine nature the Son of God?

7 Other objections answered.

They indeed find a blustering defense of their heresy in its being said, "God spared not his own Son," and in the communication of the angel, that He who was to be born of the Virgin should be called the "Son of the Highest" (Romans 8:32; Luke 1:32). But before pluming themselves on this futile objection, let them for a little consider with us what weight there is in their argument. If it is legitimately concluded, that at conception he began to be the Son of God, because he who has been conceived is called a Son, it will follow, that he began to be the Word after his manifestation in the flesh, because John declares, that the Word of life of which he spoke was that which "our hands have handled" (1 John 1:1). In like manner we read in the prophet, "Thou, Bethlehem Ephratah, though thou be little among the thousands of Israel, yet out of thee shall he come forth that is to be a ruler in Israel; whose goings forth have been from of old, from everlasting," Micah 5:2).

How will they be forced to interpret if they will follow such a method of arguing? I have declared that we by no means assent to Nestorius, who imagined a twofold Christ, when we maintain that Christ, by means of brotherly union, made us sons of God with himself, because in the flesh, which he took from us, he is the only begotten Son of God. And Augustine wisely reminds us, that he is a bright mirror of the wonderful and singular grace of God, because as man he obtained honor that he could not merit. With this distinction, therefore, according to the flesh, was Christ honored even from the womb—viz. to be the Son of God. Still, in the unity of person we are not to imagine any intermixture, which takes away from the Godhead what is peculiar to it. Nor is it more absurd that the eternal Word of God and Christ, uniting the two natures in one person, should in different ways be called the Son of God, than that he should in various respects be called at one time the Son of God, at another the Son of Man. Nor are we more embarrassed by another cavil of Servetus—viz. that Christ, before he appeared in the flesh, is nowhere called the Son of God, except under a figure. For though the description of him was then more obscure, yet it has already been clearly proved, that he was not otherwise the eternal God, than as he was the Word begotten of the eternal Father. Nor is the name applicable to the office of

Mediator, which he undertook, except in that he was God manifest in the flesh. Nor would God have thus from the beginning been called a Father, had there not been even then a mutual relation to the Son, "of whom the whole family in heaven and earth is named" (Ephesians 3:15).

Hence, it is easy to infer that under the Law and the Prophets he was the Son of God before this name was celebrated in the Church. But if we are to dispute about the word merely, Solomon, speaking of the incomprehensibility of God, affirms that his Son is like himself, incomprehensible: "What is his name, and what is his Son's name, if thou canst tell?" (Proverbs 30:4). I am well aware that with the contentious, this passage will not have sufficient weight; nor do I found much upon it, except as showing the malignant cavils of those who affirm that Christ is the Son of God only in so far as he became man. We may add, that all the most ancient writers, with one mouth and consent, testified the same thing so plainly, that the effrontery is no less ridiculous than detestable, which dares to oppose us with Irenaeus and Tertullian, both of whom acknowledge that He who was afterwards visibly manifested was the invisible Son of God.

8 Conclusion of the former objections. Other pestilential heresies of Servetus.

But although Servetus heaped together a number of horrid dogmas, to which, perhaps, others would not subscribe, you will find, that all who refuse to acknowledge the Son of God except in the flesh, are obliged, when urged more closely, to admit that he was a Son, for no other reason than because he was conceived in the womb of the Virgin by the Holy Spirit; just like the absurdity of the ancient Manichees, that the soul of man was derived by transfusion from God, from its being said, that he breathed into Adam's nostrils the breath of life (Genesis 2:7). For they lay such stress on the name of Son that they leave no distinction between the natures, but babblingly maintain that the man Christ is the Son of God, because, according to his human nature, he was begotten of God. Thus, the eternal generation of Wisdom, celebrated by Solomon (Proverbs 8:22), is destroyed, and no kind of Godhead exists in the Mediator: or a phantom is substituted instead of a man. The grosser delusions of Servetus, by which he imposed upon himself and some others, it would be useful to refute, that pious readers might be warned by the example, to confine themselves within the bounds of soberness and modesty: however, I deem it superfluous here, as I have already done it in a special treatise.

The whole comes to this, that the Son of God was from the beginning an idea, and was even then a preordained man, who was to be the essential image of God. Nor does he acknowledge any other word of God except in external splendor. The generation he interprets to mean, that from the beginning a purpose of generating the Son was begotten in God, and that this purpose extended itself by act to creation. Meanwhile, he confounds the Spirit with the Word, saying that God arranged the invisible Word and Spirit into flesh and soul.

In short, in his view, the typifying of Christ occupies the place of generation; but he says that he who was then in appearance a shadowy Son, was at length begotten by the Word, to which he attributes a generating power. From this it will follow, that dogs and swine are not less sons of God, because created of the original seed of the Divine Word. But although he compounds Christ of three untreated elements, that he may be begotten of the essence of God, he pretends that he is the first-born among the creatures, in such a sense that, according to their degree, stones have the same essential divinity. But lest he should seem to strip Christ of his Deity, he admits that his flesh is of the same substance with God, and that the Word was made man, by the conversion of flesh into Deity. Thus, while he cannot comprehend that Christ was the Son of God, until his flesh came forth from the essence of God and was converted into Deity, he reduces the eternal personality (*hypostasis*) of the Word to nothing, and robs us of the Son of David, who was the promised Redeemer. It is true, he repeatedly declares that the Son was begotten of God by knowledge and predestination, but that he was at length made man out of that matter which, from the beginning, shone with God in the three elements, and afterwards appeared in the first light of the world, in the cloud and pillar of fire. How shamefully inconsistent with himself he always becomes, it would be too tedious to relate.

From this brief account sound readers will gather, that by the subtle ambiguities of this infatuated man, the hope of salvation was utterly extinguished. For if the flesh were the Godhead itself, it would cease to be its temple. Now, the only Redeemer we can have is He who, being begotten of the seed of Abraham and David according to the flesh, truly became man. But he erroneously insists on the expression of John, "The Word was made flesh." As these words refute the heresy of Nestorius, so they give no countenance to the impious fiction of which Eutyches was the inventor, since all that the Evangelist intended was to assert a unity of person in two natures.

Chapter 15

THREE THINGS BRIEFLY TO BE REGARDED IN CHRIST—
VIZ. HIS OFFICES OF PROPHET, KING,
AND PRIEST.

The principal parts of this chapter are—I. Of the Prophetical Office of Christ, its dignity and use, sections 1, 2. II. The nature of the Kingly power of Christ, and the advantage we derive from it, sections 3–5. III. Of the Priesthood of Christ, and the efficacy of it, section 6.

Sections

1. Among heretics and false Christians, Christ is found in name only; but by those who are truly and effectually called of God, he is acknowledged as a Prophet, King, and Priest. In regard to the Prophetical Office, the Redeemer of the Church is the same from whom believers under the Law hoped for the full light of understanding.

2. The unction of Christ, though it has respect chiefly to the Kingly Office, refers also to the Prophetical and Priestly Offices. The dignity, necessity, and use of this unction.

3. From the spirituality of Christ's kingdom, its eternity is inferred. This twofold, referring both to the whole body of the Church, and to its individual members.

4. Benefits from the spiritual kingdom of Christ. A. It raises us to eternal life. B. It enriches us with all things necessary to salvation. C. It makes us invincible by spiritual foes. D. It animates us to patient endurance. E. It inspires confidence and triumph. F. It supplies fortitude and love.

5. The unction of our Redeemer heavenly. Symbol of this unction. A passage in the apostle reconciled with others previously quoted, to prove the eternal kingdom of Christ.

6. What necessary to obtain the benefit of Christ's Priesthood. We must set out with the death of Christ. From it follows, A. His intercession for us. B. Confidence in prayer. C. Peace of conscience.

D. Through Christ, Christians themselves become priests. Grievous sin of the Papists in pretending to sacrifice Christ.

1 Among heretics and false Christians, Christ is found in name only; but by those who are truly and effectually called of God, he is acknowledged as a Prophet, King, and Priest. In regard to the Prophetical Office, the Redeemer of the Church is the same from whom believers under the Law hoped for the full light of understanding.

Though heretics pretend the name of Christ, truly does Augustine affirm that the foundation is not common to them with the godly, but belongs exclusively to the Church: for if those things which pertain to Christ be diligently considered, it will be found that Christ is with them in name only, not in reality. Thus in the present day, though the Papists have the words, Son of God, Redeemer of the world, sounding in their mouths, yet, because contented with an empty name, they deprive him of his virtue and dignity; what Paul says of "not holding the head," is truly applicable to them (Colossians 2:19). Therefore, that faith may find in Christ a solid ground of salvation, and so rest in him, we must set out with this principle, that the office, which he received from the Father, consists of three parts. For he was appointed Prophet, King, and Priest; though little were gained by holding the names unaccompanied by knowledge of the end and use. These too are spoken of in the Papacy, but frigidly, and with no great benefit, the full meaning comprehended under each title not being understood.

We formerly observed, that though God, by supplying an uninterrupted succession of prophets, never left his people destitute of useful doctrine, such as might suffice for salvation; yet, the minds of believers were always impressed with the conviction that the full light of understanding was to be expected only on the advent of the Messiah. This expectation, accordingly, had reached even the Samaritans, to whom the true religion had never been made known. This is plain from the expression of the woman, "I know that Messiah cometh, which is called Christ: when he is come, he will tell us all things" (John 4:25). Nor was this a mere random presumption, which had entered the minds of the Jews. They believed what sure oracles had taught them. One of the most remarkable passages is that of Isaiah, "Behold, I have given him for a witness to the people, a leader and commander to the people" (Isaiah 54:4); that is, in the same way in which he had previously in another place styled him "Wonderful, Counselor" (Isaiah 9:6). For this reason, the apostle commending the perfection of Gospel doctrine, first says that "God, at sundry times and in divers manners spake in times past unto the prophets," and then adds, that he "has in these last days spoken unto us by his Son" (Hebrews 1:1, 2).

But as the common office of the prophets was to hold the Church in suspense and at the same time support it until the advent of the Mediator, we read that the faithful, during the dispersion, complained that they were deprived of that ordinary privilege. "We see not our signs: there is no more any prophet, neither is there among us any that knoweth how long" (Psalm 74:9). But when Christ was now not far distant, a period was assigned to Daniel "to seal up the vision and prophecy" (Daniel 9:24), not only that the authority of the prediction there spoken of might be established, but that believers might, for a time, patiently submit to the want of the prophets, the fulfillment and completion of all the prophecies being at hand.

2 The unction of Christ, though it has respect chiefly to the Kingly Office, refers also to the Prophetical and Priestly Offices. The dignity, necessity, and use of this unction.

Moreover, it is to be observed, that the name *Christ* refers to those three offices: for we know that under the law, prophets as well as priests and kings were anointed with holy oil. Whence, also, the celebrated name of Messiah was given to the promised Mediator. But although I admit (as, indeed, I have elsewhere shown) that he was so called from a view to the nature of the kingly office, still the prophetical and sacerdotal unctions have their proper place, and must not be overlooked. The former is expressly mentioned by Isaiah in these words: "The Spirit of the Lord God is upon me: because the Lord has anointed me to preach good tidings unto the meek; he has sent me to bind up the broken-hearted, to proclaim liberty to the captive, and the opening of the prison to them that are bound; to proclaim the acceptable year of the Lord" (Isaiah 60:1, 2). We see that he was anointed by the Spirit to be a herald and witness of his Father's grace, and not in the usual way, for he is distinguished from other teachers who had a similar office. And here, again, it is to be observed, that the unction which he received, in order to perform the office of teacher, was not for himself, but for his whole body, that a corresponding efficacy of the Spirit might always accompany the preaching of the Gospel. This, however, remains certain, that by the perfection of doctrine, which he brought, an end was put to all the prophecies, so that those who, not contented with the Gospel, annex somewhat extraneous to it, derogate from its authority. The voice that thundered from heaven, "This is my beloved Son, hear him," gave him a special privilege above all other teachers. Then from him, as head, this unction is diffused through the members, as Joel has foretold, "Your sons and your daughters shall prophesy, your old men shall dream dreams, and your young men shall see visions" (Joel 2:28).

Paul's expressions, that he was "made unto us wisdom" (1 Corinthians 1:30), and elsewhere, that in him "are hid all the treasures of wisdom and knowledge" (Colossians 2:3), have a somewhat different meaning, namely, that out of him there is nothing worth knowing, and that those who, by faith, apprehend his true character, possess the boundless immensity of heavenly blessings. For which reason, he elsewhere says, "I determined not to know anything among you, save Jesus Christ and him crucified" (1 Corinthians 2:2). And most justly: for it is unlawful to go beyond the simplicity of the Gospel. The purpose of this prophetical dignity in Christ is to teach us, that in the doctrine that he delivered is substantially included wisdom, which is perfect in all its parts.

3 From the spirituality of Christ's kingdom, its eternity is inferred. This twofold, referring both to the whole body of the Church, and to its individual members.

I come to the Kingly office, of which it would be in vain to speak, without previously reminding the reader that its nature is spiritual; because it is from thence, we learn its efficacy, the benefits it confers, its whole power, and eternity. Moreover, in Daniel an angel attributes eternity to Christ's office (Daniel 2:44). In Luke, an angel justly applies eternity to the salvation of his people (Luke 1:33). But this is also twofold, and must be viewed in two ways: the one pertains to the whole body of the Church; the other is proper to each member. To the former is to be referred what is said in the Psalms, "Once have I sworn by my holiness, that I will not lie unto David. His seed shall endure forever, and his throne as the sun before me. It shall be established forever, as the moon, and as a faithful witness in heaven" (Psalm 89:35, 37). There can be no doubt that God here promises that he will be, by the hand of his Son, the eternal governor and defender of the Church. In none but Christ will the fulfillment of this prophecy be found; since immediately after Solomon's death the kingdom in n great measure lost its dignity, and, with ignominy to the family of David, was transferred to a private individual.

Afterwards decaying by degrees, it at length came to a sad and dishonorable end. In the same sense are we to understand the exclamation of Isaiah, "Who shall declare his generation?" (Isaiah 53:8). For he asserts that Christ will so survive death as to be connected with his members. Therefore, as often as we hear that Christ is armed with eternal power, let us learn that the perpetuity of the Church is thus effectually secured; that amid the turbulent agitations by which it is constantly harassed, and the grievous and fearful commotions, which threaten innumerable disasters, it remains safe. Thus, when David derides the audacity of the enemy who attempt to throw off the yoke of God and his anointed, and says, that kings and nations rage "in vain" (Psalm 2:2-4), because he who sitteth in the heaven is strong enough to repel their assaults, assuring believers of the perpetual preservation of the Church, he animates them to have good hope whenever it is occasionally oppressed. So, in another place, when speaking in the person of God, he says, "The Lord said unto my Lord, Sit thou at my right hand, until I make thine enemies thy footstool" (Psalm 110:1), he reminds us, that however numerous and powerful the enemies who conspire to assault the Church, they are not possessed of strength sufficient to prevail against the immortal decree by which he appointed his Son eternal King.

Whence it follows that the devil, with the whole power of the world, can never possibly destroy the Church, which is founded on the eternal throne of Christ. Then in regard to the special use to be made by each believer, this same eternity ought to elevate us to the hope of a blessed immortality. For we see that everything which is earthly, and of the world, is temporary, and soon fades away. Christ, therefore, to raise our hope to the heavens, declares that his kingdom is not of this world (John 18:36). To conclude, let each of us, when he hears that the kingdom of Christ is spiritual, be roused by the thought to entertain the hope of a better life, and to expect that as the hand of Christ now protects it, so it will be fully realized in a future life.

4 Benefits from the spiritual kingdom of Christ. A. It raises us to eternal life. B. It enriches us with all things necessary to salvation. C. It makes us invincible by spiritual foes. D. It animates us to patient endurance. E. It inspires confidence and triumph. F. It supplies fortitude and love.

That the strength and utility of the kingdom of Christ cannot, as we have said, be fully perceived without recognizing it as spiritual, is sufficiently apparent, even from this, that having during the whole course of our lives to war under the cross, our condition here is bitter and wretched. What then would it avail us to be ranged under the government of a heavenly King, if its benefits were not realized beyond the present earthly life? We must, therefore, know that the happiness which is promised to us in Christ does not consist in external advantages—such as leading a joyful and tranquil life, abounding in wealth, being secure against all injury, and having an affluence of delights, such as the flesh is wont to long for—but properly belongs to the heavenly life. As in the world the prosperous and desirable condition of a people consists partly in the abundance of temporal good and domestic peace, and partly in the strong protection which gives security against external violence; so Christ also enriches his people with all things necessary to the eternal salvation of their souls and fortifies them with courage to stand unassailable by all the attacks of spiritual foes.

Whence we infer, that he reigns more for us than for himself, and that both within us and without us; that being replenished, in so far as God knows to be expedient, with the gifts of the Spirit, of which we are naturally destitute, we may feel from their first fruits, that we are truly united to God for perfect blessedness; and then trusting to the power of the same Spirit, may not doubt that we shall always be victorious against the devil, the world, and everything that can do us harm.

To this effect was our Savior's reply to the Pharisees, "The kingdom of God is within you." "The kingdom of God cometh not with observation" (Luke 17:21, 22). It is probable that on his declaring himself that King under whom the highest blessing of God was to be expected, they had in derision asked him to produce his insignia. But to prevent those who were already more than enough inclined to the earth from dwelling on its pomp, he bids them enter into their consciences, for "the kingdom of God" is "righteousness, and peace, and joy in the Holy Ghost" (Romans 14:17).

These words briefly teach what the kingdom of Christ bestows upon us. Not being earthly or carnal, and so subject to corruption, but spiritual, it raises us even to eternal life, so that we can patiently live at present under toil, hunger, cold, contempt, disgrace, and other annoyances; contented with this, that our King will never abandon us, but will supply our necessities until our warfare is ended, and we are called to triumph: such being the nature of his kingdom, that he communicates to us whatever he received of his Father. Since then he arms and equips us by his power, adorns us with splendor and magnificence, enriches us with wealth, we here find most abundant cause of glorying, and also are inspired with boldness, so that we can contend intrepidly with the devil, sin, and death. In fine, clothed with his righteousness, we can bravely surmount all the insults of the world: and as he replenishes us liberally with his gifts, so we can in our turn bring forth fruit unto his glory.

5 The unction of our Redeemer heavenly. Symbol of this unction. A passage in the apostle reconciled with others previously quoted, to prove the eternal kingdom of Christ.

Accordingly, his royal unction is not set before us as composed of oil or aromatic perfumes; but he is called the Christ of God, because "the Spirit of the Lord" rested upon him; "the Spirit of wisdom and understanding, the Spirit of counsel and might, the Spirit of knowledge and of the fear of the Lord" (Isaiah 11:2). This is the oil of joy with which the Psalmist declares that he was anointed above his fellows (Psalm 45:7). For, as has been said, he was not enriched privately for himself, but that he might refresh the parched and hungry with his abundance. For as the Father is said to have given the Spirit to the Son without measure (John 3:34), so the reason is expressed, that we might all receive of his fullness, and grace for grace (John 1:16). From this fountain flows the copious supply (of which Paul makes mention, (Ephesians 4:7) by which grace is variously distributed to believers according to the measure of the gift of Christ. Here we have ample confirmation of what I said, that the kingdom of Christ consists in the Spirit, and not in earthly delights or pomp, and that hence, in order to be partakers with him, we must renounce the world. A visible symbol of this grace was exhibited at the baptism of Christ, when the Spirit rested upon him in the form of a dove.

To designate the Spirit and his gifts by the term *"unction* is not new, and ought not to seem absurd (see 1 John 2:20, 27), because this is the only quarter from which we derive life; but especially in what regards the heavenly life, there is not a drop of vigour in us save what the Holy Spirit instills, who has chosen his seat in Christ, that thence the heavenly riches, of which we are destitute, might flow to us in copious abundance. But because believers stand invincible in the strength of their King, and his spiritual riches abound towards them, they are not improperly called Christians.

Moreover, from this eternity of which we have spoken, there is nothing derogatory in the expression of Paul, "Then cometh the end, when he shall have delivered up the kingdom to God, even the Father" (1 Corinthians 15:24); and also, "Then shall the Son also himself be subject unto him that put all things under him, that God may be all in and" (1 Corinthians 15:28); for the meaning merely is, that, in that perfect glory, the administration of the kingdom will not be such as it now is. For the Father has given all power to the Son, that by his hand he may govern, cherish, sustain us, keep us under his guardianship, and give assistance to us. Thus, while we wander far as pilgrims from God, Christ interposes, that he may gradually bring us to full communion with God.

And, indeed, his sitting at the right hand of the Father has the same meaning as if he was called the vicegerent of the Father, entrusted with the whole power of government. For God is pleased, mediately (so to speak) in his person to rule and defend the Church. Thus, also, his being seated at the right hand of the Father is explained by Paul, in the Epistle to the Ephesians, to mean, "he is the head over all things to the Church, which is his body" (Ephesians 1:20, 22). Nor is this different in purport from what he elsewhere teaches, that God has "given him a name which is above every name; that at the name of Jesus every knee shall bow, of things in heaven, and things in earth, and things under the earth, and that every tongue should confess that Jesus Christ is Lord, to the glory of God the Father" (Philippians 1:9-11). For in these words, also, he commends an arrangement in the kingdom of Christ, which is necessary for our present infirmity. Thus, Paul rightly infers that God will then be the only Head of the Church, because the office of Christ, in defending the Church, shall then have been completed. For the same reason, Scripture throughout calls him *Lord*, the Father having appointed him over us for the express purpose of exercising his government through him. For though many lordships are celebrated in the world, yet Paul says, "To us there is but one God, the Father, of whom are all things, and we in him; and one Lord Jesus Christ, by whom are all things, and we by him" (1 Corinthians 8:6).

Whence it is justly inferred that he is the same God, who, by the mouth of Isaiah, declared, "The Lord is our Judge, the Lord is our Lawgiver, the Lord is our King: he will save us" (Isaiah 33:22). For though he everywhere describes all the power which he possesses as the benefit and gift of the Father, the meaning simply is, that he reigns by divine authority, because his reason for assuming the office of Mediator was, that descending from the bosom and incomprehensible glory of the Father, he might draw near to us. Wherefore there is the greater reason that we all should, with one consent, prepare to obey, and with the greatest alacrity, yield implicit obedience to his will. For as he unites the offices of King and Pastor towards believers, who voluntarily submit to him, so, on the other hand, we are told that he wields an iron scepter to break and bruise all the rebellious like a potter's vessel (Psalm 2:9). We are also told that he will be the Judge of the Gentiles, that he will cover the earth with dead bodies, and level down every opposing height (Psalm 110:6). Of this, examples are seen at present, but full proof will be given at the final judgment, which may be properly regarded as the last act of his reign.

6 **What necessary to obtain the benefit of Christ's Priesthood. We must set out with the death of Christ. From it follows, A. His intercession for us. B. Confidence in prayer. C. Peace of conscience. D. Through Christ, Christians themselves become priests. Grievous sin of the Papists in pretending to sacrifice Christ.**

With regard to his Priesthood, we must briefly hold its end and use to be, that as a Mediator, free from all taint, he may by his own holiness procure the favor of God for us. But because a deserved curse obstructs the entrance, and God in his character of Judge is hostile to us, expiation must necessarily intervene, that as a priest employed to appease the wrath of God, he may reinstate us in his favor. Wherefore, in order that Christ might fulfill this office, it behooved him to appear with a sacrifice. For even under the law of the priesthood it was forbidden to enter the sanctuary without blood, to teach the worshipper that however the priest might interpose to deprecate, God could not be propitiated without the expiation of sin. On this subject, the Apostle discourses at length in the Epistle to the Hebrews, from the seventh almost to the end of the tenth chapter.

The sum comes to this, that the honor of the priesthood was competent to none but Christ, because, by the sacrifice of his death, he wiped away our guilt, and made satisfaction for sin. Of the great importance of this matter, we are reminded by that solemn oath which God uttered, and of which he declared he would not repent, "Thou art a priest forever, after the order of Melchizedek" (Psalm 110:4). For, doubtless, his purpose was to ratify that point on which he knew that our salvation chiefly hinged. For, as has been said, there is no access to God for us or for our prayers until the priest, purging away our defilements, sanctify us, and obtain for us that favor of which the impurity of our lives and hearts deprives us. Thus, we see that if the benefit and efficacy of Christ's priesthood is to reach us, the commencement must be with his death. Whence it follows, that he by whose aid we obtain favor, must be a perpetual intercessor. From this again arises not only confidence in prayer, but also the tranquility of pious minds, while they recline in safety on the paternal indulgence of God, and feel assured, that whatever has been consecrated by the Mediator is pleasing to him. But since God under the Law ordered sacrifices of beasts to be offered to him, there was a different and new arrangement in regard to Christ—viz. that he should be at once victim and priest, because no other fit satisfaction for sin could be found, nor was anyone worthy of the honor of offering an only begotten son to God.

Christ now bears the office of priest, not only that by the eternal law of reconciliation he may render the Father favorable and propitious to us, but also admit us into this most honorable alliance. For we though in ourselves polluted, in him being priests (Revelation 1:6), offer ourselves and our all to God, and freely enter the heavenly sanctuary, so that the sacrifices of prayer and praise which we present are grateful and of sweet odor before him. To this effect are the words of Christ, "For their sakes I sanctify myself" (John 17:19); for being clothed with his holiness, inasmuch as he has devoted us to the Father with himself (otherwise we were an abomination before him), we please him as if we were pure and clean, nay, even sacred. Hence, that unction of the sanctuary of which mention is made in Daniel (Daniel 9:24). For we must attend to the contrast between this unction and the shadowy one which was then in use, as if the angel had said, that when the shadows were dispersed, there would be a clear priesthood in the person of Christ. The more detestable, therefore, is the fiction of those who, not content with the priesthood of Christ, have dared to take it upon themselves to sacrifice him, a thing daily attempted in the Papacy, where the mass is represented as an immolation of Christ.

Chapter 16

HOW CHRIST PERFORMED THE OFFICE OF REDEEMER IN PROCURING OUR SALVATION. THE DEATH, RESURRECTION, AND ASCENSION OF CHRIST.

This chapter contains four leading heads—I. A general consideration of the whole subject, including a discussion of a necessary question concerning the justice of God and his mercy in Christ, sections 1–4. II. How Christ fulfilled the office of Redeemer in each of its parts, sections 5–17. His death, burial, descent to hell, resurrection, ascension to heaven, seat at the right hand of the Father, and return to judgment. III. A great part of the Creed being here expounded, a statement is given of the view, which ought to be taken of the Creed commonly ascribed to the Apostles, section 18. IV. Conclusion, setting forth the doctrine of Christ the Redeemer, and the use of the doctrine, section 19.

Sections

1. *Everything needful for us exists in Christ. How it is to be obtained.*

2. *Question as to the mode of reconciling the justice with the mercy of God. Modes of expression used in Scripture to teach us how miserable our condition is without Christ.*

3. *Not used improperly; for God finds in us ground both of hatred and love.*

4. *This confirmed from passages of Scripture and from Augustine.*

5. *The second part of the chapter, treating of our redemption by Christ. First generally. Redemption extends to the whole course of our Savior's obedience, but is specially ascribed to his death. The voluntary subjection of Christ. His agony. His condemnation before Pilate. Two things observable in his condemnation. A. That he was numbered among transgressors. B. That he was declared innocent by the judge. Use to be made of this.*

6. *Why Christ was crucified. This hidden doctrine typified in the Law, and completed by the Apostles and Prophets. In what sense Christ was made a curse for us. The cross of Christ connected with the shedding of his blood.*

7. *Of the death of Christ. Why he died. Advantages from his death. Of the burial of Christ. Advantages.*

8. *Of the descent into hell. This article gradually introduced into the Church. Must not be rejected, nor confounded with the previous article respecting burial.*

9. *Absurd exposition concerning the Limbus Patrum. This fable refuted.*

10. *The article of the descent to hell more accurately expounded. A great ground of comfort.*

11. *Confirmation of this exposition from passages of Scripture and the works of ancient Theologians. An objection refuted. Advantages of the doctrine.*

12. *Another objection that Christ is insulted, and despair ascribed to him in its being said that he feared. Answer, from the statements of the Evangelists, that he did fear, was troubled in spirit, amazed, and tempted in all respects as we are, yet without sin. Why Christ was pleased to become weak. His fear without sin. Refutation of another objection, with an answer to the question, Did Christ fear death, and why? When did Christ descend to hell, and how? What has been said refutes the heresy of Apollinaris and of the Monothelites.*

13. *Of the resurrection of Christ. The many advantages from it. A. Our righteousness in the sight of God renewed and restored. B. His life as the basis of our life and hope, also the efficacious cause of new life in us. C. The pledge of our future resurrection.*

14. *Of the ascension of Christ. Why he ascended. Advantages derived from it.*

15. *Of Christ's seat at the Father's right hand. What meant by it.*

16. *Many advantages from the ascension of Christ. A. He gives access to the kingdom, which Adam had shut up. B. He intercedes for us with the Father. C. His virtue being thence transfused into us, he works effectually in us for salvation.*

1 Everything needful for us exists in Christ. How it is to be obtained.

All that we have hitherto said of Christ leads to this one result, that condemned, dead, and lost in ourselves, we must in him seek righteousness, deliverance, life and salvation, as we are taught by the celebrated words of Peter, "Neither is there salvation in any other: for there is none other name under heaven given among men whereby we must be saved" (Acts 4:12). The name of Jesus was not given him at random, or fortuitously, or by the will of man, but was brought from heaven by an angel, as the herald of the supreme decree; the reason also being added, "for he shall save his people from their sins" (Matthew 1:21). In these words, attention should be paid to what we have elsewhere observed that the office of Redeemer was assigned him in order that he might be our Savior. Still, however, redemption would be defective if it did not conduct us by an uninterrupted progression to the final goal of safety. Therefore, the moment we turn aside from him in the minutest degree, salvation, which resides entirely in him, gradually disappears; so that all who do not rest in him voluntarily deprive themselves of all grace.

The observation of Bernard well deserves to be remembered: The name of Jesus is not only light but food also, yea, oil, without which all the food of the soul is dry; salt, without which as a condiment whatever is set before us is insipid; in fine, honey in the mouth, melody in the ear, joy in the heart, and, at the same time, medicine; every discourse where this name is not heard is absurd. But here it is necessary diligently to consider in what way we obtain salvation from him, that we may not only be persuaded that he is the author of it, but having embraced whatever is sufficient as a sure foundation of our faith, may eschew all that might make us waver. For seeing no man can descend into himself, and seriously consider what he is, without feeling that God is angry and at enmity with him, and therefore anxiously longing for the means of regaining his favor (this cannot be without satisfaction), the certainty here required is of no ordinary description, — sinners, until freed from guilt, being always liable to the wrath and curse of

God, who, as he is a just judge, cannot permit his law to be violated with impunity, but is armed for vengeance.

2 Question as to the mode of reconciling the justice with the mercy of God. Modes of expression used in Scripture to teach us how miserable our condition is without Christ.

But before we proceed further, we must see in passing, how can it be said that God, who prevents us with his mercy, was our enemy until Christ reconciled him to us. For how could he have given us in his only begotten Son a singular pledge of his love, if he had not previously embraced us with free favor? As there thus arises some appearance of contradiction, I will explain the difficulty. The mode in which the Spirit usually speaks in Scripture is, that God was the enemy of men until they were restored to favor by the death of Christ (Romans 5:10); that they were cursed until their iniquity was expiated by the sacrifice of Christ (Galatians 3:10, 13); that they were separated from God, until by means of Christ's body they were received into union (Colossians 1:21, 22).

Such modes of expression are accommodated to our capacity, that we may the better understand how miserable and calamitous our condition is without Christ. For were it not said in clear terms, that Divine wrath, and vengeance, and eternal death, lay upon us, we should be less sensible of our wretchedness without the mercy of God, and less disposed to value the blessing of deliverance.

For example, let a person be told, Had God at the time you were a sinner hated you, and cast you off as you deserved, horrible destruction must have been your doom; but spontaneously and of free indulgence he retained you in his favor, not suffering you to be estranged from him, and in this way rescued you from danger, —the person will indeed be affected, and made sensible in some degree how much he owes to the mercy of God.

But again, let him be told, as Scripture teaches, that he was estranged from God by sin, an heir of wrath, exposed to the curse of eternal death, excluded from all hope of salvation, a complete alien from the blessing of God, the slave of Satan, captive under the yoke of sin; in fine, doomed to horrible destruction, and already involved in it; that then Christ interposed, took the punishment upon himself and bore what by the just judgment of God was impending over sinners; with his own blood expiated the sins which rendered them hateful to God, by this expiation satisfied and duly propitiated God the Father, by this intercession appeased his anger, on this basis founded peace between God and men, and by this tie secured the Divine benevolence toward them; will not these considerations move him the more deeply, the more strikingly they represent the greatness of the calamity from which he was delivered?

In short, since our mind cannot lay hold of life through the mercy of God with sufficient eagerness, or receive it with becoming gratitude, unless previously impressed with fear of the Divine anger, and dismayed at the thought of eternal death, we are so instructed by divine truth, as to perceive that without Christ God is in a manner hostile to us, and has his arm raised for our destruction. Thus taught, we look to Christ alone for divine favor and paternal love.

3 Not used improperly; for God finds in us ground both of hatred and love.

Though this is said in accommodation to the weakness of our capacity, it is not said falsely. For God, who is perfect righteousness, cannot love the iniquity that he sees in all. All of us, therefore, have that within which deserves the hatred of God: first, our corrupt nature, and secondly, the depraved conduct following upon it. We are all offensive to God, guilty in his sight, and by nature the children of hell. But as the Lord wills not to destroy in us that which is his own, he still finds something in us, which in kindness he can love. For though it is by our own fault that we are sinners, we are still his creatures; though we have brought death upon ourselves, he had created us for life. Thus, mere gratuitous love prompts him to receive us into favor. But if there is a perpetual and irreconcilable repugnance between righteousness and iniquity, so long as we remain sinners we cannot be completely received. Therefore, in order that all ground of offense may be removed, and he may completely reconcile us to himself, he, by means of the expiation set forth in the death of Christ, abolishes all the evil that is in us, so that we, formerly impure and unclean, now appear in his sight just and holy.

Accordingly, God the Father, by his love, prevents and anticipates our reconciliation in Christ. Nay, it is because he first loves us, that he afterwards reconciles us to himself. But because the iniquity, which deserves the indignation of God, remains in us until the death of Christ comes to our aid, and that iniquity is in his sight accursed and condemned, we are not admitted to full and sure communion with God, unless, in so far as Christ unites us. And, therefore, if we would indulge the hope of having God placable and propitious to us, we must fix our eyes and minds on Christ alone, as it is to him alone it is owing that our sins, which necessarily provoked the wrath of God, are not imputed to us.

4 This confirmed from passages of Scripture and from Augustine.

For this reason Paul says, that God "has blessed us with all spiritual blessings in heavenly places in Christ: according as he has chosen us in him before the foundation of the world" (Ephesians 1:3, 4). These things are clear and conformable to Scripture, and admirably reconcile the passages in which it is said, that "God so loved the world, that he gave his only begotten Son"

(John 3:16); and yet that it was "when we were enemies we were reconciled to God by the death of his Son" (Romans 5:10). But to give additional assurance to those who require the authority of the ancient Church, I will quote a passage of Augustine to the same effect: "Incomprehensible and immutable is the love of God. For it was not after we were reconciled to him by the blood of his Son that he began to love us, but he loved us before the foundation of the world, that with his only begotten Son we too might be sons of God before we were anything at all. Our being reconciled by the death of Christ must not be understood as if the Son reconciled us, in order that the Father, then hating, might begin to love us, but that we were reconciled to him already, loving, though at enmity with us because of sin. To the truth of both propositions we have the attestation of the Apostle, "God commendeth his love toward us, in that while we were yet sinners, Christ died for us," (Romans 5:8). Therefore he had this love towards us even when, exercising enmity towards him, we were the workers of iniquity. Accordingly, in a manner wondrous and divine, he loved even when he hated us. For he hated us when we were such as he had not made us, and yet because our iniquity had not destroyed his work in every respect, he knew in regard to each one of us, both to hate what we had made, and love what he had made." Such are the words of Augustine.

5 The second part of the chapter, treating of our redemption by Christ. First generally. Redemption extends to the whole course of our Savior's obedience, but is specially ascribed to his death. The voluntary subjection of Christ. His agony. His condemnation before Pilate. Two things observable in his condemnation. A. That he was numbered among transgressors. B. That he was declared innocent by the judge. Use to be made of this.

When it is asked then how Christ, by abolishing sin, removed the enmity between God and us, and purchased a righteousness which made him favorable and kind to us, it may be answered generally, that he accomplished this by the whole course of his obedience. This id proved by the testimony of Paul, "As by one man's disobedience many were made sinners, so by the obedience of one shall many be made righteous" (Romans 5:19). And indeed he elsewhere extends the ground of pardon which exempts from the curse of the law to the whole life of Christ, "When the fullness of the time was come, God sent forth his Son, made of a woman, made under the law, to redeem them that were under the law" (Galatians 5:4, 5). Thus, even at his baptism he declared that a part of righteousness was fulfilled by his yielding obedience to the command of the Father.

In short, from the moment when he assumed the form of a servant, he began, in order to redeem us, to pay the price of deliverance. Scripture, however, the more certainly to define the mode of salvation, ascribes it

470

peculiarly and specially to the death of Christ. He himself declares that he gave his life a ransom for many (Matthew 20:28). Paul teaches that he died for our sins (Romans 4:25). John Baptist exclaimed, "Behold the Lamb of God, which taketh away the sin of the world" (John 1:29). Paul in another passage declares, "that we are justified freely by his grace, through the redemption that is in Christ Jesus: whom God has set forth to be a propitiation through faith in his blood" (Romans 3:25). "Again, being justified by his blood, we shall be saved from wrath through him" (Romans 5:9). Again, "He has made him to be sin for us, who knew no sin; that we might be made the righteousness of God in him" (2 Corinthians 5:21).

I will not search out all the passages, for the list would be endless, and many are afterwards to be quoted in their order. In the Confession of Faith, called the Apostles' Creed, the transition is admirably made from the birth of Christ to his death and resurrection, in which the completion of a perfect salvation consists. Still there is no exclusion of the other part of obedience, which he performed in life. Thus Paul comprehends, from the beginning even to the end, his having assumed the form of a servant, humbled himself, and become obedient to death, even the death of the cross (Philippians 2:7). And, indeed, the first step in obedience was his voluntary subjection, for the sacrifice would have been unavailing to justification if not offered spontaneously.

Hence, our Lord, after testifying, "I lay down my life for the sheep," distinctly adds, "No man taketh it from me" (John 10:15, 18). In the same sense Isaiah says, " Like a sheep before her shearers is dumb, so he opened not his mouth" (Isaiah 53:7). The Gospel History relates that he came forth to meet the soldiers; and in presence of Pilate, instead of defending himself, stood to receive judgment. This, indeed, he did not without a struggle, for he had assumed our infirmities also, and in this way it behooved him to prove that he was yielding obedience to his Father. It was no ordinary example of incomparable love towards us to struggle with dire terrors, and amid fearful tortures to cast away, all care of himself that he might provide for us. We must bear in minds that Christ could not duly propitiate God without renouncing his own feelings and subjecting himself entirely to his Father's will. To this effect, the Apostle appositely quotes a passage from the Psalms, "Lo, I come (in the volume of the book it is written of me) to do thy will, O God" (Hebrews 10:5; Psalm 40:7, 8). Thus, as trembling consciences find no rest without sacrifice and ablution by which sins are expiated, we are properly directed thither, the source of our life being placed in the death of Christ.

Moreover, as the curse consequent upon guilt remained for the final judgment of God, one principal point in the narrative is his condemnation before Pontius Pilate, the governor of Judea, to teach us, that the punishment to which we were liable was inflicted on that Just One. We could not escape the fearful judgment of God; and Christ, that he might rescue us from it, submitted to be condemned by a mortal, nay, by a wicked and profane man. For the name of Governor is mentioned not only to support the credibility of the narrative, but to remind us of what Isaiah says, that "the chastisement of our peace was upon him;" and that "with his stripes we are healed" (Isaiah 53:5). For, in order to remove our condemnation, it was not sufficient to endure any kind of death. To satisfy our ransom, it was necessary to select a mode of death in which he might deliver us, both by giving himself up to condemnations and undertaking our expiation. Had he been cut off by assassins, or slain in a seditious tumult, there could have been no kind of satisfaction in such a death. But when he is placed as a criminal at the bar, where witnesses are brought to give evidence against him, and the mouth of the judge condemns him to die, we see him sustaining the character of an offender and evil-doer.

Here we must attend to two points, which had both been foretold by the prophets, and tend admirably to comfort and confirm our faith. When we read that Christ was led away from the judgment-seat to execution, and was crucified between thieves, we have a fulfillment of the prophecy, which is quoted by the Evangelist, "He was numbered with the transgressors" (Isaiah 53:12; Mark 15:28). Why was it so? That he might bear the character of a sinner, not of a just or innocent person, inasmuch as he met death on account not of innocence, but of sin. On the other hand, when we read that he was acquitted by the same lips that condemned him (for Pilate was forced once and again to bear public testimony to his innocence), let us call to mind what is said by another prophet, "I restored that which I took not away" (Psalm 69:4).

Thus, we perceive Christ representing the character of a sinner and a criminal, while, at the same time, his innocence shines forth, and it becomes manifest that he suffers for another's and not for his own crime. He therefore suffered under Pontius Pilate, being thus, by the formal sentence of the judge, ranked among criminals, and yet he is declared innocent by the same judge, when he affirms that he finds no cause of death in him. Our acquittal is in this that the guilt which made us liable to punishment was transferred to the head of the Son of God (Isaiah 53:12). We must specially remember this substitution in order that we may not be all our lives in trepidation and anxiety, as if the just vengeance, which the Son of God transferred to himself, were still impending over us.

6 Why Christ was crucified. This hidden doctrine typified in the Law, and completed by the Apostles and Prophets. In what sense Christ was made a curse for us. The cross of Christ connected with the shedding of his blood.

The very form of the death embodies a striking truth. The cross was cursed not only in the opinion of men, but by the enactment of the Divine Law. Hence, Christ, while suspended on it, subjects himself to the curse. And thus, it behooved to be done, in order that the whole curse, which because our iniquities awaited us, or rather lay upon us, might be taken from us by being transferred to him. This was also shadowed in the Law, since the word by which sin itself is properly designated, was applied to the sacrifices and expiations offered for sin. By this application of the term, the Spirit intended to intimate, that they were a kind of kaqarmavton (purifications), bearing, by substitutions the curse due to sin. But that which was represented figuratively in the Mosaic sacrifices is exhibited in Christ the archetype. Wherefore, in order to accomplish a full expiation, he made his soul a propitiatory victim for sin (as the prophet says, (Isaiah 53:5, 10), on which the guilt and penalty being in a manner laid, ceases to be imputed to us.

The Apostle declares this more plainly when he says, that "he made him to be sin for us, who knew no sin; that we might be made the righteousness of God in him" (2 Corinthians 5:21).

The Son of God, though spotlessly pure, took upon him the disgrace and ignominy of our iniquities, and in return clothed us with his purity. To the same thing he seems to refer, when he says, that he "condemned sin in the flesh" (Romans 8:3), the Father having destroyed the power of sin when it was transferred to the flesh of Christ. This term, therefore, indicates that Christ, in his death, was offered to the Father as a propitiatory victim; that, expiation being made by his sacrifice, we might cease to tremble at the divine wrath. It is now clear what the prophet means when he says, that "the Lord has laid upon him the iniquity of us all" (Isaiah 53:6); namely, that as he was to wash away the pollution of sins, they were transferred to him by imputation. Of this the cross to which he was nailed was a symbol, as the Apostle declares, "Christ has redeemed us from the curse of the law, being made a curse for us: for it is written, Cursed is everyone that hangeth on a tree: that the blessing of Abraham might come on the Gentiles through Jesus Christ" (Galatians 3:13, 14). In the same way Peter says, that he "bare our sins in his own body on the tree" (1 Peter 2:24), inasmuch as from the very symbol of the curse, we perceive more clearly that the burden with which we were oppressed was laid upon him. Nor are we to understand that by the curse, which he endured, he was himself overwhelmed, but rather that by enduring it he repressed broke, annihilated all its force. Accordingly, faith apprehends acquittal in the condemnation of Christ, and blessing in his curse.

Hence, it is not without cause that Paul magnificently celebrates the triumph, which Christ obtained upon the cross, as if the cross, the symbol of ignominy, had been converted into a triumphal chariot. For he says, that he blotted out the handwriting of ordinances that was against us, which was contrary to us, and took it out of the way, nailing it to his cross: that "having spoiled principalities and powers he made a show of them openly, triumphing over them in it" (Colossians 2:14, 15). Nor is this to be wondered at; for, as another Apostle declares, Christ, "through the eternal Spirit, offered himself without spot to God" (Hebrews 9:14), and hence that transformation of the cross which were otherwise against its nature. But that these things may take deep root and have their seat in our inmost hearts, we must never lose sight of sacrifice and ablution. For, were not Christ a victim, we could have no sure conviction of his being our substitute-ransom and propitiation. And hence mention is always made of blood whenever scripture explains the mode of redemption: although the shedding of Christ's blood was available not only for propitiation, but also acted as a laver to purge our defilements.

7 Of the death of Christ. Why he died. Advantages from his death. Of the burial of Christ. Advantages.

The Creed next mentions that he "was dead and buried." Here again it is necessary to consider how he substituted himself in order to pay the price of our redemption. Death held us under its yoke, but he in our place delivered himself into its power, that he might exempt us from it. This the Apostle means when he says, "that he tasted death for every man" (Hebrews 2:9). By dying, he prevented us from dying; or (which is the same thing) he by his death purchased life for us. But in this he differed from us, that in permitting himself to be overcome of death, it was not so as to be engulfed in its abyss but rather to annihilate it, as it must otherwise have annihilated us; he did not allow himself to be so subdued by it as to be crushed by its power; he rather laid it prostrate, when it was impending over us, and exulting over us as already overcome.

In fine, his object was, "that through death he might destroy him that had the power of death, that is, the devil, and deliver them who through fear of death were all their lifetime subject to bondage" (Hebrews 2:14, 15). This is the first fruit, which his death produced to us. Another is that by fellowship with him he mortifies our earthly members that they may not afterwards exert themselves in action, and kill the old man, that he may not hereafter be in vigour and bring forth fruit. An effect of his burials moreover is that we as his fellows are buried to sin. For when the Apostle says, that we are engrafted into the likeness of Christ's deaths and that we are buried with him unto sin, that by his cross the world is crucified unto us and we unto the world, and that we are dead with him, he not only exhorts us to manifest an example of his death, but declares that there is an efficacy in it which should appear in all Christians, if they would not render his death unfruitful and useless.

Accordingly in the death and burial of Christ a twofold blessing is set before us—viz. deliverance from death, to which we were enslaved, and the mortification of our flesh (Romans 6:5; Galatians 2:19, 6:14; Colossians 3:3).

8 Of the descent into hell. This article gradually introduced into the Church. Must not be rejected, nor confounded with the previous article respecting burial.

Here, we must not omit the descent to hell, which was of no little importance to the accomplishment of redemption. For although it is apparent from the writings of the ancient Fathers, that the clause which now stands in the Creed was not formerly so much used in the churches, still, in giving a summary of doctrine, a place must be assigned to it, as containing a matter of great importance which ought not by any means to be disregarded. Indeed, some of the ancient Fathers do not omit it, and hence we may conjecture, that having been inserted in the Creed after a considerable lapse of time, it came into use in the Church not immediately but by degrees. This much is uncontroverted, that it was in accordance with the general sentiment of all believers, since there is none of the Fathers who does not mention Christ's descent into hell, though they have various modes of explaining it. But it is of little consequence by whom and at what time it was introduced.

The chief thing to be attended to in the Creed is that it furnishes us with a full and every way complete summary of faith, containing nothing but what has been derived from the infallible word of God. But should any still scruple to give it admission into the Creed, it will shortly be made plain, that the place which it holds in a summary of our redemption is so important, that the omission of it greatly detracts from the benefit of Christ's death.

There are some again who think that the article contains nothing new, but is merely a repetition in different words of what was previously said respecting burial, the word Hell (Infernis) being often used in Scripture for sepulcher. I admit the truth of what they allege with regard to the not infrequent use of the term *infernos* for *sepulcher*; but I cannot adopt their opinion, for two obvious reasons. First, What folly would it have been, after explaining a matter attended with no difficulty in clear and unambiguous terms, afterwards to involve rather than illustrate it by clothing it in obscure phraseology? When two expressions having the same meaning are placed together, the latter ought to be explanatory of the former. But what kind of explanation would it be to say, the expression, *Christ was buried*, means, *he descended into hell*? My second reason is the improbability that a superfluous tautology of this description should have crept into this compendium, in which the principal articles of faith are set down summarily in the fewest possible number of words. I have no doubt that all who weigh the matter with some degree of care will here agree with me.

9 Absurd exposition concerning the Limbus Patrum. This fable refuted.

Others interpret differently—viz. That Christ descended to the souls of the Patriarchs who died under the law, to announce his accomplished redemption, and bring them out of the prison in which they were confined. To this effect, they wrest the passage in the Psalms "He hath broken the gates of brass, and cut the bars of iron in sunder." (Psalm 107:16); and the passage in Zechariah, "I have sent forth thy prisoners out of the pit wherein is no water" (Zechariah 9:11). But since the psalm foretells the deliverance of those who were held captive in distant lands, and Zechariah comparing the Babylonish disaster into which the people had been plunged to a deep dry well or abyss, at the same time declares, that the salvation of the whole Church was an escape from a profound pit, I know not how it comes to pass, that posterity imagined it to be a subterraneous cavern, to which they gave the name of *Limbus*. Though this fable has the countenance of great authors, and is now also seriously defended by many as truth, it is nothing but a fable. To conclude from it that the souls of the dead are in prison is childish. And what occasion was there that the soul of Christ should go down thither to set them at liberty? I readily admit that Christ illumined them by the power of his Spirit, enabling them to perceive that the grace of which they had only had a foretaste was then manifested to the world. And to this not improbably the passage of Peter may be applied, wherein he says, that Christ "went and preached to the spirits that were in prison" (or rather "a watch-tower") (1 Peter 3:19).

The purport of the context is that believers who had died before that time were partakers of the same grace with ourselves: for he celebrates the power of Christ's death, in that he penetrated even to the dead, pious souls obtaining an immediate view of that visitation for which they had anxiously waited; while, on the other hand, the reprobate were more clearly convinced that they were completely excluded from salvation. Although the passage in Peter is not perfectly definite, we must not interpret as if he made no distinction between the righteous and the wicked: he only means to intimate, that the death of Christ was made known to both.

10 The article of the descent to hell more accurately expounded. A great ground of comfort.

But, apart from the Creed, we must seek for a surer exposition of Christ's descent to hell: and the word of God furnishes us with one not only pious and holy, but replete with excellent consolation. Nothing had been done if Christ had only endured corporeal death. In order to interpose between God's anger and us, and satisfy his righteous judgment, it was necessary that he should feel the weight of divine vengeance. Whence also it was necessary that he should engage at close quarters with the powers of hell and the horrors of eternal death. We lately quoted from the Prophet, that the "chastisement of our peace was laid upon him" that he "was bruised for our iniquities" that he "bore our infirmities;" expressions which intimate, that, like a sponsor and surety for the guilty, and subjected to condemnation, he undertook and paid all the penalties which must have been exacted from them, the only exception being, that the pains of death could not hold him. Hence, there is nothing strange in its being said that he descended to hell, seeing he endured the death, which is inflicted on the wicked by an angry God. It is frivolous and ridiculous to object that in this way the order is perverted, it being absurd that an event, which preceded burial, should be placed after it. But after explaining what Christ endured in the sight of man, the Creed appropriately adds the invisible and incomprehensible judgment which he endured before God, to teach us that not only was the body of Christ given up as the price of redemption, but that there was a greater and more excellent price—that he bore in his soul the tortures of condemned and ruined man.

11 Confirmation of this exposition from passages of Scripture and the works of ancient Theologians. An objection refuted. Advantages of the doctrine.

In this sense, Peter says that God raised up Christ, "having loosed the pains of death: because it was not possible he should be holden of it" (Acts 2:24). He does not mention death simply, but says that the Son of God endured the pains produced by the curse and wrath of God, the source of death. How small a matter had it been to come forth securely, and in sport to undergo death. Herein was a true proof of boundless mercy, that he shunned not the death he so greatly dreaded. And there can be no doubt that, in the Epistle to the Hebrews, the Apostle means to teach the same thing, when he says that he "was heard in that he feared" (Hebrews 5:7). Some instead of "feared," use a term meaning reverence or piety, but how inappropriately, is apparent both from the nature of the thing and the form of expression. Christ then praying in a loud voice, and with tears, is heard in that he feared, not to be exempted from death, but so as not to be swallowed up of it like a sinner, though standing as our representative. And certainly, no abyss can be imagined more dreadful than to feel that you are abandoned and forsaken of God, and not heard when you invoke him, just as if he had conspired your destruction. To such a degree was Christ dejected, that in the depth of his agony he was forced to exclaim, "My God, my God, why hast thou forsaken me?"

The view taken by some, that he here expressed the opinion of others rather than his own conviction, is most improbable; for it is evident that the expression was wrung from the anguish of his inmost soul. We do not, however, insinuate that God was ever hostile to him or angry with him. How could he be angry with the beloved Son, with whom his soul was well pleased? Or how could he have appeased the Father by his intercession for others if He were hostile to himself? But this we say, that he bore the weight of the divine anger, that, smitten and afflicted, he experienced all the signs of an angry and avenging God.

Hence, Hilary argues, that to this descent we owe our exemption from death. Nor does he dissent from this view in other passages, as when he says, "The cross, death, and hell are our life." And again, "The Son of God is in hell, but man is brought back to heaven." And why do I quote the testimony of a private writer, when an Apostle asserts the same thing, stating it as one fruit of his victory that he delivered "them who through fear of death were all their lifetime subject to bondage?" (Hebrews 2:15). He behooved therefore, to conquer the fear, which incessantly vexes and agitates the breasts of all mortals; and this he could not do without a contest. Moreover, it will shortly appear with greater clearness that his was no common sorrow, was not the result of a trivial cause. Thus by engaging with the power of the devil, the fear of death, and the pains of hell, he gained the victory, and achieved a triumph, so that we now fear not in death those things which our Prince has destroyed.

12 Another objection that Christ is insulted, and despair ascribed to him in its being said that he feared. Answer, from the statements of the Evangelists, that he did fear, was troubled in spirit, amazed, and tempted in all respects as we are, yet without sin. Why Christ was pleased to become weak. His fear without sin. Refutation of another objection, with an answer to the question, Did Christ fear death, and why? When did Christ descend to hell, and how? What has been said refutes the heresy of Apollinaris and of the Monothelites.

Here some miserable creatures, who, though unlearned, are however impelled more by malice than ignorance, cry out that I am offering an atrocious insult to Christ, because it would be most incongruous to hold that he feared for the safety of his soul. Then in harsher terms they urge the calumnious charge that I attribute despair to the Son of God, a feeling the very opposite of faith. First, they wickedly raise a controversy as to the fear and dread, which Christ felt, though the Evangelists openly affirm these. For before the hour of his death arrived, he was troubled in spirit, and affected with grief, and at the very onset began to be exceedingly amazed. To speak of these feelings as merely assumed, is a shameful evasion. It becomes us, therefore (as Ambrose truly teaches), boldly to profess the agony of Christ, if we are not ashamed of the cross. And certainly had not his soul shared in the punishment, he would have been a Redeemer of bodies only. The object of his struggle was to raise up those who were lying prostrate; and so far is this from detracting from his heavenly glory, that his goodness, which can never be sufficiently extolled, becomes more conspicuous in this, that he declined not to bear our infirmities.

Hence, also that solace to our anxieties and grief which the Apostle sets before us: "We have not an High Priest who cannot be touched with the feeling of our infirmities; but was in all respects tempted like as we are, yet without sin" (Hebrews 4:15). These men pretend that a thing in its nature vicious is improperly ascribed to Christ; as if they were wiser than the Spirit of God, who in the same passage reconciles the two things—viz. that he was tempted in all respects like as we are, and yet was without sin. There is no reason, therefore, to take alarm at infirmity in Christ, infirmity to which he submitted not under the constraint of violence and necessity, but merely because he loved and pitied us. Whatever he spontaneously suffered detracts in no degree from his majesty.

One thing, which misleads these detractors, is that they do not recognize in Christ an infirmity, which was pure and free from every species of taint, inasmuch as it was kept within the limits of obedience. As no moderation can be seen in the depravity of our nature, in which all affections with turbulent impetuosity exceed their due bounds, they improperly apply the same standard to the Son of God. But as he was upright, all his affections were under such restraint as prevented everything like excess. Hence, he could resemble us in grief, fear, and dread, but still with this mark of distinction. Thus refuted, they fly off to another cavil, that although Christ feared death, yet he feared not the curse and wrath of God, from which he knew that he was safe.

But let the pious reader consider how far it is honorable to Christ to make him more effeminate and timid than the generality of men. Robbers and other malefactors contumaciously hasten to death, many men magnanimously despise it, and others meet it calmly. If the Son of God was amazed and terror-struck at the prospect of it, where was his firmness or magnanimity? We are even told, what in a common death would have been deemed most extraordinary, that in the depth of his agony his sweat was like great drops of blood falling to the ground. Nor was this a spectacle exhibited to the eyes of others, since it was from a secluded spot that he uttered his groans to his Father. And that no doubt may remain, it was necessary that angels should come down from heaven to strengthen him with miraculous consolation. How shamefully effeminate would it have been (as I have observed) to be so excruciated by the fear of an ordinary death as to sweat drops of blood, and not even be revived by the presence of angels? What? Does not that prayer, thrice repeated: "Father, if it be possible, let this cup pass from me" (Matthew 26:39)—a prayer dictated by incredible bitterness of soul—show that Christ had a fiercer and more arduous struggle than with ordinary death?

Hence, it appears that these triflers, with whom I am disputing, presume to talk of what they know not, never having seriously considered what is meant and implied by ransoming us from the justice of God. It is of consequence to understand aright how much our salvation cost the Son of God. If anyone now asks, Did Christ descend to hell at the time when he deprecated death? I answer, that this was the commencement, and that from it we may infer how dire and dreadful were the tortures, which he endured when he felt himself standing at the bar of God as a criminal in our stead. And although the divine power of the Spirit veiled itself for a moment, that it might give place to the infirmity of the flesh, we must understand that the trial arising from feelings of grief and fear was such as not to be at variance with faith. And in this was fulfilled what is said in Peter's sermon as to having been loosed from the pains of death, because "it was not possible he could be holden of it" (Acts 2:24). Though feeling forsaken of God, he did not cease in the slightest degree to confide in his goodness. This appears from the celebrated prayer in which, in the depth of his agony, he exclaimed, "My God, my God, why hast thou forsaken me?" (Matthew 27:46). Amid all his agony, he ceases not to call upon his God, while exclaiming that he is forsaken by him.

This refutes the Apollinarian heresy as well as that of those who are called Monothelites. Apollinaris pretended that in Christ, the eternal Spirit supplied the place of a soul, so that he was only half a man, as if he could have expiated our sins in any other way than by obeying the Father. But where does the feeling or desire of obedience reside but in the soul? And we know that his soul was troubled in order that ours, being free from trepidation, might obtain peace and quiet. Moreover, in opposition to the Monothelites, we see that in his human he felt a repugnance to what he willed in his divine nature. I say nothing of his subduing the fear of which we have spoken by a contrary affection. This appearance of repugnance is obvious in the words, "Father, save me from this hour: but for this cause came I unto this hour. Father, glorify thy name" (John 12:27, 28). Still, in this perplexity, there was no violent emotion, such as we exhibit while making the strongest endeavors to subdue our own feelings.

13 Of the resurrection of Christ. The many advantages from it. A. Our righteousness in the sight of God renewed and restored. B. His life as the basis of our life and hope, also the efficacious cause of new life in us. C. The pledge of our future resurrection.

Next follows the resurrection from the dead, without which all that has hitherto been said would be defective. For seeing that in the cross, death, and burial of Christ, nothing but weakness appears, faith must go beyond all these, in order that it may be provided with full strength. Hence, although in his death we have an effectual completion of salvation, because we are reconciled to God by it, satisfaction is given to his justice, the curse is removed, and the penalty paid. Still, it is not by his death, but by his resurrection that we are said to be begotten again to a living hope (1 Peter 1:3). He, by rising again, became victorious over death, so the victory of our faith consists only in his resurrection. The nature of it is better expressed in the words of Paul, "Who (Christ) was delivered for our offenses, and was raised again for our justification" (Romans 4:25); as if he had said, By his death sin was taken away, by his resurrection righteousness was renewed and restored. For how could he by dying have freed us from death, if he had yielded to its power? How could he have obtained the victory for us, if he had fallen in the contest?

Our salvation may be thus divided between the death and the resurrection of Christ: by the former sin was abolished and death annihilated; by the latter righteousness was restored and life revived, the power and efficacy of the former being still bestowed upon us by means of the latter. Paul accordingly affirms that he was declared the Son of God by his resurrection (Romans 1:4). He then fully displayed that heavenly power, which is both a bright mirror of his divinity and a sure support of our faith. He elsewhere teaches, that "though he was crucified through weakness, yet he liveth by the power of God" (2 Corinthians 13:4). In the same sense, in another passage, treating of perfection, he says, "That I may know him and the power of his resurrection" (Philippians 3:10). Immediately he adds, "...being made conformable unto his death." In perfect accordance with this is the passage in Peter: that God "raised him up from the dead, and gave him glory, that your faith and hope might be in God" (1 Peter 1:21). Not that faith founded merely on his death is vacillating, but that the divine power by which he maintains our faith is most conspicuous in his resurrection. Let us remember, therefore, that when death only is mentioned, everything peculiar to the resurrection is at the same time included, and that there is a like synecdoche in the term *resurrection*, as often as it is used apart from death, everything peculiar to death being included. But as, by rising again, he obtained the victory, and became the resurrection and the life, Paul justly argues, "If Christ be not raised, your faith is vain; ye are yet in your sins" (1 Corinthians 15:17). Accordingly, in another passage, after exulting in the death of Christ in opposition to the terrors of condemnation, he thus enlarges, "Christ that died, yea rather, that is risen again, who is even at the right hand of God, who also maketh intercession for us" (Romans 8:34).

As we have already explained that the mortification of our flesh depends on communion with the cross, so we must also understand, that a corresponding benefit is derived from his resurrection. As the Apostle says, "Like as Christ was raised up from the dead by the glory of the Father, even so we also should walk in newness of life" (Romans 6:4). Accordingly, as in another passage, from our being dead with Christ, he inculcates, "Mortify therefore your members which are upon the earth" (Colossians 3:5); so from our being risen with Christ he infers, "seek those things which are above, where Christ sitteth at the right hand of God" (Colossians 3:1). In these words we are not only urged by the example of a risen Savior to follow newness of life, but are taught that by his power we are renewed unto righteousness.

A third benefit derived from it is that, like an earnest, it assures us of our own resurrection, of which it is certain that his is the surest representation. This subject is discussed at length (1 Corinthians 15). But it is to be observed, in passing, that when he is said to have "risen from the dead," these terms express the reality both of his death and resurrection, as if it had been said, that he died the same death as other men naturally die, and received immortality in the same mortal flesh, which he had assumed.

14 Of the ascension of Christ. Why he ascended. Advantages derived from it.

The resurrection is naturally followed by the ascension into heaven. For although Christ, by rising again, began fully to display his glory and virtue, having laid aside the abject and ignoble condition of a mortal life, and the ignominy of the cross, yet it was only by his ascension to heaven that his reign truly commenced. This the Apostle shows, when he says that he ascended "that he might fill all things" (Ephesians 4:10). Thus, he reminds us that under the appearance of contradiction, there is a beautiful harmony, inasmuch as though he departed from us, it was that his departure might be more useful to us than that presence which was confined in a humble tabernacle of flesh during his abode on the earth.

Hence, John, after repeating the celebrated invitation, "If any man thirst, let him come unto me and drink," immediately adds, "the Holy Ghost was not yet given; because that Jesus was not yet glorified" (John 7:37, 39). This our Lord himself also declared to his disciples, "It is expedient for you that I go away: for if I go not away the Comforter will not come unto you" (John 16:7). To console them for his bodily absence, he tells them that he will not leave them comfortless, but will come again to them in a manner invisible indeed, but more desirable. They were then taught by a surer experience that the government, which he had obtained, and the power, which he exercises, would enable his faithful followers not only to live well, but also to die happily. And, indeed we see how much more abundantly his Spirit was poured out, how much more gloriously his kingdom was advanced, how much greater power was employed in aiding his followers and discomfiting his enemies. Being raised to heaven, he withdrew his bodily presence from our sight, not that he might cease to be with his followers, who are still pilgrims on the earth, but that he might rule both heaven and earth more immediately by his power. By his ascension, he fulfilled the promise that he made to be with us even to the end of the world. As his body has been raised above all heavens, so his power and efficacy have been propagated and diffused beyond all the bounds of heaven and earth.

This I prefer to explain in the words of Augustine rather than my own: "Through death Christ was to go to the right hand of the Father, whence he is to come to judge the quick and the dead, and that in corporal presence, according to the sound doctrine and rule of faith. For, in spiritual presence, he was to be with them after his ascension." In another passage, he is more full and explicit: "In regard to ineffable and invisible grace, is fulfilled what he said, Lo, I am with you always, even to the end of the world (Matthew

28:20). But in regard to the flesh, which the Word assumed in regard to his being born of a Virgin, and in regard to his being apprehended by the Jews, nailed to the tree, taken down from the cross, wrapped in linen clothes, laid in the sepulcher, and manifested on his resurrection, it may be said, "Me ye have not always with you." Why? Because, in bodily presence, he conversed with his disciples forty days, and leading them out where they saw, but followed not, he ascended into heaven, and is not here: for there he sits at the right hand of the Father: and yet he is here, for the presence of his Godhead was not withdrawn. Therefore, as regards his divine presence, we have Christ always: as regards his bodily presence, it was truly said to the disciples, "Me ye have not always." For a few days, the Church had him bodily present. Now, she apprehends him by faith, but sees him not by the eye."

15 Of Christ's seat at the Father's right hand. What meant by it.

Hence, it is immediately added, that he "sitteth at the right hand of God the Father;" a similitude borrowed from princes, who have their assessors to whom they commit the office of ruling and issuing commands. Thus Christ, in whom the Father is pleased to be exalted, and by whose hand he is pleased to reign, is said to have been received up and seated on his right hand (Mark 16:19). It as if he was installed in the government of heaven and earth, and formally admitted to possession of the administration committed to him. Not only was he admitted for once, but to continue until he descends to judgment. For so the Apostle interprets, when he says that the Father "set him at his own right hand in the heavenly places, far above all principality, and power, and might, and dominion, and every name that is named not only in this world, but also in that which is to come; and has put all things under his feet, and given him to be the head over all things to the Church." You see to what end he is so seated, namely, that all creatures in both heaven and earth should reverence his majesty, be ruled by his hand, do him implicit homage, and submit to his power. All that the Apostles intends when they so often mention his seat at the Father's hand, is to teach, that everything is placed at his disposal. Those, therefore, are in error, who suppose that his blessedness merely is indicated.

We may observe, that there is nothing contrary to this doctrine in the testimony of Stephen, that he saw him standing (Acts 7:56), the subject here considered being not the position of his body, but the majesty of his empire, *sitting* meaning nothing more than presiding on the judgment-seat of heaven.

16 Many advantages from the ascension of Christ. A. He gives access to the kingdom, which Adam had shut up. B. He intercedes for us with the Father. C. His virtue being thence transfused into us, he works effectually in us for salvation.

Faith derives manifold advantages from this doctrine. First, it perceives that the Lord, by his ascension to heaven, has opened up the access to the heavenly kingdom, which Adam had shut. For having entered it in our flesh, in our name, it follows, as the Apostle says, that we are in a manner now seated in heavenly places, not entertaining a mere hope of heaven, but possessing it in our head.

Secondly, faith perceives that his seat beside the Father is not without great advantage to us. Having entered the temple not made with hands, he constantly appears as our advocate and intercessor in the presence of the Father. He directs attention to his own righteousness, to turn it away from our sins. He reconciles him to us, as by his intercession to pave for us a way of access to his throne, presenting it to miserable sinners, to whom it would otherwise be an object of dread, as replete with grace and mercy.

Thirdly, it discerns his power, on which depend our strength, might, resources, and triumph over hell, "When he ascended up on high, he led captivity captive" (Ephesians 4:8). Spoiling his foes, he gave gifts to his people, and daily loads them with spiritual riches. He thus occupies his exalted seat. By transferring his virtue to us, he may quicken us to spiritual life, sanctify us by his Spirit, and adorn his Church with various graces; by his protection, preserve it safe from all harm; and by the strength of his hand, curb the enemies raging against his cross and our salvation. In fine, that he may possess all power in heaven and earth until he has utterly routed all his foes, who are also ours, and completed the structure of his Church. Such is the true nature of the kingdom, such the power that the Father has conferred upon him, until he arrives to complete the last act by judging the quick and the dead.

17 Of the return of Christ to judgment. Its nature. The quick and dead who are to be judged. Passages apparently contradictory reconciled. Mode of judgment.

Christ, indeed, gives his followers no dubious proofs of present power, but as his kingdom in the world is in a manner veiled by the humiliation of a carnal condition, faith is most properly invited to meditate on the visible presence, which he will exhibit on the last day. For he will descend from heaven in visible form, in like manner as he was seen to ascend, and appear to all, with the ineffable majesty of his kingdom, the splendor of immortality, the boundless power of divinity, and an attending company of angels. Hence, we are told to wait for the Redeemer against that day on which he will separate the sheep from the goats and the elect from the reprobate, and when not one individual either of the living or the dead shall escape his judgment. From the extremities of the universe shall be heard the clang of the trumpet summoning all to his tribunal; both those whom that day shall find alive, and those whom death shall previously have removed from the society of the living.

There are some who take the words, quick and dead, in a different sense; and, indeed, some ancient writers appear to have hesitated as to the exposition of them; but our meaning being plain and clear, is much more accordant with the Creed which was certainly written for popular use. There is nothing contrary to it in the Apostle's declaration, that it is appointed unto all men once to die. For though those who are surviving at the last day shall not die after a natural manner, yet the change, which they are to undergo, as it shall resemble, is not improperly called, death (Hebrews 9:27).

"We shall not all sleep, but we shall all be changed" (1 Corinthians 15:51). What does this mean? Their mortal life shall perish and be swallowed up in one moment, and be transformed into an entirely new nature. Though no one can deny that that destruction of the flesh will be death, it still remains true that the quick and the dead shall be summoned to judgment (1 Thessalonians 4:16); for "the dead in Christ shall rise first; then we which are alive and remain shall be caught up together with them in the clouds to meet the lord in the air." Indeed, it is probable, that these words in the Creed were taken from Peter's sermon as related by Luke (Acts 10:42), and from the solemn charge of Paul to Timothy (2 Timothy 4:1).

18 Advantages of the doctrine of Christ's return to judgment. Third part of the chapter, explaining the view to be taken of the Apostles' Creed. Summary of the Apostles' Creed.

It is most consolatory to think, that judgment is vested in him who has already destined us to share with him in the honor of judgment (Matthew 19:28); so far is it from being true, that he will ascend the judgment-seat for our condemnation. How could a most merciful prince destroy his own people? How could the head disperse its own members? How could the advocate condemn his clients? For if the Apostle, when contemplating the interposition of Christ, is bold to exclaim, "Who is he that condemneth?" (Romans 8:33), much more certain is it that Christ, the intercessor, will not condemn those whom he has admitted to his protection. It certainly gives no small security, that we shall be seated at no other tribunal than that of our Redeemer, from whom salvation is to be expected; and that he who in the Gospel now promises eternal blessedness, will then as judge ratify his promise. The end for which the Father has honored the Son by committing all judgment to him (John 5:22) was to pacify the consciences of his people when alarmed at the thought of judgment.

Hitherto, I have followed the order of the Apostles' Creed, because it states the leading articles of redemption in a few words, and may thus serve as a tablet in which the points of Christian doctrine, most deserving of attention, are brought separately and distinctly before us. I call it the Apostles' Creed, though I am by no means solicitous as to its authorship. The general consent of ancient writers certainly does ascribe it to the Apostles, either because they imagined it was written and published by them for common use, or because they thought it right to give the sanction of such authority to a compendium faithfully drawn up from the doctrine delivered by their hands.

I have no doubt, that, from the very commencement of the Church, and, therefore, in the very days of the Apostles, it held the place of a public and universally received confession, whatever be the quarter from which it originally proceeded. It is not probable that some private individual wrote it, since it is certain that, from time immemorial, it was deemed of sacred authority by all Christians. The only point of consequence we hold to be incontrovertible—viz. that it gives, in clear and succinct order, a full statement of our faith and in everything that it contains is sanctioned by the sure testimony of Scripture. This being understood, it would be to no purpose to labor anxiously, or quarrel with anyone as to the authorship, unless, indeed, we think it not enough to possess the sure truth of the Holy Spirit, without, at the same time, knowing by whose mouth it was pronounced, or by whose hand it was written.

19 Conclusion of the whole chapter, showing that in Christ the salvation of the elect in all its parts is comprehended.

When we see that the whole sum of our salvation, and every single part of it, are comprehended in Christ, we must beware of deriving even the smallest portion of it from any other quarter. If we seek salvation, we are taught by the very name of Jesus that he possesses it. If we seek any other gifts of the Spirit, we shall find them in his unction: strength in his government, purity in his conception, and indulgence in his nativity. He was made like us in all respects, in order that he might learn to sympathize with us. If we seek redemption, we shall find it in his passion; acquittal in his condemnation; remission of the curse in his cross; satisfaction in his sacrifice; purification in his blood; reconciliation in his descent to hell; mortification of the flesh in his sepulcher; newness of life and immortality in his resurrection; the inheritance of a celestial kingdom in his entrance into heaven; protection, security, and the abundant supply of all blessings in his kingdom; and secure anticipation of judgment in the power of judging committed to him. In fine, since in him all kinds of blessings are treasured up, let us draw a full supply from him, and none from any other quarter. Those who, not satisfied with him alone, entertain various hopes from others, though they may continue to look to him chiefly, deviate from the right path by the simple fact, that some portion of their thought takes a different direction. No distrust of this description can arise when once the abundance of his blessings is properly known.

Chapter 17

CHRIST RIGHTLY AND PROPERLY SAID TO HAVE MERITED GRACE AND SALVATION FOR US.

The three leading divisions of this chapter are, —I. A proof from reason and from Scripture that the grace of God and the merit of Christ (the prince and author of our salvation) are perfectly compatible, sections 1 and 2. II. Christ, by his obedience, even to the death of the cross (which was the price of our redemption), merited divine favor for us, sections 3–5. III. The presumptuous rashness of the Schoolmen in treating this branch of doctrine, section 6.

Sections
1. Christ not only the minister, but also the author and prince of salvation. Divine grace not obscured by this mode of expression. The merit of Christ not opposed to the mercy of God, but depends upon it.

2. The compatibility of the two proved by various passages of Scripture.

3. Christ by his obedience truly merited divine grace for us.

4. This grace obtained by the shedding of Christ's blood, and his obedience even unto death.

5. In this way, he paid our ransom.

6. The presumptuous manner in which the Schoolmen handle this subject.

1 Christ not only the minister, but also the author and prince of salvation. Divine grace not obscured by this mode of expression. The merit of Christ not opposed to the mercy of God, but depends upon it.

A question must here be considered by way of supplement. Some men, while they admit that we obtain salvation through Christ, are too much given to subtlety and will not hear of the name of merit, by which they imagine that the grace of God is obscured. They therefore insist that Christ was only the instrument or minister, not the author or leader or prince of life, as he is designated by Peter (Acts 3:15). I admit that if Christ were opposed simply, by himself and to the justice of God, there could be no room for merit, because there cannot be found in man a worth that could make God a debtor. Nay, as Augustine says most truly, "The Savior, the man Christ Jesus, is himself the brightest illustration of predestination and grace: his character as such was not procured by any antecedent merit of works or faith in his human nature.

Tell me, I pray, how that man, when assumed into unity of person by the Word, co-eternal with the Father, as the only begotten Son at God, could merit this." And, "Let the very fountain of grace, therefore, appear in our head, whence, according to the measure of each, it is diffused through all his members. Every man, from the commencement of his faith, becomes a Christian, by the same grace by which that man from his formation became Christ." Again, in another passage, "There is not a more striking example of predestination than the mediator himself. He who made him (without any antecedent merit in his will) of the seed of David a righteous man never to be unrighteous, also converts those who are members of his head from unrighteous into righteous" and so forth. Therefore, when we treat of the merit of Christ, we do not place the beginning in him, but we ascend to the ordination of God as the primary cause, because of his mere good pleasure he appointed a Mediator to purchase salvation for us.

Hence, the merit of Christ is inconsiderately opposed to the mercy of God. It is a well-known rule, that principal and accessory are not incompatible, and therefore there is nothing to prevent the justification of man from being the gratuitous result of the mere mercy of God, and, at the same time, to prevent the merit of Christ from intervening in subordination to this mercy. The free favor of God is as fitly opposed to our works, as is the obedience of Christ. Christ could not merit anything except by the good pleasure of God, but only inasmuch as he was destined to appease the wrath of God by his sacrifice and wipe away our transgressions by his obedience. Since the merit of Christ depends entirely on the grace of God (which provided this mode of salvation for us), the latter is no less appropriately opposed to all righteousness of men than is the former.

2 The compatibility of the two proved by various passages of Scripture.

This distinction is found in numerous passages of Scripture: "God so loved the world, that he gave his only begotten Son, that whosoever believeth in him might not perish" (John 3:16). We see that the first place is assigned to the love of God as the chief cause or origin, and that faith in Christ follows as the second and more proximate cause. Should anyone object that Christ is only the formal cause, he lessens his energy more than the words justify. For if we obtain justification by a faith which leans on him, the groundwork of our salvation must be sought in him. This is clearly proved by several passages: "Herein is love, not that we loved God, but that he loved us, and sent his Son to be the propitiation for our sins" (1 John 4:10). These words clearly demonstrate that God, in order to remove any obstacle to his love towards us, appointed the method of reconciliation in Christ. There is great force in this word "*propitiation;*" for in a manner that cannot be expressed, God, at the very time when he loved us, was hostile to us until reconciled in Christ.

To this effect are all the following passages: "He is the propitiation for our sins;" "It pleased the Father that in him should all fullness dwell, and having made peace by the blood of his cross, by him to reconcile all things unto himself;" "God was in Christ reconciling the world unto himself, not imputing their trespasses unto them;" "He has made us accepted in the Beloved," "That he might reconcile both into one body by the cross." The nature of this mystery is to be learned from the first chapter to the Ephesians, where Paul, teaching that we were chosen in Christ, at the same time adds, that we obtained grace in him. How did God begin to embrace with his favor those whom he had loved before the foundation of the world, unless in displaying his love when he was reconciled by the blood of Christ? As God is the fountain of all righteousness, he must necessarily be the enemy and judge of man so long as he is a sinner. Wherefore, the commencement of love is the bestowing of righteousness, as described by Paul: "He has made him to be sin for us who knew no sin; that we might be made the righteousness of God in him" (2 Corinthians 5:21). He intimates that by the sacrifice of Christ, we obtain free justification and become pleasing to God, though we are by nature the children of wrath and by sin estranged from him. This distinction is also noted whenever the grace of Christ is connected with the love of God (2 Corinthians 13:13); whence it follows, that he bestows upon us of his own which he acquired by purchase. For otherwise there would be no ground for the praise ascribed to him by the Father: that grace is his and proceeds from him.

3 Christ by his obedience truly merited divine grace for us.

That Christ, by his obedience, truly purchased and merited grace for us with the Father is accurately implied by several passages of Scripture. I take it for granted, that if Christ satisfied for our sins, if he paid the penalty due by us, if he appeased God by his obedience; in fine, if he suffered the just for the unjust, salvation was obtained for us by his righteousness; which is just equivalent to meriting. Now, Paul's testimony is, that we were reconciled, and received reconciliation through his death (Romans 5:11). But there is no room for reconciliation unless where offense has preceded. The meaning, therefore, is that God, to whom we were hateful through sin, was appeased by the death of his Son, and made propitious to us. And the antithesis, which immediately follows, is carefully to be observed, "As by one man's disobedience many were made sinners, so by the obedience of one shall many be made righteous" (Romans 5:19). For the meaning is—As by the sin of Adam we were alienated from God and doomed to destruction, so by the obedience of Christ we are restored to his favor as if we were righteous. The future tense of the verb does not exclude present righteousness, as is apparent from the context. For he had previously said, "the free gift *is* of many offenses unto justification."

4 This grace obtained by the shedding of Christ's blood, and his obedience even unto death.

When we say that grace was obtained for us by the merit of Christ, our meaning is that his blood cleansed us, and that his death was expiation for sin. "His blood cleanses us from all sin." "This is my blood, which is shed for the remission of sins" (1 John 1:7; Luke 22:20). If the effect of his shed blood is, that our sins are not imputed to us, it follows, that by that price the justice of God was satisfied. To the same effect are the Baptist's words, "Behold the Lamb of God, which taketh away the sin of the world" (John 1:29). For he contrasts Christ with all the sacrifices of the Law, showing that in him alone was fulfilled what these figures typified. But we know the common expression in Moses—Iniquity shall be expiated, sin shall be wiped away and forgiven. In short, we are admirably taught by the ancient figures what power and efficacy there is in Christ's death.

The Apostle, skillfully proceeding from this principle, explains the whole matter in the Epistle to the Hebrews, showing that without shedding of blood there is no remission (Hebrews 9:22). From this he infers that Christ appeared once for all to take away sin by the sacrifice of himself. Again, that he was offered to bear the sins of many (Hebrews 9:12). He had previously said, that not by the blood of goats or of heifers, but by his own blood, he had once entered into the holy of holies, having obtained eternal redemption for us. Now, when he reasons thus, "If the blood of bulls and of goats, and the ashes of an heifer sprinkling the unclean, sanctifieth to the purifying of the flesh: how much more shall the blood of Christ, who through the eternal Spirit offered himself to God, purge your consciences from dead works to serve the living God?" (Hebrews 9:13, 14).

It is obvious that too little effect is given to the grace of Christ, unless we concede to his sacrifice the power of expiating, appeasing, and satisfying. As he shortly adds, "For this cause he is the mediator of the new testament, that by means of his death, for the redemption of the transgressions that were under the first testament, they which are called might receive the promise of eternal inheritance" (Hebrews 9:15). But it is especially necessary to attend to the analogy, which is drawn by Paul as to his having been made a curse for us (Galatians 3:13).

It had been superfluous and therefore absurd, that Christ should have been burdened with a curse, had it not been in order that, by paying what others owed, he might acquire righteousness for them. There is no ambiguity in Isaiah's testimony, "He was wounded for our transgressions, he was bruised for our iniquities: the chastisement of our peace was laid upon him; and with his stripes we are healed" (Isaiah 53:3). For had not Christ satisfied for our sins, he could not be said to have appeased God by taking upon himself the penalty which we had incurred. To this corresponds what follows in the same place, "for the transgression of my people was he stricken" (Isaiah 53:8).

We may add the interpretation of Peter, who unequivocally declares, that he "bare our sins in his own body on the tree" (1 Peter 2:24), that the whole burden of condemnation, of which we were relieved, was laid upon him.

5 In this way, he paid our ransom.

The Apostles also plainly declare that he paid a price to ransom us from death: "Being justified freely by his grace, through the redemption that is in Christ Jesus: whom God has set forth to be a propitiation through faith in his blood" (Romans 3:24, 25). Paul commends the grace of God, in that he gave the price of redemption in the death of Christ; and he exhorts us to flee to his blood, that having obtained righteousness, we may appear boldly before the judgment-seat of God. To the same effect are the words of Peter: "Forasmuch as ye know that ye were not redeemed with corruptible things, as silver and gold," "but with the precious blood of Christ, as of a lamb without blemish and without spot" (1 Peter 1:18, 19). The antithesis would be incongruous if he had not made satisfaction for sins by this price. For which reason, Paul says, "Ye are bought with a price." Nor could it be elsewhere said, there is "one mediator between God and men, the man Christ Jesus; who gave himself a ransom for all" (1 Timothy 1:5, 6), had not the punishment which we deserved been laid upon him.

Accordingly, the same Apostle declares, that "we have redemption through his blood, even the forgiveness of sins" (Colossians 1:14); as if he had said, that we are justified or acquitted before God, because that blood serves the purpose of satisfaction. With this, another passage agrees—viz. that he blotted out "the handwriting of ordinances which was against us, which was contrary to us" (Colossians 2:14). These words denote the payment or compensation, which acquits us from guilt.

There is great weight also in these words of Paul: "If righteousness come by the law, then Christ is dead in vain" (Galatians 2:21). For we hence infer, that it is from Christ we must seek what the Law would confer on anyone who fulfilled it; or, which is the same thing, that by the grace of Christ we obtain what God promised in the Law to our works: "If a man do, he shall live in them" (Leviticus 18:5).

This is no less clearly taught in the discourse at Antioch, when Paul declares, "That through this man is preached unto you the forgiveness of sins; and by him all that believe are justified from all things, from which ye could not be justified by the law of Moses" (Acts 13:38, 39). For if the observance of the Law is righteousness, who can deny that Christ, by taking this burden upon himself, and reconciling us to God, as if we were the observers of the Law, merited favor for us?

Of the same nature is what he afterwards says to the Galatians: "God sent forth his Son, made of a woman, made under the law, to redeem them that were under the law" (Galatians 4:4, 5). For to what end that subjection, unless that he obtained justification for us by undertaking to perform what we were unable to pay? Hence, that imputation of righteousness without works, of which Paul treats (Romans 4:5), the righteousness found in Christ alone being accepted as if it were ours. And certainly, the only reason that Christ is called our "meat" (John 6:55) is that we find in him the substance of life. And the source of this efficacy is just that the Son of God was crucified as the price of our justification; as Paul says, Christ "has given himself for us an offering and a sacrifice to God for a sweet-smelling savor" (Ephesians 5:2); and elsewhere, he "was delivered for our offenses, and was raised again for our justification" (Romans 4:25).

Hence, it is proved not only that Christ gave us salvation, but also that because of him the Father is now propitious to us. For it cannot be doubted that in him is completely fulfilled what God declares by Isaiah under a figure, "I will defend this city to save it for mine own sakes and for my servant David's sake" (Isaiah 37:35). Of this, the Apostle is the best witness when he says "Your sins are forgiven you for his name's sake" (1 John 2:12). For although the name of Christ is not expressed, John, in his usual manner, designates him by the pronoun "He."

In the same sense also our Lord declares, "As the living Father has sent me, and I live by the Father: so he that eateth me, even he shall live by me" (John 6:57). To this corresponds the passage of Paul, "Unto you it is given in the behalf of Christ, not only to believe in him, but also to suffer for his sake" (Philippians 1:29).

6 The presumptuous manner in which the Schoolmen handle this subject.

To inquire, as Lombard and the Schoolmen do, whether he merited for himself, is foolish curiosity. Equally rash is their decision when they answer in the affirmative. How could it be necessary for the only Son of God to come down in order to acquire some new quality for himself? The exposition, which God gives of his own purpose, removes all doubt. The Father is not said to have consulted the advantage of his Son in his services, but to have given him up to death, and not spared him, because he loved the world

(Romans 8). The prophetical expressions should be observed: "To us a Son is born;" "Rejoice greatly, O daughter of Zion: shout, O daughter of Jerusalem: behold, thy King cometh unto thee" (Isaiah 9:6, Zechariah 9:9). It would otherwise be a cold commendation of love, which Paul describes, when he says, "God commendeth his love toward us, in that, while we were yet sinners, Christ died for us" (Romans 5:8). Hence, again, we infer that Christ had no regard to himself; and this he distinctly affirms, when he says, "For their sakes I sanctify myself" (John 17:19). He, who transfers the benefit of his holiness to others, testifies that he acquires nothing for himself. Surely, it is most worthy of remark, that Christ, in devoting himself entirely to our salvation, in a manner forgot himself. It is absurd to wrest the testimony of Paul to a different effect: "Wherefore God has highly exalted him, and given him a name which is above every name" (Philippians 2:9). By what services could a man merit to become the judge of the world, the head of angels, to obtain the supreme government of God, and become the residence of that majesty of which all the virtues of men and angels cannot attain one thousandth part? The solution is easy and complete. Paul is not speaking of the cause of Christ's exaltation, but only pointing out a consequence of it by way of example to us. The meaning is not much different from that of another passage: "Ought not Christ to have suffered these things, and to enter into his glory?" (Luke 24:26).

End of Book Second

One Hundred Aphorisms

CONTAINING, WITHIN A NARROW COMPASS,
THE SUBSTANCE AND ORDER OF THE
FOUR BOOKS OF THE

Institutes of the Christian Religion

Book 1

1. The true wisdom of man consists in the knowledge of God the Creator and Redeemer.

2. This knowledge is naturally implanted in us, and the end of it ought to be the worship of God rightly performed, or reverence for the Deity accompanied by fear and love.

3. But this seed is corrupted by ignorance, whence arises superstitious worship; and by wickedness, whence arise slavish dread and hatred of the Deity.

4. It is also from another source that it is derived namely, from the structure of the whole world, and from the Holy Scriptures.

5. This structure teaches us what are the goodness, power, justice, and wisdom of God in creating all things in heaven and earth, and in preserving them by ordinary and extraordinary government, by which his Providence is more clearly made known. It teaches also, what are our wants, that we may learn to place our confidence in the goodness, power, and wisdom of God, to obey his commandments, to flee to him in adversity, and to offer thanksgiving to him for the gifts, which we enjoy.

6. By the Holy Scriptures, also, God the Creator is known. We ought to consider what these Scriptures are; that they are true, and have proceeded from the Spirit of God; which is proved by the testimony of the Holy Spirit, by the efficacy and antiquity of the Scriptures, by the certainty of the Prophecies, by the miraculous preservation of the Law, by the calling and writings of the Apostles, by the consent of the Church, and by the

steadfastness of the martyrs, whence it is evident that all the principles of piety are overthrown by those fanatics who, laying aside the Scripture, fly to revelations.

7. Next, what they teach; or, what is the nature of God in himself and in the creation and government of all things.

8. The nature of God in himself is infinite, invisible, eternal, almighty; whence it follows that they are mistaken who ascribe to God a visible form. In his one essence, there are three persons, the Father, the Son, and the Holy Spirit.

9. In the creation of all things there are chiefly considered, A. Heavenly and spiritual substances, that is, angels, of which some are good and the protectors of the godly, while others are bad, not by creation, but by corruption; B. Earthly substances, and particularly man, whose perfection is displayed in soul and in body.

10. In the government of all things, the nature of God is manifested. Now his government is, in one respect, universal, by which he directs all the creatures according to the properties, which he bestowed on each when he created them.

11. In another respect, it is special; which appears in regard to contingent events, so that if any person is visited either by adversity or by any prosperous result, he ought to ascribe it wholly to God; and with respect to those things which act according to a fixed law of nature, though their peculiar properties were naturally bestowed on them, still they exert their power only so far as they are directed by the immediate hand of God.

12. It is viewed also with respect to time past and future. *Past*, that we may learn that all things happen by the appointment of God, who acts either by means, or without means, or contrary to means; so that everything which happens yields good to the godly and evil to the wicked. *Future*, to which belong human deliberations, and which shows that we ought to employ lawful means; since that Providence on which we rely furnishes its own means.

13. Lastly, by attending to the advantage, which the godly derive from it. For we know certainly, A. That God takes care of the whole human race, but especially of his Church. B. That God governs all things by his will, and regulates them by his wisdom. C. That he has most abundant power of doing good; for in his hand are heaven and earth, all creatures are subject to his sway, the godly rest on his protection, and the power of hell is restrained by his authority. That nothing happens by chance, though the causes may be concealed, but by the will of God; by his secret will which we are unable to explore, but adore with reverence, and by his will which is conveyed to us in the Law and in the Gospel.

Book 2

14. The knowledge of God the Redeemer is obtained from the fall of man, and from the material cause of redemption.

15. In the fall of man, we must consider what he ought to be, and what he may be.

16. For he was created after the image of God; that is, he was made a partaker of the divine Wisdom, Righteousness, and Holiness, and, being thus perfect in soul and in body, was bound to render to God a perfect obedience to his commandments.

17. The immediate causes of the fall were—Satan, the Serpent, Eve, the forbidden fruit; the remote causes were—unbelief, ambition, ingratitude, and obstinacy. Hence, followed the obliteration of the image of God in man, who became unbelieving, unrighteous, and liable to death.

18. We must now see what he may be, in respect both of soul and of body. The understanding of the soul in divine things, that is, in the knowledge and true worship of God, is blinder than a mole; good works it can neither contrive nor perform. In human affairs, as in the liberal and mechanical arts, it is exceedingly blind and variable. Now the will, so far as regards divine things, chooses only what is evil. So far as regards lower and human affairs, it is uncertain, wandering, and not wholly at its own disposal.

19. The body follows the depraved appetites of the soul, is liable to many infirmities, and at length to death.

20. Hence, it follows that redemption for ruined man must be sought through Christ the Mediator; because the first adoption of a chosen people, the preservation of the Church, her deliverance from dangers, her recovery after dispersions, and the hope of the godly, always depended on the grace of the Mediator. Accordingly, the law was given, that it might keep their minds in suspense until the coming of Christ; which is evident from the history of a gracious covenant frequently repeated, from ceremonies, sacrifices, and washings, from the end of adoption, and from the law of the priesthood.

21. The material cause of redemption is Christ, in whom we must consider three things; A. How he is exhibited to men; B. How he is received; C. How men are retained in his fellowship.

22. Christ is exhibited to men by the Law and by the Gospel.

23. The Law is threefold: Ceremonial, Judicial, and Moral. The use of the Ceremonial Law is repealed; its effect is perpetual. The Judicial or Political Law was peculiar to the Jews, and has been set aside, while that universal justice which is described in the Moral Law remains. The latter, or Moral

Law, the object of which is to cherish and maintain godliness and righteousness, is perpetual, and is incumbent on all.

24. The use of the Moral Law is threefold. The first use shows our weakness, unrighteousness, and condemnation; not that we may despair, but that we may flee to Christ. The second is that those who are not moved by promises may be urged by the terror of threatening. The third is, that we may know what is the will of God; that we may consider it in order to obedience; that our minds may be strengthened for that purpose; and that we may be kept from falling.

25. The sum of the Law is contained in the Preface, and in the two Tables. In the Preface we observe, A. The power of God, to constrain the people by the necessity of obedience; B. A promise of grace, by which he declares himself the God of the Church; C. A kind act, on the ground of which he charges the Jews with ingratitude, if they do not requite his goodness.

26. The first Table, which relates to the worship of God, consists of four commandments.

27. The design of the First Commandment is that God alone may be exalted in his people. To God alone, therefore, we owe adoration, trust, invocation, and thanksgiving.

28. The design of the Second Commandment is that God will not have his worship profaned by superstitious rites. It consists of two parts. The former restrains our licentious daring, that we may not subject God to our senses, or represent him under any visible shape. The latter forbids us to worship any images on religious grounds, and, therefore, proclaims his power, which he cannot suffer to be despised, —his jealousy, for he cannot bear a partner, —his vengeance on children's children, —his mercy to those who adore his majesty.

29. The Third Commandment enjoins three things: A. That whatever our mind conceives, or our tongue utters, may have a regard to the majesty of God; B. That we may not rashly abuse his holy word and adorable mysteries for the purposes of ambition or avarice; C. That we may not throw obloquy on his works, but may speak of them with commendations of his Wisdom, Long-suffering, Power, Goodness, Justice. With these is contrasted a threefold profanation of the name of God, by perjury, unnecessary oaths, and idolatrous rites; that is, when we substitute in the place of God saints, or creatures animate or inanimate.

30. The design of the Fourth Commandment is that, being dead to our own affections and works, we may meditate on the kingdom of God. Now there are three things here to be considered: A. A spiritual rest, when believers abstain from their own works, that God may work in them; B. That there may be a stated day for calling on the name of God, for hearing his word,

and for performing religious rites; C. That servants may have some remission from labor.

31. The Second Table, which relates to the duties of charity towards our neighbor, contains the last Six Commandments. The design of the Fifth Commandment is, that, since God takes pleasure in the observance of his own ordinance, the degrees of dignity appointed by him must be held inviolable. We are therefore forbidden to take anything from the dignity of those who are above us, by contempt, obstinacy, or ingratitude; and we are commanded to pay them reverence, obedience, and gratitude.

32. The design of the Sixth Commandment is that, since God has bound mankind by a kind of unity, the safety of all ought to be considered by each person; whence it follows that we are forbidden to do violence to private individuals, and are commanded to exercise benevolence.

33. The design of the Seventh Commandment is that, because God loves purity, we ought to put away from us all uncleanness. He therefore forbids adultery in mind, word, and deed.

34. The design of the Eighth Commandment is that, since injustice is an abomination to God, he requires us to render to every man what is his own. Now men steal, either by violence, or by malicious imposture, or by craft, or by sycophancy, etc.

35. The design of the Ninth Commandment is, that, since God, who is truth, abhors falsehood, he forbids calumnies and false accusations, by which the name of our neighbor is injured, —and lies, by which anyone suffers loss in his fortunes. On the other hand, he requires every one of us to defend the name and property of our neighbor by asserting the truth.

36. The design of the Tenth Commandment is, that, since God would have the whole soul pervaded by love, every desire averse to charity must be banished from our minds; and therefore every feeling, which tends to the injury of another is forbidden.

37. We have said that Christ is revealed to us by the Gospel. In addition, first, the agreement between the Gospel, or the New Testament, and the Old Testament is demonstrated: A. Because the godly, under both dispensations, have had the same hope of immortality; B. They have had the same covenant, founded not on the works of men, but on the mercy of God; C. They have had the same Mediator between God and men—Christ.

38. Next, five points of difference between the two dispensations are pointed out. A. Under the Law the heavenly inheritance was held out to them under earthly blessings; but under the Gospel, our minds are led directly to meditate upon it. B. The Old Testament, by means of figures, presented the image only, while the reality was absent; but the New Testament exhibits the present truth. C. The former, in respect of the Law, was the ministry of condemnation and death; the latter, of righteousness and life. D. The former

is connected with bondage, which begets fear in the mind; the latter is connected with freedom, which produces confidence. E. The word had been confined to the single nation of the Jews; but now it is preached to all nations.

39. The sum of evangelical doctrine is, to teach, A. What Christ is; B. Why he was sent; C. In what manner he accomplished the work of redemption.

40. Christ is God and man: *God*, that he may bestow on his people righteousness, sanctification, and redemption; *Man*, because he had to pay the debt of man.

41. He was sent to perform the office, A. Of a Prophet, by preaching the truth, by fulfilling the prophecies, by teaching and doing the will of his Father; B. Of a King, by governing the whole Church and every member of it, and by defending his people from every kind of adversaries; C. Of a Priest, by offering his body as a sacrifice for sins, by reconciling God to us though his obedience, and by perpetual intercession for his people to the Father.

42. He performed the office of a Redeemer by dying for our sins, by rising again for our justification, by opening heaven to us through his ascension, by sitting at the right hand of the Father whence he will come to judge the quick and the dead; and, therefore, he procured for us the grace of God and salvation.

Book 3

43. We receive Christ the Redeemer by the power of the Holy Spirit, who unites us to Christ; and, therefore, he is called the Spirit of sanctification and adoption, the earnest and seal of our salvation, water, oil, a fountain, fire, the hand of God.

44. Faith is the hand of the soul, which receives, through the same efficacy of the Holy Spirit, Christ offered to us in the Gospel.

45. The general office of faith is, to assent to the truth of God, whenever, whatever, and in what manner soever he speaks; but its peculiar office is, to behold the will of God in Christ, his mercy, the promises of grace, for the full conviction of which the Holy Spirit enlightens our minds and strengthens our hearts.

46. Faith, therefore, is a steady and certain knowledge of the divine kindness towards us, which is founded on a gracious promise through Christ, and is revealed to our minds and sealed on our hearts by the Holy Spirit.

47. The effects of faith are four: A. Repentance; B. A Christian life; C. Justification; D. Prayer.

48. True repentance consists of two parts: A. Mortification, which proceeds from the acknowledgment of sin, and a real perception of the divine displeasure; B. Quickening, the fruits of which are—piety towards God, charity towards our neighbor, the hope of eternal life, holiness of life. With this true repentance is contrasted false repentance, the parts of which are, Contrition, Confession, and Satisfaction. The two former may be referred to true repentance, provided that there be contrition of heart because of the acknowledgment of sin. It must not be separated from the hope of forgiveness through Christ. The confession must be either *private* to God alone or made to the pastors of the Church willingly and for the purpose of consolation, not for the enumeration of offenses, and for introducing a torture of the conscience; or *public*, which is made to the whole Church, or to one or many persons in presence of the whole Church. What was formerly called Ecclesiastical Satisfaction, that is, what was made for the edification of the Church on account of repentance and public confession of sins, was introduced as due to God by the Sophists; whence sprung the supplements of Indulgences in this world, and the fire of Purgatory after death. But that Contrition of the Sophists, Auricular Confession (as they call it), and the Satisfaction of actual performance are opposed to the free forgiveness of sins.

49. The two parts of a Christian life are laid down: A. The love of righteousness; that we may be holy, because God is holy, and because we are united to him, and are reckoned among his people; B. That a rule may be prescribed to us, which does not permit us to wander in the course of righteousness, and that we may be conformed to Christ. A model of this is laid down to us, which we ought to copy in our whole life. Next are mentioned the blessings of God, which it will argue extreme ingratitude if we do not requite.

50. The sum of the Christian life is denial of ourselves.

51. The ends of this self-denial are four. A. That we may devote ourselves to God as a living sacrifice. B. That we may not seek our own things, but those which belong to God and to our neighbor. C. That we may patiently bear the cross, the fruits of which are—acknowledgment of our weakness, the trial of our patience, correction of faults, more earnest prayer, and more cheerful meditation on eternal life. D. That we may know in what manner we ought to use the present life and its aids, for necessity and delight. Necessity demands that we possess all things as though we possessed them not; that we bear poverty with mildness, and abundance with moderation; that we know how to endure patiently fullness, and hunger, and want; that we pay regard to our neighbor, because we must give account of our

stewardship; and that all things correspond to our calling. The delight of praising the kindness of God ought to be with us a stronger argument.

52. In considering Justification, which is the third effect of faith, the first thing that occurs is an explanation of the word. He is said to be justified who, in the judgment of God, is deemed righteous. He is justified by works, whose life is pure and blameless before God; and no such person ever existed except Christ. They are justified by faith who, shut out from the righteousness of works, receive the righteousness of Christ. Such are the elect of God.

53. Hence follows the strongest consolation; for instead of a severe Judge, we have a most merciful Father. Justified in Christ, and having peace, trusting to his power, we aim at holiness.

54. Next follows Christian liberty, consisting of three parts. A. That the consciences of believers may rise above the Law, and may forget the whole righteousness of the Law. B. That the conscience, free from the yoke of the Law, may cheerfully obey the will of God. C. That they may not be bound by any religious scruples before God about things indifferent. But here we must avoid two precipices. A. That we do not abuse the gifts of God. B. That we avoid giving and taking offense.

55. The fourth effect of faith is Prayer; in which are considered its fruits, laws, faults, and petitions.

56. The fruit of prayer is fivefold. A. When we are accustomed to flee to God, our heart is inflamed with a stronger desire to seek, love, and adore him. B. Our heart is not a prey to any wicked desire, of which we would be ashamed to make God our witness. C. We receive his benefits with thanksgiving. D. Having obtained a gift, we more earnestly meditate on the goodness of God. E. Experience confirms to us the Goodness, Providence, and Truth of God.

57. The laws are four. A. That we should have our heart framed as becomes those who enter into converse with God; and therefore the lifting up of the hands, the raising of the heart, and perseverance, are recommended. B. That we should feel our wants. C. That we should divest ourselves of every thought of our own glory, giving the whole glory to God. D. That while we are prostrated amidst overwhelming evils, we should be animated by the sure hope of succeeding, since we rely on the command and promise of God.

58. They err who call on the Saints that are placed beyond this life. A. Because Scripture teaches that prayer ought to be offered to God alone, who alone knows what is necessary for us. He chooses to be present, because he has promised. He can do so, for he is Almighty. B. Because he requires that he is addressed in faith, which rests on his word and promise. C. Because faith is corrupted as soon as it departs from this rule. But in calling on the saints, there is no word, no promise; and therefore there is no faith; nor can the saints themselves either hear or assist.

59. The summary of prayer, which has been delivered to us by Christ the Lord, is contained in a Preface and two Tables.

60. In the Preface, the Goodness of God is conspicuous, for he is called *our Father*. It follows that we are his children, and that to seek supplies from any other quarter would be to charge God either with poverty or with cruelty; that sins ought not to hinder us from humbly imploring mercy; and that a feeling of brotherly love ought to exist amongst us. The power of God is likewise conspicuous in this Preface, for he is *in Heaven*. Hence, we infer that God is present everywhere, and that when we seek him, we ought to rise above perceptions of the body and the soul; that he is far beyond all risk of change or corruption; that he holds the whole universe in his grasp, and governs it by his power.

61. The First Table is entirely devoted to the glory of God, and contains three petitions. A. That the *name* of God, that is, his power, goodness, wisdom, justice, and truth, *may be hallowed*; that is, that men may neither speak nor think of God but with the deepest veneration. B. That God may correct, by the agency of his Spirit, all the depraved lusts of the flesh; may bring all our thoughts into obedience to his authority; may protect his children; and may defeat the attempts of the wicked. The use of this petition is threefold. (1). It withdraws us from the corruptions of the world. (2). It inflames us with the desire of mortifying the flesh. (3). It animates us to endure the cross. C. The Third petition relates not to the secret will of God, but to that which is made known by the Scriptures, and to which voluntary obedience is the counterpart.

62. The Second Table contains the three remaining petitions, which relate to our neighbors and ourselves. A. It asks everything, which the body needs in this sublunary state; for we commit ourselves to the care and providence of God, that he may feed, foster, and preserve us. B. We ask those things which contribute to the spiritual life, namely, the *forgiveness of sins*, which implies satisfaction, and to which is added a condition, that when we have been offended by deed or by word, we nevertheless forgive them their offenses against us. C. We ask *deliverance from temptations*, or, that we may be furnished with armor and defended by the Divine protection, that we may be able to obtain the victory. *Temptations* differ in their *causes*, for God, Satan, the world, and the flesh *tempt*; in their *matter*, for we are tempted, on the right hand, in respect of riches, honors, beauty, etc., and on the left hand, in respect of poverty, contempt, and afflictions: and in their *end*, for God tempts the godly for good, but Satan, the flesh, and the world, tempt them for evil.

63. Those Four effects of faith bring us to the certainty of election, and of the final resurrection.

64. The causes of election are these. The *efficient* cause is—the free mercy of God, which we ought to acknowledge with humility and

thanksgiving. The *material* cause is—Christ, the well-beloved Son. The *final* cause is—that, being assured of our salvation, because we are God's people, we may glorify him both in this life and in the life which is to come, to all eternity. The effects are, in respect either of many persons, or of a single individual; and that by electing some, and justly reprobating others. The elect are called by the preaching of the word and the illumination of the Holy Spirit, are justified, and sanctified, that they may at length be glorified.

65. The final resurrection will take place. A. Because on any other supposition we cannot be perfectly glorified. B. Because Christ rose in our flesh. C. Because God is Almighty.

Book 4

66. God keeps us united in the fellowship of Christ by means of Ecclesiastical and Civil government.

67. In Ecclesiastical government, three things are considered. A. What is the Church? B. How is it governed? C. What is its power?

68. The Church is regarded in two points of view; as Invisible and Universal, which is the communion of saints; and as Visible and Particular. The Church is discerned by the pure preaching of the word, and by the lawful administration of the sacraments.

69. As to the government of the Church, there are five points of inquiry. A. Who rule? B. What are they? C. What is their calling? D. What is their office? E. What was the condition of the ancient Church?

70. They that rule are not Angels, but Men. In this respect, God declares his condescension towards us: we have a most excellent training to humility and obedience, and it is singularly fitted to bind us to mutual charity.

71. These are Prophets, Apostles, Evangelists, whose office was temporary; Pastors and Teachers, whose office is of perpetual duration.

72. Their calling is twofold: *internal* and *external*. The *internal* is from the Spirit of God. In the *external,* there are four things to be considered. A. What sort of persons ought to be chosen? Men of sound doctrine and holy lives. B. In what manner? With fasting and prayer. C. By whom? Immediately, by God, as Prophets and Apostles. Mediately, with the direction of the word, by Bishops, by Elders, and by the people. D. With what rite of ordination? By the laying on of hands, the use of which is threefold. (1). That the dignity of the ministry may be commended. (2). That he who is called may know that he is devoted to God. (3). That he may believe that the Holy Spirit will not desert this holy ministry.

73. The duty of Pastors in the Church is, to preach the Word, to administer the Sacraments, to exercise Discipline.

74. The condition of the ancient Church was distributed into Presbyters, Elders, Deacons, who dispensed the funds of the Church to the Bishops, the Clergy, the poor, and for repairing churches.

75. The power of the Church is viewed in relation to Doctrine, Legislation, and Jurisdiction.

76. Doctrine respects the articles of faith, none of which must be laid down without the authority of the word of God, but all must be directed to the glory of God and the edification of the Church. It respects also the application of the articles, which must agree with the analogy of faith.

77. Ecclesiastical laws, in precepts necessary to be observed, must be in accordance with the written word of God. In things indifferent, regard must be had to places, persons, times, with a due attention to order and decorum. Those constitutions ought to be avoided which have been laid down by pretended pastors instead of the pure worship of God, which bind the consciences by rigid necessity, which make void a commandment of God, which are useless and trifling, which oppress the consciences by their number, which lead to theatrical display, which are considered to be propitiatory sacrifices, and which are turned to the purposes of gain.

78. Jurisdiction is twofold. (A). That which belongs to the Clergy, which was treated of under the head of Provincial and General Synods. (B). That which is common to the Clergy and the people, the design of which is twofold that scandals may be prevented, and that scandal which has arisen may be removed. The exercise of it consists in private and public admonitions, and likewise in excommunication, the object of which is threefold. (1). That the Church may not be blamed; (2). That the good may not be corrupted by intercourse with the bad; (3). That they who are excommunicated may be ashamed, and may begin to repent.

79. With regard to Times, Fasts are appointed, and Vows are made. The design of Fasts is, that the flesh may be mortified, that we may be better prepared for prayer, and that they may be evidences of humility and obedience. They consist of three things, the time, the quality, and the quantity of food. But here we must beware lest we rend our garments only, and not our hearts, as hypocrites do, lest those actions be regarded as a meritorious performance, and lest they be too rigorously demanded as necessary to salvation.

80. In Vows we must consider; A. To whom the vow is made—namely, to God. Hence, it follows that nothing must be attempted but what is approved by his word, which teaches us what is pleasing and what is displeasing to God. B. Who it is that vows—namely, a man. We must, therefore, beware lest we disregard our liberty, or promise what is beyond our strength or inconsistent with our calling. C. What is vowed. Here regard

must be had to time; to the *past*, such as a vow of thanksgiving and repentance; to the *future*, that we may afterwards be more cautious, and may be stimulated by them to the performance of duty. Hence, it is evident what opinion we ought to form respecting Popish vows.

81. In explaining the Sacraments, there are three things to be considered. A. What a sacrament is—namely, an external sign, by which God seals on our consciences the promises of his good will towards us, in order to sustain the weakness of our faith. We in our turn testify our piety towards him. B. What things are necessary—namely, the Sign, the Thing signified, the Promise, and the general Participation. C. What is the number of them—namely, Baptism and the Lord's Supper.

82. The Sign in Baptism is water; the Thing Signified is the blood of Christ; the Promise is eternal life; the Communicants or Partakers are, adults, after making a confession of their faith, and likewise infants; for Baptism came in the place of Circumcision, and in both the mystery, promise, use, and efficacy, are the same. Forgiveness of sins also belongs to infants, and therefore it is likewise a sign of this forgiveness.

83. The end of Baptism is twofold. (A). To promote our faith towards God. For it is a sign of our washing by the blood of Christ, and of the mortification of our flesh, and the renewal of our souls in Christ. Besides, being united to Christ, we believe that we shall be partakers of all his blessings, and that we shall never fall under condemnation. (B). To serve as our confession before our neighbor, for it is a mark that we choose to be regarded as the people of God, and we testify that we profess the Christian religion, and that our desire is, that all the members of our body may proclaim the praise of God.

84. The Lord's Supper is a spiritual feast, by which we are preserved in that life into which God hath begotten us by his word.

85. The design of the Lord's Supper is threefold. (A). To aid in confirming our faith towards God. (B). To serve as a confession before men. (C). To be an exhortation to charity.

86. We must beware lest, by undervaluing the signs, we separate them too much from their mysteries, with which they are in some measure connected; and lest, on the other hand, by immoderately extolling them, we appear to obscure the mysteries themselves.

87. The parts are two. (A). The *spiritual truth* in which the meaning is beheld consists in the promises; the *matter*, or substance, is Christ dead and risen; and the *effect* is our redemption and justification. (B). The visible signs are, bread, and wine.

88. With the Lord's Supper is contrasted the Popish Mass. A. It offers insult and blasphemy to Christ. B. It buries the cross of Christ. C. It obliterates

his death. D. It robs us of the benefits, which we obtain in Christ. E. It destroys the Sacraments in which the memorial of his death was left.

89. The Sacraments, falsely so-called, are enumerated, which are Confirmation, Penitence, Extreme Unction, Orders [which gave rise to the (seven) less and the (three) greater], and Marriage.

90. Next comes civil government, which belongs to the external regulation of manners.

91. Under this head are considered Magistrates, Laws, and the People.

92. The Magistrate is God's vicegerent, the father of his country, the guardian of the laws, the administrator of justice, the defender of the Church.

93. By these names, he is excited to the performance of duty. A. That he may walk in holiness before God, and before men may maintain uprightness, prudence, temperance, harmlessness, and righteousness. B. That by wonderful consolation it may smooth the difficulties of his office.

94. The kinds of Magistracy or Civil Government are Monarchy, Aristocracy, and Democracy.

95. As to Laws, we must see what is their constitution in regard to God and to men: and what is their equity in regard to times, places, and nations.

96. The People owe to the Magistrate, A. Reverence heartily rendered to him as God's ambassador. B. Obedience or compliance with edicts, or paying taxes, or undertaking public offices and burdens. C. That love which will lead us to pray to God for his prosperity.

97. We are enjoined to obey not only good magistrates, but all who possess authority, though they may exercise tyranny; for it was not without the authority of God that they were appointed princes.

98. When tyrants reign, let us first remember our faults, which are chastised by such scourges; and, therefore, humility will restrain our impatience. Besides, it is not in our power to remedy these evils, and all that remains for us is to implore the assistance of the Lord, in whose hand are the hearts of men and the revolutions of kingdoms.

99. In Two ways God restrains the fury of tyrants; either by raising up from among their own subjects open avengers, who rid the people of their tyranny, or by employing for that purpose the rage of men whose thoughts and contrivances are totally different, thus overturning one tyranny by means of another.

100. The obedience enjoined on subjects does not prevent the interference of any popular Magistrates whose office it is to restrain tyrants and to protect the liberty of the people. Our obedience to Magistrates ought to be such, that the obedience, which we owe to the King of kings, shall remain entire and unimpaired

The Rev. Dr. Wisner, in his late discourse at Plymouth, on the anniversary of the landing of the Pilgrims, made the following assertion:

"Much as the name of Calvin has been scoffed at and loaded with reproach by many sons of freedom, there is not an historical proposition more susceptible of complete demonstration than this, that no man has lived to whom the world is under greater obligations for the freedom it now enjoys, than John Calvin."

✛

An Account of the Life of
John Calvin

by John Foxe
excerpted from *The Foxe's Book of Martyrs*

The reformer John Calvin was born in France at Noyon in Picardy, July 10, 1509. He was instructed in grammar in Paris under Maturinus Corderius, and studied philosophy in the College of Montaign under a Spanish professor.

Young John's father noticed his son's marks of early piety (particularly in his reprehensions of the vices of his companions), reared him for the church, and got him presented on May 21, 1521, to the chapel of Notre Dame de la Gesine in the Church of Noyon. In 1527, John was presented to the rectory of Marseville, which he exchanged in 1529 for the rectory of Point l'Eveque near Noyon. His father afterward changed his resolution and would have him study law. John readily consented. By that time, through reading the Scriptures, he had grown to dislike the superstitions of popery. He gladly resigned the chapel in 1534. He made a great progress in law, and improved no less in the knowledge of divinity by his private studies. At Bourges he studied Greek under the direction of Professor Wolmar.

His father's death called him back to Noyon, where he stayed only a short time before he ventured on to Paris. It was there that he furnished materials for a speech delivered by Nicholas Cop, rector of the University of Paris. The speech greatly displeased the Sorbonne and the parliament, and gave rise to a persecution against the Protestants in general and Calvin in particular. He narrowly escaped being taken in the College of Forteret, and was forced to flee to Xaintonge after having had the honor of being introduced to the queen of Navarre, who had raised this first storm against the Protestants.

Calvin returned to Paris in 1534. This year the reformed met with severe treatment. He determined that he would have to leave France, particularly after publishing a treatise against those who believed that departed souls are in a kind of sleep. He retired to Basel, where he studied Hebrew: at this time he published his *Institutions of the Christian Religion*; a work well adapted to spread his fame, though he himself was desirous of living in obscurity. It is dedicated to the French king, Francis I.

Calvin next wrote an apology for the Protestants who were burned for their religion in France. After the publication of this work, Calvin went to Italy to pay a visit to the duchess of Ferrara, a lady of eminent piety, by whom he was very kindly received.

From Italy he returned to France, and having settled his private affairs, proposed to go to Strassburg or Basel with his sole surviving brother, Antony Calvin. The roads were not safe because of the war. The exception was a road that ran through the duke of Savoy's territories. The Calvin brothers chose that road. "This was a particular direction of Providence," says Bayle, "It was his destiny that he should settle at Geneva, and when he was wholly intent upon going farther, he found himself detained by an order from heaven, if I may so speak."

At Geneva, Calvin therefore was obliged to comply with the choice, which the consistory and magistrates made of him, with the consent of the people: to be one of their ministers and a professor of divinity. He wanted to serve only as a professor of divinity, but in the end he was obliged to take both offices upon him in August 1536. The year following, he made all the people declare, upon oath, their assent to the confession of faith, which contained a renunciation of popery. He next intimated that he could not submit to a regulation, that the canton of Berne had made. The syndics of Geneva summoned an assembly of the people, and it was ordered that Calvin, Farel, and another minister should leave the town in a few days for refusing to administer the Sacrament.

Calvin retired to Strassburg and established a French church in that city, of which he was the first minister. He was also appointed to be professor of divinity there. Meanwhile the people of Geneva entreated him so earnestly to return to them that at last he consented, and arrived September 13, 1541, to the great satisfaction both of the people and the magistrates. The first thing he did after his arrival was to establish a form of church discipline, and a consistorial jurisdiction, invested with power of inflicting censures and canonical punishments, as far as excommunication, inclusively.

It has long been the delight of both infidels and some professed Christians, when they wish to bring odium upon the opinions of Calvin, to refer to his participation in the death of Michael Servetus. Those who are unable to overthrow his opinions use this as a conclusive argument against his whole system. A certain class of reasoners use, "Calvin burned Servetus! Calvin burned Servetus!" as good proof that the doctrine of the Trinity is not true, that divine sovereignty is against Scripture, and that Christianity a cheat.

We have no wish to palliate any act of Calvin's, which is manifestly wrong. All his proceedings in relation to the unhappy affair of Servetus, we think, cannot be defended. Still it should be remembered that the true principles of religious toleration were very little understood in the time of Calvin. All the other reformers then living approved of Calvin's conduct.

Even the gentle and amiable Melancthon expressed himself in relation to this affair in the following manner. In a letter addressed to Bullinger, he says, "I have read your statement respecting the blasphemy of Servetus, and praise your piety and judgment; and am persuaded that the Council of Geneva has done right in putting to death this obstinate man, who would never have ceased his blasphemies. I am astonished that any one can be found to disapprove of this proceeding." Farel expressly says, "Servetus deserved a capital punishment." Bucer did not hesitate to declare, "Servetus deserved something worse than death."

The truth is, although Calvin had some hand in the arrest and imprisonment of Servetus, he was unwilling that he should be burned at all. "I desire," said he, "that the severity of the punishment should be remitted … We endeavored to commute the kind of death, but in vain.

"By wishing to mitigate the severity of the punishment," said Farel to Calvin, "you discharge the office of a friend towards your greatest enemy."

"That Calvin was the instigator of the magistrates that Servetus might be burned," says Turritine, "historians neither anywhere affirm, nor does it appear from any considerations. Nay, it is certain, that he, with the college of pastors, dissuaded from that kind of punishment."

It has been often asserted that Calvin possessed so much influence with the magistrates of Geneva that he might have obtained the release of Servetus had he not wanted his destruction. This, however, is not true. So far from it, that Calvin was himself once banished from Geneva by these very magistrates and often opposed their arbitrary measures in vain. Calvin was so against the death of Servetus that he warned him of his danger, and suffered him to remain several weeks at Geneva before he was arrested. But his language, which was then accounted blasphemous, was the cause of his imprisonment. When in prison, Calvin visited him and used every argument to persuade him to retract his horrible blasphemies without reference to his peculiar sentiments. This was the extent of Calvin's agency in this unhappy affair.

It cannot, however, be denied that in this instance, Calvin acted contrary to the kind and gracious spirit of the Gospel. It is better to drop a tear over the inconsistency of human nature and to bewail those infirmities that cannot be justified. He declared that he acted conscientiously, and publicly justified the act.

It was the opinion, that erroneous religious principles are punishable by the civil magistrate that did the mischief, whether at Geneva, in Transylvania, or in Britain. To this, rather than to Trinitarianism or Unitarianism, it ought to be imputed.

After the death of Luther, Calvin exerted great sway over the men of that notable period. He was influential in France, Italy, Germany, Holland, England, and Scotland. Two thousand one hundred and fifty reformed congregations were organized, receiving from him their preachers.

Calvin, triumphant over all his enemies, felt his death drawing near. Yet he continued to exert himself in every way with youthful energy. When about to lie down in rest, he drew up his will, saying:

"I do testify that I live and purpose to die in this faith which God has given me through His Gospel, and that I have no other dependence for salvation than the free choice which is made of me by Him. With my whole heart I embrace His mercy, through which all my sins are covered, for Christ's sake, and for the sake of His death and sufferings. According to the measure of grace granted unto me, I have taught this pure, simple Word by sermons, by deeds, and by expositions of this Scripture. In all my battles with the enemies of the truth I have not used sophistry, but have fought the good fight squarely and directly."

May 27, 1564, was the day of his release and blessed journey home. He was in his fifty-fifth year.

That a man who had acquired so great a reputation and such an authority should have had but a salary of one hundred crowns, and refuse to accept more; and after living fifty-five years with the utmost frugality should leave but three hundred crowns to his heirs, including the value of his library, which sold very dear, is something so heroic, that one must have lost all feeling not to admire.

When Calvin took his leave of Strassburg, to return to Geneva, they wanted to continue to him the privileges of a freeman of their town, and the revenues of a prebend, which had been assigned to him; the former he accepted, but absolutely refused the other. He carried one of the brothers with him to Geneva, but he never took any pains to get him preferred to an honorable post, as any other possessed of his credit would have done. He took care indeed of the honor of his brother's family, by getting him freed from an adulteress, and obtaining leave to him to marry again; but even his enemies relate that he made him learn the trade of a bookbinder, which he followed all his life after.

John Calvin was buried in the cemetery of Plain Palais, and at his own request, no monument was set up to mark his grave. The exact spot is unknown to this day.

Other historians and biographers offer personal insight into John Calvin, the man.

ERNEST RENAN, educated for the Romish priesthood, but later a skeptic, pays this striking tribute to Calvin's character:

"Calvin was one of those absolute men, cast complete in one mold, who is taken in wholly at a single glance: one letter, one action, suffices for a judgment of him. There were no folds in that inflexible soul, which never knew doubt or hesitation. Careless of wealth, of titles, of honors, indifferent to pomp, modest in his life, transparently humble, sacrificing everything to the desire of making others like himself, I hardly know of a man, save Ignatius Loyola, who could match him ... Lacking that vivid, deep, sympathetic

ardor which was one of the secrets of Luther's success, lacking the
charm, the languishing tenderness of Francis of Sales, Calvin
succeeded, in an age and in a country which called for a reaction
towards Christianity, simply because he was the most Christian
man of his generation."

GUIZOT, the French historian, concludes his biography:

"Calvin is great by reason of his marvelous powers, his
enduring labors, and the moral height and purity of his character.
Earnest in faith, pure in motive, austere in his life, and mighty in
his works, Calvin is one of those who deserve their great fame.
Three centuries separate us from him, but it is impossible to examine
his character and history without feeling, if not affection and
sympathy, at least profound respect and admiration for one of the
great Reformers of Europe and one of the great Christians of
France."

THEODORE BEZA, Calvin's close friend, confidante, and successor,
offers an intimate look at a beloved man:

"Calvin was not of large stature: his complexion was pale,
and rather brown: even to his last moments his eyes were peculiarly
bright, and indicative of his penetrating genius. He knew nothing
of luxury in his outward life, but was fond of the greatest neatness,
as became his thorough simplicity. His manner of living was so
arranged that he showed himself equally averse to extravagance
and meanness. He took so little nourishment, such being the
weakness of his stomach, that for many years he contented himself
with one meal a day. Of sleep he had almost none. His memory
was incredible; he immediately recognized, after many years, those
whom he had once seen; and when he had been interrupted for
several hours, in some work about which he was employed, he
could immediately resume and continue it, without reading again
what he had written. Of the numerous details connected with the
business of his office, he never forgot even the most trifling, and
this notwithstanding the multitude of his affairs.

"His judgment was so acute and correct in regard to the most
opposite concerns about which his advice was asked, that he often
seemed to possess the gift of looking into the future. I never
remember to have heard that anyone who followed his counsel went
wrong. He despised fine speaking, and was rather abrupt in his
language; but he wrote admirably, and no theologian of his time
expressed himself so clearly, so impressively and acutely as he; and
yet he labored as much as any one of his contemporaries, or of the

fathers. For this fluency he was indebted to the several studies of his youth, and to the natural acuteness of his genius, which had been still further increased by the practice of dictation, so that proper and dignified expressions never failed him, whether he was writing or speaking. He never, in any wise, altered the doctrine, which he first adopted, but remained true to it to the last.

"Although nature had endowed Calvin with a dignified seriousness, both in manner and character, no one was more agreeable than he in ordinary conversation. He could bear, in a wonderful manner, with the failings of others, when they sprang from mere weakness. Thus he never shamed anyone by ill-timed reproofs, or discouraged a weak brother; while, on the other hand, he never spared or overlooked willful sin. An enemy to all flattery, he hated dissimulation, especially every dishonest sentiment in reference to religion. He was therefore as powerful and strong an enemy to vices of this kind as he was a devoted friend to truth, simplicity and uprightness. His temperament was naturally choleric, and his active public life had tended greatly to increase this failing; but the Spirit of God had so taught him to moderate his anger, that no word ever escaped him unworthy of a righteous man. Still less did he ever commit aught unjust towards others. It was then only, indeed, when the question concerned religion, and when he had to contend against hardened sinners, that he allowed himself to be moved and excited beyond the bounds of moderation.

"Let us take but a single glance at the history of those men who, in any part of the world, have been distinguished for their virtues, and no one will be surprised at finding that the great and noble qualities which Calvin exhibited, both in his private and public life, excited against him a host of enemies. We ought not indeed to feel any wonder that so powerful a champion of pure doctrine, and so stern a teacher of sound morals, as well at home as in the world, should be so fiercely assailed. Rather ought we to let our admiration dwell on the fact that, standing alone as he did, he was sufficiently mighty to avail himself of that strongest of weapons, the Word of God. Thus, however numerous the adversaries, whom Satan excited against him (for he never had any but such as had declared war against piety and virtue), the Lord gave His servant sufficient strength to gain the victory over all.

"Having been for sixteen years a witness of his labors, I have pursued the history of his life and death with all fidelity; and I now unhesitatingly testify that every true Christian may find in this man the noble pattern of a truly Christian life and Christian death; a pattern, however, which it is as easy to calumniate as it would be difficult to follow."

John Calvin's Opus Magnus: The
Institutte of the Christian Religion

John Calvin

St. Peter's Church in Geneva.

John Calvin preaching at St. Peter's Church in Geneva.

Left: Theodore Beza,
Calvin's close friend, and
confidante
Middle: Michael Servetus
and John Calvin debating
before the Council of
Geneva.
Below: Calvin's friend,
Evangelist William Farel,
stands before the death bed
of Calvin.

A Defense of Calvinism

by
Charles Haddon Spurgeon
Author of *Morning by Morning* and *Evening by Evening*

The old truth that Calvin preached, that Augustine preached, and that Paul preached is the truth that I must preach today, or else be false to my conscience and my God. I cannot shape the truth; I know of no such thing as paring off the rough edges of a doctrine. John Knox's Gospel is my Gospel. That which thundered through Scotland must thunder through England again.

It is a great thing to begin the Christian life by believing good solid doctrine. Some people have received twenty different "gospels" in as many years; how many more they will accept before they get to their journey's end, it would be difficult to predict. I thank God that He early taught me the Gospel, and I have been so perfectly satisfied with it, that I do not want to know any other. Constant change of creed is sure loss. If a tree has to be taken up two or three times a year, you will not need to build a very large loft in which to store the apples. When people are always shifting their doctrinal principles, they are not likely to bring forth much fruit to the glory of God. It is good for young believers to begin with a firm hold upon those great fundamental doctrines, which the Lord has taught in His Word. Why, if I believed what some preach about the temporary, trumpery salvation which only lasts for a time, I would scarcely be at all grateful for it; but when I know that those whom God saves He saves with an everlasting salvation, when I know that He gives to them an everlasting righteousness, when I know that He settles them on an everlasting foundation of everlasting love, and that He will bring them to His everlasting kingdom, oh, then I do wonder, and I am astonished that such a blessing as this should ever have been given to me!

"Pause, my soul! adore, and wonder!
Ask, 'Oh, why such love to me?'
Grace hath put me in the number
Of the Saviour's family:
Hallelujah!
Thanks, eternal thanks, to Thee."

I suppose there are some persons whose minds naturally incline towards the doctrine of free will. I can only say that mine inclines as naturally towards the doctrines of sovereign grace. Sometimes, when I see some of the worst characters in the street, I feel as if my heart must burst forth in tears of gratitude that God has never let me act as they have done! I have thought, if God had left me alone, and had not touched me by His grace, what a great sinner I should have been! I should have run to the utmost lengths of sin, dived into the very depths of evil, nor should I have stopped at any vice or folly, if God had not restrained me. I feel that I should have been a very king of sinners, if God had let me alone. I cannot understand the reason why I am saved, except upon the ground that God would have it so. I cannot, if I look ever so earnestly, discover any kind of reason in myself why I should be a partaker of Divine grace. If I am not at this moment without Christ, it is only because Christ Jesus would have His will with me, and that will was that I should be with Him where He is, and should share His glory. I can put the crown nowhere but upon the head of Him whose mighty grace has saved me from going down into the pit.

Looking back on my past life, I can see that the dawning of it all was of God, of God effectively. I took no torch with which to light the sun, but the sun enlightened me. I did not commence my spiritual life—no, I rather kicked, and struggled against the things of the Spirit: when He drew me, for a time I did not run after Him: there was a natural hatred in my soul of everything holy and good. Wooings were lost upon me-warnings were cast to the wind-thunders were despised; and as for the whispers of His love, they were rejected as being less than nothing and vanity. But, sure I am, I can say now, speaking on behalf of myself, "He only is my salvation." It was He who turned my heart, and brought me down on my knees before Him. I can in very deed, say with Doddridge and Toplady,

"Grace taught my soul to pray,
And made my eyes o'erflow."

And coming to this moment, I can add,
"Tis grace has kept me to this day,
And will not let me go."

Well can I remember the manner in which I learned the doctrines of grace in a single instant. Born, as all of us are by nature, an Arminian, I still believed the old things I had heard continually from the pulpit, and did not see the grace of God. When I was coming to Christ, I thought I was doing it all myself, and though I sought the Lord earnestly, I had no idea the Lord was seeking me. I do not think the young convert is at first aware of this. I can recall the very day and hour when first I received those truths in my own soul-when they were, as John Bunyan says, burnt into my heart as with a hot iron, and I can recollect how I felt that I had grown on a sudden from a babe into a man-that I had made progress in Scriptural knowledge, through having found, once for all, the clue to the truth of God. One weeknight, when I was sitting in the house of God, I was not thinking much about the preacher's sermon, for I did not believe it. The thought struck me, How did you come to be a Christian? I sought the Lord. But how did you come to seek the Lord? The truth flashed across my mind in a moment- I should not have sought Him unless there had been some previous influence in my mind to make me seek Him. I prayed, thought I, but then I asked myself, How came I to pray? I was induced to pray by reading the Scriptures. How came I to read the Scriptures? I did read them, but what led me to do so? Then, in a moment, I saw that God was at the bottom of it all, and that He was the Author of my faith, and so the whole doctrine of grace opened up to me, and from that doctrine I have not departed to this day, and I desire to make this my constant confession, "I ascribe my change wholly to God."

I once attended a service where the text happened to be, "He shall choose our inheritance for us;" and the good man who occupied the pulpit was more than a little of an Arminian. Therefore, when he commenced, he said, "This passage refers entirely to our temporal inheritance, it has nothing whatever to do with our everlasting destiny, for," said he, "we do not want Christ to choose for us in the matter of Heaven or hell. It is so plain and easy, that every man who has a grain of common sense will choose Heaven, and any person would know better than to choose hell. We have no need of any superior intelligence, or any greater Being, to choose Heaven or hell for us. It is left to our own free- will, and we have enough wisdom given us, sufficiently correct means to judge for ourselves," and therefore, as he very logically inferred, there was no necessity for Jesus Christ, or anyone, to make a choice for us. We could choose the inheritance for ourselves without any assistance. "Ah!" I thought, "but, my good brother, it may be very true that we could, but I think we should want something more than common sense before we should choose aright."

First, let me ask, must we not all of us admit an over-ruling Providence, and the appointment of Jehovah's hand, as to the means whereby we came into this world? Those men who think that, afterwards, we are left to our own free-will to choose this one or the other to direct our steps, must admit that our entrance into the world was not of our own will, but that God had then to choose for us. What circumstances were those in our power, which led us to elect certain persons to be our parents? Had we anything to do with it? Did not God Himself appoint our parents, native place, and friends? Could He not have caused me to be born with the skin of the Hottentot, brought forth by a filthy mother who would nurse me in her "kraal," and teach me to bow down to Pagan gods, quite as easily as to have given me a pious mother, who would each morning and night bend her knee in prayer on my behalf? Or, might He not, if He had pleased have given me some profligate to have been my parent, from whose lips I might have early heard fearful, filthy, and obscene language? Might He not have placed me where I should have had a drunken father, who would have immured me in a very dungeon of ignorance, and brought me up in the chains of crime? Was it not God's Providence that I had so happy a lot, that both my parents were His children, and endeavored to train me up in the fear of the Lord?

John Newton used to tell a whimsical story, and laugh at it, too, of a good woman who said, in order to prove the doctrine of election, "Ah! sir, the Lord must have loved me before I was born, or else He would not have seen anything in me to love afterwards." I am sure it is true in my case; I believe the doctrine of election, because I am quite certain that, if God had not chosen me, I should never have chosen Him; and I am sure He chose me before I was born, or else He never would have chosen me afterwards; and He must have elected me for reasons unknown to me, for I never could find any reason in myself why He should have looked upon me with special love. So I am forced to accept that great Biblical doctrine. I recollect an Arminian brother telling me that he had read the Scriptures through a score or more times, and could never find the doctrine of election in them. He added that he was sure he would have done so if it had been there, for he read the Word on his knees. I said to him, "I think you read the Bible in a very uncomfortable posture, and if you had read it in your easy chair, you would have been more likely to understand it. Pray, by all means, and the more, the better, but it is a piece of superstition to think there is anything in the posture in which a man puts himself for reading: and as to reading through the Bible twenty times without having found anything about the doctrine of election, the wonder is that you found anything at all: you must have galloped through it at such a rate that you were not likely to have any intelligible idea of the meaning of the Scriptures."

If it would be marvelous to see one river leap up from the earth full-grown, what would it be to gaze upon a vast spring from which all the rivers of the earth should at once come bubbling up, a million of them born at a birth? What a vision would it be! Who can conceive it. And yet the love of God is that fountain, from which all the rivers of mercy, which have ever gladdened our race-all the rivers of grace in time, and of glory hereafter-take their rise. My soul, stand thou at that sacred fountainhead, and adore and magnify, forever and ever, God, even our Father, who hath loved us! In the very beginning, when this great universe lay in the mind of God, like unborn forests in the acorn cup; long ere the echoes awoke the solitudes; before the mountains were brought forth; and long ere the light flashed through the sky, God loved His chosen creatures. Before there was any created being-when the ether was not fanned by an angel's wing, when space itself had not an existence, when there was nothing save God alone-even then, in that loneliness of Deity, and in that deep quiet and profundity, His bowels moved with love for His chosen. Their names were written on His heart, and then were they dear to His soul. Jesus loved His people before the foundation of the world-even from eternity! and when He called me by His grace, He said to me, "I have loved thee with an everlasting love: therefore with loving kindness have I drawn thee."

Then, in the fullness of time, He purchased me with His blood; He let His heart run out in one deep gaping wound for me long ere I loved Him. Yea, when He first came to me, did I not spurn Him? When He knocked at the door, and asked for entrance, did I not drive Him away, and do despite to Ms grace? Ah, I can remember that I full often did so until, at last, by the power of His effectual grace, He said, "I must, I will come in;" and then He turned my heart, and made me love Him. But even till now I should have resisted Him, had it not been for His grace. Well, then since He purchased me when I was dead in sins, does it not follow, as a consequence necessary and logical, that He must have loved me first? Did my Saviour die for me because I believed on Him? No; I was not then in existence; I had then no being. Could the Saviour, therefore, have died because I had faith, when I myself was not yet born? Could that have been possible? Could that have been the origin of the Savior's love towards me? Oh! no; my Saviour died for me long before I believed. "But," says someone, "He foresaw that you would have faith; and, therefore, He loved you." What did He foresee about my faith? Did He foresee that I should get that faith myself, and that I should believe on Him of myself) No; Christ could not foresee that, because no Christian man will ever say that faith came of itself without the gift and without the working of the Holy Spirit. I have met with a great many believers, and talked with them about this matter; but I never knew one who could put his hand on his heart, and say, "I believed in Jesus without the assistance of the Holy Spirit."

I am bound to the doctrine of the depravity of the human heart, because I find myself depraved in heart, and have daily proofs that in my flesh there dwelleth no good thing. If God enters into covenant with unfallen man, man is so insignificant a creature that it must be an act of gracious condescension on the Lord's part; but if God enters into covenant with sinful man, he is then so offensive a creature that it must be, on God's part, an act of pure, free, rich, sovereign grace. When the Lord entered into covenant with me, I am sure that it was all of grace, nothing else but grace. When I remember what a den of unclean beasts and birds my heart was, and how strong was my unrenewed will, how obstinate and rebellious against the sovereignty of the Divine rule, I always feel inclined to take the very lowest room in my Father's house, and when I enter Heaven, it will be to go among the less than the least of all saints, and with the chief of sinners.

The late lamented Mr. Denham has put, at the foot of his portrait, a most admirable text, "Salvation is of the Lord." That is just an epitome of Calvinism; it is the sum and substance of it. If anyone should ask me what I mean by a Calvinist, I should reply, "He is one who says, Salvation is of the Lord." I cannot find in Scripture any other doctrine than this. It is the essence of the Bible. "He only is my rock and my salvation." Tell me anything contrary to this truth, and it will be a heresy; tell me a heresy, and I shall find its essence here, that it has departed from this great, this fundamental, this rock-truth, "God is my rock and my salvation." What is the heresy of

Rome, but the addition of something to the perfect merits of Jesus Christ-the bringing in of the works of the flesh, to assist in our justification? And what is the heresy of Arminianism but the addition of something to the work of the Redeemer? Every heresy, if brought to the touchstone, will discover itself here. I have my own Private opinion that there is no such thing as preaching Christ and Him crucified, unless we preach what nowadays is called Calvinism. It is a nickname to call it Calvinism; Calvinism is the Gospel, and nothing else. I do not believe we can preach the Gospel, if we do not preach justification by faith, without works; nor unless we preach the sovereignty of God in His dispensation of grace; nor unless we exalt the electing, unchangeable, eternal, immutable, conquering love of Jehovah; nor do I think we can preach the Gospel, unless we base it upon the special and particular redemption of His elect and chosen people which Christ wrought out upon the cross; nor can I comprehend a Gospel which lets saints fall away after they are called, and suffers the children of God to be burned in the fires of damnation after having once believed in Jesus. Such a Gospel I abhor.

"If ever it should come to pass,
That sheep of Christ might fall away,
My fickle, feeble soul, alas!
Would fall a thousand times a day"

If one dear saint of God had perished, so might all; if one of the covenant ones be lost, so may all be; and then there is no Gospel promise true, but the Bible is a lie, and there is nothing in it worth my acceptance. I will be an infidel at once when I can believe that a saint of God can ever fall finally. If God hath loved me once, then He will love me forever. God has a mastermind; He arranged everything in His gigantic intellect long before He did it; and once having settled it, He never alters it, 'This shall be done," saith He, and the iron hand of destiny marks it down, and it is brought to pass. "This is My purpose," and it stands, nor can earth or hell alter it. "This is My decree," saith He, "promulgate it, ye holy angels; rend it down from the gate of Heaven, ye devils, if ye can; but ye cannot alter the decree, it shall stand for ever." God altereth not His plans; why should He? He is Almighty, and therefore can perform His pleasure. Why should He? He is the All Wise, and therefore cannot have planned wrongly. Why should He? He is the everlasting God, and therefore cannot die before His plan is accomplished. Why should He change? Ye worthless atoms of earth, ephemera of a day, ye creeping insects upon this bay leaf of existence, ye may change your plans, but He shall never, never change His. Has He told me that His plan is to save me? If so, I am forever safe.

"My name from the palms of His hands
Eternity will not erase;
Impress'd on His heart it remains,
In marks of indelible grace."

I do not know how some people, who believe that a Christian can fall from grace, manage to be happy. It must be a very commendable thing in them to be able to get through a day without despair. If I did not believe the doctrine of the final perseverance of the saints, I think I should be of all men the most miserable, because I should lack any ground of comfort. I could not say, whatever state of heart I came into, that I should be like a well-spring of water, whose stream fails not; I should rather have to take the comparison of an intermittent spring, that might stop on a sudden, or a reservoir, which I had no reason to expect would always be full. I believe that the happiest of Christians and the truest of Christians are those who never dare to doubt God, but who take His Word simply as it stands, and believe it, and ask no questions, just feeling assured that if God has said it, it will be so. I bear my willing testimony that I have no reason, nor even the shadow of a reason, to doubt my Lord, and I challenge Heaven, and earth, and hell, to bring any proof that God is untrue. From the depths of hell I call the fiends, and from this earth I call the tried and afflicted believers, and to Heaven I appeal, and challenge the long experience of the blood-washed host, and there is not to be found in the three realms a single person who can bear witness to one fact which can disprove the faithfulness of God, or weaken Ms claim to be trusted by His servants. There are many things that may or may not happen, but this I know shall happen:

"He shall present my soul,
Unblemish'd and complete,
Before the glory of His face,
With joys divinely great"

All the purposes of man have been defeated, but not the purposes of God. The promises of man may be broken-many of them are made to be broken, but the promises of God shall all be fulfilled. He is a promise-maker, but He never was a promise-breaker; He is a promise-keeping God, and every one of His people shall prove it to be so. This is my grateful, personal confidence, "The Lord will perfect that which concerneth me"-unworthy me, lost and ruined me. He will yet save me; and ...

"I, among the blood-wash'd throng,
Shall wave the palm, and wear the crown,
And shout loud victory"

I go to a land, which the plough of earth hath never upturned, where it is greener than earth's best pastures, and richer than her most abundant harvests ever saw. I go to a building of more gorgeous architecture than man hath ever built; it is not of mortal design; it is "a building of God, a house not made with hands, eternal in the Heavens." All I shall know and enjoy in Heaven, will be given to me by the Lord, and I shall say, when at last I appear before Him-

"Grace all the work shall crown
Through everlasting days;
It lays in Heaven the topmost stone,
And well deserves the praise"

I know there are some who think it necessary to their system of theology to limit the merit of the blood of Jesus: if my theological system needed such a limitation, I would cast it to the winds. I cannot, I dare not allow the thought to find a lodging in my mind, it seems so near akin to blasphemy. In Christ's finished work I see an ocean of merit; my plummet finds no bottom, my eye discovers no shore. There must be sufficient efficacy in the blood of Christ, if God had so willed it, to have saved not only all in this world, but all in ten thousand worlds, had they transgressed their Maker's law. Once admit infinity into the matter, and limit is out of the question. Having a Divine Person for an offering, it is not consistent to conceive of limited value; bound and measure are terms inapplicable to the Divine sacrifice. The intent of the Divine purpose fixes the application of the infinite offering, but does not change it into a finite work. Think of the numbers upon whom God has bestowed His grace already. Think of the countless hosts in Heaven: if thou wert introduced there to-day, thou wouldst find it as easy to tell the stars, or the sands of the sea, as to count the multitudes that are before the throne even now. They have come from the East, and from the West, from the North, and from the South, and they are sitting down with Abraham, and with Isaac, and with Jacob in the Kingdom of God; and beside those in Heaven, think of the saved ones on earth. Blessed be God, His elect on earth are to be counted by millions, I believe, and the days are coming, brighter days than these, when there shall be multitudes upon multitudes brought to know the Saviour, and to rejoice in Him. The Father's love is not for a few only, but for an exceeding great company. "A great multitude, which no man could number," will be found in Heaven. A man can reckon up to very high figures; set to work your Newtons, your mightiest calculators, and they can count great numbers, but God and God alone can tell the multitude of His redeemed. I believe there will be more in Heaven than in hell. If anyone asks me why I think so, I answer, because Christ, in everything, is to "have the pre- eminence," and I cannot conceive how He could have the pre-eminence if there are to be more in the dominions of Satan than in Paradise. Moreover, I have never read that there is to be in hell a great multitude, which no man could number. I rejoice to know that the souls of all infants, as soon as they die, speed their way to Paradise. Think what a multitude there is of them! Then there are already in Heaven unnumbered myriads of the spirits of just men made perfect-the redeemed of all nations, and kindred, and people, and tongues up till now; and there are better times coming, when the religion of Christ shall be universal; when ...

"He shall reign from pole to pole,
With illimitable sway,"

... when whole kingdoms shall bow down before Him, and nations shall be born in a day, and in the thousand years of the great millennial state there will be enough saved to make up all the deficiencies of the thousands of years that have gone before. Christ shall be Master everywhere, and His praise shall be sounded in every land. Christ shall have the pre-eminence at last; His train shall be far larger than that which shall attend the chariot of the grim monarch of hell.

Some persons love the doctrine of universal atonement because they say, "It is so beautiful. It is a lovely idea that Christ should have died for all men; it commends itself," they say, "to the instincts of humanity; there is something in it full of joy and beauty." I admit there is, but beauty may be often associated with falsehood. There is much, which I might admire in the theory of universal redemption, but I will just show what the supposition necessarily involves. If Christ on His cross intended to save every man, then He intended to save those who were lost before He died. If the doctrine is true, that He died for all men, then He died for some who were in hell before He came into this world, for doubtless there were even then myriads there that had been cast away because of their sins. Once again, if it was Christ's intention to save all men, how deplorably has He been disappointed, for we have His own testimony that there is a lake which burns with fire and brimstone, and into that pit of woe have been cast some of the very persons who, according to the theory of universal redemption, were bought with His blood. That seems to me a conception a thousand times more repulsive than any of those consequences, which are said to be associated with the Calvinistic and Christian doctrine of special and particular redemption.

To think that my Saviour died for men who were or are in hell, seems a supposition too horrible for me to entertain. To imagine for a moment that He was the Substitute for all the sons of men, and that God, having first punished the Substitute, afterwards punished the sinners themselves, seems to conflict with all my ideas of Divine justice. That Christ should offer an atonement and satisfaction for the sins of all men, and that afterwards some of those very men should be punished for the sins for which Christ had already atoned, appears to me to be the most monstrous iniquity that could ever have been imputed to Saturn, to Janus, to the goddess of the Thugs, or to the most diabolical heathen deities. God forbid that we should ever think thus of Jehovah, the just and wise and good! There is no soul living who holds more firmly to the doctrines of grace than I do, and if any man asks me whether I am ashamed to be called a Calvinist, I answer- I wish to be called nothing but a Christian; but if you ask me, do I hold the doctrinal views which were held by John Calvin, I reply, I do in the main hold them, and rejoice to avow it. But far be it from me even to imagine that Zion contains none but Calvinistic Christians within her walls, or that there are none saved who do not hold our views.

Most atrocious things have been spoken about the character and spiritual condition of John Wesley, the modern prince of Arminians. I can only say concerning him that, while I detest many of the doctrines which he preached, yet for the man himself I have a reverence second to no Wesleyan; and if there were wanted two apostles to be added to the number of the twelve, I do not believe that there could be found two men more fit to be so added than George Whitefield and John Wesley. The character of John Wesley stands beyond all imputation for self-sacrifice, zeal, holiness, and communion with God; he lived far above the ordinary level of common Christians, and was one "of whom the world was not worthy." I believe there are multitudes of men who cannot see these truths, or, at least, cannot see them in the way in which we put them, who nevertheless have received Christ as their Saviour, and are as dear to the heart of the God of grace as the soundest Calvinist in or out of Heaven.

I do not think I differ from any of my Hyper-Calvinistic brethren in what I do believe, but I differ from them in what they do not believe. I do not hold any less than they do, but I hold a little more, and, I think, a little more of the truth revealed in the Scriptures. Not only are there a few cardinal doctrines, by which we can steer our ship North, South, East, or West, but as we study the Word, we shall begin to learn something about the Northwest and Northeast, and all else that lies between the four cardinal points. The system of truth revealed in the Scriptures is not simply one straight line, but two; and no man will ever get a right view of the Gospel until he knows how to look at the two lines at once. For instance, I read in one Book of the Bible, "The Spirit and the bride say, Come. And let him that heareth say, Come. And let him that is athirst come. And whosoever will, let him take the water of life freely." Yet I am taught, in another part of the same inspired Word, that "it is not of him that willeth, nor of him that runneth, but of God that sheweth mercy." I see, in one place, God in providence presiding over all, and yet I see, and I cannot help seeing, that man acts as he pleases, and that God has left his actions, in a great measure, to his own free-will. Now, if I were to declare that man was so free to act that there was no control of God over his actions, I should be driven very near to atheism; and if, on the other hand, I should declare that God so over-rules all things that man is not free enough to be responsible, I should be driven at once into Antinomianism or fatalism.

That God predestines, and yet that man is responsible, are two facts that few can see clearly. They are believed to be inconsistent and contradictory to each other. If, then, I find taught in one part of the Bible that everything is foreordained, that is true; and if I find, in another Scripture, that man is responsible for all his actions, that is true; and it is only my folly that leads me to imagine that these two truths can ever contradict each other. I do not believe they can ever be welded into one upon any earthly anvil, but they certainly shall be one in eternity. They are two lines that are so nearly parallel, that the human mind which pursues them farthest will never discover that they converge, but they do converge, and they will meet somewhere in eternity, close to the throne of God, whence all truth doth spring.

It is often said that the doctrines we believe have a tendency to lead us to sin. I have heard it asserted most positively, that those high doctrines which we love, and which we find in the Scriptures, are licentious ones. I do not know who will have the hardihood to make that assertion, when they consider that the holiest of men have been believers in them. I ask the man who dares to say that Calvinism is a licentious religion, what he thinks of the character of Augustine, or Calvin, or Whitefield, who in successive ages were the great exponents of the system of grace; or what will he say of the Puritans, whose works are full of them? Had a man been an Arminian in those days, he would have been accounted the vilest heretic breathing, but now we are looked upon as the heretics, and they as the orthodox. We have gone back to the old school; we can trace our descent from the apostles. It is that vein of free-grace, running through the sermonizing of Baptists, which has saved us as a denomination. Were it not for that, we should not stand where we are today. We can run a golden line up to Jesus Christ Himself, through a holy succession of mighty fathers, who all held these glorious truths; and we can ask concerning them, "Where will you find holier and better men in the world?"

No doctrine is so calculated to preserve a man from sin as the doctrine of the grace of God. Those who have called it "a licentious doctrine" did not know anything at all about it. Poor ignorant things, they little knew that their own vile stuff was the most licentious doctrine under Heaven. If they knew the grace of God in truth, they would soon see that there was no preservative from lying like a knowledge that we are elect of God from the foundation of the world. There is nothing like a belief in my eternal perseverance, and the immutability of my Father's affection, which can keep me near to Him from a motive of simple gratitude. Nothing makes a man so virtuous as belief of the truth. A lying doctrine will soon beget a lying practice. A man cannot have an erroneous belief without by-and-by having an erroneous life. I believe the one thing naturally begets the other. Of all men, those have the most disinterested piety, the most sublime reverence, the most ardent devotion, who believe that they are saved by grace, without works, through faith, and that not of themselves, it is the gift of God. Christians should take heed, and see that it always is so, lest by any means Christ should be crucified afresh, and put to an open shame.

The Five Points of Calvinism

With the possible exception of Martin Luther, no man has had greater influence on the theology of the Protestant Churches today than John Calvin. It's impossible to condense countless volumes of Biblical commentary of John Calvin down to a short summary, it is true that Calvin's most well-know teachings, set forth in *The Institutes of Christian Religion* are the often-quoted "Five Points of Calvinism."

The acronym used to help remember them is "T.U.L.I.P."

They are:

TOTAL DEPRAVITY OF MAN: That man's nature is basically evil, not basically good. Apart from the direct influence of God, man will never truly seek God or God's will, though he may seek the benefits of association with God.

UNCONDITIONAL ELECTION: That God sovereignly chooses or "elects" his children from before the foundation of time. God does not "look down the corridors of time to see what decision people will make"... rather, God causes them to make the decision to seek him.

LIMITED ATONEMENT: That the death and resurrection of Christ is a substitutionary payment for the sins of only those who are God's elect children... not the entire world.

IRRESISTIBLE GRACE: That when God calls a person, his call cannot ultimately be ignored.

PERSEVERANCE OF THE SAINTS: That it is not possible for one to "lose his salvation."

Index

Other Pure Gold Classics

More from John Calvin

John Calvin's **Obtaining Grace** and **The Holy Catholic Church** contains the third and fourth books of the *Institutes of the Christian Religion.* It is companion to **God the Creator** and **God the Redeemer**

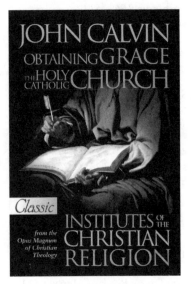

From Charles H. Spurgeon

Two powerfully crafted daily devotionals from the "Prince of Preachers." Written to enlighten, encourage, strengthen, bless and teach you.

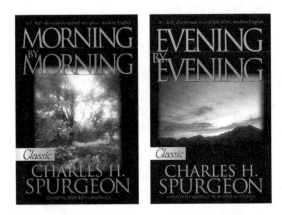